The History of Tiger Stadium:

A Love Letter to Baseball at Michigan & Trumbull

by Doc Fletcher

authorHOUSE®

AuthorHouse™
1663 Liberty Drive
Bloomington, IN 47403
www.authorhouse.com
Phone: 1 (800) 839-8640

Published by AuthorHouse 04/12/2019

ISBN: 978-1-7283-0279-9 (sc)
ISBN: 978-1-7283-0278-2 (e)

Library of Congress Control Number: 2019902640

Print information available on the last page.

The History of Tiger Stadium: A Love Letter to Baseball at Michigan & Trumbull

Book Credits & References

Proof-reader, cheerleader, ideas that made the book better, Love of my Life... Maggie Meeker

Front cover... Big Joe Braun

Photos... Doc Fletcher; Mary Kathryn Lary ('56/'58/'61 Frank Lary photos); Bobby Lewis (1968 Polaroids); Christine Verdone (1983 Brookens and Leach photo); Chucky Porta (1984 World Series photos); Pam Carroll (1986 John Hiller baseball card show); Kathy & Johnny Harcourt (Katrina Harcourt 1999 photo); Jimmy & Lisa Vollmers (Spencer Vollmers 1999 photo); Paula Brown (Andy & Willie Horton 2004 photo) Nancy Carey (Paul Carey & Ernie Harwell 2006 photo)

Additional Photos:

Courtesy of the Detroit Tigers Baseball Club, Courtesy of the Ernie Harwell Sports Collection - Detroit Public Library, Courtesy Sul Ross State (Texas) - Norm Cash photos, Topps trading card images used courtesy of The Topps Company, Inc.

Illustration... Keith Jones aka bigtimeartguy

References & cross-references...

"The Story of Baseball" by John M. Rosenburg

"Crazy '08" by Cait Murphy

"Those 1940 Detroit Tigers" by John C. Fountain

"Tuned To Baseball" by Ernie Harwell

"Hank Greenberg: The Hero of Heroes" by John Rosengren

"Yesterday's Tiger Heroes" by Jim Sargent

"The Tigers and Yankees in '61" by Jim Sargent

"The Tigers of '68" by George Cantor

"The Year of the Tiger 1968" album

"Behind the Mask" by Bill Freehan

"The 1972 Detroit Tigers: Bill Martin and the Half-Game Champions" by Todd Masters

"Tuned To Baseball" by Ernie Harwell

"A Place For Summer" by Richard Bak

"Hank Greenberg: The Story of My Life" by Hank Greenberg & Ira Berkow

"Grand Slam Baseball" (multiple contributing writers)

"Hey Kid! A Tigers Batboy Remembers" – Dan Dillman

"Sparky Anderson: The Life of a Baseball Legend" by the Detroit Free Press & Cincinnati Enquirer

Sports Illustrated

Detroit Free Press

Detroit News

Ionia Sentinel-Standard

New York Daily News

New York Times

L.A. Times

Society for American Baseball Research

(The Georgia Peach) Cobb – Norm Coleman (a one man play)

Detroit Historical Museum "The Year of the Tigers 1968" panel

www.detroitathletic.com

www.baseball-reference.com

www.baseball-almanac.com

www.si.com/vault/(year)/detroit-tigers

www.thenationalpastimemuseum.com

www.sabr.org

www.ourgamemlblogs.com

www.jackbenny.org

www.brysholm.blogspot.com

www.mlive.com

www.detroitsportsnation.com

YouTube

Introduction

Alan Trammell on Tiger fans & Tiger Stadium

They're very knowledgeable, and I'm very thankful. Obviously, I grew up out west, and was used to different venues with the (big) parking lots. I remember my first time coming to Tiger Stadium, Lou and I were coming out together in a cab, and we came around the freeway. I could see the transformers with the lights, and I'm thinking "Where do they park? You know, I'm used to… where do they park?" You know, they get 50,000 people in there, and they got the little lots, the little gas stations, and whatever, and I was just amazed by that, again coming from a different background. But, I'm just so thankful for the people in the Midwest and the way they supported… the <u>tradition</u> that they have. You know, the people… parents and grandparents, I mean they're Tiger fans, generations, through thick and thin, they're gonna support you. And not every city can say that. I've tried to thank them in the best way that I possibly can, once again, I'm just so appreciative and thankful the way they've treated myself and my family over all these years, and still… I tried to tell the young kids now, "This is what you can have. The same background, the way they support you – this is for life". And that's a very special feeling.

From the 2018 TV show "The Legends of the Olde English D"

Tiger Stadium 1999 finale: waving fans into neighborhood parking lots on Trumbull

Prologue

"Historic preservation is about keeping us in active contact with our past – the good and the bad – so that we will never forget it, and learn from it. In the long run this is why it is vital that we preserve historic places like Tiger Stadium, for what they teach us about ourselves, as well as about the game. When we preserve our past, we preserve what unites us, not what divides us, which is why cities that do preserve the best of their heritage and culture have more soul and community spirit than those that do not." Jack Walter, president of the National Trust for Historic Preservation.

This book is a fan's love letter to Tiger Stadium, the cathedral at The Corner of Michigan & Trumbull, where together with our great-grandparents, grandparents, parents, uncles, aunts, siblings, children, godchildren, and friends, we have cheered our Detroit Tigers. Although the structure is gone, the memories remain. The book is a tribute to the characters on the field, in the stands, and those in the neighborhoods surrounding the park, as well as to the broadcasters who brought the action to us when we couldn't be there. It is from those characters and those who knew them, loved them, or both, from which many of the book's stories come from. Baseball is a game of statistics, their inclusion critical to the history told, but it's the back stories that give the book its humanity, humor, and liveliness.

Some of the stories came from unexpected places - Exhibit A: while visiting my doctor, who was aware that I was working on this book, he said, *"I don't know if this is of any interest to you, but my parents were good friends with Norm Cash."* Since in 4 decades of playing softball, I'd always worn number 25 in honor of Norm, my favorite Detroit Tiger ever, my answer was, *"YEAH!"* Within 10 minutes of the appointment's conclusion, I found myself sitting in my car in the doctor's parking lot on the phone with his mother for over half an hour, recording one laugh out loud Stormin' Norman tale after another.

It is amazing the stories you can find when combing through decades of box scores – like this one: when the Tigers lost their 1956 Home Opener, a Kansas City Athletic reliever was brought in to get the final out, and he did his job well. Since it was the only save or win he posted during 3 seasons in the majors, this afternoon at The Corner was the one time in the majors that Tommy Lasorda was on the mound to receive the game ending congratulatory handshake from his teammates. Yeah, *that* Tommy Lasorda.

DDDDDDDDDDDDDDDDDDDDDDDDDDDDDDDDDDDDDDDDDDDDDDDDDDDDDDDDDDDDDDDDDDDDDDDDDDD

2121 Trumbull, the Oldest Address in American Professional Sports thru 9.27.99...

Bennett Park 1896-1911, Navin Field 1912-1937, Briggs Stadium 1938-1960, Tiger Stadium 1961-1999

American League Champions 1907, 1908, 1909, 1934, 1935, 1940, 1945, 1968, 1984

World Series Champions 1935, 1945, 1968, 1984

What fun we Detroit baseball fans have had at The Corner of Michigan & Trumbull - and at other ball fields even earlier than that. Here are snippets from some of the stories within...

- The 1887 Detroit Wolverines and their star catcher Charlie Bennett had an amazing start, winning all 30 exhibition games and beginning the regular season 19 & 2. Those National League Wolverines won the 4th ever World Series over the American Association's Louisville team, with Detroit playing their home games at Recreation Park, on the corner of Brush & Brady. Some of the best seats were not in the park, but on the roof of nearby Harper Hospital whose staff had never seen so many patients or patient visitors...

- From 1895 thru 1926, Charlie Bennett caught the ceremonial 1st pitch at every Home Opener: 1895 League Park, 1896-1911 Bennett Park, 1912-1926 Navin Field. On September 27, 1999, after the Final Game Ever was played at Tiger Stadium, Charlie's great nephew and oldest living relative, George Campbell, delivered the final pitch thrown at a MLB game at The Corner...

- On October 8, 1907, the Detroit Tigers played in their first ever World Series game, 280 miles west of The Corner at the West Side Grounds, home of the Chicago Cubs. Meanwhile, in downtown Detroit, over 12,000 fans crowded streets, leaned out of windows, and stood on rooftops to get a view of the game re-enactment taking place on a giant electronic scoreboard mounted on the Detroit Free Press building, the game situation updated after each pitch...

- Ty Cobb appeared in front of a judge for his speeding ticket, explaining to the court, *"I wasn't going any faster than when I steal 2nd base."* The judge, a Tiger fan, suspended his sentence...

- He took off his cap and, with a theatrical flourish, told the large crowd on hand, *"Ladies and gentlemen, you are now looking at Herman Schaefer, better known as Herman the Great, acknowledged by one & all to be the greatest pinch hitter in the world. I am now going to hit the ball into the leftfield bleachers. Thank you."* And damned if Germany Schaefer didn't, despite...

- In deciding game 6 of the '35 World Series, it was Mickey Cochrane, the man who molded a team of talented individuals into champions, that jumped on home plate with both feet for the Series-clinching run, Michigan exploding in joy as the Tigers won their 1st World Series ever...

- After taking an afternoon of abuse from the stands at The Corner, Yankees star pitcher Lefty Gomez had to be restrained by several teammates as he tried to jump into the crowd and throttle Patsy O'Toole, the fan known to all as the Human Earache...

- In the summer of '37, 16-year old Marion Vollmers worked a Briggs Stadium beer concession stand (it says a lot about the times that a 16-year old was working a beer stand). By the 3rd or 4th inning of most games, Marion & her fellow employees heard the distant *click-click-click* of cleats on cement grow louder until a tall figure came into view, a man wearing a trench coat with the collar turn up to cover his face. It was Schoolboy Rowe on days he wasn't pitching...

- Briggs Stadium was the first to respond to rain by covering the field with a nylon tarp, home to the first underground sprinkler system, painted the stadium's outside walls & seats every year, had attendants on hand in all restrooms, restrooms that were required to be spotless...

- Broadcaster Harry Heilmann turned the microphone toward the crowd noise, telling the radio audience, *"Listen to the voice of baseball!"*, as Gehringer...

- *"Weee-Doggies!"* Buddy Ebsen is in the Briggs Stadium crowd today, and William Frawley, too! With the future Jed Clampett AND Fred Mertz rooting for Detroit in the 1940 World Series game 3, how can we lose?

- On the eve of the Tigers-Cubs 1945 World Series game 7, the *Washington Post* implored its' readers, *"Please don't talk to us about atomic bombs, or the Russian impasse, or the strike crisis, or full employment, or such matters, until the issue of this hair-raising 1945 World Series is settled one way or the other"*...

- Dizzy Trout's pre-game ritual on days he pitched consisted of eating a carryout order from Hoot Robinson's Bar of 2 generously-sized pork chop sandwiches & 2 soda chasers. One day, when bending over to get the catcher's sign, he belched & covered the front of his jersey with tobacco juice. Catcher Bob Swift called time for a mound visit, asking Dizzy if he'd just vomited. Ol' Diz smiled and told him, *"No, but Hoot's pork chops sure taste better the second time around"*...

- Yogi Berra said of volatile Tiger pitcher Freddie Hutchinson, *"I always know how Hutch did when we follow Detroit into a town. If we got stools in the dressing room, I know he won. If we got kindling, he lost"*...

- The time-honored tradition of fans seeing their heroes flip their gloves aside and pick them up again when the opponents came to the plate, one that for decades kids mimicked at pick-up, sandlot, and high school games, would be no more...

- In 1955, his closest pursuer 21 points behind, 20-year old Al Kaline's .340 average earned him the title of youngest batting champ in MLB history. His outstanding offense AND defense earned Al the first of 13 consecutive All-Star berths and nationwide comparisons to Joltin' Joe DiMaggio. In a 1985 interview on WJR's "Focus" show, hosted by J.P. McCarthy, Mickey Mantle said that Al Kaline was the greatest player that he ever saw, adding for emphasis...

- On the eve of a series between the Tigers & Yankees, New York manager Casey Stengel was asked about a potential pitching match-up of Frank Lary vs. Whitey Ford. Casey replied, *"Naw, Whitey's not pitching against Frank Lary. He's gonna beat us anyway, so why waste Whitey?"* Frank "the Yankee Killer" Lary's 28 & 13 lifetime record against the Yankees included a 13 & 1 run during 1958 & 1959, God bless him...

- And then there was the night that Mickey Mantle & Bobby Layne went out to The Flame Bar...

- April 12, 1960, the Tigers trade Steve (not even Don) Demeter to the Cleveland Indians for Norm Cash – the Greatest Trade in Tiger History! When Tigers GM Rick Ferrell was initially offered *cash* for Demeter by Cleveland GM Frank Lane, he was surprised the Indians meant Norm & not the monetary kind...

- As a student at Alma College, Jim Northrup in '58 tossed a no-hitter against Calvin College, and in '59 was a small college All-American quarterback while 3rd in the entire USA in total offense

(1,538 yards). Both the NFL's Chicago Bears & the infant American Football League's New York Titans offered Jim contracts, but Northrup said, *"I was born to play baseball"*...

- In the 1965 All-Star game, Dick McAuliffe was at bat while Bill Freehan was in the bullpen talking to a National League catcher, who asked Bill, *"How the hell does a guy like McAuliffe hit with that type of stance?"* Before Bill could answer, Mac sent a pitch over the bullpen where the two were talking and into the stands for a 2-run homer. Freehan turned to his fellow catcher and said, *"Just like that"*...

- Gates Brown had just returned to the bench with two dogs, lathered up with mustard and ketchup, when Mayo Smith told him to grab a bat to pinch hit. Gates gobbled down one hot dog, shoved the 2nd one in his jersey, stepped up to the plate, and drove a pitch into the gap. In order to beat the throw to 2nd, Gates slid head first. The hot dog tucked near his waist had exploded into a rainbow of mustard yellow & ketchup red all over the front of his jersey...

- As the Tigers celebrated edging out Boston for the '72 East Division crown, Eddie Brinkman told sportscaster Dave Diles, *"Well, I'll tell you, it's a fantastic feeling, not so much for myself, but for the rest of the fuckin' guys.* Diles sent it back at the WXYZ studios, where anchorman Bill Bonds told listeners, *"People often ask me if Channel 7 is film or live. Well, it's live"*...

- Ron LeFlore was granted an early release from his sentence at Jackson State Prison to play for the Tigers, reporting to the farm club in Clinton, Iowa. Tiger veterans were amazed at Ron's speed, except Norm Cash, *"He can't be too fast, the cops caught him"*...

- In 1974, Norm Cash finished his career with 373 home runs. Only 3 left-handers in American League history had more homers: Babe Ruth, Ted Williams, and Lou Gehrig...

- From 1963-1975, Mickey Lolich & Bill Freehan teamed up to form a pitcher-catcher "battery" 324 times, the all-time MLB record. Lolich-Freehan is the only battery in the top ten of longevity that has neither member in the Hall of Fame...

- Reggie Jackson thought Lolich the best left-hander he'd ever seen. *"Every time I played Detroit, I had to face the son of a bitch. His fastball could knock your ass off. When he took the mound at 1PM you knew he would be there until the end. I wish he had gone into the donut business 10 years earlier"*...

- The '75 last place Tigers were awful and the outlook for 1976 was not encouraging. But baseball has a funny way of unexpectedly lifting you up just when things seem at their lowest. Who could have foreseen that 1976 would provide an emotional phenomenon that would last Tiger fans a lifetime? A quirky young man from Massachusetts, unknown to all but the most knowledgeable fans, was about to change our lives...

- Rusty Staub is the only player in major league history to have over 500 hits for 4 different teams, and one of only 4 (including Ty Cobb) to have homered before he was 20 & after he was 40. We loved to watch him tip-toe into 2nd after yet another RBI double...

- Trammell & Sweet Lou both had such an outstanding '78 spring training that Manager Ralph Houk had no choice but to bring the two north with the parent club, their first full season in the Show. Houk said, *"It's the damnedest thing. You tell one of them something & he says, 'We can do it.' Like they're a team"*...

- During the '81 strike, baseball writers were searching for ways to fill their columns. One of the most unusual stories highlighted Richie Hebner resuming his off-season grave digging job. Hebner said as a young man his father once criticized his work, complaining the boy was digging graves too shallow. Richie defense was, *"I never saw anyone get up from one of 'em"*...

- While the '84 World Series winners celebrate on the field, in the San Diego dugout Champ Summers is the only Padre sitting on the top step, taking in all the commotion in the ballpark where he had the best playing days of his career and was a Detroit fan favorite. There is a sad look in Champ's eyes, likely because his team just lost the Series, but perhaps thinking he could be, should be, out there celebrating with his old Tiger teammates, had he not been traded for...

- A sign above the visitor's clubhouse read, *"Visitors Clubhouse / No Visitors Allowed"*...

- Brian "Life" Vittes of Oak Park found no charge parking north of I-75. During the game, he was touting the virtues of his decision versus paying $3 to park at Irene Sember's, or any other pay-to-park, lot. No more forking over cash to park on game day for him. Meeting at a friend's later that same day, Life arrived a bit tardy, cursing *"the addicts who knocked out my driver's side window to get $3 in change,"* ironically the exact cost to park at Irene Sember's lot...

- '87 rookie Jim Walewander saw his favorite punk rock band, *The Dead Milkmen*, play in Hamtramck, and invited the Milkmen to the next day's Tiger game, where they posed with Sparky Anderson on the dugout steps. Sparky said later, *"One of them had on combat boots, a camouflage army shirt, and an earring. I told him, 'Son, don't take no prisoners'"*...

- As Detroit took the field for ALCS '87 game 1 at the Minneapolis Metrodome, they were greeted by jet-engine decibel sound levels. The crowd noise was described in the *L.A. Times* as, *"54,223 Scandinavian James Browns"*...

- Many of Cecil Fielder's homers, said Sparky Anderson, went *"where the big boys hit 'em."* Alan Trammell said, *"As soon as he steps to the plate, he's in scoring position."* The man known as Big Daddy led the league in RBIs from 1990 thru 1992, joining Ty Cobb and Babe Ruth as the only players with three consecutive RBI titles in American League history...

- Ann Arbor comedy troupe the Stunt Johnson Theatre penned a play entitled *"Bo & Woody"* featuring Woody Hayes coming back from the dead & instructing Bo Schembechler to do all sorts of stupid things, firing Ernie Harwell at the top of the list...

- '92... *The Good News*: Jack Morris is once again pitching at The Corner on Opening Day! *The Bad News*: he's pitching for the Toronto Blue Jays. *The Real Bad News*: the Tigers banned stadium smoking, so no more White Owl cigars while cheering on our Tigers. *Tech News*: Detroit began taking credit card ticket orders...

- At the 25-year anniversary of the 1968 Champions, Dick Tracewski told a TV reporter that Dick McAuliffe was the real leader of the '68 team. Mac was standing nearby & replied, *"Well, they always followed me into the bar, if that's what he means"*...

- On September 13, 1995, Lou Whitaker & Alan Trammell played their 1,915th game together as a double play combination, setting a new American League record. The Tigers won this day on Sweet Lou's 3-run, walk-off homer...

- Walt Terrell said of Sparky Anderson, *"I remember one time in the 8th inning, I had given up 4 runs or so when he came out to get me. He took two or three steps onto the field and I said, 'What took you so long?' And he said, 'I was in the bathroom. I didn't know you were getting beat so bad'"*...

- Joe Diroff had two big, bushy, eyebrows that met right above his nose, creating one huge, arching eyebrow, inspiring his nickname "the Brow". There's Brow hoping around on one leg, trying to get the folks fired up to cheer on our Boys of Summer, *"Strawberry Shortcake, Gooseberry Pie, V-I-C-T-O-R-Y!!!"* *"Brow,"* said Kirk Gibson, *"you're a true fan"*...

- On June 7, 1997 at The Corner, the 2nd night in a week that Tiger pitcher Justin Thompson struck out Ken Griffey Junior 3 times, 1 mile away the Detroit Red Wings were completing a four-game sweep of the Philadelphia Flyers to win their first Stanley Cup in 42 years...

- Early in the morning of September 27, 1999, Todd Jones awoke on his cot in the darken Detroit Tiger clubhouse. As someone who loves the history of baseball, Todd decided how cool it would be, on the night before the final game ever at The Corner, to sleep in Tiger Stadium...

- On 9.27.99, that Final Morning at The Corner, a roar spread through the growing crowd outside the stadium's walls. Their cheering was at the sight of the big convertible slowly making its way south on Trumbull towards Michigan Avenue, with Gordie & Colleen Howe smiling 'n waving from the front seat. Gordie had been a big Tiger fan since...

- For the Final Game, all current Tigers wore the uniform numbers of famous Tigers of the past. At the moment TV announcer Frank Beckmann told viewers, *"Here's Robert Fick, wearing Norm Cash's 25. Remember, Al Kaline told him that* (wearing Norm's number) *he'd hit a home run today"*, Rob belted it down the first base line, high into the now dark early-evening...

- As Tiger Stadium closed in 1999, Ernie Harwell wanted to take home a clubhouse urinal to use in the yard as a planter. Lulu Harwell said no.

"It's just two guys playing catch."

That was the assessment my Father, Herbert Roy Fletcher, had of the game of baseball. He felt the excitement level of the game paled in comparison to that of football, specifically that provided by his beloved Detroit Lions and their quarterback, the wildly-popular Bobby Layne, a leader of men both on and off the field… *"I ain't drunk, I'm from Texas"* is how Bobby described his condition behind the wheel to the judge, who accepted that explanation as completely reasonable coming from Layne. Dad and his Wayne State/Delta Nu fraternity brother, Hank Nickol, had Briggs Stadium season tickets to the Lions starting in the 1950s – the decade in which both the Lions (National Football League champions '52, '53 & '57) and Herb & Hank (as 20-somethings) were in their prime. It wasn't just that the Lions won championships, although that alone would create a life-long bond with fans, but it was the amazing ability to rally from behind to victory, propelled by the spectacular Robert Lawrence "Bobby" Layne, time & time again, that drove their followers to frenzied heights of excitement.

The one Tigers' era that moved Dad to reminisce fondly about baseball was the 1930s, when as a very young boy, he and his father, my Grandpa Roy Fletcher, would cheer Mickey Cochrane, aka Black Mike, the Detroiters' hard-driving catcher-manager, the team's G-Men – Greenberg, Gehringer & Goslin – and the rough 'n tumble shortstop Billy Rogell, in the 1934 World Series. There the Tigers fell just short, with redemption awaiting one year later as Cochrane emphatically jumped on home plate with the '35 World Series clinching run in game 6. As great as pitchers Schoolboy Rowe and submarine-style Elden Auker were, it was the slightly-built Tommy Bridges, a bulldog of a competitor and Grandpa Fletcher's favorite Tiger (& so a very special player to me), who was on the mound in the 1935 Series deciding game.

Detroit and the entire state of Michigan exploded in celebration with that '35 victory, people pouring into the streets, lining up at the downtown bars, shouting themselves hoarse, hugging strangers, as the cares of the Great Depression were temporarily forgotten. That was a level of sports fan euphoria for Detroiters unmet until the success of the Bobby Layne football teams.

The memories of the Lions domination of the 1950s was still fresh when, in 1965, despite his dour view of the Great Game of Baseball, Dad finally agreed to take me, his 10-year old son, to see the Tigers in person. I would attend many Lions games with Dad, but it took the arrival at Michigan & Trumbull of the great Mickey Mantle and his Damn Yankee teammates, to get us to my first-ever Tigers' game.

It was a night game, the field a shade of green that was the most beautiful color I'd ever seen, the smells, sounds, and sights of the pre-game action delightfully overwhelming… the air filled with the bouquet of hot dogs, spilt beer, and a cigar aroma much like that of the *House of Windsor* stogies preferred by my Dad. Cries of the vendors peddling those items pierced the air, while cutting through the excited crowd murmur was a toe-tappin' jazz sound created deep in centerfield by the musicians of Merle Alvey's "Tigers Dixieland Band", the 5-man band looking spiffy in their red & white striped shirts. Several Tigers were engaged in a game of pepper along the box seats down the rightfield foul line, as nearby Bill Freehan tossed a ball back 'n forth with a teammate, entertaining the fans by playfully catching the ball behind his back.

Dad and I sat between home plate and 1st base in the lower deck behind the Yankee dugout. Our initial disappointment of Mantle's absence in the starting line-up turned into the game's big moment: to a loud combination of cheers, shouts, and boos from the Tiger faithful, emerging from the dugout in front of us, swinging a couple of bats, the famous number 7 was pinch hitting. It was Mickey versus Mickey, with Mantle pinch-hitting against Lolich in what was, in the sixth, a tense 2 – 1 game, favor Tigers.

Lolich rocks and fires. Mantle does not move as that first pitch flies by – a called strike. Mick steps out of the batters' box, staring at the ground for a few seconds, then steps back in. Here comes the 2nd pitch, again the bat does not leave Mantle's shoulder, and again the ump cries *"Stee-rike!"* Mick calls time, walks away from the plate, stares at the ground for what this time feels like a full half-a-minute, every eye in the Old Ballyard glued to the legend as the stadium shakes from their full-throated joy. Number 7 steps back into the box, Lolich winds up and pitches... Mantle still does not swing his bat, but the ump decides it's *"Stee-rike 3!"*

It is now deafening at The Corner. But Mantle is not moving. He just stands there, looking down at the plate. Then slowly, but very meticulously, Mantle begins to cover home plate by pushing dirt over it with his cleats, the crowd roaring their approval. With Mick's grounds-keeping done, the plate completely buried, he calmly walks back to the dugout, while the ump – who has not moved &, as far as we can tell, not said a word (except *"Stee-rike!"*) – intently watches him. Mantle has by now disappeared into the dugout right in front of us. And then, before the next batter can step in, here comes from the Yankee dugout one cleated shoe that goes flying 20' straight up in the air. The ump continues to wordlessly watch. Then the 2nd shoe follows straight up into the night air, just like a Jerry Lumpe pop-up with runners in scoring position. Every single person in the stands will be hoarse tomorrow, but they are howling tonight! Finally, Mick's bat, following the route of his cleats, comes flying up and out of the dugout... and the umpire emphatically gives Number Seven the thumb heave-ho, the stadium girders quaking from the pandemonium!

The runs the Tigers tack on for the final 6 to 1 victory over the Damn Yankees is almost – *almost* – of secondary importance to the unforgettable show Mantle put on for us all. What an incredible initial visit to The Corner - great choice Dad!

Dedication

To my Dad, who took me to my first game at The Corner.

To my Mom who, before we left for the game, kissed her husband & 10-year old son good-bye.

1887 – 1894 Detroit Wolverines

Oh, me name it is O'Houlihan, I'm a man that in-flu-en-tial;
I mind my business, stay at home, me wants are few and small;
But the other day a gang did come, they were filled with whiskey, gin and rum
And they took me out in the broiling sun to play a game of ball

("The Day That I Played Baseball" by Mike Dean, circa 1878)

Before there was baseball at Michigan & Trumbull, there was the 1887 Detroit Wolverines, the city's first professional ballclub. Initially known as *the Detroits*, the team existed as a National League franchise from 1881 to 1888, playing their home games at Recreation Park, located at the junction of Brush & Brady. The franchise was stripped from Cincinnati & awarded to Detroit in 1880 when Cincy refused to (1) stop scheduling well-attended Sunday dates & (2) cease selling liquor at their games. The move to Detroit made sense as religious and civic leaders wanted to shut down both activities in Cincy, and it's a well-known fact that Detroiters avoid liquor on Sundays.

Also-rans during Detroit's initial 6 years of play, something special began to happen in year seven...

The hospital doctors were becoming suspicious. As the summer of 1887 dragged on, there had been a sharp increase in the number of patients checking into Detroit's Harper Hospital. Mostly men, these folk seemed like the type that would have to be on death's doorstep before walking into the front door of a hospital, but the vast majority had no outward symptoms that would seem to require medical attention. In addition, visitors to the hospital's patients rose to numbers several times beyond what the staff had ever previously seen, with an unusually large number of these men. Not only that, but after a brief visit to the patient in question, the visiting males would spend most of their hospital time on the Harper roof.

Among baseball fans in Detroit, whose numbers were growing by leaps and bounds in '87 - *winning 49 of your first 51 games will do that* - it had become an open secret that the upper floors & the rooftop of Harper Hospital offered a spectacular view of the field at Recreation Park, the home of the National League-leading Detroit Wolverines, the view being the cure for Detroiters' baseball-itis.

The Detroit Wolverines embarked on a pre-season tear that can never be exceeded, winning all 30 of their exhibition games. Once the regular season began, the Detroit 9 hardly missed a beat, comfortably occupying first place the Saturday of Memorial Day (then *Decoration Day*) weekend, with 19 wins & 2 losses.

Those 1887 Detroit Wolverines were led by 4 future Hall-Of-Famers: outfielder Sam Thompson (batting a league-leading .372 with an astounding 166 runs batted in), first-baseman Dan Brouthers (.338/team-leading 12 home runs/101 RBIs/league-leading 153 runs), third-baseman Deacon White (.303/75 RBIs), and player/manager Ned Hanlon (69 stolen bases). The fifth & sixth cogs to the hitting machine were outfielder Hardy Richardson (.328/94 RBIs) and shortstop Jack Rowe (.318/96 RBIs).

The team was an offensive dynamo, setting the National League record with 969 runs scored in the 124-game season. When you average 8 runs scored per game and your pitching staff is giving up less than 4, that's a recipe for success the Wolverines rode to a 79 and 45 first-place finish.

The supporting cast featured the ace of the pitching staff, (tie 'em in) Pretzels Getzein (29 & 13 with 41 complete games), and his battery-mate, catcher Charlie Bennett, who played on the team during every one of the Wolverines' 8 years in existence (Ned Hanlon the only other player with that distinction).

Charlie Bennett was one of the most beloved Detroit ball players of all-time and namesake of Bennett Park, the home of Detroit baseball from 1896 to 1911. Women adored Charlie at least as much as the men did – when Bennett opened a cigar shop in the city, it's estimated that one-half of all women in Detroit took up cigar smoking. Charlie was a handsome fella, think of Kurt Russell as Wyatt Earp in "Tombstone", and immensely likeable. The widely-held admiration Detroiters felt for Charlie wasn't hurt by the fact that, when Detroit was awarded their National League franchise before the 1881 season, Charlie not only was the team's first player, but became so by turning down more money from the well-established Boston Red Sox aka Red Stockings aka Beaneaters. The Boston team was an 1876 National League charter member, a 2-time champion by 1881, and based in a big city with 3 times the population of Detroit. In other words, Charlie Bennett picked the younger, down-home, small town over the older, stuffy, city slickers. He was first exposed to Detroit while playing for the minor league Detroit Aetnas in 1876 and he thought highly of the experience, the town, and its people, and it's no exaggeration to say that those very same people adored him.

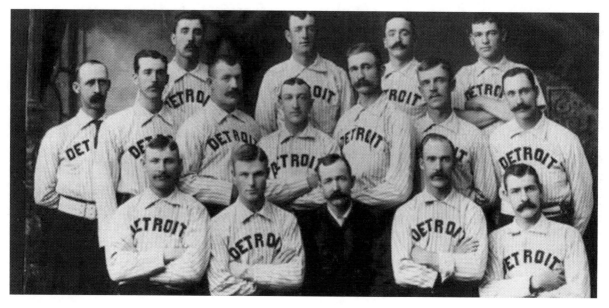

The 1887 Detroit Wolverines: back – Jack Rowe, Pete Conway, Ned Hanlon, Edward Beaton; middle – Deacon White, Harold Sutcliffe, Dan Brouthers, Henry Gruber, Sam Thompson, Charles Ganzel, Charles "Lady" Baldwin; front – Charles "Pretzels" Getzein, Larry Twitchell, manager Bill Watkins, Hardy Richardson, Charlie Bennett

Although Charlie was only 32 in 1887, 32 was old for an 1880s catcher. Though considered the dominant defensive catcher of his time, he had been playing that position for over a decade and, in an era when catcher's gloves were not yet used, a decade was a long time. A season of balls fouled off by batters, year after year, bent, broke, and bloodied fingers & hands, and by '87 the injuries slowed Charlie's big bat & limited his playing time. Bennett was, however, able to avoid broken ribs by designing the first chest protector ever used, wearing it beneath his shirt to avoid opposing fans questioning his manhood.

Even without Bennett's usual offensive production, the 1887 Detroit Wolverines packed plenty of punch, completing their extraordinary season by defeating the St. Louis Browns of the American

Association in the 4th ever World Series. Taking down the Browns was an impressive feat. St. Louis, led by manager/first baseman Charlie Comiskey, future owner of the Chicago White Sox, were champions of the two previous World Series and considered the finest team in all of baseball.

The Series of 1887 was very different than those of today, a best-of-15 affair (ending 10-5 favor Detroit) played in cities throughout the two leagues. Game 13 was the first scheduled to be played in Detroit. By then the Wolverines had already clinched the Series, and a special moment had been planned for Charlie. Well before the Series, fans had been collecting funds for a gift: in honor of his years with Detroit and all that he meant to the town, Bennett was presented with a wheelbarrow loaded with 520 silvers dollars (the equivalent of a full season's salary). The crowd stood & cheered, chanting Charlie's name, growing even louder when he came out on to the field. Shouting his thanks and waving his cap to all in attendance, Charlie then - at the crowd's urging – grabbed on to the wheelbarrow and pushed it around the base-paths to the fans' delight, while a trailing marching band added to the festive feel.

Much of the cheering was from just outside of Recreation Park, emanating from "wildcat stands", seats atop the homes and barns of private citizens. The cost of tickets to these seats was paid by fans to homeowners, of course, and not to the baseball team owners. The modern date analogy of the wildcat stands vis-à-vis Recreation Park would be the rooftop stands surrounding Wrigley Field at Cubs games. In Detroit, the wildcat stands would be a thorn in the side of the owners of various Detroit baseball clubs from the 1880s until Navin Field replaced Bennett Park in 1912 (the Cubs, after years of lawsuits and threats, reached a détente with the rooftop owners, and now get a cut of the rooftop tickets income).

Although they could not have foreseen it as the splendid magic of 1887 unfolded, baseball-mad fans of Detroit would have to wait almost half-a-century until the next Championship Season.

1888 saw the team plummet from Champions to fifth place. The pitching staff was great, as the team ERA dropped from 3.95 in '87 to 2.74, and Pete Conway had a career year at 30 & 14 with a 2.26 ERA. But while the pitchers gave up one run less per game, injuries and prolonged slumps effected just about every hitter's performance versus 1887 – except Charlie Bennett's. Despite being almost ancient for a catcher, Bennett broke his own record with a .966 fielding percentage and had the third highest on-base-percentage on the team, trailing only Dan Brouthers and Sam Thompson. Faced with a drop in ticket income, almost impossible to maintain against 1887's enormous fan appetite for seats, along with the money drain of high salary stars, ownership decided to fold the team. Several top players, including Charlie Bennett, were sold off to the Boston Red Sox – ironically, the team that Charlie rebuffed so that he could play for Detroit in 1881.

A number of teams from the minor leagues and amateur athletic clubs called Detroit home, keeping baseball fans entertained after the Wolverines were dissolved. The first steps back to the major leagues for Detroit took place in 1894 when Ban Johnson, the man who would go on to be the 1901 founder & first president of the American League, welcomed the city as a minor league franchise of his Western League. George Vanderbeck, the owner of the new Detroit team, was more showman than substance. As author Richard Bak so beautifully put it in his book, *A Place For Summer, "There appears to have been something about him that made a man want to count his fingers after a handshake."* Whether snake or just misunderstood, Vanderbeck can be credited with deciding to move the team from League Park, at Lafayette & E. Grand Boulevard (east of downtown & near Belle Island), to just west of downtown at an old hay market site located at The Corner of Michigan & Trumbull.

1895 – 1905 Bennett Park; Greatest 9th Inning Comeback Ever!

The Corner now so famous, began another way
The farmers drove to market, and there they sold their hay
From the dirt and cobblestones, an origin so humble
Emerged the famous Corner of Michigan & Trumbull

("Michigan & Trumbull" written & sung by Ernie Harwell)

As George Vanderbeck's minor league Detroit team opened play in 1895, they were known by two names, the Creams and the Tigers. The "Creams" moniker stemmed from Vanderbeck's assertion that his players would be *"the cream of the league"*. The "Tigers" byname had been associated with the city for 40 years, in connection with the community pride in the *Detroit Light Guard*. The Light Guard was heavily populated by the town's leading citizens, serving as both a social and a military society. Founded in 1855, the Light Guard had brought great honor to Detroit for their battlefield bravery in many of the most famous Civil War campaigns. Subsequent newspaper accounts of their exploits referred to them as "Tigers", and soon a tiger head insignia was added to all things related to the Detroit Light Guard and, over time, became the unofficial logo of the city and its baseball team.

1895 Haymarket at Michigan (east/west in foreground) & Trumbull –
the Tigers final year playing at League Park near Belle Isle

For the Creams, or the Tigers, 1895 home opener, the ceremonial first pitch was delivered by Civil War veteran and Mayor of Detroit, Hazen Pingree. The city never had a greater representative of its people. Pingree's leadership during the difficult economic times of the 1890s led to his being elected mayor four times and twice governor of Michigan, and the construction of a statue commemorating him as "The Idol of the People" in Grand Circus Park. As popular as Hazen Pingree was, it was the man receiving his 1895 first pitch that received the crowd's loudest cheers, retired baseball player, Charlie Bennett.

Charlie Bennett's final pro baseball season was in 1893. While boarding a train that winter, he slipped & slid beneath the train, his left foot & right leg below the knee crushed by its wheels, his baseball career over. The recovering Bennett received letters of support from all over the country, and his stoic attitude and good humor throughout brought him even greater adoration than during his time as an 1800s

Detroit Wolverine ballplayer. When he made his way to home plate to catch the 1895 Opening Day first pitch from Hazen Pingree, the fans went wild. The next pitch that Charlie would catch would be one year later, in a new ballpark with a familiar name.

April 28, 1896, Opening Day for the Detroit Tigers of the Western League, was the first ballgame ever played at The Corner of Michigan & Trumbull. The ballpark was built on the site of the former Western Hay Market and just to the east of the old Western Market (merging into Eastern Market in 1895), and would be the Tigers' home from 1896 to 1911. The new 5,000 seat wooden structure was named after the most popular man in all of Detroit, Charlie Bennett. Brand spanking new Bennett Park was filled to capacity, plus an additional 1,000 behind ropes & on trees (8 oak & elm combined) in the outfield, as Charlie walked slowly on his two artificial legs to home plate to catch the ceremonial first pitch. Every fan in the park was on their feet, many with tears in their eyes, cheering Bennett on. Charlie caught the first pitch at every Tigers' Opening Day, from 1895 through 1926, until passing away at age 72, two months before the 1927 opener. On September 27, 1999, at the conclusion of the final Tigers' game ever to be played at The Corner, George Campbell, Bennett's great-nephew, took the mound & threw a pitch to the 1999 starting Tiger catcher (and future Tiger manager), Brad Ausmus. The ball that Charlie Bennett's great-nephew tossed was used for the first pitch at the 2000 opener in new Comerica Park.

It was a glorious Opening Day in 1896. After the first pitch to Bennett, canons thundered to herald the new era of baseball at The Corner. Team captain & outfielder George Stallings hit the inaugural home run in the new park, aided by one of the fans in the crowd that overflowed on to the field of play. That spectator collided with the opposing outfielder tracking Stallings' drive as it was coming back to earth, temporarily knocking both men unconscious as the ball fell harmlessly to the outfield turf while the Tigers captain touched 'em all, just another memorable moment as the Tigers rolled over the Columbus, Ohio 9 in a 17 to 2 shellacking.

DDDDDDDDDDDDDDDDDDDDDDDDDDDDDDDDDDDDDDDDDDDDDDDDDDDDDDDDDDDDDDDDDDDDDDDDDD

Although minor league in name, the Detroit Creams aka Tigers and the other Western League franchises were pulling larger & larger crowds as the 1890s drew to a close, sometimes eclipsing in size those drawn by some in the "majors" of the National League. The National League & Western League worked together under a "National Agreement" that allowed Western players to be drafted by National clubs, that player's Western club financially reimbursed, and kept the Western League from expanding into National markets. When the N.L. reduced their franchises from 12 to 8 in 1899, one-third of their ball players had no team. The Western League, renamed the American League, now made their move. They picked up many of these National-Leaguers-without-a-home, improving the product they put on the field, moved small market teams into the larger markets of Chicago, Boston, & Philadelphia where National League teams existed, and at the end of 1900 declared themselves the 2nd major league.

Even before the Tigers magically turned from a minor to a major league team, there was a man who wore the Detroit uniform & considered by many to be the greatest pitcher of all-time, George Edward "Rube" Waddell. Rube played for Detroit just one season, in 1898, and in that year established a Western League record by striking out 11 batters in one game.

None other than Connie Mack, one of the most-highly respected baseball minds of all-time, a man whose association with the game covered 65 years, from player, manager, team executive to owner, said that Rube Waddell had more natural ability than any pitcher he had ever seen. At over 6' tall,

Waddell towered over other players of his time and, with a blazing fastball and an-almost-as-fast knee-bending curve, was virtually untouchable *when he was focused*. And therein lies the Rube, or the rub.

Perfect for a man born on Friday the 13th and leaving us on April Fools' Day, Waddell was unfocused, erratic, unreliable, and childlike, prone to wander off the field at the slightest to the most substantial distraction. His exploits were legendary and fascinated the public. As Rube was once preparing to pitch, he exited the mound and the ballpark in full flight, chasing after a clanging fire truck that drove by. He missed starts for reasons including busy fishing, shooting marbles with street kids, wrestling an alligator, bitten by a lion, and – although possibly uninvited - leading a street parade in Jacksonville, Florida one spring training.

These and other Waddell adventures were the reasons that Rube lasted only one year with Detroit in the minors, and why major league teams were so reticent to take a chance on him. Eventually though, his talent was found to be irresistible, and Rube lasted 13 seasons with 5 teams in the majors. Waddell's greatest success was from 1902 to 1907 with Connie Mack's Philadelphia Athletics. It took a man with Mack's legendary patience to get the full potential out of Rube, and Waddell's return on the investment was immediate & incredible: when he joined Philadelphia in late-June 1902, the team was 2 games over .500; Rube won 24 games for them during the season's final 3 months (his 10 wins in one month, July, has never been matched) and the Athletics finished 30 games over .500 in winning their first American League pennant. Waddell retired with 193 wins, a 2.16 ERA (10th all-time), 50 shutouts, over 300 strikeouts twice, & induction into the Hall of Fame. His 349 strikeouts in 1903, at 8.39 per every 9 innings, was the all-time record until Sandy Koufax whiffed 382 in 1965. It remains the all-time record for left-handers.

Rube Waddell was more than an immature, wild child, spectacular pitcher. He saved a woman from drowning, toured the nation acting in a stage play, asked that one year's salary be paid him in $1 bills to curb his impulsive spending, regularly assisted fire fighters on bucket brigades and ran into burning buildings multiple times to rescue people. When he died, it was due to complications from tuberculosis contracted after spending hours in armpit-deep freezing water while placing sand bags in front of flood waters from a destroyed dam in his efforts to help save a small town.

Out of many memorable games Rube pitched in, arguably the most noteworthy took place on the 4th of July in 1905, a 20-inning duel vs. Boston's Cy Young, both pitchers going the distance in the A's 4 to 2 victory. True to wacky form, after the final out, Rube joyously performed cartwheels off of the mound. Surrounded by boisterous fans post-game in a favorite watering hole, Rube bartered the game ball for free drinks for the house.

Tiger Sam Crawford said of his contemporary, *"Rube was one of a kind — just a big kid, you know. He'd pitch one day and we wouldn't see him for three or four days after. He'd just disappear, go fishing or something, or be off playing ball with a bunch of twelve-year-olds in an empty lot somewhere. You couldn't control him 'cause he was just a big kid himself. Baseball was just a game to Rube."*

DDDDDDDDDDDDDDDDDDDDDDDDDDDDDDDDDDDDDDDDDDDDDDDDDDDDDDDDDDDDDDDDDDDDDDDDDDDDDDDDD

James D. Burns was an Irishman who owned an extremely popular tavern on 14 Michigan Avenue at Woodward. His regulars included ball players & their presence agreed with him, a comfort level that may have contributed to Burns decision to buy the Tigers from Vanderbeck in 1900. It wasn't the first business transaction between Burns & Vanderbeck. In 1899, Vanderbeck agreed to allow Burns to use Bennett Park for a social gathering, may have had second thoughts, and at the appointed date Burns found the park padlocked. A locked gate isn't much of an obstruction between a thirsty Irishman and his good time, and James D. Burns always enjoyed a challenge. He had somebody locate an axe for him, and soon the invitees were stepping over the remains of what once was a gate, and a good time had by all.

In 1901, his 2nd season of ownership, Burns' team began the season for the first time as a major league squad, in its 6th season of play at Bennett Park. The park was on the same acreage as its eventual Navin Field/Briggs/Tiger Stadium replacement, but Bennett Park was positioned differently. The park's home plate was in the sun field, Tiger Stadium's right-field corner aka "Kaline's Corner". With the usual 330PM starting times at the turn of the last century, the late-afternoon sun could be brutal on hitters. Although it wouldn't change the sun-in-the-eyes issue, in preparation for its first game as a major league field, Bennett Park increased its capacity from 5,000 to 8,500 by adding outfield bleacher seats.

April 25, 1901 was a historic day at The Corner of Michigan & Trumbull, the inaugural Home Opener for the major league version of the Detroit Tigers. It was a gorgeous, sunny, warm April day, described by the *Detroit Tribune* as, *"A day to make a well man glad to be alive, and a sick man feel the tingle of returning health."* Over 10,000 fans shoehorned their way into the 8,500-seat capacity wooden park, accommodated by ownership allowing them to fill the space between the outfield bleacher seats and the outfielders themselves. The police were busy keeping out the fanatics without tickets, who tried climbing over or burrowing under the wooden fences. Before game time, thousands of these same fans joined a marching band, as well as players from both the visiting Milwaukee team and the home town Detroiters, in a parade down Michigan Avenue to The Corner.

The euphoria of the day began to dissipate as the game moved on and the Milwaukee Brewers badly outplayed our nine, the home team down 7 to nothing after only 3 innings of play. A few seats had been vacated by the time the Tigers came to bat in the bottom of the 9th, a majority of the faithful staying put. The combination of Brewer hitting and 7 Tiger errors had the home team facing a 13 to 4 deficit with only 3 outs remaining. Reporting the drama was the *Detroit Free Press, "The Tigers went at it with a determination that was admirable, and those who remained saw one of the greatest finishes ever made on a baseball diamond."* **In fact, it was THE greatest 9th inning comeback in major league history.**

The turnaround started one at bat at a time, with the aid of the overflow crowd standing in the outfield. Leading off, captain & 3rd sacker Doc Casey drove a fly ball into the crowd, counted as a ground-rule double. When outfielder Jimmy Barrett, 2nd baseman (& future 1919 Black Sox manager) Kid Gleason, and outfielder Ducky Holmes followed with hits, the score stood at 13 to 6, there were no outs, and due up was first baseman Pop Dillon. The big left-hander was Detroit's hottest hitter today with a home run and a double. As Dillon stepped up to the plate, the crowd was now fully engaged, the noise causing horses to rear up outside the park walls. *"Cracckk!"* and it's another double, 2 more runs in. 13 to 8.

When Shortstop Kid Elberfeld doubles, the lead is down to four. The bedlam in the ballpark was clearly audible beyond The Corner, drawing the early departing faithful back inside, people running towards Bennett Park from all directions. It seemed that the crowd now numbered well beyond the 10,023 paid, and the fans had to be pushed back from the Milwaukee outfielders by the Tiger players themselves. After the Brewers finally recorded the first out, catcher Fritz Buelow drew a walk and Emil Frisk, though a pitcher, the man with the highest average on the team this year at .313, singled. 13-10 with one out.

The next day's *Free Press* told its readers, *"At this stage of the game hats were being thrown in the air, coats were flying and everyone was yelling themselves hoarse."*

The batting order had now turned over, and Doc Casey laid down a bunt single. With the bases loaded, the house groaned as Jimmy Barrett went down on strikes. The Tigers are down to their last out, and up steps Kid Gleason. The Brewer third baseman couldn't handle Gleason's hard grounder, another run is in. 13-11, two outs, and runners on every base. Ducky Holmes digs in and just like Gleason before him, sends a grounder too hot to handle to third, as pitcher Frisk crosses home with the 12th run. And once again, here's the man with the smoking bat today, Pop Dillon, at the plate. Dillon sends a deep fly ball into the overflow outfield crowd, the tying & winning runs cross home plate as it seems like all 10,000 plus cover the field and engulf their heroes, especially seeking out Pop Dillon. The *Free Press* told the story, *"The big first baseman was almost torn to pieces by the fans and finally he was picked up and carried around on the shoulders of some of the excited spectators."* The competing *Detroit Tribune* was impressive in their expressive, *"The riotously jubilant vocalization of 10,000 throats let loose in one simultaneous sub-aerial explosion, making the old earth's enveloping atmosphere heave and billow clear to its surface 50 miles away, and no doubt it is tumultuous yet."*

Pop Dillon, 1901 Opener Hero

Wire reports with game updates had been making their way across Lake Michigan to Fred Gross, in the front offices of the Milwaukee Brewers. Just as Fred was ready to send a happy telegram of victory to team president Matthew Killilea, he received a phone call stating that the Tigers had won. Gross assured the caller that surely he was mistaken, as Fred held a wire with the score going into the bottom of the ninth, and a Detroit victory would've required the Tigers to score 10 runs in their last at bat. Since the caller had personally witnessed the greatest 9th inning comeback ever, Gross concluded that, *"The men all must be injured for a team to make ten runs in one inning (against them). I will wire Manager Duffy to take care of the men until they recover."* Even Dr. Sheldon Cooper could have identified this sarcasm.

For those in attendance Opening Day 1901, the miracle 10-run, bottom of the ninth rally, would be told and retold over many beers, over many years. Down 13 to 4 with only 3 outs left, yet somehow winning 14-13... if the Tigers could win under those circumstances, anything was possible. Indeed, playing for manager George Stallings, who as team captain & outfielder in 1896 hit the inaugural home run at The Corner, the 1901 Tigers had a knack for electrifying come-from-behind wins. While subsequent rallies were not on the level of the amazing Opening Day feat, the fans learned not to leave until the last out, no matter how far behind their Boys of Summer were on the scoreboard.

Although not the American League champions in 1901, Detroit had a successful first year on the field as a major league entity, finishing the season at 74 & 61 in third place, 8 & 1/2 games behind the first place Chicago White Stockings. Besides timely hitting, the '01 Tigers also had the finest rookie pitcher in the American League, Roscoe Miller. Although roughed up for 7 runs in the Tigers amazing Opening Day win, Roscoe rebounded nicely and had a record of 23 & 13 and 2.95 ERA (this was Roscoe's career year – he would no longer be a Tiger by the following July, and out of the game after 1904). Over a quarter-million came out to Bennett Park in 1901, greater attendance than 3/4s of all major league franchises.

The fun didn't last. The Tigers lost more than they won in each of the next 3 seasons, ending 1902 in 7th place in the 8-team A.L., 5th place 1903, and bottoming out with 90-losses in 1904, as only the awful 38 and 113 Washington Senators kept Detroit out of the basement. But help was on the way...

- Beginning in 1902, pitcher George Mullin spent 13 seasons wearing the Olde English D, winning 228 games (69th in MLB history) with a 2.82 ERA. Unlike most pitchers, on the days when Mullin played, there was an extra bat with punch in the line-up. For his career, George Mullin hit .262.
- From 1903 through 1912, pitcher "Wild" Bill Donovan starred for Detroit. Including his pre-1903 time in the National League, plus a 2-game/1-win return as a 41-year old in 1918, he won 185 games with an excellent 2.69 ERA (78th MLB all-time).
- After the 1902 season, a 22-year old that had been tearing up National League pitching for 4 years decided to jump to the A.L. Tigers. Wahoo Sam Crawford was just getting started.

In 1905, the Tigers spring training, held in Shreveport, Louisiana the previous two years, relocated to Augusta, Georgia. To help Detroit prepare for the upcoming regular season, two exhibition games were played against the minor league Augusta Tourists. It was during those two games that the Tigers were introduced to a raw but talented young man, Ty Cobb.

The fortunes of the Detroit Tigers had just changed in a big way.

1906 - 1911 Tyrus Raymond Cobb

The Tigers, new & feisty, took over Bennett Park
Crawford, Cobb, & Jennings, lit a civic spark
The quiet corner came alive, the town began to rumble
Baseball soon became the rage, at Michigan & Trumbull

("Michigan & Trumbull" written & sung by Ernie Harwell)

Throughout the 1970s & 1980s, arguably the best judge of talent in baseball was Bill Lajoie. During those 2 decades, serving the Tigers in roles including Scouting Director, Assistant General Manager, & General Manager, Lajoie was a major force in drafting & otherwise assembling the roster that made up the 1984 World Series Champs.

But before there was Bill Lajoie, there was Ed Barrow.

In 1896, at 28 years of age, Ed Barrow became co-owner of a Patterson, New Jersey franchise in the Atlantic League. In his first year of searching for talent to stock the team, Barrow discovered and signed a young infielder he'd seen play ball in Steubenville, Ohio, Honus Wagner. Honus was considered by many, including legendary N.Y. Giants manager John McGraw, to be the finest player to ever step foot on a baseball diamond. In 1936, along with Ty Cobb, Babe Ruth, Christy Mathewson, & Walter Johnson, Honus Wagner was in the 1st class to be inducted into the Hall of Fame in Cooperstown, New York.

In 1900, Ed Barrow purchased a quarter-interest in the Eastern League's Toronto franchise. Assuming the role of manager of this fifth-place club, Barrow uncovered a group of talented players that would drive Toronto to the league championship in 1902. One of those players was Nick Altrock, who after his Toronto days, pitched in the majors for 16 seasons, with the 71st best ERA in history at 2.69.

Tragedy in Detroit would lead to Ed's next experience. In time for the 1902 season, the Tigers acquired veteran pitcher Win Mercer, who led the team that year with 15 victories. The Tigers announced Win as their player-manager for 1903, but Mercer took his own life (the rumor was to escape his gambling debts) in January of that year. Tiger owner Sam Angus, who'd purchased the club from James D. Burns at the end of '01, hired Ed Barrow as both 1903 general & field manager. Barrow quickly began upgrading the team's talent, including enticing pitcher Wild Bill Donovan & outfielder Wahoo Sam Crawford to jump from the National League to Michigan & Trumbull (just days before the American League & the National League signed a January 1903 agreement to cease pirating each other's players).

Had Sam Angus stayed on as Tiger owner, Ed Barrow might have had a long tenure in Detroit. However, when Angus sold the team at the beginning of '04 to William Yawkey, the new owner promoted Frank Navin, Tiger bookkeeper under Angus, to the #1 position in the front office. It became impossible for two ambitious cooks like Barrow & Navin to be running one kitchen, and Barrow departed Detroit at the end of 1904.

Ed Barrow, believed by many baseball analysts to be *the finest judge of talent in the history of the game*, went on to manage the Boston Red Sox to a championship and then subsequently was hired by the New York Yankees. There, his player procurement decisions surrounded Babe Ruth with an all-star line-up and constructed a decades-long dynasty, with Barrow as the architect, from 1921 through 1945.

Though Barrow's Detroit stay lasted barely two years, it was long enough for him to create a personnel foundation strong enough to bring the Tigers 1907, 1908, and 1909 American League pennant dreams within reach. What allowed those dreams to cross over from within reach to reality was one final, albeit enormous, piece of the puzzle – Tyrus Raymond Cobb.

DDDDDDDDDDDDDDDDDDDDDDDDDDDDDDDDDDDDDDDDDDDDDDDDDDDDDDDDDDDDDDDDDDDDDDDDDDDD

During the Tigers 1905 spring training in Augusta, Georgia, they played two exhibition games against the minor league Augusta Tourists. The Tigers were immediately intrigued by one of Augusta's outfielders, Ty Cobb. He hit like nobody else on the Tourists or, for that matter, many in the major leagues. Ty was daring and creative on the base paths, *"The craziest ballplayer I ever saw,"* said Tiger infielder Germany Schaefer.

Young Tyrus was never far from the minds of Tiger players or management as they went north to start their regular season. By mid-1905, the word about Cobb had spread and other teams began to scout him at Tourists' games. Time was now of the essence and the Tigers pounced, purchasing his services in late-summer from the minor league Augusta team.

In August, while still with Augusta and 3 weeks before joining Detroit, Cobb's father, the man he respected above all others, was shot & killed. To make matters worse, the shooter was Ty's mother, who said that, in their darkened house, she mistook him for an intruder. Whatever the facts may be, it was in this fragile emotional time in his life that Ty Cobb joined the Tigers, making the usual rookie hazing difficult for him to handle, and leading to long-lasting resentments with some of the veteran players.

Ty Cobb's first game as a Tiger took place at Bennett Park in 1905 vs. the New York Highlanders, the team that would come to be known as the New York Yankees in 1913. 18-year old Ty's debut was on August 30, 1905. The hurler facing Tyrus was Jack Chesbro, who's 41 wins the year before remains the most victories by a pitcher since 1901. Ty slammed a 2-strike pitch for a run-scoring double, the perfect debut for the man who retired in 1928 owning the MLB all-time career hits record of 4,191 – until Pete Rose broke the mark in 1985 on Pete's way to 4,256. The balance of Ty's 1905 season gave little notice for what was to come, hitting only .240 in 41 games.

Playing in 98 games during '06, Cobb improved to .316, announcing his presence with a 25-game hitting streak, and was part of a fascinating side bar in Detroit baseball history. Imagine the excitement as a fan if, 8 years after he retired in 1976, Bill Freehan returned for a week or so to play for the 1984 Tiger team, 16 years after he starred for the city's previous World Series Champions. Well, that's how it felt to Detroit fans for a short 8-game stretch in the summer of 1906, when the Tigers boasted an All-Hall-of-Fame outfield of Ty Cobb, Sam Crawford, and 46-year old Sam Thompson. As a 27-year old on the 1887 Detroit Wolverines World Series juggernaut, Thompson led the way, hitting .372. 19 years later, when the 1906 Tigers were bit by the injury bug, they contacted Sam for some help. Although Thompson had retired at the end of the 1898 season, he had kept himself in great shape, and for 8 glorious days the Tigers starting outfield of Thompson, Crawford, & Cobb featured lifetime batting averages, respectively, of .331, .309, & Ty's #1 all-time .367. In his 8 games during 1906, Thompson scored 3 runs, knocked in 4, and hit .226 – not bad for a 46-year old.

DDDDDDDDDDDDDDDDDDDDDDDDDDDDDDDDDDDDDDDDDDDDDDDDDDDDDDDDDDDDDDDDDDDDDDDDDDD

"We'd play a whole game with one ball, if it stayed in the park, lopsided and black and full of tobacco juice and licorice stains." Sam Crawford

Although Honus Wagner and Babe Ruth have their own supporters on this issue, Ty Cobb is generally conceded to be the greatest player in the history of the game. He understood scientific baseball, the art of manufacturing runs through both brawn AND brains, and became its greatest practitioner. Cobb's habit of kicking the bag a few times upon reaching base was thought to be nervous energy, but instead it was his attempt to gain an extra couple of inches for his inevitable sprint, whether stealing or advancing on a teammate's hit or out, to the next base. He mastered the fade-away slide, creating space between himself and the opposition, always looking for the tiniest edge that may make the difference between safe and out. He never denied the legend spread throughout the league that he sharpened his spikes, a myth he would only deny after his playing days, believing it gave him a psychological advantage with at least some defenders who would be more concerned with their own safety than in tagging Cobb out. Four times in the same inning, Cobb stole 2nd, then 3rd, then home – a record he shares with Honus Wagner. Once, after singling, Ty stole his way around the bases on 3 *consecutive* pitches. Amazingly, Cobb stole home 54 times in his career, 21 times more than the runner-up.

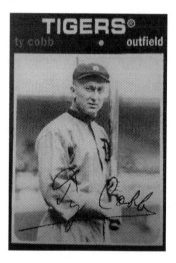

A fan favorite Cobb-maneuver was one he worked, at a high degree of success, with teammate Sam Crawford. Wahoo Sam (the byname recognizing his hometown of Wahoo, Nebraska) followed Ty in the batting order, frequently coming to the plate with Cobb perched on third base, either from hitting a triple (Cobb is #2 on the all-time triples list behind... Crawford) or doubling (#4 all-time) & stealing (#4 all-time, retired at #1) a base, or from singling (#2 all-time, retired at #1) & stealing 2 bases. If Crawford drew a base-on-balls, he would walk at a normal pace two-thirds of the way to first, and cast a glance towards Cobb at third. If given the right signal, Crawford would speed up to round the bag at a sprint and head towards 2nd. The fielders would often freeze, not knowing what to do. If they throw to 2nd, Cobb scores; if they throw home, Crawford gets to 2nd on a walk. The confusion created paralysis, working to the Tigers benefit more often than not.

Besides his brilliance on the baseball diamond, Ty Cobb was a complex individual, easily written off by some as mean, temperamental, abrasive, and a racist. That description is only partially-accurate and dismisses his intelligence, kindness, generosity, and caring-spirit. In 1945, Cobb donated $100,000, in his parents' memory, to build a hospital in Royster, Georgia. Cobb ensured that it was available to folks of all races, especially impressive back in the day, and that it would not turn away the indigent. Ty was a leading advocate of integration in the major leagues. Admired by the black players of his day, Cobb was asked to throw out the first pitch when the Detroit Stars of the Negro League began play at Hamtramck Stadium in 1930. In 1953, Cobb created the Cobb Educational Fund, endowing it with $100,000. Each year since then the fund provides financial assistance for Georgians in need who wish to attend college.

DDDDDDDDDDDDDDDDDDDDDDDDDDDDDDDDDDDDDDDDDDDDDDDDDDDDDDDDDDDDDDDDDDDDDD

Although the 1906 Tigers for the first time had Ty Cobb on the team for a full year, they still dropped 3 places in the standings from '05, ending up in sixth place at 71 & 78. George Mullin was ace of the pitching staff, posting a record of 21 & 18 with a 2.78 ERA. Pitcher Wild Bill Donovan's most noteworthy moment took place on the bases: in the fifth inning on May 7 in Cleveland, he became the second player in American League history, and the first Tiger, to steal in one inning 2nd, 3rd, and home plate (one month later, Detroit third baseman Bill Coughlin would become the 3rd American Leaguer to perform the feat; in fact, the next 3 times stealing every base in one inning took place in the A.L., a Tiger did it – Ty Cobb in '09, '11, & '12). Wild Bill's mediocre 1906 win-loss record of 9 & 15, after a successful 18 & 15 1905 campaign, was a major factor in the team's year-to-year slide.

Frank Navin was frustrated with the tumble the Tigers took in 1906, believing that the talent he and Ed Barrow assembled exceeded the results on the field. The timeless dance of replacing the manager, Bill Armour in 1905 & 1906, had begun. Navin set his sights on Hughie Jennings, player-manager the last 4 years for the Baltimore Orioles. Jennings played shortstop for the great Oriole teams of the mid-1890s as a teammate of John McGraw, Wee Willie Keeler, and Joe Kelley under manager Ned Hanlon, the same Ned Hanlon who was player-manager of the 1887 Detroit Wolverines. The Baltimore Orioles won consecutive National League pennants from 1894-1896, and Jennings, McGraw, Keeler, Kelley & Hanlon would all be eventually inducted into the Hall of Fame. As 1906 became 1907, Hughie Jennings took over the Detroit Tigers managerial reigns.

Under the heading, *"the best trades are those not made"*, during spring training of 1907, Jennings was growing irritated by the antics of the temperamental Cobb, who was getting into a series of fist fights with the veterans who hazed him so mercilessly when he first came up. Jennings offered center fielder Ty to the Cleveland Indians straight up for right fielder Elmer Flick. Although Flick was 11 years Cobb's elder, he was one of the league's best players, in '06 the A.L. leader in runs, triples, & stolen bases, by the end of 1906 he sported a career average of .318 on 1,500 hits, and – this cannot be overstated – was very popular with teammates, unlike Cobb. Cleveland rejected the offer. Bullet dodged. Elmer Flick's play declined dramatically after 1907 & he retired in 1910, while Ty played to 1928 (through 1926 with Detroit). After the trade was rejected, Cobb won all 12 of his batting crowns and led the Tigers to 3 American League titles.

The Cobb-Flick trade that didn't happen is one of 3 Michigan-Ohio trade decisions that are lopsided in favor of the Great Lakes State, along with the 1960 trade that sent Norm Cash from Cleveland to Detroit for Steve (not even Don) Demeter – Norm helped Detroit win the Series in '68 and hit 373 home runs in a Tiger uniform, while Steve played 5 games for Cleveland in 1960 and none afterward – and, of course, Michigan's trade of Toledo to Ohio for the Upper Peninsula.

It didn't take long before Hughie Jennings realized the great fortune of the failed Cobb-Flick trade. He saw that Ty's style of play was a direct descendent of Jennings 1890s Orioles & their scientific baseball... hit 'n run, bunting, stealing a base, looking for the psychological edge over an opponent, but taken by

Tyrus to another level. Instead of trying to reign him in, Jennings let Cobb be Cobb, and the results were tremendous.

DDDDDDDDDDDDDDDDDDDDDDDDDDDDDDDDDDDDDDDDDDDDDDDDDDDDDDDDDDDDDDDDDDDDDDDDDD

Baseball fever struck Tiger fans hard in 1907, as Detroit went on a tear. 20-year old Ty Cobb had his breakout year, leading the American League with a .350 average. Sam Crawford's .323 was good for 2nd in the A.L. With Ty on top, the pair finished one-two in total bases, one-four in RBIs, one-three in hits, & one-two in runs. With Sam first, the pair came in two-three in triples & one-three in extra base hits. For the first of many times to come, Tyrus led the league with 53 stolen bases. This was a daring club on the bases, with 7 regulars registering double-digits in steals.

1907 Tigers: back – John Eubanks, Claude Rossman, Sam Crawford, Bill Donovan, George Mullin, Ed Willett, Fred Payne, Ed Killian; middle – Davy Jones, Red Downs, Ty Cobb, Bill Coughlin, Germany Schaefer, Elijah Jones; front – Ed Siever, Jimmy Archer, Hughie Jennings, Boss Schmidt, Charles O'Leary

The pitching was equally as impressive. '07 was a career year for each of the two Eds... Ed Killian was terrific at 25 & 13 with a 1.78 ERA, while Ed Siever finished 18 & 11 and 2.16. George Mullin won 20 for the third year in a row, but poor run support contributed to also losing 20 despite his 2.59 ERA. Wild Bill Donovan was the staff ace, his 2.19 ERA helping him win 25 games while only losing 4. Bill's .862 winning percentage set a Tiger record that lasted for 106 years, until broken by Max Scherzer's .875 at 21 & 3 in 2013. The "Wild Bill" nom de guerre was not due to his lifestyle, but rather (1) his daring base running, underscored by stealing 2nd, 3rd, & home in a single inning the prior year (batting close to .200 lifetime, he had more base running opportunities than most pitchers and Ray Oyler) & (2) his propensity to walk batters, especially early in his career, even while being an effective mounds-man: as a 24-year old in the 1901 National League season, he led the league in both wins at 25 and walks at 152.

The Tigers captured their first American League pennant with a 92 & 58 record, scoring 162 more runs than they allowed. They were in a dog fight with Connie Mack's Philadelphia Athletics all year, several times trading places between first & second – the Tigers 3 games behind as late as September 15, until clinching the title with a 10-game winning streak stretching from September 21 to October 5, a streak that allowed Detroit to win the league by a slim one & one-half games. Michigan baseball fans had been waiting for a reason to celebrate in the 20 years since the 1887 championship won by the Detroit Wolverines, and they exploded, the state-wide party covering the gamut from painting their dogs in Tiger stripes to shouts back 'n forth between strangers to crowds dancing around enormous bonfires.

In the 1907 World Series, the Detroit Tigers faced the National League Champs, the Chicago Cubs of "Tinker to Evers to Chance" infield fame. The Cubs' 107 wins allowed them to finish a comfortable 17 games ahead of 2nd place Pittsburgh. Chicago was considered the finest team in the land, and were the odds-on favorite over Detroit.

Game 1 Chicago: In front of 24,377, the largest crowd to ever witness a World Series game, the opener match-up featured two great pitchers with two great names, the Tigers Wild Bill Donovan versus the Cubs Orval Overall. With no radio, TV, or social media, 12,000 assembled in downtown Detroit to watch the game re-enacted on a giant electronic scoreboard mounted on the Detroit Free Press building, the game situation updated after each pitch.

During a long afternoon at Chicago's West Side Grounds, it looked as though the Cubs lone run scored in the fourth would account for the final score, until a 2-run double by Sam Crawford keyed a 3-run Tiger rally in the 8th, stunning the Cub fanatics on hand and thrilling Tiger fans 280 miles away crowding the streets, windows, and rooftops around the Free Press building. Cub rooters saw visions of a 1906 Series repeat, when their heavily favored heroes fell to the cross-town White Sox. But, just as Detroit was on the verge of stealing game 1, a passed ball by Detroit catcher Boss Schmidt on what should've been the final out of the game, allowed the Cubs to tie it at 3-all in the ninth. After 12 innings of play and the score still tied, the game was called due to darkness.

The "win-that-got-away" did not dampen the spirits of the 12,000 congregated around the electronic scoreboard back in Detroit. Once the game was called, the *Free Press* reported the next day that, *"the majority surged off towards Michigan Avenue and Griswold Street, cheering so loudly that tall buildings trembled."*

Games 2 Chicago: Both teams managed 9 hits, but Chicago bunched theirs better, as the Tigers George Mullin & the Cubs Jack Pfiester both went the distance, the Cubs coming out on top 3–1. Detroit struck first as infielder Claude Rossman opened the 2nd with a triple, scampering home on a single by back-up catcher Fred Payne. The Cubs struck back immediately, starting the bottom of the frame with three consecutive singles and game tying walk, until Mullin dug-in with 2 strikeouts & a groundout to keep the score 1-1. In the 4th, Chicago clustered 3 singles, a sacrifice bunt & a stolen base to score 2, accounting for the final score.

Game 3 Chicago: The Cubs roughed up the two Eds, first Siever and then Killian, for 5 runs on 10 hits, while the Tigers still could not figure out Cubs pitchers. With a 5-1 win under their belts, the Boys from the Windy City boarded the train to Detroit with a 2 to 0 (and 1 tie) Series lead.

Game 4 Detroit: The city of Detroit hosted its first World Series game on October 11, 1907, as 11,306 ignored the rain drops to squeeze into 10,000 seat capacity Bennett Park. At Michigan & Trumbull, the two pitchers from game 1, Wild Bill & Orval, faced each other again. After 3 scoreless innings, the Tiger faithful were on their feet in the fourth as Cobb tripled and scored on first sacker Claude Rossman's single, but the Cubs took the lead in their next at bat on a 2-run single by pitcher Overall in the fifth.

When the visitors tacked on 3 in the 7th, it was all but over, final score Cubs 6 & Tigers 1. One more Chicago win and the Series was theirs.

The World Series comes to Michigan & Trumbull 1907

Game 5 Detroit: To get an idea of how deep this Cubs team was, consider that when their Hall of Fame pitcher Mordecai 3-Finger Brown took to the mound for game 5, this marked the first time they used him in the Series, despite his '07 record of 20 & 6 with a 1.39 ERA. George Mullin pitched well, giving up only solo runs in the 1st & 2nd, but Detroit could not get to 3-Finger (a childhood accident cost him parts of two fingers) for a single score. The game 5 final is 2-0 Cubs as Chicago takes the Series 4-0 & 1 tie.

For the Cubs, the Series was redemption for the totally unexpected '06 Series loss to the White Sox, not to mention gleeful contemplation at the winners' per player share of $2,142. The defeated Tigers cared not a whit about any Cubs redemption, but did get a little bounce in their step when the Series losers' share was bumped up significantly by owner William Yawkey generously tossing in $15,000 from his own pocket, boosting the players' feelings & their income to the tune of $1,946 each. The fondness of the Tigers for their boss had already been established from Yawkey's habit of rewarding exceptional play or improved production with a $100 bill subtly handed to a player OR lifting spirits, figuratively & literally, by picking up the team tab at a night at the tavern.

DDDDDDDDDDDDDDDDDDDDDDDDDDDDDDDDDDDDDDDDDDDDDDDDDDDDDDDDDDDDDDDDDDDDDDDDD

Through the spring of 1908, the nation was fixated on the Presidential campaigns of William Howard Taft versus William Jennings Bryan. But as summer turned to fall, the focus of the populace had shifted to the two great pennant races unfolding and, as late as October 1, 6 teams remained in the hunt for the two pennants: Detroit, the Cleveland Naps, & the Chicago White Sox in the American League; the Chicago Cubs, the Pittsburgh Pirates, & the New York Giants in the National League.

As in 1907, Cobb and Crawford are one-two in the 1908 American League batting race at .324 and .311, respectively, but it was a rookie hurler who makes the difference in the pennant fight versus Cleveland and the White Sox: Ed "Kickapoo" Summers and his knuckleball exploded on the scene with a sterling record of 24 & 12 and a 1.64 ERA. Like the byname of "Wahoo" for Sam Crawford's Wahoo, Nebraska upbringing, the "Kickapoo" nickname recognized the geography of the player, in Ed's case it was a reference to his Indiana region home and the Kickapoo Native American tribe that once resided there.

Ed Siever faded in 1908 to 2 & 6 from his 1907 career year of 18 & 6, but another Ed picked up the slack as Ed Willett had his breakout season, following up his 1 & 5 '07 with a 15 & 8 2.28 '08. In the tale of 4 Eds, Ed Killian was not the elite 25 & 13 of the previous year, but still chipped in with 12 wins against 9 losses, while old dependables George Mullin and Wild Bill Donovan rounded out the staff with numbers of 17 & 13/3.10 and 18 & 7/2.08.

DDDDDDDDDDDDDDDDDDDDDDDDDDDDDDDDDDDDDDDDDDDDDDDDDDDDDDDDDDDDDDDDDDDDDDDDD

In the midst of the thrilling pennant chase, one madcap Detroit Tiger forced baseball to consider a rule change no one ever imaged would come up for discussion: while standing on 2nd base, infielder Herman "Germany" Schaefer decided to steal FIRST base. The belief in scientific baseball was not restricted to Ty Cobb, for there was also a Tiger standing on third and, as bizarre as Schaefer's decision at first glance seems, he was looking to draw a throw to first in the hopes that the runner at third could score.

Let's go back a few minutes. Detroit and Cleveland were tied late in the game, with Tigers center fielder Davy Jones on third and Schaefer on first. Germany, hoping to create an opening for Jones to score by drawing a throw from Cleveland's catcher, took off for second. No throw was made. Now, Detroit has runners on 2nd & 3rd. On the next pitch, Germany Schaefer lets out a scream and bolts for first, diving in head first to beat the throw that, once again, never came. Hm. A man stole 2nd then 1st, and the only thing that has changed is that the fans are wonderfully entertained while the umpires are left scratching their heads. On the very next pitch, Germany lets out another scream, and takes off again for second. This time, the catcher DID throw to second, Germany slides in ahead of the tag while Davy Jones makes it home safely, and the Tigers take the lead.

Herman "Germany" Schaefer was one of the most fascinating individuals to wear the Olde English D. He was admired and respected by all, making people feel better than before they met him, taking time to recognize the importance in each person he encountered. Ty Cobb considered Schaefer his best friend on the Tigers; years later, Ernie Harwell called Germany one of his all-time favorites. He lit a fire under teammates. As Chicago White Sox owner Charles Comiskey noted when the Tigers acquired Germany in 1905, *"Detroit teams of recent years have been in the habit of losing heart as soon as opponents got a few runs ahead. With old Schaefer in there, fighting all the while, there has been a marked difference in their playing."* On a team with much bigger stars, it was Germany who was made team captain by manager Hughie Jennings – to the unanimous approval of his teammates.

Germany Schaefer made people feel happier, lighter. He was a comedian, whether tip-toeing the foul line like a tightrope walker on his way to first, carrying a lantern to his infield position as the day grew darker or opening an umbrella at shortstop when rain drops began to fall, which begs the question, why did he have an umbrella at shortstop?

It was common for him to, after coming up to bat, call time to loudly address the crowd, letting them know what was about to take place in the game. The most memorable such moment took place Sunday, June 24, 1906 at Chicago's Comiskey Park. The Tigers were batting in the top of the ninth, losing 2-1, one man on and two outs. On the mound for the White Sox on this day was Doc White, at year's end voted the best pitcher in the American League at 18 & 6 with a 1.52 ERA. Tiger manager Bill Armour sent up Germany to pinch hit as Detroit's final hope. Just before stepping into the batter's box, Germany called time. He took off his cap and, with a theatrical flourish, told the large crowd on hand, *"Ladies and gentlemen, you are now looking at Herman Schaefer, better known as Herman the Great, acknowledged by one and all to be the greatest pinch hitter in the world. I am now going to hit the ball into the leftfield bleachers. Thank you."* And damned if Germany Schaefer didn't, despite facing the league's best pitcher, deposit a Doc White offering into the leftfield bleachers, as promised.

There would be no simple trot around the bases. Germany squeezed every bit of joy that he could out of this triumph. Sliding headfirst into first base, he rose and shouted, *"At the quarter, Schaefer leads by a head!"* Germany then slid into second, jumped to his feet and cried, *"At the half, Schaefer leads by a length!"* After sliding into third, he announced, *"Schaefer leads by a mile!"* Sprinting towards home, he left his feet for an elaborate hook slide into home plate, screaming, *"Schaefer wins by a nose!"* Hopping to his feet, Germany dusted himself off, doffed his cap and bowed. Schaefer concluded his performance with one final proclamation in his deep baritone voice, *"Ladies and gentlemen, this concludes this afternoon's performance. I thank you for your kind attention."*

Germany came to bat 3,784 times in his 15-year career, hitting 9 home runs, or one home run every 420 at bats. And yet he hit a called shot off Doc White, the man whose record of 5 consecutive shutouts was unequaled for 62 years, until matched by Don Drysdale in 1968.

Final score: Tigers 3, White Sox 2. Best performance by a ball player: *the Amazing Germany Schaefer...*

DDDDDDDDDDDDDDDDDDDDDDDDDDDDDDDDDDDDDDDDDDDDDDDDDDDDDDDDDDDDDDDDDDDDDDDDDDDDDDDDDD

On the morning of September 25, the Tigers are in third place, 2 games behind the Cleveland Naps and one-game behind the second place White Sox. Connie Mack's Philadelphia Athletics are at Bennett Park for a double header. In a spectacular rookie season, Ed Kickapoo Summers will have his most astounding day today pitching against the Athletics – in both games. His knuckleball has great movement on this afternoon as Ed tosses a 6-hitter in the game one 7-2 victory, then goes right back out to the mound for game two, and is even more impressive in allowing only 2 hits in the 10-inning, 1 to nothing Tiger win.

In 1907, a Tigers 10-game winning streak spanning September & October allowed them to secure the American League pennant by one & one-half games over the Philadelphia A's. 1908 seems to mirror '07, as Kickapoo's double header wins versus the A's kick starts another late season Tigers 10-game winning streak, this one from September 25 to October 3. On October 1, a Tigers' off day during the streak, Henry Ford unveiled his Model T, rolling off the assembly line at the Ford Motor Company's Piquette Avenue plant, 4 miles north of Michigan & Trumbull.

Detroit is riding the 10 consecutive victories into the final series of the season at Chicago's South Side Park, with games against the White Sox on October 4, 5 & 6. The Tigers are playing their best baseball of the year, and on the morning of October 4, hold a 1 & ½ game lead on the Cleveland Naps and 2 & ½ game lead on the Sox. Chicago's two best pitchers, Doc White and spit-baller Ed Walsh (a notoriously cocky man said to strut while standing still) were set for games 1 & 2.

If Chicago takes all 3 games from Detroit, they can win the pennant, depending on what Cleveland does. For that possibility, the fans are psyched, and over 26,000, the largest crowd in the history of South Side Park, force their way into the 15,000 seat ballyard. The Tigers counter the Sox Doc White with Ed Killian. Killian pitches brilliantly, only giving up two hits all day while the Tigers garner five hits off White. The Sox, however, won a World Championship just two years ago hitting only .230 with 7 home runs for the entire season – they know how to manufacture runs. Sure enough, Chicago doesn't get a single hit in the first inning but somehow manage to score 3 runs off Killian on a walk, a Tiger error, a sacrifice bunt, a walk, and two steals. Although Wahoo Sam Crawford scores in the ninth, that's all Detroit gets today, and Chicago wins 3 to 1.

In St. Louis, Cleveland settles for a 3-3 tie with the Browns, the umpires deciding to end the game after 11 innings due to darkness. Detroit's lead is down to 1 on the Naps and 1 & ½ on the Sox.

On October 5, it's another overflow crowd on the South Side, with the Tigers 24-win rookie Kickapoo Summers facing Chicago's 39-game winner, Big Ed Walsh. It's no contest. Chicago's hitless wonders are swinging the bats well today, knocking Kickapoo around for 5 runs in his 5 innings, and tacking on one more marker against the relieving George Mullin. Walsh only yields 4 hits and 1 run while striking out 9 as he improves to 40 & 15, more importantly pulling the Sox to within one-half game of Detroit with one game remaining tomorrow.

Cleveland has lost to St. Louis, so the pennant now comes down to the winner of the October 6 game at South Side Park. The night before the finale, Sox fans congregate outside of the Tigers home in Chicago for the 3-game series, the Lexington Hotel, creating as much noise as possible throughout the night in an attempt to deprive the Detroiters of their sleep.

It's October 6, 1908, the last day of the regular season, and Detroit's Wild Bill Donovan, the man who has experienced so many big games, will pitch for the Tigers. Although he just pitched against Detroit two days ago, Sox manager Fielder Jones has chosen Doc White to tame the Tigers on just one day of rest. In front of another huge crowd of 25,000, the Tigers make two points clear in the very first inning: (1) they play very well on little sleep and (2) one day's rest is not enough for Doc White. Detroit explodes for 4 runs in the first, knocking out White before he can get the game's 2nd out & continuing the assault against Ed Walsh, crossing the plate again in the second and twice more for good luck in the ninth. The barrage against Chicago includes Crawford's 4 hits, a Cobb triple & steal of home, Herman Germany Schaefer concluding his finest all-around season - third in the league in runs, stolen bases, & sacrifice hits – with 2 more hits, and Wild Bill Donovan's magnificent outing, striking out 9 while yielding only 2 hits and zero runs in the pennant-clinching, 7 to nothing Tiger victory.

The 1908 Detroit Tigers win the American League pennant by one-half game over Cleveland & one & one-half games over the Chicago White Sox, finishing with a 90 & 63 record.

DDDDDDDDDDDDDDDDDDDDDDDDDDDDDDDDDDDDDDDDDDDDDDDDDDDDDDDDDDDDDDDDDDDDDDDDDDDDDD

The dogfight for the 1908 National League pennant was as closely contested as the American League's, with 3 teams within 1 game of each other at season's end, the Pittsburgh Pirates, the N.Y. Giants, and the Chicago Cubs. With 16 games left in the regular season, the Cubs were 4 & ½ games behind the Giants & getting back to the Series looked grim. But N.Y. Giants rookie Fred Merkle's famous misplay (as the runner on first, he failed to touch 2nd base on what should've been a game winning hit by the next batter, & is called out, causing the game against the Cubs to end in a tie instead of a Giants win) allows Chicago to stay at 4 & ½ and not drop to 5 & ½ behind first, inspiring the Cubs as they proceed to win 14 of their last 16 – including Ed Reulbach's amazing day, pitching two shutouts on September 26 versus the Brooklyn Dodgers (the only person to ever accomplish this feat).

At the end of October 3, Pittsburgh was in first, with the Cubs one-game back, the N.Y. Giants 1 & ½ games back. On October 4, the Cubs hosted the Pirates at West Side Grounds, with Chicago's Mordecai 3-Finger Brown against Vic Willis. Chicago took a 2-0 lead into the sixth, when two Buccaneers crossed the plate, tying the game at 2. The excitement is such that a lady goes into labor in the stands, and gives birth at the park. The 2-2 tie was of shorter duration than the birthing mother's labor, as the Cubs got to Pirates starter Willis and a reliever for single runs in their sixth, seventh and eighth, winning 5-2 and moving into first.

The Cubs & Pirates regular seasons were now done. The two were tied for first, but the Cubs held the tie-breaker, so Pittsburgh was eliminated. Although two rough 'n tumble teams, there's always room for classy, and the Pirates display that as their manager Fred Clarke & owner Barney Dreyfuss pay a visit to the Cubs clubhouse to offer their congratulations. The Giants had single games remaining against the Boston Doves, on October 5 & 6. If New York could win both, they would be tied with the Cubs, and force a replay of the Merkle game – and they did.

The one game playoff took place on October 8, 1908 at New York's famous Polo Grounds. The scene outside the ballyard has seemingly one-half of New York trying to squeeze, burrow, bribe, fight or scale their way inside. Two fans die in the melee. The brother of presidential candidate William Howard Taft gains entree by crawling through the sewer system, emerging victorious as his sibling would next month. The worst of people is coming out. The Giants team physician is alleged to have attempted twice a bribe of Hall-of-Fame umpire Bill Klem, including as Klem walked on to the field at the beginning of the game. By game time, with fans hanging from the grand stand roof and ringing the field of play, over 40,000 had jammed into the 23,000 seat capacity Polo Grounds. Many would not be able to see what was taking place during the game, and would have to content themselves with being present. The class that was shown by Pittsburgh after their elimination by the Cubs a few days before, was strangely (just kidding) absent from the New Yorkers, as they rained down a non-stop chorus of foul names upon the Chicago 9 until the game concluded.

The anticipated pitching match-up was to have been between two of the greatest of all-time, the Giants Christy Mathewson, 37 & 10, versus the Cubs Mordecai 3-Finger Brown, 28 & 9. However, 3-Finger has pitched in 11 of the Cubs last 14 games, and besides the Cubs have the Giant-killer ready to go, Jack Pfiester. The winner gets the Detroit Tigers in the World Series.

Much to the delight of the nervous Giants fans, and even more to Fred Merkle, New York gets to Pfiester in the very first inning with a run-scoring double. When that is followed by a walk, Cubs manager Frank Chance has seen enough, and brings in Mordecai who ends the threat with a strikeout.

Going into the third, the Giants maintain their 1-0 lead, but Chicago rallies to tie with two out. Just when it looks like Mathewson will get out of it with no further damage but the single marker, the wonderfully named Wildfire Schulte doubles in the lead run, and when player/manager Frank Chance cracks a 2-run double, the crowd has a very bad feeling, even after the third out is recorded.

The game remains 4-1 Chicago into the Giants 7th. 3-Finger Brown suddenly looks mortal, and starts the half inning by surrendering a single, single, and a walk. Bases loaded, nobody out, the noise at the Polo Grounds a deafening crescendo. When Frank Chance wanders over from his first base position to ask what's wrong, Mordecai snarls at his manager to mind his own business, and digs in. Mathewson is due up and, although Matty is a good hitter as pitchers go, N.Y. manager John McGraw must get everything he can out of this opportunity, but his pinch hitter pops out. 1 out, bases remain loaded. One run comes in on a sac fly, but that is the extent of the rally. Reducing the lead to 4-2 is not nearly enough, not with 3-Finger pitching, and he closes out the pennant-clinching game with no other concerns.

The foul epithets would not suffice for the lovable New York fans at this point. As the Cubs ran for the cover of their clubhouse, they are hit by a variety of items tossed their way. Reaching the clubhouse does not provide refuge as the Gotham vandals are breaking the windows and trying to pound the door down. The only thing that stems the mayhem is the drawn revolvers of New York's Finest.

DDDDDDDDDDDDDDDDDDDDDDDDDDDDDDDDDDDDDDDDDDDDDDDDDDDDDDDDDDDDDDDDDDDDDDDD

In the 5 years between 1906 and 1910, the Cubs won 530 games, a record that still stands today, 4 National League pennants, and 2 World Series. During that time, they were the best hitting, pitching, and fielding team in the majors. Their success led to a well-deserved confidence, succinctly expressed by Cubs' player/manager Frank Chance, *"Who ever heard of the Cubs losing a game they had to have?"*

Despite all of that, the 1908 World Series was Detroit's opportunity to exact revenge on the Cubs for 1907. The Tigers two big hitters, Cobb & Crawford, were particularly eager to atone for the previous year's clash with the Cubs, having hit only .200 & .238 respectively in the '07 Series.

Game 1 Detroit: 10,812 Tiger faithful were rockin' & rollin' Bennett Park, eager for their Boys of Summer to turn the tables on the Cubbies. The Tigers made their rooters happy by jumping out to a 1-0 lead in the first inning when Matty McIntyre singles, steals 2nd, and comes home on Ty Cobb's knock. Detroit starter Ed Killian, however, did not make it out of the 3rd, surrendering 4 Chicago runs that inning. It looked bleak when the Cubs tacked on another run off of rookie Ed "Kickapoo" Summers in the 7th, pushing their lead to 5-1.

The Tigers were a team tired of being pushed around, answering with 3 in the bottom of the 7th when Cobb & Rossman rode home on a double by little-used Red Downs, who then scored himself on pitcher Summers' single, knocking out Cubs starter Ed Reulbach. Facing the great Mordecai 3-Finger Brown in the 8th, Claude Rossman preserved, his single sending Crawford & Cobb across home plate and giving the Tigers a 6-5 lead, igniting a wall of sound reverberating around the Old Ballyard. The anticipation of victory was strong heading into the 9th, with the Detroiters 3 outs away from a Series 1-0 lead.

Johnny Evers grounds out unassisted to Rossman at first base, one out, 2 to go and Bennett Park as loud as it's ever been. And then the bottom fell out. Ed Summers painfully surrendered singles to each of the next 6 batters, as one Cub after another crossed home plate, until a groundout and a fly out mercifully ended the top of the ninth. Cubs 10 Tigers 6 going into the bottom of the ninth. The Tigers did not go down without a fight, putting 2 runners on base with Crawford & Cobb coming up, but the two great hitters were cut down by Mordecai on a flyball and a groundout. Game 1 to the Cubs.

As the Tiger faithful filed out of the park and into the Michigan Avenue pubs to relieve the pain, the two teams prepared to catch the train to Chicago for games 2 & 3.

Game 2 Chicago: Reprising their great 1907 Series game 1 pitcher's duel, Detroit's Wild Bill Donovan and the Cubs Orval Overall were exceptional once again, allowing no hits until the fifth and keeping the game scoreless going into the bottom of the 8th. After Wild Bill whiffed Harry Steinfeldt (an old Tiger from the Western League days), Cubs shortstop Joe Tinker parked a 2-run homer over the right-field fence, igniting both the home crowd and a 6-run inning. The Tigers answered with a Cobb RBI single in the ninth, but nothing more. The 6-1 Cubs victory puts Chicago up two games to one, and is their 6th consecutive World Series win against the Tigers in the last 2 years.

Game 3 Chicago: George Mullin, one of the greatest pitchers in Detroit Tiger history, holds the Cubs to zero earned runs in a complete game 8-3 Tiger victory. Hallelujah! After Cobb singles in a first inning run, Chicago capitalizes on 3 Detroit errors in a sloppy fourth, taking a 3-1 lead that they keep until the Tigers sixth, when Detroit's offense broke loose against Cubs starter Jack Pfiester. Consecutive RBI singles by Crawford & Cobb was followed by a 2-run Claude Rossman single, putting Detroit up 5-3 lead. After a double play seemed to end the rally, catcher Ira Thomas doubled in Rossman for the Tigers 6th run. Cobb opened Detroit's 8th with a double, his 4th hit of the game, raced to third on Rossman's bunt single, and scored on third sacker Bill Coughlin's sac fly. When Mullin singled Rossman in, the Tigers held a commanding 8-3 lead. George Mullin held the Cubs to one hit in the last two innings to seal the first World Series victory in Detroit Tiger history, 8 to 3, and cut the Cubs Series lead to 2-1.

Game 4 Detroit: With a decisive Series victory under their belts, Detroit was now wild for the team's return home, 12,907 filling Bennett Park to almost 3,000 over capacity. Unfortunately, 3-Finger Brown had one of his finest games, only allowing 2 hits each by Tiger shortstop Charley O'Leary and Sam Crawford. Tiger Rookie Ed "Kickapoo" Summers pitched well on a day when well wasn't going to cut it, and Detroit fell 3 to nothing. The Cubs now stood one game from their second consecutive World Series victory over Detroit.

Game 5 Detroit: In the history of this great sports town, 1908 game 5 was the Detroit fans low point. Only 6,210 came out to cheer on their Tigers on a blustery day, and the game was over in one hour & 25 minutes – the lowest crowd size <u>and</u> the shortest game ever in the World Series. Both stand as records to this day. The pitching match-up, for the fourth time in the last two World Series, pitted Wild Bill Donovan against Chicago's Orval Overall. And for the fourth time, Donovan pitched well but Orval came out on top. At least the small crowd didn't have to suffer too long. Only 3 Tigers reached Overall for a hit. Detroit's best chance came in the fifth when a Bill Coughlin single and a Matty McIntyre double gave the Tigers runners on 2nd & 3rd with one out, but a short flyout by Charley O'Leary and a strikeout of Crawford ended the lone threat. With today's 2-0 victory, the Chicago Cubs are back-to-back champions of the baseball world.

Cobb shook off his 1907 Series showing, boosting his batting average from .200 then to .368 in 1908. The rest of the Tigers combined, unfortunately, hit below .200. Solving the Cubs' pitching staff remained a mystery. Cub player/manager Frank Chance was gracious in his assessment of the Tigers and their fans, *"The Tigers, individually and as a team, are the finest lot I have ever met. They are gentlemen and never once during the five games of the series just closed did one hasty word pass between the two teams. I can't help, also, but give you my hand when I say that Detroit as a ball town is a little dandy."*

It took 108 years for the Chicago Cubs to win their 3rd World Series: in 2016, they defeated the Indians in 7 games, with the finale played in downtown Cleveland. Since the Cubs first 2 Series victories ended in both 1907 & 1908 at Bennett Park, Chicago has never celebrated a World Series title on their home field.

DDD

1909 saw the Tigers set the A.L. record of 98 victories, and establish team records that still stand: 57 home victories and a resulting .750 winning percentage. Ty Cobb was spectacular, winning the Triple Crown with a .377 average, 107 RBIs, and the only home run title of his career with 9 (his 6 homers at Bennett Park were all inside-the-park), as well as leading the league in stolen bases, hits, and runs.

Cobb was an outstanding bunter in any venue that he played in, but he had a built-in home field advantage, courtesy of the Bennett Park grounds crew. To ensure that Ty's bunts did not stray too far from the batter's box and find a fielder's glove quickly, the grounds crew saturated the area in front of home plate. This served to deaden Cobb's bunts to such a degree that the location of their watery handiwork became known as *Cobb's Lake*.

George Mullin was the 1909 pitching staff ace at 29 & 8 and a 2.22 ERA, followed in the rotation by the 3 Eds: Willett 21 & 10/2.34, Summers 19 & 9/2.24, and Killian 11 & 9 with his team-leading 1.71 ERA. Tough luck Wild Bill Donovan, despite his 2.31 ERA, had only 8 wins versus 7 losses.

After appearing in only 20 games in 1908 as a 20-year old rookie, Donie Bush became Detroit's regular shortstop in 1909, contributing 53 stolen bases, 88 walks, and 114 runs scored. Donie is found on most of the Tiger career hitting lists: #5 in runs scored (one of the few who could come between #4 Whitaker & #6 Trammell), #7 in triples, #5 in walks (between Cobb & Norm Cash), #2 in stolen bases (behind only Cobb), #8 in singles (behind Sweet Lou), #1 sacrifice bunts, #9 games played, & #8 in at bats.

And then there was, in his third season as Tiger manager, Hughie Jennings. His was a fine field general, very popular with his players, with an enthusiasm that was contagious. Never far beneath Hughie's cherry exterior was a very-1890s-Baltimore-Oriole-like trait to do whatever was necessary to win a ballgame. Sometimes this activity was clothed in a fun-loving motif. Exhibit A was whenever the Tigers faced the amazingly talented but child-like Rube Waddell. Jennings was usually stationed in the third base coaching box when the Tigers were at bat. However, with the southpaw Rube pitching and thus facing the right field foul line when he goes into his set, Hughie moved to the first base side coach's box, shouting Rube's name while looking to distract his attention by dangling toys such as rubber snakes & a jack-in-the-box, sometimes playing on Waddell's love of animals by bringing his own dog out with him to the coach's box. Umpires ran a loose ship back in the day.

The late-season 10-game winning streaks that propelled Detroit to pennants in 1907 & 1908 arrived one month early in '09, with even a few more victories, as the Tigers reeled off 14 consecutive wins from August 19 to September 2, increasing their hold on first place from one & one-half to 5 games, driven by the superlative Tyrus Raymond Cobb who hit an astounding .600 during this time.

On August 13, 1909, with the Tigers in the heat of the pennant race, management decided to make changes on the infield, saddening fans throughout Michigan by trading Germany Schaefer to the Washington Senators for Jim Delahanty. By September 21, the hard-charging Philadelphia Athletics cut Detroit's lead to 2 & ½ games as the Tigers were about to begin a crucial 4-game series with Germany's new team, the Washington Senators. A decision had been reached by American League president Ban Johnson to order Schaefer to the bench for the games against Detroit. The Tigers promised Germany that he'd receive a share of the World Series pot, and Ban was concerned that Schaefer would give less than full effort. Detroit took 3 of 4 from Washington, ending the season 3.5 games ahead of the A's.

For the World Series opener against Pittsburgh, Germany entered Bennett Park to loud cheers from the fans who would always adore him. Germany sat on the Tiger bench for each home game, and not a person in Bennett Park had to be told where he was: Germany Schaefer's voice was described as being able to penetrate six inches of chilled steel.

DDDDDDDDDDDDDDDDDDDDDDDDDDDDDDDDDDDDDDDDDDDDDDDDDDDDDDDDDDDDDDDDDDDDDDDD

The Pittsburgh Pirates brand new Forbes Field hosted a World Series in its first year of existence as the team won the 1909 National League pennant by putting away their closest competitors, the Chicago Cubs, with a 16-game September winning streak. Although the Cubs had another great season with 104 wins, the Bucs won 110 times for an outstanding .724-win percentage.

The Series matched the Pirates, winners of 4 National League pennants from 1900-1909, and Detroit, champions of the American League from 1907-1909: no National League team and no American League team had won more pennants in the first decade of the 1900s.

Leading the respective teams was the Buccaneer's 35-year old veteran, Honus Wagner, coming off of his 4th consecutive N.L. batting title, and 7th overall, against the Tigers young superstar, 22-year old Ty Cobb, A.L. winner of the 1909 Triple Crown and on his way to a .367 lifetime batting average (8 points better than the #2 all-time, Rogers Hornsby at .359). Interest in this match-up, among fans and bettors, was high all across the country.

Game 1 Pittsburgh: The opening game pitching match-up was Detroit's ace George Mullin against, not one of Pittsburgh's two 20-game winners or their 19-game winner, but against… rookie and 12-game winner, Babe Adams. Although he only had 12 regular season victories, Babe's ERA was a sparkling 1.11 and the Tigers saw why first hand. Babe was wild in the first, walking 2 of the first 3 batters, then giving up two more singles, but because a batted ball hit a runner, Adams escaped only surrendering 1 run. To paraphrase Captain Jack Sparrow, if the Tigers were waiting for their opportune moment, the first inning was it, because when the second began, Babe Adams was in a groove and the Tigers only came close to scoring once after that, when Cobb hit a long flyout to center with two on & two out in the 7th.

George Mullin went the distance for Detroit, only giving up one earned run, on a homer by Pirate player/manager Fred Clarke, but 4 Tiger errors at critical times led to 3 unearned runs, and a 4-1 Pittsburgh game 1 victory.

Game 2 Pittsburgh: After the Pirates grabbed a 2 to nothing lead in the first off of Wild Bill Donovan, the Tigers got to the Pirates ace Howie Camnitz (25 & 6/1.62 ERA) early & often, scoring 2 in the second, 3 in the third, and 2 in the fifth. Wild Bill shutout Pittsburgh after the first on 3 hits, and Detroit was on their way to a 7-2 win, knotting the series at 1-each. The first 7 Tigers in the batting order each had one hit and scored one run. Tiger catcher Boss Schmidt, batting eighth, did the most damage to the Pirates with two hits & 4 RBIs, starting with his 2-run double in the second.

Game 3 Detroit: The excitement from the game 2 victory at Forbes Field drew the hometown folks out in the largest numbers to date at The Corner as 18,277 jammed themselves into 10,000 seat Bennett Park. The fortunate ones arrived too late to witness the start of this one. Ed "Kickapoo" Summers did not survive the 1st inning, a World Series first. He was only able to record one out among the first 8 batters that he faced in the game, and once again the Tigers porous defense contributed to a Detroit pitcher's demise, committing 3 errors among these first 8 hitters. Before a Tiger came to bat, Detroit faced a 5-0 deficit. Ed Willett relieved Kickapoo, and held the Pirates to 1 run in his 6 innings of work, allowing the Tigers to get back into the game with a 4-run 7th, cutting the deficit to 6 to 4, on key hits by Tom Jones, Ty Cobb, and one of Donie Bush's 4 knocks today.

Pittsburgh got two back in the ninth off reliever Ralph Works, and that turned out to be the difference. The Tigers got those two back in their ninth to cut the deficit to 8-6. With two outs and Cobb on third, Ed Delahanty, came to the plate as the tying run. Ed was in the groove today, with 3 hits already under his belt. He picked one out that he liked, and nailed the pitch squarely. Already on their feet, the crowd now yelled as one, but Delahanty's missile was tracked down by the leftfielder to end the game. As a poor consolation to victory, many at Bennett Park enjoyed a new taste treat called Cracker Jacks for the first time, pizzas not served at The Corner for 84 more years. Sad. The Series now stood 2 to 1, Pirates.

Game 4 Detroit: With 17,036 roaring their approval, George Mullin throws 5-0 shutout. In their third World Series, the Tigers claimed their first home victory. Tiger back-up catcher Oscar Stanage had a day he would always look back fondly on, his two-run single breaking the scoreless tie in the second, to send the Tigers on their way. Run scoring doubles by Donie Bush & Ty Cobb in the 4th completed the scoring. The 1909 World Series is tied 2 to 2 heading back to the Steel City.

Game 5 Pittsburgh: In front of the home crowd at Forbes Field, Pirate rookie Babe Adams took the mound for the second time in the Series. And, once again, the Tigers got to him for a first inning run as leftfielder Davy Jones led off the game with a home run to deep center. Although they were able to add 3 more runs this time, it was not enough as Pittsburgh once again had their way with Kickapoo Ed, getting to him for all of their runs in an 8-4 win, and taking a 3-2 Series lead.

Game 6 Detroit: Tigers ace George Mullin wasn't one in the first. The fans were just getting to their seats as the Pirates first 3 batters in the game went single, single, single, 1-0 Pittsburgh. Tiger third baseman George Moriarty didn't like the way this game was starting, snatched the cap off the Pirate perched next to him on third, and slapped him about the head a few times with it, a Three Stooges-like flare up that didn't end until both players landed a few kicks to each other. Moriarty could not have felt much better when Honus Wagner stepped to the plate and doubled home 2 more runs, 3-0 Pittsburgh, nobody out. Then Mullin settled in and retired the 5th, 6th, and 7th batters without further incident. Detroit began the comeback immediately in their first at bat, Donie Bush doing what he does best, working the pitcher for a walk and then coming around to score, this time on a double by Wahoo Sam.

It stayed 3-1 Bucs 'til the Tigers fourth as Crawford walked and came home on George Moriarty's hit, Moriaty touching home on first baseman Tom Jones' knock, the game now tied at 3. In the fifth, 2nd baseman Jim Delahanty doubled in Donie Bush to give Detroit its first lead. In the very next inning, after a single by Tom Jones, it's not unusual that Cobb would double him home, so he did, building Detroit's lead to 5-3. It stayed that way until Pittsburgh's final at bat.

In the top of the ninth, the first two Pirates singled, putting runners on first & second, sending anxious rumbling through the full house at Bennett Park. The next batter, Chief Wilson, laid down a bunt. As he raced towards first, Tiger Tom Jones reached for the throw from catcher Boss Schmidt and collided with Pirate Wilson, knocking Jones unconscious as the ball rolled out to right where Cobb backed up the play. The lead runner crossed home, the Tigers lead cut to one, runners at the corners and no one out. Hang on to your fedoras!

Tom Jones is carried off the field, Crawford coming in from center to take his spot at first, Davy Jones moves from left to center, and Matty McIntyre comes off the bench to cover left. When the next Pirate grounds to Crawford at first, the runner from third breaks for home where Sam's throw cuts him down. One out, tying run at second base. As Pirate Ed Abbaticchio swings and misses at strike three, Chief Wilson tears out for third where catcher Boss Schmidt's throw to Moriarty at 3rd cuts him down in a game ending twin killing. Moriarty didn't much care for being spiked by Wilson, and lit into him, the two rolling around in a dirt pile of punchin', kickin', cussin', & blood, marking George Moriarty's Game 6 hat trick of one RBI and 2 fights. By George, that Moriarty feller is a live wire!

Tom Jones regained consciousness as his teammates tell him that they held on for the 5 to 4 victory. Its 3 games to 3 games with the deciding game 7 scheduled at The Corner in two days. Post-game, the bars, the streets, and the streetcars are filled with Tiger fever runnin' wild.

Game 7 Detroit: 17,562 very excited Detroiters filed into Bennett Park, ready to celebrate a World Series Championship. The starting pitchers were Wild Bill Donovan against Pirates rookie Babe Adams. No one any longer brings up Adams' 12 regular season victory total, but rather his 2 wins so far this Series. Make that 3. The Tigers bats were cold, the fielders made 3 errors, and Wild Bill earned his nickname, plunking the very first batter he faced & walking 6 Pirates in the 3 innings he worked. Detroit was only down 2-0 when Donovan was pulled for George Mullin, but on 2 days' rest, as great as Mullin was, he was no Mickey Lolich. He surrendered 2 Pirate runs in the fourth, 3 in the sixth, and then a final one in the eight. Meanwhile the Tiger offense could only get to Babe Adams for 6 hits and a single walk, their best threat in the second, with runners on 2nd & 3rd, left to die. The final score was Pirates 8 Tigers zero as the sad procession filed out of Bennett Park.

27 years before both would be voted into the inaugural Hall of Fame class at Cooperstown, veteran Honus got the better of young Tyrus in their 1909 World Series, head-to-head, match-up, batting .333 versus .231, respectively.

American League President Ban Johnson was not thrilled with the Tigers World Series results of 1907, 1908 & 1909, and knew who to blame, *"We do all right in the World Series, except when that damn National Leaguer, Jennings, gets into it. Then we get the hell beaten out of us."*

DDDDDDDDDDDDDDDDDDDDDDDDDDDDDDDDDDDDDDDDDDDDDDDDDDDDDDDDDDDDDDDDDDDDDDDDDDD

Frank Navin added 3,000 seats in 1910, increasing Bennett Park's capacity to 13,000. The team's success on the field excited the fans to flock in ever larger numbers to The Corner, and Frank ensured the supply met the demand.

In 1910, the Philadelphia A's ran away and hid from Detroit, earning the pennant for Philly. The Tigers had their moments this year, ending April in first, but a rough month of May had them 7 games out by Memorial Day weekend. Then, however, the Tigers excited their fans with a 15 & 3 spurt, including an early-June weekend sweep of the A's at Michigan & Trumbull, that vaulted the Boys of Summer within a single game of the league lead. A wild June 9 Sunday slugfest with Boston, the Tigers squeaking out a 10 to 9 win in 10 innings, secured 1st place for Detroit by one-half game over both the A's & the Yankees.

Tiger fans hopes were dashed as their heroes then stumbled, dropping out of first the very next day & proceeding to lose 11 of the next 17. Detroit arrived in Philadelphia for a 4-game series on July 8, trailing the A's by 6 games, with a golden opportunity to cut into the lead, but dropped all 4, leaving town 10 games back. The Tigers didn't play bad ball in 1910, finishing the year at 86 & 68, but that wasn't going to cut it against an outstanding Athletics squad, Detroit ending the year in third, 18 games out of first.

Detroit businessman & auto magnate Hugh Chalmers offered to award one of his "Chalmers 30" autos to the 1910 batting champion. With the season-ending infinitesimal difference separating 1st place Cobb's .3850687 and second place Nap Lajoie's .3840947, plus some shenanigans by the St. Louis Browns, who attempted to throw the title to Lajoie on the last day of the season, Chalmers generously awarded one car to each of the two players *(Nap on left, Ty on right)...*

DDDDDDDDDDDDDDDDDDDDDDDDDDDDDDDDDDDDDDDDDDDDDDDDDDDDDDDDDDDDDDDDDDDDDDDDDDDDD

1911 began with Detroit on fire, opening the season with a 21 & 2 tear. On July 18, after a 16-7 win over Boston, the team's ninth win in a row, the Tigers were 35 games over .500 at 59 & 24, and in first by 5.5 games. This was their high tide for the year, and Detroit's last day in first was August 5. The team finished the year with a fine record of 89 & 65, but that was only good enough for second place, 13 & one-half games back of the A's.

The Tigers were a hitting machine, batting .306 as a team, sparked by great individual performances, none better, of course, then that by Tyrus Raymond Cobb. When you say Ty Cobb had his finest year at the plate, that's quite a statement, and that he did in 1911. Cobb hit a league leading & career high .420 (including a 40-game hitting streak) for his fifth straight batting crown, and led the A.L. also in hits, runs, doubles, triples, RBIs, steals, slugging percentage while voted the league's "Chalmers Award" winner.

Starting in 1911, the Chalmers Award trophy and car would be given to *"the most important and useful player to the club and to the league"* as decided by a nation-wide vote of sports writers. The Chalmers Trophy now becomes the pre-cursor to the Most Valuable Player trophy. As the back-to-back winner, Ty Cobb's garage was getting crowded with Chalmers autos.

This was the season that Cobb tagged up and scored on a fly ball. He had been standing on second. 1911 was also the year that Ty had to appear in front of a judge for a speeding ticket he received while driving one of his Chalmers cars. Cobb explained to the court, *"I wasn't going any faster than when I steal second base."* The judge, a Tiger fan, smiled knowingly and suspended his sentence.

Detroit, not just Cobb, dominated among the American League offensive leaders. After Cleveland's Shoeless Joe Jackson, Sam Crawford was third in hitting at .378. Donie Bush was #1 in walks and 2nd in runs scored, Wahoo Sam Crawford third in hits, fourth in runs & second in RBIs, and Cobb second in home runs. 2nd baseman Jim Delahanty had his finest season in Detroit, an A.L. fifth in RBIs, sixth in both hits & batting at .339. Pitcher George Mullin, always a threat at the plate, chipped in at .286.

Besides his hitting, Mullin was staff ace at 18 wins & 10 losses with a 3.07 ERA. After Mullin, there was a noticeable drop off. Old reliable Wild Bill Donovan was the next best hurler in 1911, and he struggled to 10 & 9. The pitching could not keep up with the hitting, the reason why Detroit wasn't going to its 4th World Series in five years. The pitchers' performance was fair, but the team needed good to keep up with the back-to-back league champion Athletics.

1911 was also a good year for old friend Germany Schaefer. His second full season as a Washington Senator was the finest in his career, hitting .334 with 73 runs scored. Not bad for an old man of 35. During the Christmas season, Germany appeared at Detroit's Temple Theater, working the vaudeville circuit. While touring, Germany was sharing a compartment on an overnight train with a passenger who made clear to Schaefer that he did not care for Germany keeping a lamp on to read. After a heated exchange, Schaefer turned off the light and decided on an appropriate response to this encounter. It was only after his fellow passenger departed the train the next morning, that Germany realized he had thrown his own shoes out the window.

DDDDDDDDDDDDDDDDDDDDDDDDDDDDDDDDDDDDDDDDDDDDDDDDDDDDDDDDDDDDDDDDDDDDDDD

Although the American League Champion Tigers of 1907, 1908 & 1909 were not successful in winning a World Series, their exploits drew the fans in numbers that overwhelmed the capacity of the 10,000-seat park they played in. To meet the fans' growing demand for tickets, in the winter of 1911-1912, Bennett Park was torn down and on the same Michigan and Trumbull corner one of the first concrete and steel stadiums in the majors was constructed, with a capacity of (initially) 23,000 seats, known as Navin Field.

1910s Navin Field Is a Hit

Take me out to the ball game,
Take me out with the crowd;
Buy me some peanuts and Cracker Jack,
I don't care if I never get back.
Let me root, root, root for the home team,
If they don't win, it's a shame.
For it's one, two, three strikes, you're out,
At the old ball game.

("Take Me Out to the Ball Game" by Jack Norworth & Albert Von Tilzer, circa 1908)

Basil Kennedy, a fine Irish lad living near Navin Field, served as bat boy for the Tigers in the late-1910s. Basil was also one of the lucky kids allowed to shag balls for the team during their batting & fielding practice. One day Basil was feeling pretty good about his role at the ballpark, working hard with the other boys to field the balls that the Tiger fielders were letting go – so long as Basil and the kids stayed within their designated areas. There was one ball in particular that Basil was confident the nearest Tigers were going to pass on, and he was bound & determined to get it. The youngster was proud of the running catch he made of that ball until a split-second later when he received a swift kick in the butt from the Tiger who was also going for the same ball – Tyrus Raymond Cobb, himself...

The baseball park within which young Basil had his butt kicked was the pride 'n joy of another Irishman, the boss of the Tigers, Frank Navin. The beautiful ballyard was one befitting a team used to success, a team with arguably the finest, most creative and daring player in the game in Ty Cobb, a team that was one of the top draws in the majors, located in a city that was rapidly putting the world on wheels while its architecture earned it the nom de guerre of "the Paris of the West". Navin Field, it seemed, had something for everyone...

Pitcher's loved the additional distance a home run would have to travel at Navin Field. Bennett Park's 1911 dimensions, reduced from squeezing additional seats on to the field of play, stood at 285' down the left-field line, 390' center, and '324 down the right-field line. Contrast that to the 1912 dimensions of Navin Field of 345' left, 467' center, and 370' right (reduced in later years to 340', 440', and 325').

Hitters appreciated the Navin Field innovation of placing a large green panel in dead center, providing a wonderful background for picking up incoming pitches, and the positioning of Navin's playing field. One of the batters' biggest complaints about Bennett Park was the field's layout: home plate was set in the park's southeast corner, near the intersection of Michigan & Trumbull, and batters faced west. Since virtually every game through 1912 began at 330PM, in the late innings, they waited for each pitch while looking into a setting sun. Navin Field's home plate, however, is positioned at the southwest corner, near the intersection of Michigan & National (later Cochrane) Avenue, with the setting sun at the backs of hitters. When the famous right-field upper deck overhang was added at Navin Field along Trumbull in 1936, it became the fans' prime sun field location.

The reaction of the team's rooters to this new Navin Field was summarized in a *Detroit News* headline that appeared the day after the maiden game was played, *"Fan Verdict: SOME Park."*

DDDDDDDDDDDDDDDDDDDDDDDDDDDDDDDDDDDDDDDDDDDDDDDDDDDDDDDDDDDDDDDDDDDDDDDDDDD

Saturday, April 20, 1912 marked the inaugural game day for Detroit's new steel & concrete ball yard. The first pitch took place 5 days after the sinking of the Titanic, and hours before a first pitch took place at another brand-new ballpark, one 700 miles to the east, Boston's Fenway Park. George Mullin, son of Irish immigrants, in his 11th season with the Tigers and coming off yet another year as the Tigers ace, gets the honor of pitching the 1st game at Navin Field, spacious & spectacular compared to wooden Bennett Park, and able to meet the growing demand for tickets with twice as many seats at 23,000.

24,382 had the privilege of witnessing both the Navin Field coming out party and one very entertaining battle between the Tigers and the Cleveland Naps. The visitors from Ohio grabbed a 1st inning, 1-0, lead when center-fielder Shoeless Joe Jackson scored the new park's first run after he walked, stole second, and came home on an error by 2nd baseman Jim Delahanty. The Tigers responded immediately. Rookie left-fielder Ozzie Vitt led off Detroit's first with a single and was sacrificed to second. A Cobb single knocked Vitt in, and Ty went to second on Sam Crawford's hit. As Delahanty whiffed, Cobb & Crawford executed a double steal. With 2 outs, men on 2nd & 3rd and 1st baseman Del Gainer at the plate, Cobb & Crawford again pulled off a double steal, Ty's fade-away slide getting him across home safely. *This was the first of 8 steals of home for Cobb in 1912, still today the all-time, single-season, record.*

Detroit's 2-1 lead was short-lived as Cleveland plated two runners in the third, but just like in the first, the Tigers answered in their next at bat, scoring one in the bottom of the frame when rookie Ozzie Vitt once again touched home. Two innings later, another error by the Tigers' Delahanty helped allow the Naps to grab a 5-3 lead. It stayed that way until Detroit came to bat in the bottom of the eighth. Down to their last 6 outs, the Tigers rallied. With Cobb on third & Crawford on second, Jim Delahanty was able to offset his earlier errors with a 2-run single. End of 8, and it's all tied at 5.

Starters George Mullin and Cleveland's Vean Gregg each tossed a scoreless ninth & tenth. Mullin got into trouble in the top of the 11th, as the Naps loaded the bases with one out, but the Tiger hurler then induced two harmless groundouts. In the Tigers turn up, Donie Bush made it to third with two outs. Up to the plate stepped George Mullin. Hughie Jennings knew he had a fine hitting pitcher, and decided not to pinch hit for George – another sound decision by the manager. George Mullin didn't have to come back out to pitch the 12th, as he singled into left-field. Tigers win 6 to 5 at newly christen Navin Field!

As incredible as the 1912 celebration of the new ballpark was for the fans, the Tigers did not give their rooters the pennant race they had become accustomed to enjoying every year since 1907, as the team dropped from a second place '11 finish to sixth. There was no lack of excitement with this team, though: Cobb again owned opposing pitchers on his way to a splendid .409 season & a 6th consecutive batting crown, the team had a May date to remember on the road vs. the New York Highlanders _and_ their fans, while Detroit crowds witnessed history being made on the 4th of July at The Corner.

DDDDDDDDDDDDDDDDDDDDDDDDDDDDDDDDDDDDDDDDDDDDDDDDDDDDDDDDDDDDDDDDDDDDDDDDDDDDDDD

On the afternoon of May 15, 1912, unruly New York fans seated behind the Tiger dugout targeted the finest player in the game, pouring a stream of invectives upon Ty Cobb. Trying to get the goat of a visiting ballplayer is a cherished tradition in baseball lore, but this disparagement strayed beyond the pale. The *New York Times* reported that, *"what they have been saying to the Georgia Peach has no place in a family newspaper or even one that circulates in barber shops. The conversation yesterday got as rough as number 2 sandpaper."*

As Detroit was at bat in the 4th inning, the leather-lung perpetrators were just a few feet away from Ty's ear when he decided he'd had enough. Cobb vaulted from the Tiger dugout into the stands to confront the worst of his tormentors and a *New York Times* reporter picks it up from here, *"Cobb johnnykilbaned him right on the place where he talks, started the claret and stopped the flow of profane and vulgar words. Cobb led with a left jab and countered with a right kick to Mr. Spectator's left Weisbach, which made his peeper look as if someone had drawn a curtain over it."* (The above-mentioned Johnny Kilbane was the World Featherweight boxing title holder from 1912 to 1923).

The fan who had his left Weisbach kicked by Cobb was, ironically, a fella named Claude Lucker. As nasty as Claude's mouth was, it turns out that he was missing one hand completely and all but two fingers of his other. This gained sympathy for him - and wrath for Cobb - from another attendee at the same game, American League President Ban Johnson, who would not entertain a defense from Cobb and suspended him indefinitely.

On May 17, the entire Detroit Tiger team signed and sent a telegram to Johnson. It read, *"Feeling that Mr. Cobb is being done an injustice by your action, we the undersigned refuse to play in another game after today until such action is adjusted. He was fully justified in his action, as no one could stand such personal abuse from anyone. We want him reinstated for tomorrow's game, May 18, or there will be no game. If the players cannot have protection, we must protect ourselves."*

Ban Johnson said no, so the Tiger players walked. Frank Navin, facing a $5,000 fine if Detroit forfeited their next game, May 18 in Philly, ordered manager Hughie Jennings to assemble a team. Assisted by a local sports writer with whom Hughie was friends, he recruited Philadelphia area semi-pro and sandlot players to face the defending league champion Athletics. Detroit lost 24 to 2, the temporary Tigers paid $25 a man, $50 for the pitcher (one player, Billy Maharg, would graduate to a bag man in the bribes paid the 1919 Black Sox). It was the adventure of a lifetime for these substitute Tigers, but league president Ban Johnson was furious. The Tiger players' position was, the hell with Johnson, we could make more money on a barnstorming exhibition tour than we get paid anyways.

The universal support of his teammates was a pleasant surprise for Ty. Though appreciative of their sentiments, he urged them to end the strike. The Tigers, minus the suspended Cobb, returned to the field for their next game, each of their wallets a $100 fine lighter. Cobb paid a $50 fine (strangely, less than what each of his teammates paid) and returned from his suspension on May 26, rejoining the Tigers in Chicago, in time for a 6 to 2 Detroit victory at Comiskey Park.

DDDDDDDDDDDDDDDDDDDDDDDDDDDDDDDDDDDDDDDDDDDDDDDDDDDDDDDDDDDDDDDDDDDDDDDDD

George Mullin, the man who christen Navin Field by pitching & hitting the Tigers to victory on Opening Day, had another golden 1912 moment. It took place at The Corner in the second game of the 4th of July doubleheader. On that day, Mullin threw the first no-hitter in Detroit Tiger history, on his 32nd birthday no less, blanking the St. Louis Browns by the score of 7 to nothing. George's day at the plate was almost as good, going 3 for 4 with 2 RBIs. From his centerfield position, Ty Cobb made four fine running catches in the last 2 innings, including sealing the no-hitter by stealing a double from the game's final batter as the home crowd went wild. Amazingly, despite his Opening Day heroics and the no-hitter, George Mullin had been placed on waivers between the two events.

One of the Greatest Pitchers ever, George Mullin

1912 was a year in decline for Mullin, his 12 & 17 record producing the lowest winning percentage of a career that began with Detroit in 1902. After beginning 1913 1 & 6, though with a fine 2.75 ERA, George was sold from the only team he had ever played for to the Washington Senators on May 17, bringing down the curtain on his days with the Tigers. Mullin retired after the 1915 season, his last two years playing in the short-lived Federal League. He will always be remembered as the ace of the staff when the Tigers won their first 3 pennants in 1907, 1908 & 1909, for winning over 20 games 5 times, including a league-leading 29 wins in '09, and for being the Opening Day starter every year from 1903-1913 except in 1908. George was the winning pitcher when Detroit won their first World Series game, 1908 vs. Cubs, & defeated the Pirates twice in the 1909 Series when he tossed what remains *a single year World Series record 32 innings*. Mullin always looked for a psychological advantage over opposing batters and often found it, throwing off their timing by walking off the mound, tying & untying his shoes, starting up conversations with himself (hello Mark Fidrych), with batters and even with those in the stands. He was a pretty fair hitter, especially as pitchers go, retiring with a .262 lifetime average, and it was not unusual for Manager Hughie Jennings to bring him into a game to pinch hit, or even occasionally play outfield. George Mullin still holds the Tiger team records for most innings pitched, both in a single season and career, most games started in a season, most games completed in a single season & career, 2nd in shutouts, and retiring with the most Detroit career wins at 209. The man who is responsible for dropping Mullin to #2 all-time in Tiger career wins was a rookie in 1912...

I sat in Tiger Stadium in the late-1970s, reading the game program and perusing the all-time pitching leaders in Tiger history, when a man with an intriguing name kept popping up. Until that day at The Corner, I was unfamiliar with Hooks Dauss.

George "Hooks" Dauss byname was earned by his oft-times unhittable curve ball. Hooks made his major league debut while pitching for the Tigers on September 28, 1912, defeating Cleveland 6 to 2. Although he only appeared in two games that year, both were impressive complete game performances that convinced Manager Jennings to insert Dauss into the 1913 starting rotation. Hooks rewarded Hughie's confidence with a 13 & 12 record and a team-leading 2.48 earned run average.

Although Hooks Dauss had his breakout season, 1913 was another poor year for the team. As they did in 1912, Detroit finished again in 6th place, this time at 66 & 87. Individual successes featured Ty Cobb's 7th consecutive batting title at .390, and Sam Crawford finishing first in the league in triples & total bases, 2nd in home runs, while batting .317.

DDDDDDDDDDDDDDDDDDDDDDDDDDDDDDDDDDDDDDDDDDDDDDDDDDDDDDDDDDDDDDDDDDDDDDD

The man who was manager for 14 of Cobb's 24 seasons, and all 12 of Ty's batting titles, was Hughie Jennings. Hughie was the Tiger manager from 1907 thru 1920 and, until a colorful fella by the name of Sparky Anderson came along, no Tiger skipper had more years in or more victories during his tenure than Jennings. A natural leader, even as a youngster in his 20s on an 1890s Baltimore Orioles teams loaded with veterans he looked up to, including several Hall of Famers to be, among them the great future New York Giants manager John McGraw, it was Hughie who was chosen captain.

Hughie had great baseball ability, was fearless & intelligent, with a magnetic personality. He never hit below .328 in 5 seasons with Baltimore, including .401 in 1896 (2nd in the league), and he was the best fielding shortstop of his era. Hughie sacrificed his body for the team, still holding the MLB career (287) & single season (51) record of times hit-by-the-pitch. Rare for baseball players of his or any era, Hughie attended law school at Cornell, passed the bar, & worked at his law practice throughout his playing & managing days (and may have penned the 1912 Cobb-suspension team letter to the league President).

Jennings would get his players & the fans fired up with his famous *"Ee-yah!"* yell. It was piercing and impossible to miss if you were in or anywhere near the ballpark. Both the shout and the pose that he would strike was reminiscent of a great warrior preparing for battle, right leg raised and bent at the knee, arms waving over his head. The Hughie Jennings battle cry & pose was not only known by both league's players & their fans, but *"Ee-yah!"* was adopted as a rallying cry by U.S. Marines during World War I. Another Hughie cry was his lasting contribution to American slang: *"Attaboy!"* was said to have been his contraction of *"That's the boy!"*

Jennings was a master at flashing well-camouflaged signs to the batter from the coach's box, and is credited with being the first manager to employ platooning left-handed and right-handed hitters by position. Although Hughie was voted into the Hall of Fame as a ballplayer, the respect & accolades that he earned as an innovative & successful manager could have been his ticket into Cooperstown, also.

Firing up the boys with his "Ee-yah!" battle cry, Hughie Jennings

DDDDDDDDDDDDDDDDDDDDDDDDDDDDDDDDDDDDDDDDDDDDDDDDDDDDDDDDDDDDDDDDDDDDDDDDDD

The 1914 Tigers snapped out of their two-year slump, and brought hope back to the fans still yearning for the pennant years of 1907, 1908, and 1909. A pre-season minor league transaction that did not draw much attention at the time had a huge impact on the team's 1914 fortunes: Detroit purchased pitcher Harry Coveleski from the minor league Chattanooga Lookouts of the Southern League.

Coveleski had pitched in the National League to middling results from 1907 through 1910, compiling an overall record of 12 & 12 over the 4 years. Before '11, the Cincinnati Reds sold his rights to Chattanooga, where Harry suffered through a 22-loss '11 & a 15-loss '12. As a 27-year old in 1913, Harry finally put it all together, going 28 & 9 with a 1.44 ERA. The Tigers noticed, and acquired Harry in time for 1914. Now THAT was a good move! Over the 3 years of 1914-1916, Harry Coveleski was one of the finest pitchers in all of baseball, posting records of 22 & 12/2.49, 22 & 13/2.45, & 21 & 11/1.97. Teaming with Hooks Dauss, who won 19, 24 & 19 over the same 3 years, the Tigers presented opposing batters with an effective one-two punch that frequently overpowered them.

Detroit's '14 offense was again fueled by Cobb, his .368 average earning him batting title #8 in a row, while Wahoo Sam Crawford was the A.L. RBI king at 104. The two knocked in lead-off man Donie Bush with enough regularity to send him across the plate 97 times, good for 4th in the league.

The Tigers jumped to the head of the American League pack on Coveleski's 4-0 shutout of the Browns at Sportsman's Park in St. Louis on April 25, building their lead to 4 games by May 15 as Coveleski, Jean Dubuc, and Dauss held the Yankees to 3 runs over 3 days in the Bronx. Jean Dubuc would be the third leg of the pitching staff from 1914 to 1916, winning a total of 39 games in those 3 seasons.

A June 1 win behind little-used pitcher Marc Hall would be the final day that Detroit held first in '14. The Tigers kept their fanatics hopes up, staying in the thick of the pennant race & in second place every day but 3 from mid-June until late-July, sitting from 1.5 to 4 games out of first during that stretch. However, Detroit slumped to 13 games out by August 1st, and the final 1914 standings had Detroit in fourth place at 80 & 73, 19 games behind first place Philadelphia.

DDDDDDDDDDDDDDDDDDDDDDDDDDDDDDDDDDDDDDDDDDDDDDDDDDDDDDDDDDDDDDDDDDDDDDDDDD

And then there was 1915... oh so close. This Tiger team won 100 games, but finished 2 & ½ games behind the Red Sox, making Detroit one of only 3 teams in MLB history to win 100 or more games yet finish in second place (along with the 1954 Yankees & 1961 Tigers).

What a back-n-forth battle it was, all year long, between the clubs from Detroit & Boston. It seemed that every day of the 154-game season, both teams were winning 2 out of every 3 they played, with one team or the other in first place. Amazingly, from the 4th of July until the end of the season, never more than 4 & ½ games separated the two foes, staying within 2 games of each other for 110 of 154 games.

The Tigers Big 3 hurlers, Hooks, Coveleski & Dubuc, won 24, 22 & 17, respectively, the team earned run average a shining 2.86, and the team's offense a broken-record playing a sweet melody... Cobb taking his 9th batting title in row as well as leading the A.L. in hits, his 144 runs scored 26 beyond the next man, and - if possible - even more of a terror on the bases than ever, setting the all-time record of 28 stolen bases in one month AND a single season steals record of 96 that would last until Maury Wills 47 years later swiped 104 bags. Chicago White Sox catcher Ray Schalk had a suggestion on how to best defend against Ty's speed, *"When Cobb is on first base, and he breaks for 2nd, the best thing you can do, really, is to throw to 3rd."* Ty's fellow outfielders, Wahoo Sam & Bobby Veach, each knocked in 112 runners to tie for 1st in the league, with Ty 3rd at 99, Crawford & Veach 2nd & 3rd in hits (after Cobb, naturally), #1 doubles Bobby Veach, #1 triples Sam Crawford, tied for 2nd in walks was Donie Bush & Cobb, and the total base leaders went 1-2-3 Cobb-Crawford-Veach.

The Cobb-Veach-Crawford offensive juggernaut

1915 was the year that Bobby Veach entered his prime. In his 4th year in the majors, all with Detroit, the 27-year old's 40 doubles and 112 RBIs topped the American League. In the 4 years of 1913-1916, Veach-Cobb-Crawford was the most productive outfield in all of baseball, **called by many the greatest outfield ever put together in the majors.** Bobby Veach batted clean-up, behind 1-3 batters Donie Bush, Ty Cobb & Crawford. Physically, Bobby was as solid as the backyard brick barbeque my Dad built, strengthened from working in the Kentucky mines since the age of 12. The combination of his power, good batting eye, natural swing, and the good fortune of hitting behind 3 Tigers that always seemed to be on base, propelled Veach to drive in more runs than any other major leaguer from 1915 through 1922.

The Tigers traveled to Fenway Park for what everyone knew would be the biggest series of '15, a 4-game set that opened on Thursday, September 16. Detroit was coming off of a 4-game sweep of the Yankees in New York, arriving in Boston 2 games back, and had their ace, Hooks Dauss, ready for the opening game. Before the Fenway Faithful were settled in their seats, Donie Bush and Ty Cobb crossed home plate in the top of the first off 17-game winner Rube Foster, the Tigers adding one in the fourth & two in the fifth. The Red Sox batters could do nothing with Hooks' big bending curve, and when Detroit came to bat in the eighth, they were ahead 5 to nothing.

Detroit had knocked starter Foster from the game in the fifth, and Carl Mays pitched the final 4 for the Sox. The one thing the two had in common was hurling brushback pitches at Cobb each time he came to bat. When Cobb faced Mays in the eighth, he hit the dirt to avoid a fastball that sailed by where his head had been. Ty leaped to his feet and, returning the favor, rifled his bat in the general vicinity of Carl Mays skull. Mays got to his feet, the bat boy retrieved Ty's bat, Cobb stepped back in to hit, & felt the sting of the next pitch striking his wrist. As he strolled to first, Tyrus cursed Mays, Mays' teammates, and did not overlook the howling denizens occupying the stands. Those denizens, in turn, rifled garbage at Cobb as he stood on first. His obvious joy at scoring the Tigers' sixth run only served to further infuriate the Massachusetts Mob. When Cobb caught a Boston fly ball for the game's final out, sealing the 6-1 Tiger victory, a large group of fans pushed their way past the police, and surrounded Ty before he could get off the field. He coolly walked through the rabble, as they shared ribald stories of his mother and worse from no more than a couple feet from their target.

As Friday dawned, Detroit was within one game of Boston, with an opportunity to take over first before heading on to play the A's in Philly. Unfortunately, Tiger pitcher Bill James was rocked for 6 runs in less than 3 innings as Boston cruised to a 7-2 victory to restore their 2-game lead. On Saturday, Harry Coveleski went the distance in a 12-inning heartbreaking 1-0 loss and, after a young, 2nd year pitcher from the Red Sox outdueled Hooks Dauss 3-2 on Sunday, Detroit left town down and 3 games behind. That sophomore season pitcher, who appeared in only 4 games the year prior, burst onto the scene in 1915, winning 18 and losing only 8, with a 2.44 earned run average. That Babe Ruth kid from Baltimore could hit, too, as his .315 average could attest.

The slim difference between the two 100 game-winning heavyweights was found on the mound. As good as Detroit's Big 3 pitchers were, 5 different Boston hurlers won between 15 to 19 games. It was that slight pitching edge that allowed the Red Sox to squeak by the Tigers for the '15 A.L. pennant.

DDDDDDDDDDDDDDDDDDDDDDDDDDDDDDDDDDDDDDDDDDDDDDDDDDDDDDDDDDDDDDDDDDDDDDDDDDDDDDDDDD

In 1916, the Detroit Tigers finished third in the race for the American League pennant, 4 games behind the eventual World Champion Boston Red Sox. In an unrelated news item, Congress officially established The National Park Service as a bureau in the Department of the Interior.

Boston's Babe Ruth, in his third year in the majors, was the A.L.'s dominant pitcher of 1916. He had a record of 23 & 12, leading all league pitchers with a 1.75 ERA, 40 games started, and 9 shutouts. The balance of the Sox rotation was tough to hit, too. Dutch Leonard & Carl Mays each won 18, Ernie Shore 16, & Rube Foster 14, and the team ERA was an impressive 2.48. In contrast, Tiger pitching success was limited behind Harry Covelski & Hooks Dauss, the staff achieving its greatest notoriety for wildness: on May 9th, a Tuesday at Philadelphia's Shibe Park, Detroit mounds-men George Cunningham and Bernie Boland became part of MLB history as they combined with their A's counterparts to walk a Major League record 30 batters (18 by the Athletics) in a 16-2 Tiger victory. When 11 more Tigers received free passes in next day's game, that established another record of one team walking 29 times in two games.

The Tigers team ERA was 1/2 point higher than Boston's, leaving the offense to make up the difference. As usual, Ty Cobb had a great year at the plate, but his streak of 9 consecutive batting titles was snapped as his .371 was 2nd to the .386 of Cleveland's Tris Speaker. Cobb was still first in runs and stolen bases, and Bobby Veach was near the top, again, in runs batted in as well as doubles, triples, and runs scored. However, the bat of a man who terrorized pitchers for the last 15 years, whose bat could be counted on to produce in critical moments, had grown unusually quiet. And when it was muted, so were the Tigers' chances of catching Boston...

The Pride of Wahoo, Nebraska: Sam Crawford

1916 was the season that Wahoo Sam Crawford finally showed he was mortal. From 1901 through 1915, baseball's all-time leader for triples (309) & inside-the-park-homers (51) scored over 100 runs 3 times, hit over 30 doubles 7 times, leading the league in triples 6 times (including 1913-1915), homers twice & runs batted in 3 times (1910, 1914 & 1915). The fact that his most productive years were his most recent as a player, made his slip in 1916 an event that seemed to take the baseball world by surprise. It was the first year since '01 that Sam was not in the top 3 in any of the major offensive categories (7th in, of course, triples was his '16 best showing). After playing in a part-time capacity in 1917, Sam Crawford retired from the game at 37 years of age. Sam Crawford was built like Gordie Howe, with the same sloping shoulders, height, & quiet confidence, both letting their achievements at their sport do the talking for them. Both came from small, rural, towns, Sam from Wahoo, Nebraska, and Gordie from Floral, Saskatchewan. And each had a look in their eye during the game that told you avoid any physical confrontation with either. Sam Crawford was voted into the Hall of Fame in 1957. In the sea of Hall of Famers in their respective sports, Wahoo Sam and Gordie Howe floated to the surface.

Picking up some of the slack in '16 was a 21-year old San Francisco native enjoying his first full season in The Show, as Harry Heilmann got into 136 games and knocked in 77 runners.

DDDDDDDDDDDDDDDDDDDDDDDDDDDDDDDDDDDDDDDDDDDDDDDDDDDDDDDDDDDDDDDDDDDDDDDDD

1917 saw Ty Cobb attain the 2nd-longest hitting streak of his career, this one 35 games, to go with his 40-gamer in 1911. *To this day, only Cobb and fellow Hall-of-Famer George Sisler have more than one hitting streak of 35 or more games.* Ty seemed to be motivated in '17 by having his string of consecutive batting titles snapped the previous year: he led the American League at .383, 30 points ahead of #2 George Sisler, and was first in on base %, slugging %, hits, doubles, triples, and total bases. Cobb came in second in RBIs to teammate Bobby Veach, and he was probably mad about that. In fact, Veach led all

American Leaguers in RBIs in 1917 AND 1918. Cobb didn't dominate in as many offensive categories in '18 as he did '17, but did hit .382 to win batting crown number 10, once again by 30 points.

The individual achievements were all Tiger fans had to cheer for in those two years, as Detroit finished 21 & then 20 games back of first. The pitching support just wasn't there. Hooks Dauss continued to mow down hitters, but Harry Coveleski, the other half of Detroit's 1-2 punch on the mound, faded badly: after recording 63 wins from 1914 to 1916, he could only ring up 4 wins in '17 & zero in '18, before retiring.

DDDDDDDDDDDDDDDDDDDDDDDDDDDDDDDDDDDDDDDDDDDDDDDDDDDDDDDDDDDDDDDDDDDDDD

This was in the era of delightful, no-holds-barred, nicknames, and 1918 marked the last of 3 years as the Tiger back-up catcher for Tubby Spencer, a much kinder sobriquet than his other nickname several newspapers saddled him with, Hippo. A newspaper article noted that, *"Spencer's massiveness makes it a comparatively easy matter for him to block runners. The only chance to remove him from the plate is to use a dynamite cartridge or a derrick."* Spencer was considered to have one of the best arms in baseball, but a spring training review may have best captured the potential AND pitfalls of being Tubby Spencer, *"He worked as no man on the team has worked. He caught, ran bases, and was the life of the party."*

DDDDDDDDDDDDDDDDDDDDDDDDDDDDDDDDDDDDDDDDDDDDDDDDDDDDDDDDDDDDDDDDDDDDDD

All pretense of being competitive evaporated in 1918 when the Tigers came in at a dismal 55 & 71. They only played 126 games in '18 as the regular season was shortened one month to a September 1 ending, and the World Series between the Red Sox & Cubs begun immediately. This was to accommodate the USA's entry into World War I, and the many players departing our shores to join the fight. Reflecting the nation's patriotic fever, game 1 of the Series marked the first time that the National Anthem was heard at a sporting event – the date, September 5, 1918. The Anthem was played during the 7th inning stretch by the U.S. Navy band. Fred Thomas of the Red Sox had been granted furlough from the Navy to play in the Series, and upon hearing the song, turned to salute the flag. Other players followed suit and the already-standing Chicago fans began to sing the words to the Star-Spangled Banner. When the two team owners heard the crowd's clamorous uproar at the song's conclusion, they decided to play the anthem at the rest of the Series games, and a tradition was born. Boston's Babe Ruth threw a 1-0 shutout that day. When he also pitched, and won, game 4, Ruth hit 6th in the lineup – to this day, he remains the only World Series starting pitcher to ever hit anywhere other than ninth. The Red Sox defeated the Cubs, 4 games to 2.

The 1918 World Series pitted opponents who would endure two of the longest Series victory droughts in MLB history: it would be Boston's final Championship for 86 years, until 2004, and the Cubs were only 10 years into their 108 year, 1908 to 2016, futility. The combined Red Sox-Cub period of impotence ran 194 years. Something about Chicago... the White Sox dry spell ran 88 years, from 1917 to 2005.

DDDDDDDDDDDDDDDDDDDDDDDDDDDDDDDDDDDDDDDDDDDDDDDDDDDDDDDDDDDDDDDDDDDDDD

On May 16, 1919, Herman "Germany" Schaefer passed away much too young at 43 years old, dead from a brain hemorrhage. His loved ones said Germany was smiling as he left us. Later that year, MLB's rules committee issued a statement: *"A base-runner having acquired legal title to a base cannot run bases in reverse order for the purpose of confusing the fielders or making a travesty of the game."* The ruling is officially called Rule 52, Section 2, but most everyone refers to it as the Germany Schaefer rule.

The Tigers of 1919 improved from 16 games below .500 in '18 to 20 games above, going 80 & 60 in the 140-game season (in 1920, MLB would return to their 154-game format, the idea to play 140 games lasting only one year). Hooks Dauss had another in a string of strong years in Detroit at 21 & 9. For the first time since Harry Coveleski's 1916 performance, Detroit had a dependable number 2 pitcher as Howard Ehmke, a 166 & 166 lifetime pitcher, came through with the finest of his 15 major league seasons, winning 17 vs. 10 losses. Throw in 14-victory years each from Dutch Leonard & Bernie Boland, and the team now had the pitching to go with their usual run production, ready for a pennant race. Cobb's .384 won his 12th & final batting title (although in Ty's remaining 9 years of baseball, he never hit below .328, and that was in his final season when he was 41 years old). Bobby Veach hit .355, #2 in the league to Cobb, led the A.L. in hits, doubles & triples, and his 97 RBIs were 2nd to Babe Ruth. Cobb & Veach had help from a few youngsters to spark a potent offense. 24-year old Harry Heilmann hit his prime & .320, marking the first of his many years over .300, chipping in 92 RBIs; from the shores of Lake Michigan, Montague sent favorite son Ira Flagstead to the Tigers, and he responded by hitting .331 in his rookie year; while Chick Shorten, acquired from Boston for Ossie Vitt, contributed a .315 season.

The '19 Tigers played an exciting brand of baseball, packing the park with 643,805 fans, allowing the team to lead the league in attendance for the first time ever. After losing a 12-5 stinker to the lowly Athletics on June 21, dropping to fifth place, 9 & ½ games out of first, the Tigers reeled off 8 straight wins to end the month, outscoring the opposition 38 to 13 during the run. By the end of July, Detroit had pulled into second place, within 6 games of the White Sox. The Tigers began August on a 16 & 4 tear, Heilmann & Flagstead a house 'a fire, these young Tigers getting the fans all riled up and coming down to The Corner in droves. The problem was they were chasing the White Sox of Joe Jackson, Eddie Cicotte & Eddie Collins, who had their own 10-game winning streak in August, and the streaking Tigers could only pick up one game on Chicago during their 20-game rampage.

As much fun as the 1919 Tabbies were, they never really had a chance to flag down Chicago. The White Sox moved into first place on July 9 and would not vacate it. At the end of the regular season, those White Sox conspired with gamblers to throw the World Series, gaining fame as the Black Sox. The Detroiters, on the other hand, fought hard through their final game of the year. Tiger fans loved them for it, but their Boys of Summer ended up 8 games short of winning the 1919 pennant.

RIP Herman "Germany" Schaefer – you were one of a kind

1920s Manager Cobb Takes the Reins

Come along, join the throng, get in line, Molly mine
We are going to old Detroit town
Here we are in my car, right in town, Molly Brown
And tomorrow we'll see Ty Cobb at bat

("A Real, Live Regular Town" by Jerome Remick, circa 1912)

In 1920, the Tigers had an atrocious start, losing their first 13 games. The team tumbled from 4th place in the previous year to 7th, one team above the cellar & a not-even-shouting-distance 37 games behind the pennant-winning Cleveland Indians. Although it was a difficult decision for all involved, the much-loved Hughie Jennings resigned and Tyrus Raymond Cobb became the 1921 season player-manager.

Bobby Veach credited Jennings for the kindness & patience required to develop his raw talent into the major leagues top run producer over the last 6 years. Manager Ty Cobb, however, thought Veach could never reach his full potential unless he shed his friendly demeanor (Veach was pleasant with all players, regardless of what team they were on) and adopt a more combative personality. Since Bobby Veach drove in more runs than anyone else from 1915 to 1922, it begs the question, just how good did Cobb think Veach could be? To create the Veach he wanted, Cobb directed Harry Heilmann to heckle, tease, and otherwise heap abuse on Bobby while he was at the plate. Since Veach hit fourth and Harry fifth, Heilmann was only steps away in the on-deck circle as Bobby batted, so well within earshot.

Did Cobb's 1921 plan for work? Well, Veach did hit .338, second highest of his career, and set personal highs in hits, home runs, and RBIs. But the difference between Bobby V's production under Jennings vs. Cobb is like the difference between Miguel Cabrera's 2012 versus his 2013 – it ain't much. The cost to the relationship between Veach & Heilmann, though, was a grudge that lasted years.

The impact on the offense with Cobb as manager, however one may view some of the methods, cannot be overlooked. *In his 1921 rookie season as skipper, the Tigers as a team hit .316, still the A.L. single season team batting average record. No outfield has ever driven in more runs than the 368 Veach, Cobb, & Heilmann did that year*, and the 3 had a combined, incredible, 641 hits for a .372 batting average, with Harry's .394, and his first batting title, leading the way.

Although the Tigers scored a whopping 887 runs, they allowed almost as many at 852. The exhilaration of watching this scoring machine kept the Navin Field stands full, but as much fun as the 13-1 wins were, there were too many 11-10 losses. The pitching was mediocre with an ERA of 4.40, and the defense was just plain bad, allowing over 150 unearned runs. Despite the historic run production, the Tigers finished in sixth place at 71 & 82 in 1921.

DDDDDDDDDDDDDDDDDDDDDDDDDDDDDDDDDDDDDDDDDDDDDDDDDDDDDDDDDDDDDDDDDDDDDDDD

In 4 of Cobb's 6 years at the helm, the Tigers hit over .300. The 1920s Tigers, often called "Ty-gers", were one of baseball's all-time finest hitting clubs and, though unable to win a pennant, one of the most exciting to watch. It started with Ty's .367 lifetime average, and continued with a lineup featuring Heinie Manush (lifetime .330), Bobby Veach (.310 & RBI king), Bob "Fatty" Fothergill (.325 despite girth that drove Leo Durocher to complain to the umpires it was illegal to have 2 men in the batter's box), Lu Blue (lead-off man who hit over .300 4 of his 1st 5 years with the Tigers & a .402 career on-base percentage), and a well-deserving Hall of Famer, Harry Heilmann.

Called by Cobb *"the greatest right-handed hitter I've ever seen"*, Heilmann was a lifetime .342 hitter. Harry played for the Tigers all but the last 2 years of his career, wearing the D from 1916 to 1929, and led the American League in hitting 4 times, with averages of .394, .403, .393, & .398. If the man known as 'Ol Slug moved at more than what passed for a brisk mosey, he would have hit over .400 all four times, and might have challenged Ty Cobb's lifetime numbers.

Ol' Slug, Harry Heilmann   *MLB's top run-producer 1915-1922: Bobby Veach*

As every year with Cobb's Tygers, the team's 1922 offense fired on all cylinders. For the third time in his spectacular career, Ty hit over .400, finishing the year at .401. This was not enough to win a 13th batting crown for him though, as George Sisler of the St. Louis Browns matched Cobb's best single season at .420. Harry Heilmann's .356 average and 21 homers were both good for 4th in the league, Bobby Veach came in #9 at .327 along with his usual high number of RBIs at 126, 2nd-best in the A.L., completing his league-leading 8-year, 1915-1922, average of 107 runs batted per year. 2nd year first sacker, Lu Blue, followed up his .308 rookie season by batting .300, crossing home plate 131 times, second in the A.L. No less than 11 of Detroit's 16 position players hit .300 or more. Ah, but then there was the pitching. Hurler Herman Pillette had his moment in the spotlight, leading the staff with 19 wins against 12 losses, with a sweet 2.85 ERA, but there was little else supporting the offense. Once again, a day at The Corner would be exciting, full of fireworks by both teams, plenty of high scoring wins AND losses, as Detroit fell short of the pennant, finishing third at 79 & 75.

DDDDDDDDDDDDDDDDDDDDDDDDDDDDDDDDDDDDDDDDDDDDDDDDDDDDDDDDDDDDDDDDDDDDDDDDDD

In the Winter of 1922-1923, an infield Upper Deck that ran from first base to third base was added at Navin Field, increasing the park's seating capacity from 23,000 to 30,000. The view from the Upper Deck was new in 1923, but on the field of play below, the beat goes on in the onslaught of base hits & runners crossing home plate, for both the home team & the visitors.

Two long-time Tigers had notable seasons for different reasons. 33-year old Hooks Dauss was back in the form so familiar to his fans, his big-bender curveball once again tying batters in knots, tossing 4 shutouts in cruising to a 21 & 13 season. 34-year old Bobby Veach started the year with a salary holdout, was then sidelined with injuries, and although he still posted a fine .321 average, Manager Cobb split his playing time with 21-year old Heinie Manush, who banged out .334 in an impressive rookie season.

Standing out on a team that once again hit .300 was Harry Heilmann's .403 that gave him a 2nd batting title and the Navin Field faithful plenty to cheer for. Detroit improved to 83 & 71, but with Babe Ruth's Yankees winning 98 games, the Tigers were a distant second, 15 games back, in '23.

Late in 1923, Bobby Veach was hunting in the Fowlerville area, when some of his companions urged him to check out a local baseball player. Veach attended a sandlot game and was bowled over by the kid, arranging a tryout with the Tigers for the young Charlie Gehringer. Ty Cobb was equally impressed with Gehringer, *"I knew Charlie would hit and I was so anxious to sign him that I didn't even take the time to change out of my uniform before rushing him into the front office to sign a contract."*

The 1924 season began on a bad note for Tiger rooters. The personality conflict between Cobb's fiery intensity and happy-go-lucky fan favorite Bobby Veach prompted the January sale of Bobby to the cellar-dwelling Red Sox. On a Boston team with few runners on base when he came up, Veach still drove in a team-leading 99 in his year at Fenway. On May 18, in his first game back at The Corner, Bobby had one hit, one RBI, and was greeted home by happy & thankful fans who presented him with a diamond ring.

In early '25, Veach was traded from Boston to the Yankees and, coming off the bench, he hit .353 in 116 at bats. At 37 years of age, clearly Bobby was not done making an impact, so much so that he pinch hit for Babe Ruth that year, giving him entry into an exclusive club. On their march to the 1925 A.L. title, the Washington Senators picked up Veach for the stretch run, giving him the opportunity to get into a World Series the final year of his MLB career. With the game still a joy to him, Veach played 1926-1929 for the Toledo Mud Hens in the minor league American Association, topping the league at .382 as a 40-year old in 1928. After 75 games in 1930 with the Jersey City Skeeters, Veach called it a career, retiring with his wife to their Detroit area home.

In the history of the American League, Bobby ranks 35th all-time in batting average at .310, 62nd with 1,166 RBIs, and 75th in doubles at 393. It seems as though somewhere within the over 300 honored at Cooperstown, Bobby Veach, the majors top run-producer over an 8-year period, should reside.

DDDDDDDDDDDDDDDDDDDDDDDDDDDDDDDDDDDDDDDDDDDDDDDDDDDDDDDDDDDDDDDDDDDDDDDDDDDDD

The 1924 Tigers were a win one/lose one club through late-May, when a 10 & 3 spurt pulled them to within one game of the first place Yankees just as New York arrived in town to start a 4-game series on June 11. 2nd-year man Earl Whitehill was on the mound for Detroit in game 1. Whitehill would have a long run in the majors, pitching through the 1939 season as a 40-year old, & winning 218 games, but at this stage of his career, today was his biggest game by far. Earl pitched around the dangerous Babe Ruth, walking him twice, while Babe nicked him for a double and a run scored. That was not enough for the visitors from New York, as Ty Cobb's 3 for 3 while crossing the plate 3 times led the Tiger offense, and Whitehill went the distance in a 7-2 win that pushed Detroit into a first-place tie with the Yanks. In game 2, each team had 13 hits, but New York was more effective in bunching theirs, defeating Detroit 10-4. The third game of the series was on June 13, the day that will forever be known as *"The Brawl at The Corner"*, a 30-minute riot ignited by the long-standing Cobb-Ruth feud. This feud had its beginnings in the changing face of baseball...

The 1901-1919 *Dead Ball Era* was being replaced in the 1920s with the *Lively Ball Era*. Through 1919, pitchers had been allowed to doctor the ball, causing the baseball to travel erratically to home plate, by applying a variety of substances to it, the spitball the most popular of these "trick pitches". Pitchers were only constrained by their creativity. With the flu pandemic of 1918-1919, outlawing the spitball gained wide-spread support, as concern grew for players contacting saliva-covered baseballs. In addition, a frequent feature of the Dead Ball Era was one single ball used the entire game, no matter how greased up, black, or misshapen it had become – late in the games, players swung at a mush ball.

Then in the twenties, not only were the doctored pitches outlawed, but umpires were given several balls for each game, ensuring fresh balls were in use at all times. Perhaps, most importantly, the ball itself was much livelier: the rubber-core baseballs were replaced by cork-and-rubber center balls. As these changes took place benefitting the hitters, Babe Ruth was sold by Boston to the Yankees for $125,000 before the start of the 1920 season. In 1920 with New York, Babe hit a major league record 54 homers, more than any of the other 15 MLB *teams* hit. Babe Ruth was a colossus, far & away the biggest name in sports, in the entire country for that matter - and Ty Cobb was none too happy about it.

Ty's brand of baseball was scientific, it was creative, it was all about how to manufacture a run through smarts, daring, and psychology. No one was better at it than Tyrus Raymond Cobb. That style is reflected on the MLB sacrifice bunts career list: in the top 50, from Cobb teams were Sam Crawford, Donie Bush, Ossie Vitt, Harry Heilmann, Bobby Veach, and Ty himself. The brawn of Babe Ruth turned Cobb's world upside down, eclipsing his stature in the game. To make matters worse, even the home crowds at Navin Field adored and cheered Babe Ruth when he came to bat, as Cobb stood in the outfield and steamed. Losing to Ruth and his damn Yankees yesterday dropped Cobb's attitude from sour to rotten, and now it was time for game 3.

On 6/13/24, New York drew first blood, 3 Yanks crossing the plate in the 2nd inning. In the bottom half of the inning, the Tigers responded with 2 of their own, but the visitors came right back with 3 more in their third to take a 6-2 advantage. It stayed that way until the home team, carried by 3 RBIs off the bat of catcher Johnny Bassler, tied things up with two in the fifth and two again in the sixth. Tiger reliever Bert Cole had quieted New York's bats since he took the mound in the third, and now faced Ruth in the seventh. The Babe hit an infield grounder as Cole covered first base, and Ruth gave him a stiff-arm that roughed up Cole and would've made Jim Thorpe proud. When the Yankees proceeded to score 4 runs in the inning, the home crowd was put into a nasty frame of mind.

With the Tigers down 10-6 in the ninth, Ruth came up to bat against the man he stiff-armed two innings prior. Bert Cole delivered some chin music the Babe's way, forcing Ruth to hit the dirt. When big-hitting Bob Meusel stepped in the batter's box, Cole drilled him in the ribs. Meusel raced out to the mound, and after two wild swings that Cole ducked under, was restrained by the umpires. Both benches emptied, the two teams engaged in tossing punches and cursing each other, Ruth & Cobb goin' at it right in the middle of it all, scrapin', clawin', sluggin', spittin', wrasslin' and cursin'. It took several Yankees to pull Ruth away from the fracas and back to the dugout before New York's meal ticket could be suspended from future games.

Yankee Meusel, ejected for going after the Tiger pitcher, was leaving the field when he detoured towards the Tiger dugout and, just as the melee was winding down, all hell broke loose again. The fans, who had been shouting support for the fighting Tigers while pouring abuse down on the Yankees, now jumped the railings and were active participants in the disorder, fighting New Yorkers and the police.

The *New York Times* reported, *"The fans had now started to fight with the bluecoats, and the mob, ever-increasing in numbers, completely covered the diamond. The throng was a surging mass of straw hats and swinging fists."* The police were able to get the Yankees safely off the field and into their clubhouse, but even after the New Yorkers left the diamond, the fans would not, and the head umpire declared a forfeit & a Yankees 9-0 victory.

40,000 crammed into 30,000 seat Navin Field for the series finale, many hoping to get a swing in at someone wearing Yankee pinstripes, but no such luck in either fisticuffs or on the scoreboard, as Detroit lost for the third consecutive time, 6-2. Twice in 1924, 40,000+ attended games at Michigan & Trumbull, as the Tigers drew over 1,000,000 fans for the first time in their history. When Cobb became player-manager in 1921, his contract included (1) a base of $25,000 (3X league average) & (2) a dime for every ticket sold over 700,000, the big 1924 crowds coming to see Cobb's explosive teams doubling his salary.

The Tigers fought their way back to first place on August 3 with a 5-2 win over New York at The Corner, Earl Whitehill besting the Yankees as he did on June 11, this time with the help of Harry Heilmann's 3 for 4 plus a homer. After back-to-back losses to New York, there was that man Whitehill again, going the distance versus the Yanks for the 2nd time in 4 days, again by a score of 5-2. Earl was the Tiger ace this year, at 17 wins & 9 losses, and would be a consistent force on the hill for 9 years in Detroit, winning an average of 15 games a season through '32.

On August 10 of 1924, at the age of 38, Ty Cobb stole 2nd, 3rd, and home plate in one inning for the fourth & final time in his career, this time versus Boston at Navin Field. The feat tied his old Pittsburgh Pirate nemesis from the 1909 World Series, Honus Wagner, for a MLB record they still share today. In a wild 13-7 victory, old pro Hooks Dauss chalked up his 12th win, as the Tigers once again moved into a first-place tie.

One of the big bats keeping the Tigers in the thick of the pennant race of '24 was also one of the finest hitting catchers in Tiger history, and an often overlooked one, Johnny Bassler. Going into August, Bassler was hitting .314, but the best was yet to come. Johnny was a house 'a fire in August & September, on his way to finishing the year at .346, a career best and tied with Heilmann as Detroit's 1924 top hitter. In his 9-year career, all but the first 44 games as a Tiger, Bassler had a lifetime .304 average. Johnny always seemed to be in the middle of the team's rallies, especially this year when the only American Leaguer with a better on base percentage than his .441 was Babe Ruth.

While Johnny Bassler was one of the finest hitting catchers in Tiger history, he was one of the best defensive ones as well, once throwing out 6 runners attempting to steal in a single game. In recognition of his all-around excellence, Bassler finished in the top 10 for 3 straight seasons in voting for the league Most Valuable Player.

A 7 & 12 skid from August 10-31 dropped Detroit out of first to 5 games back going into September. Although the boys won 18 of 27 the balance of '24, and finished a respectable 86 & 68, it was not enough to win a pennant, and the Tigers ended 6 games behind the first place Washington Senators, and four behind 2nd place New York.

When Earl Whitehill shutdown the Yankees 4-3 on September 21, he recorded his fifth win against one loss versus Ruth & his mates for 1924. When the Yankees looked back on where they fell short for the flag in 1924, Earl "Yankee Killer" Whitehill might have been foremost in their thoughts.

DD

In 1925, Harry Heilmann led the league at .393 and in RBIs with 134. He had been trailing Cleveland's Tris Speaker in early-September, got red hot at the plate, and caught Speaker on the final day of the season by going 3 for 4 in the first of a doubleheader. When his teammates urged him to sit out the second game, and not risk losing his newly won lead over Tris, Harry never gave it a thought. *"I'll win it fairly, or not at all."* Heilmann went 3 for 3 in the nightcap to take the title .393 to .389.

Also in the batting race was 4th place finisher Ty Cobb at .378 and another Tiger, one-season wonder Al "Red" Wingo, 5th in the A.L. at .370. Al, short for Absalom, Wingo got into 15 games for the Philadelphia Athletics as a 21-year old in 1919, spent the next 4 years in the minors, each year hitting over .300. The Tigers were impressed, so much so that they spent $50,000 (quite a bit for the nickel-nursing Frank Navin) to purchase the rights to Red, who joined the Tigers for the 1924 season and hit .287. After his .370 '25 season, Wingo hit .282, .234, then was out of baseball in 1928.

In 1925 though, Al Wingo had quite the year. He could always tell his grandkids that he was part of the only outfield in MLB history in which every member hit .370 or better: Left-fielder Wingo .370, Right-fielder Heilmann .393, and Center-fielder Cobb .378.

After his final major league season of 1928, Al Wingo played in the minors for 6 more years, compiling a fine .320 lifetime average during his decade in the minor leagues. Once retired from the game, Al settled in Detroit, working a job at Ford's until 1964. That year, the 66-year old Wingo died when the truck he was driving was struck by a car, throwing him from his truck's cab, and crushing him under its wheels.

As spectacular as the Tigers outfield starters hit, they didn't lose much when their reserves played, as off the bench Bob "Fatty" Fothergill batted .353 & Heinie Manush .302. First baseman Lu Blue, recovering nicely from a broken ankle that cost him the last 40 games of his .311 1924 year, bounced back at .302 with 94 RBIs, 92 runs, and a team-leading 83 walks.

The staff ace, still going strong in his 14th season of wearing the Olde English D, was 35-year old Hooks Dauss. Hooks posted a 16 & 11 record, his 3.16 ERA a full point better than the Tigers next best pitcher. And therein, as in so many Tiger years under Cobb as manager, lies the problem – insufficient pitching depth beyond the top 1 or 2 hurlers to support the club's strong hitting.

At no time were the Tigers in the 1925 pennant race. From May 12 on, the team was never less than double-digit games out of first place. Even a 9-game winning streak in June only cut their deficit from 13 games to 12 games. Detroit ended 81 & 73, in 4th place, 16.5 back of Senators. In New York, not even a new, promising kid in the lineup, Lou Gehrig, could keep the New York Yankees out of 7th place, 12 games behind the Tigers.

DDDDDDDDDDDDDDDDDDDDDDDDDDDDDDDDDDDDDDDDDDDDDDDDDDDDDDDDDDDDDDDDDDDDDDDDDD

Opening Day of 1926 would be the final time that one of the most idolized Detroit ballplayers of all-time, the catcher & team leader of the 1887 World Series Champion Detroit Wolverines, and namesake of Bennett Park, Charlie Bennett, would catch the ceremonial first pitch. Despite the loss of both legs to a train accident in 1894, Charlie caught every Tigers' Opening Day first pitch since 1895, a total of 32 consecutive seasons: the final season in old League Park, all 16 seasons at Bennett Park, and the first 15 years at Navin Field. Many of those seasons, Charlie's old friend & teammate, Sam Thompson, would walk out to home plate with Bennett to hold his cane during the ceremony. With 72-year old Charlie Bennett's passing in February of 1927, baseball fans in Detroit lost a beloved community figure, a hero of the diamond, and the loss of an emotional Opening Day tradition.

Charlie Bennett

Heinie Manush will always have a soft spot in his heart for 1926. In a reserve role from 1923 to 1925, Heinie was impressive at the plate, racking up averages of .334, .289, and .302. Placed into a starting role in '26 by Manager Cobb, who gave up many of his own at bats to Manush, Heinie's stock rose from impressive to spectacular, winning the batting crown at .378 vs. 2nd place Babe Ruth's .372. This was also the year that Fatty Fothergill earned a regular spot in the outfield, taking time from Al Wingo, his .367 good for 3rd in the A.L., tied with Harry Heilmann. With the .378 of Manush, and both Fothergill & Heilmann at .367, Detroit was only .006 away from the second all-time, all .370 outfield in MLB history. In a reserve role for the first time in 21 years, the 39-year old Cobb still hit .339 in 233 at bats, while a 23-year old 2nd baseman from Fowlerville had his first full season in Detroit, as Charlie Gehringer, the kid spotted in the sandlots and brought to the team's attention by old Tiger Bobby Veach, hit 17 triples, good for third in the American League.

Cobb's star pupil, Harry Heilmann, was revered by Tiger fans on a level with Charlie Bennett. In a 1926 on-field ceremony for "Harry Heilmann Day", the fans presented Harry with an Austin Roadster that they had paid for. The Harry they knew and loved didn't let the fans down: after the game that night, Heilmann drove his new roadster down the stairs of his favorite speakeasy, pulled it up to the bar, leaned over the driver side door, laid on the horn, ordered a drink, and the place went wild. It must have been an interesting morning after for the bar owner, waking up to a tavern smelling of smoke & booze, empty bottles strewn about, and a car parked in front of the tappers.

In June of '26, Ruth, Gehrig & their buddies were in town for a series at The Corner. On June 8, pitching for the Tigers was Ulysses S. Grant "Lil" Stoner as up to the plate strode the Babe. George Herman Ruth took a mighty swing, and the ball exploded off his bat, hurtling towards right-center. Harry Heilmann, patrolling right, and Ty Cobb, defending center, stood still, looking skyward as the comet above cleared the stadium wall, cleared Trumbull Avenue, and came crashing down on a car parked on Cherry Street, 3 blocks north of Michigan Avenue. It is estimated that this longest home run in major league baseball history – 'til Mantle's 643' shot in 1960, also at The Corner - came to a stop 626' away from home plate.

It seemed that an unusually large number of the Tigers big games & big moments took place when the Yankees were the opponent at The Corner…

Ty's first game (1905)... first Tiger Sunday baseball game (1907)... the Brawl at The Corner (1924)... Babe Ruth hits the longest homer ever (1926)... Lou Gehrig ends his career (1939)... the day of the Tigers first home televised game (1947)... Mantle 643' homer sets new longest-ever record (1960)... Whitey Ford's final game (1967)... the Bird's Monday-Night-Game-of-the-Week masterpiece (1976)... and an endless number of critical pennant race match-ups.

The 1926 Tigers ended the campaign in sixth place, 79 & 75, 12 games behind the pennant-winning Yankees, bringing down the curtain on Ty Cobb's six years as player-manager. 711,914 fans came down to The Corner to watch, earning Ty only $1,191 for his attendance-base bonus of ten cents on every fan drawn over 700,000.

DDDDDDDDDDDDDDDDDDDDDDDDDDDDDDDDDDDDDDDDDDDDDDDDDDDDDDDDDDDDDDDDDDDDDDDDD

On November 3, 1926 Tyrus Raymond Cobb announced his retirement from the game that he had such an impact on for 22 seasons as a Tiger. Just 26 days later, Cobb's good friend, fellow player-manager and fellow future Hall-of-Famer, Tris Speaker, announced his retirement from the Cleveland Indians. A third announcement, this one from Baseball Commissioner Judge Kenesaw Mountain Landis shortly after those of Cobb and Speaker, shook the sports world: ex-Tiger pitcher Dutch Leonard claimed that in 1919 Ty Cobb, Tris Speaker, and Smoky Joe Wood conspired to fix a game between Detroit & Cleveland (*side note on Smoky Joe Wood:* in 1912, pitcher Walter "Big Train" Johnson, member of the inaugural 1936 Hall of Fame class at Cooperstown & whose 417 wins are #2 all-time to Cy Young, answered a reporter's question, *"Can I throw harder than Joe Wood? Listen mister, no man alive can throw harder than Smoky Joe Wood."* By 1919, when the alleged fix took place, arm problems led to Wood's conversion from pitcher to outfielder for Cleveland). With the memory of the 1919 World Series fix by the Chicago Black Sox still clear in folks' minds, these new 1919 accusations created intense national interest.

The 3 ballplayers said it was all nonsense, Ty stating Leonard's claim was retaliation for being sent to the minors by Manager Cobb in 1925. No story was discussed more in newspapers and by fans across the country, a vast majority siding with Cobb, Speaker & Wood. Humorist Will Rogers weighed-in, *"If they'd been selling out all these years, I would have liked to have seen them play when they wasn't selling."* The 3 ballplayers made a strong case for their innocence, and when Leonard didn't bother to show up for a face-to-face with Cobb & Speaker, Commissioner Landis ruled all 3 players officially innocent.

Although cleared, Ty Cobb felt the need for vindication on the ball diamond, and so accepted an offer from Connie Mack to play in 1927 for his Philadelphia A's. Tris Speaker, similarly motivated, signed with the Washington Senators. Smoky Joe Wood, coaching the Yale freshman baseball team during the whole brouhaha, happily heard the Yale Board declare it had, *"no evidence which discredits the honesty and integrity of Joe Wood's past record,"* and he would continue to coach at Yale through 1941.

DDDDDDDDDDDDDDDDDDDDDDDDDDDDDDDDDDDDDDDDDDDDDDDDDDDDDDDDDDDDDDDDDDDDDDDDD

1927 opened with a longtime Tiger pitcher missing for the first time since the 1911 season. 37-year old Hooks Dauss retired on a high note in '26, winding up an exemplary career with a 12 & 6 record. His 223 career wins wearing the Olde English D has been giving Tiger pitchers something to shoot for ever since.

more wins than Mullin, Lolich, Newhouser, Morris, Bridges or Verlander:
pitcher Hooks Dauss

The bats in the outfield once again powered the way for the Tigers in '27. Bob "Fatty" Fothergill hit .359 (with 93 runs/114 RBIs), Heinie Manush .298 (101 runs/90 RBIs), and Harry Heilmann .398. That earned Harry his fourth and final batting crown while scoring 106 runs and knocking in 120 teammates, finishing 2nd in Most Valuable Player voting to Lou Gehrig. Charlie Gehringer's .317 was his first of 13 seasons hitting over .300, crossing home 110 times. On the pitching staff, the hole left by the departure of Hooks Dauss was filled by a depth unseen in many years, as 6 different pitchers won in double digits, led by Earl Whitehill's 16 wins & 3.36 ERA.

When the 1927 schedule was released, every fan in Detroit was looking for one date – the first visit to Michigan & Trumbull by the Philadelphia Athletics and their newest player, Ty Cobb. That visit would take place May 10th. Looking nothing like a man of 40, but very much like a man on a mission, Cobb arrived in town on a hitting tear, sitting at .408. The Tigers had declared it "Ty Cobb Day", and 40,000 jammed into 30,000 seat Navin Field to welcome home the Greatest Tiger of All-Time. Before the game, Cobb & his teammates were officially welcomed to the city by Detroit Mayor John W. Smith, then honored at a testimonial luncheon followed by a police motorcycle-escorted parade from the luncheon to The Corner.

The start of today's game would be delayed by a love-fest. Ty was presented with a variety of thank-you gifts including a new car (unfortunately, the Chalmers Automobile Co. ceased production in 1923), he spoke to the crowd through a microphone set up at home plate, and signed autographs for those standing in the roped-off outfield (how you get 40,000 into a 30,000-seat ballpark). After the ceremony and during warm-ups, any fan still holding back their cheers let loose when Cobb caught a fly ball and tossed it over the screen into the crowd sitting in the right-field bleachers.

Facing Earl Whitehill as the third batter in the top of the first, Ty doubled home fellow future Hall of Famer Eddie Collins, setting off cheers every bit as loud as when he was a Tiger. The cheers re-ignited when Cobb scored on a single moments later. The *Sporting News* reported that two of Cobb's catches from his right-field position were *"distinctly spectacular"*, much to the Tiger fans delight. When Cobb was safe on a fielder's choice in the 7th, he was removed from the game for a pinch runner, giving the assembled one more chance to stand and roar for the great Tyrus. The final score of A's 6 & Tigers 3 was almost incidental to the warm homecoming celebration.

One of Ty's teammates on the '27 Athletics was 24-year old catcher, Mickey Cochrane. Much of the grit, determination, and relentless will to win that Mickey displayed 7 years later as manager of the Tigers was nurtured and amplified during his experience playing with Cobb.

On May 12, two days after Ty Cobb Day, Detroit defeated the A's to improve their record to 12 & 11, placing them 4 games out of first. The next time the team climbed over .500 was after a June 28 9-3 victory over the St. Louis Browns gave the Detroiters a 31-30 record. By then, the Tigers were a distant 13 games behind the streaking 47 & 20 Yankees. This was the great 1927 New York juggernaut, considered by many the finest team in MLB history, winning 110 times against 44 losses, producing a .714-win percentage (interestingly the number of Ruth's career home runs minus the decimal), before going on to sweep the Pittsburgh Pirates in the World Series. The Tigers 82 & 71 finish left them in fourth place, 27 games out of first.

On December 13, 1927, the Detroit Tigers pulled the trigger on one of the worst trades in their storied history, sending Heinie Manush & Lu Blue to the St. Louis Browns for Harry Rice, Elam Vangilder, and Chick Galloway. After the trade, Blue averaged a middling .270 over 5 years, but Manush was fantastic. In seven seasons after the trade, this special talent hit .378, .355, .350, .307, .342, .336 & .349 while leading the league twice in hits, twice in runs, and once in triples. New Tigers Harry Rice hit a fine and consistent .302, .304, and .305 in 3 years with Detroit, pitcher Elam Vanglider was 11 & 10 in '28, retiring after an 0 & 1 '29, while Chick Galloway hit .264 as a part-time player in '28 then retired from the game. Detroit was snookered on this deal, and would sorely miss the productive bat of Heinie Manush.

DDDDDDDDDDDDDDDDDDDDDDDDDDDDDDDDDDDDDDDDDDDDDDDDDDDDDDDDDDDDDDDDDDDDDDD

With Cobb's departure as manager after the '26 season, Frank Navin brought in another ex-Tiger to run the ship, George Moriarty. An umpire the last few years, Moriarty was a spirited sort, fondly recalled by old timers for his 1909 World Series game 6 hat trick of 2 fights & 1 RBI against the Honus Wagner-led Pittsburgh Pirates.

After a moderately successful 1927 in Manager Moriarty's first year at the helm, the '28 Tigers did not fare well. To no one's surprise, except perhaps Frank Navin's, the man who traded Heinie Manush, there was a huge hole in the offense. The team hit .279, not bad, just middle-of-the-road. It needed to be exceptional to pick up the pitching staff. A fella by the name of Ownie Carroll had his best year in the majors, winning 16 games with a 3.27 ERA, both team bests. Ownie was clearly the ace in '28, Earl Whitehill having an off-year at 11 & 16, and new acquisition Elam Vangilder, he of the Heinie Manush fiasco, won his only 11 games as a Detroiter.

The 1928 Tigers plummeted to 68 & 86, 33 games out of first place, and only 11 games out of last. Attendance, over 1,000,000 only 4 years prior, fell to 474,323. 600 miles to the east of Detroit, Ty Cobb was having a much more enjoyable '28 than his old Detroit teammates, Ty's Philadelphia Athletics in the middle of one barn burner of a pennant race against the New York Yankees. Ty was not performing like a 41-year old in the final year of a quarter-century of playing. He followed up his .357 '27 season with the A's by batting .323 in '28, 4th best on a big hitting club. Joining Cobb in the 40-and-over corner of the 1928 A's was his old buddy Tris Speaker, both on their final go-around.

On the 4th of July, Philadelphia was 13 games behind the Yankees, and going in the wrong direction, losing 9 of their last 13. That's when they caught fire. Behind the spectacular Lefty Grove, a Hall of Fame 300-game winner, enjoying a 24 & 8 year, and a barrage of timely hits by 20-year old Jimmie Foxx, Al Simmons, Mickey Cochrane, and Cobb, Philadelphia went on a major roll. They closed July on a 23 & 5 run, stayed hot through August, and finally erased that July 4, 13-game, deficit with a win September 7. Going into Yankee Stadium aka the House That Ruth Built for a mid-September showdown, Philadelphia dropped 3 of 4. That series was the determining factor as the Yankees held on to edge the 98-win A's by 2 & ½ games for the A.L. flag. Ty Cobb, once again, experienced the thrill of a pennant chase, but also experienced, once again, the agony of falling short to Ruth's Yankees, this time with another team.

After 24 years in the majors, Ty Cobb finally called it a day. In the history of Major League Baseball, he holds the highest lifetime batting average of .367 (some sources peg him at .366), the most single season batting titles at 12, including 9 in a row from 1907-1915. He hit .320 or more for 22 consecutive seasons. Cobb stole home 54 times, 21 more than the next man. Cobb is #2 in lifetime hits, #2 in singles, #4 in doubles, #2 in triples (behind old teammate Sam Crawford), #4 in steals, #2 in runs, and #8 RBIs.

When Ty Cobb retired, he held 43 major league baseball records.

Ty Cobb was a one of five in the 1936 inaugural class of inductees voted into the Cooperstown Hall of Fame, along with pitchers Walter Johnson & Christy Mathewson, shortstop & 1909 World Series adversary Honus Wagner, and perhaps Ty's greatest arch enemy on the diamond, right-fielder Babe Ruth. Of these 5, Cobb received the most votes.

Wahoo Sam Crawford said of Ty, *"He didn't outhit and he didn't outrun them. He out thought them."*

On July 17, 1963, a bronze plaque honoring Ty Cobb was unveiled on the Trumbull Avenue wall at Tiger Stadium. When Tiger Stadium was no more, the plaque was moved to Comerica Park, and may be seen on the Park's wall along Montcalm Street. The plaque reads...

Tyrus Raymond Cobb

1886-1961

Greatest Tiger of All

A Genius in Spikes

1929 – 1933 The World After Ty

They used to tell me I was building a dream
With peace and glory ahead
Why should I be standing in line
Just waiting for bread?

("Brother Can You Spare Me a Dime?" by Jay Gorney & E.Y. Harburg, circa 1930)

On September 25, 1928, only 404 fans attended that day's game at The Corner, the smallest crowd ever at Michigan & Trumbull. Fortunately, help had arrived...

In 1927, the number of Tiger fans visiting The Corner grew by one when 25-year old Mary Weider nee Vecellio emigrated from her native Auronzo, Italy to Detroit. In 1918, as World War I continued to rage, German troops entered the Vecellio family's Auronzo home with only sisters 8-year old Rose and 6-year old Mary present. The soldiers didn't want trouble, but were starving and looking for food. They came to the right place. Even at that age, Rose and Mary (who both had been taught the German language) were incredible cooks (*tortellini, ravioli, spaghetti, oh my*) and it's a wonder the soldiers ever left the house.

After emigrating from Italy to America, Mary Weider fell for the Detroit Tigers like a Michigander falls for the state's beauty. She attended Tiger games every year from 1927 to 2016, a string of 90 consecutive years, starting 1 year after Ty Cobb last wore the Olde English D, and 6 years before Mickey Cochrane became a Tiger. Once she celebrated birthday #100, Mary aka Nona (Grandma) brought a sign to 2012 games, signs updated in 2013, 2014, 2015, & 2016, starting with *"I'm 100 years old and I love my Tigers"*, with a *"Kiss Me Kinsler"* included in the mix. Among 90 years of Tiger players, Mary's favorite was that nice Italian boy, Rocky Colavito. On Labor Day 2015, at 103 years old, Mary threw out the first pitch at the Tigers' First Annual Grandparents Game, and was voted 2016's *Detroit Tiger Fan of the Year* by Major League Baseball. On 1.27.17, everybody's Nona, Mary Weider, passed away at 105 years young. Detroit's biggest fan now has a front row seat each game, while sharing sign-making tips with the Brow.

Tiger fan 1927 to 2016, from Cochrane to Cabrera: Mary Weider

In time for the 1929 season, the Tigers hired a new manager, Bucky Harris. Bucky had concluded a 10-year career in '28 as the Senators' 2nd baseman, and officially was the Tigers player-manager. However, he only played in 7 games, going 1 for 14 before wisely benching himself. Although the 1929 squad only won 2 more games than the prior year's edition, the explosive offense was back and the fans loved it, with attendance up over 80% versus '28, as 869,318 passed through the turnstiles.

Some of the production came from a dependable few: at age 26, Charlie Gehringer continued on his startling upward trajectory, this year leading the league with 131 runs, 215 hits, 45 doubles, 19 triples, and 27 stolen bases, while hitting .339; Bob Fothergill's .354 average was tied for fourth in the league, and Mister Dependable, Harry Heilmann, hit .344 and came in ninth.

Some of the hitting was from unexpected sources: in limited duty, catcher Pinky Hargrave's .330 was the best of his career; infielder Marty McManus hit 18 home runs, one more than he had in his two prior years combined, & knocked in 90 runners.

Some of the firepower came from new acquisitions: in October of '28, the Tigers traded Al Wingo to San Francisco of the Pacific Coast League for outfielder Roy Johnson. Roy had shown impressive power with San Francisco, socking 49 doubles, 16 triples, & 22 homers last season, and almost duplicated that in his rookie season against major league pitching, leading the A.L. with 45 doubles to go with 14 triples, good for 7th, 10 home runs, 20 steals (5th in A.L.), and a .314 average. Then, in a December 1928 transaction, the Tigers purchased Dale "Moose" Alexander from the minor league Toronto team. His 31 homers for Toronto caught Detroit's attention, in the hopes that he could have similar success in the majors. Moose Alexander's 1929 was all the team could ask for, as he launched 25 home runs, good for an A.L. fifth _and_ a Tiger team record, he was the league-leader with 215 hits, his 137 RBIs were good for third-best in the A.L., he was 5th in doubles at 43, and tied for 4th with 15 triples.

George Uhle's 4 Detroit seasons: 50-game winner/.284 hitter

The Tigers could score, but someone had to hold the other team. Earl Whitehill only modestly improved over his bumpy 11 & 16 of '28 by posting a 14 & 15 in '29. That record was matched by hurler Vic Sorrell, but in Vic's case it arrived with a nasty 5.18 ERA. Help was needed and it came through a December 1928 deal, when 30-year old hurler George Uhle was obtained from Cleveland. Uhle had led the league with 26 wins in '23 and 27 wins in '26, but slipped in '28 to 12 & 17. The Tigers swapped shortstop Jackie Tavener (who would hit .212 in '29 before retiring) & pitcher Ken Holloway (who in '29 & '30 combined won 7 games with an ERA over 5, then retired) for George Uhle. George was the Detroit staff ace in 1929 at 15 & 11 and would win 50 games in his 4 years wearing a Tiger uniform. Now this was a nice trade!

Even with the pickup of George Uhle to bolster the pitching corps, there was still too little help from the mound to support the impressive offense, although Uhle came with the bonus that he was one helluva hitter, and not just "for a pitcher". In 108 at bats, he had 37 hits, for a .343 average.

A 10 & 3 start to May moved the Tigers to second place, one-half game behind the Philadelphia A's, and got the excited fans showing up in larger numbers than they had in 5 years. Although the pitching was simply not good enough to keep Detroit in the race, they provided plenty of entertainment on the base paths, leading the American League in runs scored. Along with Moose Alexander's home runs providing the rare joy of the home team hitting the ball into the seats, the happy fans beat a path to The Corner, despite Detroit finishing 36 games behind the 104-win Athletics.

On October 14, 8 days after the 1929 season concluded, Frank Navin made a trade that ranks alongside dealing away Heinie Manush on the inexplicable scale, although still below the asinine decision of selling Hank Greenberg to Pittsburgh at the end of '46. The Tigers, in a straight cash deal, sold Harry Heilmann to the Cincinnati Reds. This despite the fact that, in 1929, 34-year old Harry Heilmann, in his 15th year with Detroit, proved that he remained among the major's finest by hitting .344 – 2 points above his .342 lifetime average – along with 120 RBIs. The Tigers, desperately in need of pitching, sent away Harry, who hit .333 with 90 runs batted in his first year with Cincy, not for someone who could help the rotation, but rather for… money.

On October 24, 10 days after Harry Heilmann was sold to Cincinnati, the Wall Street Crash aka the Stock Market Crash of 1929 took place. The Great Depression had begun.

DDDDDDDDDDDDDDDDDDDDDDDDDDDDDDDDDDDDDDDDDDDDDDDDDDDDDDDDDDDDDDDDDDDDDDDD

Down was the operative word for 1930. Just when the newly-unemployed victims of the stock market were most in need of a joyful diversion, their Tigers opened the year with a 5 & 10 April. In the late-20s, Frank Navin had sent away the team's 2 best hitters, swapping Heinie Manush for inferior players and selling Harry Heilmann when pitchers were desperately needed. These losses were making themselves felt as the 1930's decade opened.

The Tigers would play 1 game over .500 from May 1 until season's end, finishing 1930 in fifth place at 75 & 79, 27 games behind the World Champion, 102-win, Philadelphia Athletics and their catcher & leader, Mickey Cochrane. The Bengals had their moments, as when they finished May on a 10 & 5 run, but each run of success was followed by a 5 or 6 game losing streak. With the team never in the pennant race, as they were the first couple of months the previous year, added to the loss of discretionary income as jobs evaporated in the months since the Crash of '29, attendance dropped 25% from 869,318 to 649,450 - despite tickets for many seats available for under $1 (one 1930 dollar equals $15 in 2019).

The fans that did come to The Corner were entertained…

The '30 Tigers liked to run, and finished 1-2-3 in A.L. steals, led by Marty McManus' 23 to go with his .320 average & 89 RBIs, followed by Charlie Gehringer & Runnin' Roy Johnson. Moose Alexander bulldozed over the sophomore jinx with another power display of 20 homers & 135 RBIs along with a .326 average. The amazing Gehringer once again was near the league lead in hits, doubles, triples, home runs, steals, & base on balls while hitting .344.

In a little-noticed, late-1929, transaction, the Tigers purchased a shortstop from the St. Paul team in the American Association. Although 25-year old Billy Rogell only hit .167 in 54 games in '30, Detroit liked the determined way he approached the game, and hoped for better things from Rogell down the road. Billy was sent down to minor league Toronto for more seasoning and he responded, hitting .316 in 68 games.

Among pitchers, Earl Whitehill's 17 wins was tops on the 1930 team, matching the high-water mark in his decade with Detroit. Vic Sorrell had the finest of his 10 seasons in the majors, all with the Tigers, going 16 & 11 with a 3.86 ERA. The only other pitcher with double-digit wins was George Uhle at 12 supported by his staff-low 3.65 ERA.

Under the radar, during a year focused on a losing season in a devastated economy, a skinny rookie pitcher from Gordonsville, Tennessee made his major league debut on August 13, 1930. The Tigers were in the Bronx that day, down 10 - 6 to New York as the game moved to the bottom of the sixth. Tiger Manager Bucky Harris decided to take reliever Charlie Sullivan out of the game and insert 23-year old Thomas Jefferson Davis Bridges, better known as Tommy Bridges. The first 3 batters that Tommy would face at the very start of his career were none other than the heart of the Yankees famous "Murderers' Row", well-established stars on their way to the Hall of Fame, beginning with the Bambino himself. Following Babe were Tony Lazzeri and Lou Gehrig. Tommy got Ruth on a pop out and, although Lazzeri touched him for a single, Bridges struck out Gehrig before taking out the next batter on a ground out.

From this memorable beginning, Tommy Bridges would go on to be one of the greatest pitchers in Tiger history. Wiry, scrappy, and a bit undersized, Bridges was a bulldog, a determined competitor, and the favorite player of Detroit's Roy Fletcher, my grandfather, with fans throughout Michigan and across the country. His repertoire included an explosive fastball, a knee-bending change of pace, and a devastating curveball that Mickey Cochrane claimed was the best he ever saw (in the final inning of the 1935 World Series, with a Chicago Cub on third base representing the lead run and nobody out, Bridges threw 3 consecutive curveballs to 3-time all-star Billy Jurges; although Jurges knew what was coming, he swung & missed all 3 times – and that man on third base would never cross home). Including his August 13th debut against the Babe & Gehrig & Co., Tommy pitched 8 times in his 1930 rookie season, 3 in relief and 5 starts, completing 2 games, and chalked up the first 3 wins in a 16-year, 194-victory, career.

DDDDDDDDDDDDDDDDDDDDDDDDDDDDDDDDDDDDDDDDDDDDDDDDDDDDDDDDDDDDDDDDDDDDDDDDDD

1931 was the perfect storm for Detroit and its baseball team. As a result of the stock market crash decimating incomes across the country, Americans stopped buying autos, and the Motor City suffered from the USA's highest unemployment rate. One out of 3 Detroiters were now out of a job and the team won less than 4 out of every 10 games, matching the 1920 Tigers 93 losses (against only 61 wins) that set the team record, placing them an incredible 47 games behind the 107-wins (a MLB record at the time) of the Philadelphia A's. To no one's surprise, attendance fell dramatically, down 33% to 434,056.

The Tigers high-water mark was a May 8, 3-2, win over the Senators as Earl Whitehill won a pitcher's duel to bring the 12 & 10 Detroiters to within 1 game of first place. It quickly turned ugly for the fellas wearing the Olde English D – oh, wait a minute, in their wisdom Tiger management discarded the Olde English D in 1929 - as they finished May on a 2 & 13 run while being outscored 107 to 48. After sitting 1 game out of first after the May 8th victory, the Tigers were 13 out on May 31, dropping further behind each month until reaching 47 games back on the final day of the season. Ug-ly.

Runnin' Roy Johnson continued to show off his speed, topping the A.L. with 19 triples, tied for 9th with 37 doubles, and #2 with 33 steals. Outfielder John Stone led the Tigers in batting average at .327, good for 10th in the league. Dale "Moose" Alexander once again reached base at a high percentage in 1931, batting .320, and was a league 2nd with 47 doubles, but the man who two years ago set the Tiger single season record of 25 home runs, following that up in 1930 with 20, only connected for 3 in 1931.

Tommy Bridges felt the sophomore season sting, still trying to consistently figure out major league hitters, going 8 & 16 with a 4.99 ERA. George Uhle once again topped the staff with a 3.50 ERA, while everyone else was giving up over 4 runs a game.

As lousy as a 93-loss season feels, some of the young players provided hope that things would get better next year. 2nd year Tiger Billy Rogell was earning more playing time at short, hitting .303 in 48 games. Two rookies that excited the Tigers & their fans broke-in in '30, outfielder Gerald "Gee" Walker and infielder Marv Owen, who in limited action hit .296 & .223, respectively.

DDDDDDDDDDDDDDDDDDDDDDDDDDDDDDDDDDDDDDDDDDDDDDDDDDDDDDDDDDDDDDDDDDDDDDDDD

1932 found Detroit in the depths of the Depression, unemployment rising to 34%. Fortunately, the Tigers followed up an awful year with a little sunshine, going over .500 for the first time in five years at 76 & 75. If the fans could afford it, out to The Corner they came, and 397,157 did. Not bad, considering how folks in Detroit were scraping to get by.

Contending for the pennant through the summer was not in the cards, improved though the Tigers were. 1932 saw the American League champion Yankees win 107 games, tying the record set just the year before by Philadelphia. Although Detroit won 15 more games than they did the year prior, that still left them a distant 29 games back. In the early going, though, the Tigers were hanging tough. They came out of the starting gates cookin' at 8 & 2, and going into June the team was 24 & 16 and in 2nd place, only 4 & ½ games out of first and within striking distance of the lead. Although Detroit would get no closer to the top, the team was a fun one to watch.

2nd year outfielder Gee Walker had a fine sophomore season, registering Detroit's top batting average, sixth in the A.L., at .323, while the 30 bags he swiped was #2 in the league. Charlie Gehringer continued as the team's main cog in the line-up, in the league's top 10 in slugging percentage, runs scored, hits, total bases, doubles, & homers. Outfielder John Stone had an impressive line of .297 with 35 doubles, 12 triples, 17 home runs, & a team-leading 109 RBIs. No less than 4 Tigers placed in the A.L.'s top 10 in stolen bases, their go-go mentality keeping the opposition nervous & fans excited. Rookie Jo-Jo White, a big part of Detroit's 1934-1935 success, made his debut batting .260 in 80 games.

Among American League hurlers, Earl Whitehill was 10th with 16 wins and Chief Hogsett 7th in ERA at 3.54. All good, but 1932 was the year that Thomas Jefferson Davis Bridges, the man named after both a United States President and a President of the Confederacy, learned to harness his athletic abilities, and become a pitcher. Tommy had a 14 & 12 record, tied the great Lefty Grove for the league lead in shutouts with 4, came in fifth in ERA at 3.36, and his 108-strikeout count was good for an A.L. 8th.

One of the finest moments in Tommy's 16-year career took place August 5, 1932. It was a Friday at The Corner, and Bridges was facing the Washington Senators. His curveball, fastball, and change-of-pace were all working beautifully on this day. The Tigers broke a zero-zero tie with a 7-run onslaught in the fourth, and went on to add six more runs, as they banged out 15 hits on this afternoon. Despite the

Tigers attack, the game moved along at a brisk pace as, inning-by-inning, Tommy breezed through the Senators line-up. As the Senators came to bat in the ninth, Bridges had struck out 7, yielding no walks, and the scoreboard told the rest of the story – a story that every person at Navin Field was well-aware of - that Washington had no runs and **_no hits_**. Not a single one of the first 24 batters Tommy faced had reached base, and he was only 3 outs from tossing what would've been, as of 1932, only the sixth perfect game in MLB history.

Tommy took care of the first two batters. In every one of the tens of thousands of major league games that had been played as of 8/5/32, only once had a pitcher set down the first 26 batters and lost a perfect game on the 27th & final batter (Hooks Wiltse hit a batter with 2 outs in the ninth back in 1908). The pitcher was due up, but he would be pinch hit for. When you are playing Washington in the early-30s and a pinch hitter was called on, that meant trouble. The finest pinch hitter in all of baseball at this time was now striding to the plate. Dave Harris was Gates Brown 35 years earlier, an outfielder who rarely started but had one big hit after another coming off the bench, hitting .350 in that role so far this season. Sure enough, on the first pitch he saw, Dave Harris broke up Tommy Bridge's perfect game with a line single to left.

The first batter to go down in the 9th was Washington third sacker Ossie Bluege, a man who saw plenty of pitchers in his fine, 18-year career, but few that he admired as he did Tommy Bridges, *"He had a heart of gold. He had the courage when the chips were down, and you had to hit him and hit him hard to beat him."* After the game, Senators manager Walter Johnson defended his decision to send up his ace pinch hitter one out short of a perfect game and his team down 13-0. Johnson answered simply, *"A hitter gets paid for hitting like a pitcher gets paid for pitching."*

23 games into '32, the Tigers peddled first baseman Moose Alexander to the Red Sox for outfielder Earl Webb, who hit a league-leading 67 doubles in '31 but was fading to retirement in '33. Although Moose won the A.L. batting title at .367 in '32, his 8 homers & 60 RBIs was insufficient production for a full-time first baseman slow afoot with an iron glove, so Moose hung it up after the '33 season. Were Moose for Earl Webb the extent of the trade, it would've been considered pretty even. However, the Sox were able to snooker the Tigers into including Runnin' Roy Johnson in the deal. It's true that Roy had a slow start to the 1932 campaign, but he hit .313, .320, & .315 for Boston in '33 thru '35, was always in double digits in steals, and finished among the leaders in MVP voting in 1934 when he had 119 RBIs.

Meanwhile, word was filtering up to Detroit about something special brewing down in Texas besides Lone Star Beer (which, of course, would never be brewed during Prohibition, 'cause that would be wrong). At the Tigers class A affiliate, the Beaumont Exporters, 22-year old Hank Greenberg cracked 39 home runs, providing the promise of another big bat for the parent club in 1933.

Years later, no less an authority than Joltin' Joe DiMaggio said of Hank, *"He was one of the truly great hitters. When I first saw him at bat, he made my eyes pop out."* Hammerin' Hank was the first player in MLB history to win the Most Valuable Player Award at two different positions (1935 outfield, 1940 first base). Hank had a career OPS, on-base plus slugging, percentage of 1.017 – the only other players to exceed that figure were Ted Williams, Jimmy Foxx, Lou Gehrig, and Babe Ruth. Hankus Pankus played on four Tiger teams that went to the World Series ('34, '35, '40 & '45) and two of 'em won it ('35 & '45). As the first line on his Hall of Fame plaque simply states, *"One of baseball's greatest right-handed batters."*

But as 1932 wound down, young Hank Greenberg was just hoping that next year he would be a Tiger.

1933 began for the Tigers with a great deal of promise. To the team and most of its fans, it seemed that what the mix of up 'n coming and veteran players had in common was the talent to win - in sufficient quantity that this season would mark Detroit's return as a serious challenger for the American League title for the first time since 1924.

The kids were more than alright, upgrading the defense and giving the offense an injection of speed & extra base hits…

With only <u>one</u> previous major league at bat, rookie Hank Greenberg proved that the decision to insert him into the '33 everyday line-up was a smart one, responding with a .301 average while depositing 12 balls into the seats & knocking in 85 mates. Fellow rookie Pete Fox, with <u>zero</u> previous major league at bats, scorched 13 triples, good for 6th in the league, and a .288 average. For the second year in a row, Gee Walker was an A.L. 2nd in steals, this time with 26, while hitting .280. Fiery Billy Rogell hit at a .295 clip in year 4, his 42 doubles tied with Charlie Gehringer for 4th in the A.L. Also in his fourth year, Marv Owens played a solid third and hit .262. And good ole' Gehringer just kept bein' Gehringer, placing in the league's top 5 in batting average, hits, total bases, doubles, and runs batted in.

Outside of the kids and Charlie, there was not enough run production to boost Detroit into the pennant race; the pitching was good, but not good enough to stay close to the top teams. Tommy Bridges was quickly becoming one of the league's best on the mound, posting an A.L. #2 3.09 ERA, while his 7 hits surrendered per 9 innings was a league low; 120 strikeouts placed Tommy #4, & 17 complete games, including 2 shutouts, an A.L. 5th. Before the season began, Detroit traded pitchers with Washington – Earl Whitehill for the memorably-named Firpo Marberry, who won 16 to lead the Tigers & place a league 4th; he was #1 in the category of fewest walks/hits given up per inning, and his 3.29 ERA was an A.L. 5th.

Two rookie pitchers saw limited action but showed flashes of what could be…

Elden Auker began '33 with Detroit's minor league team in Beaumont, Texas, impressing the parent club with 16 wins and prompting a late-season call up. He won 3 games for Detroit, one a shutout, in 55 innings pitched. Elden grew up in rural Kansas, where communication was extended little beyond neighboring farms. When he was called up to the Tigers, not only had Elden never watched a major league game, he did not know what league Detroit was in. On the subject of pitching, however, Elden was worldly-wise, enough to defeat Satchel Paige in an exhibition match-up two years prior.

The other '33 rookie hurler was Lynwood Thomas "Schoolboy" Rowe, from Waco, Texas. As it did with Auker, Rowe's performance down in Beaumont – 19 wins in '32 - forced his promotion to Detroit. Unlike Auker, Schoolboy was plugged into the big-league squad's pitching rotation from day 1 in '33. He made his maiden major league start on April 15, tossing a 3-0 shutout against the White Sox for his first win in The Show. Pains of both the learning & the physical kind saddled Schoolboy with 3 losses, to go with the April 15 win, heading into a May 26 road date versus the Philadelphia Athletics & Mickey Cochrane at Shibe Park. Supported by Detroit's offensive explosion, featuring 4 hits by lead-off man and rookie centerfielder Pete Fox, Rowe went the distance in recording his 2nd win, 10 to 1. Schoolboy ran off 4 more complete game victories, took a loss, then won his 7th game on July 19, coming into the game in relief of Firpo Marberry. Schoolboy's season ended on his July 23 start, shutdown for the year when he aggravated a previously undiagnosed muscle tear, incurred while fielding a Mickey Cochrane bunt 8 days earlier. Schoolboy's rookie year ledger read 7 wins, 4 losses, a 3.58 ERA, and 8 complete games with one shutout.

The 1933 Tigers finished an A.L. fifth, 75 wins against 79 losses, 25 games behind the 99-win champion Washington Senators. Attendance dropped to 320,972, an average of only 4,115 per game. Between underachieving on the field *and* through the turnstiles, Frank Navin decided it was time to bid farewell to manager Bucky Harris in October and begin the search for his replacement.

1933 began with FDR and Adolph Hitler taking power in January. Harry Heilmann – who retired after '32 – started a new career in April as the radio broadcaster of Tiger games for WXYZ, *the first former player to ever become a play-by-play broadcaster*. The year wrapped up in December with the repeal of Prohibition. And that same month, the Tigers made one of *the most impactful team decisions in the history of major league baseball with the hiring of Mickey Cochrane to become their player-manager*.

1934 & 1935 Cochrane's Champions

During an interview, Schoolboy Rowe was asked for the secret to his success. He informed the reporter and the national radio audience listening in, "I eat a lot of vittles, climb up on that mound, wrap my fingers around the baseball and say to it, 'Edna, honey, let's go.'"

Seated behind our row at a 1995 Comerica Park game was a group of septuagenarians & octogenarians with whom we'd struck up a conversation. We were intrigued as they pulled from their pockets baggies of relish and onions, thinking it cool that this band of 70s & 80s-somethings planned ahead with their favorite brands of toppings, for the hot dogs just purchased. Bantering back 'n forth, the conversation between our rows drifted to the 60th anniversary of the 1935 World Champions Tigers. As I passionately talked about that team, chatting at length about the lineup and started in on the pitching staff, one of our new friends stopped me mid-sentence, tilted her head quizzically, & asked me, *"How old ARE you?"*

The 1935 Detroit Tigers have always held a special place in the hearts of many Detroit sports fans as the first Tiger team to win the World Series. It is almost impossible to think of '35 separately from '34.

As the 1934 campaign opened, the Tigers had not won the American League pennant in 25 years, back in 1909 when they played in old, wooden Bennett Park. But by the early 30s the Tigers, through shrewd trades – overcoming some real clunkers - and good scouting, had assembled one of the most talented, but young & still-developing, teams in the majors. As promising as the club's outlook appeared, the trajectory of the Detroit Tigers changed in an extraordinarily positive way when they negotiated a December 1933 deal with the Philadelphia Athletics. The A's catcher at that time was a special one, a force behind the plate, at the bat, and as a leader of men, future Hall-of-Famer Mickey Cochrane.

Mickey, also known as "Black Mike" or "Iron Mike" was league Most Valuable Player in 1928 and one of the main cogs on the Philadelphia Athletics teams that beat back the mighty Yankees in 1929, 1930 & 1931 for the American League pennant, continuing on to win the World Series in '29 & '30. The Great Depression had put A's owner & (with a great deal of job security) manager Connie Mack into a financial bind, and Mack began selling his star players including, in December of 1933, Mickey Cochrane for $100,000 (plus catcher Johnny Pasek, who would play 4 games for the A's in '34 before retiring) to the Detroit Tigers. Cochrane immediately became the team's new player-manager. Taking place one week after the December 5 ratification of the 21st Amendment repealing Prohibition, the glasses of baseball fans were lifted all across the state of Michigan to the Tigers – and to their - good fortune.

As it did to the Philadelphia Athletics' Connie Mack, the Great Depression negatively affected Tigers owner Frank Navin's finances. But in his case, and with the open checkbook of silent partner Walter Briggs, it prompted a search for a gate attraction to bolster sagging attendance at The Corner. Navin thought the answer lie in acquiring George Herman "Babe" Ruth as a player-manager. This was about the time that Yankees owner Jacob Ruppert was considering moving the Babe. Ruppert saw in Ruth a fading star whose antics were less & less worth putting up with. Navin saw in the Babe the biggest name in the game, still able to hit enough home runs to draw big crowds. Navin contacted Ruppert, who was receptive to making a deal, but after a couple of discussions with Babe, Navin decided the ballplayer's demands were too Ruthian for his frugal-blood, Walter Briggs money or no Walter Briggs money. This was a fortunate event for Detroit & all of Michigan as it turned out, since this forced Frank Navin to look elsewhere for his player-manager, and soon the answer was found in Mickey Cochrane.

The addition of Cochrane immediately turned around the fortunes of the team. His fighting "can do" attitude instilled in the team a belief he found lacking previously in the Tigers – a belief that they would succeed, and his work with the pitchers allowed the young staff to realize their full potential. Also, in a symbolic move that the Tiger faithful cheered, Mickey brought back the Olde English D on the jerseys, discarded since 1929.

Gordon Stanley "Mickey" Cochrane – one of his many hits against the Yankees

DDDDDDDDDDDDDDDDDDDDDDDDDDDDDDDDDDDDDDDDDDDDDDDDDDDDDDDDDDDDDDDDDDDDDDDDDDDDDDDDD

The impact of Cochrane's work with the Tiger pitching staff, through knowledge gained catching an A's staff full of 20-game winners led by Hall-of-Famer Lefty Grove (of whom journalist Arthur Baer once said *"Could throw a lamb chop past a wolf"*), was evident immediately…

*27-year old Tommy Bridges, a strong-willed bulldog of a competitor, improved from 14 & 12 to 22 & 11 (3.67 ERA/23 CG/3 shutouts/151 Ks). Mickey Cochrane called his undersized, big-hearted, right-hander *"A hundred and fifty pounds of courage."*
*23-year old Elden Auker, the submarine-style hurler, who in a 1931 exhibition won a 2-1 pitching duel for his Texas League team over the great Satchel Paige & his Kansas City Monarchs of the Negro League, made the leap from 3 & 3 in his rookie year to 15 & 7 (3.42 ERA/18 CG).
*Among relative old-timers, 35-year old Firpo Marbury improved from 16 & 11 to 15 & 5, & late-season waiver pick-up (& army veteran) "General" Alvin Crowder, a 36-year old thought to be washed-up by his previous team but not by Cochrane, helped the Tigers in the pennant stretch drive with a 5 & 1 record. General Crowder, the man known as "the Yankee Killer" two decades before Frank Lary, defeated the Yanks in 2 series openers. This crafty pitcher, who led the majors with 26 wins in '32 & tied Lefty Grove with 24 in '33, had a naked woman tattooed on to his pitching arm to break the hitters' concentration. Whether the ploy was successful or not is secondary to the fact that this makes a great story.

But Cochrane's best work may have been with 24-year old Lynwood Thomas "Schoolboy" Rowe. The nickname was from his teenage years playing against older men who warned teammates, *"Don't let that schoolboy beat you!"* Rowe blossomed from 7 & 4 in his rookie year of '33 to an outstanding 24 & 8 (3.45 ERA/20 CG/149 Ks/3 shutouts). 2nd baseman Charlie Gehringer said Schoolboy possessed, *"one of the finest fastballs I ever stood behind."* From a height of 6'4", he delivered pitches with a sweeping overhand motion and a big stride towards home that made a hitter feel he was right on top of them, releasing a heater or wicked curve with devastating effect. Despite that, he had a rough start in 1934, still suffering shoulder pain from pitching in '33 with an undiagnosed muscle tear, and did not earn his first win until May 27. From then on, though, he won 21 of his next 23 decisions, including an American League record 16 in a row. During his incredible victory streak, with a nickname hard to forget, every baseball fan in America learned who Schoolboy Rowe was.

Schoolboy was tall & lanky, personable, accessible, funny, and quirky – including always picking up his glove with his left-hand, thinking that to do otherwise was bad luck. The number of good luck charms that he carried would've burdened a weaker man. Rowe was often seen talking to the ball, or maybe himself, 4 decades before Mark "the Bird" Fidrych did. Lou Gehrig, after an unsuccessful trip to the plate versus Schoolboy, said to no one in particular, *"That's the strangest fella I've ever faced."*

Much like the wildly popular Ruth, Schoolboy Rowe could pitch AND hit, winning two games in '34 with walk-off home runs. Rowe batted in the lineup as high as 7th on a team that hit .300, occasionally pinch hitting, while finishing the year with a .303 average. His success touched a chord for folks struggling with the Depression's hard times, and when a sportswriter suggested that Schoolboy's popularity rivaled that of the Babe, many agreed.

DDDDDDDDDDDDDDDDDDDDDDDDDDDDDDDDDDDDDDDDDDDDDDDDDDDDDDDDDDDDDDDDDDDDDDDD

Mickey Cochrane becoming the Tigers player-manager was so impactful that it overshadowed the off-season acquisition of another future Hall-of-Famer: Detroit & Washington swapped outfielders, the Tigers John Stone for the Senators Leon "Goose" Goslin. Always smiling *("I'd have paid them to let me play"* he once said), the nickname "Goose" was for the unusual way he flapped his arms while tracking down fly balls from his left-field perch, for his awkward manner, and bird-beak profile. John Stone was productive for Washington in '34, hitting .315 with 7 homers/67 RBIs/77 runs, but paled in comparison to Goslin's '34 .305/13/100/106 numbers, and that's in addition to the contributions of the Goose in the 1935 regular season & World Series. His acquisition completed the big hitting "G-Men" trio of Gehringer, Greenberg & Goslin. The leadership Goose provided could not be overstated, as the young Tigers admired his career achievements and were in awe of his 3 years of World Series experience with Washington. The respect accorded Goslin allowed him to be a helpful 1st Lieutenant to Manager Cochrane in the work to ingrain a winning spirit in the team.

The '34 Tigers were a powerhouse, their 101 wins against 53 losses setting a team single season record, and leaving the Yankees in the dust, 7 games back. The Tigers averaged 6 runs scored per game, batting an even .300. Excited fans by the hundreds would greet the team with shouts & cheers as they arrived home from road trips at the Michigan Central Train Depot.

In the mid-July heat of the pennant race, the Yankees came to town for an important series, holding a slim one-half game lead over Detroit. Although the Tigers would win 3 of 4, it was their single weekend Friday the 13th loss that resides in the memories of most baseball fanatics. That match-up had two All-Star pitchers going head-to-head, Tommy Bridges and the Yanks Red Ruffing. With the game scoreless in the 3rd, the aging but still dangerous Babe Ruth dug in against Bridges, and launched career home run number 700 over the Navin Field right-field seats and rolling down Plum Street. With a *"Thanks Kid!"* Ruth paid a youngster the extremely generous amount of $20 for chasing down the milestone baseball, after bumming the Jackson from Manager Joe McCarthy. The Babe's 2-run shot was the difference as both Bridges & Ruffing went the distance in New York's 4-2 win.

On this July 13, 1934 afternoon, the record of 700 seemed safe (and was until surpassed by Hank Aaron 4 decades later). At days end, the closest lifetime home run competitors were Lou Gehrig at 323, Jimmie Foxx 248, and Al Simmons 235. Ruth would blast 8 more home runs in 1934, his final season as a Yankee, the team releasing him in the spring of '35 when the Boston Braves picked him up for one last go 'round. On May 25, 1935 the Braves were on the road playing the Pittsburgh Pirates at Forbes Field, with the 40-year old Babe hitting .153 with 3 homers & 5 RBIs, when the old magic came back one last day. Although the Pirates won the game, the Babe hit 3 home runs in the affair, the 3rd one clearing Forbes Field's right-field roof, the first time that happened since the park opened in 1909. Numbers 712, 713 & 714 would be the last home runs of Babe Ruth's career. He announced his retirement after playing his final game 5 days later, on May 30th.

DDDDDDDDDDDDDDDDDDDDDDDDDDDDDDDDDDDDDDDDDDDDDDDDDDDDDDDDDDDDDDDDDDDDDDDDDDDD

On that May 25, 1935 day at Pittsburgh's Forbes Field, a 17-year old Pirate fan named Phil Coyne was in the stands watching Babe hit the last 3 home runs of his career. The next year, Phil was hired by the Pirates to be a Forbes Field usher. As the team moved to Three Rivers Stadium and then to PNC Park, Phil Coyne continued to seat fans, finally retiring at the age of 99 in April of 2018 after 81 years as an usher, only missing 3 years while serving in the U.S. Army in Italy, France, and Germany during World War II. *"I wanted to make it to 100 but* (due to a recent fall) *I just couldn't do it. I'll still go to games and see my people* (in his old sections) *when I can."* On April 27, 2018, the Pirates celebrated Phil's 100th birthday, painting "Phil 100" on the field in front of his old third base line usher sections, 26 & 27, where a plaque honoring him was placed. Phil's favorite memory? *"Maz' home run"* to beat the Yankees in the '60 World Series. Phil Coyne's usher uniform & I.D. badge are on permanent display at the Hall of Fame Museum in Cooperstown.

DDDDDDDDDDDDDDDDDDDDDDDDDDDDDDDDDDDDDDDDDDDDDDDDDDDDDDDDDDDDDDDDDDDDDDDDDDDD

Saturday, July 14, the day after Babe's 700th, was the third of a 4-game series. After splitting the first two contests, the Yankees still held the one-half game lead they arrived in town with. The pitching match-up was less than ideal for the Tigers, sending Vic Sorrell, 6 & 9 for the year, to the hill against N.Y.'s Lefty Gomez, well on the way to a career-best 26 & 5. Sorrell had his worst day of '34, pulled after giving up 4 runs and only recording one out, while Gomez was on (although not yet invented) cruise control and holding a 9 to 1 lead, after a Ruth 3-run homer, going into the bottom of the 4th.

In a historic weekend with Babe's 700th, squaring off against the first-place Yankees, and facing an 8-run deficit against a pitcher having the best year in the majors, the Detroit 9 showed what they were made of, closing the gap to 9-8 after 6, sending the crowd into a ballpark-shaking frenzy. Frankie Crosetti's 2-run shot for the Yanks in the 7th quieted the faithful to a dull roar, and New York held an 11-8 lead into the bottom of the ninth. And that's where legends are made. Third baseman Marv Owen led-off for Detroit with his 2nd hit of the day and Cochrane singled him to second base as the potential tying run stepped to the plate. Batting for pitcher Firpo Marberry was, unusual for baseball, another pitcher – but this one the .300-hitting Schoolboy Rowe, who promptly singled the bases loaded. After a fielder's choice closed the score to 11-9, Goose Goslin doubled to tie the game, the fans full-throated shouts so loud that all concession stand transactions could only take place with hand signs. Billy Rogell was at bat, the future Detroit City Councilman and the man called "Fire Chief" due to his red-hot intensity on the field, and Billy did not throw away his shot, sending a liner through the infield, all the while shouting, *"Run Goose, run!"*, as Goslin scored the winning run in the amazing 12-11 come-from-<u>way</u>-behind victory. Everyone was delirious at Navin Field! To those in attendance, still giddy days later, recalling the game in their twilight years would bring happy tears.

The Tigers were now back in first place, building their lead over the New Yorkers to 4 & ½ games by August 14, when Detroit arrived in the Bronx for a 5-game series. This was a golden opportunity for the Yankees to make up some ground, and in the first game of a series-opening doubleheader, they got to General Alvin Crowder for 5 early runs, as their ace Lefty Gomez shutout the Tigers through the 5th. The 79,000 in attendance loved every minute of it, loudly boasting of a sweep that would send their beloved Yankees into first. Then, with one out in the Detroit sixth, the Tigers struck back. Jo-Jo White was on second when Charlie Gehringer changed the direction of a Lefty Gomez offering, depositing it among the rowdy fans in the outfield stands, cutting the lead to 5-2. After singles by Goslin & Rogell, Lefty dug in, getting the always dangerous Greenberg to pop out, and was only one out away from escaping further damage. But Marv Owens would have none of it, and his ground rule double plated the Goose, leaving runners on 2nd & 3rd for the next hitter, back-up catcher Ray Hayworth. The Yankees were relieved that they didn't have to face Cochrane, who sat himself out this game, but Ray made Cochrane look like the genius he was with a 2-run single to tie the score and knock Gomez out of the game before New York could get the third out. General Crowder, meanwhile, had settled down since the early innings, and New York's batters now could do nothing with his pitches. Detroit's 7th inning was looking an awful lot like their 6th, as they plated 4 more runs, including back-up catcher Ray Hayworth's 3rd RBI today, sealing their come-from-behind 9-5 victory.

In game 2, it was Schoolboy's turn to face the Yankees, and he quieted them on 4 hits in Detroit's 7-3 win. Although New York won games 3 & 4, on only two days rest (shades of Mickey Lolich) Schoolboy took the mound for the series finale & dominated the Bronx Bombers, going the distance in a 2-0, 3-hit, 11-strikeout, shutout. In a post-game radio interview, Schoolboy asked his bride-to-be in faraway Texas, Edna Mary Skinner, a line that immediately became famous, *"How am I doin', Edna?"* Most everyone would agree with, *"damn good!"* Detroit left New York in first by 5 & ½ games, and would stay on top through the rest of 1934, clinching their first pennant in a quarter-century.

DDDDDDDDDDDDDDDDDDDDDDDDDDDDDDDDDDDDDDDDDDDDDDDDDDDDDDDDDDDDDDDDDDDDDDDDD

In early-September, before the pennant race was settled, Hank Greenberg was mulling over what to do. Rosh Hashanah, the Jewish New Year, was approaching, and Hank spent sleepless nights debating whether to play or not that day in a game against the Red Sox at Navin Field. After consulting a rabbi, who found ancient Talmud writings of Jewish children playing on Rosh Hashanah, Hank decided to suit up. On that September 10, 1934 afternoon, Boston grabbed a 1-0 first inning lead against Elden Auker. The score stayed that way into the seventh when Greenberg stepped up to the plate and launched a game-tying home run, deep into the right-field stands. After Auker put down the Sox in the top of the ninth, once again it was Greenberg's turn at bat. Hammerin' Hank swung and the ball exploded off of his bat, a high, arching drive that Boston's right-fielder didn't even move for as it easily cleared the fence, sending the crowd into a screaming ecstasy as he rounded the bases to complete a walk-off, game-winning, home run, his teammates greeting him in a beautiful mob scene on the field. Final score, Greenberg 2 Boston 1.

Yom Kippur was 9 days later, and Hank chose to sit that holy day out. In the Detroit Free Press, a poem by Poet Edgar Guest appeared that spoke to his decision, and in conclusion said of Hank that he…

Spent the day among his people and he didn't come to play

Said Murphy to Mulrooney "We shall lose the game today."

We shall miss him in the infield and shall miss him at the bat

But he's true to his religion and I honor him for that.

Hammerin' Hank Greenberg

DDDDDDDDDDDDDDDDDDDDDDDDDDDDDDDDDDDDDDDDDDDDDDDDDDDDDDDDDDDDDDDDDDDDDDDDDDDD

At season's end, Mickey Cochrane earned the American League's Most Valuable Player award for his leadership, hitting, and defensive brilliance behind the plate, despite Lou Gehrig winning the Triple Crown, as Iron Mike hit .320 with 2 home runs & 75 runs batted in. The balance of the explosive offense read: 1B Hank Greenberg .339/26/139 RBIs/118 runs; 2B & #2 in the MVP voting Charlie Gehringer .356/11/127/135 runs/99 walks; SS Billy Rogell .296/3/99/115 runs; 3B Marv Owen .317/8/98/80 runs; OF Jo-Jo White .313/0/43/97 runs; OF Goose Goslin .305/13/100/106 runs; OF Pete Fox .285/2/44/101 runs; OF Gerald Gee Walker (Joe Louis <u>AND</u> Paul Carey's favorite player) .300/6/40/54 runs; Pitcher Schoolboy Rowe .303/6/22 RBIs… TEAM .300/74 HRs/959 runs. Besides the power display, Detroit ran wild on the bases, 5 Tigers among the league's top 10 in stolen bases, led by 3 of their 4 outfielders: Jo-Jo White 28, Pete Fox 25, & Gee Walker 20.

The Navin Field attendance improved from 320,972 in '33 to a league-leading 919,161 in '34, the team's highest total since 1924 when Ty Cobb played. Owner Frank Navin was, indeed, a happy man. If Detroit could win the impending World Series, he would be a ***very*** happy man.

DDDDDDDDDDDDDDDDDDDDDDDDDDDDDDDDDDDDDDDDDDDDDDDDDDDDDDDDDDDDDDDDDDDDDDDDDDDD

The Tigers World Series opponent was the St. Louis Cardinals. For the joyfully aggressive play that left them with dirty uniforms resembling the grease-stained clothing of car mechanics, the Cardinals were known to baseball fans everywhere as "The Gas House Gang". These guys were very good and very confident, and they had every reason to be. The Cards 1934 pennant marked their 4th National League title in the last 8 years, led by two pitching brothers, Most Valuable Player & 30-game winner Jay "Dizzy"

Dean & 19-game winner Paul "Daffy" Dean. Dizzy would be the last National Leaguer to win 30 in a season, and the last Major Leaguer to do so until Denny McLain in '68.

The offense was supplied by player-manager Frankie Frisch at second, Leo Durocher at short, Pepper Martin at 3rd, Ducky Medwick in left, and first sacker and aptly-named Ripper Collins who provided the power with 35 home runs. The Gas House Gang was a flaky bunch, and no one seemed surprised when Dizzy noted, *"The doctors x-rayed my head and found nothing."* Little changed after their playing days when some of these Cards ended up in the broadcast booth. Frankie Frisch told the radio audience, *"It's a beautiful day for a night game"*, and Dizzy suggested listeners, *"Don't fail to miss tomorrow's game."*

As the World Series began, it seemed that every Michigan household or business owning a radio was tuned to either WXYZ's Harry Heilmann, broadcasting to people in Western & Northern Michigan on into the Upper Peninsula, or to WWJ's Ty Tyson – broadcasting since the first Tiger radio game in 1927 - who described the action for folks in Southeast Michigan. Each game's first pitch was in the early afternoon, schoolkids allowed to assemble in auditoriums to listen. With the 1930's invention of car radios, Duke Ellington's *"It Don't Mean a Thing, If You Ain't Got That Swing"* was often heard from autos driving by, until channels were changed when it was time to *"Play Ball!"*

Harry Heilmann described for listeners the vast difference between the current Detroit 4-man outfield rotation of Goslin, Pete Fox, Jo-Jo White, & Gerald Walker, versus that from his playing days in the 20s, as he told it, *"the clown combination of Heilmann, Fothergill, and Wingo."* A few minutes later, Heilmann received a telegram from his old teammate Bob Fothergill that read, *"Speak for yourself, you fathead."*

Game 1 Detroit: In a surprise pick over 24-game winner Schoolboy & 22-game winner Tommy Bridges, Cochrane called on General Alvin Crowder to face Dizzy Dean in the opener, believing Crowder's World Series experience with the Senators in '33 would come into play. The General pitched well, surrendering 1 earned run on 6 hits in his 5 innings of work, but the Tigers committed 5 costly errors which their offense could not overcome against the great Dean, and St. Louis took a 1-0 Series lead, winning 8 to 3.

Game 2 Detroit: After spotting the Cardinals 2 runs in the first 3 innings, Schoolboy got into a groove, the ball responding to his sweet coaxing as he retired a then-record 22 batters in a row, and pitched all 12 frames in Detroit's 3-2 victory. The bottom of the ninth saw Detroit facing a 2-1 deficit and down to their last 3 outs. Pete Fox led off with a single, was bunted to 2nd by Schoolboy, and rode home on the pinch-hit single off the bat of Gee Walker. The game would stay 2-2 into the bottom of the 12th when the Tigers "G Men" struck: Charlie Gehringer & Hank Greenberg each walked, and Goose Goslin singled home Gehringer with the game winner. Series all even at 1-1.

Before the Tigers prepared to board a train departing for St. Louis from the Michigan Central Train Depot, most of the team stopped by Hoot Robinson's bar, next to Navin Field, to down a beer and get some sandwiches to-go that 27-year old tavern owner Hoot made up for their time riding the rails.

Game 3 St. Louis: Tommy Bridges pitched good but Daffy Dean pitched great, while St. Louis 3rd baseman Pepper Martin doubled, tripled, and scored 2 runs as St. Louis topped Detroit 4 to 1. Hank Greenberg's 9th inning triple plated the Tigers only run, but too little too late. Advantage St. Louis 2-1.

Game 4 St. Louis: Elden Auker and the Tigers offense to the rescue! Lead-off man Jo-Jo White and a parade of Tigers chipped in with 2 hits each in the Tigers 13-hit attack. Final Detroit 10 St. Louis 4. Series tied 2-2.

Game 5 St. Louis: Tommy Bridges, the Tigers bulldog, was the Great One today, out-dueling Dizzy Dean in a 3-1 Tiger win. Charlie Gehringer took Dizzy downtown in the sixth, and Detroit heads home up 3 games to 2.

Game 6 Detroit: It's Schoolboy Rowe vs. Daffy Dean facing off today before 44,551 fanatics. Since Navin Field's seating capacity is only 30,000, there are almost 15,000 shoehorned into temporary seats at the park. The two pitchers went the distance in this see-saw affair. The Tigers, down 3-1 going into the bottom of the sixth, fought back with 2 runs, had Daffy on the ropes, and probably should've had more. With men on 1st & 2nd, 1 run in & no one out, Mickey Cochrane – running from second - was forced out at 3rd on what the Tigers & their followers believe to this day was an awful call. Even the unassuming Charlie Gehringer couldn't stay quiet on the call by umpire Brick Owens, *"We should've won the sixth game. Owens called Mickey out on that play at third even though all of the photographs show that he was safe by a mile. If Cochrane had been called safe, we would've had the bases loaded with nobody out and we could've had a big inning."*

Although the rally continued to tie the game, the thought will forever be what might have been. In the St. Louis 7th, a Leo Durocher double and a Paul Dean single restored the Cards lead to 4-3. With two outs in the bottom of the ninth and no one on base, Schoolboy hit a drive to center that had all of the folks out of their seats, but it died at the fence. Series all tied at 3-3.

Game 7 Detroit: It's Dizzy Dean versus Elden Auker for the World Championship. To quote Neil Young, *"It sorta starts off real slow, then fizzles out altogether."* Ugly, ugly, ugly. Once the Cards scored 7 in the third, and it was clear that Dizzy was on his game, tempers flared and the air was thick with frustration. It peaked in the Cards 2-run 6th when Ducky Medwick slid into third base, spiking Tiger Marv Owens, the two almost getting into a fist fight. When Medwick took his left-field defensive position in the bottom of the inning, the enraged fans threw at him everything they could get their hands on, including bottles, trash, and food. Commissioner Kenesaw Mountain Landis was in attendance and ordered Medwick removed from the game *"for his own safety"*, the only time this ruling was ever made in a World Series game. Two meaningless Cardinals runs were tacked on in the seventh for a final Game 7 score of 11-0, clinching the 1934 World Series for St. Louis.

DDDDDDDDDDDDDDDDDDDDDDDDDDDDDDDDDDDDDDDDDDDDDDDDDDDDDDDDDDDDDDDDDDDDDDDDDD

A slow burn was experienced by the Detroit Tigers all through the 1934-1935 off-season, and they were determined to come out on top in '35. Spring training would be held for the second consecutive year in the small Florida town of Lakeland, the players arriving raring to go.

Despite that, the season started poorly for the Tigers, sitting in 6th place & nowhere near contention as the calendar flipped to June. Suddenly, everything changed, with General Alvin Crowder catching fire the key. His 5 victories in June included two complete game gems over the Damn Yankees. Then, on July 24, in front of a packed house of howling New Yorkers in "The House That Ruth Built", the General spun a 4-hitter, shutting out the Yanks 4-0 and quieting their faithful, boosting the Tigers for the first time all year into first place. It was a place they would not leave.

Under fiery Mickey Cochrane's direction, the entire team was jelling now. The pitching staff was led by the 21 & 10 record of undersized bulldog Tommy Bridges, named the *"Little T from Tennessee"* by broadcaster Harry Heilmann, Schoolboy Rowe's 19 & 13 (plus another fine year at the plate, hitting

.312), Elden Auker's 18 & 7 record with a league leading .720 winning percentage, and General Alvin Crowder's 16 & 10 mark. The hitters were on fire, the "G Men" – Hank Greenberg, Charlie "the Mechanical Man" Gehringer, Goose Goslin – all batting in over 100 runs each, "Hankus Pankus" aka "Hammerin' Hank" smoking at a .328 average, a league-high 36 homers (breaking his team record of 26 set last year) & 170 RBIs – a performance that would win him the MVP award, supported by Cochrane's .319 and outfielders Gerald "Gee" Walker's .301 & Pete Fox at .321 including a 34-game hitting streak.

DDDDDDDDDDDDDDDDDDDDDDDDDDDDDDDDDDDDDDDDDDDDDDDDDDDDDDDDDDDDDDDDDDDDDDDD

Recalling the fun of the Summer of '35 was Ella LoCricchio nee Fleming. That year was her 10th, living on Labrosse Street near Trumbull, 5 blocks from The Corner - so close that the family could hear the Navin Field action at their house. Ella relates, *"Thursdays were Ladies Day at Tiger Stadium. Women got in for a quarter and could bring as many kids as they wanted for free. Mom would bring us and 6 or 8 neighborhood kids to the stadium. The seats were in leftfield and the outfielder there was one of our favorites, Goose Goslin. Before the game, the Tigers would be practicing and we'd yell at him to toss us a baseball, 'Goosey! Goosey! Goosey!' Every time he turned around, he'd be throwing a ball to us. This was before the top* (the outfield Upper Deck), *was added, so the Tigers would try to hit baseballs over the low fence to the kids standing on Trumbull or Cherry Streets or to the fans on the roof of the Checker Cab Company."* Ella's continuing love affair with baseball drew her to work at the ballpark in later years, making sure that the vendors roaming the stands had enough hot dogs to keep the fans happy.

Goose Goslin, Jo-Jo White, & Pete Fox...   *and 8 decades later, Goosey Girl Ella (on left)*

Although the entire pitching staff contributed in a big way to the team's success in '35, it was General "Yankee Killer" Crowder's wins chalked up against the New Yorkers that looked huge when the final standings were tallied. His August looked much like his June, as the General again won 5 times. The biggest of Crowder's 5 August wins took place on the 17th before an overflow crowd of 32,000 at 30,000 seat capacity Navin Field, a 3-2 10-inning masterpiece over the Yankees, secured when manager Mickey Cochrane wisely put himself in as pinch hitter & knocked in the winner in the bottom half of the tenth. The Tigers last big series against their closest competitors took place mid-September, when Detroit invaded the Bronx and secured the pennant by taking 3 of 5. The final 1935 American League standings were a joy to read: first place Detroit 93 & 59, second place New York 3 games back. As important as beating New York is, what is most meaningful to the team is that taking the A.L. flag gives them a shot at redemption for the 1934 Series loss that every Tiger knows could've, perhaps should've, been theirs.

The Tigers competition in the 1935 World Series was the National League champion Chicago Cubs, who posted a 100-win season, fueled by an impressive 21-game September winning streak. Long-time Tiger fans believed that their Boys of Summer had some unfinished business against the Chicago North-Siders to take care of: in the first two World Series Detroit ever participated in, 1907 & 1908, the Tigers came up short to the Cubs.

This time around, though, the Tigers had a secret weapon by the name of Patsy O'Toole, better known around Navin Field as "the Human Earache". The Cardinals were introduced to this walking annoyance in 1934, but the Cubs never had the pleasure of experiencing a game with O'Toole in attendance. That would now change. Patsy's ear-piercing cheers were bad enough if he was on your side, every Tiger welcomed with shouts of "(fill in the blank with Tiger player name), *you're a great guy!*", while every opponent was decried as a bum or worse. To say Patsy got under the skin of more than one opponent would be an accurate statement. One afternoon, Yankee pitcher Lefty Gomez had to be restrained by several teammates as he tried to jump into the stands and throttle O'Toole.

The Human Earache's star moment was in the 1933 World Series in Washington D.C., the Senators hosting the Giants. Patsy had excellent seats as a guest of his friend, Frank Murphy, the Mayor of Detroit. In the neighboring box was President Franklin Delano Roosevelt. Mayor Murphy clearly had a sense of humor in bringing O'Toole along. FDR experienced the full Human Earache treatment, Patsy recalling with great pride, *"I never let-up for a minute!"* A member of the Secret Service was quickly dispatched to encourage Patsy to move to the opposite side of the stadium, as far away from the President as was possible, in a seat held for him by Senators' owner, Clark Griffith. This exile was the proudest moment of Patsy's life.

DDDDDDDDDDDDDDDDDDDDDDDDDDDDDDDDDDDDDDDDDDDDDDDDDDDDDDDDDDDDDDDDDDDDDD

Game 1 Detroit: The Cubs 20-game winner Lon Warneke was masterful, spinning a 4-hit shutout and quieting the Tigers big bats, if not Patsy O'Toole's lungs, for at least one day. Losing pitcher Schoolboy Rowe pitched well, allowing the Cubs two runs in the first and one in the ninth, while contributing a double to the cause, but this was Chicago's day. Final Cubs 3 Detroit 0, Chicago up 1 game to none.

Game 2 Detroit: The Tigers bats came alive immediately today, their first 4 batters delivering a single, double, single, and a Hank Greenberg home run over the left-field wall, Ty Tyson letting the radio audience know, *"That's another one out on Cherry Street."* Cubs' starter Charlie Root was knocked out before he could record an out in the game. A 2-run single by Gehringer capped a Tigers 3-run fourth inning, and Tommy Bridges limited Chicago to 6 hits as Detroit won 8-3 & evened things up at one game apiece. It was a costly win for the Tigers, though, as Greenberg was lost for the rest of the Series when he broke his wrist trying to score from 1st on a 7th inning single. Going forward, 3rd baseman Marv Owen will move to Hank's position at first, and "Flea" Clifton comes off the bench to handle third.

Game 3 Chicago: To quote Sonny Eliot, *"all the animals at the zoo are jumping up & down for you."* Today, the Goose brought a rabbit and the Tigers jumped the Cubs. Goose Goslin figured if a rabbit's foot is good-luck, why not bring an entire rabbit into the clubhouse? And wouldn't you know it, Detroit survived a deflating & game-tying 2-run Cubs 9th, taking a 6-5 thriller in 11 innings at Wrigley Field. The

Cubs other 20-game winner, Bill Lee, was in control going into the 8th, up 3-1, when the Tigers sent him to the showers with a 4-run outburst fueled by bunny-lover Goslin's two runs batted in. With a 5-3 lead going into the bottom of the 9th, Schoolboy Rowe came in to close the game out for Detroit. The Cubs had other plans, tying things up, and forcing extra innings. After a scoreless 10th, the Tigers Jo-Jo White singled home Marv Owen to make it 6-5 Detroit and Schoolboy put the Cubs down in order in the bottom of the 11th to make the Series 2-1 favor Detroit.

Game 4 Chicago: In an outstanding pitcher's duel, two nicknames beats one as "General" Alvin "Yankee-Killer" Crowder took the Cubs "Tex" Carleton 2 to 1. The General went the distance, striking out 5. The Tigers were down 1-0 when Crowder led off the 3rd with a single & came home on a Charlie Gehringer double. In the sixth, Flea Clifton (0 home runs on the year), the man replacing Hank Greenberg (36 home runs on the year) in the line-up, reached 2nd base on an error, and came around to score what turned out to be the winning run when the Cubs third-baseman could not handle General Crowder's grounder. In a tense 9th, Chicago singled twice with their best run producer, Stan Hack, at the plate, and Crowder induced a game-ending double play, shortstop Rogell to 2nd baseman Gehringer to 1st baseman Owen. With the Tigers 3rd consecutive win, they are up 3-1, and one win away from the championship.

Game 5 Chicago: In a reprise of game 1, it's Schoolboy Rowe versus Lon Warneke. Schoolboy once again pitches well, but Lon out-duels him, this time 3-1. Down 3-0, the Tigers open the ninth with singles by Gehringer, Goslin, and Pete Fox, but only can plate one run. The Series is Detroit 3, Chicago 2, as the teams take the train back to Detroit.

Game 6 Detroit: One victory away from the Detroit Tigers first ever World Series Championship, 21-game winner Tommy Bridges is matched against the Cub's Larry French. Somehow, 48,420 excited, nervous, and loud fanatics made their way into 30,000 seat Navin Field. Detroit was ready to explode. When the Tigers took the lead in their 1st, Mickey Cochrane coming home on a Pete Fox double, the stadium was so loud that the Human Earache was almost drowned out. Almost. After Chicago tied it up at 1 in the third, the Tigers again surged ahead when Gerald Gee Walker scampered home on a Bridges groundout. Detroit 2-1, but not for long. In their next at bat, a Billy Herman 2-run homer put the Cubs up 3-2. In the Tigers 6th, the first two men went down and, just as the faithful were resigned to going into the 7th behind, Billy Rogell just missed a game-tying homer down the left-field line, settling for a crowd-igniting ground-rule double. Marv Owen, in the biggest at bat of his career, got ahold of a pitch he liked and deposits it into left to score Rogell & make it 3-3, and it stayed that way into the 9th.

The entire state was on edge when the Cubs Stan Hack led off the top of the ninth with a triple to deep center-field. The lead run on 3rd with no outs. This is when legends are made, and Tommy Bridges bore down. He got a huge strikeout. One out. Then, he forced a weak grounder back to the mound, as he looked Hack back to third base before tossing the batter out at first. Two outs. Now, with Hack leading off third and the entire ballpark standing and screaming, Augie Galan lifted a flyball to left that settled into the glove of Goose Goslin. Exhale. Tigers coming to bat, bottom of ninth. Goslin turned to Elden Auker in the dugout & said, *"I have a feeling I'm going to be at the plate with the winning run on base and we're going to win the ballgame."* After a Flea Clifton strikeout, Mickey Cochrane gave Detroit a runner with an infield single to deep 2nd. Cochrane was off & running on Gehringer's groundout to first, taking 2nd. Mickey Cochrane, player-manager and the man most responsible for the Tigers surge of '34 & '35, was on 2nd with two out as up to the plate steps Goose Goslin. Goose fouls away the first pitch.

Strike 1. The wind-up and the pitch… *Goslin lines the next pitch into right-center… Cochrane races around third and jumps on to home plate with both feet! The Tigers are the World Champions of 1935!*

The *New York Daily News* described Cochrane's mad dash home, *"It was something to see, Mickey Cochrane stabbing his spikes into the plate with the winning run and then going mad, like a young colt, leaping and cavorting about, shaking his bare, dark head. When Cochrane stood on second, a lone figure in white, I have never seen such will and energy from a single person. He had to come home. He willed to come home. I believe if Goslin hadn't hit he would have stolen home from second base."*

In the middle of the celebrating madness on the field, after his single scored Cochrane with the Series clincher, Goslin hugged Auker and shouted, *"What did I tell ya? What did I tell ya?"*, as his teammates mobbed him. Tiger fans screamed, laughed and cried, in no hurry to leave Navin Field, shouting Goose Goslin's name over & over. The moment was no less jubilant for fans at home listening to Ty Tyson and Harry Heilmann describe the wild scene over the radio.

On October 7, 1935, the Tigers defeat of the Chicago Cubs secured Detroit's first World Championship since the 1887 victory by the Detroit Wolverines of the National League. Repeating a scene taking place at so many taverns across the state, many beers were lifted on this night at the bar owned by 28-year old Hoot Robinson on Trumbull Avenue, across the street from Navin Field's right-field wall. Baseball Commissioner Kenesaw Mountain Landis called the 1935 World Series *"the greatest ever"*.

How could this match-up have ended any other way? It was 1935, after all, and in any scrape Detroit & Michigan was destined to win…

- Tigers secure their 1st World Series win;
- Detroit Lions, led by quarterback Dutch Clark, win their 1st NFL title over the NY Giants in '35;
- Detroit Red Wings over Toronto Maple Leafs for team's 1st Stanley Cup win, '35/'36 season;
- and in 1935, Detroit's "Brown Bomber", Joe Louis, defeats Max Baer in the ring at Yankee Stadium – Max Baer, whose son Max Baer Jr. played Jethro Bodine in the Beverly Hillbillies. Isn't it interesting how all the major events in our lives always circle back to the Beverly Hillbillies?

A toast to Detroit, the City of Champions!

1936 – 1939 Briggs, Boots, & Breakin' Up the Old Gang

Lafayette Coney Island - Just down the street from Navin Field, at the corner of Lafayette Boulevard and Michigan Avenue, serving since 1920: the menu… Coney Dog – Loose Hamburger – Lafayette Special – Bean Soup – French Fries – Chili Fries – Chili Cheese Fries – Chili – Chili No Beans – Beer – Pop or Milk – Coffee or Tea – Pies – Doughnuts – Potato Chips

A couple of hours after Mickey Cochrane scored the 1935 World Series winning run, owner Frank Navin stood in the joyous Tiger locker room, and said, _"I can now die in peace"._

Just over one month after Cochrane passionately jumped with both feet on to home plate, securing the 1st Championship for the Detroit Tigers, setting off a state-wide celebration, Mickey and team owner Frank Navin rode horses together on Belle Isle. Rather than holding a meeting in a stuffy office, the two equestrians conferred in the fresh air, discussing strategy for the upcoming 1936 season.

The next day, Frank Navin was back in the saddle, riding this time alongside his wife Grace. The Navins were members of the Detroit Riding & Hunt Club and riding their horses together on Belle Isle was an almost daily ritual followed since 1920. Frank fell from his mount. Unconscious, he was rushed to a Highland Park hospital, and pronounced dead – not from the fall, but rather from a heart attack.

Frank J. Navin had been working towards the goal of a Detroit Tiger World Series championship every year since 1902, when he was hired as team bookkeeper by then-owner Sam Angus. In 1903, Navin bought stock in the club, becoming a minority-owner. Angus sold the team in '04 to William Yawkey, who put Navin in charge of financial operations. Before the '07 season, Yawkey sold 50% of team ownership to Navin. In 1909, Frank Navin became Detroit Tigers majority-owner.

To honor her husband's love of the Tigers, Grace secured the perfect final resting place for Frank, an above-ground mausoleum, flanked by two stone tigers facing outward, one left & one right. After her husband's burial, Grace Navin accepted a $1,000,000 offer from Walter O. Briggs, Navin's silent partner & co-owner of the Tigers, allowing Briggs to become sole owner of the team.

Briggs first to-do-list item was to expand seating to meet the increased number of fans flocking to The Corner. Over the winter of 1935-1936, he directed the extension of the Upper Deck from first base down the foul line and turning the corner into fair territory in right-field. Part of this expansion resulted in the Upper Deck in right being widened by 10' both out over Trumbull Avenue _and_ towards home plate. The 10' widening towards home plate created the famous porch hanging over the field of play in right: in the Lower Deck, its 325' from home to the wall in right, but only 315' from home to the Upper Deck porch overhang. Many a right-fielder standing near the fence below would see a certain catch taken away as descending fly-balls became home runs by landing in the first few rows of the overhang.

DDDDDDDDDDDDDDDDDDDDDDDDDDDDDDDDDDDDDDDDDDDDDDDDDDDDDDDDDDDDDDDDDDDDD

In January 1936, the Baseball Writers' Association of America voted for the first class of inductees into the brand-new Hall of Fame. Ty Cobb learned of the honor via a telegram received from his old friend, America's best-known sportswriter, Grantland Rice:

Dear Ty: Baseball's writers have elected you to the Hall of Fame. This esteemed honor is deserved and heralds your place as baseball's greatest performer and competitor. Your vote total exceeded by no one. I send my congratulations. Four others join you in the Hall of Fame. Warm regards, Grantland Rice.

Not mentioned in Grantland's telegram were the remaining inaugural class members – Babe Ruth, Honus Wagner, Walter Johnson, and Christy Mathewson. Although Cobb had the top vote total from the 226 writers, amazingly 4 left him off of their ballots & Ruth was left off of 11 ballots.

DDDDDDDDDDDDDDDDDDDDDDDDDDDDDDDDDDDDDDDDDDDDDDDDDDDDDDDDDDDDDDDDDDDDDDDDDD

The reigning *Champion Detroit Tigers* opened defense of their title April 14, 1936, on the road in Cleveland. Detroit's Brown Bomber, boxer Joe Louis, fresh off of being acclaimed the *Associated Press* "Outstanding Athlete of 1935", was asked to throw out the first pitch. Sportswriter Jimmy Cannon said of the man, *"Joe Louis was a credit to his race – the human race."* To the further delight of the fans and the players, the person on the receiving end of the pitch was Jack Benny. Jack caught the ball after his wife, Mary Livingstone, swung, missed, and fell down – the 3 participating in a salute to Detroit AND a comedic set-up to kick off the season.

In the first inning of the season opener, Hank Greenberg's 2-run double sent home Rogell & Gehringer, giving Schoolboy all the runs that he needed. Rowe tossed a complete game, 3-0, shutout and the Tigers were off to a fine start in '36. And then an incident took place that changed the course of their season. Detroit was riding a 5-game winning streak as they took the field against the Senators on April 29. Despite the wrist break suffered in the '35 World Series, Greenberg opened the season hitting .348 with 16 RBIs in the 1st 12 games. When Hank fielded a grounder on this day, Washington batter Jake Powell left the base path, charged into Greenberg, and spiked him after he hit the ground, breaking his recently healed wrist once again. The 1935 league MVP as well as home run & RBI champ was lost to the team for almost the entire final 5 months of the season. By the time Hankus Pankus returned, the Tigers were a country mile back of the Yankees, their chances for a repeat ended.

The backstory of that play and resulting injury was based in the antisemitism found throughout America in the 1930s and endured frequently by Hank, especially early in his playing career. In an interview, Greenberg shared some of that, *"How the hell could you get up to home plate every day and have some son-of-a-bitch call you a Jew bastard and a kike and a sheenie and on your ass without feeling the pressure? If the ballplayers weren't doing it, the fans were."* When a person as idolized as Henry Ford states, *"If fans wish to know the trouble with American baseball, they have it in three words – too much Jew,"* it gives small-minded people the ok they need to act in hateful ways. A few years later, when Jackie Robinson suffered through the racial slurs he had to face, Hank was a man who could empathize.

Jake Powell, the small-minded person who ran over & then spiked Greenberg, claimed it was an accident – difficult to believe by anyone who witnessed it. Years later, interviewed on a pre-game show, Powell was asked what he did to stay in shape. He replied, *"I crack niggers over the head with my nightstick."* In this one statement, Powell first lied about being a cop, and then shared how in his mind he thought a police officer should act. For these comments, he received a 10-game suspension.

When Mickey Cochrane, the only man more valuable to the Tigers success than Hammerin' Hank, went down for the year after only 44 games with a nervous breakdown, Detroit's chances in 1936 ended. Adding the responsibilities of General Manager to his roles of Field Manager & starting catcher may have simply overwhelmed him. Although the offense continued to thrive, batting .300 as a team and scoring 6 runs per contest, the loss of Hank, Mickey, and the stomach-ailment driven, mid-season, retirement of Yankee-Killing General Alvin Crowder, relegated the Tigers to a 2nd place finish with a record of 83 and 71.

Thomas Jefferson Davis Bridges tried mightily to make up for these losses, leading the league with 23 wins – his third 20+ win season in a row – and 175 strikeouts. Gerald "Gee" Walker had a bust-out year, his .353 batting average placing him right behind the .354 of 4th place finishers Charlie Gehringer and Lou Gehrig – nice company – his 55 doubles a league 2nd behind Gehringer's 60, and near the top in stolen bases, as usual. Gehringer was once again, thankfully, Gehringer. In what was one of Charlie's finest years, the stat that stands out the most is that he struck out once every 49 times at bat. Lefty Gomez is credited with coining the "Mechanical Man" nickname for Charlie, *"You wind him up in the spring and he goes all summer, hits .330 or .340 or whatever, and then you shut him off in the fall."* Goose Goslin had the last great year of his career, batting .315 and placing in the A.L. top 10 in slugging percentage, total bases, runs scored, RBIs, stolen bases, and home runs – one of those homers, on September 18, was the first ever given up by Cleveland's flame-throwing rookie pitcher and future Hall of Famer, Bob Feller.

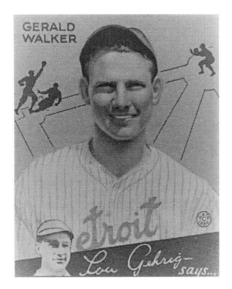

Gerald "Gee" Walker, 1/4 of the great 30s outfield of Goslin, White, & Fox
and favorite Tiger of both Joe Louis & Paul Carey

But all of these efforts were not enough to pass New York in 1936. The Yankees season was greatly aided by the contributions of a rookie sensation in center field, a 21-year old who hit .323, knocked in 125 runs with 29 homers, and who led the league in triples with 15. The rookie, a native of Martinez, California, was named Joe DiMaggio.

DDDDDDDDDDDDDDDDDDDDDDDDDDDDDDDDDDDDDDDDDDDDDDDDDDDDDDDDDDDDDDDDDDDDDDDDDDD

On May 25, 1937, the Tigers arrived in the Bronx in 2nd place, 1 & ½ games behind the Yankees. The pitching match-up that day was between Schoolboy Rowe and New York's Bump Hadley. Bump had achieved notoriety pitching for Washington in 1928 by giving up the 4,191st and final hit in Ty Cobb's career, a pinch hit double. The Yanks took an early 1-0 lead until Mickey Cochrane hit a solo homer in the third to tie the game at 1. The Tigers and their fans were encouraged by how well Cochrane had played in the season's first 2 months, seemingly fully recovered from his nervous breakdown of last year, in full control in the dugout and behind the plate, his .306 average reflective of his aggressiveness when at bat.

In Cochrane's first time up following his home run, he worked the count to 3 & 1. The next pitch was a fastball sailing directly at Mickey's head, drilling him in the temple. Mickey crumpled to the ground with a broken skull. Hadley seemed genuinely shaken, and helped to carry Cochrane off of the field. Whether Mick would survive was touch 'n go and he did not regain consciousness for over a week. Although he did pull through, this injury marked the end of Cochrane's playing days. Along with his Tiger teammates, Mick absolved Bump, who visited Black Mike twice in the hospital, of intentionally throwing at him. As happened during Cochrane's 1936 breakdown, Coach Del Baker stepped in as interim manager while Mickey recovered.

During this time, the Tigers had been trying to find a way to work a 23-year old infield prospect that they were very high on into the lineup. Rudy York hit 37 homers in the minors the previous year, but there were no positions open on the parent club for him. Cochrane's beaning created that opening, with York moving behind the plate. In only 375 at bats, Rudy hit 35 home runs, including a major league record 18 in one month (August) to go with 101 RBIs & a .307 batting average. York became a national sensation.

DDDDDDDDDDDDDDDDDDDDDDDDDDDDDDDDDDDDDDDDDDDDDDDDDDDDDDDDDDDDDDDDDDDDDDDDDDD

Navin Field neighborhood gal Marion Vollmers grew up mere blocks from the ball park. As a 16-year old in the summer of '37, she worked a beer concession in the cool shadows under the stands. Frequently during the 3rd or 4th inning of most games, Marion & her fellow employees heard a distant clicking sound of cleats on cement, growing louder 'n louder, coming towards her concession. Creating this sound was Schoolboy Rowe. Wearing a trench coat with the collar turned up to cover his face, on days he wasn't pitching, Schoolboy would order two Strohs, putting one in each pocket of his coat. He would always tip, then put his index finger to his lips and say, *"Thank you ladies. Mum's the word,"* before heading towards the team locker room, the *click-click-click* sound of the cleats gradually receding as he disappeared from sight.

DDDDDDDDDDDDDDDDDDDDDDDDDDDDDDDDDDDDDDDDDDDDDDDDDDDDDDDDDDDDDDDDDDDDDDDDDDD

Up until 1937, the sight of MLB players wearing a batting helmet was a rarity. After Cochrane's beaning, there was a league-wide outcry for their use, including from Mickey himself. On June 1, 1937, the week after Mickey was struck, the Philadelphia Athletics and the Cleveland Indians became the first teams to test helmets on game day, but it was not until 1956 in the National League and 1958 in the American League, that wearing batting helmets became mandatory.

When Mickey Cochrane was able to return to his managerial duties, the change in his personality was obvious and not good. The ability to motivate, to strategize, to focus, was missing. Mickey was mean instead of strict, unable to concentrate. The Tigers, however, played well, and their fans loved them for it, with a league-leading 1,072,276 coming out to cheer their heroes. Although from August 13 on Detroit was never below 2nd place, the balance of the year they could not get closer to first place than nine games. The Tigers 1937 record was 89 & 65, ending up in 2nd place once again to the Yankees.

Detroit's .292 team average was tops in the majors, and they again averaged 6 runs per game. The amazing Charlie Gehringer, the best 2nd baseman in the land, won the MVP award and was the A.L. batting champ at .371, prompting another great Charlie quote from Lefty Gomez, *"He's in a rut. Gehringer goes 2 for 5 on Opening Day and stays that way all season."*

Gehringer was one of 4 Tigers with over 200 hits, joined by Greenberg, Gee Walker & Pete Fox. And they kept on running, with Walker 3rd in the league in steals at 23 and Jo-Jo White & Pete Fox also in the top 10. Rudy York could not replace Cochrane's leadership skills, but he exceeded Mick's average offensive output with 35 homers & 101 RBIs. Hammerin' Hank had 183 RBIs, one short of Lou Gehrig's record of 184, and his 40 homers (once again, breaking his own team mark) was 2nd only to the 46 of DiMaggio.

Gehringer & Greenberg Day at Tiger Stadium, half-a-century later

Even beyond the loss of Cochrane for most of the year, the biggest difference between New York and Detroit in '37 was the debilitating arm troubles suffered by Schoolboy Rowe. After winning 62 games the previous 3 years, he only got into 10 games, winning once. A fella named Roxie Lawson tried to make up for Schoolboy's absence. Roxie had a career year with 18 wins & 7 losses, and Detroit scored <u>alot</u> of runs when he was on the mound. They had to in order to overcome his nasty 5.26 ERA. In Roxie's 9-year career, he never won more than 8 in any other season (see 5.37 career ERA).

DDDDDDDDDDDDDDDDDDDDDDDDDDDDDDDDDDDDDDDDDDDDDDDDDDDDDDDDDDDDDDDDDDDDDDDDDDDDD

There was a youngster called up mid-season to cover for Schoolboy's arm woes, a pitcher doing a fine job with the Tigers' minor league team in Beaumont, Texas, posting a record of 9 & 2 into June. The 21-year old's name was Cletus Elwood "Boots" Poffenberger.

To say that Boots Poffenberger was a bit of a character would be to say that Jimmy Durante had a bit of a schnoz. As one sports writer put it, *"Boots not only marched to the beat of a different drummer, he frequently heard an entirely different band."* He was a care-free child in an adult's body – he simply never grew up. Honest as the day is long, Boots was always very truthful about staying out too late (team curfews were instituted by Cochrane in '38 specifically because of Boots), or drinking too much (earning the byname "The Prince of Pilsner"), or any number of infractions. Boots Poffenberger was a genuine, irrepressible, and loveable human being. He was an eccentric who wore socks, but no shoes (except on the ball diamond), the tops & sides of those socks white as could be, the bottoms as you would figure. When a phone rang, Boots wouldn't answer it, but left the room if it rang too long.

Of most concern to the Tigers, he had an outstanding fastball & knew how to use it. The boy could pitch. Boots had his major league debut on June 11, 1937, at The Corner against the Boston Red Sox. Boots entered the game in the third inning with Detroit losing 4-2. Pitching for the Sox was one of the greatest hurlers of all-time, Hall-of-Famer Lefty Grove. The Tigers rallied to take the lead, while Boots only gave up 1 run in his 6 plus innings. Over the next couple of days, folks across the country read that some fella with the strange name of Boots Poffenberger defeated the legendary Lefty Grove, 6 to 5, and that Boots had never seen a major league park until the Tigers called him up the week before.

4 days after defeating Lefty, Boots came in to relieve in the 9th inning of an 8-8 game. He got the last out of that inning, pitched 6 innings of shutout ball, and got the win when Detroit scored the tie-breaker in the 15th. Boots began to be used for both starting & relieving, and in his third start was locked into an excellent pitcher's duel with the great Bob Feller, both going the distance, Boots getting a 3-2 walk-off victory when Rudy York knocked in Gehringer in the bottom of the 9th.

4 decades after Boots' debut, Joe Falls of the *Detroit Free Press* was shocked to find 52 press clippings in the archives on Boots. Doing some ciphering, that comes out to over 3 articles for each of his 16 wins as a Tiger, helping Boots become the most quoted player in Detroit. Once after taking a one-day hiatus from the Tigers, Poffenberger casually strolled into the clubhouse where a steamed Mickey Cochrane approached, demanding to know Boots whereabouts. Boots, given the nom de guerre of "the Baron" by sports writers due to the majestic sound of Cletus Elwood Poffenberger, replied to Cochrane, "*I refuse to reveal my identity.*"

The one & only Boots

And even the folks from Wheaties came callin', paying Boots $150 to help sell their cereal. Soon, the copy on the Wheaties boxes on breakfast tables in homes throughout America read, *"Spectacular young Tiger pitcher, Boots Poffenberger, is out to beat his 1937 record. The 'Baron' is one of a whole flock of Wheaties-eating Bengals. He says, 'You'd be surprised how many Tigers put 'em away every morning!'"* The plan was set for a live recording to push Wheaties, the company man paying Boots the night before for the live ad to run the next morning, when they met for breakfast in the lobby of a Detroit hotel. Now they were on live, and when the Wheaties fella asked Boots what he was going to have for breakfast, the nation heard him reply, *"A beer and a steak,"* exactly what he then ordered. In an interview years later, Boots protested that this story could not have been true, *"Anyone who knows me figures I'd be icing a* case *of beer in the bathtub or out at a bar."* So there.

Boots Poffenberger wrapped up his fine rookie season of '37 with a record of 10 & 5 in 29 games. In a Sporting News interview just before spring training of '38, the headlines read, *"Boots Poffenberger Decides to Be Good to Be Better: 'If I Can Win Ten Staying Up at Nights, What Can I Do In Shape?' He Asks"*. That wasn't how it worked out. In an era of all day games, Boots had plenty of time to drink at the bars and took full advantage of that fact. The season started well, but the night life wore Boots down, and the Tigers felt compelled to hire a detective to monitor his activities. Armed with the detective's findings, Walter Briggs confronted Boots with a recap of everything he'd been doing 'til the wee hours, hoping it would change the Baron's ways. Boots asked Mister Briggs how he knew about all of his activities, and Briggs told about the detective trailing him. Boots tried to be helpful, *"That's a waste of your money, Mr. Briggs. Why don't you give me the money you'd be giving to the detective, and I'll tell him where to go. All he'd have to do was go to the beer joint closest to the ballpark."*

Boots' continued poor performance in '38 earned him a demotion to minor league Toledo. Apparently, he was better able to avoid temptation with the Mud Hens under their stern manager, Fred Haney. Going 8 & 3 with a 3.92 ERA in Toledo, Boots earned a recall to Detroit in September. Before & after Toledo, Boots went 6 & 7 in 1938 at Detroit, his final win coming on September 25 at The Corner: before 19,700 cheering on the always popular Baron, he went the distance in a 7-5 decision over Cleveland. An October 1, 5-0, loss to the Tribe would be Boots final game in a Detroit uniform.

When it was time for the players to report to spring training in 1939, Boots was nowhere to be found. When he finally did arrive, he was overweight and badly out of shape, and his work at training camp didn't seem to help. When challenged about his weight, Boots told the Tiger brass that they were to blame. Why is that? *"You make me get up at 8AM for practice each day. When I get up at 8AM, I eat breakfast, lunch & dinner. If you'll let me sleep until 1PM like I want to, I'll only eat dinner."*

The Tigers had enough, and sold Baron Cletus Elwood "Boots" Poffenberger to the Brooklyn Dodgers on, appropriately, April Fools' Day. The national press had been given the wonderful gift of Boots, the zaniest man in baseball, going to the Daffiness Boys. The erratic play of the Dodgers in the 20s & 30s that earned them that nickname could best be described by this story: two Brooklyn fans sat in the bleachers, one watching the action on the field, the other working his scorecard. The Dodgers launched a sudden rally against the Giants. *"Look!"* shouted the first, *"the Dodgers have 3 men on base!"* Without looking up from his scorecard, the other said casually, *"Yeah? Which base?"*

The new Brooklyn Dodgers manager, Leo Durocher, was a stern sort, and felt insulted by the press comments, telling all that he could handle Boots. The manager was tested on the Dodgers first road trip of '39, the team staying at the Bellevue-Stratford Hotel in Philadelphia. The big clock behind the front desk was surrounded by smaller clocks giving the times from major cities all over the world. Curfew for the players was midnight, with Durocher sitting in the lobby to see if anyone came in late. Here comes Boots through the front door at 12:30AM, walking right by his manager. Leo didn't say a word that night, but the next morning approached Boots at breakfast. *"Leo, I was back by 11,"* Boots protested. "No you weren't – I was right there and it was 12:30!" *"Maybe the clock you looked at said that, but one of them little clocks said 11 and that was the one I went by."* Although he knocked around the minors for several more years, with varying degrees of success, the antics of the loveable Boots Poffenberger proved to be too great a distraction for big league managers & their bosses, ending his major league career.

Considering the prodigious amount of drinking he did, Boots greatest feat may have been in living to 84 years of age. A cousin of Boots asked him if he had any regrets about, had he lived his life differently, how his career might have played out. The Baron replied, *"Nope, I have no regrets. You gotta figure where I was at. Born and raised in Williamsport. I didn't have nothing. I didn't have a nickel! This guy got me, put me on a train, got me a suit of clothes, met me up there, bought me more clothes, and gave me $600. I was the King of Detroit for a while! No, no regrets."*

In 2003, actor Christopher Lloyd portrayed a character named *Dr. Cletus Poffenberger* on the television series "Tremors". How perfect that the man who played innocent, off-beat, Jim Ignatowski in the TV series "Taxi" would later play a character using Boots full name.

DDDDDDDDDDDDDDDDDDDDDDDDDDDDDDDDDDDDDDDDDDDDDDDDDDDDDDDDDDDDDDDDDDDDDDDD

The close of the 1937 season marked the end to their days as Tigers for two of the most popular players to wear the Olde English D...

Goose Goslin finally slowed down at 36 years of age, the lifetime .316 batter only hitting .238 in '37. With little regard for the timing, on October 3rd, the day after Goose buried his father, Detroit released Leon "Goose" Goslin. He signed with his old team, the Senators, in time for the 1938 season, but only played in 38 games while chalking up a paltry .158. Goose then retired, wrapping up an outstanding 18-year career. Goose will always have a special place in the hearts of Tiger fans for singling home Mickey Cochrane with the run that clinched the 1935 World Series for Detroit. In a fun aside, fun except for the pain of the homeowner, in 1929 with Washington, Goose hit a homer so far that it cleared the high right-field fence at Griffith Stadium by 75 feet. The ball landed in the backyard of a lady hanging laundry, striking her in the shoulder with enough force to dislocate it.

Gerald "Gee" Walker, despite an outstanding 1937 of .335, 105 runs, 113 RBIs, 42 doubles, 18 home runs, and 23 steals, was traded on December 2 along with Marv Owen to the White Sox for pitcher Vern Kennedy & outfielder Dixie Walker. In a season & one-half with Detroit, Kennedy went 12 & 12 with an ERA in the mid 5s, while Dixie, also in a season & one-half, hit .305 before both were traded. In his final full season of '38, Marv Owen hit .281, then played in only 78 games combined in '39 & '40 before he retired. Ironic for a noted base thief, Gee Walker was the steal of the trade. Although his best years were with Detroit, the player who was the favorite of both Joe Louis & Paul Carey had 3 very good years with Chicago from '38-'40, hitting respectively .305, .291, & .294, while knocking in 87, 111, & 96 runs. Gee played through 1945 and never stopped swiping bases, totaling 223 in 15 seasons, most years finishing in the league's top 10.

DDDDDDDDDDDDDDDDDDDDDDDDDDDDDDDDDDDDDDDDDDDDDDDDDDDDDDDDDDDDDDDDDDDDDDDD

At The Corner, the final pitch at the ballpark called Navin Field took place on October 3, 1937.

At The Corner, the first pitch at the ballpark renamed Briggs Stadium took place on April 22, 1938.

Between those two dates, during the winter of 1937-1938, the center field bleachers Upper Deck was begun and completed, the entire ballpark now double-decked, increasing seating capacity from 30,000 to 52,416. Since that time, 36 home runs have literally left the park. Norm Cash has the most with 4 (one in 1961 & 3 in 1962), followed by Mickey Mantle with 3.

New owner Walter O. Briggs, who made his fortune manufacturing and painting car bodies for all of the major auto companies including Ford, Chrysler, Chalmers, and Packard, directed the changes at the ballpark. Briggs was a walking contradiction. On one hand, he was a philanthropist who gave away thousands of Tiger tickets every year to Detroit-area kids. Conversely, he was a man who ran manufacturing plants believed unsafe, where men died on the job; one of the worse cases took place in 1927 when 21 perished and survivors were horribly burned in a fire at his Harper Avenue plant.

Briggs announced that his goal was to *"give Detroit the best team in the finest park in the country."* Briggs Stadium was home to the first underground sprinkler system, the first to respond to rain by covering the field with a nylon tarp; every year he had the stadium's outside walls and the seats painted, while attendants were on hand in all restrooms – restrooms that were required to be spotless. As Tiger Stadium closed in 1999, famed announcer Ernie Harwell wanted to take home a clubhouse urinal to use in the yard as a planter. Perhaps Lulu Harwell would have acquiesced had Ernie's request been made in the "spotless" restroom days of '37. Maybe not.

DDDDDDDDDDDDDDDDDDDDDDDDDDDDDDDDDDDDDDDDDDDDDDDDDDDDDDDDDDDDDDDDDDDDDDDDDDDDDD

1938 was a disappointing season for the Tigers and their fans, Detroit finishing in fourth place, 16 games back of the Yankees who finished 99 & 53. Although the Bengals ended the year on a 28 & 11 run, all it did was cut the Yanks lead over the Tigers from 23 to 16 games. After finishing 2nd to Detroit back-to-back in '34 & '35, the New Yorkers were in the middle of a 4-year run, 1936-1939, considered by many baseball analysts to be the greatest run in major league history. The Damn Yankees won the World Series in each of those 4 years, 4 to 2 over the Giants, 4 to 1 over the Giants, 4 to 0 over the Reds, and 4 to 0 over the Cubs. The man who built those Yankees' teams, and all of the Yankees' teams from 1921 to 1945, was Ed Barrow, the man who in his younger days scouted & signed many of the 1907-1909 A.L. Champion Tiger players before exiting Detroit in '04 after losing a power struggle with Frank Navin.

For the 2nd consecutive year, Schoolboy's arm miseries hampered his effectiveness, going 0 &2 in the 4 games he appeared in before being sent to the minors. Tommy Bridges led the team with 13 wins but with his highest ERA in 7 years at 4.59, a sub-par showing for a man who was an All-Star the previous 4 seasons.

August 6, 1938 was a sad day in Tiger history. Mickey Cochrane was fired as Tiger manager. Del Baker took the reins. Detroit was performing poorly through early-August, sitting at 47 & 51, when owner Briggs made the decision. Black Mike never seemed to fully recover from the 1937 cracked skull he suffered, and perhaps not even from the 1936 nervous breakdown. Maybe not, but a great deal of people in Detroit and well-beyond the Motor City thought that Walter O. Briggs wronged the man who brought hope & pride to those crushed under the weight of the Depression. Folks' passion for Cochrane was summed up in the October 7, 1935 issue of *Time* magazine with Mickey gracing the cover. A story within noted, *"Cochrane's arrival in Detroit coincided roughly with the revival of the automobile industry and the first signs of revived prosperity. His determined jolly face soon came to represent the picture of what a dynamic Detroiter ought to look like."*

As news of Cochrane's firing spread, people were shocked. Once word got out that Mickey was flying out of Detroit the next day, grief-stricken fans by the hundreds traveled to City Airport to express their love with shouts and goodbye waves to the city's hero.

Mick was fired in the middle of a series with the Boston Red Sox. One of their players was Lefty Grove, a teammate & battery-mate of Mickey's back when they were Philadelphia Athletics. Lefty was furious with Briggs, reminding the reporters and anyone else who would listen that Briggs Stadium was *"the park that Mickey built"*, reflected in the fact that attendance was 320,000 the year before Cochrane came to Detroit, the lowest in 15 years, and now, even in the down year of 1938, over 800,000 are coming through the turnstiles, creating the funds that made the recent expansion possible.

The rationale to release Cochrane can be argued, but it was inexcusable that owner Briggs never put aside a day to honor one of the most beloved men to ever wear the Olde English D. Former UAW President Douglas Fraser spoke for many when he noted, *"With the Depression, everyone was in misery and had very little to cheer about, but Cochrane and the Tigers gave us something to hang onto. It was very uplifting."* Eventually, the city renamed the street running on the west side of Tiger Stadium, the signs changed from National to Cochrane Avenue.

Mickey ready to tag out his next victim

Separate from Mickey's unique ability to inspire, teach, and make winners out of his men, Cochrane's baseball statistics are that of a great ballplayer: his .419 career on-base percentage ranks 1st among catchers and 19th among all major leaguers, right behind Shoeless Joe Jackson & Mickey Mantle; his .320 lifetime average is 1st among catchers & 50th among all players; under the category of fewest strikeouts per at bat, he ranks in the top 30. Another moniker of Mick's, Iron Mike, was a reflection of catching at least 110 games in each of his first 11 years. One of the finest defensive catchers to ever play the game, he was an outstanding influence on the pitchers he worked with, and the catcher for two of only four American League pitchers with 16-game winning streaks, Schoolboy Rowe & Lefty Grove (tied with Walter Johnson & Smoky Joe Wood).

Mickey Cochrane will always be a cherished part of Detroit's baseball lore, as the leader both on the field and in the dugout of the first Tiger team to ever earn the sobriquet World Champions. Mickey was the inspirational fulcrum for two of the game's greatest teams, the Philadelphia A's of 1928-1931 and the Detroit Tigers of 1934-1935, the well-deserving recipient of the MVP in both 1928 & 1934, leading teams to 5 A.L. pennants & 3 World Championships in 8 seasons while overcoming the great Yankee teams when Babe Ruth was in his prime.

When Major League Baseball celebrated its Centennial Year in 1969, they chose their all-time team, made up of the best player at each position. As chosen by baseball writers & broadcasters, the catcher for that team was Mickey Cochrane. The 1969 Centennial Year All-Time team by position: Lou Gehrig at first, Rogers Hornsby at second, Honus Wagner at short, Pie Traynor at third, Babe Ruth, Ty Cobb and Joe DiMaggio in the outfield, Cochrane catching, Walter Johnson the right-handed pitcher, and Lefty Grove was the left-handed pitcher (as in *"on June 11, 1937, Boots Poffenberger defeated the legendary Lefty Grove, 6 to 5, in Boots major league debut"*). John McGraw was the manager.

Gordon Stanley Cochrane was voted into the Hall of Fame in 1947, along with his old teammate and friend, Lefty Grove.

DDDDDDDDDDDDDDDDDDDDDDDDDDDDDDDDDDDDDDDDDDDDDDDDDDDDDDDDDDDDDDDDDDDDDDDDDDD

Outside of Cochrane's departure from the Tigers, the other big story of 1938, with a nation-wide audience fixated on the outcome, was Hank Greenberg's bid to equal or surpass the Babe's single season home run record of 60. Newspapers across America ran daily updates, measuring how Hank and Babe matched up after 99 games, after 100 games, after 101 games, and on and on and on. At The Corner, there was as much September excitement as during pennant-winning years, as fans flocked to the ballpark to see if Hank could do it. In the end, he fell short, finishing the year with 58 homers, tying him for the right-handed record with Jimmie Foxx but two shy of the mark everyone was keyed on. Based in part on the abuse Hammerin' Hank received over the years for his Jewish ancestry, it was speculated that many pitchers walked Greenberg to sabotage his chances. Hank himself discounted this. When one considers that working around big hitters in the lineup is a timeless baseball strategy, and that while Hank did receive a great deal of free passes at 119, the year that Ruth hit his 60 he was walked 137 times, Greenberg was probably right.

Good news came from down on the farm: Schoolboy Rowe's arm was finally coming around while in Texas with the Beaumont Exporters. Schoolie was looking good, going 12 & 2 with a 2.27 ERA (and, bein' Schoolboy, he hit .322). The arm pain plaguing him for most of 2 years was suddenly gone. In a *Sporting News* interview, he had a remarkable explanation, *"I decided I'd get my right arm around and touch my left shoulder. I took a deep breath, filled my lungs, closed my eyes, gripped the bedside with my left hand and threw my right arm as hard as I could. There was a crack like a pistol shot as the hand touched the left shoulder blade. The pain disappeared that instant."* Still only 28 years old, this piece of news offered great hope for 1939.

A couple Beaumont teammates of Rowe's gave the Tigers other reasons to be excited for the future. 23-year old Dizzy Trout was dominating batters, posting a record of 22 & 6 with a 2.12 ERA, while 21-year old Barney McCosky hit .302, spraying doubles and triples all over fields in the Texas League.

On December 15, 1938, Tiger fans said good-bye to yet another star of the 1935 Champions, pitcher Elden Auker. In '38, the submarine-style hurler went 11 & 10 with a 5.27 ERA, the highest in his 6 years with Detroit. He was traded from the only major league team he'd ever known to the Boston Red Sox for third baseman Pinky Higgins. After one year at Boston, going 9 & 10, Elden played 3 seasons with the St. Louis Browns, winning 44 games in that Mississippi River town, before retiring after 1942 with career numbers of 130 wins & 101 losses. On September 27, 1999, after the final game ever to be played at Tiger Stadium, the 89-year old Auker gave an incredibly moving speech about what it meant, what an honor it was, to wear the Olde English D. Elden's words moved every one of the 43,356 in attendance.

DDDDDDDDDDDDDDDDDDDDDDDDDDDDDDDDDDDDDDDDDDDDDDDDDDDDDDDDDDDDDDDDDDDDDDDDDD

On May 2, 1939, the day that William James "Gates" Brown was born in Crestline, Ohio, John Joseph Pienta of Ferndale decided to celebrate his impending 29th birthday by attending a Tuesday afternoon at The Corner. The Tigers had just wrapped up a weekend series versus the Indians, making the Tribe's ride back to Ohio a little longer & a little less enjoyable, with a rousing 14 to 1 spanking of Cleveland. Today, the Yankees were in town to open up a short, 2-game series against Detroit. With birthday boy John Pienta among them, an average-sized crowd of 11,379 came out for the game, anticipating more fireworks like the crushing of the Indians. Fireworks did take place, but not the kind hoped for, as New York rolled to a 22 to 2 win. Tiger fans in attendance did have one chance to stand and cheer, though, and went home with a life-long memory – unexpectedly, it was about an opposing ballplayer…

Yankee great Lou Gehrig was coming off of what was, for him, a sub-par season. In '38 he hit .295 with 29 homers and 114 RBIs – a fine year for most, but Lou's lowest batting average since his first full season in 1925, and lowest home run & RBI totals since '26. What was concerning was Gehrig's performance so far in the young 1939 season. He was hitting only .143, his strength seemed to be gone, and he played his position with a clumsiness never before seen. Before today's game began, Lou approached Yankee manager Joe McCarthy, said he was frustrated at his inability to play to the level he was used to, felt he was dragging the team down, and asked to be benched. McCarthy bowed to his wishes and assured Lou that when the warmer weather came around so would Gehrig's game.

As the game began, the crowd was surprised to see Gehrig bring the lineup card out to home plate, a job usually reserved for the manager. Then radio announcer Ty Tyson told the crowd over the p.a. system that Lou had pulled himself from the line-up, ending his record of 2,130 consecutive games played. The crowd was initially stunned, but then applause began to ripple through Briggs Stadium, building to a crescendo as all 11,379 were soon on their feet, honoring the amazing career of this humble man. It was only later that Lou, his family, friends, teammates and fans realized that Gehrig was feeling the early effects of the onset of ALS, amyotrophic lateral sclerosis, now better known as *Lou Gehrig Disease*.

DDDDDDDDDDDDDDDDDDDDDDDDDDDDDDDDDDDDDDDDDDDDDDDDDDDDDDDDDDDDDDDDDDDDDDDDDD

On May 4, 1939, 2 days after Gehrig ended his consecutive game streak at Briggs Stadium, Boston rookie right-fielder Ted Williams aka the Kid played his first game at The Corner. Ted was batting fifth behind fellow-future Hall-of-Famers Jimmie Foxx & Joe Cronin. In his first at bat, he swung on a 3 & 0 pitch from Roxie Lawson, rocketing the ball well over the head of the unmoving (why bother?) Tiger right-fielder, Pete Fox, and into the facing of the upper deck above him. Welcome to Detroit, Kid. Facing reliever Bob Harris later in the game, Ted hit the first ball to ever go over the new Briggs Stadium right-field roof, landing on Trumbull Avenue and hitting the Checker Cab building on its first bounce. As his home run trot took him by shortstop Billy Rogell, Billy asked him, *"What the hell you been eating?"*

Thomas Jefferson Davis Bridges was the comeback king in '39, once again an All-Star, among league leaders with 17 wins, a 3.50 ERA, and 129 strikeouts. Schoolboy wasn't yet the fella who won 62 times from '34-'36, but was working his way back there, going 10 & 12 including four complete game wins in a row late in the year. After Dizzy Trout's 22-wins last year in Beaumont, the Tigers found a place for him in the rotation, and Dizzy had a nice rookie year at 9 & 10 with a 3.61 ERA.

On May 13, 1939, the Tigers engineered one of the best trades in their history, sending 6 second-tier players to the St. Louis Browns for 3 guys nearing the end of their careers – and one big impact player, pitcher Bobo Newsom. The Browns GM either was fired after this swap or was the owner's son-in-law. Bobo was coming off an All-Star, 20-win, season, and immediately teamed with Tommy Bridges to give the Tigers a strong 1-2 punch at the top of the rotation, going 17 & 10 with a 3.37 ERA and 3 shutouts wearing the Olde English D. Including his 3 victories in April & early-May with St. Louis, Newsom chalked up his 2nd 20-win season in a row and 2nd consecutive All-Star selection.

Barney McCosky was a rookie sensation for Detroit in 1939. Manning centerfield and batting lead-off, he went 2 for 3 on Opening Day, and was off to the races. Barney hit .515 in his first 8 games, the amazing young man who grew up in Detroit quickly becoming a fan favorite. McCosky starred at Southwestern High School, where the house beyond the right-field fence was under assault with a series of line drives. The homeowner put up with the barrage, but finally felt the need to file a complaint when his dinner was interrupted by a ball that flew through the open dining room window and landed in his bowl of soup. The gentleman was assured that this problem would cease as today was Barney McCosky's final high school game, and nobody else in the league could hit the ball that far.

Although the rookie-of-the-year award was not in existence until 1947, newspapers and baseball executives were touting McCoskey as *"the recruit (rookie) of the year"* - in a field that included fellow rookie Ted Williams. Detroit newsmen were even comparing Barney to Ty Cobb! Always smiling, full of energy, humble, and immediately likeable, Barney finished near the top in many league categories: #4 with 120 runs scored, #4 190 hits, #6 33 doubles, #2 14 triples, #4 20 stolen bases, while batting .311.

These fine individual performances did bring the crowds out, Detroit 2nd in attendance at 836,279, but were not enough to allow the Tigers to seriously challenge for the pennant in 1939. From mid-May on, Detroit was never within 10 games of first, finishing the season in fifth place, 81 & 73, 26 games behind the 106-win Yankees.

On December 6, 1939, Billy Rogell, well-liked and a sparkplug in all 10 of his years in Detroit, was traded to the Chicago Cubs for infielder Dick Bartell. His time in Chicago lasted less than one full year before being released & retiring in August of '40, most of his short stay in the Windy City spent riding the bench and barking at his new teammates, who were still upset from losing to Detroit in the 1935 World Series. As the veteran Cubs came up with a long list of excuses for why they fell short, Rogell reminded them it was the Tigers who were without their best hitter, Hank Greenberg, for almost the entire Series after he broke his wrist in game two. Tiger fans had to smile when they heard the stories about the fiery Rogell taking on a gaggle of Cubbies and not backing down an inch. No wonder we loved him. Give 'em hell, Billy, just like he would as a member of the Detroit City Council for all but two years from 1941 to 1980.

1940 a Guy Named Bobo & the Dizziest Race in 40 Years

Mother, may I slug the umpire, may I slug him right away?
So he cannot be here Mother, when the teams begin to play?
Let me clasp his throat, dear Mother, in a dear delightful grip
With one hand and with the other, bat him several in the lip.

("Slug the Umpire" by Anonymous)

As Detroit reported to 1940 spring training in Lakeland, the Yankees were the favorite of most everyone to win the pennant. And why not, as New York was not only the league champion 4 years running, but also victorious in all four of those World Series, winning 16 games while only losing 3 to the National League in the '36-'39 Fall Classics. Schoolboy Rowe was unimpressed. In a spring training interview with the *Lakeland Evening Ledger*, he opened up, *"The Yanks are due for that long coming crack-up and the Tigers are going to have a terrific ball club. We've been playing in tough luck for several years, but we've got the ballplayers and we'll be dynamite to stop. Think of a batting order with McCosky, Gehringer, Greenberg, York, Campbell, Higgins, Tebbetts and Bartell in it. The Yankees can't offer anything to top it, and if you ask me, their pitching staff is liable to pop wide open with all those old men on it."*

Schoolboy went on to talk up the Tigers pitching staff of Bobo Newsom, Tommy Bridges, and himself, adding, *"I hear we got some mighty promising rookies who may toss a few wins in there."* One of those promising rookies was an 18-year old who starred on the sand lots of Detroit, Hal Newhouser. Manager Del Baker liked what he saw in spring training, a kid who was giving fits to veterans who'd won a World Series in '35. There were 5 Tigers from that championship team still on the roster, every one of them healthy and chompin' at the bit to win it again in 1940: Greenberg, Gehringer, Bridges, Pete Fox and the man who spoke with such conviction in that Lakeland newspaper interview, Lynwood Schoolboy Rowe.

It had been a rough last few years for Schoolie. After pulling such a big load for the team '34 thru '36, arm troubles left him a shadow of himself most of the last 3 seasons. Late last year though, Rowe threw 4 consecutive complete-game victories. He knew he was back, and could not wait to show his stuff in the middle of a pennant race once again.

The Tigers of 1940 landed on the perfect mix of talented youth hitting their stride, veterans from the pennant years of '34 & '35 - including the return of the Schoolboy of old – hungry to return to those mid-30s glory days, and the acquisition of Bobo Newsom in an early-1939 lopsided trade greatly favoring Detroit. This recipe tossed the Tigers smack dab into a delightful, nerve-wracking, 3-way pennant race that brought out a franchise record-setting 1,112,693 to The Corner.

DDDDDDDDDDDDDDDDDDDDDDDDDDDDDDDDDDDDDDDDDDDDDDDDDDDDDDDDDDDDDDDDDDDDDDD

It was Tuesday, April 16, 1940 and Opening Day in Detroit. Is there anything quite like the anticipation, spirit, and happiness that Opening Day at Michigan & Trumbull brings? Bobo Newsom was the choice of manager Del Baker to pitch the Opener, and 49,417 were on hand, cheering him on against the St. Louis Browns. Bobo was the perfect pick to start, coming off of back-to-back All-Star seasons of 20 wins each. The Tigers took the early lead, McCosky walking to lead-off the bottom of the first, working his way around to third before coming home on a Greenberg groundout. It stayed 1-0 until the Browns fifth, when future Tiger Bob Swift singled in a run before Bobo surrendered a bases loaded walk for a 2-1 St. Louis lead. Newsom was pulled in the seventh, the Tigers eventually falling 5-1. On this same April 16 afternoon, across Lake Michigan on the Southside of Chicago, 21-year old Bob Feller of Cleveland became the first man to throw an Opening Day no-hitter, leading his Indians to a 1-0 victory over the White Sox.

Hank Greenberg's Opening Day RBI was the first of a major league-leading 150 that he would drive in. The 29-year old slugger earned the 1940 A.L. Most Valuable Player Award, becoming the first major leaguer to ever win the award at two different positions, agreeing this past off-season to switch from first base (his position when he was '35 MVP) to outfield in order to make room for Rudy York at first – a position that best hid the big-hitting York's limited defensive abilities. Greenberg negotiated a $10,000 salary increase before he would make the move, adding to his sweet season. He hit .340 and led the league in slugging percentage, total bases, doubles, 40 home runs, & the afore-mentioned 150 RBIs.

Greenberg, McCosky, Bobo, Schoolboy

As mighty as Greenberg performed, Louis Norman "Bobo" Newsom aka Buck was the story of 1940. Louis could never remember anyone's name, and would always just call 'em Bobo. So, of course, Louis became "Bobo". Newsom bounced back from his Opening Day loss by reeling off 13 consecutive wins. Number 13 was a July 13 game at Washington's Griffith Park, the offense driven by 3 Barney McCosky hits, a Rudy York home run, and 2 hits, a run scored, and 2 RBIs by Bobo himself. As Bobo liked to say, *"Ol' Bobo is on the mound today, and you can put it in the win column."* At the end of July 13, the Tigers were 1/2 game behind first place Cleveland, the Yankees 6 & ½ back.

On July 17, Detroit & Cleveland were tied for first place as the day began. Bobo was starting the first of a doubleheader at Fenway Park, and in the 4th inning suffered a broken thumb while covering first base, putting him on the shelf for, the doctors said, 3 weeks. Without their ace, the Tigers left Boston for a big 3 game series in the Bronx. In game one, Hal Newhouser, a teenager facing the pressure of a pennant race, on the biggest stage in baseball, no big dog Bobo to lean on, going up against the man who started the All-Star game earlier this month – with all of that, Hal sucked it up & out-dueled Red Ruffing for a 3-1 Tiger win. And the kid who turned 19 just two months before even contributed two hits to the victory.

The 3-game series with the Yankees would conclude with a Sunday doubleheader. 20-year old Freddie Hutchinson was on the mound for Detroit in the first game. Freddie was pulled after giving up 3 runs in two innings, relieved by Archie McKain. Archie came to Detroit at the end of '38 with Pinky Higgins from Boston in the Elden Auker trade. Archie was magnificent, holding the Yankees lineup to no runs & 3 hits over 6 innings. Yankee starter Marv Breuer, meanwhile, was cruising along with the early 3-0 lead he was given, holding the Tigers scoreless through 8.

And then came the Tigers 9th. 38-year old Earl Averill stepped up to the plate to pinch hit for shortstop Red Kress. Picked up mid-1939 from Cleveland, Earl was a 6-time All-Star with the Indians, nearing the end of his career. The lifetime .318 hitter still had some of that old magic, and led-off with a single. Del Baker sent Bruce Campbell, also acquired from Cleveland, up to pinch hit for reliever McKain, and Bruce delivered with a 2-run shot into the suddenly much quieter Yankee stands. With nobody out, the score now stood at 3-2 New York. Yankee Marv Breuer gave up a single to Pete Fox, got the always dangerous McCosky to fly out, but when Gehringer doubled to right & Fox pulled into third, Breuer was replaced by Bump Hadley, the man who beaned Mickey Cochrane in 1937, effectively ending the Mick's career. Bump intentionally walked Greenberg, and coaxed Rudy York into a flyball that could not advance the runners. Just one out to a Yankee victory, but Pinky Higgins, with every Yank rooter standing & shouting, singled in both Fox & Gehringer for a 4-3 Tigers lead. Hadley induced catcher Billy Sullivan to ground out, ending the 9th, but the damage was done. The best reliever in baseball for 1940, Al Benton, came in to face Hall-of-Famer Bill Dickey, All-Star George Selkirk, and Hall-of-Famer Joe Gordon, and down they went, 1-2-3. Archie McKain picked up the victory in what would be the finest season of his 6-year career, helping the pennant run with a 5 & 0 record and a 2.82 ERA.

In doubleheader game 2, Detroit drew first blood in the fifth, Pete Fox & Barney McCosky each knocking in a run, Schoolboy surrendering a solo shot to Joe Gordon in the bottom of the frame. Each team scored a run in the 7th, Detroit on a Pete Fox home run, and with a one-run lead to protect in the ninth, reliever Dizzy Trout put down the Yankees in order to complete the Tigers sweep. Boarding the train for Detroit, the Tigers left town in first, 1 & ½ up on Cleveland and 7 up on the Yankees, and feeling a lot better about weathering the storm of Bobo's absence.

DDDDDDDDDDDDDDDDDDDDDDDDDDDDDDDDDDDDDDDDDDDDDDDDDDDDDDDDDDDDDDDDDDDDDDDDDDDDDDD

During Newsom's time on the injured list, he could not sit still. Bobo drove Schoolboy crazy by nailing his shoes to the floor. He kept his teammates in stitches with a spot-on impersonation of Amos & Andy – some of the guys walked into the clubhouse thinking that the *Amos & Andy Show* was on the radio, but then saw Bobo doing the characters' voices with the Tigers doubled over in laughter. Ty Tyson invited Newsom into the booth during games to give commentary about his teammates, and was so good that the Fox Theatre gave him a contract to do standup.

On the disabled list since his July 17 injury, Bobo kept telling everyone who'd listen that the doctors' 3-weeks-to-mend forecast was incorrect, *"When Bobo wants a fracture to heal, it's going to heal in a hurry and no doctor is going to say how long it's going to take."* Sure enough, Newsom took the ball on July 28 to face the Athletics. Tigers bats gave him a 5-2 cushion going into the sixth, but although Bobo whiffed 10 this day, the 7 walks he issued caught up to him and the A's tied it after 7. It stayed 5-5 into the 11th, but Philly rallied for 4 against Newsom & reliever McKain to take Detroit down, 9 to 5.

Bobo was soon back to his old self, winning 4 times in August, the last of the four a 6 to 0 whitewashing of the Senators, his 17th win against 2 losses. But when Charlie Gehringer was lost to the team for a couple of weeks with a pulled muscle, a huge gap was created in the lineup and in the infield. Detroit dropped 10 of 12 mid-August and Cleveland surged into first. By early September, the Tribe had put a little distance between themselves and their pursuers. With the Yanks 3 & ½ back in second, moving ahead of Detroit after winning 13 of 14, and the Tigers in third at 4 games out, Cleveland arrived in Detroit on September 4 to begin a huge 3-game series at The Corner. The Tigers would play with 3 of their best players injured and unavailable, CF Barney McCosky, RF Pete Fox & 3B Pinky Higgins, replaced in the lineup by, respectively, 38-year old Earl Averill, Bruce Campbell, & Billy Sullivan.

The game 1 matchup was Schoolboy Rowe versus the year's best pitcher, Bob Feller. The home team Tigers struck in their first at bat. With one out, Bruce Campbell singled, Gehringer doubled Campbell home, and York singled Charlie in. 2-0 Detroit. Cleveland got to Schoolie for single runs in the 2nd & the 4th to tie things up, but that's all the stingy Rowe would surrender today. Solo shots by Greenberg & Bruce Campbell put Detroit up by two, and the Tigers broke it open when Gehringer buried a 3-run homer among the wildly cheering Tiger fans. Broadcaster Harry Heilmann, as he so often did at such exciting moments, said, *"Listen to the voice of baseball!"* before turning the microphone towards the crowd noise.

After Schoolboy put down the Tribe in order in the last two innings, improving his record to 13 & 3, with back-up Bruce Campbell getting 3 hits & scoring 3 runs, Detroit moved to within 3 games of first.

Game 2 had a couple of old pros going at it, Tommy Bridges against Cleveland's Al Smith. Once again, the Tigers jumped out to an early 2-0 lead on RBIs by Rudy York & Bruce Campbell. Bridges could only get 2 outs in the fifth, getting beat up for 3 Cleveland runs, before Al Benton came in to put out the fire, shutting out the Indians the rest of the way. A 3-run homer in the sixth by Rudy York put the Tigers back on top, and the deal was sealed by a second 3-run shot, this one by suddenly-super-sub Bruce Campbell, and a 2-run triple by another player off the bench, Billy Sullivan. The result 11-3 Detroit, the Tigers now within 2 games of first.

For the final game in the series, it would be the Tribe's Johnny Allen facing Bobo. Cleveland got to Newsom for 2 first inning markers, before Detroit's newest star, Bruce Campbell, singled & scored in the Tigers half of the first. The Indians took a 3 to 1 lead into the bottom of the fourth when the delightfully-named Tuck Stainback, called up from the minors when injuries struck Detroit's outfield, singled with one out & rode home on a homer by another sub, Billy Sullivan. Birdie Tebbetts followed with a double and crossed home when Bobo singled him in. The Detroit fifth began with Campbell & Gehringer striking out, but then Greenberg walked... and Rudy York walked... and Tuck Stainback walked to load the bases. A Billy Sullivan grounder handcuffed Cleveland's first baseman for an error, scoring Hank, and a Birdie Tebbetts double sent Tuck Stainback & Billy Sullivan across home, putting Detroit ahead 8-3. Bobo surrendered 2 runs in the 7th, but then got one back himself in the bottom of the frame with a RBI single. A Greenberg solo shot in the 8th made the final score Detroit 10 Cleveland 5.

The Indians left town with their lead over Detroit shrunk to 1 game, the Yankees now in third, 2 back.

DDDDDDDDDDDDDDDDDDDDDDDDDDDDDDDDDDDDDDDDDDDDDDDDDDDDDDDDDDDDDDDDDDDDDDDDDDDDD

After the September 4 thru 6 Cleveland series, St. Louis then Boston came to The Corner for 2 games each. Detroit took 3 of 4, pushing them past Cleveland into first. On the morning of September 12, league-leading Detroit's record was 78 & 58 with Cleveland 1/2 game back in 2nd & New York 1 game back in 3rd, Mickey Lolich was born, and the Yankees had just arrived in town for 3 games.

Schoolboy took the baseball for the opener vs. New York, the Tigers 1-0 lead erased by a Joe DiMaggio 2-run triple in the third. A Hank Greenberg homer off Atley Donald in the 6th tied matters at 2-2. After the Yanks responded with a run in the seventh, it was New York 3 Detroit 2 going into the bottom of the 8th. With two out, the Tigers rallied with run scoring singles by Rudy York, the just-off-the-injured-list Pinky Higgins, Billy Sullivan, and the always dangerous at the plate Schoolboy, to win the game 6 to 3.

In game 2, Tommy Bridges was magnificent on the hill, his fastball sizzling with last-second movement and his curveball knee-bending outstanding. The Yankees never had a chance, falling to Detroit 8-0. In the series finale, the Tigers jumped out to a first inning 4-0 lead. With Bobo pitching, a sweep looked good, but it wasn't Newsom's day. The Yankee offense came out of the coma Bridges put 'em in the day before, awaking big time for a 16-7 victory to salvage one of the 3 games at Briggs Stadium.

As New York left town on September 14, the standings at day's end showed Detroit remaining in first by one-half game over the Tribe, and the Yanks 2 back.

1940 pitching staff top – Lynn Nelson, Johnny Gorsica, Al Benton, Tommy Bridges, Schoolboy Rowe, Bobo Newsom; bottom – Dizzy Trout, Hal Newhouser, Tom Seats, Archie McKain (missing from the photo is one hurler, called up from the minors in September, who'd twice come thru big time: 30-year old rookie Floyd Giebell).

On September 15, the Tigers & Yankees lost, while Cleveland swept a doubleheader from the Athletics, including Bob Feller's 25th victory. First place Cleveland, Tigers 1 back, Yankees 3 & ½ behind.

September 16 was an open one on the calendar for the Indians, while New York was pummeled 16-4 by St. Louis. The Tigers faced Washington with Bobo on the mound, and settled things early with 6 in the first 3 innings, Newsom cruising to win #19, 9-2. The Tigers now 1/2 out of first, Yankees 4 out.

September 17 and Schoolboy was handed a 4-0 first inning lead. He held Washington to two runs before turning things over to Al Benton late in Detroit's 6-3 win. The Tigers moved back into 1st when Cleveland lost a tough one, 4-3, to Philadelphia, while the Yankees pounded St. Louis, 9-0. It's first place Detroit one-game up on the Indians and 3 & ½ up on New York.

September 18 saw the Tigers split with the A's, Tommy Bridges again surrendering no runs in a 14-0 laugher before Philadelphia returned the favor, raking Tiger starter Johnny Gorsica and bullpen in a 13-6 victory. Cleveland took a pair from the Senators, including #26 for Feller, and the Yankees split with the White Sox. Today, it's the Indians turn on top, Detroit 1/2 back, New York 4 out.

September 19 marked the first major league appearance of 1940 for Detroit's 30-year old rookie pitcher, Floyd Giebell, just recalled from the minors. Floyd was up with the Tigers briefly in 1939, relieving in 9 games, but this would be his first start in The Show, pressed into service with so many doubleheaders on the schedule. Giebell was brilliant, going the distance in today's game 1, the offense driven by 3 hits each from Bartell, York & Greenberg in a 13-2 Tiger victory over the Athletics. Detroit completed the sweep as Dizzy Trout tossed a 4-hitter in the 10-1 win. With Cleveland and New York both triumphant, the day ended in a first-place tie between the Tigers & the Indians, the Yanks remaining 4 out.

In a brilliant/fortunate piece of scheduling, the two teams tied for first would play each other 6 times in the season's final 8 days.

DDDDDDDDDDDDDDDDDDDDDDDDDDDDDDDDDDDDDDDDDDDDDDDDDDDDDDDDDDDDDDDDDDDDDDDDDDDDDDDDD

Friday, September 20, Briggs Stadium: Bobo was facing Cleveland's 4-time All-Star Mel Harder. Pre-game found Bobo his usual chatty self, *"I've pitched against that Cleveland team twice this year and beat them both times. As soon as they show up, we'll take care of them."* It didn't quite work out that way.

The outstanding Indians' rookie shortstop, and Denny McLain's future father-in-law, Lou Boudreau (97 runs, 101 RBIs, .295) opened the scoring in the third with a run-scoring single off of Bobo. 1-0 Tribe. Gehringer came home on a York sac fly in the fourth, but in the next half-inning Cleveland went up 3-1 on RBIs by Roy Weatherly & Lou Boudreau. Newsom surrendered a 4th run in the sixth, and when he gave up hit #11, putting Indians on the corners, manager Del Baker pulled him for reliever Clay Smith, who ended the frame with no further damage. Indians' starter Mel Harder looked strong, and at the end of 7 had his team up 4-1 over Detroit. For the 8th, Hal Newhouser came in and held the Tribe scoreless.

Harder went back out to face the Tigers in the 8th with a 3-run cushion and needing just 6 outs for a victory. With one out, McCosky worked Mel for a base on balls, and then Gehringer singled Barney to third. With Hank Greenberg stepping in and representing the tying run, Cleveland manager Oscar Vitt pulled Mel and brought in the best pitcher in the majors, Bob Feller. As a starter, Feller was not used to coming in to relieve, and it showed as all 3 batters he faced singled, Greenberg to make it 4-2, Rudy York to tie the game at 4, and Pinky Higgins to put Detroit up 5-4, to the joyful shouts of the Tiger faithful. Manager Vitt was not popular in Cleveland to begin with, and his decision to bring Feller in for relief and the disastrous results had 'em yelling at their radios across Lake Erie. Vitt had seen enough, and replaced Feller with Joe Dobson, who the Tigers got to for one last 8th inning run on a Bruce Campbell single to put Detroit up 6-4 going into the ninth.

Al Benton came in for the ninth to close the game out for Detroit. Although he was the major's best reliever in 1940, the final frame was nerve-wracking. After getting the first batter on a foul pop to first,

2nd batter Roy Weatherly hit a foul pop to third baseman Pinky Higgins – who dropped it. Given new life, Weatherly doubled to left and Lou Boudreau singled him home, cutting the lead to one. Hal Trosky followed with another single, putting runners on the corners. A sac fly would tie it with Beau Bell, 1937 A.L. batting king, coming up. But it was 1940 not 1937, and Al Benton got a huge strikeout. Now a hit would be needed to knot things up, but it would not happen as Benton got Ken Keltner on a game-ending groundout. The Tigers go 1 up on Cleveland, the idle Yankees dropping to 4 & ½ back.

Saturday, September 21, Briggs Stadium: It was Cleveland 16-game winner Al Milnar against 15-game winner Lynwood Schoolboy Rowe. Make that *16-game* winner Schoolboy, who threw a 5-0 shutout. Being Schoolboy, he even went 2 for 3, breaking a scoreless tie in the fifth with a RBI single before scoring the game's 2nd run two batters later on Barney McCosky's sacrifice fly. In the sixth & seventh, RBIs by Pete Fox, Birdie Tebbetts, and Hank Greenberg padded the lead before Schoolboy set 'em down 1-2-3 in the eighth and again in the ninth to improve his record to 16 & 3 and, more importantly, move Detroit 2 ahead of Cleveland & stay 4 & ½ ahead of victorious, but now on life-support, New York.

Sunday, September 22, Briggs Stadium: The series finale pitted Bob Feller against Tommy Bridges. Tommy had been red hot, coming into the game on a string of 16-scoreless innings. He made it to 17 when Cleveland opened up on him in the 2nd, knocking Bridges out of the game with a 3-run inning, before adding 4 more in the third on their way to a 10-5 win. Five Indians homered, including Feller himself. It wasn't Bob's best day on the mound, but with the offensive support he had, it was plenty good enough to give him win #27 and pull Cleveland to within one of Detroit with 5 games to go, New York hanging in there at 3 & ½ games out in third place.

DDDDDDDDDDDDDDDDDDDDDDDDDDDDDDDDDDDDDDDDDDDDDDDDDDDDDDDDDDDDDDDDDDDDDDDDDD

Late in the heated pennant race, players who were with Detroit back in '37 & '38 must have had lighter hearts when they came across a *Sporting News* minor league article: their loveable old teammate, Boots Poffenberger, pitched the Nashville Volunteers to the Dixie League Championship. Boots' 29 wins were the most in organized baseball in 1940. Upon receiving this news, his ex-teammates surely raised a few glasses and told many stories about the "Prince of Pilsner", Boots Poffenberger.

DDDDDDDDDDDDDDDDDDDDDDDDDDDDDDDDDDDDDDDDDDDDDDDDDDDDDDDDDDDDDDDDDDDDDDDDDD

Monday, September 23 was an off day for Detroit, Cleveland & New York.

Tuesday, September 24 was an off day for Detroit while Cleveland lost and the Yankees won a doubleheader. The standings read Detroit first, the Indians 1 & ½ out, & New York 2 & ½ back.

Wednesday, September 25 was an open date for New York. Cleveland won their single game, and in Detroit's doubleheader with the White Sox, Bobo won both games! Game 1 was a slugfest that had the teams tied at 9 after the eighth inning. Old Bobo came in to pitch the ninth in relief of Dizzy Trout, and gave up one hit combined in the 9th & 10th before Rudy York's double in the bottom of the 10th sent home Barney McCosky with the winning run, 10-9 Tigers. Bobo started game 2, gave up two runs in the 2nd inning and then shutdown Chicago the rest of the way as Detroit got one back in the 2nd, one back in the 7th on Hank's home run, and finally took the lead in the eighth on York's sac fly. In the ninth, Bobo kept the fans on the edge of their seats by allowing runners on first & second, but got a grounder for the final out as Detroit won 3-2 on a day when Bobo won #20 & #21.

Thursday, September 26 has the Yanks winning their doubleheader, no games for Detroit or Cleveland, and the standings with 3 games left for all 3 teams: Detroit first, Cleveland 2 out, New York 2 & ½ back. Detroit boards the train for 3 in Cleveland, while New York has a date for 3 in Washington. Here we go!

DDDDDDDDDDDDDDDDDDDDDDDDDDDDDDDDDDDDDDDDDDDDDDDDDDDDDDDDDDDDDDDDDDDDDDDDDDDDDDD

Connie Mack, who has been the owner & the manager of the Philadelphia Athletics for every year since 1901, called the 1940 American League pennant race, *"the dizziest race in 40 years."* Detroit & Cleveland had changed places between first & second 17 times in this crazy season, the Yankees hanging around like a leg cramp in the middle of the night. And now, with 3 games to go in the season and 3 teams still left alive, in the biggest game of the year, the finest pitcher in the majors will go against a man who had his first major league start 8 days ago; a 21-year old who is in his 5th full season against a 30-year old rookie; a man who is #1 in the American League in ERA, strikeouts, complete games, innings pitched, shutouts, and wins with 27... will go against a man who lost 17 games in the minors this season. It will be Rapid Robert aka Bullet Bob Feller, the most famous pitcher in the game, against little-known beyond family & friends, Detroit Tiger Floyd Giebell.

September 27, Friday, Municipal Stadium: The Tigers are in a good place in the standings, needing only one win to clinch the pennant, which would seem to put manager Del Baker in a favorable position. However, as he looks at his game 1 options, he notes that Bobo Newsom & Tommy Bridges would be out until game 3 as they just pitched. Schoolboy Rowe was rested and ready to go, but if he lost to Feller, that would leave one of the youngsters versus Cleveland's tough #2, Mel Harder. You lose that one, then it's a winner-take-all finale in your opponent's ballpark before 40,000 or so rabid fans - thus the sleepless nights.

Del Baker sought council. Early on game day, the manager called a meeting of all position players, no pitchers, and asked for their vote from among 3 pitchers to face Bob Feller. The options were Dizzy Trout, Hal Newhouser, or Floyd Giebell – and the players chose Floyd.

With the roar of the crowd behind him, Feller quickly dispatched of Dick Bartell, Charlie Gehringer, and Barney McCosky, 1-2-3, to begin the game.

5,000 Detroit fans have come to support their Tigers, absorbed into a sea of 40,000 Indian fanatics. It seemed as if all of those 40,000 stopped by the West Side Market on their way to Municipal Stadium, as they were well-armed with a wide variety of fruit that they launched at Hank Greenberg as he ran out to his left-field position in the bottom of the first. Somewhere, Ducky Medwick is smiling. Time was called as the grounds crew cleared the playing field of healthy food, and play resumed. Giebell walked the first batter he faced, making the 5,000 brave Tiger fans in the stands and the tens of thousands tuned to Tyson & Heilmann back in Michigan extremely nervous. As Roy Weatherly, the number 2 batter, lofted a fly ball to left, fruit once again came flying out of the stands at Greenberg while he waited to make the catch. The head umpire got on the public address system to let the fans know that, if there is any interference with a fielder, the batter will be out, and if this behavior continues, he would forfeit the game – and thus the pennant - to the Tigers. As play resumes, Lou Boudreau hits a laser, but directly at first baseman Rudy York, who steps on the bag to double up Weatherly. Floyd Giebell has survived his initial bout with nerves and the Indians' first inning.

The Tigers threatened in the 2nd on a Greenberg double and a Bruce Campbell walk, but Feller induced a double play grounder to end the brief rally. Police are now combing the stands, looking to confiscate fruit or anything else that might be thrown at a player, and are closing in on a fella with an entire crate of fruit. From the upper grandstand, he unloads the evidence over the railing and into the Tiger bullpen below, as almost the entire contents – which includes some bottles - finds the head of catcher Birdie Tebbetts, landing with enough force to knock him out. The police catch the offender, and escort him to the Tiger's clubhouse, where they look the other way as the now revived and furious Tebbetts punches him in the face.

Giebell is cool under fire, as the Tribe opens the third with runners at the corners. With no one out, and the crowd on their feet, screaming for runs, he strikes out one batter, then another, and closes out the threat with a flyout. In the Tigers' fourth, Gehringer works Feller for a walk. With 2 outs, Rudy York launches a long fly ball towards the left-field stands, sending left-fielder Ben Chapman back, back, back, until he can go no further, helplessly looking skyward as the ball flies above him and disappears into the packed seats. 2-0 Tigers.

The Indians get two runners on in the fourth – nothing. They get two runners on in the fifth – nothing. Giebell's calm in this pressure-packed situation, in enemy territory, is extraordinary for a veteran let alone a rookie. His change-up pitch is frustrating the Cleveland batters, and he is brilliantly painting the corners of the plate. In Cleveland's 7th, the first two batters reach on an infield single and an error, and they are bunted to second & third by Feller, with the top of the order coming up. The fans sense this may be their last big chance, and are standin', stompin', and shoutin', drowning out all other sounds. As lead-off man Ben Chapman goes down on strikes, the groans are heard to Akron, & when Roy Weatherly grounds out, killing the threat, the only noise heard is from those who traveled here from Detroit.

Rapid Robert Feller had been pitching another beautiful game, only allowing 3 hits, but the 2-run homer by York will haunt him. Floyd Giebell goes through the heart of the order in the eighth, and completes his gem with a 1-2-3 ninth to end the game. Floyd is hoisted on to his jubilant teammates' shoulders and carried off of the Municipal Stadium field.

The victory eliminates both the Indians and the Yankees. The Tiger clubhouse is bedlam. There are two meaningless games to play in Cleveland, a chance for Detroit to get some innings for the young pitchers and some at bats for the back-ups. The Tigers lose both games, but nobody cares. On the night of September 27, 1940, it is celebration time. Players even hug owner Walter O. Briggs, they are so happy. Catcher Billy Sullivan is overjoyed and in awe of Giebell's effort, *"The best example of clutch pitching I ever saw. After the first inning, he put every pitch where I asked for it."*

Birdie Tebbetts is as happy as the next man, but did have one request, *"I'd like to get another pop at that so-and-so who knocked me cold."*

At the end, it was the 90 & 64 Tigers in first by one game over Cleveland and two over the Yankees. What a pennant race.

DDDDDDDDDDDDDDDDDDDDDDDDDDDDDDDDDDDDDDDDDDDDDDDDDDDDDDDDDDDDDDDDDDDDDDDDD

Bobo finished the year at 21 & 5. Gehringer said of him, *"He certainly had a great arm and a great heart for the game. Pretty good beer drinker, but other than that, he really put it out there."*

Schoolboy & Bobo were 1-2 in A.L. winning percentages at .842 & .808, Newsom's 21 wins 2nd and Schoolie's 16 wins 5th in the league; Bobo's 2.83 ERA put him at #2; in strikeouts Bobo was 2nd & Tommy Bridges 4th; when relief help was needed, the 17 saves of Al Benton, the only major league pitcher to face both Babe Ruth & Mickey Mantle in his career, were tops in the league.

6 Tigers crossed home plate per game in 1940, their 888 runs scored the best in baseball. In addition to Greenberg, the majority of the offensive punch was supplied by…

* Barney McCosky, who followed up his brilliant rookie season with an even better 1940. His .340 tied Hank for fifth in the league, and Barney led the A.L. with 200 hits and 19 triples, while his 123 runs were good for third.

* Powerful Rudy York hit .316, a league 2nd in home runs, doubles, RBIs, and total bases.

* At 37-years of age, Charlie Gehringer continued to play the finest defensive 2nd base in baseball, while hitting .313 and walking 101 times, good for 3rd in the league, against only 17 strikeouts.

* Detroit's two catchers, starter Birdie Tebbetts & back-up Billy Sullivan, combined to hit an even .300. Birdie was extremely intelligent & one of the top defensive catchers in the game. For the 2nd year in a row, he led all catchers in runners-caught-stealing & assists.

* Pinky Higgins, the third baseman Detroit obtained for Elden Auker in December '39, hit .271 and chipped in 76 RBIs, fourth on the team.

In addition, shortstop Dick Bartell, acquired for fan favorite Billy Rogell, was a stellar defensive player. Known as "Rowdy Richard" for his intensity on the diamond, though only hitting .230 in '40, he lit a fire missing with quiet teammates like Gehringer & Greenberg, and brought a badly-needed enthusiasm to the Tigers – much as the man who was traded for him had.

DDDDDDDDDDDDDDDDDDDDDDDDDDDDDDDDDDDDDDDDDDDDDDDDDDDDDDDDDDDDDDDDDDDDDDDDDDD

The 1940 World Series would pit the best offense in baseball versus the best pitching in baseball, Detroit's 6 runs scored per game against a Cincinnati staff holding teams to 3 runs per game.

This was an outstanding Cincy team that the Tigers would be facing. The previous year, they had also won the National League pennant, but were swept by the Yankees in the Series. That experience made them a more determined lot in 1940, and they rolled to the flag with a 100-win season, the best in baseball.

The Reds pitching staff was headed by an outstanding 1-2 punch, featuring the top two hurlers in the National League. The ace was Bucky Walters. In both 1939 & 1940, Bucky led all National League pitchers in wins, earned run average, complete games, & innings pitched. His 1940 line was 22 & 10, 2.48, 29, & 305. Close behind was Paul "Duke" Derringer. Paul was #2 in the N.L. with 20 victories, complete games & innings pitched, while his 3.06 ERA was good for 7th.

Cincy may not have had the firepower of Detroit, but their offense was still one to be wary of. Clean-up batter Frank McCormick was Cincy's biggest threat, tied for the N.L. lead in hits with 191, 2nd in total bases, 1st in doubles, fifth with 19 homers, and 2nd in RBIs at 127. Third baseman & lead-off man was speedy Billy Werber, a league 4th in steals with 16 and third in runs scored at 105.

Two of the biggest contributors to the Reds offense were banged up and questionable for at least some of the Series. Feisty 2nd baseman Lonny Frey led the N.L. with 22 steals, was fourth with 102 runs, and beat up from a late-season game at Brooklyn when he was injured trying to break up a double play, an injury aggravated in the fight that followed. Veteran catcher Ernie Lombardi was in his tenth year behind the plate for the Reds, an All-Star 5 years running, and 2nd in the league in batting with a .319 average. The future Hall-of-Famer had recently incurred a severe ankle injury and was questionable, at least for the first game or two.

Lombardi's injury compounded a manpower issue at catcher that the Reds were already in due to an August tragedy. Back-up catcher Willard Hershberger had committed suicide by slitting his throat with his roommate's razor. Willard was known to his teammates as "Little Slug", mostly in contrast to the man ahead of him in the depth chart, Ernie "Big Slug" Lombardi. Willard suffered from insomnia, was a bit of a hypochondriac, with a good sense of humor, and popular with his teammates. But Hershberger also carried a lingering guilt from his father's suicide 12 years earlier: as an 18-year old living with his folks, Willard returned to the house from a day of hunting, and left his shotgun out, intending to clean the gun in the morning. His father had been depressed and sleepless over family debts, wandered the house that night, came across the shotgun, and took his life. The shotgun blast awaken Willard, and it was he who found his father's body, always blaming himself for leaving the shotgun out.

The tipping point for the troubled Hershberger came when he took over at catcher from the injured Lombardi for a slate of games in July, blaming himself for the pitches he called for during a few losses. He was so despondent that he sat with manager Bill McKechnie in the manager's office and cried for an hour, told him of his Dad's suicide, and how he was considering it for himself. McKechnie held a team meeting, with Hershberger absent, to inform them of their teammate's struggles, urging the guys to look out for Willard, and do what they can to lift his spirits. It was to no avail, and a friend of Willard's found him later that day, dead on the bathroom floor. Manager McKechnie gathered the team together once more, this time to inform them of Willard's suicide, telling his crushed players, *"We must now win the pennant and give his widowed mother a full share of the World Series money, and I know you fellows will win it."*

Game 1 Cincinnati: In the bottom of the first, one Red on 2nd and 2 outs, fans huddled around radios in Detroit and outstate Michigan heard, respectively, Ty Tyson and Harry Heilmann describe a monster blast off the bat of Cincy's Frank McCormick. While holding their breaths back home, Barney McCosky took off in a sprint, the speedster catching up to the rocket just a step before he stopped himself at the center-field fence. Exhale Michigan.

In their very next at bat, the Tigers' roar was heard well beyond the confines of lovely Crosley Field. Detroit exploded for 5 runs in the second, as 7 of the first 8 Tigers that came to bat reached base, the 8th one knocking out the Red's Paul Derringer. Ol' Bobo started the opener for Detroit, and allowed one run in the 4th & one in the 8th, and between those, the Tigers plated two more of their own in the fifth on a 2-run homer by Bruce Campbell. With Bobo shutting down the Cincy bats, Detroit opened the Series with a 7 to 2 victory.

After the game, Bobo said, *"This was important because my Dad was here, and it was only the second time he'd ever seen me pitch. He has been sick in South Carolina, but he made it."* Henry Newsom had been ill with heart problems for a long time, but was determined to see his boy pitch the opening game in the World Series. When Henry left his home in the little South Carolina town of Hartsville, he was sure that his bad heart wouldn't bring him back, so sure that before leaving home he walked the nearby streets to say goodbye to his old friends, calling out to some sittin' on their porch or knocking on their doors, letting them know he was taking the train to Cincinnati to see his Buck pitch. Old man Newsom sat in that big old stadium, a ballpark that held 10 times the number of folks that call Hartsville home, and saw his boy whip those Reds. Henry got to hug his Buck, tell him how proud he was of him.

That night, in his Cincinnati hotel room, Papa Newsom passed away, departing this world a happy man.

Game 2 Cincinnati: McCosky & Gehringer score in the first to give Schoolboy a 2-run cushion, but it is not his day. Lynwood surrenders two in the 2nd, two in the 3rd, and only gets one out in the fourth before being pulled. Tiger Johnny Gorsica does a nice job in relief, holding Cincy to 1 hit and no runs over 4 & 1/3 innings, but it is too late. Reds ace Bucky Walters settles down, only giving up a Greenberg run-scoring double after the first in Cincinnati's 5 to 3 win. The Series is all even at 1 game apiece.

Game 3 Detroit: *"Weee-Doggies!"* Buddy Ebsen is in the Briggs Stadium crowd today, & William Frawley, too! With the future Jed Clampett AND Fred Mertz rooting for (we'll just assume) Detroit, how can we lose? (A favorite Fred Mertz line from *I Love Lucy:* Fred & Ricky Ricardo have to make dinner in Ethel & Lucy's absence; Ricky asked, *"Fred, what do you know about rice?"* Fred told him, *"Well, I had it thrown at me on one of the darkest days of my life."*)

52,877 rowdy fans cheer on Tommy Bridges and the Tigers. Bridges and the Reds Jim Turner are locked in a pitcher's duel, the game tied at 1 going into the bottom of the 7th, and that's when the Tigers turn it on. Hank leads off with a single to center. Up steps Rudy York, and he blasts one deep into the left-field seats. Detroit 3 Cincy 1. The next batter is Bruce Campbell. His amazing season continues with a single to left. Pinky Higgins turns on Jim Turner's next pitch, and sends a souvenir into the left-field upper deck. Detroit 5 Cincinnati 1. The crowd at The Corner is going crazy, the ballpark shakin' like it did in '35!

Cincy gets one in the 8th, but Detroit comes right back in their half of the frame. Hank leads off with a triple, and though York whiffs, Bruce Campbell (again) singles Greenberg home, and then crosses home himself on another hit by Pinky Higgins. Although the Reds get those two back in the ninth, Thomas

Jefferson Davis Bridges closes out the game with a strikeout on a devastating curveball, for his fourth consecutive World Series victory (over '34, '35, & '40).

Detroit wins 7-4 to go up 2 games to 1, the sad news for Cincinnati fans broadcast to them over 50,000-watt WLW by the announcer hired just this year to handle Reds games, the legendary Red Barber.

Game 4 Detroit: Reds Manager Bill McKechnie knew that his Reds could not go down 3 games to 1, and then have to face a well-rested Bobo in game 6, so he rolled the dice and sent out 20-game winner Paul "Duke" Derringer on only 2 day's rest. Tiger Manager Del Baker decided to give Bobo an extra day's rest, and made the daring choice to pitch 3 & 7 Dizzy Trout. Derringer hadn't made it out of the 2nd in game 1, getting pummeled for 5 runs, but was a different man this game. Dizzy would become a great pitcher one day, but not to-day.

Dizzy was knocked out of the game after giving up a single, single, and double to the first 3 batters in inning number 3, departing down 3 to nothing, and with Reds on second & third and nobody out. Impressively, reliever Clay Smith was able to get 3 outs and strand the 2 runners, limiting the damage. Detroit did get to Derringer in the next half inning when Greenberg doubled home Barney McCosky, but Derringer struck out the red-hot Bruce Campbell with two men on base to get out of the inning. A Cincy marker in the fourth made the score 4-1 in their favor. The Tigers got their faithful to their feet in the sixth on a Bruce Campbell single and a Pinky Higgins triple. With two out, Billy Sullivan walked, and up stepped the old pro, Earl Averill, to pinch hit for pitcher Clay Smith. Derringer shut the door on Detroit by coaxing Averill into a harmless fly ball to right to end the inning with Cincy up 4-2. The Red tacked on one more and Detroit could get nothing going the rest of the way, as Derringer went the distance to even the Series at 2 games apiece.

Game 5 Detroit: Ol' Bobo owned this day. Just 3 days after his father's passing, under sunny skies and 80 degrees, and before 55,189 – the largest crowd ever at The Corner up to then - Bobo only surrendered 3 hits to Cincinnati, never allowing a man past second base. Meanwhile, Detroit's offense exploded for 8 runs as Hank's 3-run shot into the left-field upper deck opened the scoring in the 3rd, and the Bengals plated 4 more in the fourth, 2 on a Bruce Campbell single. A final marker came home on a wild pitch in the eighth, making the final score Tigers 8 Reds zero.

Bobo told reporters that, when he last spoke to his Dad, he promised he would win his next game. *"I pitched this game for my Dad and I hope he knows what I accomplished. I know in my heart he wanted us to win. This is the one I wanted to win most."*

The Tigers now sit one win away from their 2nd World Series title.

Game 6 Cincinnati: It is Bucky Walters versus Schoolboy Rowe in a must-win game for the Reds. It was also critical for Detroit, for should they lose today, the only properly rested pitchers for game 7 will be one of the kids, Gorsica, Newhouser, or Fred Hutchinson, to face Paul Derringer. They needed Schoolboy to be on today. He was off, so off. After Walters set the Tigers down 1-2-3 in the first, Schoolie took the mound. The first Red, Billy Werber, doubled off the left field fence, and was sacrificed to third. Ival Goodman grounded to the right of first sacker Rudy York, but Schoolboy was late covering the bag. 1 run in, man on 1st, one out. Clean-up batter Frank McCormick lined a single past third base. Two men on. When Jimmy Ripple ripped a line single to right, a second run comes in, ending Schoolboy Rowe's day: the line read 2 runs in, men on first & third, and only one man out.

Johnny Gorsica was brought in, and Del Baker must have wondered for years what might have been had he started Gorsica. Johnny stranded the two runners, and pitched through the seventh inning, only giving up one run. But perhaps Baker did not concern himself with who he pitched in game 6, because his batters could not touch Bucky Walters, who was as impressive today as Bobo was the day before.

Dick Bartell and Rudy York each had two hits, and Pinky Higgins had one, the total of Detroit's attack. The Tigers had a mild threat in the second with two on, but that was it. To top off his day, Bucky hit an eighth inning home off of Fred Hutchinson, to make the final score 4 to nothing. This is it, all tied at 3 games each, game 7 tomorrow.

Game 7 Cincinnati: On one day rest, it'll be Bobo. After Gorsica had to bail out Schoolboy yesterday, skipper Del Baker really had no choice. Bobo was confident, as he always was. His mound opposite number, Paul Derringer, only had 2 day's rest, same as he did for game 4. If either pitcher was tired, you could not tell from their performance. Through two innings, each hurler had only allowed one runner. Then, Detroit broke through in the third. Billy Sullivan hit a hard grounder to the right of first baseman Frank McCormick, who smothered it, but his throw was late. Ol' Bobo was the next batter, as good in laying down sacrifice bunts as in getting fellas out, and soon Sullivan was standing on second. After a Dick Bartell pop-out, McCosky drew a walk, and Gehringer put the Tigers on the scoreboard when he lined a shot down the third base line, sending Billy Sullivan home. With runners at the corners, Derringer got a huge out when he whiffed Hammerin' Hank. 1-0 Detroit.

Bobo and Derringer were magnificent, and no further runs were scored through the top of the 7th. After the seventh inning stretch, Bobo was settling in to face the 4-5-6 batters. Post-game, Charlie Gehringer explained what transpired, *"We were leading 1-0 late in the game when Frank McCormick led off with a double. The next guy up, Jimmy Ripple, hit a ball over Bruce Campbell's head in right field. Campbell picked it up right away and threw it in to Bartell. Bartell thought, 'Gee, with that double McCormick must've scored,' but McCormick had waited to see whether it was going to be caught. So McCormick, who was no speed demon, was just rounding third when Bartell got the ball. I kept yelling, 'Home, home, home.' Gee whiz, with Bartell's arm, he's a dead pigeon. But he never did throw the ball. Even after he looked and still had a chance, he didn't throw. And to this day, I don't know why."*

Dick Bartell later said he'd figured McCormick had scored, and that because of the deafening crowd noise, he was unable to hear his teammates' shouts for him to throw home.

In any case, the game was now tied with the lead run standing on second, much to the delight of the Crosley Field faithful. Jimmie Wilson bunted Ripple to third base, and when Reds shortstop Billy Myers hit a long fly to McCosky in center, Ripple was able to tag up and walk home with Cincy's 2nd run.

Now pitching with the lead, Paul Derringer was able to retire the Tigers in the eighth, and then induced 3 consecutive ground outs in the ninth to secure the World Series for Cincinnati.

DDDDDDDDDDDDDDDDDDDDDDDDDDDDDDDDDDDDDDDDDDDDDDDDDDDDDDDDDDDDDDDDDDDDDDDDDDDDDD

It was an incredible, emotional season and Series. The 1940 Detroit Tigers, although falling short in their goal to be crowned World Series Champions, gave their fans possibly the wildest single-season ride in Tiger history – maybe in the entire history of major league baseball. Just the thought of the daily tension and excitement of Detroit & Cleveland *trading places between first & second place 17 times!* And then the Damn Yankees making it a crazy 3-way race the last two months. The sad suicide story of Cincinnati's

Willard Hershberger. And Bobo Newsom's Dad, weak heart 'n all, traveling north from South Carolina to witness his son win a World Series game, and then pass away that very evening. And Bobo himself, one of the most incredible figures, and true characters, anywhere in the annals of sports – any sport.

Meanwhile, during the entire season, looming in the background, was the shadow of war.

DDDDDDDDDDDDDDDDDDDDDDDDDDDDDDDDDDDDDDDDDDDDDDDDDDDDDDDDDDDDDDDDDDDDD

Late in 1940, Congress passed a bill that required all men between 21 & 31 register for the draft. The war would change life, and major league baseball, as we knew it.

On October 16, 1940, 8 days after the World Series concluded, 29-year old Henry Benjamin Greenberg registered for the draft, becoming the first professional baseball player to do so. In the spring of '41, the Detroit draft board classified Hank as 4F due to flat feet. Greenberg protested, was re-examined, and in April the draft board reclassified Greenberg. In May he was inducted into the Army. Although the United States had not yet entered the war, Hank wanted to do his part. Reporters asked him about his new salary of $21 a week, a cut in pay from his baseball salary of $55,000 a year, and he told them, *"I made up my mind to go when I was called. My country comes first."*

In the spring & much of the summer of '41, Hank trained as a tank gunner, playing in only 19 games that year for Detroit. Hammerin' Hank was discharged on December 5 – and two days later, the Japanese struck us at Pearl Harbor. In January 1942, Hank re-enlisted in the Army, became a sergeant in the Army Air Force, and when he finished officer training school in early '42, Greenberg was commissioned a first lieutenant. He was in uniform until the war's end in July 1945. Hank's final WWII service was in scouting bombing targets for B29s in the China-India-Burma Theater of Operations.

Hank Greenberg served our country for 47 months during World War II, the longest tenure of any major league baseball player. Hank left the baseball world in the prime of his career, a few months after winning his second MVP award. When he returned to the Tigers in July of '45, he played like he never left, in 78 games hitting 13 homers with 60 RBIs (projected to a full season at 26 homers & 120 RBIs) while hitting .311. He put the Tigers on his back, and took them to a World Series title, punching their ticket to the Fall Classic with a closing regular season grand slam that turned a 3-2 deficit into a 6-3 victory, followed with a home run to win Series game 1, all-told knocking in 7 runs & hitting .304 to lead the Tigers to the 2nd championship in team history.

It's often speculated what Hank's career numbers would've been had he not missed all but 19 games in 1941, all of '42, '43, '44, and '45 through June. In a *Detroit Athletic Company* article, author Dan Holmes took a crack at it, taking Hank's last two seasons before he enlisted and the first full season after he returned (i.e., 1939, 1940 & 1946). The numbers in those 3 years averaged 39 homers & 130 RBIs... multiplied by the lost 4&1/2 years, and added to his actual career output, puts Hank at (in parenthesis is where these figures would've placed Greenberg when he retired after 1947):

506 Home Runs (behind only Babe Ruth & Jimmie Foxx) & 1,859 RBIs (behind only Ruth, Foxx & Mel Ott).

Whether trying to project what might have been or enjoying what actually took place on diamonds around the major leagues, the first line on Hank's Hall of Fame plaque sums it up best, *"One of baseball's greatest right-handed batters."*

1941 – 1945 the War, Dizzy, Prince Hal... & Hank is Back!

Costello: What's the guy's name on first base? Abbott: No. What is on second. Costello: I'm not asking you who's on second. Abbott: Who's on first. Costello: I don't know. Abbott: He's on third, we're not talking about him. Costello: Now how did I get on third base? Abbott: Why you mentioned his name.

(from "Who's On First?" by Bud Abbott & Lou Costello)

Pete Fox had an excellent career with the Tigers, but with the increased playing time given in 1940 to fellow outfielder Bruce Campbell, Detroit sold Fox to the Red Sox after the '40 World Series. The Tiger fans never forgot old Pete, who hit .302 in 8 great seasons with Detroit, and they cheered him on when, though no longer wearing the Olde English D, he was included on the 1944 American League All-Star team. In 13 MLB seasons, Pete hit .298, including .295 post-Detroit from 1941-1944, before fading to .245 in '45, his last year in baseball. Bruce Campbell hit .275 in '41 & was traded at year's end. As great as Bruce Campbell played down the stretch & in the World Series in 1940, the Tigers guessed wrong when it came to Fox and Campbell.

Pete Fox was a guy often overlooked, sadly even by Tiger's GM Jack Zeller, who said he *"didn't figure Fox would make the grade this year (1941)"* before selling him to Boston. Too bad Zeller didn't read the *Chicago Tribune* article on Pete, *"Fox, many believe, is the most underrated player in baseball. His value to the team is inestimable."* The outfielder led the league in fielding average 5 times. Always a threat on the bases, the man born Ervin Fox earned the Pete moniker as a shortened version of "Peter Rabbit". He hit .327 in 3 World Series for Detroit, '34, '35 & '40, and still holds the record for doubles in a single World Series, with 6 in 1935. Tiger management may not have understood Pete's value, but the fans did and loved him.

Dick Bartell was released by Detroit 2 months into the 1941 season. His critical failure to throw home in the key play of the 1940 Series game 7 was a cloud that weighed heavy in the minds of the Tigers and their fans – every one of them knowing that Billy Rogell, the fan favorite traded for Bartell in 1939, would have made that play.

DDDDDDDDDDDDDDDDDDDDDDDDDDDDDDDDDDDDDDDDDDDDDDDDDDDDDDDDDDDDDDDDDDDDDDDD

On Monday afternoon, May 26, 1941, Bobo was on the mound in Cleveland. The game moved into the fifth inning, Bobo protecting a 2-1 lead, and facing Lou Boudreau. Newsom threw a blooper pitch, and umpire Bill Summers called it a ball. Bobo came running in, face-to-face with the ump, to plead his case. Summers wasn't looking to debate the issue with Bobo and said to him, *"Scram!"* Ol' Bobo protested, *"Scram? I ain't even had time to unwrap a cuss word."*

Two months prior, everyone knew when Bobo had arrived for spring training in Lakeland. He drove up to a group of players in a souped-up new convertible with a flashing "Bobo" sign on it, and laid on the horn that kept playing, *"Hold That Tiger".*

The excitement of Bobo showing up at Lakeland was the high point for the 1941 Tigers. The reigning A.L. champs fell to fourth place, at 75 & 79, 26 games back of the Yankees. The run production took a huge hit with Hammerin' Hank away serving the country for all but 19 games – in his final game before reporting for duty, Hank hit 2 homers to beat the Yankees in a 7-4 win. At 38, Charlie Gehringer finally showed his age, his average tumbling 93 points to .220, lowest of his career unless you count going 3 for 18 in a brief call up in 1925. The '41 offense scored 200 less runs than in '40. However, steady Rudy York led the team with 27 homers & 111 RBIs, earning him his first All-Star berth.

For $25,000 in May, the Tigers purchased 35-year old Rip Radcliff from the St. Louis Browns. It was a sound move. Although getting up in age, Rip could play left-field, a need with Hank gone, and just the year before for St. Louis had 200 hits, tied for first in the A.L. with Barney McCoskey, while batting .342, fourth best in the league. Rip was a singles guy and, though lacking Hank's power, he hit .311 in '41 for Detroit, 3rd on the team behind McCosky and rookie outfielder Pat Mullin, who in a pleasant surprise hit .345 in 220 at bats.

Team pitching took a big hit as ace Bobo dropped from 21 & 5 to 12 & 20, his ERA jumping from 2.83 to 4.60, and Schoolboy's wins fell from 16 to 8. Al Benton, however, maintained his excellence, earning his first All-Star team selection. When Benton led the league with 17 saves in 1940, he did not start a single game. In '41, Al was used in both relief and starting roles, relieving 24 times vs. 14 starts, going 15 & 6 with 7 saves & a sparkling 2.97 ERA, good for 2nd in the league, and was #1 in fewest hits per 9 innings at 7.42, ahead of #2 Bob Feller.

The kid pitchers who would be stars were still learning their craft: Hal Newhouser 9 & 11, Dizzy Trout 9 & 9, and in the minors, Virgil Trucks went 12 & 12 with a fine 3.22 ERA, earning a late-season cup of coffee (2 innings) in Detroit.

DDDDDDDDDDDDDDDDDDDDDDDDDDDDDDDDDDDDDDDDDDDDDDDDDDDDDDDDDDDDDDDDDDDDDDD

Bobo earned $45,000 in 1941. At the conclusion of his disappointing season, Newsom was informed by G.M. Jack Zeller that he would have to take a $22,500 pay cut. Zeller didn't have a great 1941 himself, hearing from baseball Commissioner Kenesaw Mountain Landis that Detroit would have to forfeit 91 of their minor leaguers, declared free agents due to illegal shenanigans by the front office. When Zeller asked Newsom to accept a 50% pay cut due to declining year-to-year performance, Bobo had a chat with the bald general manager, *"Hell Curly, you lost 91 players and I don't see you taking no pay cut."* Apparently G.M. Curly, er, Jack Zeller didn't see the humor in Bobo's remark, and 2 weeks before 1942 Opening Day, he shipped Newsom off to Washington for cash considerations.

As a member of the Senators, Bobo made the All-Star team in 1944, the 4th time he was so honored. On July 11, 1947, one month shy of his 40th birthday, Bobo was purchased from the Senators by the Yankees. Just like Ol' Bobo said he would, he came up big for New York, tossing 6 complete games including 2 shutouts, going 7 & 5 with a 2.80 ERA in helping them hold off second-place Detroit for the pennant. That fall, as a 40-year old, Bobo got the World Series ring he missed out on as a Tiger in 1940.

When Ol' Bobo hung it up in 1953, he was 46 years old. He had just wrapped up his 2nd tour of duty with the Philadelphia Athletics, the ninth team for whom he played. Bobo was traded or sold by a major league team 22 times. Newsom was with the Washington Senators 5 different stints, and enjoyed telling folks that he had more terms in Washington than FDR. His first time as a Senator, back in 1935, he was on the hill against Cleveland when Earl Averill drilled a liner off Bobo's knee in the 3rd. Washington manager Bucky Harris (note the ex-Tiger manager and 2 future Tiger teammates are the 3 principals of the story) came running out, and Newsom told him he thought the knee was broken (it was). Bucky said he'd get a reliever in the game, and Bobo looked at him kinda funny, sayin', *"I said it was broke, I didn't say I was dead."* Although he lost a tough 5 to 4 game, Newsom went on to pitch all 9 innings with his kneecap broken for the last 6+ of those, and even singled two innings after the injury. That was one tough man. As a post-script, the game recap merely says that *Averill singled to the pitcher*. Yeah, kinda.

On April 14, 1936, 11 months after he played through a broken knee, Newsom had the honor to pitch the home opener for Washington against the Yankees, with FDR in attendance. He suffered a fractured jaw on a defensive play in the fourth inning, but refused to come out. Tossing all 9 innings, he shut out New York, the 1936-1939 Yankee squad considered by many to be the greatest team in history, holding them to 4 hits in a 1-nothing victory. And, once again while injured, he even had a hit. Newsom said, *"When the president comes to see Ol' Bobo pitch, he ain't gonna let him down."*

Bobo Newsom ended his career with a record of 211 & 222, more a reflection of the sub-.500 teams that he played for than the man himself, one of only two pitchers in MLB history to win over 200 but retire with a losing record (Jack Powell the other, 245 & 255 from 1897-1912). Although Bobo would not have a plaque in the Hall of Fame, there were few pitchers that a team would rather have on the mound in a critical game than Louis Norman Bobo Newsom. Just ask a 1940 Tiger fan.

DDDDDDDDDDDDDDDDDDDDDDDDDDDDDDDDDDDDDDDDDDDDDDDDDDDDDDDDDDDDDDDDDDDDDDD

On July 8, 1941, the All-Star Game was played for the first time ever in Detroit. 54,674 crammed into Briggs Stadium, excited to see hometown heroes Al Benton, Birdie Tebbetts, and Rudy York, who all made the American League squad. Tiger Manager Del Baker skippered the team, since the Tigers were the previous season's A.L. champ.

The fans were just as thrilled to watch Ted Williams, currently hitting .405 and on his way to finishing the year at .406, making him the last major leaguer to hit over .400, and Joe DiMaggio, who by game day had hit safely in 48 straight games, already surpassing the previous MLB record of 45 games (spanning 1896 & 1897) by Wee Willie Keeler. Joe D. was on his way to at least one hit in 56 consecutive games.

In the bottom of the 9th, pitcher Claude Passeau tried to protect the National League's 5-4 lead, with two men on base and two out as Ted Williams stepped up to bat. Teddy Baseball crushed a 2-1 fastball into the right-field upper deck, clapping & dancing his way around the base paths, as the 54,000 plus on hand went crazy, almost as much as Ted's teammates, who carried him off the field, and manager Del Baker, who grabbed Ted & kissed him on the forehead. When Del was asked afterward, *"Did you kiss the Kid?"* Del replied with gusto, *"You're damn right I did!"*

DDDDDDDDDDDDDDDDDDDDDDDDDDDDDDDDDDDDDDDDDDDDDDDDDDDDDDDDDDDDDDDDDDDDDDD

On December 7, 1941, the Japanese attacked Pearl Harbor. Americans of all beliefs came together as one to meet the danger. Although Hank Greenberg may have been the first to register for the draft, he very quickly was not alone. With the homeland threatened, major and minor leaguers in droves traded their baseball uniforms for a military one. On January 14, 1942, Commissioner Kenesaw Mountain Landis sent a letter to FDR asking, *"Inasmuch as these are not ordinary times, I venture to ask what you have in mind as to whether baseball should continue to operate."* FDR's reply, the famous "Green Light" letter, said in part, *"... the final decision must rest with you & the baseball owners... I feel that it would be best for the country to keep baseball going. Everyone will be working longer hours and harder than ever before, and that means that they ought to have a chance for recreation and for taking their minds off their work..."* The president also encouraged a greater number of night games, so that more war workers could attend. The 1942 season would be played. Although many ball players enlisted into the armed services early in '42, a great majority completed the season as the machinery to fight the Great War ramped up at a surprisingly slow pace.

The 1942 Tigers had a look much different than their pennant winning season of just two years ago, and not just because they finished in fifth place, 30 games out of first. Hank Greenberg, after appearing in only 19 games in '41, was out for the entire year, and would not play again for the Tigers until July 1, 1945. Charlie Gehringer, for the first time since 1925, was not the starting second baseman, now backing up newly-acquired Jimmy Bloodworth. Gehringer's days with Detroit began in 1924 and ended on September 27, 1942 when he joined the Navy. With the amazing career that he enjoyed, everyone knew Charlie was headed for the Hall of Fame: he hit over .300 13 times, including .371 in 1937, the year that he won the MVP, had over 200 hits 7 times, over 100 RBIs 7 times, & led A.L. second baseman in fielding 8 times. Gehringer played every inning of the first 6 All-Star games (1933-1938) as the American League's starting 2nd baseman, and in those 6 Midsummer Classics hit .500 in 20 at-bats. And Charlie was a huge part of 1 World Championship and 3 pennant winners.

Two new outfielders flanked centerfielder Barney McCosky: rookie Ned Harris patrolled right, and left was manned by 34-year old Doc Cramer, a 4-time All-Star who came over with Jimmy Bloodworth from the Senators for Bruce Campbell.

The pitching staff became younger, offering promise for the future. Virgil Trucks was an outstanding rookie, going 14 & 8 with a 2.74 ERA, and fellow rook Hal White wasn't far behind at 12 & 12 with a 2.91. 21-year old Hal Newhouser had the lowest ERA on the staff at 2.45, and impressed enough to be selected to the All-Star team, but when he pitched the run support was light as he won 8 against 14 losses. Dizzy Trout continued to develop, a fine 3.43 ERA but a rough 12 & 18 win/loss mark. Among the elder statesmen, Bobo was gone, but Tommy Bridges kept on rolling at 9 & 7 with a nice 2.74 earned run average; Al Benton was by now almost exclusively a starter, and an All-Star for the 2nd year in a row – his record was only 7 & 13, but the ERA a stingy 2.90.

Lynwood Schoolboy Rowe began the 1942 season with the Tigers. On April 21, he pitched a gem against the White Sox, no earned runs and a 4-2 victory. Then, 9 days later, the Tigers sold Schoolie for $20,000 to the Brooklyn Dodgers. How sad it was to see him go. Schoolboy was a national sensation in 1934 with his record-setting 16 consecutive wins, and fought through arm trouble to be a huge contributor to the pennant winners of '34, '35 & '40. His departure, as much as Cochrane's, felt to Tiger fans like the end of an era. His new team, the Dodgers, had a solid pitching staff and many wondered what their interest in Rowe was. He only got into 9 games in the 5 months that he played with Brooklyn.

Before the '43 season, Schoolboy was traded by Brooklyn to the Philadelphia Phillies, reunited with his Tiger rookie year manager, Bucky Harris. Rowe worked on the knuckleball that he only dabbled with when he was throwing heat early in his career, now quickly mastering the knuckler along with an assortment of off-speed pitches, once again becoming a dominant pitcher, going 14 & 8 with 3 shutouts and a 2.94 ERA. And, Schoolboy being Schoolboy, not only was the best pitcher on the team, he was considered the Phillies' best hitter, batting .300 AND he led the National League with 15 pinch hits. After serving 1944 & 1945 in the military, he came back in '46 going 11 & 4 with the lowest ERA of his career, 2.12, and once in a while hearing a new nickname, "Schoolmaster", in honor of his age. As a 37-year old in 1947, Schoolboy made his third All-Star team, and first in 11 years, while posting a 14 & 10 record. In 1948-1949, his final two years, Schoolboy won 13 while losing 17, and then he hung it up.

Lynwood Rowe fought through almost continuous arm trouble in a 15-year career, but still won 158 vs. 101 defeats for an excellent .610 winning percentage to go with a 3.87 ERA. He was one of the finest hitting pitchers there ever was, batting .263 with 18 home runs and 153 RBIs in 909 at bats. From 1951 through 1960, Schoolboy was back in the Tigers organization, first as a 41-year old player-manager at class A Williamsport, going 6 & 3 with a 3.04 ERA, on to Buffalo to manage the AAA Bisons, and then roving pitching coach for a season. For two years, '54 & '55, Tiger fans got to see their old friend each game in the 1st base coaches' box, before he went on to manage Detroit's class D Montgomery Rebels. Before the 1961 season began, at only 50 years of age, Lynwood Thomas Schoolboy Rowe had a heart attack & passed away, leaving his fans with great memories & a smile at the thought of their Schoolboy.

DDDDDDDDDDDDDDDDDDDDDDDDDDDDDDDDDDDDDDDDDDDDDDDDDDDDDDDDDDDDDDDDDDDDDDDDDDDD

Major League Baseball held frequent war effort-related fund raisers in 1942 including…

* All teams donated the receipts of one regularly scheduled game to the Army-Navy Relief Fund.

* The winner of the July 6th All-Star game at New York's Polo Grounds played, the next day, an all-service squad consisting of major leaguers now in the armed forces. Since the American League defeated the National League 3-1, the following day the A.L. All-Stars traveled from New York to Cleveland's Municipal Stadium, facing off against the *Mickey Cochrane Service All-Stars* and won 5-0 in an Army-Navy Relief Fund game, raising $120,000. An excerpt from the *New York Times* coverage read:

Tanks rumbled over the field, along with jeeps, mobile anti-aircraft and anti-tank, transport and motor cycle equipment in an impressive demonstration of Uncle Sam's military might. The Great Lakes Naval Training Station and the Fort Hayes bands played martial music. A crack company of the United States Marine Corps from the Navy Pier, Chicago, gave an exhibition of precision drilling. White-clad sailors from the Great Lakes station and the Coast Guard paraded. Cheers swelled to a roar when the "Star-Spangled Banner" was played and Old Glory hoisted aloft on the field staff.

Cochrane managed the Service All-Stars, who thought that their starting pitcher, chief boatswain's mate, Bob Feller, gave them a chance. Feller, however, was not on his game this day, surrendering 3 runs in less than 2 innings, as the A.L. won 5-0. Pat Mullin, Tigers 1941 rookie, played center & batted lead-off for the Service team, who were game but out-classed by Ted Williams, Joe DiMaggio & Co.

* 70,000 fans witnessed an August 23 doubleheader between the Senators & Yankees in the Bronx, raising $80,000 for the Army-Navy Relief Fund. During downtime between the two games (one game won by each team), two members of the 1936 inaugural Hall of Fame class put on a show: Washington Senator legendary pitcher, Walter Johnson, now 54, pitched to 47-year old Babe Ruth. On the "Big Train's" fifth pitch, the Babe connected, sending the ball deep into the right-field stands, well into the third tier of the upper deck, much to the delight of the New York crowd.

DDDDDDDDDDDDDDDDDDDDDDDDDDDDDDDDDDDDDDDDDDDDDDDDDDDDDDDDDDDDDDDDDDDDDDDD

1943 was a year of transition for the Tigers and baseball in general. Players began to leave their teams in large numbers to serve our country, an average of 10 per team. The few recognizable faces remaining that continued to wear the Olde English D, at least for one more year, included the old veteran Thomas Jefferson Davis Bridges. In his 14th season with Detroit, the seemingly-ageless Bridges won 12 games and, for the 2nd year in a row, posted the lowest ERA of his career, a sweet 2.39, good for 4th in the league, as were his 124 strikeouts.

At 36 years old, Tommy was by far the elder of the 1943 pitching staff. Outside of Bridges, the range of age among the top 7 hurlers was 22 to 28 years. The next oldest pitcher was a 28-year old who was finally learning to harness his top-level talent, Paul Howard "Dizzy" Trout. Because of his poor eyesight, Trout was classified 4-F, unfit for military status, and thus eligible to play for the Tigers during World War II. Dizzy contributed to the war effort through an unrelenting schedule of public speaking in support of war bonds, the Red Cross, and the USO aka United Service Organizations, as well as working at a war plant in the off-season.

1943 was Dizzy Trout's breakout year, #1 in the league with 20 wins and 5 shutouts, #4 right behind Bridges with an ERA of 2.48, and even saving 6 games, good for #6 in the A.L. As important as any other factor in allowing Dizzy to realize his full potential as a ballplayer was getting his temper under control. His short fuse manifested itself prior to '43 on a number of occasions...

- Dizzy was pitching at The Corner when a heckler got to him. Trout went into the stands and began to batter the fan under a flurry of punches until pulled off what was left of the guy. After being ejected, Trout thumbed his nose at the crowd.
- Facing future Hall of Famer Luke Appling of the White Sox, Dizzy became furious when Appling fouled off a dozen of Trout's best pitches, and began to swear a blue streak, throwing his glove at Luke and challenging him, *"Let's see you foul that off!"*
- Tiger manager Del Baker pulled Dizzy from a ballgame, where Trout, infuriated, physically attacked Baker in the dugout until teammate Doc Cramer dragged Diz away.

As outstanding as Dizzy's fastball, curve, & sinking forkball were, until he was able to rein in the frequent outbursts, his future in the game was questionable. What turned Dizzy's fortunes around was the 1943 arrival in Detroit of veteran catcher, 34-year old, Paul Richards. Paul drew on his days as a minor league manager to help Trout get his temper under control. When Dizzy's emotions started to get the better of him, Richards delayed tossing the ball back between pitches, signaling Trout to slow down and take a breath. The transformation was immediate, and in 1943 there was no pitcher better anywhere than Dizzy Trout. Were it not for the war, Dizzy likely never would have been effected by Richards' calming influence: Detroit acquired Paul as a replacement once catcher Birdie Tebbetts was called to active duty.

Despite his temper, Dizzy had an excellent sense of humor. When asked to share his life story by *The Sporting News*, Trout told of being born on June 29, 1915, in Sandcut, Indiana, *"a town not on any map due to the fact that the wind keeps blowing the sand over and over and the town never stays in one place for very long at a time."* Explaining where the "Dizzy" nickname came from, Trout said he was caught in a storm at the Toledo ballpark and, spotting an awning on the center field wall, ran towards it, thinking it a good place to duck out of the rain. Instead, he smashed head-on into the bricks because the awning was only painted on the wall. For that, he claimed, teammates began calling him Dizzy.

DDDDDDDDDDDDDDDDDDDDDDDDDDDDDDDDDDDDDDDDDDDDDDDDDDDDDDDDDDDDDDDDDDDDDDDD

Tigers who missed entire seasons due to World War II military service included: Hank Greenberg 1942-1944, Birdie Tebbetts 1943-1945, Pinky Higgins 1945, Barney McCosky 1943-1945, Al Benton 1943-1944, Tommy Bridges 1944, Virgil Trucks 1944, Dick Wakefield 1945. Every team in the majors was affected by the loss of players, and the quality of play suffered across the league. Doc Cramer talked of so many teammates departed for military service, *"Dam, we were lucky to get nine men to put on the field sometimes. We had guys on the field, to tell you the truth, I couldn't tell you who they were."*

DDDDDDDDDDDDDDDDDDDDDDDDDDDDDDDDDDDDDDDDDDDDDDDDDDDDDDDDDDDDDDDDDDDDDDDD

1943 new manager Steve O'Neill replaced Del Baker. Although at year's end the Tigers finished in fifth as they had in Baker's final season, O'Neill's Tigers gave the Yankees a fight into the season's 2nd half, making for an interesting 4th of July weekend at The Corner.

New York arrived in town 4 & ½ games up on Detroit, with doubleheaders scheduled on both Saturday, July 3 and Sunday, July 4. The Saturday first game pitching match-up pitted two '43 All-Stars, the Yanks Spud Chandler vs. Hal Newhouser. Neither was on his best today, but Tiger bats & Yankee charity saved the day, Detroit rallying for 3 in the 8th on a 2-run double by Ned Harris and a big New York error to tie the game at 5, before Rudy York's 11th inning solo blast into the left-center field seats settled the affair.

Game 2 was a wild contest, the Yankees knocking out Tigers starter Roy Henshaw with 5 runs in the game's first 2 innings, New York stretching their lead to 9-3 as Detroit came to bat in the bottom of the eighth. The Tiger reliever who took over from Henshaw in the third was a player Detroit had just acquired 10 days prior, with the intriguing name of Prince Oana from Hawaii. Oana was a pretty good pitcher and a good enough hitter, as an outfielder, to have led the Pacific Coast League in doubles, triples, and slugging percentage in the 30s. Prince Oana came up to the plate in the 8th with two men on, and promptly deposited a 3-run shot into the stands, narrowing New York's lead to 9-6. Oana kept the Yankees scoreless in their ninth as Detroit came to bat in the bottom of the frame.

Joe Wood pinch hit for Pinky Higgins, and opened the Tigers at bat with a walk. Right-fielder Ned Harris continued his fine day at the plate with a single. New York reliever Johnny Murphy pitched carefully to big hitting and potential tying run Rudy York, and issued him a walk. Bases loaded with nobody out and the old ballpark is going crazy. Jimmy Bloodworth, the man who replaced Charlie Gehringer, doubles in two Tigers, bringing Detroit to within one run, and you can't hear yourself think. The Yankees replace Murphy with Bill Zuber, and the Tigers counter with pinch hitter Rip Radcliff, the old veteran they bought for $25,000 in May of '41 and who had 200 hits back in '40. Rip showed he still had some punch left in his bat, rifling a single into right, as York crossed the plate followed closely by Jimmy Bloodworth, tearing around third base like a bat out of hell, just beating the throw home with the winning run. The final score is Tigers 10 Yankees 9 and bedlam erupts at Michigan & Trumbull! Detroit is now just 2 & ½ games back of New York, with another big doubleheader tomorrow.

DDDDDDDDDDDDDDDDDDDDDDDDDDDDDDDDDDDDDDDDDDDDDDDDDDDDDDDDDDDDDDDDDDDDDDDDDDDDDDDD

The reliever who held back the Yankees tide in the July 3 second game, and brought the Tigers to within striking range with his 3-run homer in the eighth, was Prince Oana, signed by Detroit on June 23.

Henry Kawaihoa Oana was born in 1910 on the Hawaiian island of Oahu. On a 1928 barnstorming trip in Japan, Ty Cobb saw Hank Oana play for a California team that traveled to Japan while Cobb was there. Ty told his friend, George Putnam, owner of the San Francisco Seals, about the 18-year old Oana. Young Henry was soon a Seal, crowned with the "Prince" moniker as a publicity stunt by the Seals. Hank said, *"There's nothing to it. I'm just a kid from a sugar plantation who hopes to make good in the big leagues. I'm interested in baseball, not titles. I'm just plain Henry Oana - call me Hank."* However, the name Prince was too much fun for the fans and for the reporters – it was here to stay.

Prince Oana was a fine minor league hitter in the 30s, the outfielder frequently found in the top 10 of most categories each year. His ability had "major leagues" written all over it, but he was a playboy who enjoyed the night life too much for big league teams to take a chance with him, although the Phillies did for a short time in '33. Oana's colorful portfolio included a nightclub brawl, an overnight in jail, and games missed the day after a night of drinking. Each of those incidents scared away many teams, but Hank played extremely well during 99% of the schedule. And fans loved him! Though he spent less than a year with the Syracuse Chiefs, their fans named him the club's all-time centerfielder a decade later.

Oana ended up playing for a time with the Pacific Coast League Portland Beavers. In later years, Portland manager Spencer Abbott said of the Prince, *"I never met a player who was more willing to put out more for you than Hank Oana. He gave me many a laugh but he worried the hell out of me those two seasons I had him. But he was a team man always, and smart. Hank had many friends in every town and it was tough for him to live anything resembling the Spartan life. If he had been a less handsome fellow with the same ability, he might be a ten-year star now in the major leagues."*

When Fort Wayne picked up the young outfielder in '42, manager Rogers Hornsby saw even greater potential in Hank as a pitcher & moved him into the starting rotation. The reward was immediate. Oana threw 41 consecutive scoreless innings including 3 shutouts and one no-hitter, finishing the season at 16 & 5 with a 1.72 ERA. Manager Hornsby said, *"He throws the ball where he wants it and gives the batters nothing good to hit. He knows a lot more about pitching than most of the hitters give him credit with. He works on 'em, keeps 'em off balance and crossed up. He pitches to their weaknesses. His fastball is faster than it looks.'"* Oana told reporters, *"Of course I've got a curve ball and a specialty I call a fork ball, but it's my fast one that has made me a success. It just sails up and out on right handed batters when delivered above the belt. Pitched low it sails down and out -- a kind of slider.'"*

Milwaukee's Bill Veeck came 'a calling when the Fort Worth team, short of players due to the demands of the war, folded in early '43. Veeck acquired Oana for $5,000 to play for his minor league Milwaukee Brewers. And play he did, both baseball and banjo for manager Charlie Grimm's jug band, comprised of ballplayers entertaining fans on game days (anything is possible when you're employed by baseball's entertainment master, Bill Veeck). When financial considerations prompted Veeck to release Hank, the Tigers signed Prince Oana immediately.

For the Tigers, Prince Oana was a dual threat: he pitched in 10 games, going 3 & 2 with a 4.50 ERA, and pinch hit in 20 games. Including coming to the plate in games he was pitching in, Prince compiled a .385 average, going 10 for 26. Combined with his humble countenance, good looks, great arm & bat, Hank very quickly became a fan favorite in Detroit.

Post-script: on the 4th of July, 1943, the day after Prince Oana helped pitch & hit the Tigers to victory over the Yankees, Detroit & New York split their double-header, the Tigers remaining 2 & ½ games back of the Yankees. They would get no closer to first, eventually ending up 20 games back, at 78 & 76.

DDDDDDDDDDDDDDDDDDDDDDDDDDDDDDDDDDDDDDDDDDDDDDDDDDDDDDDDDDDDDDDDDDDDDDDDDDD

1943 was the coming out party for 22-year old leftfielder Dick Wakefield. Tiger owner Walter O. Briggs, smitten by the young slugger, made him the major league's first "bonus baby" on June 21, 1942, when Wakefield signed on the dotted line for $52,000 (in contrast, the highest paid player in 1942 was Joe DiMaggio at $43,750). For a player who never played at inning in the majors, a $52,000 bonus was a *big deal!* After spending a very successful 1942 in the minors, Dick Wakefield proved that he was ready in 1943 for The Show, coming in 2nd in the American League with a .316 batting average, first with 200 hits & 38 doubles, scored 91 runs, and had hitting streaks of 22 & 19 games. In the All-Star game, Wakefield, the American League starting leftfielder, got 2 hits & 1 RBI. In the regular season Most Valuable Player voting, he came in sixth.

Dizzy Trout joined baseball's elite pitchers in 1943, and the team & its fans were excited about how good he AND his fellow young hurlers could be in 1944. As a 24-year old rookie in 1943, Frank "Stubby" Overmire, the pride of Moline, Michigan, had a fine showing, tossing 3 shutouts while going 7 & 6 with a 3.18 ERA. Hal Newhouser, although an All-Star the last two years, was a hard-luck hurler, seemingly on the verge of reaching his full potential in '44. However, his major league record through '43 was an exasperating 34-52, something the perfectionist in him was having difficulty handling, causing Hal to question his baseball career. In the offseason, he'd worked as an apprentice draftsman at Chrysler – they liked his work & offered Hal a full-time job with a salary as good as what he earned from the Tigers. Fortunately, Hal Newhouser decided to give baseball one more shot.

The pitching staff lost 3 of their 1943 finest to the war effort in '44: veteran Tommy Bridges, promising 24-year old Hal White, and Virgil Oliver "Fire" Trucks. It was Trucks who was the biggest loss for this team, coming off his impressive first two years, 1943 16 & 10/2.84 ERA & 1942 14 & 8/2.74 ERA.

Subtracting these 3 pitchers from the rotation, as well as the absence of Dick Wakefield from the lineup due to naval flight training, along with the continued offensive hole left by the military service of Hank Greenberg, McCosky, and Birdie Tebbetts, decimated the team in early '44. But the season turned when 1st-place New York came to town May 30 for a 4-game series, and were swept by 6th-place Detroit.

In game 1, it was the Dizzy Trout Show as he tamed the Bronx Bombers 2 to 1, hitting the game-winning solo shot in the bottom of the 9th. Hal Newhouser dominated the 2nd game, a 4-1 win supported by a combined 4 hits & 3 runs scored from centerfielder Doc Cramer and 34-year old, first year Tiger, 2nd baseman Eddie Mayo. After several big league seasons, Mayo bounced around in the minors from 1939-1942, then spent one year with the Philadelphia Athletics before being acquired by Detroit in late-'43. In game 3, Stubby Overmire made it tough on New York batters, but Detroit was still losing 2-1 going into the 9th. After Rudy York began the frame reaching first on an error, Pinky Higgins doubled him to 3rd.

Left-fielder Jimmy Outlaw, a Tiger minor leaguer all but 20 games the last 4 years, was intentionally walked to set up a force anywhere on the infield. 40-year old rookie right-fielder Chuck Hostetler hit a sacrifice fly to tie the game at 2. Pinch hitter Paul Richards drew a walk to reload the bases, and up stepped Al Unser. Al Unser, a little used utility man, batted .120 in '44, going 3 for 25. Of his 3 hits, this was by far his most memorable, as he drove the pitch over the wall for a game-winning grand slam.

In the June 1 game 4 finale, New York scored a run to tie the game at 3 in the 9th, before Newhouser entered in relief to put out the fire. After throwing a complete game 2 days earlier, on just one day's rest, Hal tossed 7 scoreless innings before Detroit won it 4-3 in the 16th to complete the sweep. The four losses knocked New York from the top spot, now one-half game back of the first-place St. Louis Browns, while the Tigers jumped from 6th to 3rd-place, only 1 & ½ games back of the Browns.

DDDDDDDDDDDDDDDDDDDDDDDDDDDDDDDDDDDDDDDDDDDDDDDDDDDDDDDDDDDDDDDDDDDD

For the '44 season, Walter "Boom Boom" Beck joined the Tigers pitching staff. In his single year with Detroit, the 39-year old made a nice contribution to the bullpen with a 3.89 ERA in 28 games. One decade before his time as a Tiger, though, was a different story for Walter Beck. In 1934, he was on the pitching staff of the Brooklyn Dodgers, playing under manager Casey Stengel, experiencing a rough year with an astronomical ERA of 7.42. One 1934 day, he faced the Philadelphia Phillies and got a shellackin'. The Phillies played their games at the old Baker Bowl, Philadelphia's ball park since 1887. To fit into the Philly neighborhood that it called home, the stadium had the unusual dimensions of 342' down the left-field line, 408' to center, and only 281' to right. To compensate for the short fence in right, a 40' tall tin wall was constructed there. Balls hit off this wall made a sound unique to the Baker Bowl, and in this game, Walter gave up one rocket after another to right, each line drive explosively striking the tin wall, resulting in a forceful booming sound echoing throughout the park. Manager Stengel, seeing enough, removed Beck from the game. The upset pitcher threw the baseball off the right-field wall, creating yet another boom. Daydreaming rightfielder Hack Wilson heard the boom from Beck's toss of frustration, snapped to, thinking the game had resumed, and ran after the ball, firing it back to the infield.

From this day on, Walter Beck was forever known as Walter "Boom Boom" Beck.

DDDDDDDDDDDDDDDDDDDDDDDDDDDDDDDDDDDDDDDDDDDDDDDDDDDDDDDDDDDDDDDDDDDD

On June 23, 1944, Detroit arrived in St. Louis for 4 games, sitting 3 & ½ games back of the Browns. The Tigers proceeded to drop all 4, including a kick-in-the-pants, 10-inning, 5-4 loss that saw Detroit rally from 2-0 down with 4 in the 8th, only to have Dizzy give back 2 in the ninth to tie, and then the back-breaker fifth run in the tenth. The Tigers scuffled throughout July, dropping 9 games off the pace.

And then, the pennant race was on. The Yankees came to Detroit for 4 games from July 29 to August 1. In the first game, New York rallied for one in the ninth off of starter Rufe Gentry to tie things up 2-2, before Dizzy Trout came in to get the last two outs. After pitching a scoreless 10th, Dizzy hit the game-winning sac fly in the bottom of the inning. After the Yanks pounded Stubby Overmire, Johnny Gorsica, & Boom Boom Beck for a game two 10-2 win, the Tigers responded with 13-7 & 8-4 victories, including a victory by Newhouser – one of six that he had over New York in 1944 alone. A team can never have too many Yankee-killers. The final two victories over New York kicked off a 9-game winning streak.

The August 27 game at The Corner completed a 4-game series with first-place St. Louis, Detroit taking 3 of 4 to close to 4 games out of first, tied with Boston for third, one-half game behind New York. After splitting 2 with the White Sox, the Tigers traveled to St. Louis for 4 more with the Browns. Again, Detroit took 3 of 4, leaving town in September 3 just two games out of first.

No small part of the team's 2nd half success was the return of Dick Wakefield to the line-up. Discharged from the Navy, he played his first game back on July 13, 1944 in Chicago. Dick picked up right where he left off at the end of 1943, going 2 for 4 at Comiskey Park. Wakefield played 78 games for Detroit in '44, batting .355 with 12 home runs and 53 RBIs. Despite only playing in half the season, Dick finished fifth in MVP voting.

As much as the return of Dick Wakefield sparked the offense, it was the two Tigers who came in first and second in the Most Valuable Player voting who were the horses the Tigers rode in their 1944 pennant push, Hal Newhouser and Dizzy Trout. The two started 17 of the 28 September games as Detroit went 21 & 7 in that month to catch St. Louis for first. On September 30, Detroit beat Washington 7 to 3, "Prince Hal" Newhouser going the distance for his 29th victory, while St. Louis defeated the Yanks 2-0. The results left the Tigers and the Browns tied for 1st at 88 & 65. It would all come down to each teams' October 1st game...

In front of 45,565 at The Corner, going on just one day's rest, Dizzy Trout took the hill for Detroit. Two days ago, Dizzy was knocked around by Washington, lasting only 4 innings while surrendering 6 runs. But despite that last game and the short rest, Dizzy had to throw for Detroit today. Trout had 27 wins and a 2.07 ERA, and it was Dizzy & Hal who brung 'em here, and Dizzy had to take 'em home. The Tigers faced a very tough pitcher, Washington's Dutch Leonard. Dutch, 17 & 7 in 1945 with a 2.13 ERA, was stingy when it came to giving up runs, making this a difficult match-up.

Dizzy had one hiccup, in the 4th inning allowing 3 runs. When he gave up one more in the 8th, things got real quiet at Michigan & Trumbull. The Tigers came to bat in the ninth down 4 to 0, showing some life for the first time today. 40-year old rookie Chuck Hostetler opened the frame with a pinch hit single. The next batter, seldom-used utility man Don Ross, pinch hit for Trout. When Ross singled, sending Hostetler to third, the fans started buzzing. Doc Cramer stepped up to the plate, sending a fly ball to center, deep enough to send Hostetler home from 3rd, but that was not enough. After Eddie Mayo grounded out and Pinky Higgins flied out, ending the game, the Tigers and their fans found themselves in the extremely unusual situation of pulling for the Yankees. If New York beat St. Louis, there would be a one-game playoff tomorrow at The Corner between Detroit and the Browns.

With the Tigers straining to hear the game on the clubhouse radio, New York had an early 2-0 lead, giving the City of Detroit hope, but it was all St. Louis after that. The final score was St. Louis 5 NY 2, providing the one-game margin needed for the Browns to win the only pennant in their history.

DDDDDDDDDDDDDDDDDDDDDDDDDDDDDDDDDDDDDDDDDDDDDDDDDDDDDDDDDDDDDDDDDDDDDDDD

In the 1944 MVP voting, Hal Newhouser & Dizzy Trout finished one & two. Prince Hal led the league in wins with 29 and 187 strikeouts, Dizzy was #2 in both, 27 and 144, respectively. Trout was number 1 with a 2.12 ERA, 7 shutouts, 33 complete games, and (the most for any pitcher in 21 years) 352 innings pitched. Hal was number 2 in all of those categories, 2.22 ERA, 6 shutouts, 25 complete games, and 312 innings pitched. Dizzy contributed at the bat, too, leading all league pitchers in hits, home runs, & RBIs.

Over the season, 923,176 fans, tops in the American League, showed up at The Corner to watch the excitement of the pennant chase, the yeoman effort of these two pitchers, and to escape the reality of the war. It was a great ride, but the coveted pennant would have to wait for next year.

DDDDDDDDDDDDDDDDDDDDDDDDDDDDDDDDDDDDDDDDDDDDDDDDDDDDDDDDDDDDDDDDDDDDDDDD

The Detroit Tigers were so close in '44. They were a driven group, determined to strike gold in '45. The key was Prince Hal Newhouser. Bobo Newsom, a Newhouser fan, exclaimed *"Every time he walks to that mound, you know you'll get a good-pitched game."* Joe DiMaggio made his feelings clear, *"His curveball is the best I've ever seen."*

As a 14-year old, Hal listened to WWJ's Ty Tyson call of Goose Goslin knocking in Mickey Cochrane to win the 1935 World Series, and decided that day he wanted to pitch for his hometown Detroit Tigers. Newhouser was an ultra-competitive perfectionist, a trait that brought out an ugly side of him when his teammates let him down at the plate or on the field. Fellow Tiger pitcher Virgil Trucks, one of the nicest players in the game, said of Hal's temper, *"he may have been the most disliked fellow in all of baseball."*

Prince Hal occasionally went by another nickname, "Hurricane Hal", from the tantrums that were always just beneath the surface. During the 1940 pennant race, manager Del Baker pulled Newhouser from a game. A few minutes later in the Tiger clubhouse, every single bottle of Coke was pulled from its case and smashed against the wall.

Perhaps Hal's attitude was soured by what he missed out on during the day he joined the Tigers. In 1938, the 17-year old signed a contract offered by Detroit's chief scout, Wish Egan, a contract that came with a $500 signing bonus. Shortly after signing with Detroit, a Cleveland Indian scout pulled up next to Hal with a new car. Along with a $15,000 bonus, the car was to be Hal's. The Cleveland scout would've shown up before Wish Egan obtained Hal's signature for Detroit, but he was busy picking up the new car. Egan told his secretary, *"I've just signed the greatest left-handed pitcher I ever saw."*

Newhouser had planned to be sworn into the Army Air Force in 1942 on the mound at Briggs Stadium, and trade his Tiger uniform for a military one, but a heart murmur squashed those plans. Instead, he continued to pitch for Detroit in 1942, earning his first All-Star team berth. Once Hal committed to playing baseball, the next step in achieving his potential was accepting the direction that catcher Paul Richards provided. Step 1 was Richards teaching Hal how to throw a slider, a pitch that looked to batters just like his fastball until a devastating last-second break. Step 2 was Richards teaching, just as he had to Dizzy Trout, maturity to Hal, allowing him to get a handle on his emotions; and just like with Dizzy, the results were immediate and improved his relations with teammates, manager, and fans immeasurably. From 1943 to 1944, Hal achieved the potential that scout Wish Egan saw in 1938. What he would do in 1945 would decide if Detroit became champions or also-rans.

DDDDDDDDDDDDDDDDDDDDDDDDDDDDDDDDDDDDDDDDDDDDDDDDDDDDDDDDDDDDDDDDDDDDDDDD

When the Tigers split an April 29, 1945 doubleheader with Cleveland, they were in a 3-way tie for first with the White Sox and the Yankees. More importantly, between games Detroit reacquired a player that the Indians had soured on – Roy Cullenbine. With Dick Wakefield once again away serving our country, this move was an important one. The cost for Roy was third baseman Don Ross, which turned out to be a steal for Detroit. Cullenbine was one of the 91 minor leaguers that Commissioner Kenesaw Mountain Landis forced Detroit to forfeit in '41, when Landis declared the team guilty of rule infractions. Now Roy was back with the team he broke into pro ball with, and he & they could not be happier.

In the Tigers line-up, Roy Cullenbine batted third, right in front of Rudy York. The two tied for second in the league with 18 home runs each, and Roy was second with 93 RBIs. He was constantly on base for York to knock in, leading the A.L. with 113 walks & a .402 on base percentage. With Cullenbine and York driving the offense, and Newhouser and Trout keeping the opposition bats under wraps, Detroit ended June in first place, 1 & ½ games up on the Yankees. The next day, another bat was added to the line-up, one that would slide into the clean-up spot between Roy & Rudy, *the bat belonging to the just-released-from-military-duty Henry Benjamin Greenberg.*

On July 1, 1945, in a game at The Corner versus the Philadelphia Athletics, Hammerin' Hank aka the Hebrew Hammer aka Hankus Pankus played leftfield once again for the Detroit Tigers. It was the first time that wore the Olde English D since playing 19 games in 1941. 10,375 came out for the previous day's game – for Hank's return, 47,729 were in the stands, and they were **_loud!_** In the eighth inning, Greenberg stepped to the plate and launched a home run into the adoring masses, who then covered the field with their hats. *"They were cheering like mad,"* Hank said, *"Boy, it felt good to hit that one."* How a player doesn't have some rust on him after being out for 4 seasons is a mystery, but Hank immediately resumed where he left off. From his July 1 return to the end of the season, Greenberg hit .311, the highest average in the league (but with too few at bats to qualify for the title), along with 13 home runs and 60 RBIs, finishing tops on the team in both on-base & slugging percentages.

Joining Hank was another veteran of the 1935 & 1940 World Series. After missing all of 1944 and most of 1945 serving in the Army during World War II, Thomas Jefferson Davis Bridges aka Tommy Bridges came back to be the Tigers pitching coach during the pennant race in late-'45, but ended up seeing action as a player. Bridges pitched in 4 games, going 1 & 0 with a 3.27 ERA.

DDDDDDDDDDDDDDDDDDDDDDDDDDDDDDDDDDDDDDDDDDDDDDDDDDDDDDDDDDDDDDDDDDDDDDDD

Just in time for the stretch drive, another popular, although short-term, former Tiger returned. Prince Oana was brought back to Detroit from the minors in late-August, pitching in 3 games with a 1.59 ERA. Oana was warmly remembered for a 1943 4th of July weekend game vs. the Yankees when he relieved the starter in the third, held New York at bay for 6 innings, and hit a crucial 8th inning 3-run homer in the 10-9 Tiger win.

On September 12 of '45, the Tigers had a doubleheader at Shibe Park vs. the Athletics. Prince Oana got the starting nod in the 2nd game, the only start of his career. Oana was brilliant, holding a 1-0 lead going into the bottom of the ninth, only surrendering one hit to that point. Sandwiched between 2 flyouts, Prince allowed a walk, and now faced Philadelphia's clean-up man, Bobby Estalella. On a full count, Oana gave up a game-tying double. Prince was able to get the A's third baseman, George Kell, to line out for the 3rd out in the ninth, then pitched into the 11th before being relieved. The Tigers lost in 16, but that did not minimize Prince Oana's outstanding performance on this day. Despite the defeat, Detroit maintained their 1 & ½ game lead over the 2nd place Washington Senators.

DDDDDDDDDDDDDDDDDDDDDDDDDDDDDDDDDDDDDDDDDDDDDDDDDDDDDDDDDDDDDDDDDDDDDDDD

Each of the Tigers everyday players except one was at least 30, but these old fellas were able to hold down first place every day from June 10 on. The excitement of the pennant race drew fans in droves to The Corner, the team tops in league attendance at 1,280,341. Despite holding first place for over 3 & ½ months, as the Tigers prepared to play the final game of the year, they were in danger of losing the American League flag.

Going into that September 30 finale, the A.L. standings read Detroit in first at 87 & 65, with Washington one game back. Virgil Trucks had been discharged from the Navy just in time for this game, making the start for the Tigers versus the St. Louis Browns at Sportsman's Park. Fire Trucks went 5 innings, relieved by Hal Newhouser with the score tied 1-1. When Paul Richards singled home Roy Cullenbine with the lead run in the Tigers sixth, the outcome looked promising with Newhouser on the hill. But Prince Hal was touched up for single runs in both the Browns 7th & 8th and suddenly the possibility of a one-game, winner-take-all, match against the Senators tomorrow loomed large as Detroit stepped up to bat, down 3-2 in the ninth.

38-year old Hub Walker, batting .090 at 2 for 22, playing the last regular season game of his career, pinch hit for Newhouser and singled. Hub is now batting .130. 29-year old Red Borom, in the final regular season game of his career, came in to run for Hub. Shortstop Skeeter Webb tried to bunt Red Borom over to 2nd base, and everybody is safe when Red beats the throw on the force attempt. Eddie Mayo successfully sacrificed Borom & Webb to 2nd & 3rd. Doc Cramer worked the Browns pitcher for a walk, and up stepped Hank. The rain had been falling all day at Sportsman's Park, the drops coming down harder now. Hank swings and sends the ball high & far into the damp St. Louis afternoon, clearing the fence for a pennant-winning grand slam home run! The Detroit Tigers are back in the World Series!

DDDDDDDDDDDDDDDDDDDDDDDDDDDDDDDDDDDDDDDDDDDDDDDDDDDDDDDDDDDDDDDDDDDDDDDD

Their opponent in the Fall Classic was a familiar one to Tiger fans. In 1907 & 1908, the mighty Cubs of "Tinker to Evers to Chance" fame whipped the Tigers both years. One decade since the 1935 G-Men of Mickey Cochrane took Chicago in 6, 1945 would be Detroit's opportunity to even the all-time Series record between the two organizations at two to two.

Despite World War II concluding, celebrated with V-J Day on August 15, war-related travel restrictions remained in place. In light of this, Commissioner Kenesaw Mountain Landis decreed that the two teams would only travel once: the first 3 games to be played at Briggs Stadium in Detroit, game 4 and any additional games needed to take place at Chicago's Wrigley Field. The Tigers felt it important to take at least 2 of the 3 home games to win the Series.

Game 1 Detroit: The Cubs acquired pitcher Hank Borowy from the Yankees at the end of July. He was magnificent down the stretch, winning his final 7 games, a key reason that Chicago was able to hold off the St. Louis Cardinals to win the National League pennant. The fact that Borowy continued stifling bats today was unsurprising – the fact that the Cubs lit up Hal at The Corner was depressingly unexpected.

The 54,637 Tiger faithful had barely made it to their seats and their heroes were in a hole, the Cubs getting to Newhouser for 4 first inning runs. When Chicago added 3 more in the third, Hal was gone before he could get the final out of that frame, and an uneasy feeling spread through the ballpark. Hank Borowy, meanwhile, was rolling easily through the Tigers lineup. The only time when Borowy looked unsteady was in the first – right after Chicago scored their 4, Detroit opened up with singles by Skeeter Webb and Eddie Mayo, getting the fans to their feet early. However, when Doc Cramer's grounder to short was turned for a double play, Webb was standing on third but now two were gone. Excitement filled the stadium again when Borowy walked Hank & then Roy Cullenbine to fill the bases, with the powerful Rudy York coming up to the plate. Detroit was only one swing from a tie ball game, but York popped out to first. After a lead-off single in the sixth, the last 12 Tigers went down in order. The Cubs tacked on two meaningless runs in their seventh, producing a final score of Cubs 9 Tigers 0.

Game 2 Detroit: If there's a fire to put out, Virgil Fire Trucks is your man. In just his 2nd start since being discharged from the service at the end of September, Virgil was hot today. After giving up a single Cub run in the 4th, Trucks only surrendered two hits the rest of the way in going the distance. Virgil kept the Cubs off balance with a 95-mph fastball that occasionally touched 100, and used the same motion to throw a 75-mph change-up and an 85-mph slider. Commenting on today's masterpiece along with Virgil's 30 victories in his two seasons before leaving for the service, sports writers began referring to the elite Tiger pitching staff of Dizzy Trout, Hal Newhouser, and Virgil Trucks, as "TNT."

Down 1-0 in the fifth, the Tigers bats came alive for the first time this Series. With two outs, shortstop & leadoff man Skeeter Webb singled, Eddie Mayo walked, and Doc Cramer knocked in Skeeter with the tying run. Up stepped Hammerin' Hank, and he unloaded, the ball carrying deep into the leftfield stands for a 3-run homer, making 53,636 go absolutely nuts. Just 5 days after hitting the grand slam that propelled Detroit into the World Series, Greenberg put the Tigers up 4 to 1, the game 2 final score.

Game 3 Detroit: Today's pitching match-up in front of 55,500 featured Detroit's Stubby Overmire against Chicago's Claude Passeau, the man who gave up Ted Williams' game ending home run in the 1941 All-Star game at Briggs Stadium. Passeau had much more success in his second ever appearance at The Corner, stifling Detroit on one hit & one walk, in Chicago's 3-0 win. It was the first World Series one-hitter since another Cub, Ed Reulbach, threw one against their crosstown rival White Sox in 1906. Stubby Overmire tossed a fine ballgame, only touched for 4 hits & 2 runs in his 6 innings, but on this day that was more than enough for the Tigers to fall 3-0. As the Series moves to Wrigley Field, the Cubs are up two games to one.

Game 4 Chicago: The first '45 Series game in Chicago, in front of 42,923 was almost *42,923 and one billy goat.* Cub fan Bill Sianis, owner of the Billy Goat Tavern & Grill, had purchased a box seat for himself and one for his goat. The team, however, barred entry when the bar owner & his billy goat arrived at the Wrigley gate, the usher stating the rule that no animals are allowed in the park. Sianis appealed to Cubs owner P.K. Wrigley, who said, *"no, because the goat stinks."* It was said that Bill Sianis then shouted, *"The Cubs will never win a World Series as long as the goat is not allowed in Wrigley Field,"* aka *The Curse of the Billy Goat.* The goat lived another 20 years, during which the Cubs never finished above fifth place in the standings.

The game pitted Dizzy Trout against N.L. ERA leader Ray Prim. Dizzy was outstanding, like the Trout of '43 & '44, holding the Cubs to 5 hits, 1 run, walking 1 while striking out 6. Ray Prim didn't make it out of the fourth. After getting Skeeter Webb on a ground out to start the inning, Prim surrendered a walk to Eddie Mayo, a single to Doc Cramer, an RBI single to Hank, and a run scoring double to Roy Cullenbine before being replaced by 1940 Cincinnati Reds Series hero, Paul Derringer. Detroit had much more success against Derringer in '45 than in '40, tacking on two more runs on a Jimmy Outlaw groundout and a Paul Richards single. Final score Detroit 4 Chicago 1, the Series all knotted at 2–2. Post-game, tavern & billy goat owner Bill Sianis sent a telegram to the Cubs owner that read, *"Who stinks now?"*

Game 5 Chicago: 43,463 filled Wrigley, hoping to see a repeat of the game 1 duel that wasn't between their Hank Borowy & Detroit's Hal Newhouser, a 9-0 Cubs win. Today, the Tigers figured out Mister Borowy, drawing first blood on a Doc Cramer top of the third sac fly, matched by Chicago the next half inning on Stan Hack's RBI single off Prince Hal. And then came the sixth when the first 4 Tigers reached base off Borowy: Doc Cramer single, Hank run-scoring double, Roy Cullenbine single, and a Rudy York run-scoring single. Hank Borowy would not see a fifth batter in the sixth, replaced by Hy Vandenberg, who gave up a sac bunt to Jimmy Outlaw, moving York to 2nd & Cullenbine to 3rd.

With the pitcher on deck, Hy intentionally walked Paul Richards – perhaps if Vandenberg was up on the Tigers regular season stats, and noticed that Richards hit .256 while Newhouser hit .257, he would not have walked Paul to get to Hal, but the point quickly became moot when Hy Vandenberg issued an unintentional pass to Hal, forcing in Cullenbine with the 3rd Tiger run of the inning. A 4th & final sixth inning run came in on a Skeeter Webb RBI grounder. Paul Derringer came in to pitch to Detroit in the 7th and they greeted him with a Jimmy Outlaw sacrifice fly that brought in Hank from third, increasing Detroit's lead to 6-1. 3 late Cubs runs, and two more for Detroit on a Roy Cullenbine double, made the final score Detroit 8 Chicago 4. The Tigers are now 1 win away from their second World Series crown.

Game 6 Chicago: Two pitchers who performed brilliantly already this Series, Virgil Trucks in game 2 and Claude Passeau in game 3, would face off in front of 41,708 at Wrigley. Detroit broke the scoreless tie in the 2nd when a walk to Paul Richards forced home Roy Cullenbine. It remained 1-0 until the Cubs fifth when Stan Hack and Phil Cavarretta each stroked 2-run singles, Cavarretta's knocking Trucks out of the game as reliever George Caster stopped the bleeding, recording the final 2 outs. In the sixth, Tommy Bridges made his lone appearance in the '45 World Series, joining Hank Greenberg as the only two Detroit Tigers to play in four World Series. Bridges was touched for back-to-back doubles, making the score 5-1 Cubs, before the wily vet picked a Cub off of second base to spike the rally. The Tigers came right back in the next inning on RBI singles by Cullenbine & York, the second one knocking out Passeau and cutting the lead to 5-3, but in the next frame a run-scoring walk off Bridges & a RBI single off Al Benton restored the 4-run Cubs advantage.

Down to their last 6 outs, Detroit rallied in the eighth. Catcher Bob Swift led off with a walk, and Hub Walker pinch hit for Al Benton, doubling Swift to third. Back-up shortstop Joe Hoover reached first on an error that allowed Swift to score. An Eddie Mayo single scored Hub Walker and sent Hoover to third, but Mayo was thrown out trying for 2nd, a play that would prove critical to the game's outcome. Doc Cramer knocked in Hoover on a sac fly, and when Hank followed with a home run, it was a solo shot instead of a 2-run jack since Eddie Mayo was not on base, having been earlier tossed out at 2nd. The 8th inning ended when Cullenbine grounded out. Rather than leading 8-7, the Tigers had tied things up at 7.

Dizzy Trout came in to pitch for Detroit in the eighth, and Hank Borowy came in to pitch for Chicago in the 9th, and both put zeros up on the scoreboard through the ninth, tenth, and eleventh innings. In the top of the 12th, Tiger shortstop Joe Hoover singled with two outs, but was thrown out attempting to steal. In the Cubs 12th, Dizzy gave up a one out single to Frank Secory and, after striking out Borowy, Stan Hack ended the game when he doubled home Secory. Cubs win the long, extra inning affair, 8-7, evening the Series at 3 games apiece.

At the conclusion of Game 6, the *Washington Post* implored its' readers, *"Please don't talk to us about atomic bombs, or the Russian impasse, or the strike crisis, or full employment, or such matters, until the issue of this hair-raising 1945 World Series is settled one way or the other."* It was time for Game 7.

Game 7 Chicago: It had to be Prince Hal today. Manager Steve O'Neill had no other choice. The best player in all of baseball in 1945 had to have the ball for the final game of the year. Hal Newhouser was spectacular this season, winning the Pitching Triple Crown: 25 wins, 1.81 earned run average, 212 strikeouts; he also had 8 shutouts, 29 complete games, and 313 innings pitched. Hal was named MVP for the second consecutive season, the first pitcher to ever do so. To make all of those achievements meaningful, today Prince Hal had to outpitch Hank Borowy and secure the World Championship for Detroit. Borowy came in for the ninth inning of game 6, and stayed in 'til the end of the 12-inning classic. Today, with one day's rest after throwing those 4 scoreless innings, despite concern that he would not be rested enough for this big game, the Cubs hopes would ride on his shoulders.

41,590 attended this deciding game at Wrigley Field. Game 7 played over the airways of 300 affiliates of the Mutual Broadcasting System to servicemen & women overseas on the Armed Forces Radio Service, with Bill Slater & Al Helfer doing play by play. Helfer was a 300-pounder who was said to *"drink triples without any apparent effect and wore a cashmere cardigan that cost the lives of a herd of goats."*

To the glorious delight of the folks listening back in Michigan, the Tigers came out of the gates roaring. Skeeter Webb singled, Eddie Mayo singled, Doc Cramer singled, and it's 1-0 Detroit. Cubs skipper Charlie Grimm had seen enough of Borowy, replacing him with Paul Derringer. The first batter that Derringer faced was Greenberg. Hank held back the hammer and fooled 'em all by laying down a gorgeous sacrifice bunt that moved Cramer & Mayo to second & third. Derringer intentionally walked Roy Cullenbine to set up the double play with the heavy hitting but slow afoot Rudy York due up. Rudy popped out to Stan Hack at third for out number two, the bases remaining loaded. Jimmy Outlaw worked Derringer for a base on balls that forced in a 2nd run, bases still loaded. That's when Paul

Richards, known for his defense and adept handling of pitchers, but not for his bat, had the biggest hit of his career, a bases-clearing double into the left field corner. Newhouser grounded out to complete Detroit's batting around in inning number one, the Cub fans in a gloomy, stunned silence, as their boys came to bat down 5-0.

The Cubs immediately got one back on a Phil Cavarretta RBI single, but with two outs & nobody on in Detroit's 2nd, Paul Derringer gave up a single to Doc Cramer followed by 3 consecutive walks to make it 6-1 Tigers. For Derringer, the third walk meant the end of his day and the end of an outstanding career, as the 38-year old hung it up after this game. Hy Vandenberg recorded the final out of the inning.

A triple by Cub Andy Pafko off Newhouser scored Cavarretta to close the gap to 6-2 Detroit in the fourth, until Paul Richards continued his wonderful day with a run-scoring double in the Tigers 7th. Detroit's 8th was icing on the cake as Skeeter Webb led off with a walk and came home on Eddie Mayo's double. Mayo moved to third on a Doc Cramer grounder, and scampered home on Hank's line-out to left. The Cubs got one of those two runs back in their half of the eighth, but all that did was make the final score Detroit 9 Cubs 3 when Prince Hal Newhouser closed the Cubs out in the ninth.

For the second time in the history of the Detroit Tigers, they were World Series Champions!

The celebration swirls around Prince Hal, middle row, 3rd from left & holding his glove; standing above him are (left) Dizzy Trout (glasses) & (right) Roy Cullenbine; to right of Hal, both back this year from WWII, Virgil Trucks tips cap & Greenberg is bent over; bottom in catcher's gear is Bob Swift, bottom right is Paul Richards

After the Tigers won game 7 of the 1945 World Series, defeating the Cubs at Wrigley Field, their train pulled into the Michigan Central Station, greeted by an estimated 100,000 fans stretching from the train station to downtown. On the crush of the wildly excitable mass, Newhouser said he never experienced a more joyful & at the same time frightening evening.

Thousands of those crowded between the train depot and downtown, on that chilly but heartwarming October evening, pushed their way at some point into 38-year old Hoot Robinson's bar on Trumbull, across the street from Briggs Stadium's right-field wall. Deep into the night and early the next morning, one toast after another were lifted to our Tigers.

An article in *The Detroit News* noted, *"A strange, almost mystical connection between Detroit's fortunes in the world of sport and the state of the local mind and morale."* The 1,280,341 fans drawn to The Corner in 1945 was only 9,081 shy of the 1920 New York Yankees attendance record – and that was when Babe Ruth, in only his 2nd year with New York, created nationwide excitement as he broke his previous MLB single season home run record of 29 by hitting 54, an unimaginable figure.

Michigan could not get enough of their Tigers.

1946 – 1950 Class Sticks Out All Over Mister Greenberg; Kell is Swell

Whitey Kurowski, Max Lanier
Eddie Waitkus and Johnny Vandermeer
Bob Estalella
Van Lingle Mungo

Augie Bergamo, Sigmund Jakucki
Big Johnny Mize and Barney McCosky
Hal Trosky

("Van Lingle Mungo" by Dave Frishberg)

25 games into 1946, two of the most popular players in the history of the Detroit Tigers were traded for each other: the Tigers sent centerfielder Barney McCosky to the Philadelphia Athletics for 3rd baseman George Kell. In Barney's first 4 years in the majors, from his Detroit rookie season of 1939 through 1942, McCosky was nothing short of sensational, hitting .316, averaging 99 runs scored annually, frequently turning opposing hitters' triples into long outs while patrolling center, and in each season receiving MVP consideration. But after 3 years away from the game while serving our country, Barney was a little rusty coming out of the gates in '46, turning an ankle that slowed him on the bases, averaging .198 in his first 25 games. Factoring in his batting fall off, the promise shown by young Tiger outfielders Dick Wakefield, Pat Mullin & Hoot Evers, and the need to upgrade 3rd base, Detroit General Manager George Trautman sent Barney packing to the A's.

How is it possible that the Detroit schoolboy sensation, the player favorably compared to Ty Cobb in his athleticism, speed & style, admired and liked by all... how is it possible that Barney McCosky is gone?

The man the Tigers received for Barney was 23-year old George Kell, 6 years younger than McCosky, and a .270 hitter in his two full seasons. Initially, it appeared that the Tigers were snookered in this swap, yet both teams & their fans had to be happy with the production each squad received from 1946-1948...

Barney got healthy and caught fire with Philadelphia the balance of '46, hitting .354 in 92 games, looking like the McCosky of before the war, finishing the year at .318, Detroit & Philly combined. For an encore, Barney hit .328 in '47 – battling Ted Williams all year long for the batting title before finishing 2nd – and then .326 in 1948. George Kell had been hitting .299 in 26 games with the A's at the beginning of '46, and improved on that by batting .327 in 105 games with the Tigers, for a full year .322. In '47 & '48, Kell hit .320 & .304, respectively.

But it was after 1948 that the trade leaned heavily to the Tigers advantage.

DDDDDDDDDDDDDDDDDDDDDDDDDDDDDDDDDDDDDDDDDDDDDDDDDDDDDDDDDDDDDDDDDDDDDDDDDDDDDDDDD

The day that Detroit traded Barney McCosky, they just won their 8th consecutive game, 6-5 over the White Sox, as Hal Newhouser improved his record to 5 & 1, the Tigers now 15 & 10, 6 & ½ games back of first place Boston, 1 back of the second place Yankees. There was a noticeable lack of respect for Hal's back-to-back MVPs of '44 & '45 since they were earned with the game's best players away serving our country, and he faced many classified as 4F, or either too young or old to serve. Hal's '46 performance against the top players back from the service let those doubters know that Newhouser was a terror for any hitters at any time, his 26 wins, versus 9 losses, and 1.94 ERA tops in the league. When the Most Valuable Player voting was complete, only Ted Williams stood in Hal's way of a third consecutive award.

The balance of the pitching staff was strong, with Dizzy Trout having another fine season at 17 & 13 including 5 shutouts and a 2.34 ERA. Virgil Trucks followed up his significant late-season '45 showing with a 14 & 9 record and a 3.23 ERA. Rounding out the starting staff was Freddie Hutchinson. Freddie was 3 & 6 as a 19-year old in 1939 for Detroit, and 3 & 7 as a 20-year old. After spending '41 in the minors and '42 – '45 in military duty, the 26-year old blossomed in '46, going 14 & 11 with a 3.09 ERA. The elder of the crew, 35-year young Al Benton, started 15 games, relieved 13 times, & spun an 11 & 7 record with a 3.65 ERA.

The fans in '46 may have been more excited about Dick Wakefield's return from military service than any other aspect of the upcoming season. His last action as a Tiger was in 1944, curtailed to one-half of the season by his time in the Navy, when Dick hit .355 with 12 homers, 53 RBIs, and a .576 slugging percentage. Naval duty took him away for all of 1945, and his '46 return was hampered by a broken wrist & arm that cost Wakefield 50 games, his .268 average representing an 87 point drop & while Dick's slugging percentage plunged to .412.

The big bat of Rudy York had been traded before 1946 to the Red Sox for shortstop and Detroit's new lead-off man, Eddie Lake. Eddie knew how to draw a walk, and led the league with a .412 on base percentage in 1945 with Boston. Despite his '46 average dropping 25 points to .254, his 103 base-on-balls for Detroit got him into scoring position often enough to score 108 times, 3rd in the A.L.

The offensive load was carried by Greenberg, Roy Cullenbine & newcomer George Kell. Hank's first full year since 1940 showed that the 35-year old was not slowing down, as he led the league with 44 home runs & 127 RBIs, with only Ted Williams ahead of Hank in total bases & slugging percentage. With seven outfielders returning from the service this year, Cullenbine didn't figure to be more than part-time 'til injuries moved him into the everyday starting line-up at the beginning of July, to Detroit's good fortune. On the 4th of July in front of 51,503, the Tigers hosted Cleveland in a doubleheader, Roy entering the day batting .196. In the two games combined, he hit 3 home runs while working Tribe pitchers for 2 walks (in his career, Roy walked in 17.8% of his plate appearances, #7 in MLB history). On July 5, he hit a 3-run shot in the 7th that proved to be the winning margin in a 7-5 Tiger win. From July 4 through the final '46 game of September 29, Roy Cullenbine was tops in the league with a .391 batting average, an amazing .530 on base percentage, & a .620 slugging percentage.

With pitching and run production among the major's best, the Tigers played .600 ball, but that was not enough in 1946. Although the Tigers won 4 more games than in their World Championship 1945 season, 92 & 62 was only good for 2nd place, 12 games back of the 104-win Boston Red Sox. The Sox were led by MVP Ted Williams who, after missing all of '43 – '45, hit .342 and was #1 in the league in walks, runs, OBP, & slugging percentage, with a supporting cast of shortstop Johnny Pesky's .335, centerfielder Dom DiMaggio's .316, plus 1st baseman & ex-Tiger Rudy York's 119 RBIs and 2nd bagger Bobby Doerr's 116 RBIs; Boston's pitching featured a 1-2 punch of 25 wins from Dave Ferriss & 20 from Tex Hughson.

Though 12 games out of first in 1946, the Tigers 92 wins, driven by an explosive offense & an excellent, young pitching staff, had the team, management, and the fans excited about the upcoming 1947 season.

And then Walter Briggs made a foolish decision in a shameful way.

DD

The January 1, 1947 edition of the *Sporting News* opened with this headline, *"Hank Hints He'd Like to End Career as Yankee"*, and included a photo of Hank in a New York Yankee uniform. The only problem was that Henry Benjamin Greenberg never said such a thing. Tiger owner Walter Briggs saw the article, let his temper get the better of him, and directed new G.M. Billy Evans to send Hank packing – but to a National League team where Hank could not hurt the Tigers. The impulsive Briggs never bothered to ask Hank or the *Sporting News* about either the quote or about the photo, a photo that was 5 years old and taken during a war-time benefit game, the New York uniform the only one big enough to fit the 6'4", 215-pound, Greenberg.

On January 18, Hank Greenberg, a Tiger through & through, with the organization since he was a teen in 1930, beloved by fans, a leader on 4 pennant winners & 2 World Series Champions, the first MLB player to leave the game to defend our country, who upon his return in 1945 hit a homer in his first game back in 4 years, then hit a grand slam on the final day of the '45 season to win the pennant for Detroit, just two out of countless highlight moments as a Tiger, one of the greatest players in major league history, *found out while listening to the radio* that his Detroit Tigers had sold him to the Pittsburgh Pirates. At the very least, Walter Briggs owed Hank Greenberg a face-to-face meeting to inform him of the decision.

The headline of the *Detroit Free Press* announced the news to stunned Tiger fans, *"Greenberg Sold To Pirates"*. Nobody could believe it after all Hank had done wearing the Olde English D. Disbelief, pain, trauma, shock, & devastation were the emotions that ran though not only the fans, but also Hank's teammates: Hal Newhouser said he'd lost a friend; Virgil Trucks felt Briggs let his pride hurt the team.

The Detroit Tigers became the first team in major league history to release outright the reigning home run king. *The New York Times* Jimmy Powers wrote, *"It all adds up to a mighty flimsy excuse for the callous canning of one of the greatest sluggers of our time."* Joe Williams of the *World-Telegram* perhaps best captured the fans' sentiments, *"It is undoubtedly a tribute to the tolerance of people that Walter O. Briggs, owner of the Detroit club, plainly a man with a dark heart, was not measured for a tight-fitting collar."*

Even when Hank was away in the military from 1941 to 1945, he was our Hank serving our country while representing our Tigers. Hank was shocked. *"I left Detroit with a very harsh, bitter taste in my mouth."*

DDDDDDDDDDDDDDDDDDDDDDDDDDDDDDDDDDDDDDDDDDDDDDDDDDDDDDDDDDDDDDDDDDDDDDDDDDDD

As they did in 1946, the 1947 Tigers finished in 2nd, 12 games back of, this year, the Yankees. What did change was the number of people passing through the turnstiles at The Corner, 300,000 less than in 1946. Much of the decline in turnout was attributed to how upset the fans were at the treatment shown their hero, Hank Greenberg. And, that 300,000-drop took place with the Tigers in first place most of the first half of the '47 season, a position that they only held for two days in '46. The 1947 team led the pack from May 10 to June 10, followed by a 10-game losing skid that dropped Detroit to 7 out on June 23rd. They were never a factor the rest of the way.

It was during Detroit's time in 1st place that the first-ever televised Tiger game took place, a Tuesday afternoon clash versus New York on June 3, 1947. Unfortunately, what viewers got to see was a 3-0 loss. Fortunately, this sad news was transmitted to a limited market, as in '47 there were approximately only 2,000 TV sets in the Detroit area.

After the Tigers traded Rudy York in the '46 pre-season, Greenberg moved back from left-field to his old position at first base. In '47, with Hank wearing a Pirates uniform, Roy Cullenbine took over at first. Roy made up for some of the power lost with Hank's departure, hitting a career-high 24 homers, good for 4th in the A.L. Although he only hit .224, Cullenbine worked pitchers for 137 base-on-balls, the all-time Tiger record, including walking in 22 consecutive games, a MLB record. All those free passes allowed Roy to chalk up a league third .401 on base percentage. 24-year old George Kell made his first All-Star team, the only Tiger to hit over .300, his .320 good for 5th in the A.L., while #2 with 188 hits, to go along with 93 RBIs.

Hal Newhouser was once again among the elite pitchers in the A.L., tops in complete games, second in strikeouts & innings pitched, and fifth with a 2.87 ERA. Although he won 17 times, he also lost that many, indicative of his poor run support, the most losses for any league hurler. Freddie Hutchinson had a career-high 18 wins against 10 losses and a fine 3.03 ERA, while Stubby Overmire posted the best winning percentage of his career, going 11 & 5 with a 3.77 ERA.

DDDDDDDDDDDDDDDDDDDDDDDDDDDDDDDDDDDDDDDDDDDDDDDDDDDDDDDDDDDDDDDDDDDDDDDDDD

One of the 1947 highlights was a 4-game weekend series kicking off July 18 at The Corner with the Yankees. Although 2nd place Detroit had been playing great, winning 15 of their last 20, New York hit town looking for their 20th consecutive victory. On the mound for the Friday opener was Freddie Hutchinson. Often overlooked, at least by those on the outside, on a pitching staff loaded with Hal Newhouser, Dizzy Trout, and Virgil Trucks, Hutch was counted on in many crucial games. Today was one of those. Previously on the shelf from a bad shoulder, it was Freddie's first game in a month. Manager Steve O'Neill hoped his pitcher would not be rusty. He needn't have worried.

A pitcher must record 27 outs in a 9-inning game. Today, Hutchinson faced 1 batter over that minimum, surrendering only two singles (erasing one on a double play), striking out 8, and walking none. Hutch, a .263 lifetime hitter, often called on to pinch hit, also went 3 for 4 and knocked in two runs. There would be no American-League-record 20th consecutive win for the Yankees today, as Hutch only needed 1 hour & 43 minutes to complete his domination of the men in pinstripes: final score 8 to nothing. On a pitching staff of stars, Manager O'Neill said, *"If I needed one game upon which my whole season was based, if my career depended on that one victory, I'd pick Hutch to pitch it for me."*

Game 2 of the 4-gamer resulted in a tough 2-1 loss for the Tigers, Allie Reynolds out-dueling Dizzy Trout. Freddie Hutchinson pinch hit for Dizzy to start the Tigers ninth, but his long fly ball was tracked down by center fielder Joe DiMaggio in front of the stands.

The Sunday, July 20, doubleheader versus the Yankees was one for the books. The sale of standing-room-only tickets enabled *58,369 fans, the largest crowd to ever attend a game at The Corner*, to get in the park to cheer on their Boys of Summer. Even the third level press box took in people, and hundreds stood behind ropes strung in the outfield. Hal Newhouser was brilliant in game one, limiting the first-place Bronx Bombers to 3 hits in a 4-1 Tiger win. Game 2 was a wild affair featuring 6 lead changes, with starting pitchers Stubby Overmire & New York's Joe Page both gone by the fourth inning. In the fifth, the Tigers erased a 4-3 Yankee lead when Roy Cullenbine walked, one of his 5 base-on-balls today, & scored on a double by Dick Wakefield, who then came home on a single off the bat of rookie right-fielder Vic Wertz. In the next frame, the Yanks torched two of the finest hurlers in Tiger history, Virgil Trucks & Al Benton, for 7 runs to retake the lead, 11-5. A Pat Mullin 2-run shot in the sixth closed the gap to 11-7, and that's where things stood as the Detroiters came up to bat in the bottom of the ninth.

Pinch hitter John McHale led off with a single (his son, John McHale Jr., was Tiger President from 1995 to 2001). An Eddie Lake single was followed by a Cullenbine 3-run homer, bringing the Tigers within one & their fans to hysteria. Before New York could get the third Tiger out, Eddie Mayo walked with the bases loaded, forcing in the tying run, and sending the contest to extra innings. In the 11th, it was Eddie Mayo-time once again, as Hoot Evers came flying around from first on Eddie's game-winning double, sending 58,000 screaming with delight into the night.

It was an evening that Detroit native and 19-year old Tiger pitcher, Art Houtteman, would never forget. Art came into game 2 to start the 10th inning, and held the Yankees hitless in the 10th and the 11th to earn this future All-Star's first major league victory.

DDDDDDDDDDDDDDDDDDDDDDDDDDDDDDDDDDDDDDDDDDDDDDDDDDDDDDDDDDDDDDDDDDDDDDDDDDDDDDDDD

After a visit with his old friend, Babe Ruth, Hank Greenberg arrived at the 1947 training camp of his new team, the Pittsburgh Pirates. Pirate owner John Galbraith signed Hank to a contract that made him MLB's first player to earn $100,000 in a single season. Hank promised Galbraith that he'd hit 25 homers for the team this year. The Pirates helped out by moving the bullpen in front of the remote left field fence, shortening the distance for a home run to travel, christening the bullpen "Greenberg Gardens".

Hammerin' Hank's greatest contribution to the Pittsburgh club was the impact that he had as an unofficial hitting instructor to outfielder Ralph Kiner. He saw great power potential in Ralph, and worked with him constantly, getting Kiner to move closer to the plate, to study pitchers and what they like to throw in what situations, become more selective in what he swung at, improve the balance of his stance, and emphasized the need to work daily on all of these suggestions. Kiner said, *"It was sort of an advanced course in calculus. He was the most astute student of hitting I ever knew. Hank Greenberg was the single greatest influence on my baseball career and adult life. I remember him not as a man who taught me how to play, but as a man who showed me how to live."*

In Ralph Kiner's 1946 rookie year, although he led the National League with 23 home runs (while then Tiger Hank led the A.L. and the majors with 44), his 109 strikeouts also led the league. When the Pirates were going to send Kiner down to the minors for more seasoning at the beginning of '47, Greenberg asked for a meeting with team management, outlining his case for why Kiner should stay with the parent club, and bet the team president a new suit that Ralph would knock in 100 runs. The Pirates agreed to keep Kiner on the club, and never regretted it. Hank's star pupil hit so many balls into the leftfield seats of Greenberg Gardens that they were renamed *Kiner's Korner*. Ralph cut down on his whiffs by 25% while increasing his homer total to 51, again tops in the N.L., boosted his RBIs from 81 to 127, earning Hank a new suit, and his average rose from .247 to .313. Kiner learned his lessons so well, he was the National League home run king every year from 1946 to 1952, making the All-Star team annually from '48 thru '52. General Manager Roy Hamey said, *"Even if Hank Greenberg doesn't hit another home run, he'll be worth his salary for what he has done with Ralph Kiner."*

DDDDDDDDDDDDDDDDDDDDDDDDDDDDDDDDDDDDDDDDDDDDDDDDDDDDDDDDDDDDDDDDDDDDDDDDDDD

Aside from the fantastic job teacher Hank did with Ralph Kiner, the 1947 season was a rough one for Greenberg. He dealt with chronic back pain & bone chips in his elbow – and a base path collision with rookie Jackie Robinson. When Jackie broke the color barrier in 1947, and verbal abuse poured down on him from fans and players, he had a great deal of empathy from Hank Greenberg, who experienced similar prejudice for his Jewish faith. The collision between Jackie and Hank was painful, but historic.

The date was May 17, 1947, the place Forbes Field. It was the finale of a 3-game series between the host Pirates and the Brooklyn Dodgers and their first baseman, Jackie Robinson. It was barely one month into the integration of the game, and emotions were running high, the possibility of an on-field incident that would lead to trouble always just below the surface.

In the fourth inning, Jackie laid down a bunt that was fielded by the pitcher. His throw to Hank at first was off the mark, and drew Greenberg into the path of the on-coming Robinson. Jackie crashed into Hank and the two went sprawling, before Jackie bounced up and ran to 2nd. When Hank drew a base-on-balls the next half-inning, he spoke with Jackie, the Dodgers first baseman, *"Hope I didn't hurt you Jackie. I tried to keep out of your way, but it was impossible."* Jackie assured him he was fine. Hank continued, *"Listen, I know it's plenty tough. You're a good ballplayer, however, and you'll do alright. Just stay in there and fight back. Always remember to keep your head up."* Jackie Robinson said that Hank's comments meant a great deal to him, *"Class tells. It sticks out all over Mister Greenberg."*

In the next day's *Pittsburgh Courier*, sportswriter Wendell Clark wrote, *"If this incident had involved anyone other than Hank Greenberg, there would have been a riot."*

DDDDDDDDDDDDDDDDDDDDDDDDDDDDDDDDDDDDDDDDDDDDDDDDDDDDDDDDDDDDDDDDDDDDDDDDDDD

Hank had a number of game-winning home runs for the Pirates, just like in the old days with Detroit, and never stopped playing hard, but was falling short of the high bar he had always set for himself. No one worked harder and, just like in Detroit, he was the first one at the ball park and the last to leave. And, just like in Detroit, he was the best clutch hitter in the Pittsburgh line-up – and that included his star pupil, Ralph Kiner. Hank had a real problem picking up the ball in night games, 25% of all Pirate games in '47, something he never had to deal with in Detroit (the first night game at The Corner took place in 1948), and hit only .198 under the lights. Finally, Hank adjusted to the artificial lighting, began to get a feel for National League pitchers, and had a great August, kicking it off with 3 homers in one game and averaging well over .300 for the month. Overall, though, 1947 did not meet Hank's high standards, and he announced that the final Pirate game of 1947 would be his last as a player.

Greenberg did hit the 25 home runs he'd promised the Pirate owner, but that was the lowest in a full year in Hank's career. Injuries limited him to 402 at bats, and he only hit .249, another career low, but he did post a fine .408 on base percentage as he worked the National League hurlers for a league high 104 walks. Although the Pirates year-to-year record stayed basically the same, 63 & 91 to 62 & 92, Hank's presence was the key in driving attendance from 749,962 in '46 to 1,283,531. At the season's conclusion, the editor of the *Pittsburgh Sun-Telegraph* spoke for the team and the majority of their followers, crediting Hank's high moral character, his work with Kiner, and the increased attendance, *"Hank came in modestly amid the greatest fanfare for any player in the Pirates' history, and he's going out the same way, a man of quality and substance. Even at his great cost and tremendous salary, he was the Pirates' biggest bargain."*

In 1986, Ralph Kiner was in the broadcast booth for a New York Mets' game when he was handed a note that read, *Hank Greenberg died today.* Ralph told his listeners, *"I've just received the saddest news I could possibly have heard,"* and shared with the audience the word of Hank's passing before adding, *"Hank Greenberg made me a mensch."* (i.e., a person of honor & integrity).

DDDDDDDDDDDDDDDDDDDDDDDDDDDDDDDDDDDDDDDDDDDDDDDDDDDDDDDDDDDDDDDDDDDDDDDDDDDD

At the conclusion of 1947, Detroit sold Roy Cullenbine to the Philadelphia Phillies. Roy never played a game for Philly, as he lost his spot on the roster to a young man who exploded on to the scene and a future Hall of Famer, 21-year old Richie Ashburn. Roy then retired from the game, later scouting for the Tigers in the 50s, returning one last time to the playing field at The Corner when he was invited by the Tigers to the 1980 retirement ceremony of Al Kaline's number 6.

DDDDDDDDDDDDDDDDDDDDDDDDDDDDDDDDDDDDDDDDDDDDDDDDDDDDDDDDDDDDDDDDDDDDDDDDDDDD

On June 15, 1948, before a packed house of 54,480 at The Corner, the Detroit Tigers played their first night home game. Walter O. Briggs was not a believer, stating *"baseball belongs to the sun and the sun to baseball,"* and fought the decision for years. But the tide for night baseball was too strong, and now with only the Tigers and the Cubs holding out – the Cubs for another 40 years – Briggs approved artificial lighting for his gorgeous ballyard. Installed for this historic occasion were 8 steel edifices, each towering 150' above the playing field, supporting 1,458 incandescent bulbs.

The Philadelphia Athletics & old fan favorite Barney McCosky were the opponent on this special evening, the honor to pitch for Detroit going to Prince Hal Newhouser. After Hal surrendered a run-scoring double in the first and a harmless single in the second, he no-hit the Athletics the rest of the way. On the mound for Philadelphia was All-Star Joe Coleman, father of the Joe Coleman who won 86 games while pitching for Detroit in the 5 years from 1971-1975.

After getting the first two Tigers out in the third, Coleman had problems locating home plate, walking Eddie Lake, George Kell, & Dick Wakefield in succession. Before he could get out number 3, Hoot Evers singled in Lake & Kell for a 2-1 Detroit lead. From there, Newhouser & Coleman dueled on even terms into the Tigers 8th, when Wakefield cracked a long fly towards Philly's left-fielder, Barney McCosky. Barney made a mad dash for the ball until the concrete wall stopped him dead in his tracks, the sphere sailing over his head and into the stands for a home run. After slamming into the wall, Barney tripped on the wooden frame holding the tarp, at the wall's base, twisting his back and hit the ground hard.

Athletics center-fielder Sam Chapman sprinted over to check on the prone McCosky. Barney had a plug of tobacco in his cheek, and asked Sam to pull out the chew. Chapman did as asked moments before McCosky passed-out and was then carried from the field on a stretcher. Taking this pounding sparked something in Barney. He was hitting .265 at the time of the injury, returned 9 days later, and hit .355 in the last 3 months of 1948, ending the season fifth in the league with a .326 batting average.

Two batters after Dick Wakefield's homer & Barney McCosky's injury, Pat Mullin touched Joe Coleman for another solo shot, putting Detroit up 4-1 going into the ninth. With all 54,000 on their feet, Prince Hal put the A's down 1-2-3 as Detroit won the first night contest ever played at Briggs Stadium.

DDDDDDDDDDDDDDDDDDDDDDDDDDDDDDDDDDDDDDDDDDDDDDDDDDDDDDDDDDDDDDDDDDDDDDD

The June 15 night game victory improved the Tigers record to 27 & 25, keeping them in fourth place, 7 games behind first place Cleveland. Detroit won one game for every one that they lost the rest of the way, ending at 78 & 76 and in fifth place, 18 games out of first. Boston & Cleveland finished the regular season tied for first, both 96 & 58, forcing a one-game playoff to determine the '48 American League pennant winner, the game won 8-3 by Cleveland. The Indians went on to defeat the Boston Braves in the World Series, 4 games to 2, Cleveland's most recent World Series Championship. They were led by player-manager & All-Star shortstop Lou Boudreau's regular season .355 average and a pitching troika of Bob Feller, Gene Bearden, & Bob Lemon.

Hal Newhouser was once again the Tiger ace, leading all league hurlers with 21 victories, and near the top with 19 complete games, 143 strikeouts, and a 3.01 ERA. At age 27, he made his 6th & last All-Star team. 20-year old Tiger Art Houtteman, on the heels of a wonderful 7 & 2/3.42 ERA in '47, had a year he'd like to erase from his memory, going 2 & 16, but with a really-not-that-bad 4.66 and 10 saves. In fact, during the following season, the contending Tigers would've killed for a reliever with 10 saves.

In his first full season wearing the Olde English D, shortstop Johnny Lipon had a fine all-around year while hitting .290. Center-fielder Hoot Evers had a breakout season, earning his first of two All-Star berths (homering in the Midsummer Classic) and finished 1948 at .314 with 103 RBIs. Hoot was fast becoming a fan favorite, and when he came up to bat, the cries of "Hoooooooot!" echoed through the Briggs Stadium stands. Born Walter Evers, as a child he loved TV cowboy Hoot Gibson, and soon everyone knew Walter Evers as Hoot.

1948 was the most difficult season of George Kell's career. Although he was named to the American League All-Star team for the 2nd consecutive time, he suffered two injuries that limited him to 92 games. The first came in a May 8 doubleheader at Yankee Stadium when a pitch from Vic Raschi broke Kell's wrist, sidelining George the rest of the month. The second took place August 29, once again at the Den of Iniquity in the Bronx, when a grounder off the bat of Joe DiMaggio took a funny hop & fractured Kell's jaw, ending his season.

Much better things were in store for George Clyde Kell in 1949.

DDDDDDDDDDDDDDDDDDDDDDDDDDDDDDDDDDDDDDDDDDDDDDDDDDDDDDDDDDDDDDDDDDDDDDD

Sunny skies and 56 degrees greeted the 53,435 fans who flocked to The Corner for Opening Day 1949. For the fifth year in a row, Hal Newhouser would have the honor of pitching the opener, this year versus the Chicago White Sox. His was a dominant performance, limiting the Sox to 3 hits, and needing only 95 minutes to secure Detroit's 5 to 1 victory.

The game introduced a couple of new players to Tiger fans…

Rookie center-fielder Johnny Groth wowed the crowd with his speed and his power, doing his best Kirk Gibson impression 30 years early, hitting an inside-the-park home run in the fifth, and blasting one deep into the left-field stands in the seventh. Tiger fans got a sneak preview of Johnny late the year before when, called up after lighting up the International League as a Buffalo Bison with a .340 average, he went 8 for 17 with Detroit including a 2-run homer. After Groth's two '49 Opener home runs, he hit another the next day, and going into May was batting .449. His start was a national phenomenon, and articles soon appeared in *Time, Saturday Evening Post, Life, Newsweek,* and *Colliers,* with way too many over-the-top comparisons to Joe DiMaggio. A severe slump dropped his average to .254, prompting new manager Red Rolfe to sit the kid down a few days and allow things to settle a bit. When Groth was re-inserted into the line-up, he was rejuvenated and looked like he did back in April. Only a late-August, season-ending injury stopped him short of winning the Rookie-of-the-Year award, finishing fourth. In 103 games in 1949, Groth hit .293 & walked 65 times for a sweet on-base percentage of .407, hit 11 homers, and drove in 73 runs.

33-year old catcher Aaron Robinson made his Tiger debut a memorable one, smashing a 2-run homer in the second inning of the Opener to break a scoreless tie and send Detroit on their victorious way. In 110 games in '49, Robinson hit .269 with 13 homers. His numbers declined in '50 & he was waived in August of '51. Aaron Robinson was acquired from the White Sox in November of '48, costing the Tigers a 21-year old pitcher who went 3 & 0 for Detroit in '48, his first full year with the team, but with a bloated 6.34 ERA. That young Detroit native's name was Billy Pierce. Billy was immediately inserted into the Sox starting rotation, going 7 & 15 in year one & then 12 & 16 in year two, before his 15 & 14/3.03 ERA breakout year of 1951. Pierce made the A.L. All-Star team in 1953 and would be so honored 7 times total, was the league ERA champ in '55 at 1.97, was voted *The Sporting News* MLB pitcher of the year in '56 & '57 (20 wins in both), and from '50 through '61 never won less than 10 games in a season as a Chicago White Sox pitcher.

On November 10, 1948, when the Tigers sent pitcher Billy Pierce to the Chicago White Sox for catcher Aaron Robinson, it was one of the worst trades in the history of major league baseball. And that does not include the fact that Detroit threw in an extra $10,000 to Chicago along with Pierce.

DDDDDDDDDDDDDDDDDDDDDDDDDDDDDDDDDDDDDDDDDDDDDDDDDDDDDDDDDDDDDDDDDDDDDDD

In a preview of what was to come in 1949, George Kell hit a sizzling line single to knock in the final run of Detroit's Opening Day victory.

George Kell's ball playin' genes were handed down to him from his Daddy. From his home in Imboden, Arkansas, Papa Clyde Kell was an occasional pitcher for the team down in Swifton, 35 miles to the south. Clyde made such an impact on the success of the Swifton team when he was on the mound for them, the town made him an offer: if Clyde would move to Swifton, and pitch for them all the time, they'd buy him the barber shop in town to call his own. Clyde Kell accepted the offer, moved to Swifton, Arkansas, pitched for the town folk, cut their hair, married his sweetheart Alma, and on August 23, 1922, their first child was born, George Clyde Kell.

George grew up as a fan of the St. Louis Cardinals, the nearest major league team to Swifton, located four hours away. George would've been a 12-year old rooting against the Tigers in the 1934 World Series, but in another dozen years he'd be wearing the Olde English D and would never make that mistake again. By the time George became a Tiger in May of '46, he had only played two full seasons in the big leagues, but was already considered the finest fielding third baseman in the game. In those first two years in Philadelphia, he had compiled a modest .270 batting average, and was hitting .299 in the first 26 games of 1946 before the trade.

Playing for the Athletics in Philly's Shibe Park, George was used to plying his trade before 8,000 fans on any given day. Kell's debut with the Tigers took place Sunday, May 19, in front of 57,130 at The Corner, the Tigers hosting the league-leading Boston Red Sox. Years later, Kell shared his recollections of that day with reporter Bill Dow, *"I was scared to death. In the first inning, Johnny Pesky slashed one down third base, I made a backhand stab and threw him out, which really calmed me down. I was young, full of enthusiasm, played hard, and the Detroit fans accepted me and were so good. It was the beginning of a great romance."* George loved hitting in the gorgeous, green park, picking up two hits on that May 19 day on his way to averaging .327 the last 105 games of 1946. Between his 26 games with Philadelphia and 105 with Detroit, he hit a fourth best in the American League .322.

In '47, his .320 was good for an A.L. fifth. Injuries slowed him to a still-pretty-good .304 in 92 games for 1948. George was completely healthy when the bell rang for 1949.

At the 1949 All-Star break, the Tigers were 10 & ½ behind the 1st place Yankees. They hovered between 8 and 11 out until late-August when they started an 18 & 2 run, concluded on September 11 with a Virgil Trucks 3-hit shutout that brought the Tigers within 5 games of New York. While the battle for the flag raged on, George Kell & Boston's Ted Williams season-long battle was reaching its pinnacle.

DDDDDDDDDDDDDDDDDDDDDDDDDDDDDDDDDDDDDDDDDDDDDDDDDDDDDDDDDDDDDDDDDDDDDDDDDDDD

Going into 1949, Teddy Baseball had won the two previous batting titles and 4 overall. George Kell had never won a batting title, but was a hitter reaching his prime. Ted hit .306 in April, .343 in May, .304 in

June, and at the July 12 All-Star break, he was at .325. George hit .348 in April, .330 in May, .392 in June, and at the All-Star break was hitting .345. The race was on.

Ted was a ball 'a fire in July & August, raising his average to .356 going into September. Kell continued his first half pace, and entered September at .344. Both sluggers slowed down in September, Williams hitting .279, Kell with a broken thumb that cost him 7 games. With 10 games remaining and George still out with his injury, Ted held a 10-point lead in the race. Kell's thumb healed in time for him to play on September 23, and on his first trip to the plate, he lined a single to left off of Early Wynn, singling to right his next time up, too. With 5 games remaining, it was Ted up .349 to .342. Going into the final game of the season, the gap had closed to .344 versus .341.

On October 2, the last game of the 1949 season, Boston was playing at Yankee Stadium. These two teams had more on the line than deciding a batting champion – they were tied for first, and the winner of the game would be headed to the World Series. Ted Williams, facing 20-game winner Vic Raschi, was walked twice and went hitless in his other two at bats, as the Yankees won 5 to 3. Ted's final batting average was .3427.

That same day at The Corner, 51,714 had come out to cheer on George Kell's quest for the batting crown. It was Detroit vs. Cleveland, with the Tribe's Bob Lemon, a 22-game winner, on the hill, a man always tough on Kell. George, though, thrilled the crowd, hitting bullets off Lemon his first two times up, a double to centerfield in the first inning, and then a single to left in the third. When Kell led off the Tigers' sixth, Lemon walked him, the start of a 4-run rally that tied the game at 4 apiece. In the bottom of the 7th, with Kell scheduled to bat 2nd, the great Bob Feller was now on the mound. *"Facing Feller"*, Kell said, *"was as much fun as getting a tooth pulled without pain killer."* When George flew out to left-field, a moan rose from the crowd.

Before the Tigers came up to bat in the ninth, with George due up fourth, Tigers P.R. man, Lyall Smith, called down to the Tiger dugout to tell manager Red Rolfe the news that Ted Williams had gone 0 for 2 against the Yankees, that Kell was now ahead of Williams in the batting race, and that if George didn't bat again, he would win the batting title. Bob Feller got lead-off man Johnny Lipon on a grounder to 3rd. Dick Wakefield was the next batter, and he singled. Eddie Lake stepped into the batter's box and, to the roar of the 51,000, George Kell walked to the on-deck circle. Not one of those 51,000 knew what, today, every fan in the ballpark would know from their or their neighbor's smart phone: Kell was now ahead of Teddy Baseball, and guaranteed to win the batting title *if he did not bat again*.

As Feller was getting ready to pitch to Lake, back-up catcher Joe Ginsberg was shouting to Kell from the dugout, letting him know that Manager Rolfe wanted Ginsberg to pinch hit for George, in order to secure the crown for Kell. Joe Ginsberg was in the minors for almost the entire season and had no at bats with the Tigers in his brief stay with them in '49. Although the 23-year old Ginsberg would go on to play 11 more major league seasons, batting for George Kell at this point in the race for the batting title – heck, batting for George Kell at ANY time – would've been the highlight of his career.

As George Kell turned to hear Ginsberg's shouts, he now knew that the two hits he had off Bob Lemon had put him over the top. George also knew that, 8 years earlier, Ted Williams did not sit out when he entered the final day of the 1941 season batting .400. At the start of that day in '41, Ted's average sat at .399955, which would have rounded up to .400 if he decided to sit out the season-ending doubleheader.

There was never a doubt that Ted would play, telling his manager, *"I want to have more than my toe nails on the line,"* and being Ted Williams, he went 6 for 8 to finish 1941 at .406.

George Kell waved off his manager and the option of a pinch hitter. Sorry Joe Ginsberg. George Kell wasn't about to back into a batting title over Ted Williams. As George waited his turn to bat, Eddie Lake hit a sharp grounder to short for a tailor-made double play to end the game. When George jubilantly tossed his bat into the air, no smart phones were needed for the crowd to know that their Tiger was the league's new hitting champion. Briggs Stadium vibrated from the cheers and shouts of joy for George.

The Great 1949 Batting Title Race ended George Kell .3429, Ted Williams .3427.

DDDDDDDDDDDDDDDDDDDDDDDDDDDDDDDDDDDDDDDDDDDDDDDDDDDDDDDDDDDDDDDDDDDDDDDDD

On June 13, 1949, a ceremony at Cooperstown was held to induct Charlie Gehringer into baseball's Hall of Fame, but Charlie was not there. He was back in Michigan preparing to marry his Josephine in 5 days, saying he did not want to travel to Cooperstown and distract from the wedding. Gehringer was 46 on his wedding day, explaining he married late in life to care for his mother, a diabetic, because *"I couldn't see bringing a wife into that kind of situation."* Charlie would only consider courting and marrying a woman after his mother passed.

Charlie is the only living Hall of Fame inductee not present for his induction. From the day Charlie & Jo married, they attended every Tiger Opening Day &, ironically, every Hall of Fame induction ceremony.

DDDDDDDDDDDDDDDDDDDDDDDDDDDDDDDDDDDDDDDDDDDDDDDDDDDDDDDDDDDDDDDDDDDDDDDDD

The 18 & 2 hot streak that brought the Tigers within 5 games of New York in mid-September of '49 would be the team's high-water mark as Detroit finished 10 games back.

At year's end, the American League standings read: 1st New York 97 & 57, 2nd Boston 96 & 58, 3rd Cleveland 89 & 65, and 4th Detroit 87 & 67.

Many factors go into who wins the pennant, but one that stands out was Detroit releasing Al Benton at the end of the prior season. The decision was understandable. They saw a 37-year old, two-time All-Star's numbers go south the last two seasons, in '47 6 & 7 with 7 saves/4.40 ERA & in '48 2 & 2 with 3 saves/5.68 ERA. The old horse had something yet left in the tank, though, & shined for the Tribe in 1949, going 9 & 6 with 10 saves while posting a sparkling 2.12 ERA. Oh, could we have used Benton in 1949.

The story of the 1949 bullpen was not an unfamiliar one to long-time Tiger fans...

The 1949 Tiger starting pitchers were excellent, the 5-man rotation of Virgil Trucks, Hal Newhouser, Art Houtteman, Fred Hutchinson, & Ted Gray posting an overall earned run average in the low 3s. But unless a starter went the full 9, Detroit was in trouble: the bullpen was a sieve, ace of the staff Trucks often pressed into service to bail them out, leading the team with 4 saves. Among pitchers whose main job was relief, Dizzy Trout was the best with 3 saves, a 3 & 6 record, and an ERA of 4.40. The other relievers with the most innings pitched had ERAs of 6.16, 6.41, 9.10 & 9.87 - and those 4 without a single save.

Al Benton played through the 1952 season, going 4 & 3 with 6 saves and a 2.39 ERA for the Boston Red Sox that year. Benton's first year was Babe Ruth's last full season, and Al's last season was Mickey Mantle's first: Al broke in as a 23-year old with the Philadelphia Athletics in 1934, Ruth's final year as a Yankee, and faced the Bambino a few times back then. 18 years later, in 1952, the 41-year old Benton pitched in several games against Yankee rookie Mickey Mantle, thus becoming the only major leaguer to pitch against both Babe Ruth AND Mickey Mantle.

DDDDDDDDDDDDDDDDDDDDDDDDDDDDDDDDDDDDDDDDDDDDDDDDDDDDDDDDDDDDDDDDDDDDDDDDDD

By 1949, the shine had dulled on Dick Wakefield's career. The rookie who exploded on the scene in 1943 with 200 hits and a .316 average, sunk to .206 as a part-time player. Once a favorite of both Mister & Missus Walter O. Briggs, Wakefield's activities in creation of the players' pension fund was something that Briggs might have been able to come to terms with by a player showing a "skies-the-limit" potential & batting over .300, but not a back-up struggling to hit .200. So, in December of '49, Dick Wakefield was traded to the Yankees for 1st baseman Dick Kryhoski.

For Detroit, Kryhoski played little in '50 then had a fine '51, hitting .287 as the Tigers starting first sacker. Wakefield played from 1950-1952 spent all but 6 games (3 as a Yankee in '50 then 3 as a Giant in '52) in the minor leagues before retiring, thus ending the career of major league baseball's first bonus baby.

DDDDDDDDDDDDDDDDDDDDDDDDDDDDDDDDDDDDDDDDDDDDDDDDDDDDDDDDDDDDDDDDDDDDDDDDDD

As Detroit prepared for the 1950 season, expectations were high. The young outfield of Groth, Evers, and Wertz excited everyone, in George Kell the Tigers had the reigning batting champ & best defensive third baseman in the game today, and the pitching staff was loaded. Among so many pitching stars in '49, one stood one – at age 32, Virgil Trucks took his game to a new level, going 19 & 11, a 2.81 ERA, tops in the A.L. with 6 shutouts & 153 strikeouts, and was the winning pitcher in his long-overdue first All-Star game. Virgil gave the credit to pitching coach Ted Lyons. Ted had a fantastic 21-year career pitching for the Chicago White Sox, even as a 41-year old in 1942 leading the league with a 2.10 ERA, and was as good a teacher as he was a player. Virgil said Lyons work with him to improve his slider and curveball was the key.

Their 1949 overall performance, including an 18 & 2 run at crunch time, gave the team the confidence that they could win it all in '50. They started well, winning the season opener in front of 65,744 in Cleveland. Fred Hutchinson was banged up for 4 early Tribe runs, Detroit rallying in the 8th to go up by 2, Cleveland coming right back in the bottom of the inning to tie it up at 6, before Johnny Lipon's sac fly in the 10th knocked in the winner. In the 2nd game of the short series, Tiger pitcher Ted Gray withstood Al Rosen's 2-run shot in the ninth to hold off Cleveland 5-4. That evening, the team took the train to Detroit for the next day's home opener.

44,642 came out to soak up the Opening Day ambiance and cheer on their Boys of Spring. Virgil Trucks was given the pitching honor against the visiting White Sox, and picked up right where he left off in '49. After giving up a run in the fourth, he held the Sox to two singles in the sixth and nothing more. Johnny Groth's solo shot off Mickey Haefner in the bottom of the 7th tied things up, and Vic Wertz 3-run blast in the 8th sent the folks streaming into the bars with smiles on their faces.

Detroit was clicking on all cylinders, their hitting, pitching, & defense outstanding. After sweeping a May 11 doubleheader at Fenway, the Tigers came home for two with the Brownies, sitting in first place at 12 & 5. In front of a May 13, Saturday crowd of 16,002, Virgil Trucks opened the series hooking up in a fine pitchers' duel with future Tiger Ned Garver, both hurlers throwing a shutout into the 11th inning. With two outs in the bottom of the inning, Johnny Lipon singled, moved 90' on a single by 2nd baseman Jerry Priddy, Kell was walked to load the bases, and Vic Wertz ended the game with his RBI single.

After the game, Virgil felt pain in his throwing arm for the first time in his career. He went back out for his next scheduled start on May 18, and didn't make it out of the third, getting knocked around for 3 early runs, the pain still present. Trucks left the team to consult a specialist, and the decision was made to shut down Virgil and his pulled tendon for the rest of the year. The injury cost the Tigers the man who had become the staff ace over the last year & a half, but the decision to shut down immediately may have saved the rest of Trucks career.

DDDDDDDDDDDDDDDDDDDDDDDDDDDDDDDDDDDDDDDDDDDDDDDDDDDDDDDDDDDDDDDDDDDDDDDD

Without Trucks for most of '50, the other hurlers picked up the slack, posting the 2nd best ERA in the league. Art Houtteman had a career year, leading the staff in wins and ERA at 19 & 13/3.54, tops in the A.L. with 4 shutouts, while earning a berth on the All-Star team. Freddie Hutchinson was #2 in the rotation, going 17 & 8/3.96. The men who were 1-2 for the MVP vote in 1944 showed a little of that old mojo as Hal Newhouser and Dizzy Trout posted numbers of 15 & 13/4.34 and 13 & 5/3.75, respectively. Ted Gray, in his 3rd full season wearing the D, rounded out the rotation quite nicely, making the All-Star team with a 10 & 7/4.40 record. The starters also performed spot relief duty, earning 12 of Detroit's 20 team saves.

The Tigers hit .282 as a team, the offense a powerhouse led by George Kell whose .340 average was second in the A.L., his 218 hits and 56 doubles both tops in the league. Kell's 114 runs & 101 RBIs were career-highs. The twenty-something kids in the outfield were fantastic: Johnny Groth, Hoot Evers, and Vic Wertz combined for 60 home runs & 311 RBIs while batting, respectively, .306, .323, & .308. The ability of all 3 to draw walks pushed their on base percentages to .407, .408, & .408. Shortstop Johnny Lipon had his finest season at the plate at .293, while 2nd sacker Jerry Priddy had a .401 OBP, and 1st baseman Don Kolloway contributed a fine .289. When Freddie Hutchinson was pitching, his .326 average meant that the only weak link in the lineup was catcher Aaron Robinson's .226.

DDDDDDDDDDDDDDDDDDDDDDDDDDDDDDDDDDDDDDDDDDDDDDDDDDDDDDDDDDDDDDDDDDDDDDDD

Over the two weeks after Virgil's 11-inning win on May 13, 1950 and subsequent season-ending injury, the Tigers floundered a bit, dropping from first to third place, 4 games out on May 25. The boys then turned it on, winning 11 of 12 to pull within one-half game of first place New York on June 6, heading into the Bronx for a weekend series. After dropping the first 2 to the Yanks, Detroit salvaged the third, blowing open a tight game with an 8-run 6th inning, the big hit a 3-run triple by Johnny Lipon. From New York, the Tigers traveled to Boston for a 3-game series and rained 33 runs on the Red Sox in a sweep, retaking first with a 10-inning, 6-5 victory over the Athletics the next day at Michigan & Trumbull.

On Friday, June 23, manager Casey Stengel and his 2nd-place Bronx Bombers arrived at Briggs Stadium to begin a 4-game series. This first game was one that Tiger fans would fondly remember the rest of their days. It was played on a warm evening when night games were still the exception. The offense was as scorching as the setting sun, the two starters, Ted Gray & New York's Tommy Byrne, gone before the end of the fourth. Hank Bauer's two homers, Yogi Berra's 2-run jack, and Jerry Coleman's solo shot put the New Yorkers up 6 to nothing before a Yankee was out in the fourth. When Ted Gray followed Coleman's homer by walking the pitcher, manager Red Rolfe had finally seen enough, and pulled Gray for Dizzy Trout, a move that changed the course of the game.

Ol' Diz put down Phil Rizzuto, Cliff Mapes, and – after he'd homered in his first two trips to the plate - Hank Bauer to end the Yankees fourth, bringing Detroit to bat. After Hoot Evers led-off with a fly out to center, Johnny Groth and Don Kolloway hit back-to-back singles. When Bob Swift drew a walk, Dizzy Trout, inserted into the game to relieve half an inning ago, came to bat with the bases loaded, and cleared them all with a grand slam that brought the fans out of their seats and the Tigers to within 2 runs, 6 to 4. After pitcher Tommy Byrne recorded the 2nd out, Jerry Priddy cleared the fences, sending Byrne to the showers and bringing in Fred Sanford - not that Fred Sanford - to pitch. Well, maybe it was that Fred Sanford. The first Tiger he faced was George Kell, who singled, and Vic Wertz followed with a ball that landed on the right field roof. When the next man to bat, Hoot Evers, also homered, Detroit was up 8-6, Sanford headed to the showers before he could get an out and before Tommy Byrne had a chance to towel off.

Now with the lead, Dizzy sailed through the Yankee fifth & sixth but was touched by a 7th inning Joe DiMaggio solo blast to make the score 8-7. The home run derby continued in New York's 8th when a 2-run shot by Tommy Henrich knocked Trout out of the game and put the Yanks up 9-8, the score as the Tigers came to bat in the bottom of the ninth.

Yankee Joe Page had pitched the 8th and came out for the 9th. He was one of the toughest relievers in the game, a 3-time All-Star and last year the league-leader in saves with 27 and 3rd in MVP balloting. Page dispatched George Kell on a short fly, the Tigers down to their last two outs. They wouldn't need them. After Vic Wertz hit a booming double to center, Hoot Evers drove a Page serving over the head of Joe DiMaggio, the ball bouncing off the 440' mark in dead center. As DiMaggio raced for the ball, his back to home plate, and Wertz scored, 51,400 were on their feet, screaming & encouraging Evers as he sprinted around the bases and crossed home plate with an inside-the-park-homer, the Tigers 10th and winning run, the fans going berserk and screaming *"Hoooooooooooot!"*

The 11 home runs the two teams hit accounted for all of the scoring in the 10-9 shoot-out, and set a major league record for homers in one game, one that would stand for 45 years: in 1995, again at The Corner, the Tigers & Chicago White Sox combined for 12 round-trippers to break the 1950 mark; then in 2002, this time in Comiskey Park, Detroit & Chicago repeated their 1995, 12 homer, barrage.

Almost lost in the wild victory was the fantastic relief job that Freddie Hutchinson did, putting down in order the last 5 Yankees to bat, a Murderer's Row of Gene Woodling, Hank Bauer, Joe DiMaggio, Yogi

Berra, and Big Johnny Mize. Hutch's work boosted his record to 8 & 4, and more importantly, increased the Tigers advantage to two games on the 2nd place Yankees. The next day, Vic Wertz & Hoot Evers doubles keyed a 3-run first, and Art Houtteman cruised to a 4-1, complete game, victory. A Sunday twin bill in front of 55,628 saw the two teams split, Hal Newhouser getting rocked in an 8-2 opener loss, then Fred Hutchinson & Ted Gray flipping the Friday script, this time with Gray relieving Hutch as Hoot Evers' (there's that man again) 3-run shot in the 8th broke a 3-3 tie and propelled the Tigers to a 6-3 win.

DDDDDDDDDDDDDDDDDDDDDDDDDDDDDDDDDDDDDDDDDDDDDDDDDDDDDDDDDDDDDDDDDDDDDD

On June 25, the Yankees left town 3 games behind first-place Detroit. The two teams battled all summer for the title, Detroit's biggest lead 4 & ½ games after a July 17 doubleheader sweep at Philadelphia's Shibe Park. In their next 3 series, Detroit dropped 2 of 3 at Fenway, 2 of 3 at Yankee Stadium, then 2 of 3 back home against the Red Sox; July ending with Detroit & New York tied for first. The Tigers swept the Yankees in a 3-game series at Briggs Stadium to open August, but closed the month on a 4 & 8 slump, including losing 2 of 3 in the Bronx, and entered September two behind New York.

Detroit took 8 of their first 9 contests in September, vaulting them back over New York into first. Their big chance to take control of the pennant race was a 3-game series with the Yankees at The Corner on September 14-16. In the first game, the Tigers excited their fans with a 4-run first, but Hal Newhouser couldn't hold the lead, and lost 7-5. In game 2, Detroit rallied with 3 late runs to win 9-7. The rubber game was played before 56,548 excited fans, the pitching match-up Dizzy Trout against a rookie called up from the minors at the start of July, Whitey Ford. The two were both on their game, putting zeros on the scoreboard until Joe DiMaggio reached Dizzy for a solo shot into the seats in the sixth. It stayed 1-0 Yanks until the Tigers 8th, when 2nd sacker Jerry Priddy opened the frame with a double and scored one out later on a Vic Wertz double, tying the game at 1 going into the 9th. That's when things got ugly for the home team. Trout could only get 1 out as 4 Yankees crossed home plate, and Newhouser in relief couldn't stem the tide until 3 more runs came in. When the Tigers were retired in order in their ninth, the final score read Yankees 8 Tigers 1.

New York left Detroit on September 16 ahead by one-half game. The two teams were tied 5 days later after the Tigers completed a sweep of the Athletics, Freddie Hutchinson going the distance in the 8-2 win, with Philadelphia's Joe Coleman Sr. taking the loss.

Detroit moved on to Cleveland for 3. In game 1 Hal Newhouser & Bob Feller hooked up in a pitcher's duel as they had so many times over the past decade. A dramatic ninth inning Don Holloway homer off Feller tied the game at 3, but Joe Gordon led off the bottom of the inning with a solo shot that sent Detroit to a tough defeat. The Indians won the next day in a 10-2 romp. In the finale, Ted Gray pitched his heart out, dueling 21-game winner Bob Lemon for 10 innings, but Detroit fell short, 2-1.

The Tigers left Cleveland down 2 & ½ games with 7 to play. Detroit came home and took 3 of 4 against the St. Louis Browns, but New York also went 3 & 1 at the same time, and with 3 games to go, the Yanks were still up by 2 & ½. The Tigers closed with 3 against Cleveland at home, needing to win all 3 while New York lost their last 2. The first game versus the Indians featured the same Ted Gray-Bob Lemon match-up that produced such a magnificent duel just 5 days before. There would be no repeat of that duel and there would be no pennant for Detroit in 1950, as Gray was rocked by Cleveland's offense in a 12-2 thumping.

The 1950 A.L. final standings read: New York 98 & 56, Detroit 3 back 95 & 59, Boston 4 back in third at 94 & 60, Cleveland 6 back in fourth at 92 & 62. The outstanding rookie year of Yankee pitcher Whitey Ford, going 9 & 1 with a 2.81 ERA since his July 1 call-up, the big regular season difference maker. The Yankees faced the Whiz Kids, the nickname of the rookie-driven Philadelphia Phillies, in the World Series and swept them in four-straight.

1950 marked the third time in the last 5 seasons that the Tigers finished in second place: '46 versus Boston, and '47 & '50 versus New York. The thought of how differently 1950 might have run its course had pitching ace Virgil Trucks not been sidelined for the season's final 4 months was both a source of frustration and an inspiration for the upcoming 1951 campaign.

1951 - 1954 Bottoming Out; Hutch Leaves His Mark

"Baseball is cigar smoke, roasted peanuts, the Sporting News, winter trades, 'Down in front', and the seventh-inning stretch. Sore arms, broken bats, a no-hitter, & the strains of 'The Star-Spangled Banner.' Baseball is a highly paid Brooklyn catcher telling the nation's business leaders: 'You have to be a man to be a big leaguer, but you have to have a lot of little boy in you too.' This is a game for America, this baseball!"

("The Game For All America" by Ernie Harwell)

Detroit Tiger legend, Charlie Gehringer, the greatest second baseman in Tiger and, arguably, major league history, became the Tigers general manager in time for the 1951 season. A job that requires frequently speaking to folks seemed an unusual assignment for a man of so few words. Mickey Cochrane once said of Charlie, *"He says hello on Opening Day, goodbye on closing day, and in between hits .350."* However, the little he did say showed Charlie's sense of humor. At a banquet in his honor, his entire speech was: *"I'm known around baseball as saying very little, and I'm not going to spoil my reputation."*

1,951,474 came down to The Corner in 1950, the largest attendance in Tiger history until 1968. The excitement of the pennant race in '50 had fans eager for the 1951 season to commence, and 43,470 filed into Briggs Stadium for Opening Day '51. The pitching match-up featured two all-time greats, Hal Newhouser facing Cleveland's Bob Lemon. Hal deserved a better fate. The Indians scored an unearned run in the first inning to take the early lead. The Tigers third was a wonderful flashback to how Ty Cobb once manufactured runs: 2nd baseman Jerry Priddy led off with a double, advanced to 3rd on a ground out by Joe Ginsberg and, with Newhouser at bat, pulled off a steal of home plate to tie the game at 1.

Unfortunately, the Tigers only managed one more hit off of Lemon, when Priddy singled in the fifth. Newhouser was almost as impressive, keeping the Tribe offense under wraps until the ninth, when an error by shortstop Johnny Lipon, on what should've been out #3, allowed Larry Doby to cross the plate with the run that made it 2-1 Cleveland, the final score when Lemon put down Detroit 1-2-3 in the bottom of the 9th.

Detroit opened 1951 with losses in 4 of their first 5, stayed 3 games under .500 into early-May, then kicked off a 12 & 3 run with series wins over Boston and New York, boosting the 16 & 10 Tigers to 2 & ½ games within first on May 20. The bats went ice cold as the team lost 12 of the next 13, dropping Detroit to 10 games back by the start of June. Although the streaky Tigers turned around to take 8 of their next 9, that run only cut the deficit from 10 to 9 behind the surprising first-place White Sox.

Injuries were the main culprit in halting the steady play needed to get Detroit into the pennant race. The biggest blow to the Tigers chances was the arm woes of Newhouser. Hal's 4th of July victory over the White Sox would be his 6th and last for 1951, and when he was pulled in the 2nd inning of a July 14 loss to the Senators, Newhouser's season was done. The pain that Hal first felt in his shoulder at the end of '48 never really went away, all those innings thrown since the 30s taking their toll, and when he won in '49 & '50 he won on smarts, guts 'n grit, his fastball no longer overpowering hitters. Now in mid-1951, the pain could no longer be overcome.

Between Newhouser's last two decisions of '51, the July 4 win & the July 14 loss, the 18th Midsummer Classic returned to The Corner.

DD

1951 marked 10 years since Ted Williams' bottom of the 9th home run won the 1941 All-Star game for the American League at Briggs Stadium. And now, for the 2nd time since the game's 1933 inception, Detroit was again the host city. The excited anticipation preceding the event was interrupted by sad news on the eve of the game: Harry Heilmann had passed away after his battle with cancer. Harry had continued to broadcast Tiger games on the radio throughout the exciting 1950 season, and even came back for a bit in '51, but the sickness finally prevailed. Players from both teams wore black armbands in Harry's honor.

Harry Heilmann, 1952 Hall of Fame Inductee &
One of the Most Popular Tigers Ever

Tiger pitcher Freddie Hutchinson pitched the 4th, 5th, & 6th for the American League, giving up 3 runs. The two A.L. starters from the Tigers, Vic Wertz & George Kell, each hit solo home runs off of the New York Giants Sal "the Barber" Maglie ("the barber" nom de guerre from throwing so close to batter's heads that it seemed to shave their chins). Despite surrendering those two long balls, Maglie was the winning pitcher in the National League's 8 to 3 victory.

Heilmann's old teammate and manager, Ty Cobb, threw out the first pitch. How appropriate as on Harry's deathbed Ty was present and told his friend that Harry was going to be inducted into the Hall of Fame. Sure enough, with Cobb leading the charge, Harry was voted in to Cooperstown 6 months after his passing. Ty made sure that everybody knew he considered Heilmann the greatest right-handed hitter in major league history.

DDDDDDDDDDDDDDDDDDDDDDDDDDDDDDDDDDDDDDDDDDDDDDDDDDDDDDDDDDDDDDDDDDDDDDDD

Founded in 1925, American Legion Baseball's stated mission is promoting sportsmanship, good health, and active citizenship in young men 13 to 19 years old. Thousands of American Legion ballplayers have gone on to play college and pro ball – as of 2019, Legion alumni numbering 68 have been inducted into major league baseball's Hall of Fame.

Each Legion season culminates with a championship tournament. The American Legion National championship game of 1951 was played at Briggs Stadium. Los Angeles Crenshaw Post 715 beat out 16,000 other teams to win the title at The Corner. Their 17-year old 2nd baseman was a scrappy ball-of-fire named George Anderson. 33 years later, on this same field, George "Sparky" Anderson would lead the Detroit Tigers to their 4th World Series title, 16 years before his induction into Cooperstown.

DDDDDDDDDDDDDDDDDDDDDDDDDDDDDDDDDDDDDDDDDDDDDDDDDDDDDDDDDDDDDDDDDDDDDDDD

After the '51 All-Star break, Virgil Trucks began to heat up. Returning slowly from his May 1950 injury, Virgil opened the season in the bullpen, working on increasing his velocity. His first start was a May 27 Sunday game against the St. Louis Browns, going 8 innings in a 3-2 Tiger win. Only 2 & 2 by the All-Star game, he was the Virgil of old in the 2nd half, tossing 5 complete games in his last 6 starts, the most memorable taking place at Chicago's Comiskey Park, the 2nd game of a September 7 doubleheader. That game was a wonderful old fashion pitcher's duel, two guys in for the duration no matter how long it took: Virgil Trucks against ex-Tiger Billy Pierce, and nothing came easy for the batters on this day.

Chicago scored first, pushing across an unearned run in the fifth on one single and 2 Tiger errors. Detroit tied it in the 7th on a Vic Wertz homer. After 9 it was 1-1, the score the same after 10, 11, 12 & 13. In the top of the 14th, Johnny Groth led off with a double off Pierce and, after the next 2 batters went down, he then came home on a double by... Virgil Trucks. After knocking in the lead run in the top half of the frame, Virgil put down the White Sox 3rd, 4th, & 5th batters – Minnie Minoso, Eddie Robinson, & Ray Coleman – 1, 2, 3 to seal the 14-inning, 2-1, Detroit victory.

Manager Red Rolfe said, *"He's a better pitcher now than when he won 19 games, better control and a curve. He can set up his hitters better."* From that mid-season 2 & 2 record, Virgil ended the year 13 & 8. As nice as it was having Trucks back in the saddle in the 2nd half of the '51 season, from 10 games back at the end of June, Detroit fell to 15 & ½ at the close of July, 21 & ½ going into September and, at the end of Virgil's September 7, 14-inning, victory, the Tigers were 22 games out of first.

Just the year before, the Tigers were tied for first on September 21, and but for a couple of plays the pennant could have been theirs. To have fallen so far so fast, from 1950's 95 & 59 to 1951's 73 & 81 and 25 games out of first, no one – not the fans, not the opponents, not ownership, not least of all the players - could have foreseen it.

They ain't seen nuthin' yet.

DDDDDDDDDDDDDDDDDDDDDDDDDDDDDDDDDDDDDDDDDDDDDDDDDDDDDDDDDDDDDDDDDDDDDDDD

On January 17, 1952 Walter O. Briggs passed away. '52 would be the first season since 1918 that Briggs was not at least part of Tiger ownership. The mantle of ownership now fell to the Briggs estate, with son Walter "Spike" Briggs Jr. named president.

The 1952 campaign began April 15 as 43,112 witnessed a pitchers' duel at The Corner between Dizzy Trout and the St. Louis Browns Ned Garver. Although Dizzy only gave up single runs in the 4th & the 5th before being relieved after 8, the Tigers bats were comatose, and Detroit fell 3-0. Opening Day of 1952 was an omen of what was to come, the team starting the year 0 & 8.

The winless start was broken April 26 by a delightfully surprising 13-0 win over the 8 & 2 Indians and their All-Star pitcher, Bob Lemon. The Tiger offense awoke from its lethargic season start, but it was Art

Houtteman who was the story, taking a no-hitter into the ninth. It was a tragic month for the Houtteman family – on April 2, his wife drove a car off a mountain road in Tennessee, and their only child, 7-month old Sheryl, was thrown from the vehicle and died. How surreal this must have all seemed to Art. And now, just 3 outs to no-hit fame. With 17,922 roaring on every pitch, Jim Hegan dug in, and lofted a fly ball to left-fielder Johnny Groth. One out. Old friend Barney McCosky, slowed greatly by back injuries and now a part-time player nearing the end of his career, pinch hit for the pitcher and grounded out. Two outs. Now, lead-off man Harry Simpson stepped to the plate. For the only time the entire game, Art shook off his catcher, Joe Ginsberg, who called for a curve. Instead, Art fired a fastball, and Simpson was able to make 17,000 groan-as-one by lining the pitch into left for a single. Houtteman quickly put the disappointment behind him and dispatched Bobby Avila on a short fly, ending the contest with a one-hit shutout.

The 13-0 steamrolling was only a brief smooth patch in an otherwise terribly bumpy road. Although Ted Gray's 1-0 shutout of Cleveland the next day (the first place Tribe must have wondered what got into the winless Tigers for this two-game series) pulled Detroit out of the cellar and into 7th place, a 4-1 loss at New York on May 2 dropped the team back into the basement, and they did not vacate the cellar the rest of 1952.

On May 15, a paltry crowd of 2,215 showed up at The Corner to see their 6 & 18 Tigers take on the third place Washington Senators. Many would-be attendees were a mile east cheering a parade honoring visiting General Douglas MacArthur. Those folks missed history of another kind being made at Michigan & Trumbull. Virgil Trucks and the Senators Bob Porterfield hooked up in a fine, old-time, pitchers' duel, nothing but zeros on the scoreboard through 8 innings. Between the two teams in those first 8 innings, the batters were only able to scratch out two hits – both by Detroit. Only 24 games into the season, just 3 weeks after Art Houtteman's masterpiece against Cleveland, in one of the Tigers worst starts in their history, a 2nd Detroit pitcher was taking a no-hitter into the ninth. Virgil faced the number 2, 3, & 4 batters in the Washington line-up, and mowed 'em down. He had no-hit an opponent through 9 innings, but could not celebrate since the Tigers were as yet unable to push a run across.

George Kell led off the bottom of the ninth with a groundout to short. Pat Mullin stepped up and sent a flyball to deep center, the small crowd rising as one, hopeful, but the ball was hauled in by Jim Busby short of the wall. Now Vic Wertz was in the batter's box, and he absolutely crushed Bob Porterfield's first pitch, deep into the right field upper deck to seal Truck's no-hit victory. As so many excited Tigers did over the years, Virgil leaped up from the bench, hit his head on the dugout ceiling, shook it off and raced out on to the field, the first to congratulate Vic Wertz as he crossed home plate.

DDDDDDDDDDDDDDDDDDDDDDDDDDDDDDDDDDDDDDDDDDDDDDDDDDDDDDDDDDDDDDDDDDDDDDDDDD

Trucks no-hitter was a wonderful moment, but it was a rare success for the '52 Tigers. They struggled mightily, and after 40 games floundered 10 & ½ games out at 13 & 27. The day of game number 41, June 3, G.M. Charlie Gehringer pulled the trigger on one of the biggest post-war trades in the majors, and it was shocking. Although George Kell just came off of another great year in '51, leading the league with 191 hits and 36 doubles while hitting .319, his Detroit Tigers' career just ended. Traded to the Boston Red Sox was George, Hoot Evers, Dizzy Trout, and Johnny Lipon. In return, Detroit received 1st sacker Walt Dropo, outfielder Don Lenhardt, pitcher Bill Wight, third baseman Fred Hatfield, and shortstop Johnny Pesky.

Kell was confused and disappointed, *"I sure didn't want to leave Detroit, but the only thing that made it better was going to Boston because that's the other great baseball town in the American League."* He teamed up with Ted Williams, a man he became good friends with, to make lives miserable for pitchers throughout the American League. The year before the trade, Ted was asked who he considered his biggest rival as a hitter. He answered without hestitation, *"Kell, of course. He just goes along hitting steadily all the time. Take a look at his averages. There may be players getting more publicity for their hitting, like Gus Zernial, but Kell always is up there right near the top, and he'll stay there. He's a good hitter for he moves around in the box, pulling and punching the ball."* Gerhinger explained to George that he didn't want to trade him, but saw this swap as a way to snap the Tigers out of their funk and Boston would not ok the trade unless Kell was part of it.

First-place Boston saw immediate dividends. In the first game after the transaction, a 13-11 victory over Cleveland, Kell and Hoot Evers each homered, driving in three runs apiece. In the first 30 times that George went to the plate for Boston, he reached base 18 times, and in his 75 games with Boston in '52, he hit .319. After his days wearing the Olde English D, Kell made the All-Star team in '52, '53, '54, '56 & his final season of '57. Evers hit 14 homers for the Sox in '52 & 11 in '53, but his career faded after that. Lipon hit only .205 & .214 in '52 & '53, coming to bat only 10 times after that before retiring. Dizzy Trout helped the '52 Sox with 9 wins & a 3.64 ERA, but never won another game in the majors.

The new-look Tigers sang the same old song, losing 9 of their first 11 post-trade. Walt Dropo did provide the production that Gehringer sought, with 23 homers & 70 RBIs in 115 games while with Detroit in '52, including setting a MLB record by getting hits in 12 consecutive at bats, and in '53 hit 13 taters while knocking in 96 runs, but fell to 44 RBIs in '54 and was soon an ex-Tiger. The other key player in the trade to Charlie Gehringer's mind was Don Lenhardt, but he was a .188 bust in '52 as a Tiger and soon gone. When changing players didn't work, Gehringer tried changing managers, replacing Red Rolfe after a 4th of July doubleheader loss to Cleveland with 32-year old pitcher Fred Hutchinson. Gehringer hoped that the temperamental Hutch would light a fire under his charges. After a bad game, evidence of his fury was left both at The Corner, where after a loss he might punch out the light bulbs lining the tunnel to the Briggs Stadium clubhouse, or on the road. *"I always know how Hutch did when we follow Detroit into a town,"* Yankees catcher Yogi Berra noted. *"If we got stools in the dressing room, I know he won. If we got kindling, he lost."*

Although the win/loss ratio wasn't much affected, at least initially, when Freddie became the skipper, things sure got entertaining: 26 minutes into Hutchinson's first game as manager he was out of the dugout yelling at an umpire. Hutch wasn't tossed that day, but he was often enough that it was a fifty-fifty bet what would happen more often: a Tiger victory or Fred getting the heave-ho.

DDDDDDDDDDDDDDDDDDDDDDDDDDDDDDDDDDDDDDDDDDDDDDDDDDDDDDDDDDDDDDDDDDDDDDDDDDDD

The '52 Tigers found themselves 25 games out of first on July 22, their year-to-date low point, as the Senators arrived in town to open a 3-game series. In game 1, Virgil Trucks pitched against the team he'd no-hit 2 months prior. Perhaps curious to see if lighting might strike twice, the 2,215 who showed up in May increased on this day to 18,706 intrigued souls. There was no repeat tonight, though, as the very first batter of the game, Eddie Yost, singled to left. But, if possible, Virgil was even more dominant than he was in the May no-hitter, spinning a perfect game the rest of the way, retiring the next 27 batters in succession. Trucks again beat Washington 1-0, this time when Walt Dropo singled home Johnny Groth in the 1st.

As dawn broke on August 25, the Tigers awoke in the Bronx, 30 games behind the first place Yankees. After losing a tough 4-2 decision the day prior, in a few hours they would wrap up the short 2-game series, with Virgil Trucks facing Bill Miller. Despite Virgil's fine pitching so far this season, the Tigers feeble offense gave him little support, and his record sat at 4 & 15. It was to be another pitchers' duel today, nothing but zeros on the board until the Tigers 7th, when Walt Dropo's double was followed by an RBI single off the bat of reserve outfielder Bud Souchock. Trucks, meanwhile, was mowing down the most dangerous line-up in all of baseball inning after inning, and right in *The House That Ruth Built*. After 7, he had not allowed a hit. In the Yanks' 8th, he struck out Billy Martin, got Big Johnny Mize to pop out, and Irv Noren to fly out. In the 9th, Virgil began by striking out 20-year old & first-time All-Star Mickey Mantle for the second time in a row. First baseman Joe Collins hit next, and flew out to center. It was now down to a tough as nails Marine & another first-time All-Star, Hank Bauer, who grounded to 2nd, and Virgil Trucks had his second no-hitter of 1952.

Indicative of the run support Virgil and the entire pitching staff received in 1952, was that Trucks won each of these 3 outstanding outings (two no-hitters & a July 22 one-hitter) by the score of 1 to nothing.

DDDDDDDDDDDDDDDDDDDDDDDDDDDDDDDDDDDDDDDDDDDDDDDDDDDDDDDDDDDDDDDDDDDDDDDDDDDDD

11 days before Trucks 2nd no-hitter, trader Gehringer further changed the roster, this time shipping Vic Wertz and 3 throw-ins to the Browns for the man who beat Detroit on Opening Day, pitcher Ned Garver, outfielder Jim Delsing and 2 warm bodies. Garver was an All-Star & a 20-game winner in '51 with St. Louis, and won 11, 14 & 12 for Detroit from '53 thru '55. Delsing hit .288 in his first full season as a Bengal in '53, then slowly faded away. Tiger teammates & fans hated to see Vic Wertz go. Vic had just represented Detroit in the '52 All-Star game, and for the year had 23 homers – his 4th year in a row with over 20 long balls – and 70 RBIs. Wertz would continue to produce at a high level into the 1960s, his best post-Tiger years in '56 (32 HRs/106 RBIs), '57 (28/105) and '60 (19/103). Near the end of the 1961 season, Vic Wertz was waived by Boston and picked up for a 2nd stint with Detroit. As a 37-year old in 1962, used mostly as a pinch-hitter, Vic appeared in 112 games while hitting .324. Released early in '63 by the Tigers, Vic retired from the game shortly thereafter with career numbers of 266 home runs, 1,178 RBIs, a .277 batting average, and 4 All-Star appearances.

Virgil Trucks ended the season at 5 & 19, but his two no-hitters made Virgil only the third pitcher in MLB history to hurl two no-nos in the same season. Since that 1952 season, Nolan Ryan & Roy Halladay have joined the small fraternity of Trucks, Allie Reynolds, and Johnny Vander Meer.

Overall, 1952 was an awful year for the Tigers. For the first time in franchise history, the team sank to last place, and for the first time lost over 100 games, ending the year at 50 & 104. 1952 cost Detroit the distinction of being the only American League team to never finish in last.

Before the calendar could flip to 1953, things were about to get worse.

DDDDDDDDDDDDDDDDDDDDDDDDDDDDDDDDDDDDDDDDDDDDDDDDDDDDDDDDDDDDDDDDDDDDDDDDDDDDD

On the eve of 1953, trader Gehringer struck yet again, and as in August his trading partner was the St. Louis Browns. It was December 4, 1952 when Detroit traded Virgil Trucks, Johnny Groth, & reliever Hal White to the Browns for Bob Nieman, Owen Friend, & Jay Porter. How did that trade work out?

Virgil spent 3 months with the Browns in '53 before being traded to the White Sox, and finished his first season away from Detroit going 20 & 10 with a 2.93 ERA. In '54, the 37-year old Virgil was an All-Star for the 2nd time in his career, posting numbers of 19 & 12 with a 2.79. After going 13 & 8 in '55, Trucks was re-acquired by Detroit for utility man Bubba Phillips, went 6 & 5 in '56 before being part of an 8-player deal (no other impact players involved) with the Kansas City Athletics. Virgil went 9 & 7 with a 3.03 in 1957, finishing his career in '58 splitting the season between Kansas City & the Yankees, compiling a record of 2 & 2 with a 3.65 before hanging it up as a 41-year old.

Johnny Groth hit .257 with 10 homers & 57 RBIs in '53 for St. Louis, .275/7 HRs/60 RBIs in '54 – his last as a regular, then was a reserve until retiring after the 1960 season, from '58 thru '60 back wearing the Olde English D. The next Joe DiMaggio he wasn't, but Groth's first 4 years were nice ones, especially his rookie & sophomore seasons when his on base percentage was over .400 and he hit .293 & .306, with 11 & 12 homers, and 73 & 85 runs batted in.

Hal White was released by the Browns in May '53 and picked up by the cross-town rival Cardinals, doing a fine job for Stan Musial's team, going 6 & 5 with a 2.99 ERA and 7 saves. Hal only got into 4 games in 1954 before he called it a career.

Meanwhile, the players the Tigers received for Trucks, Groth & White performed as follows…

Infielder Owen Friend hit .177 in one-half a year in Detroit before serving as a throw-in on a June '53 trade; left-fielder Bob Nieman had a nice '53 at .281/15/69, was a reserve in '54, & was traded before '55 to the White Sox with Walt Dropo & Ted Gray for Ferris Fain & 2 others; catcher Jay Porter was away serving our country in '53 & '54, returning for '55 & '56 to hit .197.

Bottom line: the Tigers underestimated how much Virgil Trucks had left in the tank, and sorely missed the 39 games he won during his first two post-Tiger years.

DDDDDDDDDDDDDDDDDDDDDDDDDDDDDDDDDDDDDDDDDDDDDDDDDDDDDDDDDDDDDDDDDDDDDDDDDDDDDDDDDD

Trader Gehringer had transformed the Tigers to such an extent that not a single 1952 Opening Day starter was in the 1953 Opening Day line-up. The pitcher who opposed Detroit in the '52 Opener, Ned Garver, was the '53 Opener Tiger starter. As a sign of how Detroit was faring in the early-50s, while Garver defeated Detroit 3-0 in '52, he lost 10-0 while pitching for the Tigers in '53 - and the St. Louis Brown pitcher who shutout Detroit 10-0 on Opening Day 1953 was their new mound ace, ex-Tiger Virgil Trucks. When the parade of Detroit relievers made their way to the mound this day, they did not come in from beyond the centerfield gate as they had since Navin Field debuted in 1912, rather they came in from the new bullpens located down the first and third base foul lines.

Interestingly, much of the offensive damage to Detroit that day was also done by ex-Tigers, namely Johnny Groth & Vic Wertz. One could make a pretty good argument that the 3 multi-player trades made in 1952 stunk for Detroit, when you look at what George Kell, Vic Wertz & Virgil Trucks accomplished after those trades, and what the Tigers received in return.

However, in 1953 there were three Tiger player procurement decisions that did pay off…

George Moriarty was a productive scout for the team in the 50s, but back in the day he was the Tiger 3rd baseman from 1909 to 1915 and Tiger manager in '27 & '28. George was a fiery sort, a bit of a live wire. One day Ty Cobb was itching to fight Moriarty, and before they could start in on each other,

George handed Cobb a baseball bat and passed along some advice, *"A fellow like you needs a bat to even things up when fighting an Irishman."* Cobb's itch to brawl quickly dissipated. Playing 3rd in game 6 of the 1909 World Series, George didn't much care for the way things were starting, Pittsburgh leading off the 1st with 3 singles. To show his displeasure and get a fire lit under his teammates, he snatched the ball cap off the head of the runner standing on the 3rd base bag, and used it to whack the fella's noggin, the two kicking each other a few times before play resumed. That 1909 Series game ended as Moriarty tagged out the potential tying run at third while being spiked by the runner, a little 15-stitch tear, the two of them rolling & scrapping in the dirt, giving Moriarty a hat trick of 1 RBI & 2 fights in one glorious afternoon, the Bennett Park faithful howling in delight as the Tigers skirmished their way to a 5-4 win.

Old George proved to be as fine a judge of talent as he was a spark plug on the field, urging the Tigers to sign a shortstop playing at the University of Wisconsin, Harvey Kuenn. The Tigers signed Kuenn in '52 and sent him to Class B Davenport, where he hit .340. The Tigers called Harvey up to the parent club in September, and in 85 at bats he hit .325 and only struck out once – and that to Hall of Famer Bob Feller. Harvey's 1953 spring training performance ensured that he would begin the regular season as Detroit's starting shortstop and lead-off batter. What a rookie season it was! In his first year wearing the Olde English D, Harvey hit .308, leading the league with 209 hits & an American League record 679 at bats, while making the All-Star team and winning the rookie-of-the-year award.

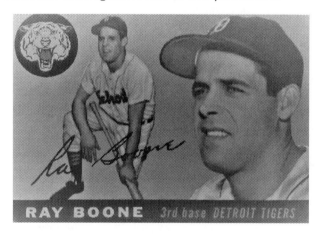

In June of '53, the Tigers sent pitcher Art Houtteman, a pitcher that Joe DiMaggio said was one of the toughest he'd ever faced, to Cleveland for third baseman Ray Boone. The change of scenery helped both players. It had been rough sledding for Art since his 1950 All-Star season: the death of his baby girl, losing a league-leading 20 games in '52, and going 2 & 6 with a 5.90 ERA in early-'53. Art's 15 wins made a nice contribution to Cleveland's 1954 pennant season, following that with 10 victories in '55. Ray Boone had been one of the best defensive third sacker's in the game, but his .241 average and low power numbers in the early-'53 going fell short of Tribe management expectations. Their impatience was surprising considering Boone just the year before posted very good numbers of .296/26/114. In Ray's 101 games as a Tiger in 1953, he was outstanding, batting .312 with 22 home runs and 93 RBIs, leading the Tigers in all 3 categories while only playing 2/3rds of the year in Detroit. Boone was one of the league's top run-producers over the next 3 seasons, with an A.L. best 116 RBIs in '55 and All-Star berths in '54 & '56.

Also in June of '53, the Tigers signed an 18-year old kid right out of Baltimore's Southern High School, Albert William Kaline. Tiger scout Ed Katalinas proved as astute a scout as George Moriarty, and prevailed over representatives from the Brooklyn Dodgers, St. Louis Cardinals, and Philadelphia Phillies in securing Al for Detroit. There would be no minor leagues for Kaline, going right from his high school graduation to a Tiger uniform, getting into 30 games in the 2nd half of 1953, often inserted into a game to pinch run. On July 21, Al stood on first base when Don Lund doubled, beating a path from first to home so quickly that he immediately earned the nickname of the "Baltimore Greyhound".

Evident to scout Ed Katalinas, during his pursuit of Kaline to a Tiger contract, was not only Al's potential greatness as a player, but also his maturity, sincerity, and humble nature. The finest day in Kaline's short '53 season with Detroit must have been when manager Freddie Hutchinson introduced Al to the great Ted Williams. Although Ted only spent 10 minutes with Al, they were 10 minutes that he would never forget and that made him a better player, as Ted shared tips on batting & off-season workout exercises that Al promptly incorporated into his game.

Al's first major league start took place on September 16, 1953 at Fenway Park, batting 8th and playing centerfield. With Ted Williams looking on, Al showed Ted that he had worked on the tips Williams shared with him, going 3 for 5 with a run scored and an RBI.

DDDDDDDDDDDDDDDDDDDDDDDDDDDDDDDDDDDDDDDDDDDDDDDDDDDDDDDDDDDDDDDDDDDDDDDDDDDDD

1953 was Freddie Hutchinson's first full season as Tiger manager. Under Hutch, Detroit did improve by 10 games over '52, but were still a dismal 60 & 94, 40 & ½ games out of first. Hutchinson was officially a player-manager, but only inserted himself into 3 games, surrendering 3 runs in 9.2 innings pitched. Although an All-Star pitcher just two years before, and only 33 years old, these were the last innings he ever tossed in the majors. In a wonderful way to close out his big league playing days, especially for a pitcher, Freddie Hutchinson hit a home run in his final at bat. It was not a surprise to many, though, as Hutch was a fine hitting pitcher, batting over .300 4 times in his career & at times called on to pinch hit.

Late-season '52 acquisition Ned Garver was considered the '53 staff ace, with an 11 & 11 record and a 4.45 ERA against an ugly team ERA of 5.25. Ted Gray, the last holdover from the 1952 Opening Day staff, went 10 & 15/4.60, the only other starter with double-digit wins. The third pitcher in the rotation was the most intriguing, 21-year old Billy Hoeft.

Hoeft was a high school phenom, winning 34 consecutive games including 3 no-hitters in '48 & '49, before losing 2-1 on a late-game unearned run, then in 1950 striking out all 27 batters in one game. Once again, it was ace Tiger scout George Moriarty, the man who landed Harvey Kuenn, securing this outstanding prospect for Detroit. Billy Hoeft signed for $55,000 and, after a 2 & 7 rookie year in '52, improved to 9 & 14 with a 4.83 ERA in 1953.

DDDDDDDDDDDDDDDDDDDDDDDDDDDDDDDDDDDDDDDDDDDDDDDDDDDDDDDDDDDDDDDDDDDDDDDDDDDDD

1953 marked the end of a wonderful era, that of Hal Newhouser as a Detroit Tiger. After injuries forced an end to his 1951 season on July 14, Hal bounced back to post a 9 & 9 record with a 3.74 ERA in 1952, the 9th victory his major league 200th. In 1953, though, Hal only made it into 7 games, going 0 & 1 along with a 7.06 ERA before being released by Detroit on July 27.

Hal was ready to accept the end of his brilliant career when his old friend, Hank Greenberg, came 'a calling. Hank was now the Cleveland Indians General Manager, and Hank convinced Hal to come to Cleveland as a relief pitcher for the 1954 season. The Tribe's starting rotation was already stacked with

23-game winners Bob Lemon & Early Wynn, and 19, 15, & 13 wins from, respectively, Mike Garcia, ex-Tiger Art Houtteman, and 35-year old Bob Feller. Hal accepted the challenge in a decision that worked out beautifully for himself and Cleveland, going 7 & 2 with 7 saves and a sparkling 2.51 ERA, mostly in long-relief. At 33 years old, Newhouser was part of an outstanding relief trio with a pair of 25-year olds and future Tigers, Don Mossi and Ray Narleski.

Interestingly, on June 1 of '54, the 111-win Indians acquired another ex-Tiger, Vic Wertz, to be their clean-up hitter for the rest of the season. It was said that Vic's 450' fly ball in the 1954 World Series, tracked down in dead center by Willie Mays, *"would've been a home run in any other park, including Yellowstone"*. 27 years later, Vic founded the "Wertz Warriors" in 1981, with the goal of 100% funding for Michigan's Special Olympics Winter Games through an annual 7-day snowmobile endurance ride through Northern Michigan.

DDDDDDDDDDDDDDDDDDDDDDDDDDDDDDDDDDDDDDDDDDDDDDDDDDDDDDDDDDDDDDDDDDDDDDDDDDD

In 1954, MLB instituted a rule that prohibited ballplayers from leaving their gloves at their defensive positions when they went in to bat. The time-honored tradition of fans seeing their heroes flip their gloves aside and pick them up again when the opponents came to the plate, one that for decades kids mimicked at pick-up, sandlot, and high school games, was no more.

DDDDDDDDDDDDDDDDDDDDDDDDDDDDDDDDDDDDDDDDDDDDDDDDDDDDDDDDDDDDDDDDDDDDDDDDDDD

The 1954 Tigers did not fare nearly as well as the 111-win Indians (a team with 3 ex-Tigers, Newhouser-Wertz-Houtteman, making major contributions), but under skipper Freddie Hutchinson, Detroit did improve their record for the 2nd consecutive season, this time by 8 victories. Their ace pitcher in '54 was ex-Cleveland Indian Steve Gromek, who came to Detroit with Ray Boone in the Art Houtteman trade of '53. As a 25-year old in 1945, Gromek had a breakout season, going 19 & 9 with a 2.55 ERA, but in the 8 years since then had only won 10 games once – until 1954 when Steve posted 18 wins, good for sixth in the league, with an A.L. fifth best 2.74 earned run average. Along with Ned Garver's 14 wins and league seventh best 2.81 ERA, the two provided the Tigers with a nice 1-2 punch on the hill. Although 22-year old Billy Hoeft slipped from 9 wins last year to 7 this year, 4 of those 7 were the first shutouts of his career, showing the good things yet to come from young Hoeft.

Al Kaline played his first full major league season, promoted from a reserve in centerfield last year to the everyday right fielder. Al began to display his amazing ability to track down fly balls and players were learning not to run on his arm. Kaline batted sixth most of the year, hitting .276, not bad for a teenager. Harvey Kuenn followed up his fabulous rookie year by again leading the A.L. in hits, this time with 201, and repeating as an All-Star, while hitting .306. And for the 2nd straight year, Ray Boone led Detroit in homers and runs batted in, logging in at 20 & 85, respectively.

With Hutchinson at the helm, the Tigers rose modestly in the standings since the 1952 debacle, and after two full seasons as manager, Hutch asked for a 2-year contract to take him through 1955 & 1956. The Tigers wished Fred to stay on, but only offered a 1-year deal. He declined Detroit's offer, and 1955 marked the first year that Freddie was not a part of the Tiger organization since his 1939 rookie year. He instead returned to his native Seattle to manage the Pacific Coast League Seattle Rainiers in '55, the team that he starred with as an 18-year old pitcher in 1938 when he won 25 games and was named *The Sporting News* Minor League Player of the Year.

Hutch would lead the Rainiers to a PCL pennant and return to the majors as manager of the St. Louis Cardinals for 1956, their improvement in '57 earning Freddie recognition again from *The Sporting News*, this time as Manager of the Year. Hutchinson had further success with the 1961 Cincinnati Reds, a team picked by most to finish among the National League's bottom dwellers, surprisingly taking the league pennant before losing to New York in the World Series. Although the Reds did not return to the Fall Classic under Hutch, they did win 98 games in '62 & 86 in '63, earning him a contract extension through 1965 (the successes of the Hutchinson-led Reds of 1961, 1962 & 1963 was considered the start of what would be Sparky Anderson's Big Red Machine). The good news was short-lived as in December of '63 Hutch felt a lump on his neck, and malignant tumors were found in his neck, chest, and lungs. As the '64 season began, Fred continued to skipper the Reds while receiving radiation treatment, but on August 13, one day after his 45th birthday, his illness forced him to turn the reins to the team over to coach Dick Sisler. Hutch's health continued to deteriorate, and he passed away on November 12, 1964.

SPORT magazine honored Hutch posthumously with their 1964 Man of the Year Award. The respect and love that Freddie received after death matched those in his life. In '57, Cardinal great Stan Musial said, *"If I ever hear a player say he can't play for Hutch, then I'll know he can't play for anybody."* In the 1959 book by pitcher Jim Brosnan, he wrote, *"Most ballplayers respect Hutch. In fact, many of them admire him, which is even better than liking him. He seems to have a tremendous inner power that a player can sense. When Hutch gets a grip on things it doesn't seem probable that he's going to lose it. He seldom blows his top at a player, seldom panics in a game, usually lets the players work out of their own troubles if possible."*

Freddie's greatest legacy is the *Fred Hutchinson Cancer Research Center* and the breakthroughs made there in cancer treatment.

1955 Al Kaline: "Mister Tiger"

"Al Kaline – he's the only guy who could make the ball come to him."

(Purple Rose Theatre play by Jeff Daniels, "The Vast Difference")

In a 1985 interview on WJR's "Focus" show, hosted by J.P. McCarthy, Mickey Mantle said that Al Kaline was the greatest player that he ever saw. *"I was no better than Kaline – he was stuck in Detroit. If he'd played in New York…"* the implication that, in the bigger market, Al would've been recognized nationally on a par with Mick, and Bob Costas might have had Kaline's card in his wallet. (*Author's note: although I'm sure that Mickey meant well with his comment, I'd much rather be "stuck" in Detroit cheering on the Tigers than living in New York City with the Damn Yankees as my team!*)

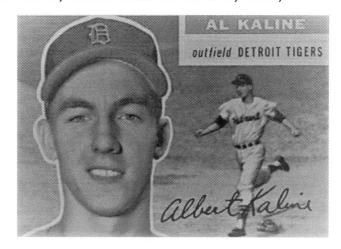

Al Kaline, the man known as "Mister Tiger", with an arm so good, it was said by many to be the equal of Pittsburgh's Roberto Clemente's. That's in the high rent district! Kaline's arm could be characterized as an accurate cannon.

He was considered a "bonus baby". Upon the June 1953 graduation from his Baltimore high school, Al was paid a $15,000 bonus to sign with the Tigers, and then another $20,000 in salary for the total of his first 2 & ½ seasons: the balance of '53, and all of '54 & '55. He graduated on June 20 and was in the Tiger line-up on June 25 – although a Briggs Stadium security guard initially turned away Kaline, assuming that this very youthful-looking young man must be a fan pulling a prank to gain entry into the ballyard.

Kaline only saw the field 30 times as a rookie in 1953, earning full-time status in '54. That's the year Al gained notoriety for his fearless defense, exhibiting a successful daring in diving on the ground, climbing fences, and slamming into walls in pursuit of balls hit to his right-field position. Few were as successful as Al in stealing hits from the opposing team. Many of these plays, however, came at a price, especially on those balls batted into the right-field corner of what was then called Briggs Stadium. In the 1954 configuration of the ball yard, box seats in the right-field corner, not far from the 325' marker, jutted out dangerously close to the foul line. In pursuit of <u>everything</u> hit his way, Al frequently crashed into these box seats, including once when his momentum caused him to slam into the seats and, after firing the ball back to the infield, pass out from the pain. Tiger president Spike Briggs weighed the income those box seats brought in against the possible loss of his budding star to injury, and had the offending box seats removed – and thus was born the name *"Kaline's Corner"*, in honor of a ballpark reconfigured for a single, albeit unusually talented, ballplayer.

Any questions about Briggs' decision ended the next year when Al, as a 20-year old in 1955, led the American League in hits with 200 and, with his .340 average, became the youngest player in Major League history to win the batting title – Al was one day younger than Ty Cobb was when Ty won the 1907 title, with a .350 average (Cobb was born on December 18, Kaline December 19). The skinny kid who only had 4 homers & 25 total extra base hits just the year before, causing concern among team management about his lack of power, slammed 3 home runs on April 17 alone, leading the league in that department through July before finishing fourth with 27 homers and first in total bases at 321. The off-season tips that Ted Williams passed on to the teenage Kaline paid off, including daily swinging of a heavy bat and squeezing a baseball, building up Al's strength as he practiced all winter long.

Despite his offensive ability, it was Kaline's defense that stood out. No one could match his ability to track a ball hit down the right-field line to the wall, surely a double, and in one motion grab the ball, turn around and – without looking – fire a strike to nip the surprised runner at second. Soon, opposing teams knew better than to take anything more than a single on a ball knocked into *Kaline's Corner*.

DDDDDDDDDDDDDDDDDDDDDDDDDDDDDDDDDDDDDDDDDDDDDDDDDDDDDDDDDDDDDDDDDDDDDDDDDD

Jimmy Vollmers remembers a warm spring morning in May 1968. His schooling that year was on a split shift, Jimmy attending Utica High on the afternoon shift while Sterling Heights Stevenson, the new school, was being completed. Though he left early for school that day to play catch and hit some balls with chums before classes started, the siren call of skipping school to attend a Tiger game won out. He jumped into friend Tony Kirkus' 1957 Plymouth Belvedere, and off to Tiger Stadium they traveled.

After purchasing fifty cent bleacher seats, but both being big fans of Al Kaline, the boys slipped past the usher to some open seats down the right field line, where Al patrolled. Jimmy thinks the usher may have chuckled as the two slid by him. Mickey Lolich was on the mound, facing the Boston Red Sox. By the 8th, the Tigers had taken a 3-2 lead when Norm Cash followed back-to-back singles by Dick McAuliffe and Kaline with a sacrifice fly to deep right.

Jimmy recalled, *"There we were, top of the ninth, up by one, two down for the Sox and Yaz singled up the middle to put the tying run on first. The next batter rifled the first pitch into the right field corner. Yaz was off on the pitch, turned at 2nd and headed for third before he even knew where the ball went. The ball came right by us, hit fair, bouncing into Kaline's Corner. Al, as usual, got a good jump on the ball & watched it bounce off the side wall, then off the back wall, and was positioned perfectly to grab the rebound. His right foot was already planted when the ball hit his mitt and in one deft, swirling motion, he pivoted, cocked his arm and threw a strike to McAuliffe, who was standing on the foul line just on the grass. Trying to tie the game, Yaz sped around third and headed home. Much to his dismay, he was met about four feet before the plate by Bill Freehan with the relay from Mac already in his mitt. He slid, but the game ended there. I will never forget the poetry in motion I witnessed that day. And the amazing thing is that we Tiger fans got to expect that type of play every day down in the right field corner. No matter what happens to the old ballpark, I will always be able to close my eyes, sit in one of those green wooden seats, smell the wafting smoke from somebody's White Owl, and watch Kaline take command out in right."*

DDDDDDDDDDDDDDDDDDDDDDDDDDDDDDDDDDDDDDDDDDDDDDDDDDDDDDDDDDDDDDDDDDDDDDDDDDD

Al Kaline spent his entire 22-year major league career wearing the Olde English D. He retired after the 1974 season with a lifetime .297 batting average, 399 home runs, and 3,007 hits. Had he hit one more homer, Al would've been the first American Leaguer to have 400 home runs and 3,000 hits (the Babe had 2,873 hits). Instead that honor went to the man that Jimmy Vollmers saw Kaline throw out at home to end the game on that warm spring day in '68, Yaz aka Carl Yastrzemski, who achieved the 400/3,000 plateau in 1979. When informed of this, Al laughed and said, *"If I'd have known that, I would've swung harder those last few games."*

When asked about his most memorable at bat, Al said, of course, it was his 1968 World Series hit in game 5 that put the team ahead, a hit crucial to the Tigers win that day and the eventual Series victory. Second, however, took place in another game at Tiger Stadium, this one against the Yankees and his good friend, Mickey Mantle. That day, Al hit two home runs and Mantle hit two home runs – but one of Al's came with a teammate on base. The headline in the next day's paper - a New York paper - read, *"Kaline 3, Mantle 2"*. For years after, Kaline got mileage kidding Mick about that one.

Albert William Kaline… 18-time American League All-Star, winner of 10 Gold Gloves in right field, voted 1980 into the Hall of Fame on the first ballot, 1968 World Series Champion, and idolized by the State of Michigan.

1955 & 1956 the K&K Kids

I'm talkin baseball, the Motor City team
Well Hal and Dizzy set 'em down
And Kaline won the batting crown
The year before he had the right to vote

("Talkin' Tiger Baseball" by Terry Cashman)

When Fred Hutchinson turned down Detroit's 1-year offer to continue as manager in 1955, returning to his native Seattle to run the minor league team in that town, he was replaced as Tiger skipper by a man familiar with both the job and the team that offered it to him, Bucky Harris. It had been 22 years since Bucky, known as the amazing "boy manager" when as a 27-year old he led the Washington Senators to their one & only World Series crown in 1924, parted ways with the Tigers near the end of the 1933 season – becoming the last man to run the Tigers before Mickey Cochrane took over 3 months later. Harris was hired to return to Detroit by the catcher from his old Washington team, and the player who scored the winning run in the 12th inning of 1924's game 7 run to clinch the Series for the Senators over legendary John McGraw's New York Giants, Muddy Ruel.

When Charlie Gehringer was promoted from general manager to team vice-president after 1953, president Spike Briggs made his first G.M. hire a good one in Muddy Ruel. Often overlooked today, Muddy was known by baseball fans everywhere in the 1950s through his long resume: considered by none other than Connie Mack to be the game's finest catcher in the mid-1920s, one of the key cogs of the back-to-back A.L. pennant winning Washington Senators 1924 & 1925 teams, earning praise later as a highly respected coach & manager, leaving those ranks to serve as special assistant to baseball commissioner Happy Chandler only to return to his love of mentoring baseball players. Muddy stated his philosophy of coaching in the Great Contest, *"This game of baseball is so beautiful, mainly because it's so simple. The Good Lord every season supplies approximately 400 men and boys in this country with the physique and the mechanical ability to play in the major leagues. Given that good health and that skill, they're sure to succeed—unless they make mistakes. So, that's the basis of my operation. I try to keep them from making mistakes."*

In his old friend Bucky Harris, Muddy Ruel hired a kindred spirit.

DDDDDDDDDDDDDDDDDDDDDDDDDDDDDDDDDDDDDDDDDDDDDDDDDDDDDDDDDDDDDDDDDDDDDDDD

The 1955 Tiger team that Bucky Harris took over from Freddie Hutchinson had some very coachable & promising young players, and Hutch had 'em headed in the right direction, but you wouldn't know it from the *Sports Illustrated* pre-season analysis, including *S.I.'s* view of the Tiger's moundsmen: *"Detroit's challenge is to find starters and relievers from an unholy mess of rookies and proven undependables."*

Detroit began the year by splitting two games in Kansas City before opening the home portion of the '55 schedule. On April 14 at Briggs Stadium, 42,684 saw 23-year old Billy Hoeft, he of only 7 wins but 4 shutouts the prior year, fail to escape the first inning in a 5-3 loss to Cleveland. The Tiger's hitting star was the number 3 batter, Al Kaline, who just turned 20 four months prior. Kaline had 2 hits and knocked in all 3 Bengal runs.

The next day's stadium beer lines shortened dramatically as a small assembly of 3,786 passed through the turnstiles. The date, April 15, 1955, and Frank Lary was on the mound for the fourth game of the young season. After two years of military duty, Frank was called up late in '54, getting into 3 games in relief for his first taste of The Show. Today was his first major league start and it would've been hard to open up a career with a bigger challenge: facing the team that won 111 times the previous year, the Cleveland Indians, and their All-Star rookie pitcher, Herb Score. Youngsters Kaline & Kuenn hit sac flies in the first & second innings, respectively, to put Detroit up early, but the Tribe responded with 3 runs to take a 3-2 lead after 5. That was the score when Frank Lary departed his first major league start, with a not-half-bad stat line that read 6 innings, 8 hits, 3 runs/2 earned, with 5 strikeouts and a loss in his first MLB decision. The only Tiger to reach Herb Score for more than 1 hit was that Kaline kid with two - a trend had begun.

Just 3 years removed from the franchise's worst-ever 104 losses, the *S.I.* labeled *unholy mess of rookies and proven undependables* began to jell. April 24 in Cleveland saw a rematch of Frank Lary against Herb Score. The RBI machine known as Ray Boone uncorked a 3-run homer off of Score in the third to break a 1-1 tie, and Lary went the distance, outpitching 4 mighty-fine pitchers - including a couple of old friends – in Score, Art Houtteman, Hal Newhouser, & Early Wynn for a 6-4 Tiger victory, the first major league win of Frank Lary's career. And Al Kaline had two hits.

Lary's inaugural win was part of the team's 7-game winning streak to end April, vaulting the 10 & 5 Tigers into first place going into May, driven by the smokin' hot Al Kaline, who wrapped up April with a 14-game hitting streak and a .453 average. Although the Tigers slipped out of first for good by May 6, they played with an enthusiasm that made things exciting for their fans, in no small part due to an offense that led the league in hits, runs scored, and came in 2nd in batting average.

One of the season's bigger moments took place on June 8, 1955, as 43,139 came out on a Wednesday night at Briggs Stadium to witness the Tigers host their favorite foe, the New York Yankees. What those 43,000 plus could not know was the significance of their young rookie pitcher, Frank Lary, facing for the first time in his career the team he would dominate so much that within 3 years, Yankee skipper Casey Stengel would hold back his ace, Whitey Ford, rather than waste him in a losing effort to Frank "Yankee Killer" Lary. The day before Frank's debut versus New York, Kaline's 3 hits pushed his league-high batting average to .378 in leading Detroit to a 12-inning win over the Yanks, sealed when part-time third sacker Fred Hatfield put a Tom Sturdivant pitch into a walk-off orbit. Today, Lary pitched for the series rubber match vs. 1954 strikeout king and All-Star, Bob Turley.

Frank fell behind New York in the third when Mickey Mantle singled in Gil McDougald. That was it for the Yankees. The Tigers surged past the Bronx Bombers in the fourth on RBIs by Harvey Kuenn and centerfielder Bill Tuttle. 2-1 Detroit. Rookie Lary mixed his fastball & curve beautifully, keeping the big bats of New York quiet. He also contributed at the plate - leading off in the Detroit sixth, Frank drew a base-on-balls, moved to third on a single by Tuttle and a walk to Kaline. Up stepped hard partyin' Ferris Fain. In one of the last games in his brief, half-season, stay with Detroit, the aging 5-time All-Star and 2-time batting champ gave Frank and the Tigers a little breathing room, pushing Lary across home plate with an RBI grounder. Yielding only a Yogi Berra single over his last 4 innings, Frank Lary struck out Hank Bauer to finish off his complete game masterpiece, recording the first of 28 lifetime victories he earned against the Yankees. The final score before a delighted Briggs Stadium crowd: Detroit 3 New York 1.

DDDDDDDDDDDDDDDDDDDDDDDDDDDDDDDDDDDDDDDDDDDDDDDDDDDDDDDDDDDDDDDDDDDDDDDDD

In need of bullpen help, Detroit made a mid-season move for a name that would be well-known to Tiger fans a generation later, signing 32-year old Joe Coleman on July 8. Joe, father of the fine Tiger pitcher of the same name in the 70s, was winding down a 10-year career that earned him a '48 All-Star team berth while with the Philadelphia Athletics. In the back half of '55, Coleman brought much-needed help to the relief staff, going 2 & 1 with 3 saves and a 3.20 ERA in 17 games, nicely complementing two youngsters holding down the fort, Babe Birrer (4 & 3 – the only decisions he had in his brief career, with 3 saves and a 4.15 ERA) and lefty Al Aber (6 & 3, 3 saves, 3.38).

Joe Coleman Sr.'s first decision with Detroit took place on Sunday, July 17, at Briggs Stadium. The day before, the Tigers won the first 2 games of a 3-game series versus the first place Yankees, Ned Garver victorious in game 1 and Billy Hoeft whipping Whitey Ford in an outstanding 2-1 pitcher's duel in game 2. On this Sunday, manager Bucky Harris sent Steve Gromek to the mound looking for the sweep. The Yanks built an early 3-0 lead against Gromek, Detroit striking back to tie things up in the third on Ray Boone's 2-run single and Charlie "Always on a Sunday" Maxwell's double chasing Boone across home plate with run number 3. A sixth inning homer by New York's Gil McDougald was matched by a Ray Boone solo shot in the 8th. Joe Coleman took over Detroit's pitching chores in the top of the eighth, throwing 3 innings of hitless ball to keep the score even as the Tigers came up to bat in the 10th.

31-year old Tiger first baseman Earl Torgeson led off the frame with a walk, the Yankees answering by bringing in starter Bob Turley in a rare relief role. Ray Boone greeted Turley with a single as Torgeson raced around to third. With the infield playing in, Turley kept the runner on third while getting catcher Red Wilson and Charlie "Paw Paw" Maxwell (the man of many nicknames) on infield grounders. As light-hitting reserve 2nd baseman Harry Malmberg stepped up to bat, it seemed Turley would be able to get out of the jam. It was then that Earl Torgeson, not your normal slow-footed first sacker as his 133 career steals would attest, bolted for home while Turley began his motion, a cloud of dust swirling around the arriving Torgeson, the arriving baseball, and Yank catcher Yogi Berra, as the ump shouted *"Safe!"*

As happy as the 33,000 Tiger fans were as they filed out of Briggs Stadium with the Tigers sweep of New York, Detroit had only cut their games-back-of-first-deficit to 9 & ½.

DDDDDDDDDDDDDDDDDDDDDDDDDDDDDDDDDDDDDDDDDDDDDDDDDDDDDDDDDDDDDDDDDDDDDDDDDDDDDD

The '55 Tigers had a rough August, playing 7 games under .500, but kid pitcher Billy Hoeft continued to shine, whitewashing two teams that month on his way to a league-leading 7 shutouts. Meanwhile, Al Kaline kept 25 to 30 points ahead of his closest batting average competition, going into September at .348. A surge in late September included a 3-game road sweep against the defending A.L. champion Indians, featuring Frank Lary outdueling 7-time All-Star, Bob Lemon, in a sweet 3-1 Tiger triumph, earning Frank his 14th and final rookie season victory. The Tigers ended 1955 in fifth place, 79 & 75, their first year over .500 since 1950.

The kids are alright, indeed. 23-year old Billy Hoeft and 25-year old Frank Lary were the club's top two hurlers. Billy's 16 wins were a league 2nd behind #1 Whitey Ford's 18, Hoeft's 17 complete games 2nd to Ford's 18, and Billy's 7 shutouts placed him tops in the A.L., all of this earning Hoeft a berth on the All-Star team. Lary wrapped up his rookie year going 14 & 15 while posting a 3.10 earned run average, 16 complete games in 31 starts, and a team-high 235 innings pitched. Another young pitcher didn't fare as well as Hoeft & Lary, getting into 15 games in his rookie season, winning 3 & losing 5 with a rough 6.35 ERA. But a 7-time All-Star career dawned for 23-year old Kentuckian Jim Bunning.

On September 25, a beautiful fall Sunday afternoon, 17,888 came out to The Corner to witness the 1955 finale, the Tigers hosting the Cleveland Indians. Minor league stats of 30 homers & 104 RBIs earned 21-year old Rocky Colavito a late-season call up to Cleveland, and today he was playing his 5th game in the big leagues. Al Kaline only had one at bat (a groundout moving a runner into scoring position), Bubba Phillips taking his place in right field in the top of the 2nd inning, Al wrapping up his amazing season early in the Tigers 6-2 win, a victory fueled by a Harvey Kuenn home run & 2 RBIs by Ray *Booooooooone!* as the Tiger faithful loved to call him, numbers 115 & 116 for Ray, winning him the league RBI crown.

In 1955, with his closest pursuer 21 points behind, 20-year old Al Kaline's .340 average crowned him the youngest batting champ in Major League history. His outstanding offense AND defense earned Al the first of 13 consecutive All-Star berths. Kaline's 200 hits & 102 RBIs made him the last Tiger to have at least 200 hits & 100 RBIs in one season until 32 years pass and Alan Trammell does that again in 1987. Kaline is 2nd to only Mantle in on base percentage & slugging percentage, and 2nd to Cleveland's Al Smith with 121 runs scored. Al is number 1 in the A.L. in hits and in total bases.

KALINE BECOMES YOUNGEST BAT CHAMP

HARVEY KUENN
shortstop DETROIT TIGERS

The other half of the K&K Kids, Harvey Kuenn, has another outstanding season in his third year. He is an American League fifth in batting average, third in hits, and first in doubles.

This off season offers the most fan excitement and anticipation for the upcoming campaign since the beginning of the 50s. To prepare for '56, Kuenn, the effusive side of the Kuenn-Kaline duo, goes back to his home in the Badger State to resume his usual winter workout regimen of bowling 3 times a week. How wonderfully Wisconsin, perfect for a man born near Milwaukee, an All-Star shortstop at the University of Wisconsin (the school's 1st ever All-American), who married a former Miss Wisconsin, and would manage the hard-hitting Milwaukee Brewers, "Harvey's Wallbangers", to the 1982 World Series.

DDDDDDDDDDDDDDDDDDDDDDDDDDDDDDDDDDDDDDDDDDDDDDDDDDDDDDDDDDDDDDDDDDDDDDDD

3 days after the 1955 season concluded for Detroit, the greatest Tiger of them all, Tyrus Raymond Cobb, spent a pleasant evening on national television. It was Wednesday night in America, and TVs across the country tuned in to the popular CBS show, *I've Got a Secret*.

The show's format, for you young-ins, consisted of four panelists asking questions in a bid to determine what the secret was of the mystery guest. Before the questions began, the guest would appear from behind the curtains and sit next to the show's chain-smoking (nothing but Winstons) host, Garry Moore. The guest would whisper to Garry his or her secret, their words flashed on TV screens for the benefit of the viewing audience. Ty's secret: *"I have the highest lifetime batting average in baseball".*

For certain well-known mystery guests, some or all of the panelists would be blindfolded. In Ty's case, the two male panelists had to put on blindfolds. When Cobb's secret could not be ascertained from the questions, the two male panelists were allowed to take off their blindfolds, but that still did not help (in their defense, the 68-year old Cobb looked different from photos of the young ballplayer). It was then that Garry Moore explained who Ty was, and revealed his secret. *"But we had a hard time in deciding what he should be known for,"* Garry said, and began to list all of the many records Cobb held. Panelist Bill Cullen had one to add to the list, *"He spiked a lot of 2nd baseman in his time."* Even Ty laughed. Sure, he wasn't a second baseman.

DDDDDDDDDDDDDDDDDDDDDDDDDDDDDDDDDDDDDDDDDDDDDDDDDDDDDDDDDDDDDDDDDDDDDDDDDD

As dawn broke on April 17, 1956, the streets, the bars, and the Ma & Pa parking lots surrounding Briggs Stadium quickly filled up. It was Opening Day in Detroit, and the annual statewide holiday was, once again, finding its legs early. The Kansas City Athletics were the Tigers guests, as Detroit sent out Frank Lary to start the season of promise. KC countered with Alex Kellner, a lefty on the downside of his career. With the game scoreless as the Tigers came to bat in their fifth inning, Frank Lary came up to the plate with one out & no one on. Frank wasn't in the class of Schoolboy Rowe or Earl Wilson when it came to outstanding hitting pitchers, but he was pretty close. Frank turned on a pitch from southpaw Kellner, and drove the ball deep to center, over the head of outfielder Harry Simpson. Now Harry was flat out fast, a man who would lead the A.L. in triples both this year & next, and as he turned to chase down Frank's wallop, he had the afterburners on. But Frank was no poke himself, and as he made the turn at 2nd, Lary didn't look like he planned to stop in 90 feet. A less determined man might have settled for a triple, but as Harry Simpson made the throw to the infield, Frank rounded third on a mad dash for home plate, beating the relay & creating work for the manual scoreboard operator: Tigers 1 Athletics 0.

Frank Lary, as fierce on the bases as on the mound, recognized
by Roger Maris as "one of the greatest competitors I've ever faced."

Frank dominated the Kansas City batters, allowing only 6 hits, striking out 4 with 1 walk – but it was that one walk that came back to bite him. With the Tigers maintaining their 1-0 lead, and the A's batting in the 7th, Frank surrendered a one out double. It was then that he issued his one & only walk, putting men on first & second, before getting out #2. With the pitcher due up, Gus Zernial grabbed a bat and strolled to the plate to pinch hit. Future Tiger Zernial, like current Tiger Ray Boone, was an RBI machine. Before the Philadelphia Athletics franchise moved to Kansas City after the '54 season, Gus knocked in over 100 runs 4 times, including a league-high 129 in '51. Though his best days were behind him, Zernial continued to be a dangerous man with a bat in his hands, as Frank was about to find out, slamming a double to left and sending both runners across home plate. The only man that Frank walked today scored the lead run. Athletics 2 Tigers 1.

Down to their final 3 outs, Detroit gave the 40,506 on hand something to cheer about. 2nd baseman Reno Bertoia led off the frame with a double off of reliever Tom Gorman. Utility man Buddy Hicks, in his one season in the majors, was sent in to pinch hit for Frank Lary. Manager Bucky Harris probably wishes he could take that move back, especially in light of (1) what a fine bunter that Lary was, increasing the likelihood of pushing Bertoia to third with (2) Harvey Kuenn, a magician with the bat, on deck, and (3) in light of what happened next – a Hicks pop out to catcher. One out, man still on second, and Kuenn flies out to right, which might have scored a man on third, but alas. With Earl Torgeson batting, Gorman uncorked a wild pitch, sending Reno Bertoia scampering to third and the crowd to their feet.

It was at this point that KC skipper Lou "I'll be Denny McLain's father-in-law in 7 years" Boudreau walked to the mound and called for the lefty warming up in the bullpen, 28-year old Tommy Lasorda. Yes, the same Tommy Lasorda who as manager of the Dodgers 32 years & 6 months later would send Kirk Gibson up to pinch hit against A's ace closer Dennis Eckersley in the 9th inning of 1988 World Series game 1, a move that minutes later prompted announcer Jack Buck to shout *"I can't believe what I just saw!"* about the game-winning Gibby home run. The 60-year old Lasorda in '88 tried to leap for joy, but his generous mass would not allow him to escape the earth's pull.

So, on Opening Day 1956, relief pitcher Thomas "Tommy" Charles Lasorda was able to get Earl Torgeson on a game-ending ground out, stranding the tying run 90' from home, to secure the Athletics victory and earn the save. Lasorda's only other major league experience was a cup of coffee with the Brooklyn Dodgers (why he "bleeds Dodger blue") in '54 & '55, 4 appearances/no decisions in each of those two seasons. The save that Tommy Lasorda earned at Briggs Stadium in the '56 Opener was his only major league save, the one time in his career a game ended with him on the mound receiving congratulations from his teammates, a career that would conclude 5 months later with an 0 & 4 record, a 6.48 ERA – and this lone save in an Opening Day that Tommy Lasorda would never forget.

DDDDDDDDDDDDDDDDDDDDDDDDDDDDDDDDDDDDDDDDDDDDDDDDDDDDDDDDDDDDDDDDDDDDDDDDD

The excitement surrounding the 1956 Tigers spread beyond the Motor City: the May 14, 1956 cover of *Sports Illustrated* featured a sitting Al Kaline and a standing Harvey Kuenn, each holding a bat and wearing the Olde English D, the heading *"Kaline and Kuenn: Detroit's Mr. Outfield and Mr. Infield"*. The *S.I.* story research came at an interesting time: as the calendar turned from April to May, both men were struggling at the plate, Kaline at .195 and Kuenn at .184. Team GM Muddy Ruel confidently dismissed any concerns about the two with a reassuring, *"They won't stay there."* Muddy Ruel was a wise man.

Early in the season, with few at bats calculated into the equation, averages can change quickly. Fighting foot & shoulder injuries during April & May, Kaline gamely pushed through the pain. Kuenn began May with 12 hits over 2 games at Yankee Stadium & 3 at Fenway and never slowed down. As the first half of

May concluded, about the time that the magazine hit the stands, Kaline was hitting .260 and Kuenn had made the amazing rebound to .357.

At the break for the Midsummer Classic, the 34 & 42 Tigers were already out of the pennant race, a distant 17 games out of first. Despite the poor start, 4 Detroiters made the All-Star team: Kuenn & Kaline were starters (hitting .354 & .283 at the break, respectively) and Charlie Paw Paw Maxwell & Ray Boone were reserves. Among the pitchers at the break, Billy Hoeft was 10 & 6 and could've made a strong argument to be an All-Star for the 2nd year in a row, Frank Lary, though, was struggling at 6 & 10.

Everything changed in the second half of 1956 for Detroit. The promise that many felt was theirs for the year was realized, not coincidentally as Kaline finally became fully healthy, shaking an early-July flu bug that cost him 7 pounds in 3 days – this on a man with little to spare. Once Al was feeling good again, *The Sporting News* quoted manager Bucky Harris as saying, *"Maybe Kaline can't repeat as the league batting champion, but it looks like he'll give someone a chase."* Both Kaline & his running mate Kuenn were fantastic after the break (in Harvey's case, pretty much like he was from the start of May), driving the Tigers to the best 2nd-half record in the American League at 48 & 30.

Kaline didn't come close to catching the batting average leaders, but did hit .314, good for a league 8th, and almost caught Mantle (who was in his Triple Crown season) in RBIs, 130 to 128. Al was also 2nd to Mick in total bases, while banging out 27 home runs. Kuenn & Kaline were 1-2 in hits at 196 & 194 – after ceding the league hits title to Kaline in '55, Kuenn was on top for the third time in 4 years - and tied for second in doubles with 32. Harvey hit .332, good for third, and finished 2nd in singles. Harvey could spray singles & doubles all over the field, and it was felt he could've chalked up a good many home runs if he chose to be that kind of hitter, but Harvey felt a long ball stroke would cost him too much in batting average.

The K&K Kids had plenty of offensive help in '56, so much so that Detroit as a team was first in the American League in batting average and second in runs scored. Ray Boone hit 25 homers (an A.L. 9th) with 81 RBIs and a .308 average. The top 3 reserves, catcher Red Wilson, 1st sacker Jack Phillips, and outfielder Jim Small hit, respectively, .289, .295 & .319. Charlie Maxwell had his breakout season, putting up numbers of .326 (just behind Kuenn for a league fourth), 28 homers (a Tigers lefty record, and an A.L. fifth, one ahead of Kaline), 87 RBIs & 97 runs scored (a league 4th, one ahead of Kaline & Kuenn's 96). The native of Lawton in southwest Michigan moved 15 minutes away from his hometown to Paw Paw in 1952, and since Charlie became a Tiger in '55, Detroit fans took to shouting *"Paw Paw!"* when he'd come to bat. Sportswriters began calling this popular player who hustled on every play and had one big hit after another, "The People's Choice".

Carrying their share of the second half load was the pitching staff. The Tigers 1-2 punch began with Frank Lary, who was simply amazing after the All-Star break, going 15 & 3 with an ERA of just over 2. Frank finished the year leading the league in victories with 21 (against 13 losses) & innings pitched, had 3 shutouts, and a league sixth 3.15 ERA. Right behind Lary was Billy Hoeft, following up his All-Star year with a 20 & 14 record, 4 shutouts (#2 in the A.L.) and a 4.06 ERA. The number 3 hurler was third-year man Paul Foytack, posting numbers of 15 wins (his first 15 major league victories) & 13 losses, a 3.59 ERA, and a league third 184 strikeouts – in fact, Foytack, Hoeft, & Lary were 3rd, 4th, and 5th on the strikeout leader board.

The fourth starter was 39-year old Virgil Trucks, who battled through injuries to post a 6 & 5 mark and a 3.83 ERA. Virgil was traded for the 2nd time by the Tigers at year's end, and as a 40-year old for the KC Athletics, turned in a fine 9 & 7/3.03 ERA '57 season. The young man primed to take Virgil's place in the rotation was 24-year old Jim Bunning, who was figuring out how to pitch in The Show, going 5 & 1/3.71.

The 1956 Tigers featured a team of young up & comers, whose 2nd half surge dominated the American League, fueled by 4 hitters over .300 & 2 pitchers with 20+ wins. Any team with this kind of starting pitching and Kaline & Kuenn driving the run-scoring machine was a legitimate contender. As the dust cleared, Detroit had an 82 & 72 record and inspired in both the team & their fans great hopes for 1957.

1956 Frank Lary: "The Yankee Killer"

Sweet Home Alabama
Where the Skies Are So Blue
Sweet Home Alabama
Lord, I'm Comin' Home to You

("Sweet Home Alabama" by Lynyrd Skynyrd)

Paddling 2011 down the Flint River through the town of Flushing (with its midstream wooden islands, fields of trillium along the river banks, and the air filled with blue herons & geese, canoeing 'n kayaking the Flint is a surprisingly delightful experience, but I digress…), I learned the river had not been running this high on a May 18 since 1956. My immediate assumption was that, on this same May Day in '56, Frank Lary defeated the Yankees and the Hungarians did not fare so well against Soviet tanks.

Checking baseball-almanac.com after the river, though no word on the Hungarian-Soviet '56 scrimmage, I learned that the Tigers did not play the Yanks on May 18, 1956, but *did* beat the Yankees 4 days later, the next time they played them. Sure enough, Frank Lary pitched as Detroit defeated New York by a score of 3-2 at Briggs Stadium, out-dueling Whitey Ford that day, both hurling complete games. Lary gave up 2 New York runs in the 1st, then nothing else; Ford allowed Detroit 1 run in the 8th before surrendering a game-winning, Red Wilson, 2-run homer in the bottom of the 9th – what a great day!

A favorite Frank Lary story involves an interview conducted by sports writers with New York Yankee manager Casey Stengel, conducted a few years after this May 1956 clash. The Yanks & Tigers were beginning a series the next day, and Casey was asked about the much-anticipated opening game pitching match-up of Frank Lary versus Whitey Ford. Ole Case replied, *"Naw, Whitey's not pitching against Frank Lary. He's gonna beat us anyway, so why waste Whitey?"* (In an unrelated Casey Stengel quote, he noted, *"It ain't sex that's troublesome, it's staying up all night looking for it."*)

DDDDDDDDDDDDDDDDDDDDDDDDDDDDDDDDDDDDDDDDDDDDDDDDDDDDDDDDDDDDDDDDDDDDDDDDDDDDD

Frank Lary came into this world on April 10, 1930 in Northport, Alabama, the 6th of 7 sons born to Mitt & Margaret Lary. There was plenty of work to do on the family's 520-acre farm, but when the chores were completed, the sons learned how to play baseball on the ball field Mitt built for them on the big front yard, complete with pitcher's mound. Mitt later told a reporter, *"I'd sit on the porch here and tell them what they were doing wrong."* Tuscaloosa was home to the high school the Lary boys attended, and where 5 of the 7 went off to college at the University of Alabama. At the university, all 5 lettered in baseball, and 2 of the 5 also in football.

As a 20-year old, Frank was the pitching ace on the 1950 College World Series Alabama Crimson Tide squad. After serving in the Korean War, Frank broke in with the Tigers in 1954, and teammates soon christened him with the nicknames of "Mule" and "Taters" as a nod to his rural 'Bama roots (once on the team train during a road trip, in his order for dinner Frank wrote "taters" instead of "potatoes").

In 1955, his first full year in the majors, Frank posted for Detroit a 14 win & 15 loss record with a very respectable 3.10 earned run average. The first half of 1956 was a rough one for Lary, and after a July 1 loss his record fell to 4 victories (3 of the 4 over the Yankees) and 10 losses. But it all came together for the 26-year old in the second half: from a July 5 win through the end of the year, Frank was a sizzling 17

& 3, victorious in his last 8 starts, and his win total of 21 was first in the American League for '56. It should be noted that he went 5 & 1 vs. New York. Lary credited part of the 2nd half turnaround to a knuckleball pitch that he'd been working on for a couple of years - by midseason he felt comfortable enough to add it to his game-day arsenal of fastball, curve & slider. As a counterbalance to this hard stuff, the knuckler effectively kept even the best hitters off balance.

A third moniker, "Bulldog", honored Frank for his toughness as a competitor, with the best nickname yet to come: "The Yankee Killer". During Frank's 9 complete seasons with Detroit, the New Yorkers won 8 pennants. Yet of his 123 victories as a Tiger, 28 of them came against the Yankees while losing to the team from the Bronx only 13 times, for a .683-win percentage. Frank's highest win total against any other team was 18 versus the Washington Senators/Minnesota Twins franchise.

It is the author's belief that the single greatest baseball card ever is the Topps 1960 Frank Lary card: on the back of the card it is noted that, in the two previous years of 1958 (when the Yankees were World Champions) and 1959, Frank had a 13 & 1 run against the Yankees. Lary's success against the New York team can be partly explained by the fact that when he pitched against them, he knew he could best 'em and, maybe more importantly, the Yankees knew that he could beat them.

On WJR's "Focus" show with J.P. McCarthy in 1985, J.P. interviewed Mickey Mantle. Mick was talking about the success the Yanks had – except with Detroit, *"In my first 15 years, we won the pennant 13 times... we had a lot of trouble here (in Detroit) though, with Frank Lary, Kaline, and Kuenn. I don't know what our record was with Detroit during those really good (for New York) years, but it couldn't a been much over .500, 'cause they beat us pretty good."* J.P. replied, *"I don't think it was. Frank Lary was known around here as 'the Yankee Killer'. I don't know what you called him in New York."* Mick laughed, *"It wasn't Yankee Killer."*

Frank Lary was chosen for the American League All-Star team in 1960 & 1961, led the A.L. in complete games in 1958, 1960, and 1961 (the only Detroit Tiger to ever do that more than twice), earned a Gold Glove in 1961, and was inducted into the Alabama Sports Hall of Fame. Frank pitched effectively through the 1961 season, but on Opening Day 1962, in a game against the Yankees at Tiger Stadium – which, of course, he won – Frank pulled a leg muscle while turning a double into a triple. Lary changed his pitching delivery to compensate for the injury, creating a series of arm problems, and was never the same again, retiring after the 1965 season.

Frank was a talented musician, a fine guitar picker and singer. During his decade with the Tigers, he performed on stage with country groups at a variety of nightclubs in town, including the old Caravan Gardens on 6 Mile Road at East Davison Street. One of the groups Lary played with around Detroit was *the Swingsters*, whose bandleader Eddie Jackson knew Frank best by his "Taters" handle. At weekend barn dances held at the U.A.W. Hall on Mack Avenue, Frank would play with *Clark's Lazy Ranch Boys*. Just about the entire Lary family knew their way around musical instruments, and in the 60s & 70s Frank and 6 of his 7 brothers played together several times on stage at the Ryman Auditorium in Nashville, the original Grand Old Opry. The group was called, perfectly, *the Lary Brothers Band* (Frank is center stage)...

Perhaps not performing on the level of *the Lary Brothers Band*, but having just as much fun, was the Tigers *Hillbilly Choir*, clubhouse country singing featuring Frank and teammates Bobo Osborne, Red Wilson, and Gail Harris. Vic Wertz, one of the many fellow Tigers who admired Lary, noted that teams need fellas like Frank, a player all the guys looked up to and someone who always had 'em laughing, to keep things loose. In a *Sport* magazine article, Joe Falls told of an early morning in the Lakeland Holiday Inn – the waitress mistakenly brought Paul Foytack a coffee, and he let her know he wanted hot tea. Frank, overhearing this exchange, shouted over, *"Just bring him a beer!"* (sounding a lot like good old Boots Poffenberger back in '38).

With Frank, you could count on a steady stream of jokes and one-liners, a personality that delighted fans as it did teammates. Combined with his successes and tenacity on the field, Lary was a big favorite with the Tiger faithful. Frank roomed with Norm Cash in the 60s, which must have been one of the most light-hearted lodging combinations in sports history. Fellow pitcher Foytack recalled *"a pre-game meeting when we were talking about a certain hitter that we didn't want to beat us. Someone said 'we should just walk him.' Frank said, 'why don't we just hit him?' "* Lary made sure opponents knew that the inside of the plate was his, leading the league in hitting batters with a pitch 3 out of 4 years in the 50s, so perhaps his comment was only partially in jest.

Frank was good friends with several country music legends. His wife Mary Kathryn fondly recalls a time in the mid-70s when she and Frank were invited to spend some time at the home of Webb Pierce, the honky-tonk man who charted more number one songs in the 50s, including "In the Jailhouse Now", than any other country artist. While Frank & Mary were visiting Opryland in the late-70s, Roy "the King of Country" Acuff was playing. Acuff spotted Frank in the audience, inviting Lary to join him on stage. Frank didn't have his guitar with him, but he sang with Roy on a few numbers, much to the delight of Mary watching her husband from the wings. Weekends at Frank & Mary's were spent with Frank's brothers on the front porch, playing & singing together, wedged in tight, until Frank built a roomier structure at the end of their driveway for the weekly musical get-togethers.

DDDDDDDDDDDDDDDDDDDDDDDDDDDDDDDDDDDDDDDDDDDDDDDDDDDDDDDDDDDDDDDDDDDDDDDDDDDDDDD

2007 found Frank back in Michigan at a baseball card show in the Detroit suburb of Redford. I stood in line waiting for my turn to speak with Frank, holding a "Yankees Suck" hat that I'd purchased outside of Fenway Park two years previous. *"Mister Lary, may I shake your hand? It's a true honor to meet you. I was wondering if you'd sign this hat for me, and include on it your lifetime record against the Yankees?"* Frank, as friendly as could be, took one look at the hat and started laughing. He'd brought along one of his buddies, turned to him and said, *"Oh, that's some hat!"* Frank then said he'd be very happy to sign the hat with both his name and his record versus New York, *"But… what was my record against the Yankees?"* Told it was 28 & 13, Frank said with a big smile, *"That's pretty good!"* When you meet your heroes, and they turn out to be kind folks like Frank Lary, it warms your heart. Like Dennis Edwards and the Temptations, I was on *Cloud Nine*.

In 2012, Frank & Mary Lary attended World Series games at Comerica Park. In the concourse, they were visiting the "Walk of Fame", a variety of displays featuring Tiger players decade by decade. They were in front of the Frank Lary display when a man alongside them kept telling Frank & Mary to look at another player displayed, *"Al Kaline is over here! Kaline is over here!"* When they replied that they were looking at the Frank Lary display first, and the man repeated himself, Mary put her hand on Frank's shoulder and said to the fella, *"No… THIS is Frank Lary."* Soon Frank was surrounded by a sea of fans who overheard the exchange, asking him to pose for photos and requesting his signature. Mary said that Frank loved his interactions with Detroit fans, signing autographs, answering fan mail, and that he often said Detroit had the greatest fans in the world.

In 2014, Frank purchased World Series tickets for games at Detroit, but unfortunately our Boys of Summer were eliminated in that year's post-season before reaching the Fall Classic.

Frank Lary passed away just before Christmas of 2017, leaving his dear wife, Mary Kathryn, family, friends, old teammates, and Tiger fans with some incredible memories. We were blessed to have this fine man representing the Tigers, the city of Detroit, and the state of Michigan. Thank you Mary and thank you Alabama for sharing your best with us.

1957 - 1960 Maddening Mediocracy - Except in the Broadcast Booth

"For lo, the winter is past, the rain is over and gone, the flowers appear on the earth, the time of the singing of birds is come, and the voice of the turtle is heard in our land – Happy New Year, Tiger Baseball!"

("Song of Solomon 2:12" – Ernie Harwell's version)

1957 brought new ownership to the Detroit Tigers through a group known as the Knorr syndicate, headed by the two men responsible for radio broadcasts of Tiger games across Michigan: Fred Knorr, owner of Tiger flagship station WKMH (since 1952 replacing WXYZ in that capacity) and John Fetzer, owner of the Tigers out-state radio stations. Financing needed for the syndicate to purchase the team came not only from Knorr & Fetzer, but also from a group of silent partners that included Bing Crosby.

Under Knorr-Fetzer, Knorr was president, Fetzer chairman of the board, Muddy Ruel transitioned from general manager to team special advisor, and Spike Briggs slid over to the vacated G.M. slot. Spike's first major move as general manager was his last major move as general manager. He fired manager Bucky Harris, not appreciating Bucky as much as the players did, and hired in his place Jack Tighe, the man in charge of the Detroit's minor league operations. John Fetzer had made it clear he wanted Spike to hire Al Lopez, the man who piloted the only two teams in the 50s to beat out the Yankees for the league pennant (the Indians in '54 & the White Sox in '59). Unhappy that his suggestion was ignored, Fetzer called a meeting of the board to discuss Spike Briggs' position in the organization. Over the objection of Spike's friend, Fred Knorr, the board agreed that Briggs would be fired, a job that fell to Knorr as team president. However, rather than fire his friend, Knorr resigned his title (while maintaining his ownership stake in the club), the hatchet job then to be handled by the new president, Harvey Hansen. Detroit-native John McHale, a little-used reserve first baseman for the Tigers in the 40s, became the new G.M.

Firing Spike Briggs from his management position in late-April of '57, severed the last vestige of the Briggs Family connection to the ball club that existed since Walter O. Briggs bought a quarter-share of the Tigers from Frank Navin in 1919.

DDDDDDDDDDDDDDDDDDDDDDDDDDDDDDDDDDDDDDDDDDDDDDDDDDDDDDDDDDDDDDDDDDDDDDDDDDDDDDDDD

The excitement felt by the new ownership, the players, and throughout the state of Michigan for the upcoming '57 season was impossible to overstate. Anticipation boiled over with the 48 & 30 second half of '56, propelled by the number one league offense, and two young 20-game winners. If you would have told folks, on top of all of the success from last year, that Jim Bunning, a 5-game winner in '56, would in '57 top the A.L. with 20 victories, they'd be making their World Series plans.

But there was no post-season for Detroit in '57. Not even close. Instead of 4 regulars hitting over .300 as in '56, no one did, and the team batting average dropped 22 points to .257. Al Kaline won his 1st Gold Glove (9 more would follow) and had a good year offensively, but below what everyone had come to expect, leading the team at .295, 90 RBIs & 83 runs scored. Harvey Kuenn hit a pedestrian .277, a full 55-point drop-off from '56. After averaging 99 RBIs in each of the last 4 seasons, Ray Boone only sent 65 runners across home plate. And although Charlie Paw Paw Maxwell's production numbers suffered only minimally, posting a team-high 24 homers with 82 RBIs, his average plummeted 50 points to .276.

The pitching could not make up for the offensive slump, despite Jim Bunning's spectacular showing as number 1 among American League hurlers with 20 wins against only 8 defeats, a shining 2.69 ERA, and topping the circuit with 267 innings tossed. Paul Foytack was the team's number 2 man on the mound in '57, following up his 15-win year with 14 victories and a 3.14 ERA, 8th best in the league. But Lary and Hoeft, who combined for 41 wins just one season before, had off years. The two posted win/loss numbers, respectively, of 11 & 16 and 9 & 11. The most pleasant surprise from the pitching staff, outside of Bunning's fantastic showing, was that of Duke Maas. Unlike Lary and Hoeft, Maas, a Utica native, came off of a horrible 1956, going 0 & 7 with a 6.54 ERA. Now in his 3rd year in The Show, the Duke rebounded smartly at 10 & 14 with a nice 3.28 earned run average, third-best on the team.

The '57 Tigers amazed with their consistent mediocrity, finishing May at 21 & 20, June 35 & 35, July 49 & 49, August 64 & 65, and the season at 78 & 76. And Frank Lary's record against the Yankees? 2 & 2.

DDDDDDDDDDDDDDDDDDDDDDDDDDDDDDDDDDDDDDDDDDDDDDDDDDDDDDDDDDDDDDDDDDDDDDDDDDDD

Just before Thanksgiving 1957, the Tigers front office pulled the trigger on a 13-player trade with the Kansas City Athletics. Never had a transaction involving so many players helped two teams so little. The principals sent packing from Detroit were pitcher Duke Maas, coming off of his best season wearing the Olde English D, centerfielder Bill Tuttle and catcher Frank House, while arriving in the Motor City were 35-year old outfielder Gus Zernial, a 4-time 100-RBI man whose best days were long gone and who would knock in only 51 runs total in '58 & '59 before retiring, Mickey McDermott, a pitcher who hit better than he pitched, and he didn't hit that well, middle-of-the-road reliever Tom Morgan who would have his best years after leaving Detroit in '60 (although with a pretty cool first week with Detroit that year), catcher Tim Thompson who spent all but 4 games of his two years in the Tiger organization as a minor leaguer, and two other players...

1) Also coming to Detroit was outfielder Lou Skizas who hit 18 homers for KC in '57 but would hit only 1 for Detroit in '58 and be out of the majors by '59. As poorly as Lou performed at the plate for the Tigers, .242 in 33 plate appearances, he may have been even worse with a glove. As Skizas himself noted, *"Manager Jack Tighe not only thought I was a terrible 3rd baseman, but also not a very good outfielder."* So we got that going for us. The man nicknamed "the nervous Greek" did, however, bring entertainment value to Tiger fans on the rare days when the manager dared write Lou's name on the line-up card. As Skizas walked from the on-deck circle to home plate, he would set his bat on the ground, cover it with dirt, then wipe the bat off by rubbing it between his legs, kiss the end of the bat, and conclude the ritual by reaching into his back pocket 3 times to touch a good-luck charm that apparently stopped working once Lou began receiving paychecks from the Tigers.

2) The main reason Detroit sought this trade was to obtain KC shortstop Billy Martin. The team brain trust saw Billy as the sparkplug the offense needed to get back to their league-leading 1956 production. Since breaking in as a rookie with the Yankees in 1950, Billy Martin was known for frequent fist fights with opponents (earning him the name *Billy the Kid*), strong defensive play, and clutch hitting. Casey Stengel, Billy's manager at New York, asked why he thought so highly of Martin as a player, said, *"If liking a kid who never let you down in the clutch is favoritism, I plead guilty."* Billy's best performances took place at World Series time, including his 1952 Game 7 spectacular catch of a Jackie Robinson wind-blown pop-up with the bases loaded and 2 outs that saved the Fall Classic for the Yanks, and in '53 when he broke Babe Ruth's record for total bases in a 6-game Series.

Why would the Yankees ever let such a player go to the Kansas City Athletics? Martin teammate and close friend Mickey Mantle explained it in his 1985 interview with WJR's J.P. McCarthy, detailing the legendary 1957 night at New York's Copacabana, when several Yankees, including Mickey, Billy Martin, & Whitey Ford, got into a bit of a brawl with a couple of bowling teams out celebrating at their year-end banquet. *"The Yankees then traded Billy, sayin' he was a bad influence on me. In 1956, I won the Triple Crown, and led the league in 6 offensive departments. In 1957 when they traded Billy, I was hitting .400 or something like that. So, when they traded him and told him it was 'cause he was a bad influence, he said, 'what do they think this guy can do anyway?'"*

Detroit felt that if Billy could light a fire under the 1958 Tiger offense, he was worth taking a chance on.

DDDDDDDDDDDDDDDDDDDDDDDDDDDDDDDDDDDDDDDDDDDDDDDDDDDDDDDDDDDDDDDDDDDDDDDDDDDDDDDDDDDD

Although his best years were with Detroit, since his trade from the Tigers to the Boston Red Sox in June of 1952, George Kell's bat never slowed down. From the moment he departed Detroit as a 29-year old, through his days paired with Ted Williams in Boston, and then as a member of the Chicago White Sox, until retiring as a 34-year old with the Baltimore Orioles at the end of 1957, Kell hit .296 over those final 5 & ½ years and earned four All-Star berths ('53, '54, '56 & '57) to go with his 6 while with the Tigers.

George had begun to consider retirement since his '54 trade from Boston to Chicago, and when as an Oriole he was hit in the head twice in '57 (once at Briggs Stadium by Tiger Steve Gromek), he likely wished he had listened to his own counsel. However, it was fortuitous that Kell stayed in the game for his May '56 trade to Baltimore, as an important person was about to come into his life, William Earnest "Ernie" Harwell. Ernie was the Brooklyn Dodgers and then the New York Giants announcer from 1949 to 1953, becoming the first-ever Baltimore Oriole broadcaster, once the St. Louis Browns franchise moved to Baltimore and became the Orioles in time for the '54 season.

Kell showed a knack for the broadcasting biz while with Detroit in the early-50s, occasionally working with Harry Heilmann on Harry's game day 15-minute baseball radio program. While Kell recuperated from the two baseballs to his head in 1957, he took the opportunity to sit in the Oriole's broadcast booth with his new friend, Ernie Harwell. Ernie told George, *"Now you're learning the art of freeloading: all the hot dogs you can eat and all the pop you can drink."* Harwell invited Kell to broadcast an inning – George liked it <u>and</u> the radio/TV audience liked him.

The Kell-Harwell friendship was now established, but working together in the booth on a regular basis was still aways down the road. When George was healthy enough to rejoin the Orioles in July of '57, he finished his final season as an active player with his 10th All-Star berth and a .297 batting average, giving Kell a career mark of .306. In his year and one-half with Baltimore, Kell showed the ropes to a teenaged 3rd baseman with tremendous potential, fellow Arkansas native Brooks Robinson. Brooks grew up 90 miles away from George's beloved Swifton, and when George went home after each season, friends told him of an amazing American Legion ballplayer from Little Rock. How ironic that George would groom the young Brooks to take over his third base position at Baltimore AND that the two, who quickly became close friends, were inducted into the Hall of Fame together in 1983.

George planned, after 1957, to spend a long retirement with his dear Charlene while tending to his Swifton farm, but CBS came a' calling, asking Kell to host a pre-game interview for their *"Game of the Week"*, a nationally-televised show running ever Saturday throughout the season, featuring different (and usually the top) teams in each week's game. He would be gone from his home only 1 night a week while getting to talk baseball with old teammates & opponents – good friend George Kell was just about the only interviewer that Ted Williams would talk to –and this opportunity proved one that Kell could not pass up. George was so good that when Tiger announcer Mel Ott died in a car crash in November of '58, Detroit offered George a partnership with Van Patrick on the radio/TV broadcasts, Kell handling the middle 3 innings, Patrick the first-third & seventh-ninth. Sorry Charlene, but your husband just signed a 5-year contract, and the quiet retirement was put on hold.

Van Patrick, the 'Ol Announcer, was let go at the end of '59 – the Tigers newest sponsor, Stroh's beer, felt that Patrick's promotional work over the years tied him too closely to Stroh's competitor, Goebbels beer, for Van to stay (no worries - Patrick had plenty of work to keep him busy, as voice of the Lions from 1950 until he passed away in 1974). The search for Van Patrick's replacement was a short one. George Kell recommended to the Tigers that they hire Ernie Harwell & Detroit made an offer to Lulu's husband: beginning with Opening Day 1960, Harwell would broadcast the first 4 & ½ innings on TV, and Kell would do the same thing on radio, then they'd swap. Ernie accepted, a beautiful marriage bloomed, and Tiger fans were the richer…

George… *It's a bunt, and it's a dandy; I don't think you can hit a ball any harder than that; It's a bright & sunshiny day.* Ernie… *He stood there like the house by the side of the road; That ball was caught by a fan from Southgate (or any other Michigan town Ernie chose to say); He kicks and deals…* just a few of the sayings spoken by these two fine southern gentlemen that warmed the hearts of Tiger fans everywhere.

DDDDDDDDDDDDDDDDDDDDDDDDDDDDDDDDDDDDDDDDDDDDDDDDDDDDDDDDDDDDDDDDDDDDDDDDDDDDDD

During the first month of 1958, the Tigers pulled off a pretty nice inter-league trade. Going to the San Francisco Giants was Bengals light-hitting reserve infielder Jim Finigan, while coming to Detroit were two players: 1st baseman and soon to be a member of Frank Lary's *Hillbilly Choir*, Gail Harris, who not only could carry a tune, but also added some nice production to Detroit's '58 lineup with 20 home runs & 82 RBIs; and a man who in his first game as a Tiger in front of the home crowd had as many hits as Finigan did in all of 1958, utility man Ozzie Virgil.

After spending the 1st two months of the season with Detroit's farm club in Charleston, on June 6, 1958, Ozzie Virgil of the Dominican Republic became the first non-white to ever wear the Olde English D. His first game at The Corner took place on June 17, and what a Briggs Stadium debut Virgil had! Ozzie went

5 for 5 versus the Washington Senators in front of 30,000 fans cheering on the newest Tiger and his teammates in Detroit's 9-2 victory, pitcher Billy Hoeft the beneficiary of the 17-hit attack.

Ozzie's arrival coincided with Detroit's rebound from a rough start to the '58 season, its nadir on May 23 when Detroit dropped their 9th in a row, the last 2 against the Yankees, falling 13 games behind red-hot New York. On May 24, the Tigers sent Frank Lary to the mound to break the streak. So, guess what happened? The losing streak ended as Frank Lary once again pitched magnificently versus the Bronx Bombers, going the distance in a 3-2 Tiger win. After falling behind to the Yanks 1-0 in the first on a Mantle RBI grounder, Detroit got to pitcher Sal "the Barber" Maglie for their own RBI grounder by Reno Bertoia along with a Harvey Kuenn homer to take a 2-1 lead in the third. Although Frank surrendered a game-tying single to Gil McDougald in the sixth, Al Kaline doubled in Frank Bolling with what proved to be the game-winner in the 7th, as Frank put down the final 6 Yankees in order.

In '58 Lary rebounded nicely from his rough '57, leading the pitching staff with a 2.90 ERA and 16 wins against 15 losses; versus the pennant-winning Yankees, Frank dominated, going 7 & 1 with two June shutouts. Mister Consistency, Paul Foytack, followed up his 15 & 14-win seasons with once again 15 victories. Billy Hoeft, although still a young man at 26, was on the downside of his career. While in '58 he won 10 games, the hurler who dominated hitters in tossing 15 shutouts over 1954 through 1956 would, from 1959 until he retired in 1966, only average 3 victories a year with one last career shutout. Jim Bunning, hampered by an early season rib injury, wasn't able to repeat his spectacular 20 win/2.69 ERA of '57, posting numbers of 14 & 12 with a 3.52, BUT did have a golden moment in 1958...

On July 20, the Tigers played a doubleheader against the Red Sox at Fenway Park. The game 1 mound match-up saw Bunning against a fine hurler, two-time All Star Frank Sullivan. Through 4 innings, the two dominated the hitters, a first-inning Billy Martin single the only blemish against Sullivan, while Bunning surrendered only a walk and a hit batsman. The Tigers broke through big time in the fifth. Vocalist and first sacker Gail Harris scorched a booming triple to right to open the frame, before coming home on a Gus Zernial double. Sullivan settled down to get Bolling on a pop fly and then struck out Ozzie Virgil. Just when it looked like he'd get out of the inning with no further damage, catcher Red Wilson singled home Zernial. After Bunning kept the inning alive with a single of his own, Kuenn sent Red home with a knock to center before a Billy Martin liner was tracked down in right by Jackie Jensen for out number 3.

Jim Bunning now returned to the mound with a 3-run cushion, and sailed through the 5th, 6th, 7th, and 8th with only one runner reaching base, that on a walk, and not one Boston batter had yet touched him today for a hit. Frank Sullivan had likewise settled in, but the 3 runs the Tigers got to him for in the fifth were 2 more than Bunning would need. The ninth would not be easy, with the top of the Sox order due up, including one of the greatest hitters in MLB history, with a lifetime .344 average, batting third, Ted Williams. Bunning bore down to get Gene Stephens on a called third strike, then put down Ted Lepcio on a swinging strike 3. Bunning stood only one out from baseball immortality, as Teddy Baseball stepped up to the plate and all 29,529 Bostonians in attendance rose to their feet. If Bunning could have picked the one defender to secure his no hit bid, it would be Al Kaline. Sure enough, Williams swings and lofts a flyball towards right field where Kaline floats towards the incoming sphere, wrapping both hands around the baseball as it lands in his glove. Jim Bunning became only the third pitcher to keep an opponent hitless at Fenway Park, his 12 strikeouts the most ever by a Tiger tossing a no hitter.

DDDDDDDDDDDDDDDDDDDDDDDDDDDDDDDDDDDDDDDDDDDDDDDDDDDDDDDDDDDDDDDDDDDDDDDD

On June 28, 1958, 3 weeks before Bunning's no-hit gem at Fenway, an amazing reunion took place at The Corner, also involving the Detroit & Boston franchises. To kick off the historic afternoon, four legends from the days when Detroit played at old Bennett Park, teammates on the Tigers first pennant-winning teams of 1907, 1908, & 1909, Ty Cobb, Wahoo Sam Crawford, Davy Jones, and George Moriarty, walked on to the field. Following was a 2-inning Old Timers game between Red Sox & Tigers players of teams spanning the 1900s thru 1940s, including the entire starting lineup of the '35 World Champion Tigers, led by their player/manager, Mickey Cochrane.

Hank Aguirre asked Al Kaline if he could have one of his bats, and then managed to have the bat signed by 5 Hall-of-Famers: the G-Men aka Hank Greenberg, Charlie Gehringer & Goose Goslin, plus Hal Newhouser, and Cochrane. Others autographing the bat were Tommy Bridges, Schoolboy Rowe, Elden Auker, Vic Sorrell, Gerald "Gee" Walker, Jo-Jo White, Pete Fox, Billy Rogell, and Marv Owen from the '35 team; pitcher Bernie Boland, who averaged 13 wins a season from 1915-1919 for Detroit; Clyde Manion, a reserve catcher in the 20s; Chet Laabs from the '37-'39 teams; the wonderful Barney McCosky & big hitting Rudy York from the 1940 pennant-winning Tigers; Dick Wakefield & his incredible 1943 & 44; from the 1945 World Series Champions were pitcher Dizzy Trout & manager Steve O'Neill; and the last man to wear number 6 before Kaline, an All-Star in 1947 & 48, Pat Mullin.

All except Cobb, Crawford & Davy Jones played in the Old Timers game, even George Moriarty – at 74 still fun 'n feisty - and every one of the 24 who played for Detroit signed Aguirre's bat. These legends of Detroit played the legends of Boston, who included Jimmy Foxx, Joe Cronin, and Lefty Grove, to a 1 to 1 tie, the Tigers run courtesy of a Jo-Jo White homer off of Grove into the lower deck in right.

In the regular season match-up that followed the Old Timers game, Boston defeated Detroit 6-5 in 12 innings, despite 4 hits by Harvey Kuenn and 3 by Gail Harris. Hank Aguirre pitched the ninth inning, 3 up and 3 down, including getting Ted Williams on strikes.

It is believed that the bat signed by so many Tiger greats remains in the Aguirre family to this day.

DDDDDDDDDDDDDDDDDDDDDDDDDDDDDDDDDDDDDDDDDDDDDDDDDDDDDDDDDDDDDDDDDDDDDDDDDDDD

Despite the contribution of newcomer Gail Harris, his 82 RBIs and team-best 20 homers, the 1958 Tiger offense was, perfect for their '57-'59 231 win/231 loss run, mediocre. Exceptions to lackluster included Kuenn, who bounced back from an unlikely .277 in '57 to bat .319 with a league-best 39 doubles, and Kaline at .313 with a team-high 85 RBIs while winning his 2nd consecutive Gold Glove. The two K&K Kids ranked 3rd & 4th in A.L. batting average. The supporting cast featured 2nd baseman's Frank Bolling's 91 runs & 75 RBIs, highs for his 12-year career, Gus Zernial chipping in a nice .323 in limited action, and catcher Red Wilson – a Paul Carey favorite – who enjoyed the finest of his 10 seasons in batting .299.

After his 5 for 5 debut at The Corner, it was downhill for Ozzie Virgil, hitting only .244 for the full year; the strong production from Charlie Maxwell in the prior two years, 28 & 24 homers with 87 & 82 RBIs, sagged to 13 & 65; the great Billy Martin experiment, despite his league leading 13 sacrifice bunts, was a failure – he was rarely on base to score, hitting .255 with a low .279 on base percentage due to drawing only 16 walks, while the hoped for spark that would ignite the team was nowhere to be found.

When the dust settled on 1958, the Tigers won exactly as many as they lost, 77 & 77, good for 5th place in the A.L. What impacted the record as much as any other single factor was that the usual contributions from Ray Boone, the #1 Tiger run producer in the fifties, were in the rearview mirror...

On June 15 of '58, the Tigers traded one of the finest third sackers in team history, when they sent Ray Boone, one month shy of his 35th birthday, along with 25-year old pitcher Bob Shaw, to the White Sox for reliever Bill Fisher and first baseman/outfielder Tito (Terry's Dad) Francona, a .250 hitter in his 3 major league seasons. The timing was good on moving Boone. Although loved by Tiger fans, his skills were waning. After knocking in 41 runs in the back half of '58 for Chicago, Ray would only plate 32 runners over the next two seasons before retiring from the game after 1960. But boy, what a '53-'57 production machine he had been for the Tigers, averaging 88 RBIs in each of those 5 years for Detroit, while flashing a glove that earned him recognition as one of the finest defensive third basemen in the 50s. Tiger fans cheer of *Boooooone!* will be heard at The Corner once again on September 27, 1999.

Now the wisdom of peddling Bob Shaw, on the other hand...

In Shaw's 1 & ½ years as a Tiger, he appeared in 18 games, all but 2 in relief, going 1 & 3 with a 5.75 ERA. After finishing out '58 as a Chicago reliever, the Sox decided to try Shaw as a starter in 1959 and did ***that*** turn out to be a fine decision: Bob Shaw had an outstanding season, going 18 & 6 with a sparkling 2.69 ERA and was 3rd in Cy Young Award balloting. Regarding the two White Sox sent to Detroit, Bill Fisher's bloated 7.63 ERA earned him only 3 months in Detroit before being waived; in Tito Francona's 45 games as a Tiger, he hit .246 and was traded in March '59 to Cleveland for Larry Doby, a once great and now over-the-hill player who will appear in 18 games in his 1 month as a Tiger and be out of the majors at year's end. As a first-year Cleveland Indian in 1959, Francona hit a no-one-saw-it-coming .363 in 443 plate appearances, not enough times at bat to qualify for the batting title, but spectacular nonetheless. As the Detroit brass and their fans watched what ex-Tigers Bob Shaw and Tito Francona did with their new Chicago and Cleveland teams in 1959, they had to think of what might have been.

By Thanksgiving, Billy Martin's days as a Tiger were over, sent away in a very good trade for Detroit with reliever Al Cicotte to Cleveland for infielder Ossie Alvarez (done as a major leaguer after 8 games as a Tiger), pitcher Ray Narleski (although a '58 All-Star, going only 4 & 12 with a 5.78 ERA in '59), and the man who made it such a fine transaction for Detroit, pitcher Don Mossi. Although only 7 & 8 with a 3.90 with the Tribe in 1958, from 1959 through 1963 with Detroit, Mossi would win 59 games.

DDDDDDDDDDDDDDDDDDDDDDDDDDDDDDDDDDDDDDDDDDDDDDDDDDDDDDDDDDDDDDDDDDDDDDDDDDDD

At the end of the 1950s, Mickey Mantle spent a night out in Detroit with the great Lions' quarterback, Bobby Layne, and spoke to J.P. McCarthy about it on WJR a quarter century later...

"One of the only games I ever got kicked out of was here in Tiger Stadium. Bobby Layne took me out to The Flame Bar. We went out to eat, I don't know if you ever been to The Flame Bar or not, it's not a good place to, well, I'm not gonna say it's not a good place, it wasn't a good – I was scared, let's put it that way. Anyway, we stayed out quite late that night, and I had a terrible hangover the next day, and ah, the first time up... I don't know who was pitchin' for Detroit, but I barely saw the ball move, swish, right by. The next pitch, I said I got no business in this game, so the next pitch I yelled at the umpire, and the catcher – you know I hardly ever yelled at the umpire – the catcher looks at me like, 'Hey Mick, that was right down the middle.' I said, "No it wasn't, and I could see that I had to say something worse, so I called the ump something and he said, 'If you're trying to get out of this game, you're gone!'"

Over the years, the story has taken on a life of its own, and been told and retold by those other than Mantle, with a slightly different ending, one in which the ump tells Mick, *"I know who you were out with last night Mickey, and you aren't going anywhere, so get right back in the batter's box."* Each version is charming in its own way.

DDDDDDDDDDDDDDDDDDDDDDDDDDDDDDDDDDDDDDDDDDDDDDDDDDDDDDDDDDDDDDDDDDDD

The Tigers '58 post-season wheeling & dealing wasn't done with the Thanksgiving-eve trade of Billy Martin to Cleveland for Don Mossi. On December 6, Detroit dramatically improved their on-base-percentage with the acquisition of "the Walking Man", Eddie Yost, third baseman from the Washington Senators. Also coming over from our nation's capital was utility man Rocky Bridges & outfielder Neil Chrisley in exchange for infielder Reno Bertoia, and minor leaguers Jim Delsing & Ron Samford.

This move was a steal for Detroit. Eddie's "Walking Man" nickname was well-deserved, having led the American League in walks 4 times while a Senator. In his two years as a Tiger, 1959 & 1960, Yost was the perfect lead-off hitter, tops in the league in both walks (135 & 125) and in on-base-percentage (.435 & .414). His 1,614 career base-on-balls placed him 11th all-time in MLB history. However, the presence of Eddie Yost at the top of the order could not overcome the team's horrible start to the 1959 campaign. The season opened at home on April 10 against the White Sox in front of 38,332, a Charlie Maxwell 8th inning 3-run homer rallying the Tigers from a 7-4 deficit and sending the game into extra innings, where Detroit lost a tough one, 9-7 in 14.

The Tigers dropped their next 5 and were 2 & 12 when Washington hit town for a 3-game series from April 30 to May 2. Not only did Detroit get swept, the third game a resounding 15-3 pounding, but the team drew only <u>8,101 total</u> to Briggs Stadium for all 3 contests. A 2 & 15 team with a disinterested fan base was cause for alarm and new GM Rick Ferrell decided the time to act was now, firing as skipper Bill Norman, who had taken over the managerial reins from Jack Tighe 50 games into the '58 campaign, and replacing Bill with Jimmy Dykes. Jimmy was an old pro who had played in baseball's first two All-Star games of '33 & '34, and managed in the majors for 18 seasons since his first in 1934 as a 37-year old player/manager for the Chicago White Sox.

For Jimmy Dykes, this was his fifth managerial stop, and he never had a finer debut then that first day on the job with Detroit. It was May 3, a Sunday, with the Yankees at The Corner as 43,438 filed in to watch the doubleheader. Up until today, Charlie Maxwell had spent most of the young season on the bench, batting a meager .182. After Charlie slumped the prior year to 13 homers & 65 RBIs, the team traded for Larry Doby as insurance in case Maxwell couldn't bounce back. Dykes thought it might be a good idea to get Charlie in the lineup today. Good thinkin' Jimmy. Game 1 was the first 1959 clash between Detroit & New York, and the pitching match-up was a doozy, pitting the reigning Cy Young winner, the Yanks' Bob Turley, against the pride of Northport, Alabama, the Yankee Killer himself, Frank Strong Lary.

Detroit drew first blood, Eddie Yost leading off the Tigers first with a walk, one of 4 for Eddie in today's twin bill. The next batter was part-time 1st sacker & Frank Lary's *Hillbilly Choir* member, Bobo Osborne. Bobo also drew a walk, pushing Yost to 2nd. Up stepped Charlie Maxwell who promptly singled Yost across home plate to put Detroit up 1-0. After the Yankees scored two unearned runs in their 2nd, a Frank Bolling home run in the Tigers half of the frame tied things up. Detroit shortstop Rocky Bridges broke the tie and at the same time knocked Turley out of the game with a third inning single that sent Kaline scurrying across home plate. 3-2 Detroit. The game stayed that way until Charlie *"Always on a Sunday"* Maxwell led off Detroit's 7th with a solo homer off of Don Larsen that gave Lary a 2-run cushion. Frank closed the game out as pinch hitter Enos Slaughter, 42-years old but still dangerous, flew out to Kaline with 2 runners on base for the game's final out. With today's win, Frank's all-time record versus New York improved to 17 & 5.

On the hill for game 2 was Don Mossi for Detroit versus ex-Tiger Duke Maas. Duke never made it out of the first inning. Eddie Yost led off for the Tigers with a homer and Bobo Osborne followed with a single. Charlie Maxwell continued to make new manager Dykes look like a genius as he lit into the Duke's next offering for a 2-run home run, putting Detroit up 3-0. Maas finally recorded an out when Kaline blasted a rocket, but right at third baseman Clete Boyer, and when next batter Larry Doby was issued a base on balls, the Duke was sent to the showers, his day done. Reliever Johnny Kucks surrendered a single to Rocky Bridges and a run-scoring base hit to Red Wilson that scored Doby before putting out the fire. At the end of one, Tigers 4 Yankees nothing.

In the fourth, the Yankees got on the scoreboard on a wild pitch, and the Tigers responded in their half of the frame on a 3-run home run by Charlie Maxwell. Charlie *"Sunday Punch"* Maxwell was loving this Sabbath. He'd homered in his last at bat in game 1, homered in his first at bat in game 2, drew a walk his 2nd time up, then homered again in the 4th. But he was not done yet, concluding the scoring with a solo shot in the 7th – his fourth home run in four official (a walk counting as no time at the plate) at bats, tying the major league record. Final score, Detroit 8 New York 2. Charlie's day was the greatest in his 14-year career: 5 for 7 with 4 home runs and 8 RBIs.

What an afternoon for the Tigers and their fans! The doubleheader sweep of first-place New York was the spark that catapulted them on a 2-month, red-hot, run. From 10 & ½ games out going into the May 3rd twin bill, the Tigers were a house 'a fire, driven by league-leading performances from Eddie Yost, tops with 115 runs scored/135 walks/.435 OBP, and the outfield of CF Kaline, RF Kuenn and LF Maxwell, as they closed in on first place.

Last year, Kuenn had moved to centerfield from shortstop to make room for Billy Martin, but manager Dykes preferred Kaline in center, although Harvey had done an amazing job patrolling that position, a major surprise to some. Long-time baseball man Leo Durocher questioned the wisdom of having Kuenn cover center – that was before he saw a play that Kuenn made at Comiskey Park, a play that prompted the amazed Durocher to state that, *"Only Willie Mays could make a play like that."* In Harvey's first year in center, he led the league's outfielders in putouts. No matter who played center, the Tigers presented an outstanding outfield defense (including Kaline's 2nd consecutive Gold Glove) and no outfield was more dangerous offensively:

Kaline's .530 slugging percentage was #1 in the A.L. & his .327 average was #2; Kuenn was #1 with 42 doubles to go with his A.L. title winning .353. And then there was *"the Sabbath Smasher"*, Charlie Paw Paw Maxwell. After Charlie's 4-home run May 3rd, he hit homers on 5 of the next 8 Sundays, every one of them either tying or winning the game, and established career highs with 31 homers (A.L. 4th) & 95 RBIs (A.L. 5th). All of this offense was solidly supported by 17-win seasons each from Bunning, Mossi & Lary. When Detroit rallied for 7 late runs to pull out a 7-4 win at Washington's Griffith Stadium on June 20, their 32nd win in their last 46 games, they were one-half game out of first place.

DDDDDDDDDDDDDDDDDDDDDDDDDDDDDDDDDDDDDDDDDDDDDDDDDDDDDDDDDDDDDDDDDDDDDDDDDD

The kids loved all the Tigers, but near the top of each one's list was Charlie Maxwell. During pre-game warm-ups, Charlie would monkey around for their entertainment, catching balls hit or thrown to him behind his back or between his legs, and then toss the balls to kids in the stands. One youngster was able to get closer to Charlie than most...

Attending a '59 game with his grandpa, Levi Mueillur, was 6-year old Johnny Harcourt of St. Clair Shores. During Tiger pre-game warmups, Grandpa Levi leaned over the railing calling out to his buddy, Charlie Maxwell. Levi was a fine enough ballplayer to have earned a tryout with Detroit some years back, and it was during this time that he had struck up a friendship with some of the Tigers including Paw Paw. Levi hollers to Charlie, *"Hey how ya doin', how ya doin'?"* Charlie waves back and during a break in the game prep wanders over to his old buddy Levi and young Johnny for a chat. After a spell, the guys in the dugout shout for Charlie to come on in, it's getting near game time. Charlie turns to head toward the dugout and flips the ball to Levi, whose grandson Johnny is excitedly distracted, looking up at his grandpa and yappin', *"I got to talk to Charlie Maxwell! I got to talk to Charlie Maxwell!"* With his attention focused on sharing his elation with grandpa, 6-year old Johnny never saw Charlie flip the ball in their direction, and "Bonk!" the ball goes off the side of his head. *"Oh man, Charlie Maxwell talked to me AND tossed a ball off my head – wait 'til my friends hear about this!"*

DDDDDDDDDDDDDDDDDDDDDDDDDDDDDDDDDDDDDDDDDDDDDDDDDDDDDDDDDDDDDDDDDDDDDDDDDD

One-half game out on June 20 was as close as the Tigers would get to first place in '59. Detroit dropped 6 of their next 7, and had a rough 12 & 18 July. Too many injuries and too little bullpen dragged the team down, although the individual performances of Maxwell, Kaline, Kuenn, Yost, and Bunning (201 Ks tops in the A.L.) were entertaining for Tiger fans – as was Frank Lary's August 4 win at Yankee Stadium, his fifth straight win over New York this year and 13th in his last 14 decisions versus the team from the Bronx, ending the year with a 21 & 6 lifetime record versus the Yanks.

The Tigers finished in fourth place at 76 & 78, but just 3 games behind the Yankees – this was only the 2nd time in the fifties that New York didn't win the American League pennant. That honor in '59 went to the surprising Chicago White Sox, in no small part due to two pitchers that Detroit gave them in two bad trades from the Tigers perspective: Bob Shaw, whose 18 & 6 mark resulted in an A.L. tops .750 winning percentage, and Detroit-native and an All-Star for the fifth year in a row, all since being traded by the Tigers, Billy Pierce.

The White Sox also had a 2nd year player who got into 58 games, contributing 16 runs scored, 4 homers, 16 RBIs and a great sense of humor that kept his teammates loose, a 24-year old named Norm Cash.

After the '59 season concluded, Chicago included Norm in a December 6 trade with Cleveland. Norm's stay in Cleveland would be a brief one.

DDDDDDDDDDDDDDDDDDDDDDDDDDDDDDDDDDDDDDDDDDDDDDDDDDDDDDDDDDDDDDDDDDDDDDDDDD

Paul Pienta of Huntington Woods had his first Briggs Stadium encounter when, *"I was probably eight or nine years old. That would be 1959 or 1960. My dad took me to a Sunday Tiger double-hitter. I can't remember who won, but I think it was a split. What happened to the Tiger pennant, scorebook and Tiger 'bat-pen' I got as souvenirs is anyone's guess. What I do remember is that before we ever got to our seats, I saw the greenest, most well-kept grass I had ever seen in my entire life - and that was through a haze of smoke. I say the greenest because my dad's free time was always spent tending to the care of his lawn at our house or keeping the flowerbeds weed-free. I always thought that was the color of green grass. I was wrong. The green grass at Briggs Stadium far surpassed the "green, green grass of home". After the shock of seeing someone with a green thumb that was better than my dad's and the field mowed criss-cross pattern, my sense of smell came into effect. My nose picked up the smell of the cigars - that explained the haze between the ball field and myself. But then I smelled hot dogs! What I remember most is the taste of that hot dog on a steamed bun with mustard. It makes my mouth begin to salivate. The best dog in the world came from those metal containers being served at your seat."*

DDDDDDDDDDDDDDDDDDDDDDDDDDDDDDDDDDDDDDDDDDDDDDDDDDDDDDDDDDDDDDDDDDDDDDDDDD

For 13 months, from September 1959 to October 1960, Bill DeWitt served as president of the Tigers. Prior to his hire by Detroit, DeWitt was the assistant general manager of the Yankees for 3 years in the late-50s. As Tiger President, Bill DeWitt reinstated 50 cent *Ladies Day* games after a 16-year hiatus and created a policy giving kids a "Tiger contract" if they grabbed a foul ball. On the frown side, he had the Olde English D removed from player uniforms, replaced by "Detroit" written in script across the front – the Olde English D was brought back permanently in '61.

Above and beyond those moves, Bill DeWitt's short tenure was best known for the 3 huge (2 historic) trades that Detroit made in '60 with the Cleveland Indians GM, Frank "Trader" Lane...

1. April 12: one week before Opening Day, the Tigers trade Steve (not even Don) Demeter to the Cleveland Indians for Norm Cash – the Greatest Trade in Tiger History!

When Tigers GM Rick Ferrell was initially offered *cash* for Demeter by Cleveland GM Lane, he was surprised that the Indians meant Norm and not the monetary kind. Ferrell most likely expected a modest sum of money, not a promising slugger, to be offered for a man who hit .111 the prior year.

Until April of 1960, the *Toledo War Peace Settlement of 1836*, resulting in the State of Ohio trading the Upper Peninsula to the Territory of Michigan in exchange for Michigan's southern strip of land including Toledo, was considered the most lopsided trade between the 2 neighbors (the 1836 settlement was believed to be one-sided even *before* the U.P. discovery of billions of tons of copper & iron ore).

With the April 12, 1960 deal that sent the Detroit Tigers Steve (*not even Don*) Demeter to the Cleveland Indians for Norm Cash, we have a new Buckeye State champion for worst Ohio-to-Michigan trade ever.

After the trade, Steve played in 4 games for Cleveland in 1960, went to bat 5 times, had no hits, and his MLB career was concluded in May of that year. Norm soon became the Tigers everyday first baseman, a position he held for 15 years, made four All-Star teams, was the only American Leaguer with over 20 homers every year from 1961-1969, and retired with 373 homers in a Tigers uniform, 2nd only to Al Kaline (when left-handed Norm retired in '74, his 377 lifetime homers – including 4 with the White Sox – placed him 4th among lefties in A.L. history, behind only Babe Ruth, Ted Williams, & Lou Gehrig). In '61, Norm had an MVP-worthy year, hitting .361 with 41 home runs and 132 runs batted in. 7 years later in the World Series, Norm led the Tigers with a .385 batting average.

Norman Dalton Cash was one of the most popular players in Detroit sports history, loved by teammates and fans alike. Norm reflected the blue-collar Tiger fans who cheered him on - work hard, play hard.

Norm Cash for Steve (*not even Don*) Demeter… God bless their little Buckeye hearts.

2. April 17: 2 days before the Opener, the Tigers trade Harvey Kuenn to the Indians for Rocky Colavito.

Trading the reigning batting champion for the reigning home run champion had never been done – until now (Harvey will be greatly missed by Tiger fans, as Rocky will be by the Tribe faithful). It was Kuenn's .353 average for Colavito's 42 home runs. Colavito homered in his first home at bat with Detroit, then did so again the next day, finishing the year with 35 homers (equaling Rocky's per year average in his four Detroit seasons), the most for the Tigers since Hank Greenberg hit 44 in 1946. In Kuenn's single season with the Tribe, he hit .308 and made the All-Star team, before being swapped to San Francisco. New Detroit Tiger Rocky Colavito would now wear Harvey Kuenn's old number 7.

3. August 3: the teams trade managers, Detroit's Jimmy Dykes in exchange for Cleveland's Joe Gordon.

This was the only trade of managers in MLB history. The effect on each team was amazingly similar: under Joe Gordon, Detroit's record was 26 & 31; under Jimmy Dykes, Cleveland's record was 26 & 32. Gordon's stay in Detroit was brief, and he was replaced by Bob Sheffing as Tiger skipper before the 1961 season began. In an interesting footnote to this manager swap, 4 days after it occurred, coaches from the two teams also traded places to follow their managers: Luke Appling went to Cleveland and Jo-Jo White came to Detroit. This was a homecoming for Jo-Jo, the starting centerfielder for the 1935 World Series Champion Tigers under Mickey Cochrane, and star of the 1958 Old Timers Game. White played for Detroit from 1932 through 1938, rooming with Hank Greenberg on road trips during those years. The two were great friends, though Greenberg said New Yorker Hank & Georgia native Jo-Jo *"fought the Civil War every evening"* and Jo-Jo admitted to Hank he'd thought (before they were roomies, it's assumed) that all Jews had horns on their heads.

DDDDDDDDDDDDDDDDDDDDDDDDDDDDDDDDDDDDDDDDDDDDDDDDDDDDDDDDDDDDDDDDDDDDDDDDDD

The 1960 Detroit season opened on April 19 before 52,756 in Cleveland, the first game worked by the Tiger broadcast pairing of Ernie Harwell & George Kell. With a freezing wind blowing in off of Lake Erie, Ernie recalled it as one of the coldest days he'd ever experienced, and one that felt like it would never end. The game had a strange aura about it in light of the 2 trades between the teams that took place in the past week, Norm Cash-Steve Demeter & Harvey Kuenn-Rocky Colavito. The game turned out to be one of the great Opening Day pitcher's duels. Frank Lary and the Tribe's Gary Bell, who would be All-Star teammates in 3 months, tossed one shutout inning after the other, through the 8th, the 9th, the 10th, with both still on the mound into the 11th. Finally, the Tigers broke through in the top of the 11th. Catcher Lou Berberet drew a one-out walk & Johnny Groth ran for Lou. Frank Lary, as he so often did, helped his own cause by singling Groth to 3rd base. "The Walking Man", Eddie Yost, walked to load the bases as Gary Bell was relieved by Bob Grim. Pinch hitter Neil Chrisley kept Grim grim, with a single scoring both Groth & Lary as the game moved into the bottom of the 11th with Detroit up 2-0.

Cleveland fought back, opening their half of the frame with a Tito Francona single & a Russ Nixon double as Jim Bunning relieved Lary. A fielder's choice grounder that gets Francona out at home is followed by a walk to load the bases and then a fly out. Just 1 out to go to a Tiger victory, but Jimmy Piersall comes through for the home crowd with a 2-run single before Bunning can get out number 3. After 11, it's all tied up at 2.

Now it's Cleveland's Mudcat Grant and Detroit's Pete Burnside's turn to duel away through a scoreless 12th, 13th, and 14th. In the Tigers' 15th, Mudcat surrenders a walk to Burnside and a double to Red Wilson before Kaline doubles home both runners to put Detroit up 4-2. In the bottom of the inning, Pete Burnside completes his impressive 4-inning scoreless relief performance with 3 strikeouts, including whiffing Steve (*not even Don*) Demeter for the game's final out, to secure Detroit's Opening Day win. Four hours & 54 minutes after the 1st pitch, Ernie said goal #1 was getting back to the hotel to thaw out.

How did the recently traded do? Harvey Kuenn went 2 for 7; Rocky Colavito, in front of his adoring fans freshly crushed at his departure from Cleveland just 2 days ago, goes 0 for 6 with a walk & 4 strikeouts; Norm Cash pinch hit in the 12th and drew a walk; third baseman Steve (*not even Don*) Demeter entered the game in extra innings, flying out in the 13th & whiffs in the 15th. On May 6, just 16 games into his time with the Indians (appearing in 4 of their 16 games), Steve flies out to center in the 7th inning in Baltimore, completing his 0 for 5 season and, as it turned out, his major league career. After the May 6, 1960 game, Steve Demeter was sent down to AAA Toronto, and he would continue playing in the minors until retiring at age 37 after the '72 season, racking up 272 home runs in 19 years as a minor leaguer.

DDDDDDDDDDDDDDDDDDDDDDDDDDDDDDDDDDDDDDDDDDDDDDDDDDDDDDDDDDDDDDDDDDDDDDDDDDDDDD

Before there was Jon Warden in 1968 there was Tom Morgan in 1960. In 1968, the Tigers lost the first game of the year, then reeled off 9 wins in a row – Warden, a little-known relief pitcher who would win 4 games the entire season, was the winning pitcher in 3 of those 9 April victories. In 1960, the Tigers won their first 5 games of the season, and reliever Tom Morgan, who would only win 4 games all year, was the winning pitcher in two of those five.

The 1st of Tom Morgan's 4 victories in '60 occurs in the season's 2nd game. The Home Opener crowd of the previous day at Cleveland's Municipal Stadium, 52,756, has shrunk to 4,836. No beer or bathroom lines today. The Tribe draws first blood, getting to Don Mossi for 3 in the third. Detroit comes right back in the next half inning on a 3-run homer by Rocky Colavito. Cleveland takes a 4-3 lead in the fifth, and that remains the score until Detroit's 8th. With one out and Mossi due up, Norm Cash grabs a bat to face Indian starter Jim Perry. Norman Dalton Cash gets ahold of one, driving it deep into the rightfield stands; his 1st homer as a Tiger ties the game. Since Norm drew a walk as a pinch hitter in yesterday's Opener, this game-tying pinch-hit homer takes place on his 1st official at bat as a Tiger – nice start! After reliever Tom Morgan gets a 1-2-3 eighth, Al Kaline opens the ninth with a home run and newcomer Steve Bilko's triple plates Colavito before Paul Foytack saves the 6-4 win for winning pitcher Tom Morgan.

It's Opening Day 1960 at Michigan & Trumbull, and a fine crowd of 53,563 comes out to welcome home the 2 & 0 Tigers as they open a 3-game series versus the Chicago White Sox. Rocky Colavito gets on the fans good side in his first at bat on the home field with a 2-run homer in the 2nd to put Detroit up 2-1.

But Jim Bunning is not on his game today, and the Tigers soon find themselves down 5-2. The offense to the rescue! A 2-run shot by Eddie Yost in the 5th and a Steve Bilko solo homer in the 6th tie things up at 5-5, and the score stays that way as Tiger reliever Tom Morgan comes in for the ninth and gets 3 outs – becoming the winning pitcher when Lou Berberet's 2-out single sends Al Kaline across the plate with the winning tally.

The Tigers are 3 & 0, and Tom Morgan has 2 of the 3 wins putting him on a pace to finish 1960 at 103 wins and zero losses. This will establish a single season mark more difficult to catch than DiMaggio's 56 game hitting streak. Best wishes, Tom Morgan.

Home runs by Colavito, his 3rd in 4 games, and Steve Bilko provide all the support that Frank Lary needs to win the 2nd game of the series. The next day, the Tigers complete the sweep with a blowout 12-4 win, led by 4 hits off the bat of 2nd baseman Casey Wise on the greatest day of his career. Casey, who hit .174 in 126 games over 4 big league seasons, will have but 6 more hits in a major league career that ends after he goes 0 for 2 this July 3rd. Casey will be sent down to the minors on the 4th of July *(Happy Holiday Casey!)* and retire at the age of 30 after hitting .215 for the Jacksonville Suns in 1963.

DDDDDDDDDDDDDDDDDDDDDDDDDDDDDDDDDDDDDDDDDDDDDDDDDDDDDDDDDDDDDDDDDDDDDDDDDDD

With the 5 & 0 Tigers in first place, Colavito & Kaline on fire, this Tom Morgan guy already with 2 wins, and contributions coming from a variety of guys we'd never expect (Lou Berberet? Steve Bilko? Casey Wise?), the fans are wildly excited. Sadly, the bottom then falls out.

The team proceeds to lose 10 games in a row – even (gasp!) Frank Lary lost to the Yankees during this skid – as the 5 & 10 Detroiters sank to seventh place. The Tigers righted the ship in our nation's capital, snapping the losing streak with back-to-back, 1 to nothing, shutouts over the Senators by Don Mossi & Frank Lary on May 10 & 11. Colavito's 9th inning homer was the difference in the first game (Norm Cash, starting to get a little more playing time, had 2 of Detroit's 5 hits), and Kaline's 11th inning homer won the 2nd game pitcher's duel between Lary & Pedro Ramos. 2 weeks later, the Yanks came to The Corner for a pair of games, and Mossi & Lary again won back-to-back, Mossi tossing a 4-0 shutout as Charlie Paw Paw Maxwell supplied the power with a 3-run homer, the next day Frank Lary hurling a complete game in a 9-3 win over the Yanks propelled by Frank Bolling's 4 RBIs.

The Red Sox came to town for a 3-game series that kicked off June 14. Jim Bunning only gave up one run on 4 hits through 7, but future-Tiger Bill Monbouquette kept Detroit scoreless as the Tigers came to bat after the 7th inning stretch. Monbouquette got Kaline & Red Wilson out on flyballs, but Chico Fernandez kept the inning alive with a base hit. Bunning was called back from the on-deck circle as pinch hitter Norm Cash grabbed a bat and stepped up to the plate. Norm changed the direction of a Monbouquette fastball, and deposited his 4th homer of the year deep into the right field upper deck to give the Tigers a 2-1 lead. No other Tigers would reach base today, but the damage was done. Detroit reliever Pete Burnside put down the Sox in order in the 8th & 9th, including strikeouts of Ted Williams & Vic Wertz, ending the game by enticing pinch hitter & old friend Ray Boone to ground out to short.

With this 2-1 victory, Detroit improved to 27 & 23, moving to within 2 & ½ games of the first place Baltimore Orioles. Unfortunately, this would be the nearest to the A.L. pennant that the 1960 Tigers would get, as the team won 44 and lost 60 from here on out.

DDDDDDDDDDDDDDDDDDDDDDDDDDDDDDDDDDDDDDDDDDDDDDDDDDDDDDDDDDDDDDDDDDDDDDDDDDD

Looking back on the '60 Tigers, the pitching staff as a whole was average, their ERA 4th in the 8-team league, and Tom Morgan fell 99 wins short of his projected 103 victories. Bummer. Frank Lary is the team's ace and makes his first of two consecutive All-Star teams, going 15 & 15 with a 3.51 ERA, leading the A.L. in innings pitched, complete games, and – for the 4th time in 5 years – in hitting batters with the pitch, this time with a career-high 19 (don't mess with Frank). Jim Bunning led the league in strikeouts for the 2nd year in a row with 201 (the same as in '59) and is the only other Tiger to post double-digit wins with 11 against 14 losses, although with a sweet 2.79 ERA. Don Mossi's middling 9 & 8 looked great compared to Paul Foytack's nosedive from 14 wins last year to 2 & 11 with a 6.14 ERA. On the plus side, in his 6th season in The Show and his 3rd as a Tiger, 29-year old Hank Aguirre has his finest year yet, posting a 2.85 ERA (a sign of things to come) to go with his 5 & 3 record and a team-leading 10 saves.

The offense, on the other hand, is bad, ranked next-to-last in run scoring to go along with a team batting average of .239, the Tigers worst since 1904 – the year before Ty Cobb arrived on the scene. Not a single starting position player hit .300. Even Kaline slumped to .278, Al's lowest average since his first full season in 1954. No one had 90 RBIs as Rocky Colavito's 87 and Charlie Maxwell's 81 topped the team. The one category that Detroit did rank highly in was home runs, finishing #2 in the league, led by Colavito's 35, Maxwell's 24, and – despite only 353 at bats – 18 from newcomer Norm Cash.

Norman Dalton Cash was the unexpected offensive bright spot. He earned increased playing time as the season progressed, hitting 12 of his 18 homers after the All-Star break. Norm also began to display a trait that would play out throughout his career, the ability to draw walks and frequently get on base. Among 1960 regulars, only Eddie "the Walking Man" Yost had a higher on base percentage, .414 to .402, than Cash. Norm's performance in his first year with Detroit gave cause for optimism in 1961, but no one could have foreseen the performance that was coming.

A December 7, 1960 trade added speed to the lineup & bullpen depth: 2B Frank Bolling and OF Neil Chrisley went to the Milwaukee Braves in exchange for CF Billy Bruton and relief pitcher Terry Fox. Incoming manager Bob Sheffing installed Bruton as the everyday centerfielder, moved Kaline from that position back to right field (where he was before Jimmy Dykes became skipper) and moved Colavito from right to left. 34-year old Bruton was a 3-time National League base stealing champ with plenty left in the tank, as shown by topping the N.L. in 1960 with 13 triples and 112 runs scored. His addition to the line-up moved long-time fan favorite Charlie Maxwell to a pinch hitting & reserve OF role. Separate from the outfield, shipping Frank Bolling to Milwaukee opened up a spot at 2nd base for a kid who had been lighting up the minors for 3 years running, including the 1960 season in Denver with a .306 average, 101 runs, 18 triples, and 34 stolen bases – Jake Wood. With Eddie Yost lost to the Los Angeles Angels in the pre-1961 expansion draft, Wood was penciled in as the team's lead-off man for the upcoming season.

DDDDDDDDDDDDDDDDDDDDDDDDDDDDDDDDDDDDDDDDDDDDDDDDDDDDDDDDDDDDDDDDDDDDDDDDDDDDDDDDDD

In October 1960, co-owner John Fetzer decided to part ways with Bill DeWitt, and assumed Bill's role as team president. On the day after Christmas 1960, co-owner Fred Knorr, only 47 years old, died of burns suffered when he accidentally fell into a bathtub of scalding water while vacationing in a Fort Lauderdale hotel. With the passing of Knorr, Fetzer became the Tigers majority owner.

The final game at the ballpark known as Briggs Stadium took place on September 25, 1960. The first game at the ballpark known as Tiger Stadium took place on April 11, 1961. Over the winter of 1960-1961, seating capacity increased from 52,416 to 52,904.

1961 The Great Pennant Race: Stormin' Norman, the Surprising Tigers & the Damn Yankees

Although the author did not order a custom license plate for his new vehicle, one of his Guardian Angels did, the issued license plate number DFY6861. DFY surely stands for the "Damn F-in' Yankees" and "68" & "61" the two years that the Tigers won their most games in the 1960s - '68 when the 103-win Tigers were World Series Champs and '61 when the 101-win Tigers were... well...

On a gorgeous, sun-drenched morning one Lakeland spring training day in March 1961, the national media wrapped up a session of interviews and photographs with the Tiger team. With Detroit having finished 1960 in 6th place, 26 games behind the 97-win, first place, New Yorkers, little was expected of the Tigers in 1961. No experts and few fans predicted a contending squad, and the media treatment of the Detroiters was curt. As the last few newsmen took their leave, first year Tiger skipper Bob Sheffing exclaimed, *"Hey, you guys didn't get pictures of Norm Cash."* When one cameraman asked, *"Who?"*, soothsayer Sheffing replied, *"Norm Cash - the guy who just might be this year's batting champ!"*

Norman Dalton Cash, born 11.10.34 in Justiceburg, Texas, was just weeks away from introducing himself and his smoking hot bat in a big way to the baseball-loving world. Ernie Harwell, having been the Orioles announcer from 1954 thru 1959, met in Baltimore a man named Norman Almony, a fella that already went by the nickname "Stormin' Norman". When Norm Cash lost his temper with an umpire, Ernie anointed our Norm with the "Stormin' Norman" moniker. Soon both Harwell & fellow Tiger broadcaster George Kell used the *Stormin' Norman* name on the air every time Cash stepped up to bat or had a big hit. It wasn't long before the handle appeared on home-made signs brought by fans into Tiger Stadium.

The last two years had been quite a blur for Norm...

He got his first taste of the majors in a 13-game debut with the Chicago White Sox in 1958. That earned him a spot on the Sox in 1959, when in 58 games Cash hit .240 with 4 homers, enough to keep him on the roster when the White Sox reached the World Series that year. Although the Sox lost the Series to the Dodgers in 6 games, Norm received a $7,000 check, the loser's share, with which he bought cattle for the Texas ranch of his wife Myrta's parents. By Christmas of '59, Norm was part of a multi-player trade that sent him from the White Sox to the Cleveland Indians. Norm never played a regular season game as a Cleveland Indian. On April 12, 1960 – 4 months after being traded from Chicago to Cleveland

& one week before Opening Day – Norm was dealt by Cleveland to Detroit for Steve (*not even Don*) Demeter. At age 25, Norm played has first full Major League season in 1960, and proved an immediate boon to the Tigers' offense, hitting a solid .286 with 18 home runs and 63 RBIs in 121 games.

1961 would take Norm's game and, as a result, the success of the Detroit Tigers, to a new level.

And his teammates and the team's fans loved him.

DDDDDDDDDDDDDDDDDDDDDDDDDDDDDDDDDDDDDDDDDDDDDDDDDDDDDDDDDDDDDDDDDDDDDDDDDDDDD

In the Great Pennant Race of '61, counterbalancing the impact Norm Cash had on the Tigers' fortunes was the new pitching coach for their rival New York Yankees, Johnny Sain. In his playing days during the 1940s & 50s, Sain was an outstanding pitcher, particularly as a 2-time All-Star for the National League Boston Braves in the late-40s. In 1948 the Braves won their first N.L. pennant since 1914, and the importance to the team of Johnny Sain and fellow pitcher and future Hall-of-Famer Warren Spahn, the Pride of Broken Arrow, Oklahoma, was summed up in a famous poem penned by *Boston Post* writer, Gerry Hern: *"First we'll use Spahn, then we'll use Sain, then an off day, followed by rain. Back will come Spahn, followed by Sain, & followed, we hope, by two days of rain."*

In 1968, however, Johnny Sain was a popular man with Tiger fans. He was the Tiger team's pitching coach & considered a key element in the club's '68 World Championship. Simply put, Johnny Sain was thought by many to be the greatest pitching coach in baseball history. In 1961, however, Sain was not the Tigers friend. The year before, the Yankee's 31-year old Whitey Ford, ace of New York's pitching staff, began to show his age, posting the lowest winning percentage of his career, .571 with 12 wins and 9 losses. Before the 1961 season began, the Yankees hired Johnny Sain as pitching coach. Under Sain's tutelage, Whitey was put through a series of arm-strengthening exercises and, of more importance, Sain taught Whitey a new pitch – the slider. Amazed at the effect the slider had on his pitching performance, Whitey believed it lengthened his career by 5 years. A very effective 5 years (damn you, Sain!).

In this great Tigers-Yankees 1961 chess match, the Tigers countered the Yanks' Whitey Ford 2.0 upgrade with an All-Star performance by the Yankee-Killer himself, Frank Lary. Frank's dominance over New York was well-established before this season, but 1961 held some extra-special fan moments of Lary over the Yanks, including a Tiger road trip in mid-May that took them to Yankee Stadium for a 4-game weekend series, Detroit holding down first place and the Bronx Bombers in 2nd, Frank pitching the Friday night opener opposite Yankee hurler Art Ditmar.

The game held scoreless until the 4th when Rocky Colavito tripled and trotted home on 3rd baseman Steve Boros sac fly. The Yanks came back with 2 homers driving in 3 runs, one round-tripper each by Hector Lopez & Yogi Berra, the Detroiters replying with another Boros sacrifice fly to make it 3-2 Yankees going into the 7th. Frank Lary, *"One of the better-hitting pitchers in the league"*, George Kell told the faithful listening back home, led off the Tigers half of the inning with a hit to left, sliding head-first into 2nd base, barely beating the throw from the outfield, stretching a single into a double. Such daring base running drove Frank into position to score when the next batter, Jake Wood, followed with a single to tie the game at 3-all. In the ninth, Frank Lary took his Yankee-beatin' ways to the next level, smashing his 6th career home run deep into the left field stands, providing the final margin in the Tigers 4-3 win at Yankee Stadium.

The May 12 box score read: Frank "game-winning hit" Lary, 2 for 4, 1 run-batted-in, 2 runs scored, a complete game win improving his season record to 5 & 1. Detroit & New York split the 4-game series, the Tigers leaving town the way they came in – with a 3 & ½ game lead over N.Y. The Detroit Tigers had not been a serious contender for the American League title since 1950, so the players and their fans savored every minute of this.

DDDDDDDDDDDDDDDDDDDDDDDDDDDDDDDDDDDDDDDDDDDDDDDDDDDDDDDDDDDDDDDDDDDDDDDDDDDD

Expansion took place in 1961, the American League growing from 8 to 10 teams thru the addition of the Los Angeles Angels & the Washington Senators. Detroit & the rest of the established 8 teams could each only protect 25 players on their 40-man roster, the other 15 eligible to be drafted by either Los Angeles or Washington. Drafted by L.A. was the Tigers 1960 third baseman, 34-year old Eddie "the Walking Man" Yost, left unprotected because of a 23-year old 3rd sacker who was a 1960 minor league MVP with the Tigers Denver farm club, Steve Boros. The youngster hit .317 and, due to his ability to draw walks, had a .404 on base percentage, along with 128 runs, 30 homers, & 119 RBIs. Steve's dominant performance earned him a promotion to the Tiger roster in '61. Boros repaid the team's confidence in him by having what turned out to be his MLB career year, batting .270 with a .382 OBP, 51 runs & 62 RBIs, *despite* losing 6 weeks in '61 with a broken collarbone suffered July 24, sidetracking for a time his outstanding year. When injured, Boros already had 53 RBIs, one more than Kaline.

Steve Boros was a Flint native and a star shortstop at the University of Michigan in 1956 & 57 before accepting an offer to sign with the Tigers. His time in The Show was brief, a disappointing .228 average in '62 prompting Detroit to trade Boros to the Cubs for pitcher Bob Anderson (who played 1 quiet year in Detroit before retiring), and his last at bats in the majors were with the Cincinnati Reds as a 27-year old in 1964 – in spite of the fact that Steve set a Cincy club record with 50 consecutive errorless games at third in '64.

Boros played AAA ball from 1965 through 1969, retiring just short of his 33rd birthday. The cerebral Steve coached, managed & scouted from the 70s through the 90s, and championed the "scientific" stolen base, documenting the tendencies of each pitcher and catcher in the game to give his runners that extra split-second advantage. The San Jose Bees team he managed set the all-time minor league single-season record of 372 stolen bases, while his coaching in the majors was credited with assisting the KC Royals team and then Tim Raines of the Montreal Expos in leading their respective leagues in steals multiple times. Boros effort as a scout for the Los Angeles Dodgers in the 1988 World Series was acknowledged as contributing to one of the greatest moments in the history of the Fall Classic: he and fellow scout Mel Didier pinpointed A's relief ace Dennis Eckersley's inclination of throwing a backdoor slider on a full count versus left-hand batters – exactly the pitch that Dennis threw to lefty Kirk Gibson for Gibby's 2-run, walk-off, game 1 winner.

DDDDDDDDDDDDDDDDDDDDDDDDDDDDDDDDDDDDDDDDDDDDDDDDDDDDDDDDDDDDDDDDDDDDDDDDDDDD

The '61 Memorial Day game was rained out, rescheduled as the front end of a Tuesday doubleheader. The 51,791 who congregated at The Corner that day witnessed one to remember. Don Mossi pitched a fine game, but left with Detroit down to Kansas City 2-1 after 7 innings. When ex-Tiger Bill Tuttle singled in a run off of Tiger reliever Bill Fischer in the Athletics 8th, the Tigers were down to their last 6 outs while looking up at a 2-run deficit. After opening the next frame by getting Jake Wood on a pop fly, tiring KC starter Jim Archer walked Billy Bruton and surrendered a single to Al Kaline before being relieved by

Bill Kunkel who promptly walked Colavito to load the bases. Another KC pitching change to Bud Daley had no effect on the standing & screaming fans, the noise rising at the sight of Stormin' Norman swinging two bats over his head before stepping up to the plate. Daley winds and pitches… and Norm drives his delivery deep into the upper deck in right, a grand slam that sends the packed house into ecstasy and Bruton, Kaline & Colavito across home, all waiting to congratulate Norm on his blast. The Athletics got the potential lead run to the plate in their 9th, but Bill Fischer left two runners stranded when he secured out number 3 in Detroit's 5-3 victory.

May 1961 ended with the Tigers in first place, Cleveland 2 games back in 2nd, and the Yankees in 3rd, 4 games behind Detroit.

Rocco Domenico Colavito Jr.: the Rock in "Rock & Sock"

"Rock & Sock" was the nickname given in '61 to the Tigers two big power hitters, Rocky Colavito and Norm Cash. On April 17, 1960, when Cleveland swapped home run king Colavito to Detroit for batting title king Harvey Kuenn, Tribe GM Frank Lane believed that he got the better of the deal, saying he got a steak for a hamburger. Well, we Detroiters DO love our Top Hats, Telways, Bray's, Travis, Greene's, White Castles & Bates Burgers! As fond as Tiger fans were of Harvey Kuenn, and hated to see him go, that Rocky "hamburger" banged out 139 homers for Detroit from '60 to '63, while Kuenn – an All-Star every year from '53 thru '59 - had his best years (though still a 1960 All-Star) behind him.

"Rock & Sock" played some impressive long ball in early June. On June 2nd, "Rock" Colavito made a serious bid to become the first player ever (since the second deck was added to left-field in 1938) to clear Tiger Stadium's left-field roof, instead smashing one off the facing of the upper deck, while on June 11, "Sock" Cash made history as the first Tiger ever to hit a ball over the right-field roof, a feat only opponents Ted Williams & Mickey Mantle had previously achieved.

DDDDDDDDDDDDDDDDDDDDDDDDDDDDDDDDDDDDDDDDDDDDDDDDDDDDDDDDDDDDDDDDDDDDDDDDDD

July 4th in the Bronx was electric. The 1st place Tigers were in town for a doubleheader and 74,246 fans jammed into Yankee Stadium, the ballpark's largest crowd since 1947. The teams split the twin bill, with New York winning game 1 by a count of 6 to 2, 14 & 2 Whitey Ford out-pitching 9 & 1 Don Mossi – who deserved a better fate as Detroit made 5 errors behind him.

Fondly etched in the minds of Tiger fans is game 2. Once again, it was Mister Reliable, Frank Lary (they must hate him in New York), winning in the Big Sour Apple, improving his season record to 12 & 4 in a 10-inning nail biter, 4 to 3. The excitement included pinch runner Chico Fernandez stealing home in the 9th inning with 2 outs and big hitting Colavito at bat. *"If I don't make it, I'm in Denver,"* (Denver being the Tigers' minor league affiliate) said Chico of the play that put the Tigers up 3-2. Then, after allowing the Yankees to tie it in the bottom of the 9th, Frank Lary made amends when his 10th inning, 2-out/2-strike, bunt single drove in the game winner from 3rd. George Kell, doing the TV broadcast in the 10th, kept yelling into the mic, *"'Ol Taters'll find some way to beatcha! 'Ol Taters'll find some way to beatcha!"*

The Pride of Northport, Alabama: Frank Lary
aka Bulldog aka Taters aka Muke aka Yankee Killer

In the book, *Roger Maris at Bat*, Maris said Lary was *"one of the greatest competitors I've ever faced."* Tiger Manager Bob Scheffing said of Lary, *"I'll take him over any pitcher in either league."* The *New York Times* John Drebinger summed it up simply, *"Frank Lary, the Yankees arch tormentor these past six years, really did a job on the Bombers. The right hander was the winning pitcher and it was his daring bunt that pushed across the winning run."*

DDDDDDDDDDDDDDDDDDDDDDDDDDDDDDDDDDDDDDDDDDDDDDDDDDDDDDDDDDDDDDDDDDDDDDDDDDD

In 1959, Chico Fernandez was the shortstop in the Philadelphia Phillies double-play combination with a rookie second baseman who only played one year in the majors, George "Sparky" Anderson. The Tigers acquired Chico in a trade before the 1960 season. Chucky Porta, the pride of East Detroit and a man with a keen eye for talent, was not enamored by Chico's defense, unfailingly referring to him as Chico "I got a hole in my glove" Fernandez.

DDD

Seeking to raise additional money for the players' pension fund, MLB played two annual All-Star games 1959 thru 1962 (the idea of two Midsummer Classics was not well-received by fans, feeling the game's importance minimized, and by 1963 was again once a year, owners agreeing instead to increase pension funding from the single game). The 1961 games were played July 11 at San Francisco's Candlestick Park, the Nationals winning 5-4, and July 30 at Fenway Park, ending in a 1-1 tie. The roster was the same in both games, the American League squad featuring 5 Tigers: pitchers Jim Bunning & Frank Lary, along with Kaline, Cash & Colavito. In the 1st All-Star game 5-4 loss, the A.L. was held to 4 hits, Cash and Kaline with one each. The 2nd All-Star game ended in a 1-1 tie, the A.L. team again had 4 hits including 2 by Kaline & a home run by Colavito that accounted for the team's only run. Detroit claimed the top 3 spots in the starting American League batting order: Cash, Colavito, and Kaline, while the Tigers Jim Bunning started and allowed no hits in 3 innings pitched.

As mid-July arrived, after the first of the two All-Star games played, the Tigers & the Yankees jockeyed back 'n forth between first & second place. A look at statistics on the morning of July 15 showed some notable individual achievements on the two teams: Whitey Ford, a pitcher who had to date enjoyed a stellar career but had never won 20 games in a single season, had 16 wins chalked up and was considered a threat to win 30, a feat not accomplished since Dizzy Dean in 1934; Norm Cash was sitting at .355 with 24 homers & 70 runs batted in, and considered a long-shot Triple Crown candidate; the great Babe Ruth's single season home run record of 60 was in danger, with the Yanks Roger Maris at 33 & Mickey Mantle at 29, as baseball purists began to feel uneasy about the possibility of Babe's record, set in a 154-game season, being broken in a 162-game season.

DDDDDDDDDDDDDDDDDDDDDDDDDDDDDDDDDDDDDDDDDDDDDDDDDDDDDDDDDDDDDDDDDDDDDDDDDDDDDDDDD

On July 17, 1961, Ty Cobb, passed away at 74 years of age. In time for that evening's game at The Corner, the Tigers asked Ernie Harwell if he'd write a eulogy to be broadcast to the fans by public address announcer Joe Gentile over the P.A. system. Ernie's eulogy read...

Baseball's greatest player, Tyrus Raymond Cobb, died today in his native Georgia. Cobb was genius in spikes. His mind was the keenest ever to solve the strategy of the diamond. He was fiery and dazzling on the base paths. For 24 years of high-tensioned baseball action, his name led all the rest. He was the best – in hitting, base-stealing, run-making – in everything. Cobb's rise to fame in the early 1900s kept step with the progress of baseball as a national spectacle. His dynamic spirit was a symbol for the ever-growing industrial community he represented – Detroit, Michigan. And now, here in a baseball stadium where the cheers were the loudest and longest for this greatest of all Tigers, let us stand and pay final tribute to him in a moment of respectful silence.

After all stood in a moment of silence for Ty, Norm Cash wasted no time in giving the Ty-gers a lead, slamming a 3-run homer in the first. What Cobb, the man who idealized scientific baseball, would've appreciated even more was how Detroit scored in the eighth: Cash walked, moved into scoring position on a Steve Boros sacrifice bunt, and crossed home plate on a Jake Wood single in the Tigers 7-4 win.

Tyrus set 90 major league records during his career. In the "Line-Up for Yesterday" Ogden Nash wrote,

> *C is for Cobb, Who grew spikes and not corn,*
> *And made all the basemen, Wish they weren't born.*

DD

The Tigers suffered a critical loss when catcher Dick Brown, in his first year as a starter, went down for over a month with injuries in mid-July – within a few days of Steve Boros' broken collarbone. Brown had connected for 11 home runs at that point, many in key situations, one of several Tigers below star-status contributing to the team's success. Although his primary successor at catcher, Mike Roarke, couldn't supply the same offense as Brown, he was top-notch defensively. After hitting .353 in 64 games at minor league Denver, 21-year old Dick McAuliffe was called up to Detroit for the 2nd half of the season, filling in nicely for the injured Steve Boros.

Rookie Jake Wood & first year Tiger Billy Bruton provided speed at the top of the order, and always seemed to be on base whenever Kaline, Cash & Colavito delivered an extra-base hit. Bobo Osborne, beyond his singing contribution to Frank Lary's *Hillbilly Choir*, was the poor man's Gates Brown, with the ability to come into a game cold as a productive pinch hitter. Beyond Osborne, off the bench to deliver hits at key moments in '61 were Bubba Morton and, of course, Charley Paw Paw Maxwell. Hank Aguirre, Terry Fox, and Ron Kline provided what Detroit teams over the years had so often lacked, an effective bullpen.

As August came to a close, the Yankees held a 1 & one-half game lead over the Tigers. The New Yorkers were hot in August, but the Tigers stayed within striking distance by winning 6 of their last 8 games in the month. Detroit ended August with a 14-hit attack, including home runs by Billy Bruton & Norm Cash, with Stormin' Norman's mammoth blast landing upstairs, to the right-field side of the 75-cent-per-ticket upper deck bleacher seats. This offensive explosion supported what was pitcher Paul Foytack's finest outing of the year, as he struck out 7 White Sox in a complete game 8 to 2 Tiger victory. That same evening, August 31, the Tigers boarded a plane for New York City to play the biggest series of the 1961 regular season, 3 games in the Bronx on Labor Day weekend.

DDDDDDDDDDDDDDDDDDDDDDDDDDDDDDDDDDDDDDDDDDDDDDDDDDDDDDDDDDDDDDDDDDDDDDDDDDDDDD

Each of the Tigers "Big 3" of Don Mossi, Frank Lary, and Jim Bunning were in a pitching groove, the hitters were hot, and every man on the team felt the Tigers were peaking at just the right time. Mossi was on the mound for the Friday night opener, facing the Yankees ace, Whitey Ford. Each hurler was at the top of their game, continuously frustrating the opposing batters. A pulled muscle caused Ford's departure in the 5th, but the Tigers offense could do as little with the Yankees bullpen as the Yanks hitters could do with Mossi, and the game was scoreless going into the 8th.

In the 8th, the Detroiters began to get to reliever Bud Daley. With one out and Bruton on first, Al Kaline scorched a rocket into the left-field corner, where long-time catcher Yogi Berra was playing today, and about to make the play of the series. Yogi played the carom off the wall beautifully, spun and rifled a perfect throw to 2nd, the ball arriving just in time to beat the sliding Kaline. Instead of Tigers at 2nd & 3rd with only one out, two Tigers were out with Bruton on third. Still, "Rock & Sock", Detroit's best clutch hitters were coming to the plate, but after a walk to Colavito, Daley got Cash on a pop-out to Elston Howard, and the Tiger threat was extinguished.

The Yanks came to bat in the bottom of the ninth, the game still a zero-zero deadlock. Mossi retired first Maris on a fly out to Kaline, and then the folks back home heard Ernie Harwell tell them that Mantle *"stood there like the house by the side of the road and watched that one go by"* for a called strike 3. Two outs, nobody on. Then, with sickening speed, Howard, Berra & Moose Skowron singled in succession off Mossi, and the Yankees left the field with a 1-0 victory. The Tigers & their faithful followers in Michigan could take heart: Frank "Yankee Killer" Lary would be on the mound tomorrow.

As game 2 began, the Tigers got to Yanks' starter Ralph Terry early, on a 1st inning 2-run homer off the bat of Rocky Colavito. In the bottom of the 2nd, the man who knocked in yesterday's game-winner, Skowron, doubled home Mantle to make it 2-1 Detroit. As the game moved to the fourth, the M&M Boys, aka Mantle & Maris, proved that they could play small ball, too, as Mickey bunted Roger in from third. The 2-2 tie was broken by a Maris solo homer in the sixth, and things stood 3-2 NY going into the bottom of the 8th. Frank Lary was able to get the first batter, but 3 singles knocked him out. Hank Aguirre in relief could not stem the tide, surrendering Maris 2nd homer of the game, a 2-run jack, that made the final score 7-2 New York.

The Sunday final paired Detroit's Jim Bunning against New York pitcher Bill Stafford. As on Saturday, the Tigers opened the scoring in the top of the 1st, this time on an RBI single off the bat of Colavito. And, as on Saturday, New York quickly responded. Back-to-back bottom-of-the-first homers by Mantle, a 2-run shot, and Berra, sent the game into the second 3-1 Yanks and their fans into a frenzy. A Cash 6th-inning solo home run offset a 4th NY run in the fifth and, after another Detroit marker in the 8th, the game was 4-3 Yankees heading into the 9th inning. The never-say-die Detroiters rallied to take the lead on a 2-run Jake Wood single, the news giving renewed hope to the thousands huddled around their transistors back home, but a Mantle lead-off homer in the bottom of the 9th quickly tied it, and with two outs, an Elston Howard 3-run homer off reliever Ron Kline completed the weekend disaster for Detroit. The Tigers arrived in the Bronx an excited 1 & ½ games back, exiting New York deflated and in a 4 & ½ game hole.

DDDDDDDDDDDDDDDDDDDDDDDDDDDDDDDDDDDDDDDDDDDDDDDDDDDDDDDDDDDDDDDDDDDDDDDDDDDD

The Tigers finished the year with a flourish, winning 12 of their last 16 games, including a Tiger Stadium split of the final series of the year with the Yankees in mid-September. Within those 4 games, Frank Lary improved his 1961 record to 21 & 9 with an 8-strikeout, 10-4 win, Lary's 27th victory all-time versus the Yankees against 10 losses. 10 days later, on September 26, a 19-year old rookie catcher from the University of Michigan – where he played both football & baseball - made his Tiger debut going 2 for 4 after earlier in the year at U of M setting the all-time Big Ten conference play batting average of .585 (a record previously held by Purdue's - and current Yankee - Moose Skowron), a teenager by the name of Bill Freehan. Bill played all of his 16 Major League seasons wearing the Olde English D, was an 11-time

All-Star, Gold Glove winner every year from '65 – '69, retired with the MLB record for catchers in fielding percentage, total chances & putouts, and ***should be*** in the Hall of Fame at Cooperstown.

All of this was very nice, but the Yanks followed their Labor Day weekend sweep of Detroit with 10 consecutive wins, and it was much too late for Detroit to catch New York for the pennant.

On October 1, the day that Detroit chalked up win 101, Stormin' Norman Cash finished his greatest season by hitting home run 41, notching RBI 132, and by going 2 for 3 to finish with a league-leading .361 batting average AND an astounding on base percentage of .487 – almost once every two at bats! Norm's .487 OBP is the 33rd MLB all-time best single season ranking, one ahead of Ty Cobb's 1915 .486. From this season on, the author was one among thousands of Michigan kids who would wear Norm's number 25 on every baseball & softball jersey they would ever play in.

On the same day, New York's Roger Maris hit homer number 61, breaking Babe Ruth's single season record of 60, a September injury sidelining Mantle (whose season ended with 54) from the home run race. Roger's accomplishment, taking place in a 162-game season, was always diminished by baseball purists since the Babe's occurred in the 154-game 1927 season (although ignoring that Maris hit his 60 in 3 less plate appearances than it took Ruth), so much so that both Ruth's and Maris' feats are noted separately (but without the supposed asterisk) in baseball's record books.

The American League pennant won, the Yanks moved on to the World Series and took the Cincinnati Reds in 5 games. The final A.L. standings had 1st-place New York at 109 & 53 and 2nd-place Detroit at 101 & 61. The Tigers were left in the unsatisfying position as one of the greatest 2nd place teams in Major League Baseball history, only the third team to win 100 or more games and not win the pennant, after the 1915 Tigers & their 100 triumphs (behind 101-win Boston) and the 103-win Yankees of 1954 (behind Cleveland's 111 victories). The 101 wins of '61 tied the team record set by the great '34 Tigers, later broken by the 103 wins of the '68 champs & then the 104 wins of the kings of '84.

Detroit finished atop the American League in hitting with a .266 average and in runs scored with 841. Kaline, Colavito, and Cash – Detroit's 3, 4 & 5 batters - struck fear in the hearts of pitchers who had the unenviable task of facing them: besides Norm's MLB leading .361 average, .487 OBP & 193 hits, Al was number 2 in the A.L. with a .324 average, first with 41 doubles, and 5th with 116 runs scored; Rocky was an A.L. 5th at 45 homers, 2nd with 140 RBIs, and his 129 runs were good for 3rd. The top 2 in the lineup, Jake Wood & Billy Bruton, were a league 3rd & 4th in stolen bases at 30 & 22, respectively, ensuring that they were in scoring position for the Big 3 hitting behind them, Jake crossing home 96 times, with an A.L. tops 14 triples, and Billy scoring 99 runs.

The '61 Tigers top 3 starting pitchers, in combined stats, were #1 in wins, innings pitched, complete games, and shutouts. Staff ace Frank Lary had a spectacular season, number 2 in A.L. wins at 23 & 9, with a 3.24 ERA, tops in complete games at 22, winning his first Gold Glove, earning his 2nd consecutive All-Star berth, finishing 3rd in Cy Young balloting, in addition to winning games with his bat, his base running, and daring. Fellow All-Star Jim Bunning was a great number 2, fourth in the A.L. in wins at 17 & 11, a 3.19 ERA, and a league third at 194 strikeouts. Don Mossi completed the triumvirate, his 15 wins 6th most in the A.L., finishing 15 & 7, Don's 2.96 ERA third in the league.

DDDDDDDDDDDDDDDDDDDDDDDDDDDDDDDDDDDDDDDDDDDDDDDDDDDDDDDDDDDDDDDDDDDDDDDDDDDD

1961 was the first year that I have a clear recall of cheering on the Tigers, the earliest game impressed on my mind the 4th of July victory over the Yankees by Frank Lary, and I can easily (thank you God) call up the memory of sunshine & listening to the game from the Bronx on the family transistor radio in our Detroit yard that day. The Tigers efforts were heroic in '61, but they were up against a machine that stockpiled players: the Yankees 3rd string catcher, Johnny Blanchard, batted .305 with 21 home runs – one homer every 12 times at bat. Their 3rd string catcher. I have detested the New York Yankees ever since that year.

On 11.16.11, 50 years after this wild 1961 season concluded, I came home to an answering machine birthday song message left by Jacksonville, Florida friends and native Michiganders Kathy & Johnny Harcourt and Rich Magyar. Perhaps a part-birthday-song and part-ode-to-1961 (oh, face it, an ode to every baseball season) the original composition is quite catchy and easy to learn…

"The Yankees Suck, The Yankees Suck, The Yankees Suck, The Yankees Suck… they really, really, really, really, really, really suck… the Yankees SUCK!"

1962 - 1967 Building a Champion

The lights are much brighter there
You can forget all your troubles, forget all your cares
So go downtown, things'll be great when you're
Downtown, no finer place for sure
Downtown everything's waiting for you

("Downtown" by Petula Clark)

1962 began with a very bad omen.

6 months & a few days after the Great 1961 Pennant Race concluded, Frank Lary was pictured on the cover of the April 9, 1962 *Sports Illustrated*. Based on the '62 Tigers' injuries and performance falloff versus '61, the *S.I.* curse proved as strong as ever. On the magazine cover date, Detroit opened a 3-game series in our nation's capital. Don Mossi & the Tigers suffered a 4-1 loss to the Washington Senators on April 9, and the team watched the pouring rain postpone games 2 & 3. The curse had just begun.

On a rainy & chilly Friday the 13th, of course, Opening Day 1962 at Michigan & Trumbull pitted the home team against the World Champion New York Yankees, the pitching match-up Frank Lary versus N.Y.'s Bill Stafford. In the early going, the Yanks got to Frank for 2 runs in the 2nd and added an Elston Howard solo home run in the 4th. Down 3-0 to NY, Detroit rallied for 2 in the 6th then, in the 7th, Frank Lary's triple tied the game at 3-all. But, in an incident that foreshadowed what lie ahead for the Tigers this year, Frank pulled a leg muscle while running in the muddy base path to make third base. Reno Bertoia came in to pinch run for Lary, and scored what ended up the difference-maker in the Tigers 5-3 win. Frank improved his all-time record versus NY to 28 & 10, but...

The 1962 Home Opener ranks as one of the costliest victories in Tiger history: in an effort to compensate for the leg muscle pull, Frank changed his pitching delivery in subsequent outings, which created a series of arm problems. He was he never the same pitcher again. Frank's outstanding 23 & 9 of 1961 fell to 2 & 6 in '62 and 4 & 9 in '63. Pitching in 6 games with an 0 & 2 record early in '64, Lary was sold by the only major league team he'd ever played for to the New York Mets on May 30, who then traded Frank to the Milwaukee Braves on August 8, ending 1964 with a combined 3 & 5 for his three '64 teams. After a 2nd go with the Mets in the first half of '65, he was traded to the Chicago White Sox, ending 1965 with an overall 2 & 3 win-loss record, Frank retiring that fall.

After the 1962 Opener, Frank had 3 more lifetime decisions against the Yankees, all losses (clearly, he was not his old self), the "Yankee Killer" ending his career with a 28 & 13 record versus New York. The Pride of Northport, Alabama was here with us in Michigan for one glorious decade, creating a lifetime of love among Tiger fans for *Frank Strong Lary*.

DDDDDDDDDDDDDDDDDDDDDDDDDDDDDDDDDDDDDDDDDDDDDDDDDDDDDDDDDDDDDDDDDDDDDDDDD

Frank Lary's injury was one of two the Tigers suffered that had the biggest impact on their hopes in '62. On May 26 in Yankee Stadium, Al Kaline made a diving, game-saving, catch, ensuring the Tigers 2-1 victory. However, Al broke his collarbone on that play, causing him to miss the next 2 months of the season. Going into this game, Kaline was enjoying the best start of his career, leading the league in home runs & runs batted in, while batting .345. Al returned for the last two months of the year and, impressive playing in only 100 of the season's 162 games, hit 29 homers with 94 runs batted in – but what might have been...

And, oh how the Tigers of '62 needed Frank Lary and Al Kaline at their best: although Stormin' Norman still continued to rain homers in ballparks all over the American League with 39 (including his 2nd, 3rd, and 4th over the Tiger Stadium right-field roof), his RBIs dropped by 43 (132 to 89) and his batting average plunged like a boat going over the Upper Tahquamenon Falls, from a MLB-leading .361 to .243. The 118-point drop is the biggest by a batting champ in major league history, but he scored 94 runs and was on base plenty with 104 walks, allowing Cash to be an A.L. 4th in on-base plus slugging percentage. The other half of "Rock & Sock", Rocky Colavito, dropped from '61's 45 homers & 140 RBIs to 37 & 112, still very good (& an A.L. first in total bases & 5th in on-base plus slugging %), but declines nonetheless, in a year the Tigers could not afford any.

One bright spot for the Tigers in '62 was the pitching of Hank Aguirre, the 6'4" man known as "High Henry". A favorite of both teammates and fans, Hank had a year that was a wonderful surprise: he was the American League leader in both earned run average at 2.21 & in giving up the fewest hits per every 9 innings at just over 6. Hank's record of 16 wins vs. 8 loses allowed him to form one-half of a fine one-two pitching punch for Detroit along with Jim Bunning's 19 & 10 showing.

In Hank Aguirre's rookie season of 1955, he was able to get the great Ted Williams out on strikes. Hank immediately requested that the ball be taken out of play for safekeeping in the dugout. When the game was concluded, Williams graciously signed the ball for the excited young pitcher. The next time the two players squared off, Ted teed off on a Hank offering, sending the ball deep into the stands. As Williams rounded third, he shouted to Aguirre, *"Hey kid, if you find that baseball, I'll sign it, too."* Years later, Ted Williams visited Detroit in support of *the Jimmy Fund*, his favorite charity, and while in town accepted Bill Reedy's invitation to visit his tavern. Ted, upon arriving, spied Aguirre already in Reedy's Saloon, calling out to him, *"I remember you rook,"* as he proceeded to relate to the delighted crowd the story of the strikeout, the signed ball, and the long home run from those many years ago. No one in Reedy's packed saloon had a bigger smile on their face than the old rook himself, Hank Aguirre.

DDDDDDDDDDDDDDDDDDDDDDDDDDDDDDDDDDDDDDDDDDDDDDDDDDDDDDDDDDDDDDDDDDDDDDDDDDD

On June 24, 1962, the longest game ever played at Michigan & Trumbull took place. The opponents, again, were the Yankees, the pitchers Frank Lary & NY's Bob Turley. Lary, struggling with the arm troubles that would plague him the rest of his career, was roughed-up for 6 runs in the first, the Tigers bouncing back with 3 in the bottom of the 1st, Turley pulled after only getting one out. Both starters were gone after Frank gave up a 7th run in the 2nd. The home team pulled within 1 with a 3-run, 3rd inning outburst, and then tied it up in the 6th when Billy Bruton scored after a Colavito single. The Rock stood at first base after his hit, when NY first-baseman Moose Skowron sidled over shaking his head, *"Did you have to do that? I thought we were finally going to beat Frank Lary."*

Then the relief pitchers took over, neither team able to score the tie-breaker through the ninth and on into extra innings, despite Rocky Colavito's 7 for 10 day, as runners were frequently left in scoring position by both teams. Yanks pitcher Tex Clevenger threw 6 innings of shutout ball from the 7th through the 12th, while the home team's Hank Aguirre came on to get the last out in the 7th and kept the Bronx Bombers stifled for 5 additional frames. Terry Fox followed Aguirre on the mound, tossing 8 shutout innings, and in the process lowered his earned run average for the year to 0.96.

At the top of the 22nd, the Tigers 7th hurler of the game was pitching, Phil Regan. After a walk to Roger Maris, up to bat for New York was a rarely used, reserve outfielder, Jack Reed. Jack usually got into a game when Mantle's ever more painful legs gave out, and had the distinction of being one of only four people to ever play in a major college football bowl game (1953 Sugar Bowl with Ole Miss) and in a World Series game (1961 with New York). Phil Regan delivered to the plate, and Reed jacked a 2-run homer, the only home run that Jack Reed hit in his 3 years of major league ball, giving New York a 9 to 7 lead. As the Tigers came to bat, a rookie took over mound duties for the Yanks, Jim Bouton, a young man who would go on to have 2 very good years (21 wins '63 & 18 in '64), little other baseball success, but then write a best-selling book, "Ball Four". Despite giving up Colavito's seventh hit, he held the Tigers without a run, final score 9-7 New York, and the 22-inning game was over in exactly 7 hours.

DDDDDDDDDDDDDDDDDDDDDDDDDDDDDDDDDDDDDDDDDDDDDDDDDDDDDDDDDDDDDDDDDDDDDDDDDDDDDDD

On June 28, 1962, 4 days after the 22-inning game versus the Yankees, 59-year old Mickey Cochrane passed away. An editorial in the *Detroit Free Press* read, *"To a depression ridden Detroit, Cochrane's baseball leadership brought an interest, an enthusiasm, an élan that somehow kept hearts high and grins going despite life's daily discouragements. It has been said that Mickey Cochrane licked the depression in Detroit. That's overstating it, naturally. But the man had a magic about him that made it easier for Detroit to ride out those early '30s."*

God bless you Gordon Stanley Cochrane. What a blessing you always will be to Detroit and to Michigan.

DDDDDDDDDDDDDDDDDDDDDDDDDDDDDDDDDDDDDDDDDDDDDDDDDDDDDDDDDDDDDDDDDDDDDDDDDDDDDDD

The Tigers finished 1962 4th in the A.L., at 85 & 76, 10.5 games behind the pennant-winning Yankees. What difference would a healthy Frank Lary, his 23-win total of '61 only 2 in '62, have made in the race? What difference would a healthy Al Kaline, having his single best run-producing season with 29 homers and 94 RBIs in only 100 games, available all year, have made? Without these two season-changing losses, 1962 might have been the year that 1961 was not.

Although *Sports Illustrated* and their damn front cover curse infected this team, the inside article about our Boys of Summer allowed us to look back at 1962 on a humorous note: *"The Tigers desperately need a shortstop who can at least field his position. Chico Fernandez is poor on the double play, but on the other hand he can't hit."* (So we got that goin' for us.)

DDDDDDDDDDDDDDDDDDDDDDDDDDDDDDDDDDDDDDDDDDDDDDDDDDDDDDDDDDDDDDDDDDDDDDD

The first pack of baseball cards I ever bought was in the spring of 1963. I was 8 years old and on the way home from a day in 3rd grade at McKenny Elementary School in Detroit. The cards were purchased from the truck of Marv the Ice Cream Man, who always parked on the same SW corner of Pembroke & Trinity. Marv sold packs of Topps baseball cards for a nickel each. In each pack was a piece of frequently stale gum and 5 baseball cards. What do I get in the very first pack of baseball cards that I ever purchase in my life? A team photo of the 1963 New York Frickin' Yankees! What helped ease the pain was the sound from the car parked across the street – with its engine running, windows down, radio on & tuned to WJR, a rare song was going out over 760AM's airwaves, Herb Alpert's *"The Lonely Bull".* The tune put a smile on the face of everyone within listening distance - even those who unsuspectingly spent their lawn cutting money on a New York Yankee team photo.

DDDDDDDDDDDDDDDDDDDDDDDDDDDDDDDDDDDDDDDDDDDDDDDDDDDDDDDDDDDDDDDDDDDDDDD

1963 was pitcher Paul Foytack's final year with Detroit. In mid-season of '63, Paul was traded with Frank Kastro to the Los Angeles Angels for George Thomas. After brief stints in the Motor City in '53 & '55, Paul became a regular part of the Tiger pitching rotation in 1956, and was most effective from '56 through '59, racking up victory total in those years of 15, 14, 15 & 14. Foytack was a favorite of Tiger rooters, but his biggest fan may have been the Yankee's Mickey Mantle. Mick hit some of his longest home runs off of Paul Foytack, including one at Tiger Stadium on September 10, 1960, 1 of 3 Mantle hit over the right-field roof at The Corner – 2 of the 3 off Foytack - this one traveling 643' and landing over the Checker Cab Company on Trumbull, the longest home run in MLB history.

Paul Foytack & Mickey Mantle became good friends, and hung out together when traveling to each other's towns. After Foytack retired from the game in 1964, the Yankees came to Detroit for a series. Post-game, Mickey was out late at the bars and called his old friend at 4AM, *"Hey Paul, come on down and have a drink!" "Mickey, I can't - I have to be at work at 7."* Mantle, doing some quick ciphering, exclaimed, *"Great, you still have 3 hours!"*

DDDDDDDDDDDDDDDDDDDDDDDDDDDDDDDDDDDDDDDDDDDDDDDDDDDDDDDDDDDDDDDDDDDDDDD

John Fetzer was a 1957 member of & moving force behind the 11-man Knorr syndicate that purchased the Tigers from the Briggs Family Trust. He was a fine athlete in his youth, but an even more impressive scientist, acknowledged as primarily responsible for developing & standardizing the directional antenna, improving radio signals at night, allowing you to hear Ernie, George, Ray Lane, & Paul Carey announce those late-night Tiger games so clearly. Fetzer's combination of invention and business acumen led to great success in the broadcasting field, including financially, and by 1960 majority ownership of the Tigers. One of his first decisions in this position changed the ballpark name from Briggs Stadium to Tiger Stadium. Interestingly, Fetzer also negotiated MLB's first-ever national TV contract in 1967.

The Fetzer-Campbell partnership began in 1962, when owner Fetzer hired Jim Campbell to be his general manager. Campbell lived up to the Scottish tradition of frugality, and it may not have been an exaggeration to say he threw nickels around like manhole covers. Jim Campbell never gave away a dollar needlessly, but also knew how to build a champion, and did so twice for Detroit, in 1968 and 1984.

Campbell's 1949-1962 years working in the Detroit minor league system convinced him that developing home-grown talent would be the key to success.

Supported by John Fetzer, Campbell felt confident that he had the scouts and the young talent in place to build a champion through the Tiger farm system, ensuring trades would only be a supplement to the core that came up through Detroit's minor league affiliates.

The team's top minor league squad by 1963 was the AAA Syracuse Chiefs, and Detroit was so successful in cultivating & promoting their young talent that by the mid-60s the Tigers were known as *"The Boys from Syracuse"*. One of the first of those young Syracuse men to be called up was Detroit-native, Willie Horton. While attending Northwestern High, Willie's school earned a spot in the '59 Detroit Public High School title game hosted by Briggs Stadium. Willie homered to clinch the game for Northwestern over Cass Tech, his mammoth blast one of the most memorable homers ever hit at The Corner, the right-handed Horton hitting the same light tower that lefty Reggie Jackson hit in the 1971 All-Star Game.

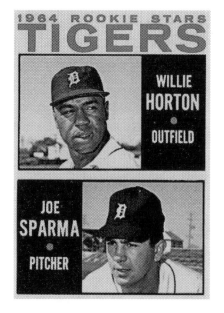

Willie had always been a catcher growing up, and when he first reported to the Tigers minor league camp, they placed him with the outfielders. Confused, Willie called his Dad, *"Something's going on down here. They have me with the outfielders – they're not giving me the opportunity to catch."* His Dad told him, don't ever call home to complain. Willie called it the best advice he'd ever had, and started rolling. After hitting .315 and 16 homers against minor league pitching for the first 5 months of '63, 20-year old "Willie the Wonder" broke in with Detroit on September 10, 1963, and hit .326 in 43 at bats. A slow start in '64 found Willie sent back down to Syracuse for more seasoning, and Horton responded with 28 of the longest home runs ever seen in International League play, earning him a late-season call up and a permanent place on the Tigers roster. Willie was one of many versatile athletes in the Tigers minor league system, and a Golden Gloves boxer as a 17-year old – whenever tempers rose on the diamond and benches emptied, opponents made sure that they always knew where Willie Horton was, and kept themselves a long way from there.

Joe Sparma pitched for minor league clubs Knoxville & Syracuse before the Tigers called him up in 1964, but prior to his baseball days, Joe started for Ohio State at quarterback under Woody Hayes in '60 & '61.

Bill Freehan played against Joe's Buckeyes in the 1960 UM-OSU game as an end for the University of Michigan, then played catcher the following spring for the UM baseball team, setting the all-time Big Ten single season hitting mark of .585. Duly impressed, the Tigers signed Freehan to a contract with a $125,000 bonus (huge money in the day, and not half bad now) and, after he hit .310 with 11 home runs in 258 at bats in the low minors during the summer, called Bill up to the parent club on September 26 of '61. By then, it was too late to catch the Yankees in the Great Pennant Race of '61, but Freehan did get a taste of The Show, getting into 4 games and going 4 for 10 to bat an even .400. After Bill's assignment to the minors for all of '62, Freehan was in Detroit to stay as 1963 began until 1976 ended.

Freehan & Horton knew each other since they were 11 years old. As teenaged opponents in a Detroit-area late-50s Little League All-Star game, future Tiger teammates Bill Freehan & Willie Horton shared a moment when catcher Freehan blocked home plate as Horton steamed around third, resulting in a thunderous collision at the plate (Bill had more success denying Lou Brock home a decade later). Together, they led a team representing Detroit in a Babe Ruth League World Series tournament where the Detroit squad defeated a Cincinnati, Ohio team that had on its roster star pitcher and eventual Boston Celtics great John Havlicek, Pete Rose, and future Tiger shortstop Eddie Brinkman. When the man who coached Pete Rose in high school was asked about Rose by a scout, he replied, *"Rose is good, but not a Brinkman"*.

Mickey Lolich & Gates Brown were teammates in the Tigers minor leagues, first during '62 with the AA Denver Bears and then in '63 as AAA Syracuse Chiefs. Back then, when the teams were on the road in a southern town, Gater wasn't welcome in restaurants since his skin was considered by some the wrong color. Mickey knew what carryout order to bring back to the team bus for his friend 'cause it never changed: cheeseburger, fries & a vanilla shake. Gates' 13 homers at Syracuse in 1963 earned him a late-season call up to the Tigers, where he stayed for 13 seasons, creating a long list of special moments for the fans. Lolich, like his buddy the Gater, was called up to the parent club in late '63 and stayed 13 seasons. In Mickey's first full season of 1964, he was a terrific 18 & 9.

Jim Northrup was called up to Detroit in 1964 after his season in Syracuse concluded where he posted numbers of 18 homers, 92 RBIs (sounds a lot like his 1968), and hitting .312. While attending Alma College from 1957-1960, Northrup set the college broad jump mark, a record he held for several years, was a star basketball player, and a small-college All-American quarterback while 3rd in the entire USA in total offense for '59 (1,538 yards). Both the NFL's Chicago Bears & the infant American Football League's New York Titans offered Jim contracts, but Northrup said, *"I was born to play baseball"*. For the Alma Scots baseball team, he threw a no-hitter against Calvin in 1958. Upon his graduation from Alma College, Jim signed with the Tigers in the spring of '60. As fine a college pitcher as Jim was, it was as an outfielder that he broke into the Tigers starting line-up in 1965.

"The Boys of Syracuse" was a farm system fraternity that grew into major leaguers together (though some jumped right from AA Denver to the Tigers): Freehan, Horton, Sparma, Gater, Lolich, Northrup, Ray Oyler, Dick McAuliffe, Denny McLain, Tom Matchick, Wayne Comer, Fred "the Bear" Gladding, Pat Dobson, Daryl Patterson, Jon Warden, and the man that was perhaps the best pure athlete of the group, a trait that led to a daring World Series managerial move in 1968, Mickey Stanley.

While playing together in the minors, a close friendship between Mickey Stanley and Willie Horton blossomed. After a ballgame concluded in Asheville, North Carolina, Willie began walking to lodging arranged for the non-white players, a black hotel in Asheville. Before he knew it, a teammate was walking alongside him – Mickey Stanley – to keep Horton company. When the two arrived at the hotel, Mickey intended to stay with his comrade in arms, but the hotel turned Stanley away. This experience not only created a bond between the two young men, but began efforts by both to bridge the gap between black & white players.

Thru the Tiger farm system to '68 World Series Champion
Mac was a team leader & a fierce competitor

DDDDDDDDDDDDDDDDDDDDDDDDDDDDDDDDDDDDDDDDDDDDDDDDDDDDDDDDDDDDDDDDDDDDDDDDDDDDDD

Cash & Mantle were chatting one day during batting practice at Tiger Stadium. They were talking about the cozy right-field roof, when Norman says, *"Mick, I've hit as many balls over that roof as you have,"* and Mick replied, *"Yeah, but you play here all the time!"*

DDDDDDDDDDDDDDDDDDDDDDDDDDDDDDDDDDDDDDDDDDDDDDDDDDDDDDDDDDDDDDDDDDDDDDDDDDDDDD

Detroit's record from 1962 through 1967 reflected gradual, sometimes painful, growing pains as they built a championship team...

1962: 85 & 76, 1963: 79 & 83, 1964: 85 & 77, 1965: 89 & 73, 1966: 88 & 74, and 1967: 91 & 71.

Detroit certainly had the pieces from within their own system to be challenging for the pennant each year. There was plenty of good, young, pitching and hitting, and two outstanding veterans (featured together on a Topps 1967 baseball card as "Bengal Belters") in future Hall of Famer Al Kaline and power hitting Norm Cash, the only American Leaguer with over 20 home runs every year from 1961 to 1969. On top of all that, the Tigers had throughout the 60s & beyond, arguably the finest field general in all of baseball in Bill Freehan. In 1964, his 2nd full season as a Tiger, Bill became the first Detroit catcher since Mickey Cochrane in '35 to hit .300. He led by example and by early '64 even the veteran pitchers were letting Freehan call the game. GM Jim Campbell commented, *"We put the full load on Freehan's shoulders, and he didn't stumble."* The recognition of what Bill Freehan meant to the Tigers was league-wide, and he was the only A.L. player to finish both 1967 & 1968 in the top 3 for Most Valuable Player voting.

Beyond the development of the young talent in the farm system, there was one trade that had a huge impact on building towards a championship: on June 14, 1966, the Tigers traded Don Demeter to the Boston Red Sox for pitcher Earl Wilson. The debonair Mister Wilson was known to his teammates as the Duke of Earl. From his acquisition on June 14 through the balance of '66, Earl was 13 & 6 for Detroit, giving them the critical 4th starter in a rotation with McLain, Lolich & Sparma. Wilson had an even more impressive 1967, going 22 & 11 as the ace of the staff.

This is the 2nd lopsided trade in Detroit's favor that involved a Demeter, following the theft of Norm Cash for Steve Demeter in pre-season 1960. The two Demeters are related only in the booty their departures brought back to the Tigers. Although Don Demeter hit a very respectable .292 for Boston in '66, he was out of baseball by the end of 1967, while the *Duke of Earl* Wilson was a major contributor to the Tigers fortunes through the summer of 1970, playing a big role in the team's 1968 success.

DDDDDDDDDDDDDDDDDDDDDDDDDDDDDDDDDDDDDDDDDDDDDDDDDDDDDDDDDDDDDDDDDDDDDDDDDDD

During the early-60s, Mark Alwood, a St. Clair Shores youth, recalled, *"Lutheran Night at Tiger Stadium with a bunch of my school chums and our dads as chaperones. I attended St. Thomas and St. Peter school on 9 Mile and Kelly from '63-'66. One game we were sitting way up in the LF upper deck when the tiny figure of Bill Freehan swung & seemingly minutes after the bat crack a fuzzy white object appeared heading straight for us. Time slowed down and then-**bang!**-the object knocked the Coke out of Paul Neffs' hands sitting next to me. The mad scramble went on and all I remember is someone other than Paul got the ball."*

DDDDDDDDDDDDDDDDDDDDDDDDDDDDDDDDDDDDDDDDDDDDDDDDDDDDDDDDDDDDDDDDDDDDDDDDDDD

Charlie Dressen took over as manager of the Tigers in the middle of 1963, when upper management decided the team was underperforming with Bob Scheffing at the reins. Funny how Scheffing, the genius that led the '61 team to 101 wins, suddenly was found lacking. Dressen had an almost 3-decade long track record of managerial success with both minor & major league teams, including as skipper of the Los Angeles Dodgers teams in the early-50s. In the Tigers 102 games in 1963 under Dressen, the team was 55 & 47, continuing to be competitive in '64 at 85 & 77.

However, Charlie Dressen's greatest contribution during his time with the Tigers was of a humanitarian nature. On New Years' Day 1965, both of Willie Horton's parents died in a car accident, and Charlie spent a great deal of time with the grieving Horton, becoming a surrogate father to the young man. The comfort that Dressen brought to Willie's life may well have contributed to the break-out, 29 homer/104 RBI All-Star season that Willie achieved in '65. In May of that year, Horton went on a tear that received national attention, hitting six 400' or longer home runs in 4 games against the Red Sox & Senators, forever securing his nickname of *"Willie the Wonder"*.

In spring training 1965, Charlie Dressen suffered a heart attack. Coach Bob Swift filled in until Dressen's return after 42 games, the '65 team winning 4 more games than the prior year. Dressen suffered a 2nd heart attack one month into the 1966 season, and coach Bob Swift once again stepped in to run the club. A kidney infection complicated Charlie's recovery, and he suffered a third, this time fatal, heart attack on August 10. Interim Manager Bob Swift was stricken by a fast-moving cancer that took his life in October, the team managed the final few games of '66 by another coach, Frank Skaff.

The 1966 Tigers had been through the sad & bizarre experience of playing under 3 managers & seeing two die during the season. Despite this, '66 marked the third year in a row that the team had won 85 or more games. In the standings, their 88 & 74 record earned them a 3rd place finish, 10 games behind the World Champion Baltimore Orioles.

DDDDDDDDDDDDDDDDDDDDDDDDDDDDDDDDDDDDDDDDDDDDDDDDDDDDDDDDDDDDDDDDDDDDDDDDDDDDDD

Does anyone here tonight
Remember those times?
Somebody call the riot police
There's trouble down on 12th Street

("Detroit '67" by the Sam Roberts Band)

Before the 1967 season, Mayo Smith was named manager of the Detroit Tigers. He inherited a group of talented young veterans ready to win. But if '66 was the year of bizarre, '67 was the year of frustration.

Beyond the '67 career-bests of 22 & 11 for Earl Wilson and 16 & 9 for Joe Sparma, the pitching was erratic. After Denny McLain's 20 victory breakout '66 season, both teammates and Tiger management believed he had the stuff to become one of the game's best. Although Denny did win 17 games, that was only 1 more than he lost, and he did not transform into the elite mound presence that many expected – not just yet. Mickey Lolich finished the year with a flourish, but a combination of tough luck and rough outings saddled him with a 10-game losing skid that lasted through mid-season. The bullpen, throughout long stretches of Tiger history an Achilles heel, frequently lost leads in critical games.

Willie Horton, coming off another outstanding season of 27 home runs & 100 RBIs in '66, missed 40 games in '67 with injuries, limiting his contributions to 19 homers & 67 RBIs. Upset after striking out in a June game, Kaline missed 26 games after slamming his bat into the bat rack, suffering a broken thumb.

Although beset by injuries and pitching woes, the Tigers fought through it all to be in the thick of one of the greatest pennant races in history. Four teams, the Tigers, Twins, Red Sox, and White Sox, took turns going in and out of first place all season long.

DDDDDDDDDDDDDDDDDDDDDDDDDDDDDDDDDDDDDDDDDDDDDDDDDDDDDDDDDDDDDDDDDDDDDDD

The excitement of the season-long pennant fight brought the crowds out in large numbers. One regular was Southgate's Carol Hunter. Carol always dressed sharp for a game at the stadium, her outfit including elbow-length white gloves. At one 1967 ballgame, with 13-year old son Rick Rice by her side, Carol sat in the 3rd row between home plate & third base when a foul ball off the bat of Minnesota Twin rookie Rod Carew rocketed her way. Sitting several rows behind Carol was a friend who had no idea that Carol was in attendance – until a long, white-gloved, arm reached up to snag the ball, prompting a good-natured shout, *"Hey! That must be Carol!"* Carol Hunter still owns and treasures the ball to this day – the gloves, *Loooong-Gone!*

DDDDDDDDDDDDDDDDDDDDDDDDDDDDDDDDDDDDDDDDDDDDDDDDDDDDDDDDDDDDDDDDDDDDDDD

In late-July, with all four teams no more than 2 games of 1st place, an event took place that put the importance of baseball in perspective…

In the early morning hours of July 23, 1967, Detroit Police raided an illegal after-hours bar 'n gambling house on 12th Street, 3 miles north of Michigan & Trumbull. Arrests were made, attracting a crowd that grew large & confrontational. Shouting led to rocks thrown at the cops. Soon windows were broken and homes & stores set ablaze. The unrest took place too late to make the early morning Sunday editions of the *Detroit News* & *Detroit Free Press*, and – at least at first – television & radio stations downplayed the seriousness of what was taking place on 12th Street, while information obtained via social media was a phenomenon still 30+ years away. With this as a backdrop, fans unaware of the violence made their way down to The Corner for the Tigers & Yankees Sunday doubleheader.

The American League standings as July 23 dawned reflected an amazingly tight pennant race, with 5 of the league's 10 teams – the Angels now joining Detroit, Boston, Chicago & Minnesota - within 3 & ½ games of 1st place. The Yankees, not the juggernaut that they used to be, were 13 games back. In game 1 of the twin-bill, Mickey Lolich faced New York's young ace, Mel Stottlemyre. Mickey pitched well, but did not break out of his 2-month winless slump, as Detroit lost 4-2 in Mick's 10th consecutive loss. In game 2, reliever John Hiller picked up his first win of the year when the Tigers rode home runs by Willie Horton and little-used right-fielder Jim Landis to a 7-3 victory.

"Bus lines outside the stadium will not be operating - please drive safely", the Tiger public address announcer informed 43,000 fans at the conclusion of the doubleheader. Over 90% of the crowd could not see from their seats the smoke rising 3 miles north on 12th Street. Only when departing the park and looking north, did this curious announcement make sense.

That night, a phone call at his home notified a tired Mickey Lolich to trade his Tiger uniform for full combat gear. Along with his fellow National Guardsmen, he was mobilized for riot duty, assigned to patrol downtown Detroit. Willie Horton, meanwhile, kept his Tiger uniform on after the game, racing to the 12th Street & Clairmount neighborhood, the heart of the riot and where he grew up. Willie stood on a car, begging the crowd to stop the madness. The bravery of these two Tigers, and many like-minded folks, changed a few minds, but the tragedy would not end for 5 more days, in the process taking 43 lives, injuring 342, with 1,400 buildings torched.

The Tigers were in and out of first, the final two months of the pennant race, until it came down to the last weekend of '67. In order to make up early season rainouts, back-to-back double-headers for both Saturday and Sunday, September 30 & October 1, were scheduled against the California Angels. If the Tigers could win all 4, they would be the American League champions outright. If they could win 3 of 4, that would force a one-game playoff, at The Corner, versus Boston. In Saturday's game one, Mickey Lolich took the mound, the poster child for this up & down year, and won for the 9th time out of his last 10 decisions, after losing his previous 10, improving to 14 & 13 in a 5 to nothing shutout. In game 2, however, the bullpen was handed a 6-2 lead going into the 8th, and was raked for 6 runs, as the Tigers fell 8-6. It now came down to Sunday – win both, and they host Boston in a 1 game playoff for the American League crown.

In Sunday's first game, the Tigers offense staked Joe Sparma to an early 5-1 lead, and he coasted to a 6-4 win to up his record to 16 & 9. The final game of the year, and Detroit's fate, was in the hands of Denny McLain. After Denny's 20 wins the previous season, everyone had high hopes for him in '67, but it was a strange year for McLain. Today was Denny's first game in two weeks, a twisted ankle keeping him on the bench, an accident Denny said was due to rising from a couch too fast after his foot had fallen asleep. McLain, his 17 & 16 record, and his healthy ankle faced the Angels in this must-win game. A 2-run homer by Jim Northrup keyed an early 3-1 Tiger lead, but Denny could not get out of the third, and when John Hiller surrendered a 2-run bomb to Don Mincher, California's 3rd inning ended with a lead that they eventually built to 8-3. The Tigers got two back in the 7th, giving the fans hope, and in the 9th had two on, nobody out, and the tying run at the plate. The crowd implored their heroes to make some magic. After a pop out, up stepped Dick McAuliffe, who had only hit into one double play all year. In 1968, the man everyone knew as Mac would have hit a 3-run homer to tie things up. But... this was 1967. Mac hit the ball as hard as you can, right at the Angels 2nd baseman, for a season-ending double play.

The shock of a pennant lost they thought was theirs kept the Tigers sitting stunned in front of their lockers for a long, long time that night. Building a determination for 1968 had begun.

1968 We Win!

We're all behind our baseball team – Go Get 'Em Tigers!
World Series bound and pickin' up steam – Go Get 'Em Tigers!
There'll be joy in Tigertown, we'll sing you songs,
When the Bengals bring the pennant home, where it belongs
We're all behind our baseball team – Go Get 'Em, Detroit Tigers
Go Get 'Em... Tigers!

("Go Get 'Em Tigers" by Don Rondo & Mary Lou Simons Zieve)

Detroit Tigers 1968 featured a pitching staff led by 31-game winner Denny McLain & World Series hero Mickey Lolich, the American League's finest defensive team, a league-topping offense in homers at 185 (by 50 over the next closest team) and runs scored at 671, led by Willie Horton (#2 A.L. 36 homers), Al Kaline (#4 at .287), Bill Freehan (25 HRs), Norm Cash (25 HRs), Jim Northrup (#3 90 RBIs), Dick McAuliffe (#1 95 runs) and pinch-hitter extraordinaire Gates Brown (.450 as a pinch-hitter, 8th best in MLB history) who told folks that, *"I'm square as an ice cube and twice as cool."* The excitement the team generated brought 2,031,847 through the turnstiles, the first time in franchise history the Tigers drew 2,000,000+ to the park in a single season.

Northrup, Stanley, Kaline, Matthews, McAuliffe

But one piece of information more than any other signaled that this was the year our Boys of Summer would finally become champions: a member of the much-maligned bullpen was the winning pitcher in 3 of Detroit's first 8 games. Few fans had heard of Jon Warden at the year's beginning. He had impressed management with a fine '67 showing in A ball, 19 wins with a 2.73 ERA, had an outstanding spring training this year, and became the last man to make the team before breaking camp for Detroit. The Tigers knew that the bullpen could not be a repeat of 1967 if the team was to be a winner, and Warden was one of several young arms who had earned a larger role in 1968 from their success in the farm system, among them Pat Dobson, Daryl Patterson, and Fred Lasher. It was Warden, though, who had such an incredible start, the first & only reliever in MLB history to win his first 3 career appearances, letting all know that this year would be special.

Sadly, Jon Warden secured the final roster spot at the expense of the immensely popular Hank Aguirre. To make room for Jon on the team, exactly one week before the April 10 season opener, High Henry was traded to the Los Angeles Dodgers for Frederick Moulder, a minor league utility man who never made the big leagues. As Aguirre's fans back in Detroit cheered him on, Hank pitched in 25 games for L.A. in '68 and in 39 innings of relief went 1 & 2 with 3 saves and an outstanding 0.69 ERA. In '69, Aguirre signed as a free agent with the Chicago Cubs, and in two seasons as a reliever he threw 59 innings, going 4 & 0 with 2 saves and a 3.05 earned run average before retiring from the game at 39 years of age.

What should not be overlooked in assessing the '68 pitching performance was the effect Pitching Coach Johnny Sain's tutelage had on the young staff AND on the veterans, including teaching McLain to perfect the straight change-up and the pitch that allowed him to realize his full potential, the same pitch taught by Sain to Whitey Ford in '61 that may have cost the Tigers the pennant that year, the slider.

DDDDDDDDDDDDDDDDDDDDDDDDDDDDDDDDDDDDDDDDDDDDDDDDDDDDDDDDDDDDDDDDDDDDDDDDDDDD

The 1968 team lost their first game of the season, and then proceeded to reel off 9 straight victories (including Jon Warden's 3). Four of those 9 were won in the Tigers final time at bat. Although Detroit had a fine month of April at 12 wins & 5 losses, after losing 4-0 to Baltimore on May 6 - their 4th defeat in 5 games - Detroit found themselves in second place, 2 & ½ games back of the first place Orioles. But the Tigers bounced back the next two days at Baltimore's Memorial Stadium.

On May 7, Mickey Lolich & the O's Tom Phoebus both hurled shutout ball for the game's first 8 innings before Willie Horton drew a base on balls to start the Tigers 9th. After Norm Cash laid down a sacrifice bunt to move Willie to 2nd, Phoebus intentionally walked Don Wert to set up force plays at 2nd & 3rd. Mayo Smith sent out Gates Brown to pinch hit for Dick Tracewski, and although Gater grounded out, he did move the runners up a base. Now it was Lolich's turn to bat, but instead Mayo again chose to pinch hit, this time sending up Tommy Matchick to hit for Mickey, and Matchick came through with a double to right field, sending both Horton and Wert across the plate. Phoebus was able to get McAuliffe out on a ground ball to second, but the damage was done. Although Boog Powell scorched a 2-out home run off of reliever Fred Lasher in the Orioles 9th, and Davey Johnson followed with a single, Jon Warden came in to get the save on a Don Buford ground out to Mac at 2nd to secure the Tigers 2-1 victory.

On May 8, the rubber game of the series, the pitching match-up was the Duke of Earl Wilson against Baltimore's Dave McNally. Detroit got to McNally early, on a Jim Northrup solo homer in the first, and the Tigers 2nd started with a Horton single, a Wert double, and a Tracewski sacrifice fly to center that scored Willie before Ray Oyler & Wilson went down on strikes. 2-0 Detroit. In Detroit's 6th, an Al Kaline double & a Horton 2-out single padded the lead to 3-0, as the Duke kept Baltimore scoreless thru 8. In the O's ninth, Boog Powell & Davey Johnson led off with singles to put runners on 1st & 2nd, before Jon Warden came into the game to relieve Wilson. Two fly ball outs moved Powell to third base, and Boog scored as Wert bobbled Andy Etchebarren's ground ball. Warden overcame the unearned run by getting Paul Blair on strikes to chalk up Jon's 2nd save in two days, nailing down Detroit's 3-1 win and allowing the team to depart Baltimore's Memorial Stadium only one-half game behind the Birds.

Detroit traveled to nearby Washington to continue their road trip with 3 games against the Senators. Game 1 on May 10 was a 12-1 laugher powered by homers off the bats of Bill Freehan, Wert, & Kaline, propelling the Tigers back into first place, a position they would not leave the rest of 1968.

Before the end of May, Denny McLain already had put the league on notice that this was his year. He had complete game wins in 8 of his first 11 starts, and after his 13-strikeout, 3-0 shutout of the Angels on May 29, his record stood at 8 & 1. With this torrid pace, talk had begun that Denny just might be the major's first 30-game winner since Dizzy Dean back in 1934.

On May 31, Willie Horton's 7th inning home run off of the Yankees Mel Stottlemyre broke up a scoreless pitcher's duel between Stottlemyre and Mickey Lolich in Detroit's 1-0 win, sending the team into June with a 28 & 16 record and a 2 & ½ games advantage over Baltimore. The bulge grew to 7 & ½ by June 30, and the Orioles could never get closer than 4 games to first the rest of the season, finishing 12 games back of the 103 & 59 American League Champion Detroit Tigers.

DDDDDDDDDDDDDDDDDDDDDDDDDDDDDDDDDDDDDDDDDDDDDDDDDDDDDDDDDDDDDDDDDDDDDDDDDDDDD

Fannie Coffman of Detroit cheered for the Tigers since back in the days when the ballpark they played in was known as Navin Field, before 1938. In later years, when a Tiger game was being broadcast, the only way Fannie could be enticed to leave the house to join family gatherings was after her kin bought her a transistor radio. But with Fannie's ear glued to the Tiger game on the air, there wasn't much in the way of conversations taking place.

Once, Fannie was a little miffed at Ernie Harwell, probably the only person on the planet that ever got mad at Ernie, and she wrote him a letter. Her missive informed Ernie, *"I feel like you've forgotten that we're all Tiger fans, and not Ernie Harwell fans",* feeling he had been getting a little full of himself. So, one Sunday afternoon, after Fannie had listened to that day's game, the doorbell rang. Ernie himself stood at her Linnhurst Street front door on Detroit's east side. *"Mrs. Coffman?"* *"(slowly) Yeah... Mister Harwell?"* as Mrs. Coffman turned 30 shades of red. Ernie told Fannie, *"I didn't mean to offend you."* A lovely conversation ensued, and as Ernie took his leave, Mister Harwell had another fan for life.

DDDDDDDDDDDDDDDDDDDDDDDDDDDDDDDDDDDDDDDDDDDDDDDDDDDDDDDDDDDDDDDDDDDDDDDDDDDDD

It was the *Year of the Comeback* for our never-say-die Tigers, who won an incredible 28 games in their last at bat. An argument over which of those 28 comebacks were the most dramatic could provide such happy flashbacks that no one would lose. Two, no make that three (can't break up _this_ particular August doubleheader), worthy candidates are...

First, July 19, a Friday night with 2nd place Baltimore in town to start a 4-game series, 7 games back of the 58 & 33 Tigers, as 53,208 crammed into the Old Ballyard. While Lambertville's Herb & Mary Fletcher slept on the other side of my bedroom wall, their 13-year old son lay in bed in the dark, listening with the volume down low on the transistor radio next to his pillow. The Tigers were losing 4 to 2, down to their last 3 outs. After Jim Northrup singled to open the Tigers 9th and Kaline followed with a base on balls, the excitement in the old ballpark was deafening as Stormin' Norman Cash stepped up to the plate. Norm grounded to Brooks Robinson at third, allowing the O's to get the force at 2nd on Kaline while Northrup moved to third & Cash was safe at first. Bill Freehan – not the fastest of Tigers – was now at bat. Freehan hit a grounder that felt like a game-ending double play, yet by the smallest of margins, Bill beat the relay to first base. Fans at the stadium and those listening on the car radio or at home could exhale. On Bill's grounder, Northrup ran home from 3rd to cut the margin to 4-3 Orioles.

Then, Tommy Matchick, a role player and .215 lifetime hitter, walked from the on-deck circle to the batter's box. Pitching for the Orioles was their relief ace, a man who struck out a World Series record for relievers of 11 batters in one (1966) Series game, he of the 1.54 ERA, Moe Drabowsky. Despite Tommy's 2-run ninth inning double that defeated Baltimore 2 months earlier, this was not the ideal match-up for Detroit. Matchick was able to work the count to 3 & 2, and we'll let Ernie Harwell's broadcast tell the rest of the story… *"2 out, a man on first – that's Freehan – Tigers are trailing by one run, 4 to 3 behind Baltimore, Matchick now waiting on a full count pitch from Drabowsky. Swung on… there's a fly ball to right… its deep, it might be… back is Robinson… and it is a HOME RUN! THE TIGERS WIN IT! A 2-RUN HOMER BY MATCHICK! HERE COMES FREEHAN TO SCORE! MATCHICK IS ROUNDING SECOND, HEADED FOR THIRD… ALL THE TIGERS ARE OUT AT HOME PLATE TO MEET HIM! HERE HE COMES! AND THE TIGERS WIN THE BALLGAME, BY A SCORE OF 5 TO 4!"* I was screaming into the pillow, muffling my enthusiasm as best I could so as not to wake up the folks, and instantly becoming a life-long Tommy Matchick fan.

(Maybe the most amusing story from '68 featured another surprise hero: on June 23, .156 hitter Dick Tracewski had the game's biggest hit in a 4-1 Tiger victory, a 3-run homer, off of perennial All-Star and one of the league's toughest hurlers, with a 1.81 ERA, Cleveland's Sudden Sam McDowell. At 2AM that morning, Sam found a place to ponder life's mysteries sitting atop a downtown Detroit statue.)

Second, August 11, Boston in town for a double header. In game 1, Tiger pitcher Earl Wilson did not have his best stuff, and the home team was quickly down 4 to nothing after 1. Wilson, after getting only the 1st two outs of the game, was replaced by Joe Sparma who was replaced by Jon Warden who was replaced by Don McMahon who was replaced by Fred Lasher – all four relievers held the Red Sox scoreless while the Tigers chipped away with 4 one-run innings, and it was all tied up at 4 after 9. With the bullpen exhausted from use in the previous day's game, when 6 hurlers were used in the 4-3 Tiger victory (won on a Norm Cash 8th inning solo shot), Manager Mayo Smith turned to normally-a-starter Mickey Lolich to take the mound in the 10th – even though Lolich got the last 5 outs a day earlier. As Mickey would show today and once again in the World Series, he can give a lot of innings on little rest.

From the top of the 10th until the bottom of the 14th, Lolich and Red Sox relievers Sparky Lyle and Lee Stange kept the game at 4 to 4. In Detroit's 14th, Stange retired the first two Tiger batters when Gates Brown emerged from the dugout to pinch-hit for Mickey Lolich. A roar sprung from the crowd. In a year of magic finishes for Detroit, no one batter was having a more magical year than the Gater, enjoying one of the best seasons as a pinch hitter in major league history. Ray Lane was at the microphone, *"Now, the 2 – 0 pitch. LONG DRIVE TO RIGHTFIELD! BACKING UP IS HARRELSON! IT'S GONE!!! HOME RUN!"* (for 15 seconds, a loooooooong deafening roar, that Ray wisely does not try to speak over) *"Gates Brown clears the fence downstairs in right field, a home run! His third of the year, to win the ballgame for the Tigers, 5 to 4, in 14 innings."*

Third, still August 11, the second game of the doubleheader matched John Hiller against Boston's Gary Bell. Scoreless through 6, the Sox scored 2 in the top of the 7th, the Tigers answering after the 7th inning stretch with a 2-run single by Norm Cash, knocking in Mickey Stanley & – in a rare start for the unrivaled pinch hitter – Gates Brown. The Sox broke the tie by roughing up relievers John Wyatt and Jon Warden in the top of the 9th for 3 runs, leaving the Tigers facing a 5 – 2 deficit and down to their last 3 outs.

However, this was 1968. Jim Price led off with a walk, Wayne Comer flied out, Bill Freehan had a pinch hit single and, when Dick McAuliffe singled in Price, Tiger Stadium shook from the crowd excitement! With 2 runners on & one run in to make it 5 - 3, Mickey Stanley came up to bat, with Ernie Harwell calling the play, *"2-2 count on Mickey, here it comes… he taps one over the mound, into center field for a base hit. Freehan rounding third, he's coming home! McAuliffe goes for third. Another run in for the Tigers. 5 to 4 the score.* <u>And these Tigers just won't quit!</u> *They have a man at first and third with one out, and that man at third is the tying run. 5 to 4 the Red Sox lead in the last half of the 9th inning. On third is McAuliffe, man on first is Stanley. The set, the pitch to Kaline. Swung on – a looping drive to right, it's in! The ballgame's tied, McAuliffe scores. Racing for third is Stanley. Kaline's safe at first. It is a tie game, 5-5 in the 9th."* And here comes the Gater to the plate. *"The set… and Brown waits… the pitch… swung on, a bounding ball to first base… IT'S THROUGH FOR A BASE HIT! THE TIGERS WIN THE BALLGAME! The Tigers stream out of the dugout, mob Gates Brown… the crowd is going berserk as the Tigers win the doubleheader, getting the second game with a rally of four runs in the 9th inning to win it by a score of 6 to 5. And what a mad mob this is at Tiger Stadium tonight!"*

<u>Gates Brown!</u> <u>Gates Brown!</u> <u>Gates Brown!</u> Two game winners in one day! As incredible as the Gater-driven doubleheader win was, the most delightful Gates Brown story ever took place on a different 1968 day. Gates was not in the lineup, and left the bench for the clubhouse in search of hot dogs. He had just returned to the bench with two dogs, lathered up with mustard and ketchup, when Mayo Smith told him to grab a bat to pinch hit. Damn. Gates quickly gobbled down one hot dog, shoved the 2nd one in his jersey, stepped up to the plate, and drove a pitch into the gap. In order to beat the throw to 2nd, Gates slid head first. As he stood up, it was clear that the hot dog tucked near his waist had exploded into a rainbow of mustard yellow & ketchup red all over the front of his jersey. As Gater later described it, *"The fielders took one look at me, turned their backs and damned near busted a gut laughing. My teammates in the dugout went crazy. Mayo fined me $100 and asked, 'What the hell were you doing eating on the bench in the first place?' and I told him, 'I was hungry. Besides, where else can you eat a hot dog and have the best seat in the house.'"*

DDDDDDDDDDDDDDDDDDDDDDDDDDDDDDDDDDDDDDDDDDDDDDDDDDDDDDDDDDDDDDDDDDDDDDDDDD

In late-June of '68, after what was no doubt some unruly fan behavior, GM Jim Campbell announced that beer could no longer be brought into Tiger Stadium from the outside. A moment of silence, please, before the narrative continues.

DDDDDDDDDDDDDDDDDDDDDDDDDDDDDDDDDDDDDDDDDDDDDDDDDDDDDDDDDDDDDDDDDDDDDDDDDD

Beginning in the summer of 1968 through that of 1972, teenage Southgate sisters Laura and Kathy (daughters of Ella – see 1935 *"Goosey! Goosey! Goosey!"*) LoCricchio and their cousins worked the popcorn room at Tiger Stadium, under the guidance of the wonderful lady who ran the room, their Aunt Helen Lemelin. Kathy recalled, *"It was a great job with lots of perks. There were lots of cute boys working there - an important thing when you are in high school - & you could eat popcorn non-stop from when we started at 730AM until we finished each day. We could go out on the field during lunch breaks and run the bases as long as no one was around, and when we weren't too busy we could catch quick glimpses once the game began. The entrance to our work area was adjacent to where the Tigers parked their cars and entered the stadium. I watched faithfully for Bill Freehan who was my personal baseball hero in those days. The stadium is a pretty cool place to be when hardly anyone is around. We felt like we were celebrities being able to go "behind the scenes" where most people couldn't go. I cherish those fun times with my sis & my cousins & my favorite aunt. Oh, to have a job like that today!"*

Laura reminisced, *"As the players walked from their cars to the clubhouse, it was impossible for them to ignore the aroma of freshly made popcorn, and they'd stick their heads in the room and we'd get to talk to them. In one of the '68 World Series games, in the popcorn room there was nothing to do. They said "nobody's eating popcorn today!" No fans wanted to leave their seat to go buy any and miss the action, so I got to bring box lunches up to the Press Box. I'm like, 'Woo-hoo, I get to go to the Press box!' I shared an elevator ride to the Press Box with Ernie Harwell's Tiger radio broadcast partner Ray Lane - wow! But the most amazing thing was that Aunt Helen had a key to Tiger Stadium!"*

DDDDDDDDDDDDDDDDDDDDDDDDDDDDDDDDDDDDDDDDDDDDDDDDDDDDDDDDDDDDDDDDDDDDDDDDDD

The '68 Tigers had offensive threats all up & down their lineup (Ray Oyler... not so much), with 8 regulars homering in double-digits. But it was the man at the top of the order that keyed the attack, best known to his teammates for his intensity as "Mad Dog", Dick McAuliffe. Among the fans, though, he was Mac, the man who led the league with 95 runs scored, and always seemed to be on base at critical points in the game, a major reason for the RBI totals of Freehan (84), Horton (85) and Northrup (90).

On the evening of Wednesday, July 31, at The Corner, my father Herb Fletcher & I witnessed first-hand the impact Mac could have on a game. Against the Washington Senators & their home run king, Frank Howard, McAuliffe went 4-for-4, scoring all 4 Detroit runs, including 1 on his 14th homer of the year. The Tigers won 4 to nothing and Denny McLain improved his record to 21 & 3.

Mac's value to the Tigers march to the pennant was never more apparent than at the end of August. On the 22nd, the White Sox were in town for the final game of a series, as McAuliffe faced their ace, Tommy John. Perhaps frustrated that his team was used as a Tiger punching bag all year, or from the Sox losing a tough, 10-inning affair the night before on Jim Price's walk-off homer, Tommy John's throws forced Mac to hit the deck 3 times on pitches that buzzed by McAuliffe's head. The 3rd brushback pitch was ball four and, as Mac walked to first, John barked at him, and Mad Dog charged the mound. The two wrestled to the ground as the dugouts emptied, both teams pushing and shoving, the White Sox players making sure to keep their distance from the muscular, ex-gold glove boxer, Willie Horton.

Tommy John was injured in the skirmish and lost for the balance of the season. McAuliffe was fined and suspended for 5 days, covering 6 games. The Tigers only won one of the 6 during Mac's suspension, but then reeled off 8 wins in his first 10 games back. With McAuliffe back and the team rolling, it was only a matter of time 'til Detroit clinched the pennant. On September 16, the Tigers whipped the Yankees 9-1, the offense led by Stormin' Norman's 3-run homer & 5 RBI day, reducing to 1 the team's magic number to win their first American League flag since 1945.

46,512 Tiger fanatics were in a buoyant mood as they filed into Tiger Stadium on Tuesday, September 17, hopeful that they would see their heroes make history this evening. Joe Sparma was on the mound for Detroit facing New York's Stan Bahnsen. Both pitchers were excellent tonight, putting nothing but zeroes on the scoreboard until the Tiger fifth. Bill Freehan singled to start the frame, and was standing on 2nd with two outs as his roommate on the road, Joe Sparma, came up to bat. After Joe's 16 & 9 breakout year in 1967, he'd struggled most of '68, his record 8 & 10 going into today. How deserving for a class act like Sparma that Joe's biggest day of the year would take place on one of the biggest days in Tiger history. Not only was he sparkling on the hill, only surrendering 5 hits and an uncharacteristically-low one walk, but with Freehan in scoring position in the scoreless affair, Joe Sparma promptly singled to centerfield, thrilling the crowd as his hit sent Bill across home plate and put Detroit up 1-0.

The game stayed 1-0 until the top of the ninth. With the fans on their feet, clapping & screaming, their celebration was temporarily put on hold when, with 2 outs, Yankee Jake Gibbs singled in the tying run before Sparma struck out Mickey Mantle to send the contest into the bottom of the ninth. New York reliever Steve Hamilton replaced Bahnsen and started the frame by fanning Northrup & getting Horton to ground out. Two outs, nobody on, and it was starting to look like extra innings, but just as quickly as the fans calmed down, they were up 'n shouting as Kaline drew a walk and Freehan singled Al to third. The Gater pinch hit for Jim Price and the new Yankee reliever, Lindy McDaniel, pitched to Gates very carefully before ball four was called, the bags now jammed for the next batter, Don Wert. Could it have been scripted any better that, when Wert singled to right, it was Al Kaline, the man who waited 16 years for this day, the longest of any of these Tigers, who crossed home plate with the pennant-winning run?

The next day's *Detroit News* reported that, *"Detroit had a riot last night – 1968 style. It started at Michigan and Trumbull, inside Tiger Stadium, as Detroit clinched its first American League pennant in 23 years. The Tigers celebrated the 1968 pennant win blue-collar style with champagne and a few cases of Stroh's beer."* It wasn't long before the celebration moved from The Corner several blocks east to the Lindell A.C. pub where Tiger players and thousands of fans, inside & outside the Lindell, assembled as several Tigers got behind the bar and poured beers all night long to the happy, thirsty partiers. Lindell A.C. owners Jimmy & Johnny Butsicaris were honored that the team chose their bar to celebrate at, but would have been just as happy if the Tigers tending bar had charged money for at least a few of the drinks that they poured.

After a very long night of celebrating went deep into the next morning, when the following day's game was called due to rain storms, not a single Tiger player was upset.

DDDDDDDDDDDDDDDDDDDDDDDDDDDDDDDDDDDDDDDDDDDDDDDDDDDDDDDDDDDDDDDDDDDDDDDDDDDDD

15-year old Mick Robinson of Redford recalled the pennant-clinching evening, *"My mom, dad, brother, and I had been to the game on Monday when they could have, but didn't, clinch the pennant (since the Orioles also won). The next day, my brother and I were outside playing catch after dinner and decided to beg mom and dad to take us to that night's game - they caved in and off we went. Parking was at a premium and we were directed to park at the back of a lot near an alley between two telephone poles. After buying what were probably the last four upper deck general admission tickets, we found our seats (one obstructed view) in left field. When Don Wert singled home Al Kaline in the bottom of the ninth to win the game, the fans went crazy! The celebration spilled out of the stadium and out on the streets. As we walked back to the parking lot, people were everywhere with celebratory screaming, horns honking and yeah, they were dancing, dancing in the streets. It was great - right up to the time to get in our car, which was not where we left it. Turns out the parking attendant had us park in the alley (not in the lot) and our car was towed. After a couple phone calls to the police, we learned that our car had been towed only a few blocks away. It made for a memorable moment on a very memorable evening. Go Tigers!*

DDDDDDDDDDDDDDDDDDDDDDDDDDDDDDDDDDDDDDDDDDDDDDDDDDDDDDDDDDDDDDDDDDDDDDD

September 19, 1968, 5 days after McLain won his 30th & two days after the Tigers clinched the pennant against the Yankees, the 3-game series with New York wrapped up. As everyone knew, it would be the last time that the legendary Mickey Mantle would play in Tiger Stadium. As the sun rose on 9.19.68, Mantle was tied with Jimmie Foxx in lifetime home runs with 534 each, behind only Babe Ruth & Willie Mays. Denny McLain, who had already won his 30th, was pitching to back-up catcher Jim Price. McLain called time and walked towards home plate to talk with Price, stopping just a few feet from Mantle. As Mickey told the story in an interview with J.P. McCarthy 17 years later, *"I could hear Denny tell him, 'Let's let him hit one, this is his last game here' But you know McLain. You don't know if he's really gonna let you hit one or hit you in the back. So anyway, the first pitch I took. So, he gestured like, what's the matter?"* J.P. asked, *"Was it a fat one?"* *"Well, yeah, right down the middle!"* (laughter) *"And I looked at Freehan* (actually, it was Price) *and he said, 'Yeah! He wants you to hit one.' "So, I hit it into the upper deck. As I was rounding third, I looked out at him, and he gave me a big wink & a grin, and I tipped my hat to him."* J.P. said of Denny, *"That was a nice gesture."* Mick replied, *"That WAS a nice gesture... but I'd a probably hit one off him anyway."* It should be noted that the colorful Joe Pepitone followed Mick to the plate, and asked Denny to be as kind to him as he was to Mantle. Denny laughed and, as he said years later, *"I threw a fastball behind his head, all you could see was elbows and his butt before he hit the ground."*

The 6-2 victory over New York, powered by 2 home runs off the bat of Norm Cash, improved Denny's win total to 31 – it would be his final win of the regular season. McLain finished 1968 at 31-6 with an earned run average of 1.96, 28 complete games, and 6 shutouts in 336 innings pitched. Denny won the American League MVP and Cy Young Awards in this spectacular year. While Denny was the first to win 30 since Dean in '34, the last hurler to win 30 or more <u>all as a starting pitcher</u> was Grover Cleveland Alexander way back in 1917.

As Mickey and the Yankees flew home to the Bronx, Mantle was now sitting at 535 lifetime homers, one ahead of Foxx, and would finish the year, and his career, at #3 all-time with 536. Another Mickey made news in that same September 19 game, as the Tigers regular centerfielder, Mickey Stanley, started the game at shortstop – which leads to the next story...

In May, Kaline was hit by a pitch and suffered a cracked wrist, keeping him out of action until July. When once again healthy, Al was called into Manager Mayo Smith's office to talk about getting him back in the line-up. Kaline argued that the team couldn't take Jim Northrup out of right field, Al's usual position, since Jim was having too good a year. Mayo and Al agreed that Kaline, his whole career an All-Star outfielder, would start taking balls at third base, allowing the current outfield of Northrup in RF, Mickey Stanley in CF, & Willie Horton in LF to continue. Third didn't agree with Al, so he was utilized as a part-time first-baseman/outfielder and pinch hitter. Willie was soon injured, and Al moved into Horton's spot in left. As soon as Kaline was back in the line-up, his bat caught fire, leading to – when Willie got healthy – a meeting Mayo called of team veterans Kaline, Norm Cash, & Bill Freehan to figure out how all 4 bats in the outfield could play at the same time in the upcoming World Series. According to a 2018 interview with Kaline, in the meeting all agreed that Mickey Stanley was the Tigers best athlete and it was also noted, interestingly, that during daily fielding practice, Mickey often took grounders & throws from the outfield while manning the shortstop position.

On the eve of the Series, Manager Mayo Smith, in one of the gutsiest decisions in baseball history, decided to move Mickey Stanley, the team's starting - and defensively outstanding (a 1968 Gold Glove recipient with zero errors while tracking down every fly ball in sight) - centerfielder to shortstop. This decision was reached despite the fact that Stanley never played an inning at shortstop in the majors (until the rare game this year) or even in the minor leagues. This bold move allowed the bats of the four-outfielder rotation, Kaline (RF), Horton (LF), Northrup (CF) & Stanley (SS), to be in the line-up at once, and took the bat away from the team's offensive weak-link, shortstop Ray Oyler. Ray was defensively a vacuum as the team's primary shortstop, but only managed a .135 season batting average and, as noted in a Joe Falls' *Detroit Free Press* column, was *"0 for August"*. The days when Earl Wilson was pitching, it was only out of courtesy, and maybe a sense of tradition, that the Duke of Earl (hitting .227 with 7 home runs in only 88 at bats vs. Ray's .135 with 1 homer in 215 times at the plate) remained at the bottom of the batting order, and not batting ahead of Oyler.

DDDDDDDDDDDDDDDDDDDDDDDDDDDDDDDDDDDDDDDDDDDDDDDDDDDDDDDDDDDDDDDDDDDDDDDDDD

The 1968 World Series pitted the American League Champion Detroit Tigers, in their first Series since 1945, against the National League Champion St. Louis Cardinals, victors of the prior year's Series…

Game 1 St. Louis: It was a short-sleeve, muggy, day in Busch Stadium for the Series Opener. The Bob Gibson vs. Denny McLain pitching match-up received the bulk of the game 1 national pre-game hype. Gibson & McLain both won their respective leagues Cy Young awards and Most Valuable Player awards – the only time two pitchers have won both awards in the same season.

McLain, the first 30-game winner since Dizzy Dean in '34… Gibson, he of the regular season microscopic 1.12 ERA (third-lowest since 1900) & 13 shutouts, and winner of 3 games in the 1967 World Series. The anticipated game 1 pitching duel never took place. What did take place was a pitching clinic put on by Bob Gibson, setting a single game Series strikeout record of 17, whiffing 6 of the first 7 Tigers including Kaline-Cash-Horton, back-to-back-to-back, then polishing off the Detroiters by striking out the same 3 in the 9th, driving the Cardinals to a 4 to 0 opening game victory. Gibson's game 1 performance was one of the greatest displays of power pitching in World Series history – and to become champions, the Tigers would have to find a way to beat him at least once.

Cash called Kaline's room after the game, *"Thanks Al!" "Thanks for what, we lost." "Yeah, but your 9th inning strikeout tied the record, and mine broke it – I'm going to go on local TV tomorrow morning and get paid $500!"*

Despite the game 1 loss, Detroit's grand experiment of moving Gold Glove Centerfielder Mickey Stanley to short went well. He played flawless defense, and even had 2 of Detroit's 5 hits. Stanley though, was a bundle of nerves. *"Norm Cash told me that I was so tight you couldn't have pulled a pin out of my ass with a tractor."* Stanley never got comfortable at short during the Series, but it did not show in his play.

Game 2 St. Louis: The Tigers slipped 'em a Mickey, Lolich that is, in game 2, and Tiger fans could breathe again. The Detroit offense, put into a game 1 coma by Bob Gibson, awoke for 13 hits, including 3 by Stormin' Norman Cash and (you coulda got great odds in Vegas on) the only home run of Mickey Lolich's major league career. Whenever Lolich hit a ball, his focus in running the bases was to avoid an injury that would hurt his pitching. Assuming that most anything he hit would be an out, when striking the ball he would step *over* first base, to avoid turning an ankle or incurring a sprain on the bag. When Mickey hit his home run, he'd lost sight of the ball once it was in the air towards left, and chalked it up as a fly out. Following his practice of stepping <u>over</u> first, Tigers first base coach Wally Moses instructed Lolich to circle back and step on the base. Mickey asked Wally *"why?"* and when Moses informed Mickey that he had reached the seats, Mick said to him, *"Are you shittin' me?"* Lolich, winner of 17 regular season games, fired a complete game 6-hitter as the Motor City's heroes earned an 8 to 1 win that evened the Series at 1 game apiece.

Game 3 Detroit: My Uncle Henry took his one-month-shy-of-14-year-old nephew to game 3 of the World Series. The mental images remain strong of awe, upper deck infield reserved seats, beautiful sunshine, and red, white & blue bunting hanging everywhere. The Duke of Earl, Big Earl Wilson, was on the mound for us, and our heroes took a 2-0 lead into the 5th – when Cardinal Tim McCarver hit a 3-run homer that turned the tide in a 7-3 Cards victory.

Game 4 Detroit: This is getting ugly. On a gloomy, rainy day at Tiger Stadium, 53,634 fans witnessed menacing Bob Gibson out-pitch Denny McLain once again. The final score 10 to 1 Cardinals, our Tigers now down 3 games to 1. We're in a tight spot, boys.

DDDDDDDDDDDDDDDDDDDDDDDDDDDDDDDDDDDDDDDDDDDDDDDDDDDDDDDDDDDDDDDDDDDDDDDDDDDDD

On Monday, October 7, 1968, the morning of Game 5, 14-year old Laz Surabian was in his 8th grade Latin class at Berkshire Junior High in Birmingham, Michigan. Suddenly his Mom was at the classroom door, *"I have to take Laz out of class – it's an emergency."* As mother & child walked together down the hall, the concerned teenager got no answer to his inquiry, *"Mom, what is it? What's wrong?" "Just be quiet. Get your items out of your locker."* As they walked out of the school together, Laz saw his sister, who Mom also pulled out of class, in the car. Mama Surabian then informed her children that they were about to experience something that, today anyway, was more important than school: Dad was able to get tickets just this morning for Game 5.

Game 5 Detroit: the day began with the beloved Ernie Harwell finding himself in an unusual position – in trouble. Ernie suggested to Tiger management that the team allow Jose Feliciano (who in '68 had a very popular cover of the Doors "Light My Fire") to sing the pre-game National Anthem. Jose's version had a non-traditional, modest Latin touch to it and was met with light applause and some boos in the stands, while the Tiger Stadium phone lines lit up with complaints (a feeling pervasive enough that many local radio stations would no longer play Feliciano songs - until his 1970 Christmas hit "Feliz Navidad").

Mickey Lolich had just finished his warm-up tosses as the National Anthem began. To Mickey, Jose's version ran a little long (although he was quoted as saying it was *"fantastic"*), so much so that in the October chill it created the need for Mickey to warm-up again – but there was no chance for that as the game was about to begin. For whatever the reason or reasons, Lolich had a rough start, and the Tigers found themselves down 3 to nothing after the first inning. This was no way to end a great season – and the fighting Tigers clawed their way back in this one. Lolich settled down, giving up no further runs. In the 4th, Stanley & Horton scored to narrow the deficit to 3 to 2 (as 14-year old Laz Surabian was clicking away with his new Instamatic camera). In the fifth, the Cards Lou Brock hit a one-out double. Brock's speed had been an effective weapon for St. Louis all through this World Series, and with Lou in scoring position at such a critical juncture in the game, the feeling in the stadium was anxious and electric. This was *a shared Michigan moment* with the entire state tuned into the game at home, at work, or in any school with an electrical outlet, extension cord, & television wheeled into the classroom.

Julian Javier was next up, and hit a shot to left-field. Willie Horton fielded the ball on one hop and fired it towards home plate. Here comes Brock around third, arriving at home as the ball does. Lou decides not to slide, believing he can score standing up. Catcher Bill Freehan, though, had effectively positioned his foot to block the plate, denying Brock the opportunity to touch home as Freehan put the tag on him – and Lou is called "Out!" by the ump in one of the great plays in World Series history. Milt Richman of

United Press International told a national newspaper audience that Freehan met Brock at home plate *"like the towering Washington Monument."*

2 innings later, the Tigers - still a run behind and in need of a rally, got one when Al Kaline had one of the biggest (if not hardest) hits of his career, a 2-run single into short-center, giving the Detroiters their first lead of the game, 4 to 3. After tacking on an insurance run, courtesy of a Norm Cash run batted in, the Detroiters completed their 5-3 comeback, forcing the Series back to St. Louis for a game 6.

Al Kaline's single produced the go-ahead runs as Mickey Lolich won his 2nd game of the series for Detroit.

Jim Northrup's bases loaded home run off Larry Jaster topped 10-run Detroit rally in 3rd inning of Game #6.

Game 6 St. Louis: Kaline, Cash & Horton came home on Jim Northrup's grand slam, part of a 10-run explosion (a Series single inning record) in the third inning of the Tigers 13 to 1 victory. Today was Northrup's 5th grand slam of '68 (two of the 5 came in back-to-back innings June 24 at Cleveland). Denny McLain was the beneficiary of that June game & today. McLain pitched well in game 6, but although the Tigers ensured there would be a game 7, it would be without their 31-game winner on the hill. As game 6 concluded, Manager Mayo Smith motioned Lolich to meet him at the end of dugout by the tunnel, and Mayo asks, *"Can you pitch tomorrow?"* *"Well sure Mayo, there's no problem. You need me to pitch a couple innings for you, I can pitch in relief."* Smith says, *"No, no, not relief. I want you to start."* *"What?"* *"Can you give me 5 innings tomorrow?"* *"Sure I can."*

Game 7 St. Louis: The year before, in the 1967 Series vs. Boston, Bob Gibson pitched and won games 1, 4 & 7, surrendering only 3 runs total, all complete game victories. Based on Gibson's total dominance of Detroit in games 1 and 4 this year, all of St. Louis - and most baseball fans across the nation - had every reason to believe that he would do it again. In addition, Mickey Lolich, Detroit's starting game 7 pitcher, was going on only 2 day's rest instead of his normal 4. Mayo assembled the Tigers for a pre-game prep talk. *"Fellas, we have another shot at Bob Gibson today. He's a pitcher, not Superman."* Norm Cash spoke up, *"Ah, Mayo, I just seen him changing clothes in a phone booth."*

Mickey matched Bob Gibson, shutout inning for shutout inning, and entered the dugout after retiring the Cardinals in the fifth, figuring his day was done. But Mayo asked Mick for one more inning, so back out he went. After Lou Brock led off the bottom of the 6th with a single, Bill Freehan called time and walked to the mound, asking Lolich, *"You alright? Anything I can do for you?"* *"Yeah,"* Mickey said, *"could you get me a couple of hamburgers between innings?"* When play resumed, Lolich picked Brock off of first. With two outs, Curt Flood singled – and Mickey then picked <u>him</u> off of first to end the 6th. Curt Flood's day was about to get much worse.

After the first two Tigers made outs to start the 7th, Norm Cash & then Willie Horton singled, and up to the plate stepped the man who hit the game 6 grand slam, the Silver Fox aka the Gray Fox, the pride of Alma College, Jim Northrup. Gibson pitched and Northrup connected, the ball rocketing towards deep, straightaway centerfield. 7-time Gold Glove-winning outfielder Curt Flood took a step in towards the infield, realized his err and turned, but too late. It didn't really matter. Years later, Curt Flood said he was never going to catch this one, no matter how he played it. Northrup's laser screamed over Flood's head for a 2-run triple, breaking the scoreless tie. After Bill Freehan's double to left-center scored Jim, the 7th inning stretch found the Tigers in front 3 to nothing. That's when Lolich told Mayo, *"Now I'll finish it for you."* Mayo replied, *"That's exactly what I wanted to hear."*

Mickey Lolich blanked St. Louis in the 7th and the 8th, old reliable Don Wert aka the Coyote knocked in the team's 4th run in the top of the 9th (both of his Series hits were off Gibson), and then Lolich took the mound to close out the game. With the Cards down to their last out, Mike Shannon hit a solo home run to make it 4 to 1. As Harry Caray made the call for the national television audience, next batter Tim McCarver's foul pop settled into Bill Freehan's glove for the final out. In an instant, Lolich is lifted off the ground by the exuberant Freehan, and carried into the fast closing mob of teammates, their yelling and laughing echoing across the Busch Stadium field and its mostly – except for pockets of euphoric Tiger fans - quiet stands, the folks back home in a state of hysteria. 23 years since their last World Series win in 1945, Detroit was the Champion of the Baseball World once again. ***Sock It To 'Em Tigers!***

The Sporting News

1968 WORLD SERIES SPECIAL

TIGERS CELEBRATE THEIR VICTORY

Detroit's Heroes Go Wild

Detroit's Dick McAuliffe, Denny McLain and Willie Horton spent happy times after winning 1968 World Series.

12-year old Toni LaPorte of River Rouge rode bikes through the neighborhood with her friends, chanting over & over, *"Tigers won, four to one, Bye Bye Birdies!"*

My Dad was home in bed for Game 7, released after hospitalized for a heart attack he'd suffered, coincidently, after Game 3. Dad created a score card for me to fill in as the game progressed, and together we cheered our boys on. After Freehan squeezed the last out of the game, my Dad & I yelled and hugged, then I excused myself so that I might go outside and race several times around the house, stopping to jump 'n skip several times, while screaming for joy.

DDDDDDDDDDDDDDDDDDDDDDDDDDDDDDDDDDDDDDDDDDDDDDDDDDDDDDDDDDDDDDDDDDDDDDD

In what is arguably tied with the '35 Tigers for the most memorable sports championship in the city's history, the 1968 Detroit Tigers became only the 3rd team in World Series history to come back from a deficit of 3 games to 1 (along with the 1925 Pirates & the 1958 Yankees), the perfect ending for a team that came back to win 28 times in their last at bat. In the clubhouse afterward, Bill Freehan said, *"A lot of people must have been praying for us."* Norm Cash hit .385, Al Kaline hit .379, and Jim Northrup & Kaline each knocked in 8 runs to lead the offense, while Mickey Lolich became only the 8th pitcher in Major League history to win 3 games in a single World Series (interestingly, the only one of the 8 against 3 different opposing pitchers – Nelson Briles, Joe Hoerner & Bob Gibson) and no other pitcher since has tossed 3 complete game wins in a Series.

The State of Michigan was awash in grins, goose bumps and tears.

Ernie Harwell called the celebration that broke out back home, *"Probably the biggest, spontaneous celebration in peacetime history."* Within hours of the final out settling into Bill Freehan's glove, an estimated 150,000 had gathered to celebrate in downtown Detroit. One year after the riots in the Motor City, blacks hugged whites, strangers danced with strangers, sirens screamed, horns honked, and folks in general just went crazy.

The morning after the game 7 victory, a slightly hungover Freehan heard the sweet sounds of a distant choir coming from outside. He wandered to the window and saw a beautiful sight on his front lawn: a large group of nuns & kids from the nearby Catholic school were facing the house and singing a song with the repeating chorus of, *"We love you, Freehan!"*

"I guess you could say I'm the redemption of the fat man. A guy will be watching me on TV and see that I don't look in any better shape than he is. 'Hey Maude,' he'll holler, 'Get a load of this guy and he's a twenty-game winner.' "   Mickey Lolich

DDDDDDDDDDDDDDDDDDDDDDDDDDDDDDDDDDDDDDDDDDDDDDDDDDDDDDDDDDDDDDDDDDDDDDDDDDDDD

To celebrate the 50-year anniversary of *The Year of the Tiger 1968*, in 2018 folks gathered at the Detroit Historical Museum to hear stories being told by Willie Horton, Mickey Lolich, radio/TV broadcaster Ray Lane, & the old Detroit News columnist, Jerry Green. Late in the program, Mickey shared this story…

I was signing autographs at a show, when a fellow came up and asked, *"Would you have time when you get done to talk to me for a few minutes? I have a story I want to tell you."*

It was the day of the 7th game of the '68 World Series, and this man was serving his country in the jungles of Vietnam. It was day time in St. Louis, and night time in Vietnam. The man was from Detroit and went to his Lieutenant… *"We were going out on a night time ambush that night. Pitch-black in the jungle… I had a transistor radio with ear phones… both the Lieutenant and I were from Detroit."* He told his officer, *"We gotta listen to the 7th game of the World Series."* The Lieutenant says, *"You're crazy. The Vietcong hear any noise at all, they'll know there's an ambush waiting for them."* He replied, *"Let me take my radio, you sit right alongside me, you hear anything, I'll turn my radio off."* After a couple of seconds, the Lieutenant leans over and tells him, *"I can't hear anything."*

Prior to going out into the jungle, a system of soundless signals was set-up by these two Tiger fans. When Detroit is at bat, the soldier would lean over to the Lieutenant next to him and touch his chest where the Tiger "D" is on the uniform. When St. Louis is at bat, he'd draw his finger across the uniform, to mimic the longer "Cardinals" spelling. When the Tigers scored, he'd touch where the "D" was, and tap the lieutenant on the knee. When St. Louis scored, he'd tap his helmet. *"When you guys won"*, he told Mickey, *"we both turned and hugged each other, mouths wide open in a silent scream, our heads bobbing up and down in joy."*

1968 Willie Horton: "Willie the Wonder"

Few athletes in the history of Michigan sports are as loved by fans as much as Willie Horton. In 2013, on the 50th anniversary of his first call-up to the Tigers, some of those fans shared their thoughts about "Willie the Wonder"...

35th District Judge Michael Gerou – Canton MI

I believe Willie Horton had a shot at the US Olympic boxing team in 1960 in Rome. In any event he was a good boxer who won a Gold Glove in boxing and no one wanted a piece of him if the Tigers got into a skirmish.

Johnny Steck – Ann Arbor MI

My Willie memory was watching on TV. The first, last, and only time I ever saw a baseball player break a bat on a checked swing...didn't even touch the ball!

Mark (Yankee fan) Alwood – Lambertville MI

Shortly before our buddy Goobs (aka Dave Guba) passed, and was strugglin' at home towards the end, I noticed an autographed "To Goobs" Willie Horton photo by his bed. Our long-time, goodhearted, Lambertville boy Smitty had somehow sought out Willie, I believe at Willie's home, during one of his sales assignments, relayed the Goobs story and his Cleveland baseball love and left with a great memory and momento of Willie's caring nature. God bless my great buddy Goobs - nobody did a better and sometimes relentless Yannkeeeees SUUUUUUCK!!!!!!!

Paula Brown – New Boston MI

In 2004, I read in the newspaper that Willie would be signing autographs on a Saturday at the Home Depot in Canton. Imagine my surprise when my son Andrew and I showed up and there were only 3 people in line (it must have been a slow readership day at the Free Press) BUT great for us! Willie talked and talked to Andy about Little League and baseball in general. He signed a bunch of stuff that Andy keeps as his "treasures." Willie couldn't have been nicer, even to mom!

New friends: Andy and Willie

Vicky Zande – Livonia MI

My Grandpa, Joe D'Arigo, was a Boston native & played 3 years of minor league ball for the Boston Red Sox. He was a big Willie Horton fan, and from his years in Michigan he was the most loyal and devoted Tigers fan. Even when the Tigers went through their losing years, Joe would sit and watch just about every game rooting them on. He moved to Florida and his next-door neighbor Bill Gudioso, a nice Italian man who was from New York, used to spar back and forth through their living room windows when the Tigers would be playing the Yankees. Grandpa would be laughing about the Yankees getting beat by the Tigers telling Bill, "Boy, those Yankees are getting a schlakin!" Love you Grandpa... Vicky

Jimmy Vollmers – Dexter, MI

My favorite memory of Willie Horton is almost non-baseball related. I was 14 years old and mowing city lots with my cousin during the summer. We each made $2 per lot, but we didn't have to pay for the gas for the tractor. My uncle covered that. One day we were going about our business when we saw my uncle's Mercury Marauder drive over the curb and come careening through the field. He yelled, "Get off that tractor and get in the car. NOW!" As we drove away, he explained that there were riots going on and people were burning the city down.

That night we were watching the news, like everybody else that wasn't looting, burning and rioting. One of the TV cameramen got some footage of Willie Horton pleading with people in the streets to stop the madness and return to their homes. Willie had left the ballpark, still in his Tiger uniform, to try to restore calm to the city that he loved. As we now know, he wasn't successful as the city burned. But it showed Willie's courage and the love he had for his home town and the people here. Willie's boyhood home was destroyed by those fires.

Paul Carey, Tiger broadcaster – Rochester MI

Great to see so many wonderful memories of Willie... and I have many, too. Like listening to him talk about his Club 23 bar on Livernois while riding a bus into Tiger Stadium at 3 a.m. to pick up our cars after a road trip. Watching his buttons pop off his jersey when being restrained by teammates after being brushed off by a flame-throwing Frank Tanana in the mid-70s. Remember, Willie was always in the very front of the batters' box, trying to take his cut before the pitch broke. Seeing how distraught he was upon being traded to Texas for Steve Foucault--a nice guy who could never replace Willie and wound up going back to Texas and becoming a Deputy Sheriff. Willie is known for that throw to Freehan in the '68 Series but I remember Willie as being so fundamentally sound as an outfielder, never missing the cut-off man. He didn't play LF with his back to the wall as did his replacement Steve Kemp...nor were balls hit at him an adventure as you old-timers will remember Dick Wakefield made them. Remember the game in the Kingdome after Willie joined Seattle and was having a really good year at the plate? He hit a towering drive toward left and stayed near the plate admiring it when the ball hit a speaker and dropped in front of our left-fielder and Willie managed to get to first base. One last thought... after retiring, Willie did some coaching and spent a short time with the Yankees. Ernie and I visited their clubhouse to see Willie and I sensed a feeling of embarrassment as he sat in those pin-stripes. To this day, Willie still worships Sam Bishop, his coach and mentor at Detroit Northwestern while the rest of us hold Willie in the highest esteem.   Paul Carey

1969 - 1970 Pennant Flying at The Corner; Denny & the Bets

Home folks think I'm big in Detroit City
From the letters that I write they think I'm just fine, yes they do
But by day I make the cars and by night I make the bars
If only they could read between the lines

("Detroit City" by Bobby Bare)

In the afterglow of the 1968 Championship, to the Tiger faithful, the future looked bright. The teams in Detroit's farm system, the pipeline that provided so many of the key players for the 1968 World Series victors, had never been so successful. The Tigers AAA affiliate Toledo Mud Hens (who replaced Syracuse as Detroit's AAA crew in 1967) were, like their parent team at Michigan & Trumbull, 1968 champs of their league. Even the AA Montgomery squad had strong back-to-back 1967-1968 2nd place finishes.

The '68 Mud Hens, victors of the International League, were driven by an outstanding pitching staff featuring their Big 3: Mike Marshall had 15 wins against 9 losses with a 2.94 earned run average, Jim Rooker was 14 & 8 with a 2.61, and Dick Drago posted a 15 & 8 record and a 3.36 ERA.

But the chances of keeping these 3 with Detroit were dim. The 1969 season opened with two American League expansion teams, the Seattle Pilots and the Kansas City Royals, now playing and a late-1968 expansion draft was held to help stock those 2 new entries. For the draft, each team in the American League was allowed to protect only 25 players, the parent club together with their minor league affiliates, in their system. The Tigers had to make some tough choices regarding who to expose in the draft. They decided that the young pitchers who helped Detroit win it all in '68, for the most part, would be protected – but not the 3 Mud Hens pitchers.

As a result, the Tigers lost to the draft included...

Ray Oyler, all glove/no bat & the first Tiger chosen, picked by the Seattle Pilots. Although no one likes to lose a long-time member of their baseball club family, when this choice was made team management must have exhaled in relief. But they couldn't stay that fortunate. In subsequent rounds:

Jim Rooker, *Toledo Mud Hen pitcher #1*, was the 2nd Tiger system player drafted, chosen by the Kansas City Royals. Jim was actually lost to Detroit 2 weeks before the draft, as the player-to-be-named-later (knowing they would likely lose him in the upcoming draft) in the June '68 acquisition from the Yankees of a reliever who would be out of baseball before the end of May '69, John Wyatt. Rooker was traded by the Royals to the Pittsburgh Pirates at the end of '72, where he was a key contributor from '73 thru '78, reeling off victory totals of 10, 15, 13, 15, & 14 while in the National League top 10 in ERA '74, '75, & '79.

The third Tiger lost was reliever Jon Warden, taken by Kansas City. The man who was 3 & 0 before the Tigers had played two weeks in 1968, had arm issues that halted his baseball career by the end of 1969.

Kansas City also drafted from Detroit pitcher Dick Drago, *Toledo Mud Hen pitcher #2*. Drago was a 17-game winner by 1971, and an effective contributor his entire 13-year MLB career.

It was very late in the draft, and no one had yet chosen Toledo pitcher Mike Marshall. The Tigers were hopeful, but just before the draft concluded, Seattle chose Mike, *Toledo Mud Hen pitcher #3*. This loss hurt the most. After elite-level years in '72 & '73 (4th & 2nd in Cy Young voting, respectively) with the

Montreal Expos, as a L.A. Dodger in '74 Marshall became the first relief pitcher in history to win the Cy Young Award.

As the calendar turned to the 70s, many key players from the '68 Tigers were getting long in the tooth but they had enough gas left in the tank for an East Division title in '72. Although all the argument can be is speculative, it's worth considering how many titles our Boys of Summer might have won, or at least the number of pennant-races they'd have been in, had no expansion draft taken place in 1968.

DDDDDDDDDDDDDDDDDDDDDDDDDDDDDDDDDDDDDDDDDDDDDDDDDDDDDDDDDDDDDDDDDDDDDDDD

Charlie "Boss" Schmidt, was the starting catcher during the Tigers first 3 World Series, in 1907 to 1909. Charlie, an Arkansas native, passed away on November 14, 1932 at the age of 52, of an acute intestinal obstruction. The dirt-poor Schmidt was buried in an unmarked grave in the town of Altus, Arkansas. In 1969, residents of Altus contacted the Tigers about Charlie's final resting place, and Jim Campbell took the reins in correcting the situation. Early in 1970, with Charlie's fellow Arkansas native George Kell in attendance, a stone was laid on Charley Schmidt's grave. Beneath his name and birth & death dates, an inscription read: *"A Detroit Tiger 1906-1911."*

Boss Schmidt's finest moments took place in the 1909 World Series versus Pittsburgh. In game 2, on a team with Ty Cobb & Sam Crawford, it was Charlie who propelled the offense, his 2-run double in the 2nd starting the scoring, Schmidt's two hits & 4 RBIs the keys to Detroit's 7-2 victory. In the game 6 recap by the famous Ring Lardner in the *Chicago Daily Tribune*, Ring noted, *"Schmidt rose brilliantly to the occasion."* In the bottom of the ninth inning, with the Pirates rallying, Boss Schmidt blocked the plate, absorbing Bill Abstein's spikes in the process, preventing the tying run. Then, to end the game, he pegged out Chief Wilson coming into third on the front end of a double steal to seal Detroit's 5-4 win.

Rest in peace Charlie "Boss" Schmidt.

DDDDDDDDDDDDDDDDDDDDDDDDDDDDDDDDDDDDDDDDDDDDDDDDDDDDDDDDDDDDDDDDDDDDDDDD

Boss Schmidt was one in a long line of strong catchers that the Detroit teams and their fans have been blessed with. From Charlie Bennett of the 1887 World Series Champion Detroit Wolverines through Boss Schmidt on the early Ty Cobb teams to Johnny Bassler on the later Cobb squads, through 1935 World Champion player/manager & Hall of Famer, a leader of men and two-time MVP, Mickey Cochrane, through great receivers Lance Parrish, Mickey Tettleton, and Pudge Rodriquez.

But in the middle of all of those, the dominant American League catcher for the decade of the 60s and into the 70s, is the one and only Bill Freehan. Willie Horton believed that Bill Freehan was *"the best catcher in baseball"* during Horton's time in the game, and Willie said that includes Johnny Bench. After his playing days, Mickey Lolich said, *"If you're a good pitcher, you call your own games, and Freehan and I worked together. He knew what I wanted to throw in every situation. In the 13 years that we played together, there was only two times – two times – that I shook my head because he called the wrong pitch. He knew me like a book, knew what pitch I wanted to throw in what situation. I highly respect that man."* Detroit News sports writer, Jerry Green, said, *"Bill Freehan was the consummate football player in a baseball uniform."* In the fifth inning of game 5 in the '68 Series, Lou Brock saw that first-hand.

11 time All-Star - same as the number on his uniform, defensive stalwart, 5-time Gold Glove recipient, retired with the MLB record for catchers in fielding percentage, total chances & putouts, hit 200 career

home runs, clutch hitter, a 2nd & a 3rd in MVP voting, inspirational leader – William Ashley Freehan is a Hall of Fame worthy candidate. *Bill's 11 All-Star games is the most for any player not in the Hall.* As of 2018, 18 catchers are in Cooperstown. Sabermetrician Jay Jaffe has developed a system to measure a player's Hall of Fame worthiness, and Jaffe ranks Bill #14 among all catchers who've ever played.

As 1969 began, Freehan was – as were his Tiger teammates – basking in the glow of being a 1968 World Series Champion, and wanting that feeling once again. Perhaps inspired by the great '68 experience, Bill decided to keep a diary during the '69 season, believing that his position of catcher provided him with the most distinct perspective on the diamond, as the only defensive position that has direct contact with the pitcher, the hitter, and the manager. That diary would become a 1970 book, *"Behind the Mask"*.

The season that Freehan was recording would bring him his 6th consecutive All-Star team berth, his 5th consecutive Gold Glove, and a lot of quotes from Norm Cash including: coming back to the dugout after striking out, Norm said, *"Boy, things got so bad out there even my wife was booing.";* *"The only way to keep from losing money with bad investments is to spend it.";* Cash hit a little chop down the first base line that he believed foul, but when the umpire called it fair and Norman was thrown out at 1st, Norm told the ump, *"I hope you guys all go out on strike. We'll do better on the honor system."*

Even when Stormin' Norman wasn't the one speaking, he frequently found himself in the middle of humorous moments. One such 1969 moment took place when Detroit hit two mammoth home runs to build their lead to 12-0 over the California Angels as Cash came to bat. California manager Bill Rigney called time and, instead of walking to the mound, as might be expected, Rigney strode towards Norm at home plate, and asked to look at the ball in play. When the umpire asked why, Rigney explained, *"I just want to make sure these are the same balls that my team is trying to hit."*

Besides giving the reader an inside look at how sometimes wildly divergent personalities work together as a team and progress through a major league season, Freehan's diary recorded great frustration. Bill suffered a spring training broken nose while getting in some extra batting practice – he was at home plate, adjusting his batting stance & looking down while Jim Northrup (the one-time star collegiate pitcher at Alma College) threw a fastball towards him, and it hit Bill square on the bridge of the nose. Although the injury healed quickly, Freehan had other concerns, foremost despair at how poorly the team was performing the fundamentals they executed so well in '68: when to bunt, when to hit away, when to cut off a throw or let it through – the mental errors that can mean the difference between a good season or a championship season.

As a team leader, Freehan took the squad's concerns upon himself more than most of the guys did, but he also knew how to lighten the mood. Late in spring training, when manager Mayo Smith had to make the tough decisions on who to cut and who to take north for the regular season, outfielder Ron Woods got the good news that he'd made the Tigers. Ron was 26, had been in the minors for 8 years, and never had a single major league at bat in all that time – and now he was crying tears of happiness. Bill sat with Ron for a while, listening to Woods tell his story, before leading Ron to the Gatorade jug that Freehan had spiked with a fifth and a half of vodka. Pretty soon Ron, Bill, and anyone else who drank from the jug was laughing and found the world around them a happier place.

DDDDDDDDDDDDDDDDDDDDDDDDDDDDDDDDDDDDDDDDDDDDDDDDDDDDDDDDDDDDDDDDDDDDDDDDDDDDD

Opening Day 1969 at Michigan & Trumbull was played April 8, a Tuesday, in front of 53,572 fans still giddy from the incredible 1968 Year of the Tiger season. It all felt like a wonderful dream from which no one wanted to wake. Before the first pitch, Commissioner Bowie Kuhn passed out the World Series rings to each player at home plate, none more excited to receive his than the man who played so hard and so well 16 years for the Tigers waiting for this day, Mister Tiger, Al Kaline.

The opponents for the first two '69 games were the Cleveland Indians, and they trotted out two fine pitchers to face Detroit, Luis Tiant and Sudden Sam McDowell. But Denny McLain, who else but the 31-game winner would get the Opening Day nod, was on his game, surrendering single runs in the first and the second, and only gave up one hit all day after that, while the Tiger bats boomed. Stormin' Norman doubled home the tying runs in the 3rd, Kaline broke the tie with a 2-run blast in the 5th, and Denny himself singled in run number 5 to knock out Tiant and salt the game away. By the time that Don Wert drew a walk in the bottom of the 7th with the bases loaded, forcing in the day's 6th run, the party that is Opening Day in Detroit couldn't have been more fun if Freehan was spiking the concession stand drinks.

Mickey Stanley manned shortstop on Opening Day, as he did in the World Series. With the loss of Ray Oyler in the expansion draft to the Seattle Pilots, the plan was to have Tommy Matchick and Dick Tracewski compete for the position. Neither, though, firmly grabbed the job in spring training and – for now - the primary shortstop would be Stanley.

Game 2 saw Mickey Lolich opposite Sam McDowell. The expected pitcher's duel between the two flame-throwers never materialized as Detroit exploded for 12 runs, Freehan's 5th inning grand slam sending Sudden Sam to a sudden shower. The more whimsical among the crowd asked if 162 and 0 was possible.

It wasn't, of course, but even worse was that the old bullpen bugaboo, a '67 plague overcome in '68, poked out its ugly head once again in '69. Exhibit A was witnessed in game 3, with the Yankees in town. These were hardly the big, bad Bronx Bombers of old and yet... with the game still close in the 9th, Tiger reliever Dick Radatz, whose off-season acquisition led to the release of John Wyatt, faced 5 batters and 4 scored in a 9-4 loss. The 6'6" Radatz, known as "the Monster" due to his frame and the fear he once put into batters, leading the A.L. in saves in '62 & '64, was past his prime and released by mid-June.

Following Yankee Mel Stottlemyre's shutout of the Tigers on 1 hit, Detroit avoided a 3-game sweep when Joe Sparma somehow only gave up 1 run on 5 hits and 8 walks before being pulled in the 7th, the Tigers 6-2 win powered by Kaline's 2-run homer & Horton's 2-run double. It said something about Mayo Smith's lack of trust in his bullpen that he brought in starter Lolich in relief of Joe to finish the game. Sparma is a tough pitcher to hit but wild – Joe shut out the Senators later in April, giving up only 2 hits but also 8 walks; at the end of May, he tosses a no hitter for 8 & a third innings, surrendering only a Don Mincher 9th inning double in a 1-hitter, but also issues 7 walks in a 3-2 complete game victory. For the season, Joe will pitch 92 innings and give up 77 walks, almost one per inning. The other 3 main starters, Lolich/Wilson/McLain, combined to give up 2.5 base on balls per 9 innings in '69.

When Detroit lost the final game in April, 3-2 to first place Baltimore, their closest competitors in '68, it evened their record at 10 & 10 and dropped them 4 & ½ games back of the Orioles. They managed a split of the short two-game series the next day in a great pitching duel between McLain & Jim Palmer. Each team could only get 3 hits on the day, but Bill Freehan connected for a 2-run homer in the fifth off Palmer for the game's only runs in the quick 1 hour & 49-minute, 2-0 Tiger victory, pulling Detroit back to within 3 & ½ of first.

On May 13 at The Corner, Mickey Lolich defeated the White Sox by a score of 3 to 1. Besides Mickey, the big Tiger star of the game was Norm Cash. Norman had 3 hits on the day, scored the Tigers first run, and was standing on first base after singling in the bottom of the 7th when Willie Horton came to bat. It was then that the rains started coming down and the game was delayed. When play resumed, Norm was standing on 2nd base. The nearest ump asked Norm, *"What are you doing over there?"* *"I stole second,"* Norm told him. *"When did that happen?"* the ump asked. *"During the rain delay."*

McAuliffe's signature foot-in-the-bucket batting stance

Two days later, in the finale of the White Sox series, Earl Wilson pitched brilliantly, only surrendering 1 run on 4 hits with 9 strikeouts in his 9 innings. Tommy John is on the mound for Chicago, marking the first time that John faces Dick McAuliffe since their fight last August. There is no flare-up between the two today, in fact the only fireworks in the first 9 innings from anyone in a Detroit uniform takes place when Jim Northrup hits a solo home run off John in the 7th to tie the game at 1. When Earl draws a walk in the bottom of the ninth, John Hiller goes in to pinch run for Wilson, but is left stranded as the game moves on to the 10th. Reliever Pat Dobson sets down the only 3 White Sox batters he faces and gets credit for the win when McAuliffe leads off the bottom of the 10th with a walk-off home run served up by Chicago reliever Bob Locker. In the post-game clubhouse, the Duke of Earl sees winning pitcher Dobson walk by, laughs and announces to his predominately Caucasian teammates, *"You're all a bunch of prejudiced bastards. You wait until the white pitcher comes along until you score."*

This comfort level, camaraderie, the ability to joke, among the white & black teammates was further underscored when Detroit traded Ron Woods in June for the Yankees Tom Tresh. Norm Cash explained the transaction to Earl Wilson, *"Hey, I thought that was a great trade – when you get one white guy for one colored guy even up"*, and the entire clubhouse broke up in laughter.

DDDDDDDDDDDDDDDDDDDDDDDDDDDDDDDDDDDDDDDDDDDDDDDDDDDDDDDDDDDDDDDDDDDDDDD

Mickey Lolich frequently spoke of the high regard in which he held Bill Freehan, and May 23, 1969 offered a fine example of how well this pitcher-catcher battery functioned. Mick was struggling to hold on to a 4-3 lead over the Angels, and his last 4 warm-up pitches prior to the 5th inning were in the dirt. Before the first batter of the inning stepped in, Freehan asked Lolich if he'd like to hear his thoughts. Mickey said yes, and Bill suggested that he keep his front shoulder in and not rear back so far on each pitch. Mick adopted the recommendation and proceeded to set a team single game record of 16 strikeouts while limiting California to 2 hits the rest of the way in the 6-3 Tiger win.

Including Mickey's May 23 victory, Detroit won 11 of their last 13 in May – and only picked up one-half game on the red-hot Orioles who led the Tigers by 6 at the end of the month. From June 1 to June 26, Detroit went a pedestrian 13 & 10 and found themselves 11 & ½ back as they arrived in Baltimore for a 4-game series with the Orioles, a golden opportunity to cut into the Birds lead. Instead, the Tigers lost 3 of the 4, the crusher was the 2nd game of the series, and again it was the bullpen that cracked. Daryl Patterson came on in relief of McLain in the 6th with Detroit up 4-2...

In 1968, Detroit arrived in 2nd place Baltimore for a big, late-July, 3-game series. Daryl Patterson came in to relieve in as tough a situation as could be: bases loaded & nobody out, the Tigers holding a slim 2-0 lead. Daryl proceeded to strike out the next 3 batters, including Hall of Famer Brooks Robinson and 4-time All-Star, Davey Johnson. But that was the magical season of 1968. *This, however, was 1969,* and today, Daryl faced 5 Orioles and gave up 4 runs in the Tigers 6-4 loss. June ended with Detroit 39 & 32 – not bad, but 13 & ½ behind the high flying 55 & 21 Orioles.

DDDDDDDDDDDDDDDDDDDDDDDDDDDDDDDDDDDDDDDDDDDDDDDDDDDDDDDDDDDDDDDDDDDDDDDDDD

The decision to make Mickey Stanley the primary shortstop for '69 started badly when he injured his throwing arm on the very first grounder of the very first day of spring training, throwing it to first base off of the wrong foot. Mickey fought through the injury amazingly well, and led the team with 149 games played, 59 of those at short. It wasn't until shortstop Tom Tresh was acquired from the Yankees on June 14 that Stanley returned to his old position as Detroit's regular center fielder, running his Tiger outfielder record of errorless games to 220 on the way to his 2nd consecutive Gold Glove award.

Years later, Stanley said that the 1969 spring training arm injury plagued him for the rest of his career, *"It definitely took the fun out of baseball for me, because that* (his arm) *was my biggest asset."* Mickey overcame the injury to shine defensively, while finishing 2nd on the team with a career best 70 runs batted in. Perhaps it was Stanley's frustration over his damaged wing or how the pennant chase was developing or some other issue or all of the above, but after leading off the June 11 game with a fly out and returning to the dugout, Mickey loudly reduced the bat rack to kindling.

Baltimore, 11 games up on Detroit, came to The Corner for a 4th of July holiday weekend 3-game series, another big opportunity for the Tigers to gain ground. Friday's game 1 pitted 10 & 1 Mickey Lolich against 7 & 7 Mike Cuellar. Stormin' Norman Cash got the home team off to a great start with a 3-run homer in the 1st inning. When Mickey Stanley's single in the 2nd sent Don Wert home, Cuellar was knocked out of the game. But the rainy day threatened to cancel the game before the required 4 & ½ innings were played to make it official. Frank Robinson led off Baltimore's 5th with a solo shot, but Mick clamped down and got Merv Rettenmund on a fly ball and both Brooks Robinson & Davey Johnson on strikes, making the game official, just before the grounds crew was directed by the umpires to cover the field with tarp as play was halted.

At this point, the Tigers wanted the rain to go on & on until the game was called and a win was in the books. Daryl Patterson, part Native American, walked out on to the field to perform a rain dance. With umpire Emmett Ashford's hands tucked into his back pockets, Norm Cash snuck up behind Emmett, slipped his arms around the ump's waist extending them outward, making a gesture to the television cameras that the game was now over. Although funny stuff, Norman's efforts were insufficient to halt play until the umpire crew finally called the day game near 530PM. The Tigers had now pulled to within ten games of the first place Orioles.

Ten games out of 1st was as close as the Tigers got from here on out in '69, splitting the final two games of this series. In game 2, Dave McNally improved to 12 & 0 in the Orioles decisive 9-3 win. The Tigers mounted a comeback in game 3, as they so often did with Denny McLain on the mound, overcoming Boog Powell's 2-run homer over the right field roof, becoming the 5th player to accomplish that feat (along with Norm Cash, Ted Williams, Mickey Mantle, & Don Mincher). On Powell's next at bat, Freehan went out to the mound to see how McLain wanted to pitch him. Denny shared his plan, *"The best thing I can do is give the sign of the cross before I throw the ball,"* and then wisely walked Boog. Dick McAuliffe & Tom Tresh hit back-to-back home runs to break a 3-3 tie and provide the winning margin in a 5-4 win.

The July 15, 1969 Tigers game at Washington, D.C. was attended by 2 people who ran for President the previous year: Senator Eugene McCarthy & the man who won the election, President Richard Milhous Nixon. Bill Freehan met McCarthy when the senator covered the '68 World Series as a *Life* magazine special correspondent, the two discussing sports and Vietnam while developing a mutual admiration for each other. Al Kaline campaigned for Nixon in '68, and in '69 joined the advisory staff of the President's Council on Physical Fitness. Although Detroit turned a triple play, they fell 7-3 to the Senators.

As interesting as these political leaders are, the fellow in town that most excited the Washington Senators fans in '69 was first year manager Ted Williams, the man with the highest on base percentage in major league history, .482 (Babe Ruth is 2nd at .474), amazingly getting on base almost one out of every two times at bat. Williams knew not only how to get on base himself, but as a manager had success in teaching this to his team. The Senators last had a winning season in 1952, but in 1969, his rookie year as team skipper, Washington finished at 86 & 76, up from 65 & 96 in '68, their team batting average rising from .221 to .251 (even defensive wizard & future Tiger Eddie Brinkman, a career .224 batter, hit .266 in 1969). At season's end, Ted won the Associated Press Manager of the Year Award.

745PM was the starting time for the July 18 game in Cleveland, McLain the scheduled starter. Mayo Smith often allowed Denny to operate under a separate set of rules, including flying his own plane to road games, traveling apart from the rest of the Tigers. When a team is in 1st place and all is well, allowances made for the big shots are more easily accepted... when a team is suffering through a frustrating year, not so much. Denny had trouble with a plane's engine midway between Detroit and Cleveland, circled back for repairs, and did not arrive at Municipal Stadium until 710PM. As Denny hurriedly dressed, Norm Cash came in from fielding practice, grabbed McLain and walked him into Mayo's office announcing, *"This is a guy named Dennis McLain. He'd like to pitch tonight."* Denny, to no one's surprise, threw a complete game shutout, 4 to nothing, improving his record to 14 & 5.

Jim Campbell, upset that Denny's business ventures outside of pitching a baseball were becoming a distraction, summoned McLain to his office. What bothered Campbell specifically at this time was Denny's involvement in promoting a paint company, that had McLain everywhere but at the ballpark. Jim recalled, *"I really chewed him out. McLain stood there in front of my desk and took it without a word before leaving my office. Then the door opened, and Denny leaned in saying, 'I like your style. When my paint company becomes a success, I'll let you run it for me.'"*

3 days after Apollo 11's Neil Armstrong became the first man to walk on the moon, All-Stars Freehan, Lolich & McLain were back in our nation's capital for the July 23 Midsummer Classic. On game day, players spoke with President Nixon at a White House reception for both All-Star teams, the President shaking each player's hand in the receiving line. During Bill Freehan's turn, the President told him, *"I've watched your career, and admired your comeback in the Series last year."* Bill thanked him and acknowledged that he'd be catching the ball when the President threw out the first pitch of this evening's game, kiddingly adding, *"I hope you have good stuff tonight."* The good-natured bantering continued, the President replying, *"Well, be alive, because I've been getting my arm in shape."*

Since Detroit won the A.L. flag the previous year, Mayo Smith would be the '69 American League All-Star team manager. Dennis Dale McLain, Cy Young recipient in '68 and well on his way to repeating in '69, was the obvious choice to start on the hill. The only problem being that, with an hour 'til game time, Denny was nowhere in sight, running late due to a dentist appointment back in Detroit, compounded by engine problems with his private plane. Replacement starter, Yankee Mel Stottlemyre, gave up 3 runs in the first 2 innings, and the next A.L. pitcher, Blue Moon Odom, was rocked for 5 runs in the 3rd. Denny arrived 20 minutes after the first pitch and was inserted into the game to pitch the fourth, surrendering 1 run, leaving the game with the National League leading 9-2 on their way to a 9-3 victory. Starting catcher Freehan played 'til the 7th inning, going 2 for 2 with a solo homer off of Steve Carlton in the third and a run-scoring single off Bob Gibson in the 4th for the game's final run.

Mickey Lolich, the third Tiger All-Star, did not play – part of a rough day. He and his wife were guests on Denny's plane and, with McLain's dentist appointment and engine trouble delays, left Detroit too late to make the White House visit or the beginning of the All-Star game. About mid-game, Denny informed Mick that he'd have to find his own way home as McLain was now going on to Florida. Fortunately, Lolich was able to get seats for his spouse and himself on Freehan's flight back to Metro Airport.

DDDDDDDDDDDDDDDDDDDDDDDDDDDDDDDDDDDDDDDDDDDDDDDDDDDDDDDDDDDDDDDDDDDDDDDDDDDDD

Ted Williams wasn't the only 1969 rookie manager making his mark in the American League. When the Minnesota Twins defeated Detroit at The Corner on August 6, the surprising Twins under Billy Martin's guidance were in front of the West Division by 3 games, and on their way to the divisional title. Post-game, two Twins players were at the Lindell A.C. pub, pitcher Dave Boswell and outfielder Bob Allison. Boswell was loudly critical of Twins' manager Billy Martin. When Allison tried to calm him down, Boswell punched him, and that's when Billy entered the bar. Martin and Boswell were barking back 'n forth, Billy suggested that they take it outside, and ended up beating Boswell into a condition that required 20 stitches and 2 weeks to heal.

In his book, *"Behind the Mask"*, Freehan assesses this Lindell A.C. incident, *"Billy always was a good street fighter. I'd like to play for him. You've got to respect that man. He can keep you on your toes and keep you hustling. He'll go out and have a couple of drinks with the boys. I like that."*

Bill Freehan did get his wish to play for Billy, and the Tigers would win a '72 East Division title with him as manager, but as always with Martin, the welcome quickly wears thin. By 1973, Freehan's attitude about Martin had soured as his manager was second-guessing Bill's game-calling & began platooning the 11-time All-Star who both Mickey Lolich & Willie Horton called the greatest catcher of their time.

DDDDDDDDDDDDDDDDDDDDDDDDDDDDDDDDDDDDDDDDDDDDDDDDDDDDDDDDDDDDDDDDDDDDDDDDDDDDDDD

With the team 14 games behind the Orioles, the Tigers sent reliever Don McMahon to the San Francisco Giants on August 8 for a player-to-be-named-later. The guys felt this showed management had given up on the season, a disheartening development. McMahon was the most dependable man out of the Tigers bullpen, a veteran who led the team in saves. Pitching Coach Johnny Sain was none too happy about this, complaining to an Associated Press scribe that there was no communication between Mayo and himself. Once G.M. Jim Campbell confirmed with Sain that he was quoted correctly, Campbell fired the man who was the pitching coach on World Series teams 5 of the last 8 years, the man who Whitey Ford credited with adding 5 years to his career, and who the majority of baseball analysts consider to be the greatest pitching coach in MLB history. A man with this well-earned reputation can find work again if he wishes, and Johnny Sain would coach for the Chicago White Sox & the Atlanta Braves thru the 70s & 80s.

Despite the turmoil surrounding the loss of Sain and McMahon, the Tigers continued playing winning baseball, but with the incredible pace that the Orioles won at, it made little difference. Going into August, Detroit was 14 games behind Baltimore, and after going 21 and 9 that month they could only shave 1 & ½ games off of the deficit.

The Tigers had one last big chance to gain ground on Baltimore: on September 4, the O's arrived in town for a 4-game series. A sweep pulls Detroit to within 8 & ½ with 20 more games to play before the year's final 3 at Baltimore. Tonight, the Duke of Earl pitched against the O's Tom Phoebus, who never saw the end of the first inning. Detroit's Tom Tresh led off with a home run and 5 batters later Tommy Matchick singled in Northrup and Kaline. End of 1, Detroit 3 Baltimore 0. Through 8 innings, Wilson only yielded one run on a sacrifice fly in the third. When Al Kaline deposits a Pete Richert offering deep into the left-center stands in the 8th, it seems like the Tigers have all the insurance they will need, now with a 4-1 lead as the Orioles come to bat in the 9th. Shockingly, Frank Robinson, Boog Powell, & Brooks Robinson, the first 3 batters in the top of the 9th, all hit solo home runs off of Earl to tie the game at 4. The rowdy crowd now sits in stunned silence as Mayo finally comes to get the tired Wilson out of the game. Davey Johnson greets reliever Tom Timmerman with a double, and comes around to score on a flyball and a groundout. Baltimore 5 Detroit 4, Tigers coming up to bat, but Willie Horton, Jim Price, and Bill Freehan go down 1-2-3 as the fans quietly file out. The spectacular late-game comebacks that were the Tigers trademark in '68 now belong to the Orioles in '69.

Detroit would take only one of 4 games with Baltimore, the Orioles leaving town with a 14 & ½ game lead and the pennant race, for all practical purposes, over. The single Tiger victory is a 5-4 win on Tom Tresh's 11th-inning walk-off home run. Tresh was playing right field on this day instead of his usual shortstop position. Playing short for the Tigers was the newly arrived player-to-be-named later from the August Don McMahon trade to San Francisco, Cesar Gutierrez. In his Tiger debut, Cesar hit in the lead-off spot, going 2 for 5 and showing speed that the Tigers often lack. On June 21 of next year, "Cocoa" Gutierrez would have a day he'd never forget.

DDDDDDDDDDDDDDDDDDDDDDDDDDDDDDDDDDDDDDDDDDDDDDDDDDDDDDDDDDDDDDDDDDDDDDDDDD

In Freehan's *"Behind the Mask"* book, the diary of the 1969 season, his August 7 entry talks about how much he'd like to someday play for Billy Martin. In the September 8 entry, with the Yankees in town, Bill meets their manager Ralph Houk, and Freehan says, *"Of all the managers in the league, Ralph is the one I'd most like to play for."* Bill Freehan must have been psychic as he would finish his career under first Martin & then Houk. Interestingly, Freehan also is impressed by a young catcher the Yankees brought up in early-September, Thurman Munson, and how he feels old when Thurman addresses him as <u>Mister</u> Freehan. *"I thought it was only a couple of spring trainings ago I was calling Yogi Berra 'Mr. Berra'."*

The 2nd place Tigers had a fine season by most measures, but their 90 & 72 record left them 19 games behind the 109-win Orioles, at the time the 5th-most wins by a team in any single season. No matter how well Detroit performed in '69, Baltimore was one step ahead: typical was when the Tigers won 7 of 9 in August & they lost one-half game in the standings to the Birds. Injuries placed further road blocks in the way, losing sparkplug McAuliffe the 2nd half of the year to knee damage the most-costly infliction. The number of wounded grew so great that guys began calling the trainer's room "Mayo's Clinic".

The 1969 season's final game was a 2-1, 10-inning, loss in Baltimore. Jim Palmer, now 16 & 4, outdueled Mickey Lolich, now 19 & 11. On the plane ride back to Detroit, several Tigers took over the p.a. system, and sang to their teammates *Auld Lang Syne*.

Better things were surely in store for the team in 1970.

DDDDDDDDDDDDDDDDDDDDDDDDDDDDDDDDDDDDDDDDDDDDDDDDDDDDDDDDDDDDDDDDDDDDDDDD

Denny McLain's 1969, like his 1968, was an outstanding one. He led all American League pitchers with 24 wins, 325 innings pitched, and 9 shutouts – 3 more than the #2 hurler. Denny's performance earned him his 2nd consecutive Cy Young Award. As 1970 dawned, Dennis Dale McLain was on top of the sports world. At only 25 years old, he was often referred to as the best pitcher in the game. Denny's salary from the Tigers was $90,000 and he earned that much again, and then some, from his outside interests: a variety of product endorsements, not to mention performing on his Hammond organ as a headliner in Las Vegas – even playing on the Ed Sullivan Show. Combining income from the Tigers and from other sources, no baseball player earned more. Denny was living large, flying his private plane to wherever his busy, profitable schedule took him. *And then Denny McLain's life suddenly changed.*

There's never been any like Denny

The February 23, 1970 issue of *Sports Illustrated* hit the newsstands on the eve of Tiger spring training in Lakeland. The front cover had a photo of Denny next to the headline, *"Baseball's Big Scandal: Denny McLain and the Mob"*. <u>The article claimed</u> that early in 1967, Denny invested in a Flint-based Syrian mob bookmaking operation. A gambler named Edward Voshen placed a bet on a horse race with this group, his horse came in, and he was due $46,000. The man who took the bet could not pay, and directed

Voshen to get his money from one of the bookie's partners – Denny being one of those. Voshen sought the help of mobster Tony Giacalone, who met with Denny in September '67. The mobster stomped on McLain's toes, dislocating them, and threatened much worse if his man wasn't paid (just about the time that Denny, during the down-to-the-wire pennant race, couldn't pitch for 2 weeks due to an injury from, he told the Tigers, rising too fast from a couch when his foot fell asleep). According to the article, after this visit with Denny, Giacalone bet large sums of money on Boston and Minnesota to win the pennant and then put down big money on the final game of the year, betting against the Tigers, who were starting McLain, versus the California Angels (Denny pitched poorly in the 8-5 loss that ended Detroit's pennant hopes). The article included *Sports Illustrated* conceding that the sources for much of the story were criminals.

When this story came out, Commissioner Bowie Kuhn met with Denny. McLain said, yes, he did invest $15,000 in the Flint bookie operation, but after a dispute he severed ties with them before Voshen placed his $46,000 winning bet – although Denny still loaned $10,000 to one of the partners to help pay the $46K debt. The Commissioner also was told by McLain that he'd never met mobster Tony Giacalone and told Kuhn the story of his foot falling asleep.

After the Kuhn-McLain meeting, Denny was indefinitely suspended while the story was investigated. On April 1, 1970, the Commissioner announced his decision: McLain's suspension would run until July 1 and he continued, *"While McLain believed he had become a partner in this operation and has so admitted to me … it would appear that he was the victim of a confidence scheme. His own gullibility and avarice had permitted him to become a dupe of the gamblers with whom he associated. I thus conclude that McLain was never a partner and had no proprietary interest in the bookmaking operation."* Bowie Kuhn added that Denny was exonerated from charges that his actions had any effect on baseball games or the 1967 pennant race.

Once the decision was read to a room full of reporters, the Commissioner took questions. One newsman asked Bowie to explain the difference between a person attempting to become a bookie, and becoming one. Kuhn answered, *"I think you have to consider the difference is the same as between murder and attempted murder."* The reaction in Detroit reflected that of most of the country, summed up in Dick McAuliffe's comment, *"If Denny's innocent, it should be nothing. If he's guilty, then this is not enough."*

DDDDDDDDDDDDDDDDDDDDDDDDDDDDDDDDDDDDDDDDDDDDDDDDDDDDDDDDDDDDDDDDDDDDDDDDDD

For the first 3 months of the 1970 season the Tigers were without their ace and at the same time without an annoying double standard for one player above all others. Mickey Lolich stepped into the ace role, while other hurlers beyond Earl Wilson would have to pick up the slack left by Denny's absence. In December of '69, Detroit traded Pat Dobson & Dave Campbell to Seattle for pitcher Joe Niekro, who served as an effective starter, as did 22-year old Les Cain in his first full year in the majors.

The Tigers began the season with 3 against Ted Williams' Washington Senators on the road at RFK Stadium. Mickey Lolich was outstanding in the opener, tossing a 10-strikeout, 5-0 shutout. In Cesar Gutierrez first Opening Day with the Tigers, he had 3 hits and scored the team's first run. In game 2, the Duke of Earl Wilson was banged around, headed to the showers before the third inning was done, leaving Detroit down 5-3 on their way to a 14-4 defeat. The Tigers took the rubber match as Joe Niekro had a fine Detroit debut, shutting out the Senators 3-0 behind a 2-run Freehan homer.

Traveling to nearby Baltimore for 3, Lolich & Wilson dropped two close ballgames before Joe Niekro salvaged the finale for his new team, a 7-2 win. The offense was powered by 3 hits each from Horton & Gutierrez, the big hit a 2-run triple by Niekro himself. Tom Timmerman picked up the save, the 1st of what would be a surprising 27 saves for him this year, good for third in the league. Now 30 years old, Tom was called up to Detroit early in '69 after spending all of '61 to '68 in their minor league system.

Opening Day at The Corner took place on April 14 in front of an Opener-small crowd of 26,891. Mickey Lolich had the honors, and the Tiger offense gave him plenty of support in the 12-4 victory, Stormin' Norman leading the way with a 2-run homer among his 3 hits. Powered by an 8-game winning streak, Detroit's record in April was 12 & 6, good for 2nd place and one-half game behind the Orioles. The good times did not last, though. May was unkind to the team, victorious only 9 times against 17 losses. However, in a 162-game season we can always find reason to celebrate...

On May 30, 1970 the Tigers played the Brewers at Milwaukee's County Stadium. In the Tigers top of the 1st, Willie Horton singled home Al Kaline, staking Les Cain to a 2-0 lead. But Cain was wild, walking the first two Brewers that he faced, then surrendering a run-scoring single before giving up yet another walk to load the bases. When Les struck out the next 2 hitters, it looked like he might be able to escape without any further damage. However, 7th batter Roberto Pena sent a Cain pitch deep into the right-center gap. Both right fielder Kaline & center fielder Northrup were racing towards each other in an attempt to catch the fast falling smash on the fly, and the 2 Tigers and the baseball arrived at the same place at the same time, the outfielders slamming into each other as the ball ticked off the top of Northrup's glove and bounced to the wall. That all 4 runners scored on the inside-the-park grand slam was secondary as Kaline lay motionless on the ground.

Jackie Moore, an old Tiger teammate of Al and Willie's from 1965 (and with Willie before that in the minors) and now the Brewer's bullpen coach, sprinted out to Al. Jackie told a reporter later, "I could hear him gasping for air, he was choking and turning blue. I realized he had swallowed his tongue and I tried to pry his jaw open, but the best I could do was get two fingers between his teeth." Horton raced over from his position in left field, arriving only seconds after Jackie Moore did, pushing him aside and quickly forcing Kaline's jaw to unclench, then moving Al's tongue out of the way so he could breathe again. Kaline's jaw immediately tried to snap shut again, clamping down on Horton's hand and leaving a permanent scar as a reminder (as if one was needed) of likely saving Al's life. Kaline was helped off the field, missed only one game, and then was right back in the lineup. Jim Northrup stayed in the game and, although he and Horton scored the Tigers 4th and 5th runs to tie the game, the Brewers won 9-7.

DDDDDDDDDDDDDDDDDDDDDDDDDDDDDDDDDDDDDDDDDDDDDDDDDDDDDDDDDDDDDDDDDDDDDDDDDDDDD

On June 21, Cesar "Cocoa" Gutierrez went 7 for 7 against the Indians at Cleveland's Municipal Stadium, setting a new record for most consecutive hits in an extra-inning game. Mike Kilkenny started for Detroit, the Tribe sending him to the showers early with a 5-run outburst in the 1st. The Tigers rallied, winning 9 to 8 in 12 innings. Cesar entered the game batting .218, and at day's end was hitting .249. To say that Cesar's 7 for 7 day was an unusual outburst is like saying Don Larsen's perfect game in the 1956 World Series was unforeseen – a gigantic understatement: in 4 seasons in the majors, Cesar hit .235.

Detroit played at a .630 clip in June, closing the gap to first place from 11 to 7 games during the month and giving their fans cause for hope that with Denny's scheduled July 1 return, there will be a pennant race to watch in late-summer. That anticipation, and the excitement of the return to the team of the man who won 55 while only losing 15 the last 2 years, has 53,863 pushing their way into the Grand Old Ballpark on this warm July 1 evening. The feeling is akin to Opening Day, and Hoot Robinson's bar was typical of the saloons surrounding Michigan & Trumbull, overflowing with a party atmosphere for several pre-game hours. Unlike Opening Day in Detroit, the national press is here in World Series numbers, and there is little chance of snow.

The opponent for Denny's comeback is the New York Yankees. Isn't it always the New York Yankees? Throughout the history of the Detroit Tigers, an overwhelming percentage of the big games has been versus the Bronx Bombers. And the Tigers more than hold their own in those games. 2 days ago, Detroit was 5 games behind 2nd place New York and 7 & ½ behind 1st place Baltimore. Defeating the Yanks 5-3 last night, in the first game of a 3-game series, was the perfect appetizer for McLain's return. Young Les Cain improved to 7 & 2, taking matters into his own hands by breaking a scoreless tie in the 3rd with a solo home, followed in the same at bat by homers from Mickey Stanley & Al Kaline, all off of, to date, 10-game winner & first-year All-Star, Fritz Peterson.

To the roar of the crowd, McLain puts down the Yankees in the top of the first, 1-2-3. As so often occurs with Denny on the hill, the Tigers put runs on the board quickly, on 2 hits, 1 NY error, and 2 sac flies. 2-0 Detroit after 1. But Denny is not sharp this evening, and home runs by Jerry Kenney & Thurman Munson put the Yankees up 3-2. Cesar Gutierrez singles in Bill Freehan to even things up after 4, but in the sixth McLain allows a Bobby Murcer lead-off home run, gets the next man out, but is nicked for a Danny Cater double and a Curt Blefary RBI single, before Mayo Smith strolls to the mound to get Denny out of the game to a standing ovation. Daryl Patterson induces Thurman Munson to hit into a double play grounder to end the inning at 5-3 New York. RBIs by Stanley & Kaline tie the game in the 7th, and 3 shutout innings of 1-hit ball by Tom Timmerman in the 9th, 10th & 11th hold New York at bay until the Tigers win it 6-5 on Mickey Stanley's 11th inning RBI single.

The consensus is that, sure, Denny wasn't Denny, but after the rust is off, he'll be the McLain we all know. What almost – almost – overshadows Denny's return was Joe Niekro's near no hitter the very next day against the Yankees. Niekro took his bid into the 9th, but with one out Horace Clarke singled to deep 2nd to break it up. Joe got the final 2 outs on grounders and had to settle for a 5-0 shutout to complete the sweep of the New Yorkers, improving his record to 9 & 6 with a 3.03 ERA. Joltin' Joe Niekro also provided a key hit, breaking up a scoreless tie with a 2-run single in the 2nd. The Tigers hot June, Denny's return to the rotation, Niekro's near no hitter, and a sweep of 2nd place New York has the city in an upbeat mood about our Boys of Summer. Detroit is now only 2 games behind the Yankees and have closed to 6 games – only 4 in the loss column - behind Baltimore.

DDDDDDDDDDDDDDDDDDDDDDDDDDDDDDDDDDDDDDDDDDDDDDDDDDDDDDDDDDDDDDDDDDDDDDDDDD

There was little time to celebrate Niekro's gem, as the next day began a 3-game series in Baltimore, an immediate chance to gain ground. Lolich-Cuellar faced off in game 1, and although only giving up 6 hits, Mickey took a 4-0 loss. When Tigers game 2 starter Mike Kilkenny was pounded for 5 runs in 5 innings and the O's Dave McNally cruised into the 9th up 5-1, it looked bleak for the Detroiters. But, down to their last 3 outs, the Tigers played like it was 1968: when Horton and Northrup opened the ninth with singles, O's manager Earl Weaver replaced McNally with reliever Dick Hall, but that did not slow Detroit. Freehan singled home Willie and Wert followed with a sac fly to score Northrup, Baltimore 5 Detroit 3. Norm Cash came off the bench to pinch hit for shortstop Ken Szotkiewicz and that brought Weaver back out of the dugout to bring in lefty Pete Richert to face lefty Cash, and Stormin' Norman sent one of

Pete's pitches to the deepest part of Memorial Stadium in left center for a game-tying 2-run homer. Before Richert could get out number 3, Mickey Stanley took him over the fence to put the Tigers up 6-5. Tom Timmerman came in to get 3 outs to nail down the victory and his 10th save.

The series finale was the one that everyone was looking towards – Denny McLain's 2nd game back and facing one of the best, Jim Palmer. Denny looked much sharper than against the Yankees, striking out Don Buford and Frank Robinson in the first inning and striking out the side in the 2nd. The Tiger offense was stymied by Palmer, not getting their first base runner until the fifth. Baltimore broke through for single runs in the fifth & sixth, but that was it, Denny leaving after a 1-2-3 seventh. McLain's outing was a strong one, but Detroit could only reach Jim Palmer for 3 hits as he spun a 2-0 shutout.

McLain's next outing was a no decision versus Boston in a Tiger 7-3 win. He followed that with a blow-out loss to the Orioles - it was the July 12 finale of a 4-game series, and a chance to cut the O's lead to 5 games, but Denny was rocked for 7 runs in 5 innings, and took the loss in the 13-3 thrashing. In the middle of *Denny's Comeback Tour*, the Tigers swept a July 19 doubleheader at Kansas City to pull within 3 games – 2 in the loss column – behind Baltimore. The game 1 pitching match-up, Joe Niekro versus ex-Toledo Mud Hen Dick Drago, was a dandy. Norm Cash knocked in both Tiger runs, first on a sac fly that scored Kaline, then with a single to plate Horton. Niekro, meanwhile, only allowed 3 hits and when he tired in the 9th, Timmerman came in to get the final 3 outs to secure the 2-0 victory, his 14th save and Niekro's 10th win against 7 losses. In game 2, Detroit trailed 4-0 and was down to their last 6 outs when the KC bullpen lent a helping hand, walking 4 of the first 5 batters. The Royals defense then kindly kicked away a grounder to third base, allowing the 2nd & 3rd runs of the inning to cross home plate. At this point, the Tigers offense decided to join the party, a Gates Brown single driving in Cash and a Don Wert double sending Horton & Gater home. Tom Timmerman pitched the 8th & 9th, locking down the 6-4 win with save number 15. Pulling to within 3 of Baltimore with this July 19 doubleheader sweep was the high-water mark for Detroit in the 1970 pennant chase. *Now, back to Denny...*

After a no decision at Comiskey Park, McLain posted his first 1970 win, versus 2 losses, at Minnesota on July 21, pitching 7 innings of the 5-2 win. 4 days later, before 30,080 at The Corner, Denny pitched well for the third consecutive outing and picked up his 2nd win, departing after surrendering his 3rd run in the 8th, Tigers 9 White Sox 4. On the final day of July, Denny cruised along against the Twins, up 3-0 going into the sixth, when Minnesota rallied. After the first 4 batters reached him for a single, homer, a walk, and a single, Denny was pulled from the game with Detroit up 3-2. McLain would not win today, though, as reliever Daryl Patterson allowed both inherited runners to score, before the Tigers rallied to pull out a 10-9 win to end July in 2nd place, 6 & ½ games back of Baltimore. Out of character for Denny, he had yet to toss a complete game.

DDDDDDDDDDDDDDDDDDDDDDDDDDDDDDDDDDDDDDDDDDDDDDDDDDDDDDDDDDDDDDDDDDDDDDDDDDDDDD

With McLain's return to the rotation, the Tigers parted ways on July 15 with the Duke of Earl, big Earl Wilson. This was a straight cash transaction with the San Diego Padres. Earl was now 35, slowing down a bit – although he did shutout the Damn Yankees, God bless him, as recently as May 26. The Duke was a big part of the team's successes the last few years, winning 64 games for Detroit over 4 seasons (mid-'66 through mid-'70) and always a power hitting threat, unusual for a pitcher, hitting 7 home runs in '68 alone and 17 overall for the Tigers. Earl retired at the end of 1970, wrapping up a 121-win, 11-year career, and will always be known as a 1968 World Series Champion.

August 2 was a day for Mister Tiger, as the Tigers celebrated *"Al Kaline Day"* at Tiger Stadium. The man also known as "Six" for his jersey number – he would be the last Tiger to ever wear that number – was in his 18th season with the only major league team he'd ever play for. The Tigers last celebrated a "Day" 30 years prior, in 1940 for Charlie "the Mechanical Man" Gehringer. 40,113 came out to cheer Kaline, along with his old teammate from the 50s, Harvey Kuenn, the great Gordie Howe aka Mister Hockey, Commissioner Bowie Kuhn, A.L. President Joe Cronin, Governor Bill Milliken, Mayor Roman Gribbs, and Mel Torme who sang for Al, "Thanks for the Memories" with customized lyrics. Cherry Street, running along the northern edge of Tiger Stadium, became "Kaline Drive".

Overwhelmed by the outpouring of love, Al wept while sharing his thoughts with the fans, *"This is the greatest day of my life. There have been so many people who have helped me to get to the big leagues and who have helped me stay there, it would be impossible for me to acknowledge them all. I can still remember back to June of 1953, and I can honestly say I thank God I chose to play for the team here in Detroit, as I did. I will always remember this day, and I will always remember you, the fans, and the support you have given me, and I say that from the bottom of my heart."*

DDDDDDDDDDDDDDDDDDDDDDDDDDDDDDDDDDDDDDDDDDDDDDDDDDDDDDDDDDDDDDDDDDDDDDDDDD

Unfortunately, after their 19 & 12 July, Al's special day was near the beginning of a bad month for the team. Willie Horton was enjoying one of his finest seasons (.305/17 HRs/69 RBIs) until he was lost for the year with a late-July ankle injury. The team record in August was 12 & 18 as they fell 16 & ½ games back of the Orioles; before the month was done, not only were they be out of the pennant race, but Denny McLain will have played his final game as a Tiger.

Denny's first August mound assignment was August 4 versus the Senators. Before many in the crowd even made it to their seats, Detroit fell behind 3-0 after half an inning. McLain pitched much better in the rest of his 8-inning outing, but still dropped a 4-1 decision to fall to 2 & 3. Win number 3 had to wait until a 5-2 win over Milwaukee on August 22. Denny's last game in the Detroit Tiger organization turned out to be Wednesday, August 26, before 16,143 at The Corner versus the California Angels where McLain was roughed up in his 8 innings, giving up 6 runs in Detroit's 6-3 defeat.

Two days later, on August 28, McLain poured buckets of ice water on two Detroit sports writers, Jim Hawkins of the *Detroit Free Press* and Watson Spoelstra of the *Detroit News*. In 1968, when you're the dominant pitcher for a World Series-bound team, this episode might have been laughed off as an "oh, that rascal" moment, but when you've already been associated with underworld figures and are 3 & 5 with a 4.63 ERA... not so much. Tiger management did not see this as the harmless prank that Denny did, suspending him from the team for 7 days. Before the 7-day suspension was completed, Commissioner Bowie Kuhn suspended Dennis Dale for the rest of the season when it was discovered that McLain had carried a gun on a team flight in August.

One man who would not be taking Denny's spot in the rotation was Joe Sparma. In December of '69, the Tigers had traded Joe to the Montreal Expos for another pitcher, Jerry Robertson (who tossed 14 innings for Detroit in 1970, his final 14 innings in the majors). Joe Sparma was a nice guy with a blazing fastball, a nasty overhand curve, & long stretches of wildness, who will always be remembered for winning the '68 pennant-clinching game. Joe only played into May of '70 for Montreal, appearing in 9 games and going 0 & 4 with a 7.06 ERA. He spent the balance of the year on the Expos AAA team, and in 1971 the Toledo Mud Hens signed Joe. Although he did fire a one-hitter for the Hens, he was wilder than ever, walking 5 consecutive men in one game, missing the plate with 15 straight pitches. After a 2 & 5, 5.88 ERA, season, Toledo released him in August of '71, ending Sparma's baseball career.

DDDDDDDDDDDDDDDDDDDDDDDDDDDDDDDDDDDDDDDDDDDDDDDDDDDDDDDDDDDDDDDDDDDDDDDDDDD

After starting September 7 & 9, Detroit went into a complete collapse, losing 11 of their last 14 for a final season record of 79 & 83. For many Tigers, it was the first time they'd ever been on a team below .500 – 1963 was the last year that Detroit lost more than they won. In the disappointing season, Mickey Stanley had his finest individual performance, leading the team in runs, hits, stolen bases, & triples, and topping league outfielders with a 1.000 fielding percentage in winning his third Gold Glove. Jim Northrup topped the team with 24 homers & 80 RBIs. Joe Niekro had the best of his 3 years pitching for Detroit as the number 2 in the rotation with a 12 & 13 record with 2 shutouts including the near no-hitter. Tom Timmerman enjoyed his first full season in the majors & also the finest of his 6-year MLB career, with 6 wins and 27 saves, while being acknowledged as one of the major's finest relievers of '70.

The final Tiger game of the 1970 season took place on October 1, and the very next day Manager Mayo Smith was fired. Upon learning his fate, Mayo spent some time at a local watering hole, chatting with the press, famously telling them, *"The baseball fans in this town are ignorant. They couldn't tell a baseball player from a Japanese aviator. And that's a quote."* As the team fell apart in August and September, the blame was laid at Mayo's feet. He cannot be blamed though for the loss of McLain – how do you replace the game's top pitcher? - OR the loss in late-July for the balance of the season of their top first half hitter Horton to an ankle injury OR the loss for a quarter of the year including all of September of perennial All-Star and team leader Freehan to spinal surgery (even when he did play it often was with a numb leg). Mayo Smith took over the team before the 1967 season and led them in that first year to within 1 game of a pennant – despite a sieve of a bullpen, to a '68 World Series crown, and to a 1969 90-win/2nd place finish before the 1970 season.

Mayo should be credited with hiring brilliant pitching coach Johnny Sain, who worked wonders with the staff; for recognizing that McAuliffe's skills were better suited to second than short and bringing in Ray Oyler as Mac's replacement at shortstop, creating an outstanding defensive pairing up the middle; for one of the gutsiest calls in World Series history by moving Mickey Stanley to shortstop to make room in the lineup for Kaline, who hit .379 in the Fall Classic. Mayo Smith treated men as men and let his players play, a trait appreciated by those on his teams. He received kudos from both players and writers for his coolness in pressure-packed situations. On the down side, he created tension by allowing Denny to live by his own set of rules. But did you hear that he hired Johnny Sain?

Barely had Mayo paid his bar tab than Jim Campbell let players and fans know that the atmosphere around here was about to change dramatically – he replaced Mayo Smith as skipper with Billy Martin, Mayo's polar opposite. Just as folks were getting used to the idea of Billy Martin, the GM made one other move that would dramatically change the team.

On October 9, 1970, Detroit pulled the trigger on arguably the 2nd most lopsided trade, in the Tiger's favor, in team history – ranked only behind Detroit's swap of Steve (*not even Don*) Demeter to Cleveland for Norm Cash – when they traded to the Washington Senators former 31-game winner & royal pain-in-the-ass Denny McLain, the loveable but aging third-baseman Don Wert, pitcher Norm McRae, and OF Elliott Maddox; in return the Tigers received pitcher Joe Coleman (who in 1971-1973 won 20, 19, & 23 games for Detroit), and an outstanding pairing for years to come on the left-side of the infield: shortstop

Eddie Brinkman & 3rd baseman Aurelio Rodriguez. This trade was a shot of adrenaline for an aging team, announcing Detroit's return to the pennant chase.

Tiger fans gave their enthusiastic blessing to the Denny trade

What might Denny McLain have achieved in the game of baseball if he put in the work to maximize his talents? Bill Freehan said Denny told him that he was an organist first and a baseball player second. Freehan's thought was, *"but without baseball he would be – well, how many organists can you name?"*

Joe Falls claimed that, upon Denny's departure, he saw Tiger GM Jim Campbell walking down Trumbull and tossing his pack of Rolaids away. Jim's Rolaids decision may be a hasty one with Billy Martin in town.

1971 & 1972 Long In the Tooth & Billy Ball

In blew a Texas storm, Norman Cash
Jimmy Northrup, smash after smash
Can't take it away, Stanley's plays
Horton & Kaline, well what can ya say
But, from 60 feet out on that hill
Stood a man with a great big job to fill
Roly Poly Mickey Lolich, Roly Poly Mickey Lolich
Roly Poly Mickey Lolich, Roly Poly Mickey Lolich

("Roly Poly Mickey Lolich" by The Fans)

As 1971 dawned, a Detroit Tiger ballplayer had never been paid a $100,000 salary from the team for a single season's worth of performance. Tiger GM Jim Campbell was prepared to change that, and had forwarded a $100,000 contract to Al Kaline for the upcoming season. Al reflected on his play for the prior year, a .278 average with 16 homers & 71 runs batted in, and told Campbell thank you, but *"I'd prefer to get that much money when I rate it,"* and played 1971 for a lesser figure. Al Kaline's decision was noble but, under the heading of unintended consequences, when other players were negotiating their salaries, the message they heard was we can't pay you more than we pay Kaline.

The Denny trade to the Washington Senators took place on the eve of the 1970 Baltimore-Cincinnati World Series opener, the first Series game for Reds rookie manager Sparky Anderson. Once the Series concluded (Baltimore in 5) and folks reflected on the trade, it was thought to be even more of a heist for Detroit than at first glance. Washington manager Ted Williams was disgusted, declaring, *"The price was too high"*, refusing to attend the press conference announcing the deal. Senator's owner Bob Short saw McLain as the draw needed to get butts into the seats; the Tigers saw Aurelio Rodriguez at third & Eddie Brinkman at shortstop as the answer to the left side of their infield and 24-year old Joe Coleman – who defeated Detroit 3 times in their '68 championship year - as the ideal long-term number 2 pitcher behind Lolich.

The hiring of the 42-year old Alfred Manuel Martin aka Billy Martin to manage the talented but aging Tigers was seen almost universally as a shrewd move by Jim Campbell. Always lurking in the background was the volatility factor with the volcanic Martin. In 1969 with the Minnesota Twins, during his single season of managing thus far, he had a physical altercation with the team's traveling secretary, punched out his star pitcher, and feuded with the owner. However, he also led the Twins to the playoffs. To the Tigers, the plusses outweighed the risks. *"Looking to light a fire under the club"* was the constant theme when anyone from the front office was asked about the hiring of Martin.

DDDDDDDDDDDDDDDDDDDDDDDDDDDDDDDDDDDDDDDDDDDDDDDDDDDDDDDDDDDDDDDDDDDDDDDDDDDDDDD

The reworked Tigers sat at 15 & 15 as the '71 season moved into mid-May, despite a combined 8 & 3 start of the Big 2, Lolich & Coleman. Ike Brown, when he could get on the field, excited fans by hitting over .450, but what received the most press was the first game of a road trip that was to begin in our nation's capital. On May 14, 1971 at RFK Stadium, the Tigers faced Denny McLain. Denny was 3 & 5 in the young season, and his mound rival on this day was a pitcher the Tigers acquired from the Twins in the off-season, Bill Zepp, a reliever getting a rare start. Zepp did a nice job in his 5 innings, surrendering only 2 runs, one on a ground out and the other on a home run by Frank Howard, no crime there as that was one of 382 Big Frank mashed in his career. Denny, meanwhile, had the adrenaline flowing against his old teammates. Jim Northrup reached him for a 2-out first inning double, but then McLain reared back and fired a called strike 3 against Number 6, the folks back home hearing from Ernie that *"Al was called out for excessive window shopping."* Detroit finally had a major threat in the top of the sixth when Dalton Jones led off with a single and was doubled to third by Dick McAuliffe. But Denny dug in to get Aurelio Rodriguez and Northrup on strikes before keeping the Tigers scoreless by dispatching Kaline on an inning ending pop-up, as the Washington fans roared their approval.

The score remained 2-0 Senators as McLain took the mound for the ninth. The large number of Tiger fans in front of their TVs back home, watching the broadcast by George Kell & Larry Osterman, were encouraged as Stormin' Norman led off with a single to center, moving to 2nd with Horton safe at 1st when Washington center fielder Del Unser could not handle Willie's flyball to center. Nobody out and the tying runs on base. Jim Price flies out and the runners hold as Eddie Brinkman is due up, but Martin pinch hits for Eddie with Kevin Collins, an infielder the Tigers picked up late last season. Collins comes through with a single to load the bases as reliever Tom Timmerman is due up, but the hot Ike Brown pinch hits instead, and Ike keeps his early season magic going with a 2-run, game-tying single, sending Cash & Horton across the plate, while raising his average to .500. Minimizing the damage, Denny strikes out McAuliffe for his 7th K of the game and then induces Aurelio Rodriguez to ground out, keeping the game at 2-2. When with one out in the Senators ninth, Toby Harrah tags up at third and beats the throw home on a sacrifice fly, a satisfied Denny is now 1 & 0 all-time versus the Detroit Tigers.

The Tigers had another shot at Denny just 8 days later, when a jam-packed crowd of 53,337 made their way into Tiger Stadium to see a classic match-up of McLain versus Mickey Lolich in the first game of a twin bill. The fans roared the entire game, and the hometown heroes turned the noise up a notch in the third. Eddie Brinkman led off with a knock to left and Lolich followed with a sacrifice bunt that moved Eddie to 2nd. After Denny got Mac on strikes, Kaline drilled a pitch from his old friend deep into the left field stands to put Detroit up 2-0. Mick followed that up by striking out the side in the 4th, & dominated as he cruised through the Washington line-up inning after inning. Although Denny made it through the 7th, a Norm Cash 2-run shot in that frame settled the outcome, had there been any question. Mickey tossed a 4-hit, 5-0 shutout, the 27th and final out appropriately a strikeout, his 10th of the day, much to the delight of the overflow crowd. In game 2, the Tigers cruised 11-0 to complete a bad day for Ted Williams' fellas, as Stormin' Norman continued his torrid first half with 2 home runs and 5 runs batted in. Norm was on fire and now up to 11 homers with several days still to go in May – versus the 15 home runs he'd hit in all of '70.

Despite the big trade, the new manager, the games versus Denny (Lolich defeated McLain again on July 10), and some individual achievements, in the standings little had changed versus last year. Detroit was in third place at the start of June and were still mired there as the calendar flipped to July, 6 games behind the Orioles. However, generating a great deal of excitement was the anticipation of July 13, 1971, the 3rd time that baseball's All-Star game would be played at The Corner (along with 1941 and 1951). Four Tigers made the American League squad: besides starters Norm Cash and Bill Freehan, Al Kaline came off the bench to single and score, while Lolich earned the save. In a fun side note, the '71 All-Star game marked the first time ever that future-Tiger Sparky Anderson managed a game at Tiger Stadium, today wearing a Cincinnati Reds hat as the National League skipper.

Before a crowd of 53,559, the A.L. defeated the National League 6 to 4, the American League's first All-Star win since 1962. Rosters of the two combined teams featured 21 future Hall-Of-Famers, including Kaline, and an All-Star game record 6 home runs, all hit by players who would be inducted one day into Cooperstown: Roberto Clemente (his homer was the only hit off of Lolich), Johnny Bench, Hank Aaron, Harmon Killebrew, Frank Robinson, and the man who hit the monster shot that stands out in everyone's mind, Reggie Jackson of the Oakland A's.

Reggie pinch hit for A.L. starting pitcher Vida Blue in the bottom of the 3rd. Facing him on the mound for the N.L. was Pittsburgh's Dock Ellis. On the 2nd pitch, Reggie swung and drove the ball to deep right-center, over the right field roof, *the ball still rising* as it slammed into the light tower transformer atop the roof, to the 1st base side of the center field bleachers. Curt Gowdy and Tony Kubek told the national TV audience that until Reggie's hit (& referring to the time since the upper deck was completed in '38), *"Only 13 times had a ball been hit out of Tiger Stadium, 4 of the 13 times by Norm Cash, who was responsible for the longest drive at 560'"* (omitting Mantle's 643' shot on 9.10.60 off Paul Foytack that cleared the Checker Cab Co. building on Trumbull). Kaline said Reggie's home run was the hardest hit ball he'd ever seen, anywhere. Frank Howard believed, had it not hit the lights, it would've carried 600'.

DDDDDDDDDDDDDDDDDDDDDDDDDDDDDDDDDDDDDDDDDDDDDDDDDDDDDDDDDDDDDDDDDDDDDDDDDDDDD

Paul Pienta of Huntington Woods recalled the day Tiger Stadium hosted the 1971 All-Star Game. *"I used to date a young lady whose dad, Gus, worked the turnstiles. We'd probably go to 20-25 games each summer, just walk up to Gus and he'd let us walk right through. We'd usually sit in the upper deck until the third inning or so when Gus would find us and take us to better seats to watch the rest of the game. He got us tickets to the All-Star game when Reggie Jackson hit the light tower – I still have the tickets tucked away in a safe place and hope yet to get Reggie's autograph. We were sitting in left field upper deck, close to the overhang. That home run was a rocket! I have never seen a ball travel faster than that one, a line drive that never went down until it hit the light tower. It was great! Mickey Lolich pitched nothing but fastballs to save the game for an American league win. He was humming those fastballs for strikes until it was finally over."*

DDDDDDDDDDDDDDDDDDDDDDDDDDDDDDDDDDDDDDDDDDDDDDDDDDDDDDDDDDDDDDDDDDDDDDDDDDDDD

Nothing Martin did to *"light a fire under the club"*, as management sought to have happen, took – at least through July, whether flipping over a post-game buffet after a tough loss, heckling opposing players, benching fan favorite Willie Horton after questioning his hustle, or appealing to the team's pride during a clubhouse meeting: *"The world is full of quitters, people looking for a way out. Let's play so that we can be proud of the name 'Detroit' across our chests."*

After the All-Star game, Detroit went 8 & 10 the balance of July, but then the light switched on. The August charge was led by 5 wins from Mickey Lolich, the noticeable impact on team defense by the stellar play of Brinkman and Rodriguez, the continued carnage Norm Cash's bat inflicted on opposing pitchers, with 27 homers & 74 RBIs going into September, and Gates Brown stepping up when Horton's playing time was limited by injuries, ending August with a year-to-date batting average of .388 and an on base percentage of .455 while introducing himself to one and all with his, *"Hi, I am the Gator."* Baltimore however, continued their hot pace, and although Detroit moved up to 2nd place, as August concluded Detroit remained a distant 11.5 games back. Although the Tigers won 91 games on the year, playing nearly .700 ball in September, they did not catch the Orioles for the '71 East Division pennant, finishing 10 games out of first as the O's won their final 11 games of the year. The Tigers entertained their fans with a league leading 179 homers, but more importantly they built confidence for the following season by defeating Baltimore 5 consecutive times in September. 1972 would be a battle.

In addition to his 1971 All-Star team selection, Stormin' Norman won the American League Comeback Player of the Year Award (to go along with his '65 Comeback Award). Cash finished 2nd in league home runs with 32 and said, *"If I hadn't been in the Lindell A.C. every night, I coulda hit 64."* The prior year of 1970, Norm had hit 15 homers, although in a limited 370 at bats, after being the only A.L. player from 1961 to 1969 to hit a minimum of 20 homers each year. Complimenting his 32 homers in '71, *Comeback Cash* finished a league 8th in RBIs at 91, and 3rd in slugging percentage at .531 while batting .283.

Michael Stephen Lolich made a strong case of his own for the 1971 Comeback Player of the Year Award, but what he should have won was the 1971 Cy Young Award. In 1970, the Pride of Portland, Oregon, led the league with 19 defeats – although he was 2nd with 230 strikeouts. 1971 turned that completely around, starting with Billy Martin's year-opening announcement that Mickey would be his ace and start every 4 days no matter what. Lolich won 25 games against 14 losses, with a 2.92 ERA, started 45 games and hurled 376 innings, averaging an amazing 8.3 innings per start. Mick threw 29 complete games (or 29 more than Max Scherzer had when he won the Cy Young in 2013) - *the most complete games since Bob Feller in 1936*. The 376 innings are the 2nd most since the "live ball era" began in 1920 (only Wilbur Wood had more, by 2/3rds of one inning, in 1972). Mickey had been a great pitcher for years, as many American League batters and the 1968 St. Louis Cardinals would attest, but it wasn't until spring training of 1971 that a teacher's lesson finally sunk in, making Lolich an even more dominant pitcher: while warming up one day, his fastball had an unusual amount of movement to it and Mickey suddenly became aware that he had begun to unconsciously implement the *cut fastball* delivery Johnny Sain had been trying to teach him. For the '71 season, he was #1 in the American League in wins, strikeouts, innings pitched, games started, complete games, and batters faced (Mickey faced 1,538 batters, Vida Blue faced over 300 fewer) – yet finished 2nd in the Cy Young Award race to Vida Blue.

Kaline finished 1971 with a .294 average, 8th best in the league, and made the All-Star team for the 14th time in his career. Based on that kind of a season, when the Tigers sent him his contract for '72, offering

Al the opportunity to become the first Tiger to make $100,000 in a single year, Kaline now felt his play worthy of the milestone, and signed it. What a nice way to celebrate his 20th season in a Tiger uniform.

As the Tigers looked back on 1971 and the 1972 season approached, they could be thankful for many things. They believed that Billy Martin as manager was one of them, and they rewarded him with a new contract and a raise; the McLain trade in general and specifically that, while still a Senator, Joe Coleman had a falling out with manager Ted Williams, the reason why Washington was willing to include Joe in the trade. Joe had a breakout year in '71, among A.L. leaders with 20 wins, 236 Ks, innings pitched, and complete games - the perfect right-hand compliment to lefty Lolich, arguably the game's best 1-2 punch. And then there was a Christmas gift from an unlikely source, the Baltimore Orioles, who in December '71, traded All-Star/team leader/clutch hitter Frank Robinson to the Dodgers for 4 prospects including a young Doyle Alexander.

Billy Martin was hoping for another gift: an off-season trade that would bring an established veteran pitcher to add to the rotation. It didn't happen, not yet anyway. But there was hope that the arm woes of the immensely talented Les Cain were behind him, and that Les could make the Big 2 of Lolich and Coleman a Big 3. In '71, Les wasn't healthy until late-May, then had the Tigers and their fans salivating with a 7-game 5 & 1/1.10 ERA run, but soon re-injured the arm and struggled to the finish line at 10 & 9. When questioned by a reporter about options for the 4th 1972 starter, Lolich asked, *"Have we found the 3rd starter yet?"* If Detroit could figure a way to get the game to the bullpen, they would be in good shape. Fred Scherman was coming off of an 11-win/20-save year, all but 1 of his 69 appearances in relief, and steady Tom Timmerman was just one year removed from a 27-save season.

1972, however, was delayed. Ballplayers staged the first-ever major league strike at midnight on March 31, demanding more owners' funding of player pensions. The 2 sides reached a compromise settlement thus resuming the league schedule on April 15, with no make-up of any games prior to that date. The number of games lost prior to April 15 varied by team, as would the number of games that would constitute the '72 season – the most a team would play was 156, the fewest 154. Fans, players, and owners were all happy to get this behind them and *"play ball!"*

DDDDDDDDDDDDDDDDDDDDDDDDDDDDDDDDDDDDDDDDDDDDDDDDDDDDDDDDDDDDDDDDDDDDDDDDDDD

Detroit was determined to shake the trend that had existed since the 1969 season: falling behind the Baltimore Orioles at the start of the year, then spending the rest of the season playing catch-up ball. And in '72, they were able to do just that. After 4 weeks of play, fresh from defeating the KC Royals 3-1 May 13, Detroit fans enjoyed reading the next day's *Detroit Free Press* or *Detroit News*, seeing their Tigers tied for first with Cleveland, the O's in third, 2 games back, and then read under *American League batting leaders* the name of Norm Cash listed first, next to his .371 average – shades of 1961 – and Bill Freehan right behind Norm at .343, with Bill's 17 RBIs a league 2nd. *American League pitching leaders* led-off with Mickey Lolich at 6 & 1. On May 14, Joe Coleman improved to 5 & 0 when Dick McAuliffe's 8th inning 2-run shot lifted Detroit to a 3-2 win.

This same week, Denny McLain was sent to the minors. He went 10 & 22 in his single season of playing for the Washington Senators in 1971. Shortly after the franchise moved to Texas, becoming the Texas Rangers for the 1972 season, they traded Denny to Oakland (A's owner Charlie Finley always interested in sensationalism) for 2 pitchers, Jim Panther (5 & 9 in '72, retiring after '73) and rookie Don Stanhouse (an All-Star closer for Baltimore in the late-70s). Denny pitched in 5 games for Oakland, going 1 & 2 with a 6.04 ERA before his May demotion to the minors, then was traded from Oakland to Atlanta for '68 Series opponent Orlando Cepeda on June 29. McLain posted a 3 & 5/6.50 ERA record for the Braves, who would release McLain in March 1973, ending Denny's big-league career at age 28; the man he was traded for, 34-year old Orlando Cepeda, got little playing time at Atlanta or Oakland, and was thought to be at the end of his Hall of Fame career. Boston signed him as a free agent in March '73, and Cepeda had one fine season left in him, hitting .289 with 20 homers and 86 RBIs for the Red Sox.

DDDDDDDDDDDDDDDDDDDDDDDDDDDDDDDDDDDDDDDDDDDDDDDDDDDDDDDDDDDDDDDDDDDDDDDDDDDD

Tom Timmerman, now the Tigers 3rd starter, pitched well but with little run support when he took the mound. That changed as Detroit opened an unusual-in-length 5 game series at Yankee Stadium on '72 Memorial Day weekend, the Tigers taking the opener 8-2 while Timmerman improved to 3 & 4 with a 1.95 ERA. The next day, Joe Coleman outpitched Mel Stottlemyre, 2 to 1, to win his 7th game. Detroit's game 3 starter, Les Cain, walked the first batter of the game on 5 pitches, re-injured his shoulder and was replaced by Phil Meeler, whose major league career would consist of 7 games in 1972 for Detroit. Meeler tossed 2 innings before being replaced by rookie Chuck Seelbach, who threw 6 innings of 1 run ball in Detroit's 5-4 win. Seelbach got the win to improve to 2 & 1 with a 2.42 ERA, becoming a reliever Billy Martin felt he could count on. Although no one knew it at the time, today marked the end of Les Cain's once promising career, as he could no longer pitch over his arm and shoulder problems. After winning the first 3 games in the Bronx, the Tigers dropped the final two. The road trip moved on to Cleveland, game 1 the final day of May, Detroit winning 5-4 in 10. It was another Tom Timmerman fine outing, but the win went to Fred Scherman who threw 2 innings of 1-hit ball, his ERA now 2.12. Going into June, Detroit held a one-half game edge over 2nd place Baltimore and 2 games over the Indians.

Minnesota, jockeying for the lead of the West Division with Reggie Jackson's Athletics, came to The Corner for 3 in early June for a bit part in the Gates Brown Show. The Gater doubled home Mickey Stanley in the 10th inning to win game 1, 5-4, and in the 1st inning of game 2 hit a 2-run homer in the Tigers 5-3 win, Dick McAuliffe's 3-run blast accounting for the winning margin. Gates had been getting plenty of playing time while Horton was on the DL, providing an offensive force and batting .319 at day's end. In game 3, Tom Timmerman completed the sweep with a beautiful 3-0 shutout, improving to 4 & 4 with a 1.78 ERA, Stanley's two-run homer in the 7th breaking the scoreless tie.

After an off day, the Angels came to town for 3. The opening game was a slugfest, the Tigers winning 8-6 with the big hit from an unexpected source, defensive stalwart Eddie Brinkman's 3-run homer, as Lolich won his 9th. Although Detroit dropped the 2nd game of the twin bill, at day's end they led the East by 4 games over Cleveland & Baltimore, what would turn out to be the Tigers biggest lead of the '72 season.

Then, Baltimore caught fire, winning 9 games in a row to tie Detroit for first, a tie broken June 18 when the O's finally lost while Detroit was trying to finish off a 3-game sweep in Anaheim. That Sunday battle vs. the Angels was a classic duel between two of the best pitchers in major league history, Mickey Lolich & Nolan Ryan. The scoreboard showed nothing but goose eggs through 6 innings as the Tigers came to bat in the 7th. With one out, Jim Northrup turned on a Ryan fastball and deposited it into the right field seats. Norm Cash added an insurance run with a 9th inning drive into the stands in right, giving Detroit the margin of victory in the 2-0 game, win 11 for Mickey, the team back in first by one over the Orioles.

A nationwide TV audience saw Northrup rob Davey Johnson
of a game-tieing homer in the ninth on 6.30.72

One of the most amazing plays of the entire 1972 MLB season took place on the final play of the June 30 game between Detroit and host Baltimore. The Saturday game, televised nationally on NBC, featured a match-up between Lolich and the always tough Dave McNally. The two allowed no runs until Kaline hit a solo homer off McNally in the 6th. It stayed 1-0 Detroit until the top of the ninth when the Tigers tacked on a 2nd run against a young reliever who came to the Orioles in the Frank Robinson trade, Doyle Alexander. In the bottom of the 9th, with 1 out, Lolich walked Brooks Robinson. The next batter, Davey Johnson, hit a deep drive to left where Jim Northrup was playing. As soon as the ball was hit, it appeared to be gone, a 2-run, game-tying, home run. Northrup drifted back to the 365' sign at the wall, grabbed the screen above the wall with his right hand and pulled himself over the 9' tall fence to snag the ball with the very tip of his outstretched glove. Jim crashed to the ground, the ball still securely in his mitt, quickly got to his feet, and rifled the ball to relay man Eddie Brinkman, who fired a strike to double up the runner at first, ending the game.

From the Lolich-Ryan June 18 match-up to the July 25 All-Star game, Detroit went 20 & 15, holding a 1 game lead over Baltimore going into the Midsummer Classic break. The bats had gone cold over these 35 games: the 3 hitters providing so much of the early firepower, Freehan, Cash & Gates, now batting .256, .254 & .233, respectively. Only Tony Taylor, sharing time at 2nd with McAuliffe & playing some 3rd, was over .300 at mid-season, hitting .328. To make up for the power outage, the guys played *Billy Ball* –

hit & run, hard slides to break up double plays, sacrifice bunts, & suicide squeeze plays - manufacturing runs to eke out wins in low-scoring games.

The pitching staff also picked up the slack, not just the Big 2 of Lolich & Coleman, but Tom Timmerman continued to be an effective third, and the kids were coming through – Fred Scherman (3 & 1 with 9 saves/2.76) and Chuck Seelbach (6 & 4 with 7 saves/2.90). A third youngster, Bill Slayback, called up from Toledo June 26, had trouble with the directions to Tiger Stadium. Bill finally found the park near game time, where he was informed by Manager Martin that he'd be starting against the Yankees that night. While Detroit's offense built a 4-0 lead after 6 innings, Slayback couldn't figure out why his new teammates weren't speaking to him, unaware of the situation: he was throwing a no-hitter into the 8th, and the guys were respecting a time-honored tradition of silence when a pitcher was working on one.

Veteran Johnny Callison led off the Yanks' 8th with a sharp single to right when Kaline made a play Bill Slayback had never seen, charging in & rifling the ball to first in an attempt to get the batter. When back in the dugout, Bill complimented Al on his hustle play and Kaline said, *"Kid, you don't know what's going on, do you?"* Al had to inform Slayback that he had a no-hitter going, and explained the silent treatment he'd been getting. After Callison's single, Bill gave up a single to the next man up, Thurman Munson, but then quickly got out of trouble by getting a double play and a strikeout from the next two batters as 30,961 roared their approval. Bill came back out for the ninth, and after a walk, single, double, a ground out, and 2 runs in, left to a standing ovation in Detroit's 4-3 win. During the next month, Bill Slayback pitched even better: in a span of 9 July days, he won 3 complete games while only giving up 2 runs total, and then in the final game before the All-Star break, he pitched 4 innings of shutout relief. After only 4 weeks in the majors, Slayback's record was 4 & 3 with a 1.40 ERA.

John Frederick Hiller picked up his first save of 1972 on July 10. John suffered 3 heart attacks before the '71 season began, missing all of that year, and hadn't pitched since the final game of 1970, the last game under manager Mayo Smith, when Hiller tossed a complete game, 2-hit, 1-0 shutout against the Indians. Not until a year & 9 months later, in July of '72, were the Tigers ready to see what John could do. On July 7, Billy Martin set up a pre-game competition between Hiller and Les Cain. Whoever threw better would be kept on the team. The winner was Hiller, and he pitched his first game since 1970 the next night, on 7.8.72, throwing 3 innings of 4-hit, 2-run, relief. John appeared in 24 games between July 8 and season's end, going 1 & 2 with 3 saves and a sterling 2.03 ERA in 44 innings pitched.

Detroit's defense was outstanding. The acquisition of Brinkman & Rodriguez gave Detroit the best left-side defense in all of baseball. Aurelio's quick glove and the way he cocked his arm to (almost literally) rifle a throw to beat a hapless runner at first was eaten up by the Tiger faithful. Eddie, the number 1 defensive shortstop in the game in 1972, set the all-time record of 72 consecutive errorless games at short. Despite hitting only .203 for the season, he was runaway choice as "Tiger of the Year", the one indispensable player on the team. Overall, Detroit was tops in the league with a .985 fielding average, their 96 errors one short of tying the MLB record. In addition to Aurelio & Eddie, Bill Freehan, Al Kaline, Mickey Stanley, Jim Northrup, Norm Cash, Dick McAuliffe, and Tony Taylor were defensive stars, the recipients of a combined 21 Gold Gloves. Tiger fans couldn't get enough of this team, their blue-collar manager, and the excitement of being back in a pennant race. The July 17-19 series with the White Sox, the week before the All-Star game, pushed attendance over 1 million, the earliest that plateau had ever been reached in franchise history.

DDDDDDDDDDDDDDDDDDDDDDDDDDDDDDDDDDDDDDDDDDDDDDDDDDDDDDDDDDDDDDDDDDDDDDDDDDDDD

For the 1972 All-Star game, the fans voted in Bill Freehan as the starting catcher, and A.L. manager Earl Weaver added Norm Cash, Mickey Lolich, and Joe Coleman to the team. Freehan scored the game's first run, drawing a lead-off walk in the third off the Pirate's Steve Blass, was bunted to 2nd by Jim Palmer, and scored on Rod Carew's single. With his Tiger teammate Freehan still behind the plate, Lolich came in to pitch shutout ball in the 4th & 5th. In Norman's one plate appearance, Tug McGraw struck him out in the 9th, while Joe Coleman saw no action. The National League scored a run in the 9th to tie the game at 3 apiece, and won it in the 10th on a Joe Morgan RBI single.

When regular season play resumed, the Tigers picked up where they left off, sweeping a doubleheader in Milwaukee, a dramatic ninth-inning 3-run Norm Cash homer, his 19th, lifting Detroit from behind to a 3-2 win in game 1. In the nightcap, 20-year old Fred Holdsworth made his major league debut, 1 of only 2 1972 games he appeared in, leaving after 5 with Detroit down 5-4. John Hiller kept Milwaukee off the scoreboard in the 6th, followed to the mound by Chris Zachary who tossed a shutout 7th. When the Tigers rallied for 4 in the next frame, Zachary got the win, his last of 10 in a 9-year major league career. Zachary was effective for the Tigers in '72, his only season with Detroit, going 1 & 1 with a save and a 1.41 ERA in 38 innings. July ended with 1st-place Detroit 2 & ½ up on Baltimore, the Yanks 6 & Boston 7 behind. Detroit closing the month by taking 2 of 3 from the Red Sox loomed large when these two teams met in October to decide the East Division champion.

August started with two player acquisitions that had a huge impact on the Tigers 1972 fortunes. The first took place on the 2nd of the month, when 32-year old pitcher Woodie Fryman was picked up on waivers from the Philadelphia Phillies. The second acquisition took place on the 4th when Detroit made waiver move number 2, signing 31-year old reserve catcher/outfielder Duke Sims from the L.A. Dodgers.

Both Woodie Fryman & Duke Sims had their first big moment as Tigers on the Saturday, August 5, game at Cleveland's Municipal Stadium. Detroit had lost the first 4 games of August, and Tiger rookie pitcher Bill Slayback was in early trouble in this one. After retiring the first two Indians in the bottom of the first, Slayback issued a double, a walk, a 2-run double, then 2 more walks to load the bases, prompting Billy Martin to go to the bullpen much earlier than planned. Waiting longer wasn't an option as Detroit could not expect to score too many on 18-game winner Gaylord Perry - the rally had to be stopped now. Martin chose the newly-acquired Woodie Fryman to relieve. It turned out to be an excellent decision. Fryman struck out the first batter he faced, ending the 1st inning stranding 3 Indians on base, and kept the Tribe scoreless over the next 6 innings of 3-hit, 4-strikeout, relief. While Woodie pitched, Detroit got one run back when Duke Sims, making his Tiger debut, nicked Gaylord Perry for a 7th inning solo homer. Cleveland got that run back, restoring their 2-run margin, with a run off of Fred Scherman in the bottom of the 8th. Detroit was behind 3-1 and down to their last 3 outs when two all-time favorite Tigers came up big, as Gates Brown and Stormin' Norman Cash led off the ninth with solo homers, number 21 for Norm, silencing the stunned Cleveland crowd and tying the game at 3. It stayed that way 'til newcomer Duke Sims struck again, following an Aurelio Rodriguez 11th inning double with a run-scoring single that held up for an unlikely come-from-behind 4-3 Detroit victory.

Duke Sims was a .239 lifetime hitter, a reserve in each of his 9 seasons. Woodie Fryman was in his 7th big league year, an underrated .500 pitcher who was having a rough 4 & 10 season with the Phillies thus far in 1972. As unspectacular as the two seemed to most, the Tigers saw something in them that convinced the team to make the waiver acquisitions (although Detroit wasn't alone in their belief in Woodie: Larry Bowa once said that *"trying to hit Fryman was like eating soup with a fork"*). In their short time with Detroit in the '72 season, both players exceeded the expectations of even their strongest supporters: Sims hit .316 in 98 at bats, many of his hits clutch ones; Fryman was even better, going an outstanding 10 & 3 with a 2.06 ERA in the pennant race stretch drive.

Echoes of the '72 Woodie Fryman transaction took place (1) 15 years later when the 1987 Tigers traded for Doyle Alexander that August, and Doyle went 9 & 0 down the stretch, and (2) 39 years later in the end-of-July pick-up of Doug Fister, who went 8 & 1 in 2011's last 2 months. All 3 pitcher acquisitions were key to pushing their respective teams over the finish line to win division titles in '72, '87 & '11.

DDDDDDDDDDDDDDDDDDDDDDDDDDDDDDDDDDDDDDDDDDDDDDDDDDDDDDDDDDDDDDDDDDDDDDDDD

Despite the August 5 heroics of newcomers Sims & Fryman in helping break a 4-game losing skid, and notwithstanding a Fryman 6-0 shutout victory at Yankee Stadium on the 9th, his first start as a Tiger, the team began the month by losing 10 of 13 games to tumble 1 & ½ games behind the division-leading Orioles, with New York and Boston right on Detroit's heels. The situation seemed to require something out of the ordinary, so Billy Martin came up with an idea to change the team's luck: pulling the line-up out of a hat for game 1 of an August 13 twin bill vs. Cleveland! Billy asked Al Kaline to pick out the names one at a time, and when the first name was pulled, Norm Cash found himself in the unusual position of batting lead-off – Norm last hit lead-off in the 2nd 1961 All-Star game. After Kaline pulled the names of Northrup and Horton, the luck-of-the-draw placed Eddie Brinkman in the clean-up position for the only time in his .224 career. The silliness seemed to loosen the boys up, and wouldn't you know it, Eddie's 6th inning double off of Gaylord Perry knocked in the game-tying run. After Tony Taylor followed with a single to score Brinkman, Woodie Fryman set the last 9 Indians down in order, completing his 4-hitter and securing the Tiger's 3-2 win.

Number 6 was ready to do more than just cheerlead and pull names out of a hat. Kaline, injured since July 27, was taken off the DL on August 15. He promptly went on a hitting tear, increasing his batting average from .271 to .296 in leading Detroit on an 8 & 3 spurt that sent the team back into 1st, 1 & ½ games up on Baltimore, 3 & ½ ahead of New York and Boston, as of August 27. As the calendar flipped to September, the Tigers purchased the contract of Frank Howard from Texas. Howard was a giant of a man known as the Washington Monument, and well past his years of hitting 40 plus homers, but Detroit was hopeful that a change of scenery and the adrenaline rush of a pennant race would ignite some of that old magic. Frank joined the team in the midst of a 1 & 5 slump that, after the Sunday, September 3 games, left the East Division standings with Baltimore, New York, Detroit & Boston all within one-half game of first place. After Mickey Lolich outpitched Jim Palmer 4-3 on the 6th for his 20th victory, Detroit was back in sole possession of first place for the last time in the month, although they would share the top spot on 3 more September dates.

By September 12, Detroit had slipped to 4th place, two games behind 1st place Boston as Baltimore arrived at The Corner for the teams' final two '72 meetings. The Tigers hottest pitcher took the mound for game 1, and Woodie Fryman didn't let them down. The offensive punch came from light-hitting Eddie Brinkman, whose few hits counted big in '72. Eddie hit a 2-run homer in the third, to allow Detroit to overcome Paul Blair's 1st inning solo shot, then scored the Tigers third run in the 7th on McAuliffe's double. With the Tigers up 3-1 in the 9th, Fryman hit the first batter with a pitch, got the next man out, but gave up another walk and then a run-scoring single to make the score 3-2. The tiring Fryman was relieved by Chuck Seelbach, but Seelbach issued a walk to load the bases as the always-dangerous Boog Powell stepped up to the plate. Martin called on John Hiller to put the fire out. John was magnificent, whiffing Boog and ending the game by getting Blair on a ground out. Hiller had been spectacular since he rejoined the team on July 7 and saw his first action the very next day, his fastball, breaking pitches, & change-up better than ever. Post-game he told reporters, *"When I had the heart attack* (in spring '71), *the doctors told me that I could pitch again. They said it was all up to me. That's all I needed to know. Now I'm just trying to do a job."* Eddie Brinkman said of his big home run, *"Well, I sure wasn't trying to hit it out. I just did what I always do – put the bat on the ball and put it into play."* On this same September 12 day that John Hiller continued to resurrect his career, another '68 Tiger, Denny McLain, was making his final MLB appearance. Called on by yet another '68 teammate, Eddie Matthews, now manager of the Atlanta Braves, to pitch the 9th of a 3-3 game versus Cincy, Denny's first pitch landed '400 away, followed by 2 singles before being pulled. McLain's line for '72 was 4 & 7 with a 6.37 ERA.

Joe Coleman drew the September 13 assignment in the Orioles series finale. Joe's teammates gave him an early lead in the 1st when Big Frank Howard doubled in Bill Freehan. But Coleman was not his usual sharp self today, surrendering a solo homer the next half inning and a grand slam to Boog Powell in the third. Orioles 5 Tigers 1. Against the O's Dave McNally, Detroit rallied in the 5th. With two outs, Mac on with a single & Freehan with a walk, Frank Howard, the man known as Hondo and – from his days with the Washington Senators - the *Capital Punisher* & the *Washington Monument*, strode to the plate. Frank had that old hoodoo this evening, driving a McNally offering deep into the right-field lower deck for a 3-run homer, cutting the deficit to one. When McNally proceeded to allow a single to Horton and a walk to Stanley, Earl Weaver replaced him with Doyle Alexander. Aurelio Rodriguez messed up that strategy with a single to score Willie, and then Doyle issued a balk to send home the tie-breaking run before getting the final out. Tigers 6 Orioles 5. Fred Scherman came in for Coleman and pitched a perfect 6th, 7th, 8th, and 9th inning – 12 men up, 12 men down, to secure Detroit's 6-5 win while earning his 12th save. Martin told the press afterward, *"This game tonight makes getting Howard worthwhile. His influence among the other players has been tremendous even if he doesn't hit. He's a very unselfish guy."* The 2-game sweep of Baltimore pulled Detroit to within 1 of the current 1st place team, Boston.

DDDDDDDDDDDDDDDDDDDDDDDDDDDDDDDDDDDDDDDDDDDDDDDDDDDDDDDDDDDDDDDDDDDDDDDDDDDD

The '72 Tigers were looking more & more like the '68 squad in how often they could overcome a late-inning deficit. They traveled to Milwaukee for 3, winning the 1st in come-from-behind fashion, 2 to 1, on an 8th inning pinch hit RBI by Duke Sims and a 9th inning, 2-out, game winning single by Cash. The 2nd game against the Brewers was a 2-1 *Billy Ball* victory, the first run set up by a hit 'n run single, the second run coming home after Mickey Stanley stole 2nd and scored on Eddie Brinkman's hit. In the finale, Duke Sims put Detroit up 2-0 with a 2-run first inning single, and Dick McAuliffe had a huge day with a solo homer & a 3-run shot, powering the Tigers 6-2 win. Detroit left Milwaukee tied for first with Boston, Baltimore 1 & ½ out, New York 2 & ½ out.

On to Cleveland for 3, Detroit dropped the first 2, but rallied to win game 3, 4-1, behind Woodie Fryman's complete game, the Tigers breaking a 1-1 tie in the 9th on Duke Sims double to knock in the Gater, and – after Eddie Brinkman was intentionally walked - Fryman himself finishing the scoring with an insurance 2-run single before extinguishing the Tribe in the bottom of the 9th. Detroit departed Cleveland for a 4-game series in Fenway, arriving with Boston in 1st, Detroit 1 back, Baltimore 2 & ½ back, and New York starting to drop out of the race, 3 & ½ games back.

As large as the games at Boston seemed, after splitting the 4, the September 24 standings looked almost identical to when the series began, except the Yankees were 1/2 game closer to 1st. Detroit was coming home for their final 8 games, the Yankees in for 2, Milwaukee in for 3, and then 1972 would conclude with 3 versus Boston. The game 1 pitching match-up against New York featured Joe Coleman vs. Steve Kline. The Yankees exploded for 3 first inning runs, then knocked Joe out when he put 2 runners on base in the 2nd. Fred Scherman escaped the jam, but gave up 2 runs in the top of the third, Detroit getting one back in their half of the inning. The score would stay Yankees 5 Tigers 1 until the 8th when that late-inning mojo from '68 returned: Al Kaline singled in Willie Horton, Frank Howard came through with a big pinch-hit RBI single, and Mickey Stanley hit a sac fly. Yankees 5 Tigers 4 going into the ninth and the crowd emotions changed from nervous to expectant. After Chuck Seelbach kept New York scoreless, the Tigers came up to bat, down to their final 3 outs, and facing the year's sensation, reliever Sparky Lyle. Eddie Brinkman came through as he had all year, this time leading off with a single. Willie followed with a seeing-eye hit through the hole to left. Tony Taylor was called upon to pinch hit for Mac, and laid down a gorgeous bunt single to load the bases and drive the standing, shouting, foot-stomping fans crazy, as up stepped the legend, Number 6. Al hit a fly ball deep enough to straight-away center to score Eddie with the 5-5 run. It was Sparky Lyle versus Duke Sims with the game on the line, and Duke lined a bullet into center that scored pinch runner Marvin Lane with the game-winning run, as Tiger Stadium exploded in celebration. *Don't close that beer window just yet!*

Lyle got his revenge the next day, pitching the final 3 innings of a 12 inning, 3-2 Yankee victory. Lolich went the distance, but made one big mistake – surrendering a 9th inning homer to a pitcher who was in his 18th season and who in all of those years only hit 2 previous home runs, Lindy McDaniel – a mistake that kept Detroit from winning in 9. It was a costly defeat for the Tigers, keeping them 1 & ½ back of Boston and 2 out in the loss column, while the win kept the 3rd place Yankees faint hopes alive as they sat 3 & ½ out, with Baltimore 4 behind. Now Milwaukee was in for 3 at The Corner, the final series before Boston hit town. So long as Detroit swept the Brewers, even if Boston swept the 3 they were playing in Baltimore, the worst that the Tigers would be going into the Boston series was 1 & ½ back, and that meant Detroit controlled their own fate: the Tigers would be crowned East Division champs by taking all 3 from the Red Sox.

Detroit's bats were on fire against Milwaukee. Game 1 was a 12-5 Tiger clobbering led by Jim Northrup's 4 hits and 5 RBIs; game 2 opened with a 6-run Detroit first propelled by an Eddie Brinkman 3-run homer and closed with a 5-run 8th powered by Kaline & Duke Sims homers, as Joe Coleman breezed to win number 19; game 3 had special meaning for long-time Tiger fans, as John Hiller got a spot start and tossed a complete game 5-1 gem on October 1, 1972 for his first win since October 1, 1970. Billy Martin would hold John up as an example to his other pitchers, referencing his Lazarus-like comeback from three '71 pre-season heart attacks, *"Hiller's back from the dead and can throw strikes – why can't you."*

As Detroit defeated the Brewers in each of their first two games, Boston was also beating the Orioles. Baltimore and New York were now eliminated from the race as the Tigers remained 1 & ½ games back. But shortly after John Hiller dusted off the Brew Crew in the October 1 finale with Milwaukee, Detroit received the good news from Baltimore: a game-ending double play killed Boston's ninth inning rally as the Red Sox fell 2-1. This meant that Detroit no longer needed to sweep Boston to win the East as the difference in the standings between the two combatants had been reduced to one-half of one game. For all intents and purposes, the teams were tied for first and a simple 2 out of 3 would decide the division champion. The regular season-ending, 3-game series, between two franchises that had been in the American League since its founding in 1901, would open the next day at The Corner.

Monday October 2: Before dawn had broken, long lines formed down Trumbull & Michigan Avenues, full of fans waiting for the box office to open, hoping that seats would be left for today, tomorrow, or Wednesday's game by the time they made it to the ticket window. The pitching match-up for this evening's game 1 was Mickey Lolich against John Curtis. The Red Sox lefty was basically a rookie, having appeared in only 6 games in '70 & '71 combined, though he performed well this year. Coming into this battle, Lolich was 21 & 14, the kid 11 & 7.

37-year old Al Kaline, in his 20th season as a Tiger, brought the 51,518 to their feet early, launching a first-inning solo home run into the left field seats. Detroit 1 Boston 0. Number 6 was in an amazing hot streak, raising his average from .271 on August 15, when he came off the disabled list, to .304 going into this game. Today's home run was Kaline's third in 3 days. In Boston's 3rd, they threatened. After Mickey struck out his counterpart Curtis to open the frame, Sox lead-off man Tommy Harper hit a line single to left. Shortstop & old pro Luis Aparicio, in his 17th season and on his 10th All-Star team this year, ground a single through the hole as Harper raced around to third. One out, men at the corners, and stepping up to the plate the great Yaz, Carl Yastrzemski, future Hall of Famer, 3-time batting champion, past Triple Crown winner, and on a tear since the beginning of September, hitting 8 home runs & driving in 24 runs. Yaz lit into a Lolich offering, sending a rocket over Mickey Stanley's head in center, as Harper crossed home with the tying run and, just a few seconds behind, Aparicio was rounding third, ready to score the lead run BUT here's where the game and the series took a turn. Luis tripped on the 3rd base bag, fell to the ground, popped up, saw the throw coming into home, realized that it was now too late to score, and scampered back to third. This turned out to be a problem as Yaz was cruising into the very same base, on what should've been an easy stand-up triple. Catcher Duke Sims fired the ball to Aurelio Rodriguez at third who applied the tag to Yaz for the 2nd out since the rule book says, *"Two runners are not allowed to occupy the same base. If two runners are touching the same base, the lead runner* (Aparicio, in this case) *is entitled to the base."* Instead of one out, two runs in, and a man on third, Boston had two outs, one run in, man on third. When Mickey took down the next hitter, Reggie Smith, on a called strike 3, the inning was over with a 1-1 tie instead of Boston leading at least by 2-1 and maybe by more.

From here on out, it was the Aurelio, Al, & Mickey Show. Rodriguez broke the tie with a solo homer in the fifth, then in the sixth, after Kaline's 2nd hit of the game, he singled in Al for a 3-1 lead, and finally in the bottom of the 8th, after Kaline's 3rd hit of the game (though forced at 2nd on a fielder's choice), Aurelio singled in Duke Sims to give Detroit a 4-1 lead going into the ninth. The crowd was on its feet this inning, cheering & shouting every pitch as Lolich picked up strikeout #15 in dispatching the Red Sox in their last at bat, chalking up his 22nd win and placing Detroit one victory away from the division title.

Tuesday, October 3: Since yesterday's final out, an excited anticipation gripped the city & the state. As the 8PM first pitch approached for game 2, 50,653 boisterous fans passed through the Tiger Stadium turnstiles to cheer their heroes on, and radios throughout the Lower & Upper Peninsulas and a good chunk of the Midwest were tuned to 760AM to hear Ernie Harwell and Ray Lane paint a picture for them of the action taking place at The Corner.

El Tiante, the amazing Luis Tiant, the pitching ace of the Red Sox, was the Tigers challenge today. As a Cleveland Indian in 1968, Luis was 21 & 9 and topped the A.L. with a 1.60 ERA. Multiple injuries and two trades later, he was back to his old form by this July. Luis was as dramatic as he was effective. Going into his wind-up... slowly raising his arms above his head, pivoting on his right foot as he turned his back to the plate, then spinning towards the batter, he released his pitches from a variety of delivery points.

Tiant would have a big victory cigar clenched between his teeth after a win, a frequent occurrence since an 11 & 1 run from the start of August – including 6 shutouts among 8 starts - on his way to a 15 & 6 record and a league-best 1.91 ERA. Lined up against El Tiante was a man who had been almost every bit as effective since becoming a Tiger on August 2, Woodie Fryman. Without Fryman's 9 & 3 record since that time, today's game would be much less meaningful.

The first batter of the game, Boston's Tommy Harper, singled then stole 2nd and held there as Luis Aparicio grounded out to Aurelio at third. Woodie pitched around Yaz, issuing a walk, and seemed to be out of the inning when Reggie Smith hit a tailor-made double play ball to Brinkman. Eddie flipped the ball to Mac at 2nd, but McAuliffe dropped the throw as Harper scored and the runners at 1st & 2nd were safe. Instead of Detroit coming to bat in a scoreless game, Boston had a run in, two on, and only one out. But Fryman bore down, got Rico Petrocelli on a called third, and Kaline saved the day with a diving grab on a sinking bloop hit to right by Rookie of the Year Carlton Fisk. 1-0 Boston.

Tiant & Fryman dueled away, putting goose eggs on the scoreboard into the sixth. In Detroit's half of the frame, Stormin' Norman led off with a walk before Willie Horton laid a beautiful sacrifice bunt down the 3rd base line to advance Norm to 2nd. Jimmy Northrup hit a bullet between center & right field to send Cash across home with the tying run. After the 7th inning stretch, with one out, McAuliffe atoned for his first inning error with a liner to the fence in right-center for a stand-up double. The crowd was now standing and cheering as one 'cause the man they know as Mister Tiger or simply Six was stepping up to hit. One of the finest clutch hitters in major league history, the hottest hitter in the ballpark, with one hit already today, believed – like most everyone else – he'd receive an intentional pass with first base open. But Sox manager Andy Kasko decided to pitch to him. Bad move Andy. Kaline rifled a single to left, Mac easily beating the throw to home by rookie Dwight Evans. As the lead run scored and Al cruised into 2nd on the throw home, Tiger Stadium became synonymous for deafening. 2-1 Detroit.

Tiant was pulled and replaced by Bill Lee (who'd later be better known as Bill "Spaceman" Lee, famous for quotes like, *"I said I believed in mandatory drug testing a long time ago. All through the Sixties I tested everything."*). The first batter Spaceman faced was Duke Sims, who squibbed an infield single that moved Kaline to 3rd and brought Norm Cash to bat with still only one out. Norman hit a chopper to Carl Yastrzemski at first and, as Kaline streaked for home, Yaz grabbed the ball from his mitt to throw home, but it slipped from his hand to the ground as Al scored the run that made it 3-1 Detroit. With Boston down to their last 6 outs, Yaz led off the 8th with a single and advanced to 2nd on a wild pitch. Fryman got Reggie Smith on a flyout to Kaline, but then Rico Petrocelli hit a much longer fly ball to right that had 50,000 fans holding their collective breathes, as Kaline drifted back, back, back until he caught the drive while leaning against the right-field wall. Billy Martin had seen enough, and replaced Woodie with Chuck Seelbach, Fryman leaving the game to an extremely vocal standing ovation. A tough out was at the plate, Carlton Fisk, and he hit a screamer down the third base line, but a diving Rodriguez snagged the missile to extinguish Boston's rally. 3 outs to go.

Detroit went down 1-2-3 in their 8th, but that did nothing to dampen the roar building in the ballpark. Seelbach went back out for the ninth, and slipped a third strike past Dwight Evans. A future star in only his 26th major league game, Cecil Cooper, pinch hit, and he took a called third as Ernie told us, *"home plate umpire Nestor Chylak said so."* With one out to go, the third rookie to bat this inning, and a man that these same fans would someday be cheering for as a Tiger, Ben Oglivie, was up. Ben hit the 2nd pitch to shallow right as Kaline raced in to make the catch. The Tigers are the 1972 East Division champs!

The Amazing Al Kaline had gone 22 for his last 44, and today he made what were quite possibly the 3 biggest defensive plays of the game. Manager Martin was gushing to reporters about Al, *"He sure doesn't look like an old man, does he?"* Although the game was not televised, every Detroit station was live in the Tiger clubhouse to broadcast the team's post-game celebration to Metro Detroiters. Big Frank Howard led cheers that almost the entire team participated in, spelling out as they chanted back *"T-I-G-E-R-S!"* WXYZ newsman Dave Diles interviewed Eddie Brinkman in one of the most celebrated and talked about interviews in Detroit sports history, *"Eddie, I don't know of an acquisition the Tigers have made in recent years that has been more important than the acquisition of Eddie Brinkman. That has to give you a good feeling, knowing that you have contributed so very much to this club."* Brinkman told Dave, *"Well, I'll tell you, it's a fantastic feeling, not so much for myself, but for the rest of the fuckin' guys. Just one of those years, we had to struggle the whole fuckin' time, and we're just fortunate we won the thing."* *"Ok, Eddie Brinkman, thank you very much."* Diles sent it back at the WXYZ studios, where anchorman Bill Bonds told listeners, *"People often ask me if Channel 7 is film or live. Well, it's live."*

Big Frank Howard leads the '72 East Division Champions in a "T-I-G-E-R-S!!!" chant, the pure joy on their faces a delight to behold (foreground L to R – Fryman, Kaline, Hiller, Mac, Ike, Gater, Willie)

On the Eastern Michigan University campus in Ypsilanti, as the clock passed 11PM on 10.3.72, the author and his roommate, East Detroit's Chuck Porta, were pacing their Phelps Hall dorm room floor. The radio had been switched at 8PM from WRIF *"the Home of Rock & Roll! BABY!"* to WJR *"the Great Voice of the Great Lakes",* Ernie Harwell & Ray Lane bringing us the action from Tiger Stadium. 3 hours later, as the final out settled into Al Kaline's glove, these two freshmen jumped for joy, bolted out the door, running down the hall to join the bedlam that was spreading through campus. Word was out that celebrating students were gathering to whoop it up at the McKenny Hall student union. Let's Go!

It is a short 10-minute walk across the EMU campus from the Phelps dorm to McKenny Hall, and we arrived there to a student throng numbering well into the hundreds that was growing each second. After a session of chanting over & over, *"Ti-gers! Ti-gers! Ti-gers!"*, and joyous commotion, a senseless consensus had developed that we should walk to Ann Arbor. Everyone was so giddy, why not. So, the happy, loud mob was soon on Washtenaw Avenue heading west for reasons not needed. When folks fall into an age range of 17 to 22, they feel invulnerable even when straddling the only two westbound lanes in a 45 miles per hour highway. After perilously sharing several blocks with traffic, our vanguard reached Richardson's Pharmacy when the police appeared out of nowhere, fortunately in a mood as exuberant as ours. They returned our shouts of, *"Go Tigers!"*, and we told them of our intended celebratory walk to Ann Arbor. Rather than suggesting to us that we turn back, they pointed out that we'd be safer if we kept to the slow lane, providing us with a passing lane multiple police car escort, flashers on, waving the midnight traffic around us, and joined our westward crusade.

The herd, while as lighthearted as ever, was gradually thinning, many circling back to continue the party on campus at Hungry Charlie's pub. By the time those soldiering on had reached the Kmart at Golfside Road, a bit over 2 miles from the EMU McKenny Hall starting point, the horde had shrunk in half. The most wonderful encounter that most of us will ever have with those who serve & protect had come to an end as our escort vanished into the night, perhaps heeding the siren song of (mm-mm!) Dom Donuts.

Singing hosannas to Al Kaline as we passed the Emerald City Chinese Restaurant, mysteriously outlined by the bright moonlight, soon there was but a dozen of us continuing the westward trek. A few minutes later, only Chucky & I remained. *"We have to do this! On to US23 for our Tigers!"* And, finally, just shy of 2AM, we stood on Washtenaw Avenue beneath US23, the eastern boundary of Ann Arbor, cheering for our Boys of Summer. Ubers & Lyfts only in the distant future, we retraced the 3 mile walk back to EMU, in our dorm and to bed by 4AM, ready to sink into a deep sleep, thankful for our comeback Tigers and this incredibly wonderful college experience – but questioning the wisdom of attending 8AM class.

DDDDDDDDDDDDDDDDDDDDDDDDDDDDDDDDDDDDDDDDDDDDDDDDDDDDDDDDDDDDDDDDDDDDDDDDDDD

October 4 brought one last game to the 1972 Tiger schedule. In a meaningless contest played primarily with back-ups, Boston defeated Detroit 4 to 1. Kaline did not play, ending the regular season with a .313 batting average, 2nd highest in the American League. Lolich was 3rd in Cy Young voting, behind Gaylord Perry and Wilbur Wood, after coming in 2nd the previous year. The final East Division standings read 1st place Detroit 86 & 70, 2nd place Boston 85 & 70.

The 1968 Tigers were MLB's last team to win the World Series before each league was split into two divisions in 1969, necessitating a playoff to determine both an American League & a National League combatant for the Series. On October 6 of this 1972 season, the Tigers boarded a flight to California to begin the American League Championship Series, a best 3 of 5, against the champions of the West Division, the Oakland Athletics, for the right to represent the A.L. in the World Series.

Oakland, considered the finest team in the league, had speed, power, & an outstanding starting pitching staff led by Catfish Hunter and ace relief pitcher Rollie Fingers. Their excellent hitting corps started with one of the greats, Reggie Jackson, and included Joe Rudi, Gene Tenace, Sal Bando, and speedy lead-off man, Bert "Campy" Campaneris. The interest level in this series rose from both the irritating one-sided nature of their meetings this season, 8-4 favor Oakland, and the bad blood between the teams, the result of an August 22 bench-clearing brawl at The Corner. Unusual for a baseball skirmish, several punches were not only thrown but landed, the unfortunate Mike Epstein being the Oakland A nearest Gold Gloves champ Willie Horton. When the A's retreated to their dugout, some nearby Tiger fans tossed beers on the opposing players. Billy Martin continued the theme a bit longer at the next day's game, when he brought a line-up card to home plate that included the names of Joe Louis, Rocky Marciano, and Sugar Ray Robinson.

Game 1 Oakland: 22-game winner Mickey Lolich versus 21-game winner Catfish Hunter opened the ALCS. The Tigers grabbed the early lead when Stormin' Norman Cash sent a 2nd inning offering from Catfish on a long journey over the right field wall. 1-0 Detroit. Oakland tied things up in the third on a Joe Rudi sac fly, but for the next several innings Hunter & Lolich were overpowering, and the game stayed at 1-1 into the ninth. Duke Sims, who had hit .316 since joining the Tigers in August, opened the frame with a double into the right-center gap. With Cash due up next, the man who had already tagged Catfish for a homer today, A's manager Dick Williams replaced Hunter with Vida Blue to get a lefty-lefty match-up. For this short series, both managers went to a 3-man starting rotation. Blue, after holding out for the first month of the season in a salary dispute, had not been able to regain his Cy Young Award-winning form of '71 upon his return, and was 4th in the rotation behind Catfish, Blue Moon Odom, and Ken Holtzman. As the 4th man in a 3-man starting staff series, he was the first lefty out of the bullpen. Despite Norm's power, Billy Martin decided to have Cash try to bunt the lead-run to 3rd, and he laid a beauty down the third base line, Sims easily cruising into third, and Norm himself safe when the throw to first was mishandled. Tigers were at 1st & 3rd with nobody out, and Willie Horton due up.

Dick Williams did not want left-handed Vida Blue to face Horton, so right-handed relief ace Rollie Fingers took the mound. Once Fingers was officially announced in the game, Billy Martin had lefty Gates Brown pinch hit for Willie. To paraphrase Gates himself, imagine sending somebody up to pinch hit for Willie. The Gater could not get the lead run in, fouling out to third. After Northrup failed in his attempt to send Sims home on a suicide squeeze, Jimmy hit into a threat-ending double play. Mickey pitched a perfect 9th and 10th, and Fingers tossed a perfect 10th before facing Detroit in inning number 11. After striking out McAuliffe, the ageless Al Kaline drilled a Rollie pitch deep into the left field stands to excite the Tigers dugout and put his team up 2-1. When Duke Sims followed with a triple, it looked like Detroit was poised to put the game away, but Fingers bore down and got Cash & Stanley on ground ball outs to send the game into the bottom of 11. After the tiring Lolich gave up back-to-back singles to the first two men he faced, Chuck Seelbach came in to pitch.

Gene Tenace laid down a bunt towards third to move the runners over, but Aurelio Rodriguez was on it in a flash, firing the ball to Brinkman covering third to force the lead runner. Eddie's relay to first just missed the double play. A's on 1st & 2nd, one out. 32-year old rookie Gonzalo Marquez was sent up to pinch hit in this critical situation. After knocking around in the minors & the Mexican League for years, Gonzalo finally made it to The Show late this season. He appeared in 23 games for the A's, 21 as a pinch hitter, and was a very effective 8 for 21 in that role, hitting .381. Now, in the biggest at bat of his life, Gonzalo Marquez lined Seelbach's 1-2 pitch for a single to right. Mike Hegan, the runner at 2nd, scored easily to tie the game. Gene Tenace raced around 2nd heading for 3rd as the charging Kaline came up with the ball and rifled a one-bounce strike to Rodriguez, but the sliding Tenace arrived at the same time as the throw, the ball glancing off of Gene and past Aurelio. By the time it was retrieved, Tenace had crossed home with the winning run, the dejected Tigers walking past the celebrating Athletics.

Even before this game, it was clear that Jim Northrup and Billy Martin had no use for each other. Northrup felt Martin took all the joy out of the game, saying, *"We got sick & tired of reading Martin say in the papers, 'I manage good, and they play bad.' 'I'd like to bunt, but my players can't do it.' 'I'd like to hit & run, but my players can't do it.' It was all, "Me, me, me."* As reporters surrounded Billy post-game, he told 'em, *"We should have never played extra innings. We should have won it in 9 innings. The suicide squeeze beat us."* It was Northrup who missed a suicide squeeze in the 9th that Billy was referring to.

Worse news was headed Detroit's way before play resumed.

Game 2 Oakland: Eddie Brinkman had a pinched nerve in his back, incurred on a play late in game 1. Today, he could not feel his left foot. The Tiger of the Year was out for the balance of the series. McAuliffe moved to short and Tony Taylor to 2nd. Taking the mound for the two teams was Woodie Fryman and Blue Moon Odom. The bad continued. In Oakland's first, Campy Campaneris singled, stole 2nd, stole 3rd, and scored on a Joe Rudi single. The score stayed 1-0 A's going into the fifth. It was then that Woodie surrendered singles to 3 of the first 4 batters he faced, one run was in, and Fryman was pulled for reliever Chris Zachary. Although Chris only pitched to one batter, Rudi, he made quite a mess, throwing back-to-back wild pitches, allowing one more run to score and putting a runner on third, before walking Rudi and being pulled for Fred Scherman. Reggie Jackson's double plated two more A's before Scherman got the final two outs. Oakland 5 Detroit 0.

Tiger Lerrin LaGrow relieved, facing the A's in the sixth. Outside of 10 games in 1970, LaGrow's time in the Detroit organization had been in the minors from '69 until late this year. His fine '72 season with the Toledo Mud Hens earned the 6'5", 200 lb., Lerrin a call-up, and in 16 games as a Tiger, he picked up 2 saves while posting a 1.32 ERA. LaGrow dispatched the A's in order in the 6th and then came back out for the 7th to face lead-off man Campaneris. Lerrin's first pitch was *"hard stuff down, the way I always pitch him"* LaGrow told the press later. The hard stuff down was a fastball that Campy tried to jump out of the way of, but it drilled him in the left ankle. After he hit the ground, Campy rose up, still holding the bat, reached back with his right arm and flung the bat at LaGrow's head, Lerrin ducking just low enough to avoid being hit.

Home plate umpire Nestor Chylak put Campaneris in a bear hug just in case Campy had any thoughts of charging the mound. Nestor's hug quickly changed to protective as Billy Martin charged from the dugout towards Campy with murder in his eyes. The other 3 umpires restrained Billy long enough to calm his desire to maim, and then tossed both LaGrow & Campaneris from the game *"to keep order in the ball park"* according to ump Chylak. John Hiller came in, pitched to 5 guys and got 6 outs, hard to do much better than that, inducing the first batter he faced to hit into a double play – thus erasing Campy's pinch runner - in tossing 2 perfect innings, but the 5-0 score he inherited would be the final score as Blue Moon Odom was brilliant all day on the hill, holding Detroit to singles by Northrup, Cash & Kaline.

The next morning's *Detroit Free Press* featured an article on the incident by Joe Falls. Billy Martin gave his view on Campy's actions, *"I don't know what that idiot was thinking. He may have to talk to his psychiatrist to find out. You can bet your ass I was going out there for him. I'm not going to get after him now, but if there's ever another fight out there, I'm going out there and find him and beat the shit out of him."* (Ironically, when Billy was managing the Yankees in '83, he brought the 41-year old Campy out of his 1-year retirement from the majors to cover for the injured Willie Randolph; Campy hit .322 in 60 games – and Billy did not beat the shit out of him).

The explanation given from Campaneris sounded like someone trying to dodge a suspension, *"I did not try to hit him with the bat. If I wanted to hit him, I would throw it more sidearm than overhand. I just wanted to warn him not to do that again to me."* Nice try, but before game 3, League President Joe Cronin fined Campaneris $500, suspending him for the remainder of the ALCS and the first seven games of the 1973 regular season. When Campy did play again, he needed a new bat: Ike Brown took his anger at Campaneris out on Campy's bat, reducing it to kindling before throwing it towards the A's dugout.

Game 3 Detroit: Joe Coleman took the mound today, the Tigers needing his "A" game to avoid elimination. They got it, although the game's start sent an uneasy feeling throughout Tiger Stadium. Oakland right fielder Matty Alou, normally the line-up number 2, moved up to lead-off replacing Campaneris, and lined a double into the right field corner, <u>barely</u> beating Kaline's throw into 2nd. Dal Maxvill, the old St. Louis Cardinal picked up late season by the A's, today playing Campy's shortstop position and batting 2nd, drew a walk. 2 on and nobody out before the fans were barely in their seats. But then Joe Coleman cranked it up a notch, and struck out Joe Rudi, Reggie Jackson (although the A's pulled a strike 3 double steal, to put runners at 2nd & 3rd), and Mike Epstein to squash the threat.

With one out in the Detroit 4th, Kaline walked and was doubled to third by Freehan. This was Bill's first start since breaking his thumb while tagging Yaz out at home plate on September 21, and his return was a huge lift for the Tigers. After Freehan's double, Horton followed with a walk to load the bases with one out. When A's pitcher Ken Holtzman got Stanley out on a short fly to center, too shallow to score Kaline, it seemed like the Tigers were going to miss their chance, but Ike Brown, the man who destroyed Campy's bat in game 2, came through with a clutch single right up the middle to knock in Mister Tiger and Bill Freehan. As Ike said afterwards, *"It was the biggest hit of my career,"* and one the team needed so badly. 2-0 Detroit. Michigan's day became even brighter when Freehan's 8th inning rocket hit the facing of the upper deck in left, building Detroit's lead to 3-0.

Joe Coleman never pitched better, making the hitters look foolish as they flailed away at his darting forkballs and fastballs. Joe piled up the strikeouts, including fanning the side in the first and the fifth. With the crowd on their feet, Coleman ended the shutout with strikeouts 13 & 14. Oakland's Mike Epstein paid tribute to Joe's masterpiece, *"The way he pitched today, he could have beaten any one of the last 15 All-Star teams."*

Game 4 Detroit: The Tigers and their fans were excited, feeling that the series was turning their way. The two staff aces, Lolich versus Hunter, dueled once again as in game 1. Leading off the Tigers third, Dick McAuliffe broke the scoreless tie with a home run that hit the facing of the upper deck in right. Mickey put down 13 batters in a row, from the 3rd into the 7th inning, where the score remained 1-0 Detroit. In the top of the 7th, with one Oakland Athletic out, Mike Epstein turned on a Lolich pitch and slammed it against the facing of the right field upper deck, knotting the score at 1. The Tigers missed an opportunity to take the lead in the 8th when Mac led off with a double, took third on Mickey Stanley's infield single, but was out at home when Bill Freehan could not execute the suicide squeeze Martin called for. The game went into extra innings, the two starters both relieved. Chuck Seelbach struggled on the mound for Detroit in the top of the 10th, coughing up 2 runs on a single, double, single after getting the first out before John Hiller came in to stop the rally.

Detroit had their backs to the wall, only 3 outs left to them, needing two runs to tie and 3 to win. The A's bullpen excelled, and a good one was on the hill, Bob Locker, 6 & 1 with 10 saves and a fine 2.65 ERA. A nervous buzz ran through the stadium as Dick McAuliffe came to bat. When Mac lined Locker's very first pitch for a single to right, the crowd shouted as one, rising to their feet to give a standing ovation for the man striding up to the plate, Albert William Kaline. Al sent a frozen rope to left, making it impossible to hear the person next to you above the roar. A's manager Dick Williams replaced Locker with veteran Joe Horlen to face Stanley, and Martin brought in the Gater to bat for Mickey. A wild pitch moved Mac and Al into scoring position before ball four was issued to Gates. Bags jammed and nobody out. Freehan hit a hard grounder that 3rd baseman Sal Bando fired to 2nd in hopes of trading one run for a double play – except that Gene Tenace dropped the throw. One run in, all runners safe, no one out. Deafening. With two lefties due up in Cash & Northrup, Williams brought in rookie left-hander Dave Hamilton. Norm faced a 2-2 count before fouling off 3 consecutive pitches, and then drew balls 3 and 4 to force in Kaline with the run that tied the game. Bedlam. When Jimmy Northrup drove a pitch over the head of the drawn-in outfield, the Tigers had completed a seemingly impossible 4-3 comeback reminiscent of 1968. The fans went crazy, celebrating on the field as if Detroit had won the series, not a must-have game.

The writers crowded around Stormin' Norman who said, *"I knew we had 'em all the way... like hell I did! I thought it was all over for us."* Al Kaline just kept smiling and shaking his head, *"I can't remember anything that's ever been this exciting!"* As the two 37-year old veterans spoke, an army of cots and sleeping bags began to form a line starting at the ticket window, belonging to fans hopeful to snag a seat for tomorrow's deciding contest.

Game 5 Detroit: Woodie Fryman took the mound before 50,276 electrified Tiger faithful, and he looked like a man in command, putting down the A's 1-2-3 in the first. The already amped fans stomped their feet even more when McAuliffe led off the Tigers first with a base hit to right and, after Blue Moon Odom whiffed Kaline, Duke Sims drew a walk. With Freehan at the plate, one of Odom's pitches got by Gene Tenace for a passed ball, and suddenly there were two Tigers in scoring position. Bill hit a hard grounder to shortstop Maxvill, who had no chance to get Mac breaking for home, so he settled for throwing out Freehan at first. Stormin' Norman hit a rocket to rightfield that had those in attendance rising to their feet as one, only to have it snagged on the run by Matty Alou. Detroit 1 Oakland 0.

In the Athletics 2nd, Fryman walked lead-off man Reggie Jackson. Reggie promptly stole second base and then advanced to third as Sal Bando hit a sacrifice fly. Woodie hit Mike Epstein with a pitch, putting runners at the corners with one away, and then bore down to get a big strikeout of Tenace. With light-hitting infielder Dick Green at bat, Epstein broke for 2nd base. Freehan took a quick glance at Jackson on third, and fired to second. He likely wishes he hadn't. Reggie broke for home as Tony Taylor jumped in front of the bag at 2nd to cut off Bill's throw and fired a strike home to Freehan, but too late to nab Jackson as he slid in safe while colliding with Bill as the ball squirted loose. The impact of the two large men slamming into each other took Reggie out of the game with a torn hamstring muscle. Despite his loss to Oakland, without benefit of a hit, the A's had manufactured the tying run.

The deciding moment of the game took place in the top of the fourth. Reggie was due up, but in place of the injured Jackson, George Hendrick stepped in, a 2nd year player with the A's who would go on to be a 4-time All-Star, twice with Cleveland in the 70s & twice with St. Louis in the 80s. Woodie delivered and Hendrick hit a grounder to McAuliffe at short. Mac fielded the ball cleanly, and although his throw to Cash at first beat Hendrick by 2 steps, first base ump John Rice claimed that Norm pulled his foot off the bag to make the catch. Norm argued the call, incensed, kicking dirt and yelling to the skies, Freehan protesting alongside him. Frank Howard, who joined the Tigers too late in the season to be eligible for the post-season, but given the green light to coach first, put up such a beef that he was thrown out of the game. Jimmy Northrup asserted that the call was so erroneous the ump must have been paid off.

The TV replay <u>did not</u> show that Norm had pulled his foot off the bag, but the call was not reversed. So, with George Hendrick on first and no one out, Bando bunted him to second. Fryman struck out Epstein for out number 2, but Gene Tenace singled sharply to Duke Sims in left as Hendrick rounded third. Although Sims did take an extra split second to grab the ball out of his glove before firing home, his throw was true and seemed to beat the runner, but Freehan could not hold Duke's throw. Bill had broken his thumb only 3 weeks before today's game, and since his inspirational return to the lineup for game 3, Bill's hitting helped the offense, but gripping the ball may have been an issue for him. Bases were stolen which might not normally have been, and this was the 2nd time today that a throw home was jarred loose from Freehan. Northrup later said, *"If we had Duke behind the plate where he belonged and Willie out in left field, I believe we'd have won Game 5, 1-0."*

Woodie got the third out of the 4th, and closed the door on Oakland in the fifth, sixth, seventh & eighth. Detroit's problem was that from the time the Athletics took the 2-1 lead until the Tigers 8th, the only offense the Tigers could muster against Odom and then Vida Blue was a walk and single, both by Northrup. Fryman was due to lead-off in the 8th, but Detroit needed to generate some offense quickly, so Horton was sent in to pinch hit for Woodie. Willie got the fans up on their feet when he slammed a single to right-center. Rookie infielder John Knox, a speedier player, ran for Horton. McAuliffe attempted to bunt Knox into scoring position, but Vida Blue defended the bunt perfectly, firing a strike to 2nd to get the lead man. Still, with Mister Tiger coming to bat and then late-season spark, Duke Sims, due up, Tiger Stadium was rockin' and ready to explode, but there was too much Vida Blue, and he got Kaline on a foul pop to third and Sims on a pop-up to short, ending the 8th.

After John Hiller pitched a perfect top of the ninth, 50,000 rose from their seats once again to make some serious noise as Detroit's turn to bat arrived. Fresh in each fan's mind was yesterday's terrific 10th inning, 2-run, comeback. We can do this again! Although Freehan popped out to first, Stormin' Norman lined a shot into center to put the tying run on base. Maddening shouting, chanting, & cheering ripped through the stands. Although Jim Northrup was hitting .357 in the series AND was yesterday's batting hero AND left-handed Cash just ripped a single off of lefty Blue, Billy Martin sent Mickey Stanley out to pinch hit for Northrup to get a right-handed bat facing left-handed Blue. Stanley hit the ball hard to deep short, but Cash was forced at 2nd. Only one out was left to Detroit as Tony Taylor came to bat. Tony did a fine job for the Tigers in '72, hitting .303 in 228 at bats, and now he battled Blue well, fouling off several 2 & 2 pitches before getting good wood on a fly to deep center, forcing George Hendrick back, back… but… it was not to be as Hendrick caught up to the blast for the series-ending out.

DDDDDDDDDDDDDDDDDDDDDDDDDDDDDDDDDDDDDDDDDDDDDDDDDDDDDDDDDDDDDDDDDDDDDDDDDDDDDD

The 1972 Detroit Tigers hold a special place in the hearts of their dedicated following. The core of the '68 World Champs, the very thought of whom cheered our souls, were intact for one more run, a run that featured many of its own improbable, late-inning, comebacks. The guys were a little older, but so were we, and their names we knew as dear friends: Kaline, Cash, Freehan, Lolich, Horton, Gater, Mac, Stanley, Northrup, Hiller. By association with these heroes, and through their own efforts, even the new-bees became family: Brinkman, Aurelio, Coleman, Big Frank, Woodie & Duke – as were the announcers that brought the contests into our homes and our cars: Ernie Harwell, Ray Lane, George Kell. And love him or hate him, Billy Martin was the manager that made it work. They brought us to The Corner in droves, over 2M including the 3 ALCS contests, only the New York Mets drawing more fans in '72.

There is no one right way to prepare for a ballgame
(Eddie Brinkman & Stormin' Norman)

The result on the field fell short of 1968's ultimate achievement, but no team in Tiger history ever wore the Olde English D with more honor than 1972's Boys of Summer.

1973 - 1975 Uncle Ralph; Should Auld Acquaintance Be Forgot

Move over Babe, here comes Henry, and he's swinging mean
Move over, Babe, Hank's hit another; he'll break that seven fourteen
Here's a man from Alabam "Hamm'rin Henry" is his name
Mister Aaron, "King of Slam," nailing down his all-time fame

("Move Over Babe" by Ernie Harwell & Tiger pitcher Bill Slayback)

Folks awoke January 1, 1973 to news of the tragic New Year's Eve death of baseball great Roberto Clemente. He was aboard an airplane that crashed attempting to bring relief supplies to earthquake-stricken Nicaragua. The Pittsburgh Pirate and future Hall of Famer recorded his 3,000th career hit on September 30, 1972, then returned to his Puerto Rican home to manage a team that traveled to the Amateur Baseball World Series in Nicaragua, from November 15 to December 5. Two days before Christmas, word reached Roberto in Puerto Rico that a 6.2-magnitude earthquake severely damaged Nicaragua's capital of Managua. Roberto Clemente died trying to help the people he'd recently met.

DDDDDDDDDDDDDDDDDDDDDDDDDDDDDDDDDDDDDDDDDDDDDDDDDDDDDDDDDDDDDDDDDDDDDDDD

Coming off of his 3rd All-Star selection in the last 4 years, and acknowledged as one of the top pitchers in the game (2nd & 3rd in Cy Young voting '71 & '72), Mickey Lolich negotiated his 1973 salary from a position of strength, and for the first time in his career earned $100,000 in annual salary. Interestingly, even while making $100 grand at baseball, it was a second job offer that could've set him up for life. No, not from the income his Lake Orion donut shop eventually brought in, but rather a business proposal that he turned down. Early in Mick's career, a businessman of Macedonian origin wanted to bring Lolich, a Croatian and a Macedonian ethnic cousin, in as a junior partner. Lolich, however, didn't think that selling pizzas had much room to grow, certainly not like donuts, so he turned down Mike Ilitch's offer.

The 1973 Detroit Tigers sported a new WJR radio broadcast team. Ray Lane, who had shared the radio booth with Ernie Harwell since 1967, departed to host a late-night sports show on WJBK TV Channel 2. Ray was replaced on Tiger games by a man who'd been on the WJR staff since 1956, a man with a deep baritone that had been referred to as the *"Voice of God"*, a native of Mount Pleasant, Michigan, Paul Carey. It was the start of 19 wonderful years in the booth for Ernie & Paul, the finest broadcast team in all of baseball.

The Tigers opened their third season under Billy Martin on April 7 in Cleveland. Despite a home run off the bat of Mickey Stanley, Detroit lost a 2-1 pitchers duel between Lolich and Gaylord Perry. This was the inaugural game for both squads under the American League's brand-new Designated Hitter rule, a regulation allowing teams to replace the pitcher in the batting order with a stronger hitter (though the Gater went 0 for 4 batting for Lolich today). When Mickey Mantle, now retired for 5 years, was asked if he liked the D.H. rule, he replied, *"Yeah. Would you rather see Harmon Killebrew bat or (laughing) Hank Aguirre?"* Harmon, who hit 573 lifetime homers, was able to stretch his career out a couple more years with the rule; pitcher Hank Aguirre was notoriously bad at the plate, hitting .085 in his 16 years with zero home runs.

Joe Coleman took the mound for the 2nd of 2 games in Cleveland, tossing a 4-0 shutout, looking almost as brilliant as his last time out, 1972 ALCS game 3 against Oakland. The third game of 1973, the home opener for Detroit, pitted Woodie Fryman against the Orioles Jim Palmer. After 9 it was all tied up at 1 run apiece, the Tigers on the board courtesy of a Norm Cash home run, his 2nd homer in two games. The O's won in 12 when they got to Lerrin LaGrow for 2 runs that inning.

April 14, two days after Lolich's 2nd tough loss of the young season, 1-0 to Baltimore in 10, and one day after Joe Coleman's 2nd win, marked the debut of off-season acquisition Jim Perry from the Twins. The 36-year old Perry, though hardly an injection of youth for the aging Tigers, won 54 games from '70 thru '72, and was the hopeful answer for the number 4 spot (after Lolich, Coleman, and Woodie Fryman) in the rotation. Gaylord's brother won his first Tiger game, looking good in an 8-2, complete game, 7-hitter.

Detroit moved into 1st after a 10-inning win over the Red Sox May 16, and stayed on top of the East Division every day from then through June 8, led by Joe Coleman's 10 wins and the hot bat of Willie Horton, hitting over .370. A 2 & 11 skid mid to late-June dropped the team into fifth place, 7 games behind the division leading Yankees. Going into July, although still in fifth, the Tigers closed to 5 & ½ games out and, cut that deficit to 1 & ½ out July 14 when they rallied for 2 in the 9th in a 2-1 Coleman complete game win over the Angels. In this streaky season, Detroit then lost 6 of 7 in the next week leading up to the All-Star break, falling to 6 back of New York.

Amazingly, despite Joe Coleman's 15 first-half victories, the American League All-Star team manager, Dick Williams of Oakland, did not pick Joe for the club. Coleman, on the way to his third excellent season in a row, focused less on being overlooked for the All-Star squad and more about crediting his skipper for the success he realized on the mound. *"Pitching under Billy Martin has made all the difference in the world. He gave me a free rein with my pitches. He said 'You're a pro. You know what's best for you. You pitch that way.'"* Bill Freehan, chosen for his 10th consecutive All-Star game, had a different view of Billy, who was platooning Bill and Duke Sims at catcher, with some time at first base thrown in. *"I was never platooned before, not even part-time. I wouldn't have minded if the figures showed I couldn't hit right-handers. But they don't. I wouldn't mind losing my job if I was doing a lousy job."* Billy Martin often complained to reporters about the pitches that Freehan called, strangely even some of the pitches that were ordered from the bench, bothering Freehan even more.

DDDDDDDDDDDDDDDDDDDDDDDDDDDDDDDDDDDDDDDDDDDDDDDDDDDDDDDDDDDDDDDDDDDDDDDDDDDD

The Tigers emerged from the All-Star break a house 'a fire, now streaking in the opposite direction, starting with back-to-back wins over Boston, both overcoming 8th inning deficits and each credited to John Hiller. The first victory wrapped up with an Eddie Brinkman 9th inning home run, 6-5 Tigers. The second featured a 3-run 8th in a 3-2 win, the big hits by Kaline and Frank Howard, Hiller hurling the last 4 innings, improving to 6 & 3 with a 1.55 ERA. This kicked off an 11 of 13 run to re-take first on August 6 after winning 3 of 4 from the Yankees; Detroit bounced back from the lone loss with an 8-6 offensive barrage including Jim Northrup's 4 for 4 raising his average over .300, Horton's 2 hits keeping him at .335, and homers by Northrup, Mac & Stanley, as Coleman eased to victory 18, Hiller gaining save #24.

After the games of August 6, four teams were bunched within one game of first: Detroit, Baltimore 1/2 back, New York & Boston both 1 back. The faithful packed the stadium, an average of 46,000 per game in the stands for the 4 Yankee games, folks excited about the come-from-behind victories the team was racking up. Once back in first, Detroit won 6 of 8, topped off with an August 12 6-2 win over the White Sox on *"Norm Cash Day"* before 43,211 cheering fans. Among the many pre-game laughs & gifts was a special one from the Detroit sports writers: they'd borrowed one of Norm's bats and drilled a series of holes in it to give it a Swiss cheese look, with a plaque attached commemorating his place as Detroit's all-time strikeout leader. Norm commented about reaching 1,000 career whiffs, *"Pro-rated at 500 at bats a year, that means that for two years out of the 14 I've played, I never touched the ball."* The love and adoration teammates & fans – and even sports writers – held for Norm was on full display on this day held in his honor. How wonderful that this great ballplayer and human being, who made everyone feel special, always kept us laughing, thrilling us with his play on the diamond, was so enthusiastically showered with love at this celebration.

The day after the great joy of *Norm Cash Day*, the Tigers rallied for another late-inning comeback win in Minnesota, and then… the bottom fell out for our Boys of Summer. The balance of August, Detroit lost 12 of 17, finding themselves 7 & ½ games out of 1st going into September. They also found themselves with a new manager.

On August 30, Cleveland came to town, the game 1 pitching match-up Joe Coleman vs. Gaylord Perry. Billy Martin, upset with the umpire crew, claimed they were not checking Perry sufficiently for throwing spitballs, and ordered Coleman to retaliate in kind. Billy told reporters post-game that he directed his pitcher to apply illegal substances – in this case, Vaseline - to the ball, prompting A. L. President Joe Cronin to suspend Martin for 3 games. Jim Campbell had enough of Billy's antics and, when his suspension was complete, fired Martin. Coach Joe Schultz managed Detroit the balance of '73.

Detroit played 14 & 13 ball in September, slowly sliding further out of the race. They were not alone. The tight battle for the East that existed in early-August, with 4 teams within one game of each other, ended up a Baltimore runaway, with 2nd place Boston 8 out, 3rd place Detroit 12 out, and the badly fading Yankees 17 behind. Detroit did finish tops in the league in attendance with 1.7 million fans cheering on the team at The Corner.

Billy Martin's experience in Detroit was the same as it was in Minnesota, and what it would be in Texas, New York (several times), and in Oakland: leading teams to new heights in the standings while rubbing too many people the wrong way to stay long, and quickly hired by the next team waiting in line for his services. Whatever ones view of Billy, he will always he considered a critical part of a 1972 team that excited the entire state of Michigan.

DDDDDDDDDDDDDDDDDDDDDDDDDDDDDDDDDDDDDDDDDDDDDDDDDDDDDDDDDDDDDDDDDDDDDDDD

On the strength of his amazing defense, Eddie Brinkman made the only All-Star team of his career in '73. Willie Horton earned a spot on the 4th & final All-Star team of his career, for the full year hitting a team-high .316 to go with 17 homers. Mickey Stanley led the team in hits & runs scored, won the 4th and final Gold Glove of his career, and on July 13 tied the American League record with 11 putouts in center field.

Joe Coleman racked up 23 victories, the most in his career and one behind league-leader Wilbur Wood, and was the most effective of Detroit's main 4 starters. Mickey Lolich had a drop-off from his usual dominant performance, posting a record of 16 & 15. Jim Perry contributed a 14 & 13 season in his only year wearing the Olde English D, and would be packed off to Cleveland in March '74 as part of a 3-team trade, the Tigers receiving back-up catcher Jerry Moses. Woodie Fryman could not replicate his splendid 10 & 3 run in '72 with Detroit, falling to 6 & 13 with a 5.36 ERA.

Linked in the minds of so many Tiger fans to Woodie is the other sparkplug that Detroit picked up in August '72, hitting .316 in the last weeks of that campaign, Duke Sims, who was waived on September 24 of '73. 4 weeks later, the Tigers released Frank Howard. As Tom Timmerman said of Frank, *"When pitching to Howard, I just kind of throw the ball up there and hope for the best."* Big Frank hit 12 home runs in only 227 at bats in '73, wrapping up his career with 382 lifetime homers. In the short time since his September '72 arrival in Detroit, the man known as Hondo contributed key hits, clubhouse leadership, and an enthusiastic presence. Tiger fans will fondly remember Frank Howard.

The biggest story for the Detroit Tigers in 1973, even bigger than the firing of Billy Martin, was the spectacular performance of John Hiller. In his first full season after 3 pre-season 1971 heart attacks, Hiller went 10 & 5 with a sterling 1.44 ERA, leading American League pitchers in appearances with 65 and saves with 38. The '73 effort landed Hiller 4th in both MVP and Cy Young voting.

DDDDDDDDDDDDDDDDDDDDDDDDDDDDDDDDDDDDDDDDDDDDDDDDDDDDDDDDDDDDDDDDDDDDDDDDDDDDDDDD

Two weeks after the '73 season ended, the Tigers hired their new manager, an old enemy combatant, Ralph Houk. Ralph had been manager of the Yankees from 1961 (when the Tigers won 101 games yet came in 2nd to 109-win New York) through 1973, the first MLB manager since Hughie Jennings of the 1907-1909 Tigers to win a pennant in each of his 1st 3 seasons at the helm of a team. Houk had been a coach for the Yankees from 1958 thru 1960, then promoted to manager, replacing *"The Old Perfessor"*, Casey Stengel, who was fired immediately after New York lost the 1960 World Series to Pittsburgh. In an earlier life, Ralph was a Yankee reserve catcher, making his major league debut at the start of '47 and served as player/coach through the '54 season. In 1955, at the age of 35, Houk became manager of the Yankees minor league Denver Bears team for 3 years until returning to the Yankees as coach in '58.

Ralph Houk was known as "the Major", the rank he achieved in the army after serving our country in World War II, earning the Bronze Star, Silver Star, & Purple Heart for his courage at battles including the D-Day landing at Omaha Beach and the Battle of the Bulge. One very noticeable difference between Houk and the man he replaced, Billy Martin, was that Ralph would not criticize his ballplayers publicly, saying, *"I don't think you can humiliate a player and expect him to perform."*

The end of '73 also heralded the beginning of the end for the core of the 1968 World Champions. Many of those players came up together through the farm system and together they reached the pinnacle of success in the Major Leagues. Bill Freehan said, *"If you saw one Detroit Tiger, you saw 25 Detroit Tigers. After the ballgame, we'd all be in the same restaurant, or bar, or back at the hotel suite or something like that. If someone won the card game on the plane going out to Los Angeles, that guy upgraded to a suite. Instead of going down to the bar after the game, everybody would bring a beer or a cocktail and come back to the suite. If you've got a group of guys who work with each other and keep each other up and focused on where you want to be – we had that kind of camaraderie."*

After hitting .274, the highest batting average of his career, Dick McAuliffe was traded to the Red Sox for Ben Oglivie on October 23, 1973. McAuliffe was a favorite in Detroit, Tiger fans saddened to see him go. The lefty had an unorthodox stance, referred to as *foot in the bucket,* bat held high over his head, left knee towards the catcher & right knee towards the pitcher, knees spread apart as far as possible. Mac broke in with the team mid-season '61, making his first of 3 consecutive All-Star teams in '65. In the 1965 Midsummer Classic, Mac was at bat while Bill Freehan was out in the bullpen talking to one of the National League catchers, who asked Bill, *"How the hell does a guy like McAuliffe hit with that type of stance?"* Before the inquiry could be answered, Mac got ahold of a pitch and sent it over the bullpen where Freehan and the N.L. catcher were talking and into the stands for a 2-run homer. Freehan turned to the catcher and said, *"Just like that."* Sad as the loss of Mac was, the trade was a good one for a Tiger team needing an injection of talented youth. While Dick would only be a .210-hitting reserve for Boston in '74, gone from baseball after 7 games in '75, Ben Oglivie played a solid left-field in Detroit for 4 years while batting .270, .286, 285, & .262 '74-'77, with 21 homers & 61 RBIs in '77. Traded to Milwaukee at the end of '77 for pitcher Jim Slaton, in the 80s Ben knocked in over 100 runs twice as a 3-time All-Star.

DDDDDDDDDDDDDDDDDDDDDDDDDDDDDDDDDDDDDDDDDDDDDDDDDDDDDDDDDDDDDDDDDDDDDDDDDDDDDDD

On April 8, 1974 Hank Aaron hit career home run 715, breaking Babe Ruth's all-time record of 714. In anticipation of this feat, the previous summer Tiger pitcher Bill Slayback and Ernie Harwell collaborated on a song entitled, *"Move Over Babe (Here Comes Hank),"* Ernie wrote the lyrics, Bill the music. As Aaron closed in on 714 late in 1973, whenever he came to the plate in a nationally televised game, Tony Kubek & Curt Gowdy would play their tune. Since Hank's homer count sat at 713 as '73 ended and through the off-season, the song received a long run of air time, both in the USA and in baseball-crazy Japan.

Beyond baseball, Slayback was a renaissance man of many interests and talents, including musician (a good day for Bill was to play his guitar for hours on end), portrait painter, woodworker, & professional photographer. He was excellent at each. Bill built his own recording studio, could play any instrument he picked up, wrote commercials for Nike, Budweiser & Miller, toured for one year with Jose Feliciano, wrote songs for the Sandpipers of *"Guantanamera"* fame, and wrote several songs with Ernie beyond *"Move Over Babe"*.

Slayback had a "slurve" pitch that he often used in critical situations, a combination slider-curve, that completely messed up the batters. While trying to keep a runner close at first, Bill mistakenly threw a slurve to Norm Cash that broke at the last second and hit Norm's ankle. Cash called time, went to the mound, and told Slayback to never, ever, under any circumstances, send a pickoff throw his way again.

Many in the Tiger organization felt Billy Martin ruined Slayback's arm from overuse. He had experienced arm problems in the minors, and perhaps extra caution was called for with Slayback when be reached Detroit. Instead, in '72, just 3 days after throwing 3 complete games, only yielding 2 runs, in 9 days, he pitched 4 shutout innings in relief, dropping his ERA to 1.40. Slayback's arm was never quite the same after that. He'd never thrown more than 125 innings in one season, and just threw 60 innings in less than a month. Bill struggled the rest of '72, posting for the season a record of 5 & 6 with a 3.20 ERA, in

'73 tossed only 2 innings in Detroit while pitching most of the year with the Toledo Mud Hens, spent all of '74 with the Tigers going 1 & 3 with a 4.77 in 54 innings, and retired after spending '75 (rooming with Mark Fidrych on the Evansville Triplets) and '76 in the minors.

After his baseball days, Slayback remained close friends with many of his old teammates, including Al Kaline, and even with the umpires: in 2012, Bill worked on a music project with umpire Joe West, while in 2013 he entertained patrons at a bar 'til 430AM, jamming with umps Phil Cuzzi & Ed Montague. On June 26, 2011 at Comerica Park, the day that the Tigers retired Sparky Anderson's number, and in front of his old Lakeland teammate & now Tiger manager, Jim Leyland, Bill Slayback played guitar as he sang the national anthem for the fans.

DDDDDDDDDDDDDDDDDDDDDDDDDDDDDDDDDDDDDDDDDDDDDDDDDDDDDDDDDDDDDDDDDDDDDDDDDDDDDD

Before the 1974 Home Opener at Michigan & Trumbull, the Tigers opened with 4 in Baltimore. Detroit split the series with the reigning East Division champs, John Hiller gaining the victory in both 10-inning wins. In game 2 of the new season, Hiller relieved Joe Coleman in the 7th of a 2-2 tie, holding the O's to 2 hits and no runs, getting the last 3 outs after Al Kaline's third hit & second RBI of the day in the top of the 10th for the 3-2 win. In the series finale, Hiller pitched a no hit/no run 9th & 10th as Detroit rallied behind 2 Bill Freehan RBIs for an 8-4, 10-inning, victory. Two weeks later, on April 21, Hiller entered the game in the 7th to relieve Mickey Lolich, giving up only 1 run in 7 & 2/3rds innings to get the win in Detroit's 14-inning, 6-5 defeat of Milwaukee, when Kaline singled in Northrup to end the marathon.

By the end of April, John Hiller had 3 saves to go with his 3 wins, and a microscopic 0.36 ERA, on his way to a record of 17 & 14, 13 saves, & a 2.64 ERA. Every one of his 59 appearances was in relief, his 17 wins the 2nd most in baseball history for a reliever, behind only the 18 by Pittsburgh's Roy Face in '59.

The '74 Tigers, with many heroes of '68, were the oldest team in the league: Kaline and Cash would be 40 before the calendar turned to 1975, while on the over-30 list were Freehan, Northrup, Gater, Lolich, and Stanley. And the old gang had one last push in them, riding a 12 & 5 run into 1st place on May 18, up by one game over tied-for-2nd Baltimore & Milwaukee, after two Lolich wins sandwiched around two Hiller saves. Although Detroit dropped out of first two days later, they doggedly stayed within 2 to 4 games of the division lead throughout June. The Tigers opened July with 3 straight victories over the Yankees, showing that '68-style, come-from-behind, grit. Down 3-1 in the first meeting with New York, solo shots by Ben Oglivie, Gater, and Northrup, in the 6th, 7th, and 8th respectively, pulled out a 4-3 win, John Hiller tossing 2 shutout innings for his 10th victory. In game 2, 30-year old pitcher Luke (Sky) Walker, a late '73 purchase from the Pirates, improved to 4 & 0 (5 & 5 full year) as the Tigers rallied for a 4-2 win, the big hit a 2-run double by new 2nd baseman Gary Sutherland. The third straight victory featured 5 late Tiger runs in another comeback victory, 8-6, Hiller tossing the final 2 innings for win number 11, secured when Jimmy Northrup hit a 2-run, walk-off, homer in the bottom of the ninth.

On July 5, the White Sox were in town for a twi-night doubleheader. In game 1, Detroit outscored Chicago 9-6, and in game 2 overcame a 3-0 deficit on the strength of home runs by Stormin' Norman, Gates Brown & Eddie Brinkman (amazingly, homer #7 for Eddie on his way to a career high 14) as Lerrin LaGrow chalked up his 7th win in the 7-4 victory. The July 5 sweep pulled the Tigers to within 1 game of the two teams tied for first, Cleveland & Boston. But Detroit then nose-dived, dropping 13 of their next 15 before the break for the July 23 All-Star game, pushing them 5 games behind the leaders.

DDD

Ron LeFlore, a young man from the east side of Detroit, was arrested in 1970 for armed robbery at the age of 21, and sentenced to 5-15 years in Michigan's Jackson State Prison. It was there that he first played organized baseball, and his extraordinary play caught the attention of an inmate who passed the word to a friend, Lindell A.C. co-owner Jimmy Butsicaris. Jimmy was best man at the wedding of Tiger manager & Lindell A.C. regular Billy Martin, so Martin very quickly paid a visit to Jackson Prison. A June 1973 tryout with Detroit during a weekend furlough was arranged for Ron, one so impressive that an early release was granted and LeFlore found himself playing by July for the Clinton, Iowa Tiger farm club under manager Jim Leyland. Ron later recalled, *"We played mostly night games at Clinton and I had never played under the lights. They had other uses for the floodlights in Jackson."* After Mickey Stanley was hit by a pitch and suffered a broken hand on July 30, 1974, Ron was called up to the majors to stay, taking Mickey's place in centerfield on August 1, 1974, 11 months after Martin was fired by the Tigers.

His unique prison-to-baseball experience was the subject of the 1978 movie, *"One in a Million: The Ron LeFlore Story"*. In a scene filmed in Lakeland, Al Kaline, Bill Freehan, Jim Northrup, and Norm Cash are sizing up LeFlore during his first day after being released from prison, amazed at his speed – all except Norm who drawled, *"He can't be too fast, the cops caught him."*

When LeFlore joined the Tigers in late-'74, Gates Brown took Ron under his wing. The Gater & LeFlore had similar life experiences: much as Billy Martin scouted LeFlore in prison, Gates was scouted by Tiger coach Frank Skaff while Brown served time in an Ohio penitentiary. When asked how he acquired the Gates nickname, Gater said his Mom gave it to him for reasons unknown. Legend has it, however, that his Gates byname was given to him because he went in and out of the prison gates so many times. Gater alluded to his past in a 2013 interview with Baseball Almanac, *"In high school I took a little English, a little math, some science, a few hubcaps, and some wheel covers."*

DDDDDDDDDDDDDDDDDDDDDDDDDDDDDDDDDDDDDDDDDDDDDDDDDDDDDDDDDDDDDDDDDDDDDDDDD

The '74 All-Star team included two Tigers on the roster, John Hiller and - selected for the 18th and final time in his glorious career – Al Kaline. After the July 23 game, a 7-1 National League victory, the Tigers played .500 ball in the last week of July and the first week of August, better than their awful first 3 weeks of July, but not enough to halt the team from dropping further out of the race. *There were 3 games of note in those two weeks…*

August 1 Detroit defeated Milwaukee 2-0. Woodie Fryman was brilliant, only surrendering one hit, a 7th inning single by outfielder Bobby Mitchell. Stormin' Norman Cash knocked in both Tiger runs, in the 2nd on a solo homer and in the 9th with a run-scoring single. Norm's home run was his 7th of the year and number 373 in a Detroit uniform.

August 6 was a Tuesday night game versus Cleveland, played before 14,234 at Tiger Stadium. Going into the bottom of the 9th, the Tigers were down 9-7 with catcher Jerry Moses due to lead-off. Manager Ralph Houk called on Norm Cash to pinch hit, and Norm rifled a single to left. In only his first week as a Tiger, Ron LeFlore stepped up and singled to left as Cash took 2nd and, with the tying runs on base, excitement spread through the crowd. Gary Sutherland was up next and he was hot, with two hits today including a run-scoring double, but Gary's infield grounder forced Norm at third base. The fans were hopeful with Kaline and Northrup coming up next, 5 hits today between the two of them, but Al flew out to left and Jim grounded to 2nd to kill the threat. With this loss, Detroit was now 8 & ½ out of first.

August 7 the 2nd of a 3-game series vs. the Indians, was a 3-2 Tiger win as Detroit rallied from a 2-0 hole with a 3-run 7th on run-scoring singles by LeFlore, Sutherland, and Kaline. The big news, though, took place before the game when Norm Cash was told _over the phone_ by GM Jim Campbell that, after 15 seasons of wearing the Olde English D, Norman Dalton Cash was being released. Norm was shocked, _"I thought at least they'd let me finish out the year. Campbell just called and said I didn't have to show up at the park."_ Jim Campbell did many good things for the Tigers. This episode was not on that list. Notifying Norm of his departure from the team deserved more than a phone call.

Norm's August 1 homer was his last home run and the August 6 single his final hit. With Norman's unceremonious release, his major league career was at an end. For all that Cash did for Detroit on the field and what he meant to the fans, the Tigers should have at least allowed him to play out the season. As Stormin' Norman's playing days came to an abrupt halt, he had the 4th highest home run total among left-hand batters in American League history, behind only Babe Ruth, Ted Williams, and Lou Gehrig. That's a high rent district, indeed. His 373 homers in Tiger history is 2nd only to Kaline's 399.

The same day as Norm's release, the Tigers sold Jim Northrup to Montreal. Jim considered retirement, until Baltimore obtained him for the final month of the '74 season. Besides serving as a late-inning defensive replacement, Northrup went 4 for 7 (a sweet-sounding .571 for the man sometimes called "sweet lips" for his acid tongue) with 1 homer and 3 RBIs, helping Baltimore win the East Division. Northrup played for the Orioles all of 1975, getting into 84 games and contributing his usual excellent outfield play and a .273 average, before hanging it up at 35 years of age. Jim said that Baltimore's Earl Weaver was the greatest manager for whom he'd ever played. It is shocking to think that Jim Northrup, the grand-slam kid, was never was picked for an All-Star team. The man who said of baseball, _"I felt like I was born to play the game,"_ was inducted into the Michigan Sports Hall of Fame in 2000.

DDDDDDDDDDDDDDDDDDDDDDDDDDDDDDDDDDDDDDDDDDDDDDDDDDDDDDDDDDDDDDDDDDDDDDDDDD

After the August 7 release of Cash & Northrup, the Tigers continued to slide in the standings, but the one thing that kept bringing the faithful out to Tiger Stadium was to watch Al Kaline in his final season of play. 1973 had been a year full of injuries for Al, limiting him to 91 games as he struggled to hit .255, his lowest average since .250 in 30 games as an 18-year old. Going into 1974, Kaline was 139 hits shy of 3,000, a mark that only 8 players in major league history had reached to that point, and there were concerns that lingering injuries might be too much of an obstacle to overcome in reaching that lofty plateau. To minimize the time spent standing on his aching legs, the Tigers made Al their full-time designated hitter in 1974. Playing the DH had a wonderful effect on Kaline's health, allowing him to play not only in 147 games, the most for Al since 1961, but compete at an All-Star level: Al's 146 hits were good for 2nd on the team, the most for him since '64, and Kaline led Detroit with 65 walks, 28 doubles, and 64 RBIs. As fine a season as Al was having, it was the anticipation of hit number 3,000 that had everyone's attention.

On September 15 versus the Yankees, Kaline had one hit, an RBI single in the 7th, career hit 2,992. The next day, the Tigers embarked on an 8-game road trip to Boston, Milwaukee & Baltimore. In 3 days at Fenway Park, Al collected 5 hits including smashing career home run no. 399 off of Boston's Reggie

Cleveland. In Milwaukee, Kaline had hits 2,998 & 2,999 as the team headed to Baltimore for two games before leaving for Tiger Stadium to play 1974's last 7 contests.

The date, September 24, 1974; the place, Memorial Stadium in the city of Baltimore, Albert William Kaline's home town; sitting in the front row Naomi & Nicholas Kaline, Al's Mom & Dad. If hit 3,000 could not be in front of the Tiger fans in Detroit, this was where it should take place. Dave McNally was on the mound for the Orioles, always a challenge for batters, and in the first Kaline grounded out against him. Al's next time up was leading off Detroit's 4th inning. Al swung, that picture-perfect Kaline swing, and connected, lining the ball into the right-field corner, as he glided into 2nd base with a stand-up double to join the 3,000 Club as of the end of 1974: Ty Cobb, Hank Aaron, Stan Musial, Tris Speaker, Cap Anson, Willie Mays, Nap Lajoie, Paul Waner, and the ninth major leaguer to ever achieve this goal, Al Kaline.

Play halted to take time and commemorate the achievement. Al ran over to where his folks sat to hug them and pose for photos with Mom, Dad, Jim Campbell, and A.L. President Lee MacPhail. The 3,000-hit bat & ball were handed to MacPhail so that they could be transported to the Hall of Fame, with Kaline to follow them in the minimum 5-year wait from retirement to induction – a retirement officially announced at the end of today's game to take effect at season's conclusion.

Unfortunately, Al would not hit another home run the rest of 1974, leaving him with 3,007 hits and 399 homers. In 1979, Carl Yastrzemski would become the first American Leaguer to reach both 3,000 hits and 400 home runs. Despite that, Al seemed very satisfied with a career spanning 22 years, a 1968 World Series Champion, an 18-time All-Star, a .297 career batting average, and Hall of Fame bound.

DDDDDDDDDDDDDDDDDDDDDDDDDDDDDDDDDDDDDDDDDDDDDDDDDDDDDDDDDDDDDDDDDDDDDDDDDDDD

Outside of Kaline's chase for 3,000, the Tigers focus was on rebuilding the team, infusing it with youth. Ben Oglivie slid over to first with Norm gone and, with Northrup released, Kaline the full time DH, and Horton and Stanley on the disabled list the later stages of '74, during the last few weeks of the season the outfield consisted of LeFlore in center, 21-year old Dan Meyer in left, and 23-year old Leon Roberts in right, occasionally spelled by 27-year old Jim Nettles. Meyer, Roberts, and Nettles played much of '74 together at AAA Evansville, and the end of '74 was serving as their job audition for 1975. A fan who was incommunicado from mid-July to mid-September would have a hard time believing the starting lineup upon his or her return.

The '74 Tigers came in last place for the 2nd time in franchise history (1st time 1952), finishing 72 & 90. Included in the few bright spots on the team was a fine offensive season for Bill Freehan, his .297 average the highest of his career since hitting .300 in '64, to go along with 18 homers and 60 RBIs. Freehan was not selected for the All-Star team for the first time since '63, quite possibly from spending the majority of his time at 1st, where he was mediocre defensively, rather than catcher, where he was a stud. Willie was having a great season, hitting .298 with 15 homers until knee surgery cut his year short in July. John Hiller's magnificent 17 wins, 13 saves, 2.64 season was the lone pitching staff positive. Each of the 4 main starters and every reliever other than Hiller had ERAs north of 4 with the exception of Vern Ruhle, who was brought up at the tail end of '75, got into 5 games, and went 2 & 0 with a 2.73.

Ike Brown played all but two games of '74 down at Evansville, his first time in the minors since '69, and was released October 8, 1974, his career in baseball over. Not much room for a 32-year old utility man on a team starting over. Built like Detroit Lions linebacker & Hall-of-Famer Joe Schmidt, Ike Brown was a character, popular with teammates and fans alike. Ike is in a unique club along with Willie Mays and Hank Aaron: the last 3 big leaguers who had once been in the Negro Leagues, and Ike has the distinction of being the last Negro League alum to make the majors, having played with the Kansas City Monarchs in 1961 before the Tigers signed him in '62. Brown spent 7 years in Detroit's minor league system, twice an International League All-Star third baseman, before getting his first shot at The Show in 1969, filling the role of a valuable reserve for the next 5 years – a role Ike referred to as a "designated sitter". In '70 & '71, his first 2 full seasons as a Tiger, Ike hit .320 as a pinch hitter. He was a happy, bubbly presence, starting every morning with the words, *"Its beautiful day!"* With Brown's effervescent personality, Billy Martin would call for Ike when he wanted to interject some life into the game, requesting him from the bullpen where he'd often be warming up pitchers: *"Let's get 'Boat' back on the bench,"* Martin would shout, referring to Ike's "Showboat" nickname. The thought of Ike Brown in the '72 ALCS grabbing the bat that Campaneris flung at Lerrin LaGrow, reducing it to splinters and throwing it at the Oakland bench, is one that could warm the coldest Tiger heart. God bless you Ike Brown!

The sad news of lost heroes continued into November of '74: Eddie Brinkman, a man who had a special way with words and as a defensive wizard at shortstop, was traded to San Diego for Nate Colbert, who had been a 3-time All-Star, in '71, '72 & '73, but was coming off of a rough '74. The Tigers thought they'd take a chance on Nate, to see if he could regain his hitting stroke of the early-70s. Instead, it turned out that 1974 was just the beginning of a slide into awful. Detroit's patience was gone after 45 games which produced a .147 average with only 4 homers. Colbert was sold to Montreal on June 15, 1975, and retired by the end of 1976. The very same day Eddie was traded to the Padres, they sent him to the Cardinals for Sonny Siebert. Brinkman played a minor role for 3 teams in '75, St. Louis, Texas, and the Yankees before retiring at the end of '75, only 33 years old. Eddie Brinkman will always be a star in the memories and the hearts of Tiger fans everywhere.

Woodie Fryman, such a critical component of the Tigers '72 division title stretch drive, was traded to Montreal in December for a couple of minor players. The ageless Fryman will make his 2nd All-Star team in '76 at 36 years old, and pitch for the Expos through '83, finally retiring at age 43. Although he only pitched in 6 games in 1983, in the previous 3 years, at ages 40, 41 & 42, Woodie went 7 & 4 with a 2.25, 5 & 3 with a 1.88, and 9 & 4 with a 3.75.

Finally, at the end of '74, Tiger fans dodged a bullet: a proposed trade of Bill Freehan and Mickey Stanley to Philadelphia for catcher Bob Boone was called off by the Phillies at the last minute. Although Bob Boone was a franchise legacy, his father Ray one of the Tigers greatest-ever third basemen, and a look into the future shows that Boone was on the verge of becoming a special player, the thought of Freehan & Stanley playing for anyone other than Detroit is too sad to consider. Besides, there's a young catcher named Lance Parrish who just finished his first year in the Tiger organization that looked promising.

DDDDDDDDDDDDDDDDDDDDDDDDDDDDDDDDDDDDDDDDDDDDDDDDDDDDDDDDDDDDDDDDDDDDDDDDDD

April 10, 1975 was as ugly an Opening Day game as can be recalled by even the oldest of Tiger fans, with 40,139 on hand to celebrate the annual return of baseball to The Corner. Baltimore was in town, the pitchers Joe Coleman vs. Jim Palmer. Before many could get into their seats, Detroit was down 3-0, Coleman surrendering a 3-run, 1st inning, homer to Lee May. Who are these guys wearing Detroit uniforms? Art James in right? Nate Colbert playing Norm's position at first? Dave Lemanczyk out of the pen? Thank God Bill Freehan is behind the plate. The new-look Tigers could only scratch out 3 hits in a lopsided 10-0 shutout.

Based on how 1975 began, and how the Tigers would play later in the year, it's hard to believe that they would end any month of the year in first place. But, after sweeping Boston and then Baltimore in late-April, the 10 & 6 Detroiters had climbed on top by 1 game going into May. The sweet days were few, however, in 1975, and the reality of the rebuild came down full bore during a franchise-record 19-game losing streak that spanned July and August. Detroit finished 1975 in last place for the second year in a row and to date the third time in franchise history, their .358 winning percentage, on a 57 & 102 record, ahead of only .325/50 & 104 in 1952.

The few old-timers left on the roster taught the youngsters the ropes, while keeping the boat afloat as best possible. Mickey Stanley, although he would never get his centerfield starting position back from Ron LeFlore, may have been the most valuable player on the '75 team, playing 5 different positions – 1st, 3rd, left, center, and DH, and every one of them well (rookie John Wockenfuss would be called up later in '75 and follow in Stanley's jack-of-all-trades footsteps). Manager Houk said of Mickey, *"He's done everything we could want him to do. He's just been great. No moaning or groaning. He's worked as hard as anybody. He's a great guy to have on the club."* Willie Horton took over Kaline's role as full-time designated hitter, allowing Willie to stay injury-free for a full season for the first time since '69, and he responded with a career high of 169 hits, while knocking in 92 runs (Aurelio Rodriguez a distant team 2nd at 60) with 25 home runs (Freehan 2nd with 14), earning Willie *The Sporting News* pick as league's best DH. Bill Freehan was back to where he was meant to be, starting catcher, and named to the All-Star team for the 11th time in his illustrious career. Al Kaline called Freehan the best teammate he'd ever played with, saying Bill was the leader of the Tigers, and years later adding that Freehan should not only have his number on the Comerica Park outfield wall, but should be in the Hall of Fame at Cooperstown.

John Hiller and Mickey Lolich were the two pitchers who stood out on the '75 staff. Hiller had his third outstanding season in a row, going 2 & 3 with 14 saves and a sparkling 2.17 ERA in 36 games. Lolich had the only ERA below 4 among the starters, and his record of 12 wins (including his lifetime 200th) versus 18 losses had more to do with a lack of run support than his performance: on July 11, he was 10 & 5 with a 3.31 ERA; over his next 14 starts, through September 13, the Detroit offense only scored 14 runs for him. With only 1 run per game on average in support, Mickey went 1 & 13/3.88 over these 2 months. Finally, on September 20, Tiger batters came to life with Mickey on the mound, backing him with 5 runs as Lolich went the distance vs. Luis Tiant in defeating the Red Sox 5 to 1.

DDDDDDDDDDDDDDDDDDDDDDDDDDDDDDDDDDDDDDDDDDDDDDDDDDDDDDDDDDDDDDDDDDDDDDDD

As soon as the 1975 season came to an end, 36-year old William James Brown, known to all as Gates or the Gator, decided to call it a career. One of the greatest pinch hitters in major league history and one of the most popular men to ever pull on the Olde English D could not stay away from the game for even a month, and became a scout for the club before October was out.

Mickey Lolich's 5-1 victory on September 20 turned out to be the final game that Mick would ever pitch in a Detroit Tiger uniform. On December 12, 1975, the Tigers traded Mickey to the New York Mets for 1st baseman/outfielder Rusty Staub. In little over a year, Norm, Northrup, Al, Gator, and now Lolich, gone from the '68 team we loved so much – Mick's loss seemed like a cruel Christmas present to Tiger fans. Mickey pitched 13 seasons for Detroit, winning 207 games plus 3 *never to be forgotten* World Series contests.

Mick's September 8 game versus the Yankees is noteworthy because Bill Freehan was the catcher, the 324th and final time that the two teamed up to form a pitcher-catcher "battery". From 1963 thru 1975, their 324 games as a battery is the all-time MLB record. The next longest running battery is the 316 games of Braves pitcher Warren Spahn & catcher Del Crandall. Lolich-Freehan is the only battery in the top ten of longevity that has neither member in the Hall of Fame.

On June 6, 1975 Mickey Lolich set the MLB all-time career strikeout mark for left-handers with 2,586. His 4 Ks that day moved him ahead of the previous record of 2,583 held by Warren Spahn. Mickey retired after the 1979 season with 2,832 strikeouts, striking out 200 more than 7 times, including 308 in 1971.

Reggie Jackson thought Lolich the best left-hander he'd ever seen. *"Every time I played Detroit I had to face the son of a bitch. His fastball could knock your ass off. He was a gallon of ice cream when you only wanted a cone, and when he took the mound at 1PM you knew he would be there until the end. I wish he had gone into the donut business 10 years earlier."*

Does Lolich deserve serious consideration for the Hall of Fame? Mickey has more strikeouts than Cy Young, Christy Mathewson, Lefty Grove, Bob Feller, Sandy Koufax, Warren Spahn, Dizzy Dean, Carl Hubbell, Whitey Ford - in fact, through the 2018 Hall of Fame inductees, Lolich has more strikeouts than 67 of the 72 pitchers in the Hall.

DDDDDDDDDDDDDDDDDDDDDDDDDDDDDDDDDDDDDDDDDDDDDDDDDDDDDDDDDDDDDDDDDDDDDDDDDDDDDD

Only 3 years after being 1 win from the World Series, Tiger fans experienced cheering for back-to-back last place teams, the '75 squad losing every game for 3 weeks, none of the new kids likely to install confidence in anyone outside of their immediate family, and almost all of the heroes gone from the '68 Champs. The outlook for 1976 was not encouraging. But baseball has a funny way of unexpectedly lifting you up just when things seem at their lowest.

Who could have foreseen that 1976 would provide an emotional phenomenon that would last Tiger fans a lifetime? A quirky young man from Massachusetts, pitching in 1975 for Detroit's minor league affiliate in Evansville, unknown to all but the most knowledgeable fan, was about to change our lives.

1976 the Bird

Well-a bird is a word, a-well-a bird bird
B-bird's the word now well-a
Don't you know 'bout the bird
Well ev'rybody knows that the bird is a word

("Surfin Bird" by the Trashmen)

Mark "the Bird" Fidrych RIP 4.13.09.

On April 13, 2009 my good friend the Moth and I attended a Tigers game, and stopped at El Zocalo's Restaurant in Mexican Village afterward to grab a bite. There we saw our buddy Roland, who asked if we'd heard about the Bird. No, we hadn't. A sad look spread across Roland's face. *"He died today."* The Bird lost his life due to an accident while working under his truck. Driving home, Moth kept asking me if I was ok because I couldn't stop crying. The excitement of the Tigers winning the World Series in 1968 and 1984 was goose-bump amazing, but the most wonderful part of being a Tiger fan, in our lifetimes, was experiencing the Bird in 1976.

The Bird was everywhere in '76...

Got down and did the Gator, dancing while lying on the floor at Captain Ahab's Pub in Wyandotte; walked into a party in Belleville with a 6-pack ring of 3 full and 3 empty beers; was on the cover of *Time*, *Sporting News*, & (to this day, the only baseball player ever on its cover) *Rolling Stone*; Ernie Harwell's favorite ball player of all-time; *"We want Bird! We want Bird!"* thundered in the background while Bird beat the Yankees on the *Monday Night Game of the Week* in front of millions on TV & with Lambertville brother Smitty & I watching from the left-field upper deck - two of the last tickets available in a sea of bird-lovers at Tiger Stadium. After recording the last out, the Bird shook the hands of each of his fielders & announcer Bob Uecker exclaimed, *"He's shaking the policeman's hand!"* Rock Music writer Dave Marsh declared, *"He was a new kind of athlete the way John Lennon was a new kind of musician."*

For Tiger fans, Mark Steven Fidrych came out of nowhere in 1976. We were immediately smitten. Before he began pitching, Mark got down on one knee to manicure the mound to his liking, then kept up a steady dialogue with either the ball, himself, or both, while keeping his pitches low and his bouncy enthusiasm high, shaking the hands of fielders after a good play, as victories piled up and the crowds grew. While playing in the minors, a teammate thought the tall, lanky pitcher with the floppy, curly hair reminded him of Sesame Street's Big Bird, and gave Fidrych his nickname of "the Bird".

Yes in '76 he went 19 & 9, yes he had a 2.34 earned run average, yes he started the All-Star game, yes he was the rookie of the year, yes he meant hope to a hopeless team and a struggling city, but the Bird was more than that to the city of Detroit & the state of Michigan. Honest, charming, boyish, goofy, innocent, genuine, unaffected, a glowing meteor that brightened our lives & began a life-long love-affair between a young man from Northborough, Massachusetts and the entire Great Lakes State, one that even death could not end. The Bird had an endearing way of expressing himself, once admitting, *"Sometimes I get lazy and let the dishes stack up, but they don't stack up too high. I only have 4 dishes";* cheerleading from the dugout, he urged his teammates, *"C'mon gang! Remember, a hit is as good as a walk";* and when Mickey Stanley was thrown out at third base, reminding the guys, *"All right team, let's capitalize on that now!"*

Starting with that June 1976 *Monday Night Game of the Week* victory over the Yankees, whenever the Bird pitched it was a sellout at Michigan & Trumbull. 1,058,836 attended Tiger games in 1975 – in 1976, attendance jumped to 1,467,020, a 40% increase. Usher Mark Pouch happily experienced a 5X increase in tips for games Fidrych was on the hill, well beyond the increase in fans, perhaps indicating the fans were not only greater in number but also lighter in their mood. The attendance spike was the same when the Tigers were the visiting team. The front offices of Tiger opponents would ask if the Bird was scheduled to pitch in their parks, begging the Tigers to adjust the rotation if he was not. Bird-mania was a national phenomenon!

His agent was also the agent for Frank Sinatra, Steve Pinkus from the William Morris Agency. Sinatra phoned Pinkus to invite him, and the Bird of course, to Frank's 61st birthday party in December '76. With all the bigtime celebrities at the soiree, no one attracted the guests' – and Sinatra's – attention more than the Bird.

During 1977 spring training, Rusty Staub and the Bird were standing next to each other in the outfield, shagging fly balls, Fidrych bouncing around in his normal, excited state. Right after Rusty asked him to drop it down a few notches, a fly ball came nearby, the Bird dove for it, and came up limping. What may have initially hurt just as much was Rusty's glove banging against the back of Bird's head, *"What did I just say to you?"* The Bird's season would be delayed while he recuperated from torn knee cartilage.

The Bird bounced back from his spring training injury, returning to the mound on May 27. Although he lost his first two starts, he soon looked as sharp as ever, reeling off wins in all of his 6 June decisions and earning a spot on the All-Star team for the 2nd year in a row. Then, it all suddenly changed. On the 4th of July, the Tigers were in Baltimore for a series against the Orioles, with Fidrych pitching this day. He was coasting with a 2-0 lead heading into the sixth inning when he said his arm went dead. Baltimore scored 6 runs before 3 were out in that frame, knocking the Bird out of the game. He lost this day and one more time before he was shut down for the season on July 12th.

1978 began with high hopes for a full recovery. 52,000 fans packed Tiger Stadium for the April 7 Opener, the first Opener with Lou Whitaker at 2nd & Alan Trammell at short, and the Bird sent them all home happy with a commanding performance in a 6-2 victory. At Texas on April 12, the Bird fell behind 2-0 in the 1st, but shutout the Rangers over the next 8 innings, as Ron LeFlore's 3 hits & a Lance Parrish home run provided the offense in the 3-2 win. Two Fidrych starts, two complete game wins, and the team and the fans began to feel comfortable – and then on his 3rd start, after only giving up two runs in 4 innings, the Bird was pulled from the game since the arm didn't feel quite right. The plan was for Fidrych to pitch on April 22, his next scheduled start, but as the crowd settled in, the p.a. announcer informed them, *"Ladies & gentlemen, Mark Fidrych will not be pitching today. The starting pitcher is Jack Morris"*. Poor Jack, thrust into this situation in only his 8th career major league game, received a "standing boo" from the disappointed fans. Fortunately, the Tigers won 7-6 in 10.

The Bird's arm had gone dead, once again. Visits to a series of doctors, and cures suggested by well-meaning fans, could not fix the problem, whatever it was. Another year, another comeback in 1979, but 4 starts resulted in a 0 & 3 record with a miserable ERA of 10.43.

The Bird's final year in the majors was with Detroit in 1980. Still struggling to regain his past form, the Bird won 2, lost 3, and posted a 5.68 ERA. After spending much of the year in the minors, August 12, 1980 marked his return to Michigan & Trumbull. Between attendance numbers of 28,000 August 11 & 24,000 on August 13, over 48,000 fans turned out to see their beloved Bird. Despite a Champ Summers home run, the Tigers lost 5-4 to Boston. The Bird pitched well, settling down after giving up 4 runs in the first two innings, and lasting through the 8th. After a loss and 2 no decisions, the Bird of old returned one final time at The Corner: on September 2, Mark threw a complete game in an 11-2 win over the White Sox, supported by homers off the bats of Champ Summers, Alan Trammell, and Tim Cochran. This would be the Bird's last victory at Michigan & Trumbull. On October 1, in a game broadcast to a large viewing audience back in Michigan, Fidrych pitched in Toronto against the Blue Jays and gained the last win of his major league career in an 11-7 slugfest. At age 25, his lifetime MLB record was complete at 29 wins, 19 losses, an earned run average of 3.10, 2 All-Star game selections, and the lifetime love of Tiger fans everywhere.

Unable to crack the Tigers roster in 1981, Fidrych spent the season pitching for their AAA affiliate in Evansville, chalking up a record of 6 & 3 with a rough ERA of 5.75. Released from the Tigers after the '81 season, the Boston Red Sox decided to give Fidrych another opportunity, signing him for '82 & '83 to pitch for their minor league Pawtucket, Rhode Island affiliate. On June 14, 1982, the Pawtucket Red Sox were in Toledo, a short drive for Bird-Lovers from all over SE Michigan & NW Ohio, for a series against the Mud Hens. Within the packed house of 8,236 at Ned Skeldon Stadium were Lambertville Sid, Maggie & me, our seats directly behind home plate.

As Fidrych took his pre-game warm-ups, an ear-splitting welcome from the crowd washed over him, the adulation for the Bird flowing throughout the ballgame. The Bird was hit hard, but it seemed that almost every one of those Toledo rockets were frozen-rope outs hit directly at a Pawtucket player. He departed the game to a roaring standing ovation after 6 innings, having given up two unearned runs on just 3 hits. Post-game, hundreds of fans gathered outside of the Pawtucket clubhouse, chanting *"We want Bird! We want Bird!"* over & over. Fidrych emerged to visit with his fans, and it was hard to tell who was more delighted with the encounter, the crowd or the Bird, who stayed to kibitz with the folks as long as they wanted to talk and until every autograph request was fulfilled.

The Bird finished the '82 season with Pawtucket at 6 & 8 and a 4.98 ERA. In '83, he pitched in 12 games, going 2 & 5 with a 9.68 ERA, before retiring at the end of July from the game he loved & loved him back. In 1985, it was finally determined that Fidrych had a torn rotator cuff. Surgery was successful, but at 30 years old, one more comeback was not in the cards.

In the mid-80s, his career as a baseball player behind him, the Bird was hired by the short-lived (1983-1985) ONTV cable channel to do color on Tiger games. After one of these games, I departed Tiger Stadium for post-game grub 'n grog at nearby Porter Street Station. Soon, in through the door, greeted by happily shouting patrons, was the Bird. After a few minutes, I approached the table he was seated at, *"Hi Mark! I don't want to interrupt, but just want to thank you for all of the joy you've brought me and Tiger fans everywhere and..."* At this point, the Bird exuberantly jumped up from his table, clasping both of his hands around my extended right hand, *"Oh man... Detroit... it's like a love-affair! Every time I come to Detroit or around Michigan, what a great feeling! It's a love-affair, man! It's wonderful!"* pumping my hand the entire time he spoke.

Mark Fidrych went back to his Northborough, Ma. home town & became a pig farmer & a commercial truck driver. He married Ann in 1986, and the two had a daughter, Jessica. The Bird was as bright a light as ever, always thankful for how lucky he was, *"I got a family, I got a house, I got a dog. I would've liked my career to have been longer, but you can't look back."*

Those off us fortunate enough to witness 1976, over 40 years later, will still cry while watching a TV story on the Bird. The Bird is Still the Word. He always will be.

1976 – 1979 Bird Watching

Broadcaster Curt Gowdy, out for a beer with Yankee Manager Casey Stengel, noticed Stengel emptied his beer in a single gulp. Gowdy asked Casey why he drank so fast. Casey told him, "I drink like that ever since the accident." "You were in an accident, Casey?" "Yeah, once somebody knocked over my beer."

(Charles Dillon Stengel, July 30, 1890 – September 29, 1975; Rest In Peace Casey, you were one of a kind)

Excitement was back at The Corner! Over 400,000 additional Tiger faithful poured through the turnstiles in '76 versus '75, as Bird-mania gripped the town, the state, and the nation. However, early in the 1976 season, no Tiger fans referred to Mark Fidrych as the Bird, and few even knew who he was. Fidrych's major league debut on April 20 was brief & unsuccessful, giving up a 9th inning, game winning, single to the only man he faced, an excellent hitter, Don Baylor. Mark's 2nd appearance was also in relief, this time on May 5 vs. the Twins, brought in to pitch the ninth in a mop-up role of an 8-2 Tiger loss, giving up two hits, one to Rod Carew (joining a long list of pitchers), and no runs. Interestingly, Bill Freehan caught for Fidrych these two games, the only two relief appearances Mark made in '76 AND the only times that Freehan, in his last major league season, caught the rookie.

On May 15 at The Corner, Joe Coleman played the role of Wally Pipp and Mark Fidrych the role of Lou Gehrig: Joe was due to pitch against Cleveland but came down with the flu and Fidrych became the last-minute replacement. Few of the 14,583 in attendance on this Saturday afternoon knew much about the young pitcher who seemed to effortlessly carve up the Indian line-up, putting down the first 14 batters he faced until giving up a walk in the fifth. Mark's no-hitter ended when the first two 7th inning hitters singled, one scoring when the next batter grounded out, but he then erased the final 8 batters for his first major league decision, a 2-hit, 2-1 victory. After Fidrych won back-to-back, 11-inning/8 strikeout, complete games and Coleman was rocked for 7 runs in early-June to go 2 & 5, Joe "Wally Pipp" Coleman was considered expendable and sold to the Cubs on June 8. Joe won 86 games as a Tiger from '70 thru '75, not including his amazing game 3 shutout of the A's in the '72 ALCS, earning the life-long admiration of Tiger fans everywhere.

In Fidrych's June 16 start, old reliable Mickey Stanley hit a game-winning single in the bottom of the 9th for a 4-3 Tiger win, allowing Mark, by now known to all Tiger fans as "the Bird", to improve his record to 5 & 1 with a 1.86 ERA. Although Bill Freehan and rookie Bruce Kimm each caught 61 games this year, Kimm not only caught the Bird's June 16 win but, except for the two Fidrych relief outings with Freehan behind the plate, was also the starting catcher for all 29 of the Bird's starts, 246 of 248 total innings (Johnny B. Wockenfuss handling the 9th in 2 of Mark's 29 starts after Kimm was pinch hit for). Bruce Kimm was best known in his career as the Bird's personal catcher. Perhaps Ralph Houk decided that, after Kimm caught Fidrych's first start & win, why mess with a good thing OR maybe Kimm himself had the answer when he told the *Sports Illustrated* reporter, *"Every time I catch, we draw 50,000 people."*

On June 28, when Bird beat the Yankees 5 to 1 on the Monday Night Game of the Week, it was the deliriously wonderful conclusion to a 6 & 0 June for Mark that introduced him to that part of America beyond Michigan – and those folks fell for Fidrych like his fans in the Great Lakes State had. On July 22, 1976, the author wrote Maggie, his future bride, who was visiting a friend in Monterey, California, *"The Bird reigns supreme. He was pitching at Minnesota Tuesday night. On Monday night it was Beer Night at Minnesota's ballpark and 5,000 fans showed up. For the Bird, 30,000 plus fans attended. Does that mean six times as many people in Minnesota prefer Bird-watching to beer drinking?"* Folks everywhere could not get enough of the endearing young man who talked to the ball and just kept winning. The Bird's complete game 8-3 victory over the Twins improved his record to 11 & 2 with a 1.71 ERA.

The 1976 All-Star game featured 3 Tigers in the American League starting line-up: the Bird was on the mound, Ron LeFlore patrolled center, and Rusty Staub was in right. What a change from 1975 when Detroit was represented by one player in a reserve role: Bill Freehan, making his 11th and final All-Star game appearance.

On August 17, the Bird was involved in an excellent duel with the California Angels 100 mph throwing, and Detroit-native, pitcher Frank Tanana. Frank & fellow flame-throwing Nolan Ryan were the twin aces on the Angels' staff, their importance to the team inspiring the rhyme *"Tanana & Ryan and two days of cryin"*, the offspring of the 1940s Boston Braves ode *"Spahn & Sain, then pray for rain."* The Bird-Tanana battle was in a 2-2 deadlock when Bruce Kimm, not known for his offense, stepped to the plate in the 8th and hit the one home run in his 4 major league seasons, before 51,822 excited fans at The Corner, the difference in a 3-2 Tiger win. East Detroit's Chuck Porta was impressed: while playing baseball for Notre Dame High School, Chuck hit against Detroit Catholic Central's Frank Tanana in 1970, *"Tanana threw 3 pitches and I didn't see a single one of them. After 2 called strikes, I just swung at where I thought the third pitch was, and then walked back to the dugout."*

Notre Dame High's Chuck Porta – one of Frank Tanana's many strikeout victims

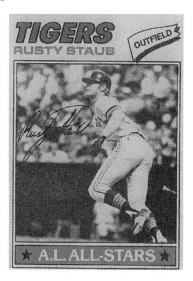

Rusty Staub, the only player in MLB history with over 500 hits for 4 different teams

Kimm's homer off of Tanana helped secure the Bird's 14th victory on Fidrych's way to a finish of 19 wins (including two on walk-off hits by Willie Horton, the 2nd a homer off of Gaylord Perry) against 9 losses with a 2.34 ERA, chosen as the All-Star game starter, Rookie of the Year award winner, and #2 in the Cy Young voting (behind Jim Palmer). Despite the Bird's astounding performance, the Tigers did not have enough overall talent to compete for the division title in '76, but there was plenty of excitement generated by individual players to entertain the fans, starting with the Bird's fellow All-Stars...

The 1968 Champion Tigers as a team stole 26 bases. In 1976, Ron LeFlore alone stole 58 bases. Ron was the Tigers best base stealer in half-a-century, not since Ty Cobb ran wild at Bennett Park & Navin Field. '76 was LeFlore's breakout season, hitting .316 while crossing home plate 93 times, his 58 steals putting him into scoring position for many of those 93 runs. Ron had a hit in the final game of 1975, then had at least one in each of the first 30 games of 1976, during those 30 games batting .392 with 52 hits and 12 steals, earning the A.L. May player-of-the-month award. In the Tigers history, only Ty Cobb had longer hitting streaks (40 in 1911 & 35 in 1917). In '78, Ron led the American League with 68 steals, and in '80 with Montreal he was king in the National League with 97 swipes, becoming the first player in MLB history to lead both leagues at least once in that category.

As sad as the faithful were to see Mickey Lolich leave after the '75 season, the man he was traded for immediately became a fan favorite, the hitting & RBI machine known as Rusty Staub. In his first year as a Tiger, Rusty had a .299 batting average, 15 homers, and a league 4th 96 runs batted in. Rusty is the only player in major league history to have over 500 hits for 4 different teams, and one of only 4 (including Ty Cobb) to have homered before he was 20 & after he was 40. Staub played for Detroit in '76, '77, '78, and on into mid-'79. In those first 3 seasons, his home run/runs batted in totals were 15/96, 22/101, & 24/121. This man could hit the ball.

Even from a seat far away, you could pick out Rusty. He was built a little like Babe Ruth, thick in the middle with skinny arms & legs, striped socks pulled up high, sporting black batting gloves that seemed the perfect accessory to the bright reddish-orange hair that gave him his "Le Grande Orange" nom de guerre. Next thing you knew, he had tip-toed into 2nd base after knocking in yet another run on yet another double.

DDDDDDDDDDDDDDDDDDDDDDDDDDDDDDDDDDDDDDDDDDDDDDDDDDDDDDDDDDDDDDDDDDDDDDDDDDDD

The '76 Tigers finished 74 & 87, a 17-game improvement over '75, with a great deal of help on the way. Drafted in 1976, either directly by genius Scouting Director Bill Lajoie or under his direction, were Steve Kemp in January, and in June Jack Morris, Alan Trammell, and Dan Petry. Drafted previously by Lajoie were Fidrych, Jason Thompson, Lou Whitaker, Lance Parrish, Tommy Brookens, and Howard Johnson. Although time in the minors for many of these kids was yet needed, GM Jim Campbell and Bill Lajoie were building the future champions that would take the baton from the '68 squad.

One of those '68 warriors, Bill Freehan, found his playing time reduced in '76, his 15th year with Detroit, catching 61 games while splitting time behind the plate with Johnny Wockenfuss and Bruce Kimm, plus getting in another 10 games at DH and 1st. Bill turned 35 in '77, as the catcher position was getting more crowded, especially with Lance Parrish projected to join the club after one more year of minor league seasoning, leading Detroit to release Bill on 12.12.76. The Tigers offered Freehan a job managing the Montgomery (Alabama) Rebels, but Bill declined, letting the team know that *"I can't feed my family on a minor league manager's salary."* Bill did stay on for a short while, coaching Lance Parrish on the nuances of handling the catching position, and would return to his University of Michigan alma mater as the head coach of the Wolverine baseball team from 1989 to 1995. Tiger fans all look forward to the day that the Veterans' Committee elects Bill Freehan to the Hall of Fame where he belongs.

Another Tiger World Series champ, Willie Horton, lost the battle when there were simply not enough designated hitter at bats for both he & Rusty Staub. Rusty played primarily right field when he first arrived in Detroit, but as great a hitter as he was, Staub's defense was average at best and DH made sense for him, especially with the emergence of Steve Kemp in the outfield. After Horton played all of 1975 & 1976 as a DH, on Opening Day '77 in front of 46,807 adoring fans at Tiger Stadium, Willie played one final game as a Tiger in left field, while collecting an 8th inning single – his final hit in a Detroit uniform. After watching from the bench as Steve Kemp played left the next 3 games, Horton was traded on April 12 to Texas for relief pitcher Steve Foucault. Willie hit 15 homers with 75 RBIs for Texas in '77, played for 3 teams in a disjointed '78, then had a very happy 1979 in Seattle. The Mariner fans loved him, nicknaming the 36-year old Horton the "Ancient Mariner", and Willie responded with 29 homers and a career high 106 RBIs, winning the A.L. Comeback Player of the Year award. Injuries, the old bugaboo, hampered Willie in '80 and, after being traded to Texas, he was released by the Rangers before the '81 season began. Willie played two years in the minors and one year in the Mexican League, never making it back to the majors. Willie returned to Detroit, where he belongs, when the Tigers hired him as a special instructor in 2000, and he has been with the team in one capacity or another ever since. *And then there were two left from the '68 Champs: Mickey Stanley and John Hiller.*

The Bird's torn knee cartilage kept him off the mound until May 27 in '77, and arm ailments shut him down for the year after July 12, reducing his '76 19-win contribution to 6. Dave Rozema had a rookie season almost as good as Fidrych's, picking up the slack in the Bird's absence, going 15 & 7 with a 3.09 ERA. However, the number two starter in wins was Fernando Arroyo with 8, and that was coupled with 18 defeats. The offense carried most of the 1977 load, as LeFlore & Staub had years equal to their '76 All-Star seasons, and two 22-year olds began to shine in 1st baseman Jason Thompson, 31 homers & 105 RBIs, and left-fielder Steve Kemp, 18 homers & 88 RBIs. Four late-season call-ups held much promise, but it was impossible in '77 to see just how much they would mean to the team's future: 21-year old Lance Parrish, 20-year old Lou Whitaker, 19-year old Alan Trammell, and 22-year old Jack Morris. On August 10, 1977, Jack's first major league victory was saved when Mickey Stanley, playing right field, leaped above the fence with two outs in the ninth to take away a potential game-tying 2-run homer by Milwaukee's Cecil Cooper.

Although Detroit's record changed but one-half game from 74 & 87 in 1976 to 74 & 88 in 1977, the team and their fan's excitement level for the upcoming '78 season was sky-high, 'cause the Bird would be flying again.

DDDDDDDDDDDDDDDDDDDDDDDDDDDDDDDDDDDDDDDDDDDDDDDDDDDDDDDDDDDDDDDDDDDDDDDDDDDD

The 1978 Home Opener, delayed one day by rain, welcomed the largest crowd since 1971, rocking the stadium with the chant: *"We Want Bird! We Want Bird!"* Mark Fidrych, in his first game since being shut down last July with arm problems, dominated Toronto batters, spinning a 5-hitter. The Tigers won 6-2, Bird's pitching supported by a Milt May home run, a 3-run shot by Phil Mankowski, and a mammoth blow by Jason "Rooftop" Thompson that landed, of course, on the right field roof top. Jason's home run was one of several he would hit on or over the right field roof during his time in Detroit.

Toronto 020 000 000 – 2 runs/5 hits/0 errors

Detroit   011 300 10x – 6 runs/10 hits/1 error

Attendance 52,528; weather – sunny & 67; time – 2 hours & 4 minutes (a typically short Bird game)

1978 marked the first Opening Day for the middle infield combination of Lou Whitaker at 2nd & Alan Trammell at short. From their September 9, 1977 debut as Tigers, through the '95 season (Lou retired after '95, Alan after '96), the two played 1,918 games together, the longest-running double-play combination in baseball history. Playing side-by-side on their first Opening Day in '78, as so often occurred in their careers, their play mirrored each other: both went 1 for 3 and scored a run.

The attendance might have been 52,528 plus one, but for the saga of Ann Arbor's Johnny Steck...

"Opening Day 1978... I was attending school at Michigan, living in the South Quad dorm. On Opener-Eve, a term paper had come due, and I'd spent the previous 60 hours working on it - I never did like to plan too far ahead. Actually, I was writing, then tearing up, then rewriting the term paper, to be exact. I finished typing it about two hours before the bus was to leave for the game, and high-tailed it to my professor's office to turn it in. Although it was pouring out & the Opener likely to be postponed, I explained to the prof that I wouldn't be in class today. I'm sure this must have been a great source of amusement to him for many years to come as I was not what you would call a regular attendee. The chances of the Tigers playing in the rain today was about the same as me attending every lecture."

"So, I get back to the dorm to find out that, yes, the Opener was postponed until the next day. Well, I was still a little wired from writing the paper, the eight thousand or so cups of coffee I drank having a little to do with it I'm sure. I stayed up a few more hours before finally crashing at around one o'clock in the afternoon. When I woke up it was one o'clock – 24 hours later! I missed the bus. I missed the game. My best Tiger Stadium story was the Tiger Opener I never saw, but I did get a "B" on my paper."

DDDDDDDDDDDDDDDDDDDDDDDDDDDDDDDDDDDDDDDDDDDDDDDDDDDDDDDDDDDDDDDDDDDDDDDD

On Monday, April 17, the Chicago White Sox were in town to start a series at The Corner, with Mark Fidrych scheduled to pitch for Detroit. This was the Bird's 3rd start of 1978, and he looked brilliant the first two games, going the distance both times while allowing only 2 runs in each win. The excitement generated by the great '78 start of the first place Tigers AND the Bird, lured Lambertville's Greg Sulewski & Don "Smitty" Smith, Southgate's Marc Weaks, East Detroit's Chucky Porta, and the author, to Tiger Stadium. Fidrych fared well, but when Milt Wilcox replaced him on the mound in the 5th, concerns and questions about the Bird's fragile wing ran through the stands. In a 1985 interview, Fidrych spoke about this game, "(after throwing 4 innings) *I just came out, and he* (Houk) *said, 'Oh, you must be...', and I said 'I think I'm hurt. I'm gonna have to give in. You know, there's something wrong with my shoulder.' He said, 'Yeah, I guess so.' And after that, it was never the same."*

Wilcox allowing 4 of the first 5 batters he faced to score didn't help the ballpark vibe. *But it was Rusty to the rescue!* Down 6-0 going into the bottom of the 5th, Detroit loaded the bases with 1 out as Rusty stepped in to face knuckleballer Wilbur Wood. Loud enthusiasm rolled through the crowd, and it seemed like every single person in the old ballyard was on their feet, cheering, shouting, many chanting *"Rusty! Rusty!"* In order to have any chance to be heard, you had to yell directly into your neighbor's ear, but anything that had to be said would be spoken by what was about to take place on the diamond. Rusty turned on one of those Wilbur Wood floaters, driving it deep into the right field stands for a grand slam, sending the place into ecstasy! We'd been keeping up a game-long dialogue with the very large, Esther "Good Times" Rolle look-alike the row in front of us, and at this moment she turned around, and pulled us into a group hug as together we jumped up & down with her, shouting *"Rusty! Rusty! Rusty!"* With one blow, the man who was known as one of the major league's best clutch hitters had pulled us back into the contest.

The game's back 'n forth climaxed as the Tigers came to bat in the bottom of the ninth. Down 9 to 6, Detroit began to rally one more time. Lead-off batter Lance Parrish singled to left. Aurelio Rodriguez followed with a single, his fourth hit of the game. 1st and 2nd, nobody out, and the fans are already on their feet, clapping & yelling. We all put our hands on the shoulders of the big gal in front of us, as if she was a faith healer. Phil Mankowski pinch hits and he comes through with a single, loading the bases. When Ron LeFlore doubles home two runs, Mankowski pulls up at third, Detroit now within one run, and the old ballpark never more beautiful in the thunderous crescendo engulfing everything.

Whitaker steps up to bat, announced by a chorus of *"LOOOOOO!"*, and singles to right as Mankowski crosses home to tie the game - *and here comes LeFlore, being waved around third!* Right fielder Bobby Bonds comes up with the ball, and may have a play on the speedy LeFlore, but the throw is wild *AND THE TIGERS WIN THE GAME!!!* We are but a small bit of the crazy taking place everywhere around us, as we scream & jump for joy, sharing our 2nd group hug today with the very big gal in front of us, fortunate to be among 20,000 that ventured to The Corner that day.

The Bird pitched in 3 April games, then suddenly out for the rest of 1978, ending his season at 2 & 0 with a 2.45 ERA. Two veterans acquired before the season began helped to make up for Mark's loss, turning out to be the top two on this year's staff, 17-game winner Jim Slaton & 15-game winner Jack Billingham. These were short-term fixes, with Slaton leaving as a free agent at year's end, and the 35-year old Billingham giving the team one more good year, going 10 & 7 in '79. At 35, John Hiller was a rock out of the bullpen for the 7th consecutive year since his return from a heart attack, on the mound at the end of 46 games, posting a record of 9 & 4 with a 2.34 ERA and 15 saves.

Detroit stayed in first through May 21, and despite a fine record of 86 & 76, from mid-June on were never a factor in the race for the East Division title. '78 was the first full year in the majors for Jack Morris (going 3 & 5 as a spot starter & reliever), Lance Parrish (who began to seriously push starting catcher Milt May for playing time), Whitaker & Trammell. The calls of *"Loooo!"* were frequently heard at The Corner, as Whitaker won the American League Rookie-of-the-Year award and Tram, 4th in balloting, was not far behind: the 2 turned double plays like they'd been together for years, while Lou hit .285 & Alan .268. Rooftop Thompson had another fine season at 26 HR/96 RBI/.287 as did Steve Kemp at 15/79/.277, all strong offensive supporting pieces to Ron LeFlore's 126 runs/68 steals and Rusty Staub's best season in Detroit with 24 HR/121 RBI.

DDDDDDDDDDDDDDDDDDDDDDDDDDDDDDDDDDDDDDDDDDDDDDDDDDDDDDDDDDDDDDDDDDDDDDDDDDDDDDDDDDD

On Sunday, August 27, 1978, Keego Harbor's Matthew Rose and the author attended the ballgame versus Milwaukee, preceded by a 10-year reunion of the 1968 champs. 43,000 fans came out to say thanks, standing & cheering wildly for their World Series heroes. The entire '68 team attended – except the unpredictable McLain. Just 10 days before, Denny promised he would participate. Only Denny could steal the spotlight with his absence. The old ballyard looked odd today in its transformation, one-half of the park still with its long-time green wooden seats, while the new blue plastic seats have been installed in the other half. In the spirit of transition, rookie *"Loooo!"* led the way, knocking in 3 of the team's 4 runs in Detroit's 4-2 win.

Ricki Rice from Southgate sez, *"Having gone to baseball games at a number of different states, major & minor leagues, one of the many features that set Tiger Stadium apart was their wooden seats. I'm not talking about if they are comfortable or not, but rather how much noise there was when you had a packed house and there was excitement or drama on the field. The fans would stand up from their seat or take the empty seat next to them and bang it up & down. Wasn't it deafening? I remember you could hear the noise & even feel the rumble if you were in the bathroom or on the ramp going up to your seat.*

No matter where I was, that noise made me want to hurry up & get to the stands so I could see what was happening."

DDDDDDDDDDDDDDDDDDDDDDDDDDDDDDDDDDDDDDDDDDDDDDDDDDDDDDDDDDDDDDDDDDDDDDD

At the age of 36, Mickey Stanley was released by the Tigers on December 12, 1978. In Stanley's final year, he played first base and all 3 outfield positions, and in 53 games made his usual number of outstanding plays with a minimum of errors – 2, while hitting .265. During Mickey's 15 years with the Tigers, he was arguably the best centerfielder in the game, winning 4 Gold Gloves. George Cantor said of Mickey's ability to get a jump on the ball: *"Whereas other center fielders excelled at sheer speed, Stanley seemed to be operating on clairvoyance, getting to many balls simply on anticipation."*

Mickey Stanley, Jim Northrup, & Willie Horton were all members of the Boys of Syracuse, the minor leaguers who came up through the Detroit organization together and together won the '68 Series. All 3 were close friends: Mickey & Jim were roommates, and Mickey & Willie had a special relationship that started in the minors when Stanley accompanied Willie to the non-white-players motel in North Carolina. When Willie would get riled up, Stanley had a calming influence on him, including a memorable time in Puerto Rico when he stepped between Horton and another player ready to rumble. *"I got in front of him…and Willie grabbed my uniform in two places by my waist, lifted me off the ground and walked me completely off the ball diamond. He was a strong, strong man…not a mean guy…not a mean bone in his body."* Mickey said of that great '68 season, *"The chemistry was so doggone good. Everybody had good years, not great years. Even the guys who didn't play much had big days where they contributed - a bunch of good guys. There were no bad apples."* Jim Campbell summed up how Mickey Stanley is viewed by just about any Tiger fan you ask, *"Mickey is one of the finest all-around athletes ever to wear a Tiger uniform, but more important he has been an exemplary individual."*

By 1979, it was clear that any comeback by the Bird would be a bonus, and not to be counted on, going 0 & 3 in 4 games all year. What a wonderful time for Jack Morris to become the Jack we all know: 17 & 7 and a 3.25 ERA. But despite the emergence of Black Jack, the team started slowly, going 13 & 17 in their first 30 games under new manager Les Moss, who was hired after Ralph Houk stepped down at the end of the '78 season. Although a 4-game winning streak through June 13 improved the record to 29 & 26, Jim Campbell fired Moss because the Tiger GM believed that he saw an opportunity to upgrade. At the end of the '78, the Cincinnati Reds had fired Sparky Anderson, the man who, since 1970, managed the Reds to 4 National League pennants and two World Series titles. Tiger TV announcer George Kell knew Sparky, thought Anderson might be interested in managing in Detroit and, with Campbell's blessing, met Sparky to discuss the possibility. On June 14, 1979, 24 hours after the meeting, George Lee "Sparky" Anderson was named the Tigers new skipper (Les Moss, who had very successfully managed Tiger minor league teams since 1975, was offered another position in the organization, but instead took a job as the Cubs minor league pitching instructor).

The first 4 weeks of the Sparky-era concluded with one of the wildest days in Tiger baseball history. On July 12, Detroit was in the Southside of Chicago for a doubleheader. In game 1, Pat Underwood, who broke in with the Tigers on May 31, improved his record to 4 & 0 in the 4-1 victory (despite the fine '79 start, Underwood would be out of baseball by early 1984). Before game 2, an on-field promotion, *"Disco Demolition Night"*, rained havoc, an event approved by the Chicago White Sox delightfully-inventive owner, Bill Veeck, and the brain child of Chicago (formerly Detroit) disc jockey, Steve Dahl, who earned a national reputation for his crusade against disco music. The promotion was wildly-popular, the reason that all 59,000 seats in Comiskey Park were sold for the twin bill. The promo & the price were too good to pass up: if you brought a disco album to the game, your ticket was 98 cents. Between games, Steve Dahl blew up a large crate of disco albums in the outfield, inciting thousands of fans to jump the fences, tear up large chunks of the field, set fire to advertising signs, & knock over the batting cages. Disco albums not yet blown up were tossed like Frisbees. 37 arrests were made, the grounds considered unfit to play on, and game 2 awarded by forfeit to the Tigers. Welcome to the American League Sparky!

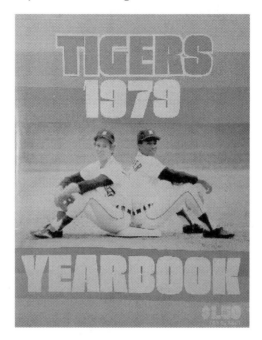

After his magnificent 1978 season, Rusty Staub wanted pay comparable with similar A.L. run-producers, did not get that from GM Jim Campbell, sat out until (with his demands unfulfilled) May 3, and started slowly until sent away in July, in one of the worst Tiger trades in team history. 68 games into 1979, the popular & productive Staub was shipped to Montreal for money and a player-to-be-named-later who turned out to be the very forgettable (except to God, family & friends) Randall Schafer, a utility man who never played a day above AA ball.

After playing the 2nd half of '79 with Montreal, batting a fair .267, Rusty bounced back in 1980 as a Texas Ranger, hitting .300. Staub signed as a free agent before the '81 season with the New York Mets, the team he played for before being traded for Mickey Lolich at the end of '75, and a town in which Rusty was extremely popular. In Staub's 2nd go around with the Mets, he stayed there 5 years before retiring at age 41 when the 1985 season concluded, hitting .317 and .296 in his best two years while being used primarily as a pinch hitter and occasionally at first or in the outfield.

Rusty Staub was an outstanding hitter, one of the best of his time, but an even better humanitarian. Much of his work was in New York City. He founded and helped raise over $140M for the *NYC Police & Fire: Widows' & Children's Benefit Fund*, providing support to families of first responders killed in the line of duty. In the first game after 9-11, New York Mets players and coaches donated their entire salaries to Rusty's charity, close to half-a-million dollars. Rusty has helped serve meals to the hungry & homeless throughout the greater NYC area through Catholic Charities, with funds from his annual golf tournament and wine auction dinners.

Ahh, and then there are other categories in which to excel. The author, as a 24-year old in the summer of 1979, set his all-time Tiger Stadium record for most beers carried back to the seats in one trip, at 18. Helpfully, concessions in '79 had no arbitrary limits to beers purchased, even providing the necessary trays to promote sales of 6 at a time, trays constructed of sturdy cardboard that allowed stacking of beers 3-high. I reached the head of the long line and placed my order for the 18 beers, and distinctly remember (1) the concession lady raising an eyebrow with a one-word confirmation question of, "18?", and (2) the muttering & cursing that broke out from those lined up behind me. The Tigers charged $1.10 for a Stroh's in '79, so 18 beers cost $19.80, or what two stadium beers cost today. I slid a twenty-dollar bill across the counter, and two dimes were slid back to me from the concession gal. Departing the beer line, I recall clearly the face of one fella standing several folks back from the window as I walked by him with the 3-stacked tray, 18-beer, booty. His face projected a look caught between admiration & a desire to trip me. Before his mind could sort it all out, I took one step to the side and strode lively past him. I am uncertain to this day, being young & stupid at 24 in '79 (versus old & immature in my 60s now) if I properly tipped, or tipped at all, the beer concession lady. It is my hope that one of the beer ladies that I tipped well in later years was this helpful gal.

The Tigers never seriously challenged for the 1979 A.L. pennant, and despite a very respectable record of 85 & 76 (1 rainout never replayed), were in 5th place every day but 3 from April 26 to September 17, improving to 4th from September 18 thru 21 before returning to 5th place for the duration of '79 and finishing 19 games behind first-place Baltimore.

Balancing the lost contributions of the traded Staub and the injured Bird, and the relative off-year for Jason Thompson at .246 with 20 homers, were ever-improving youngsters Loooo & Tram, .286 & .276 respectively, Parrish at .276 with 19 home runs, and Steve Kemp's finest year in Detroit: .318/26 home runs/105 RBIs. 31-year old Ron LeFlore swiped 78 bases, hit .300, & scored 110 runs, and the man with the all-time best name for a baseball player, Champ Summers, came up big slamming 20 home runs in only 246 at bats, hitting .313. Tiger fans acquainted themselves to a first year Tiger, a fellow from south of the border, 30-year old Aurelio Lopez aka Senor Smoke, who won 10 vs. 5 losses & saved 21 games with a sparkling 2.41 ERA. Smoke broke into the majors the year before, playing with St. Louis, after spending a decade pitching in the Mexican Leagues.

Sparky Anderson went 56 & 50 in his partial first season as Tiger manager. He was excited enough about the team's promising talent & farm system to guarantee a championship within 5 years of his arrival. Some of that promise was in the form of a young man who was first called up to the Tigers at the end of 1979, a player drafted after he played only one year of college baseball, and someone announced by Sparky to be the next Mickey Mantle (introducing Tiger fans to Anderson's gift for hyperbole), Michigan State University's – and Waterford, Michigan's - Kirk Gibson.

In Kirk's one year of MSU baseball, in only 48 games, he hit 16 home runs while batting .390. It was as a flanker on their football team that he was best known, making several All-American teams, breaking team records, and leading the Spartans to a Big Ten title while on the receiving end of throws from quarterback Eddie Smith's strong arm. Although drafted by the NFL Cardinals, Kirk chose baseball & his hometown Tigers.

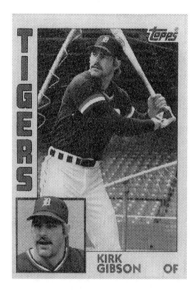

DDDDDDDDDDDDDDDDDDDDDDDDDDDDDDDDDDDDDDDDDDDDDDDDDDDDDDDDDDDDDDDDDDDDDDDDDDDDDDDDDDDD

Cindy & Ed Cohen of West Bloomfield first met Norm Cash 5 years after his final Tiger game. Cindy shared memories of their time together...

"We met Norman in 1979, down at Marco Island at a 'Champagne' Tony Lema Memorial golf outing - Tony was the first Marco Island pro - to raise funds for the hospital. The event organizer, another friend, introduced us to Norm. We became good friends, although we had a rather odd relationship with Norm as we didn't drink. He would only call us when he was on the wagon, which didn't happen very often. But when it did, we had so much fun! Ed & I belonged to the Wabeek Golf Course in Bloomfield Hills, and Norm & his wife Dot belonged to Edgewood in Commerce Township. Ed asked Norm when he was going to take him golfing at the exclusive Edgewood club. Norm's answer... well, we embraced his sense of humor. Now, most people call my husband Eddie, except Norm who called him (in Stormin's fine Texas drawl) *Ay-dee*. *'Well, Ay-dee,'* Norm kidded him, *'we don't have too many Jews out at Edgewood, we only allow one at a time, so I'll have to call & make sure there's not already one out there.'* He was just a nut! Later, we were going out to golf in Fenton, but we had to stop at Edgewood to get Norm and Dot's clubs. As we're leaving Edgewood, Norm said, *'Ok Ay-dee, now I've taken you out to Edgewood.'"*

"Or the time Norm and Dot were building their new home down the street from us on Pontiac Trail, and we were out to dinner with the two of them when, of all people, Mickey Mantle walks by. Norm shouts out, *'Hey ugly!'* and Mantle stops, looks back, & with an exasperated look says, *'Why do I always look?'"*

"Or the day Norm & Dot called and wanted to go skiing, well, it was Dot who really wanted to go skiing with us, and we belonged to a private ski resort at the time out in Fenton. The resort pretty much had no amenities at all, and we go to pick them up, and Norm looks like he's going to go ice fishing. He had yellow rubber boots up to his knees, really weird looking ski attire. I said, *'Ah… we're skiing'*, and Norm says, *'Well, I don't have any gear. I'll just rent some when I get there.' 'Norm, it's a private club, they don't have anything to rent.' 'Oh, well I'll just sit in the bar then.'* But, there really was no bar. You'd just bring your own booze 'cause it was a private club. Though we stopped by a friend's to borrow some equipment for Norm, we also stopped to get some liquor for him, at which point Norm decided to just sit there and drink while we skied."

"Once we put in a pool about the time Norm & Dot were building their home, and we were having trouble with the pool equipment, so Norm came over to look at it. My nephew was down to visit from Traverse City, and he walks in and said, *'Aunt Cindy, do you have Norm Cash out there fixing your pool?'* We were just so used to having him around! Norm threw some wild and crazy parties at his new home… Jim Northrup and Al Kaline were always there, everybody just having fun. But Dot calls one day, and says *'I don't know what to do. We're supposed to have this big party, and we just had a big fight, and I threw every plate in the house at him, and now I don't know what to do.'* I said, *'Send out a bring-your-own-plate invitation.'* The way that they lived was so foreign to us, we'd just laugh."

"There was the time Norm had his boat docked on Round Lake in Charlevoix. The city had a summer fair and when we arrived, Norm's boat was filled with about 60 stuffed animals. Turns out some poor chap had set up a *knock over the milk bottles* pitching contest, and Norm came along and cleaned him out!"

"Well, Norm was such a kind person. People would often approach him when he was out with his family and friends, but he always took the time to sign an autograph or say hello. He was just there for them."

1980 - 1983 Lajoie's Boys Come of Age

You're all invited back next week to this locality,
to have a heapin helpin of their hospitality.
Hillbilly that is, set a spell, take your shoes off.
Y'all come back now, y'hear?

("The Ballad of Jed Clampett" aka "The Beverly Hillbillies Theme Song" by Flatt & Scruggs)

As the calendar turned from March to April of 1980, the eager anticipation for Sparky's first full season stepped into a few puddles. The Tigers opened on the road in Kansas City, and all started well enough. It was the first of eleven consecutive Opening Day pitching assignments (during which he went 7 & 4) as a Tiger for Jack Morris. He rewarded Sparky's decision to start him with a 3-hit, no earned runs, 5 to 1 gem against the Royals. Off season grave digger Richie Hebner *("I like to tell people I'll be the last person to ever let them down")*, newly acquired from the N.Y. Mets for Phil Mankowski, made his Tiger debut at third base, contributing a hit & knocking in a run, while Lance Parrish and Kirk Gibson hit solo shots to power the offense.

Interestingly: Phil Mankowski retired after the '82 season, and was cast in the 1984 movie "The Natural" to be one of Roy Hobbs' (Robert Redford's) teammates on the fictional New York Knights team. Phil's starring role on the big screen has him playing third baseman Hank Benz, being distracted by a pretty lady in the stands, and taking a hard grounder in the gonads (which can be watched again & again at the 50 second mark of the movie's trailer). As Phil lay on the ground, it was believed he was heard to moan, "What do you mean another take?!"

Sparky sent first-year Tiger, Dan Schatzeder, to the mound for game 2. Schatzeder broke into the majors in '77 with Montreal, and impressed the Tigers so much in '79 with his 10 & 5 record & 2.83 ERA for the Expos that Detroit traded Ron LeFlore in December for him. Dan Schatzeder's Tiger debut was fair, but K.C.'s Larry Gura was excellent, and Detroit lost 4-0. This defeat was the first of 6 consecutive road losses before the Tigers limped back to Michigan to begin the home portion of the '80 schedule.

A gorgeous 65-degree April day greeted the 50,687 who filled Tiger Stadium for the 1980 Home Opener. The year's first game at The Corner had the same result as the final game of the season-opening 7-game road trip: an 11-inning loss. This one was particularly hard to swallow as Detroit went into the 9th up 6 to 4, powered by 3 hits each from Alan Trammell and 2nd year man Tommy Brookens, but relievers Pat Underwood & Jack Billingham gave up the two game-tying runs, before Aurelio "Senor Smoke" Lopez surrendered 3 more in the 11th, as the Tigers sank to 1 & 7.

Reflecting on the '80 Opener, Detroit's Indian Village resident Kirk Baxter spoke of *"the beautiful spring-like day, with bright blue skies. 20 family & friends from work walked to Nemo's Bar for lunch & a few beers, enjoying Nemo's Opening Day street party, both inside & outside of their facility. After lunch, we walked one block to Tiger Stadium for the game. We were to sit in a section of the outfield, down the third base line, referred to as 'Vietnam' due to its raucous spectator behavior, rivaling the better-known Bleacher Creatures, in their variety of style and dedication to the Detroit Tigers."*

"As we settled into our seats amongst the throng, in our workday attire of collared shirts and spring dresses, we kind of stood out. The outfield crowd was rocking as the beer and food vendors kept us stuffed and silly. I sat next to our corporate lawyer, one John Lebowski, and we repeatedly toasted the

Tigers, our great gang of friends, and the beautiful day. Directly in front of us sat a family of four, one that put the Clampetts to shame. Their half-filled beer cups, missing teeth, and disheveled appearance, was enough to keep us in our seats."

"As the game against Kansas City progressed, so did our playfulness. By about the fifth inning... a few rows down to my left sat a flower-child-like-woman with long hair and wearing a hippie tube-top. She began to flash her breasts to the outfield crowd. She would take a swig from her Jack Daniels bottle and then flash the crowd again & again. As the crowd became more interested in her than the game, people began to point and stand to get a better look."

"It didn't take long before the cops moved in to remove the hippie distraction. People began to jeer the police. The Clampett family in front of me stood with their beers and joined in the chorus of boos from the crowd. As the police were escorting the lady out, the Clampett boy, directly in front of me, threw his beer onto the police sergeant overseeing the ejection. It hit on top of his hat and began running down his uniform. The Clampett boy quickly realized what he had done and sat down, leaving me standing there with a half-empty beer, somewhat laughing, and staring directly at the cops."

"As I slunk back down, two officers came over to me and asked that I stand up and why had I thrown my beer on the sergeant? I explained, with my friends help, that it wasn't me. They dismissed that explanation, took me by my arms, and escorted me through the crowd and down to the police sub-station located in the basement of Tiger Stadium. It was a closet of a space and it was here they handcuffed me to the metal waiting bench. After being yelled at and slapped across the face by the sergeant with his hat, I was written up and informed I was being arrested for Disorderly Conduct. My friends were knocking at the door with the corporate lawyer in the lead. They asked what was happening and what could they do? The police slammed the door in their faces."

"From there, I was escorted to a waiting squad car and placed in the back seat. The officer & I sat there a few minutes and then came another officer with the hippie woman flasher in tow. He placed her in the front seat. She turned around & smiled at me, but she could hardly sit up straight due to her inebriation. The hippie flasher and I were hauled off to Detroit's Precinct 2 Police Station - which had just been revealed to be using cattle prods on their prisoners! Standing in front of a judge, I was booked and charged with Disorderly Conduct. I sat in the 10' by 10' jail cell with other inmates for a few hours, until my Tiger Stadium friends were able to post bail and I was released. From there, my friends took me directly to the Downstairs Pub, our favorite watering hole, where other friends were waiting to celebrate my release, yelling FREE KIRKSTER! FREE KIRKSTER!"

"To make a long story short, I had to hire a criminal attorney and make two court appearances with witnesses (some who came in from as far away as Kalamazoo) to back up the correct side of the story. In November 1980, 7 months after the Opener incident, my name & record were cleared of the Disorderly Conduct conviction and I was free to go on about my life, knowing situations aren't always what they seem."

DDDDDDDDDDDDDDDDDDDDDDDDDDDDDDDDDDDDDDDDDDDDDDDDDDDDDDDDDDDDDDDDDDDDDDDDD

The '80 Home Opener loss that dropped the Tigers record to 1 & 7 was followed the next day by a much sweeter sound, an 8 to 6 win that broke the losing skid, a victory powered by 3 Steve Kemp hits and 2 hits each from Tom Brookens and Alan Trammell. The occasional win was overshadowed by the team's sluggish play into late-May, with Jason Thompson a casualty. After slamming 94 home runs from '76 through '79, as of May 27 Jason had just 4 home runs in 142 at bats while hitting a paltry .214, and the Tigers packed him off that day to California for outfielder Al Cowens who, while lacking Jason's power, averaged .295 over the previous 3 seasons.

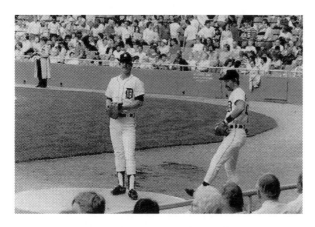

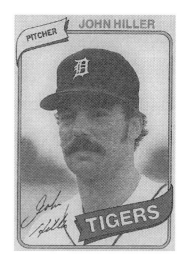

Ex-Michigan QB Rick Leach warms up alongside Tommy Brookens   *The Iron Man from Iron Mountain*

As the 1980 season unfolds, one last member of the 1968 World Series Champs plays on, a native of Toronto and long-time Iron Mountain resident, pitcher John Hiller. After only getting into 6 games for Detroit in '65 & '66 combined, the majority of those 2 seasons in the minors, Hiller's first full year in the big leagues was in the pennant race of '67. That year Hiller became a pitcher that manager Mayo Smith could depend on at 4 & 3 with a 2.63 ERA. During the championship year of '68, Hiller moved from the bullpen to the starting rotation in August. Against Cleveland on August 6, he struck out the first 6 batters he faced, tying an MLB record, on his way to numbers of 9 & 6 and 2.39. John bounced between the pen and the starting rotation throughout '69 & '70, saving his best for the final game of 1970, Mayo Smith's last game as Tiger manager. That day he tossed a 2-hit, complete game, 1-0 shutout of Cleveland, tying a major league record by striking out 7 in a row mid-game.

A month before 1971 spring training, John suffered 3 hearts attacks in one day. Hiller missed the entire '71 season and was faced with the fact that his baseball career may be over. Instead of going down a "woe is me" path, he reviewed his life, gave up smoking & drinking, worked out, lost 45 pounds, and came back in July of '72 better than ever. Hiller was a rock in Manager Billy Martin's bullpen, and Billy would hold John up as the example to his other pitchers with a line worthy of repeating, *"Hiller's back from the dead and can throw strikes – why can't you."* In 24 games for the East Division champs, Hiller struck out 26 with a 1 & 2 record and a 2.03 ERA; in the '72 A.L. playoffs he tossed 3 shutout innings over 3 games and was the winning pitcher in game 4. In 1973, John was the dominant reliever in all of baseball, establishing (at the time) the major league mark of 38 saves, led the A.L. with 65 games while going 10 & 5 with a sterling 1.44 ERA. This effort landed him a 4th place finish in both MVP & Cy Young voting, and the winner of two well-deserved honors, (1) the Comeback Player of the Year Award and (2) the Hutch Award, named for Fred Hutchinson, the former Detroit pitcher and manager who passed from lung cancer, an award given annually to the Major League Baseball active player who *"best exemplifies Hutch's fighting spirit and competitive desire".*

From his return in 1972 through 1978, John Hiller was the one indispensable man in the Tiger bullpen, in those 7 years racking up 103 saves and a 2.42 ERA. In 1979 at age 36, John started to lose a little off the fastball, his ERA rising to 5.22. 1980 was the final year for Hiller, going 1 & 0 with a 4.40 in 11 games during April & May, and he retired from his amazing career on May 30th. John played all of his 15 big league years with Detroit, departing as the team's lifetime leader with 125 saves & 545 games pitched.

DDDDDDDDDDDDDDDDDDDDDDDDDDDDDDDDDDDDDDDDDDDDDDDDDDDDDDDDDDDDDDDDDDDDD

In 1980, it took until June 21, a 4-1 victory over the White Sox, for the Tigers to get back to .500, the 2nd of 9 consecutive wins. Richie Hebner was the first half offensive leader, racking up one big hit after another, entering the All-Star break with 60 RBIs. The 9-game win streak brought the Tigers to within 6.5 games of the East Division leading New York. Detroit would never get closer to first place. They were 8.5 behind on July 1, the same entering August, and slipped to 11.5 out by September 1. The 1980 edition of the Tigers finished the year at 84 & 78, 19 games behind the 103-win, first place, Yankees.

The trade of LeFlore to Montreal for pitcher Dan Schatzeder did not work out as Detroit had hoped. The man with the 10 & 5/2.83 '79 record in Montreal ended his first season as a Tiger 11 & 13 with a 4.02 earned run average, while the newest Montreal Expo, Ron LeFlore, led the majors with 97 stolen bases.

DDDDDDDDDDDDDDDDDDDDDDDDDDDDDDDDDDDDDDDDDDDDDDDDDDDDDDDDDDDDDDDDDDDDD

Brothers Craig & Willie Weaks of Southgate attended a Tiger game together in 1980. Willie was born with Mongoloid Down Syndrome, nothing that interfered with his love of the Tigers, and especially his love of Al Kaline. Craig & Willie had seats down the third base line, along the rail, when a member of the grounds crew stopped by to give a ball to Willie. Willie tossed the ball on to the field of play, yelling *"Kaline! Catch!"* It didn't matter that Al was long retired and nowhere in sight – Number 6 was Willie's favorite and he had a baseball to throw on the field Kaline owned for 22 years, so *"Kaline! Catch!"* it is!

On August 17, 1980, the month after his Hall of Fame induction, Al Kaline became the first Tiger to have his number retired. Surrounded by teammates from the '68 team, also attending the Tiger Stadium ceremony stood Pat Mullin, the last person before Al to wear the number 6, and Roy Cullenbine, a Tiger from the 30s & 40s. *"When you think about Al Kaline, one thing comes to mind,"* said former teammate Bill Freehan, *"Plenty of ballplayers have played right field through the years. None played it any better than Al Kaline."*

DDDDDDDDDDDDDDDDDDDDDDDDDDDDDDDDDDDDDDDDDDDDDDDDDDDDDDDDDDDDDDDDDDDDD

On January 26, 1981, Ray Oyler had a heart attack & became the first member of the 1968 World Series Champions to pass away. That week, WJR morning man, J.P. McCarthy, had Bill Freehan on the line to talk about Ray. Freehan spoke fondly of his old teammate, and observed, *"Well, Ray liked to burn the candle at both ends"*. Johnny Sain said that Oyler was one of best fielders he saw in his 50 years in the game, an observation of just about everyone who ever played with or against him, none more than double play partner, Dick McAuliffe. Mac noted that Ray played grounders and delivered the ball to him so perfectly that he made his job easier. His weak hitting, however, was legendary, going "0 for August" in '68 with a lifetime average of .175. When Ray arrived one spring training wearing glasses in hopes of improving his hitting, Norm Cash said he looked like a German tank commander. Ray was the ultimate "good field, no hit".

In the George Cantor book, "The Tigers of '68: Baseball's Last Real Champions", Mickey Stanley said of Ray, *"He never carried a grudge about my replacing him during the Series. He was simply a great guy. To get into the Series and then have some guy moved entirely out of position to take your place. He'd take me out there during workouts and tried to give me a crash course in shortstop. He was such a great competitor. He played hurt, he played hungover. He never complained. We all loved that guy."*

DDDDDDDDDDDDDDDDDDDDDDDDDDDDDDDDDDDDDDDDDDDDDDDDDDDDDDDDDDDDDDDDDDDDDDD

The 1981 Tigers had a bizarre beginning to a bizarre season. Opening Day, however, was its usual, beautiful self. 51,452 fans packed the old ballyard, and Richie Hebner sent them home happy, hitting a 7th inning, tie-breaking, 3-run homer as Jack Morris went the distance in the 6-2 victory. Detroit won 7 of their first 8 games, in first by 2.5 games on April 18 – and then proceeded to lose 10 in a row and fall 4.5 games out before the calendar turned to May. In late-May, the MLB Players Association voted to go out on strike over the owners' demand on limits to free agency. So, after the games of June 11 – a night that Detroit won for the 7th time out of its last 8 – the players went on strike. Again.

During the strike, baseball writers were searching for ways to fill their columns, and spent much of their time looking for stories of how players spent their unexpected "summer vacation". One of the most unusual and colorful stories highlighted Richie Hebner resuming his off-season grave digging job. Alongside photos of Hebner shoveling out a 4' deep grave, were stories Richie shared including when, as a young man, his father once criticized his work, complaining the boy was digging graves too shallow. Richie defense was, *"I never saw anyone get up from one of 'em."*

Two months of the 1981 season were lost before a compromise settlement could be reached, including restricting free agency to players with 6 or more years of major league service. Play resumed August 10, a full two months lost to the strike. For post-season play, the owners decided on a split-season format, with the 1st half (season start through June 11) first-place team playing the 2nd half (August 10 through last game) winner in a best-of-five before heading on to a league championship series.

The Tigers were in 4th place when play halted June 11, so they needed to win the 2nd half to make the first round of the playoffs. However, Detroit ended the regular season dropping 2 of 3 to Milwaukee in October, finishing 1 game behind the 2nd half champion Brewers at 29 & 23, despite Kirk Gibson's A.L. third-best .328, Morris league-best 14 wins (remember, shortened season), and the bullpen one-year wonder, Kevin Saucier, who in 38 games went 4 & 2 with 13 saves and a 1.65 ERA.

DDDDDDDDDDDDDDDDDDDDDDDDDDDDDDDDDDDDDDDDDDDDDDDDDDDDDDDDDDDDDDDDDDDDDDD

Vic Wertz, who last played for the Tigers in 1963, founded in '81, the "Wertz Warriors". Since the winter of '82, the Warriors annually assemble for a 7-day, 900-mile, snowmobile endurance ride fund-raiser from Mount Clemens to Petoskey. Each year, the goal of the event is 100% funding of Michigan's Special Olympics Winter Games. The Wertz Warriors became the favorite charity of Mark Fidrych, and The Bird participated the last 17 winters of his life, flying in for the event each year from Boston. Bird said in '06, *"They showed me how to ride* (a snowmobile) *in 1993, and I still don't know how. The Special Olympics is a worthy cause. When you get up there Wednesday it's awesome. You have all these boys and girls who cling to you. They need the Wertz Warriors."* The Bird added, *"The group is real tight. They're all nice and know what they're doing. They have mechanics if you break down, all kinds of volunteer help. And the towns* (the 20 or so visited) *are just crazy."* Besides riding to raise money for the Special Olympians, the

Warriors participate in the Olympics opening ceremony, signing autographs and giving rides on their snowmobiles to approximately 900 Special Olympics Michigan athletes.

When Bill Freehan stepped aside as the Wertz Warriors Honorary Chairman, the Bird accepted the role. He'd never ridden a snowmobile before, but said he'd like to get involved. Mark's dedication to the cause is exemplified by his generous nature: in the middle of the 7-day event, at the end of a long, cold day of riding, Fidrych and the other Warriors were tucked in for the night when a phone rang in one of their Elba-area rooms. 50 miles away, a group of people were waiting to see the Bird that the Warriors hadn't known about, so Fidrych said, *"Let's go"*, got dressed &, with several other Warriors, drove their snowmobiles to these folks, the Bird staying to talk with them & sign autographs until the last person left. To this day, the place Bird visited late at night donates $20,000 or more annually to the Warriors.

Interestingly: in the 1954 World Series, Vic Wertz' Cleveland Indians were matched against the New York Giants, game 1 played at New York's Polo Grounds. In the top of the 8th in a 2-2 game, Vic Wertz hit his famous '420 fly ball that centerfielder Willie Mays tracked down with an over-the-shoulder catch. It was said that Wertz' drive "would've been a home run in any other park, including Yellowstone."

DDDDDDDDDDDDDDDDDDDDDDDDDDDDDDDDDDDDDDDDDDDDDDDDDDDDDDDDDDDDDDDDDDDDDD

As 1981 came to a close, the Tigers engineered two trades that would have a dramatically positive effect on their efforts to build a World Champion...

On November 27, Detroit traded left-fielder Steve Kemp to the Chicago White Sox for center-fielder Chet Lemon. Kemp, Trammell, Morris and Dan Petry were all part of Bill Lajoie's 1976 draft, considered one of the baseball's best ever. During Kemp's 5 years in Detroit, he hit .284 with 89 homers & 422 RBIs and was selected for one All-Star game; over the same time period, besides being one of the finest defensive outfielders in all of baseball, Chet hit .296 with 69 homers & 309 RBIs as a two-time All-Star. The swap was seen by most as even, Kemp with more power, Lemon better defensively. What the trade did for Detroit was give them the #1 up-the-middle defense in the majors: Parrish behind the plate, Lou & Tram patrolling the middle infield, and now Chet in center.

On December 9, 1981, the Tigers swapped pitcher Dan Schatzeder, 6 & 8 with a 6.06 ERA in '81, to the Giants for left-fielder Larry Herndon. While the Kemp-Lemon trade brought talent to both teams, this one was a steal for Detroit, Schatzeder going on to enjoy 3 good years as a bullpen set-up man while Herndon became a major contributor both defensively & offensively to the Tigers for the next 7 years.

With the Tigers new outfield line-up of Lemon, Herndon, Kirk Gibson and Lynn Jones, Al Cowens was sold to Seattle just before 1982 play began. There was simply no room left on the roster for Cowens – not with the Detroit at bats earned by a young outfielder who tore up the minors with 30 homers in a season & a half, rocket-armed Glenn Wilson.

DDDDDDDDDDDDDDDDDDDDDDDDDDDDDDDDDDDDDDDDDDDDDDDDDDDDDDDDDDDDDDDDDDDDDDDD

3 months after the Tigers sent Schatzeder to the San Francisco Giants for Herndon, the two teams made another swap. On March 8, 1982, the Tigers traded popular Champ Summers to the Giants for 1st baseman/3rd baseman Enos Cabell. Detroit opened the season on the road in Kansas City with a 4-2 loss, going 2 & 4 on a 6-game trip through KC and Toronto, before returning to The Corner for the home opener on April 15. The 51,038 on hand had a wonderful first impression of the 32-year old Cabell, the

man known to the young Tigers as "Old Dude", his two RBI singles keying a come-from-behind 4-2 win over the Toronto Blue Jays.

Continuing their Opening Day post-game tradition, Ferndale's Debbie & Ted Theodoroff and friends wandered across Trumbull Avenue to keep the party going inside Hoot Robinson's pub. After a few toasts to the Tigers, Debbie - with friends Mary & Debbie - stepped outside to soak up the beautiful, crisp, early evening air. A stranger commented that the man across Trumbull, standing at the parking entrance for Tiger players, was Dave Rozema. Debbie reminisced, *"My beautiful blonde friend Mary proceeds to shout 'Hey Dave! Come on over!' It took a few shout-outs before Dave decided to check these 3 girls out. From our van, parked in Hoot's lot, we offered Rozema a beer, which he accepted, and proceeded to share a few laughs with us. By that time our husbands came out of Hoot's and Dave's bubble burst! Knowing now this was not what he expected, Dave told us he had to leave or he'd be late to a Prince concert. But before departing, he graciously left a signed autograph for the 3 ladies. After the good-byes we read his note: 'To Mary, Debbie, and Debbie - thanks for the 3-way! Dave Rozema'. That autograph hung on the wall of our van until we sold it."*

The Home Opener victory kicked off a 9 of 10 run featuring 5 wins over the Damn Yankees, catapulting the 11 & 5 Tigers into first place by 2 games. Over the next 2 weeks, Detroit played .500 ball & dropped out of the top spot, but followed that up with an 8-game winning streak that tied them with Boston for first in the East Division. Capping off the 8 wins was a May 20th, 11-3 win over the Athletics, fueled by a 5 for 5 performance by Larry Herndon and a two homer/5 RBI day for Mike Ivie, a free agent signed on May 6. Ivie showed some pop in his bat during 9 years in the National League, and he hit 14 homers in 265 plate appearances for Detroit in '82.

The Tigers were in first through June 12, when they overcame an early deficit behind homers by Tommy Brookens and Herndon for a 7-3 win in Milwaukee. But the next day started an awful slide that ran to the end of June, Detroit only winning 2 of the next 15 games to fall to third, 5 games behind the division-leading Red Sox.

DDDDDDDDDDDDDDDDDDDDDDDDDDDDDDDDDDDDDDDDDDDDDDDDDDDDDDDDDDDDDDDDDDDDDDDDDDDDDD

On Saturday night, July 3 of '82, the Tigers hosted Baltimore at Michigan & Trumbull for the 2nd of a 3-game series. Making the drive north from the Good Side of the Michigan-Ohio border was Lambertville's Don "Smitty" Smith, Doug Pompili & Greg Sulewski, meeting East Detroit native Chucky Porta and the author for some pre-game fun at Hoot Robinson's bar. Directly across Trumbull from Hoot's sits Gate 1 where ticket man Pete scored us seats in the row directly behind the Oriole dugout, the dugout making a fine foot rest, as we kicked back sipping beers while rooting on our Tigers. These seats were ideally located for razzing every Oriole in sight, our focus directed for most of the game on the O's first base coach, Jimmy Williams, who minutes after we took our seats was christen by us as "No Neck" Williams. After several innings of our good-natured but non-stop torrent of barking, who sticks his head above the dugout, but future Hall of Fame pitcher, Jim Palmer. In the space of less than 10 seconds, Palmer has pretended to count our empties stacked on his team's dugout, before rendering a verdict of *"Well, no wonder!"* as in *"based on the number of drained beer cups, no wonder you're so obnoxious"*, before disappearing back into the dugout.

Well, now the beer-drinkers have been acknowledged, by one of the greats, no less, and our barkin' gets louder 'n louder, much of it now directed at Palmer, for selling out as a mercenary huckster in print and TV ads for Jockey brand shorts. Our serenade of the all-things Orioles reaches a fever pitch until the next inning when Palmer reemerges from the dugout with a soaking wet towel, firing it into the chest of Greg Sulewski. Startled, and before thinking it through, Greg throws it back at Palmer but misses, as his target has immediately ducked back into the dugout, while his friends lament, *"Greg! That was a Hall of Fame towel you threw away!"*

DDDDDDDDDDDDDDDDDDDDDDDDDDDDDDDDDDDDDDDDDDDDDDDDDDDDDDDDDDDDDDDDDDDDDDDD

The Young Tigers of 1982 were not yet ready to win, playing one game under .500 from July 1 through season's end, going 83 & 79 for the year. One other A.L. team, though, *was* able to catch the Red Sox and stay with the surging Orioles – the Milwaukee Brewers, skippered by an old Detroit fan favorite, former batting champion and one-half of the "K&K Kids" with Al Kaline, the man we traded to Cleveland for Rocky Colavito, Wisconsin-native Harvey Kuenn. In 1980, Kuenn had a blood circulation disorder that required his right leg be amputated below the knee, but that did not slow Harvey down. When the '82 Brewers began the season 23 & 24, the team fired manager (not that) Buck Rodgers and, with Harvey as his replacement, finished the season on a 72 & 43 run, the big-hitting Brew Crew known as *"Harvey's Wallbangers"*. In game 162, Milwaukee was at Baltimore with the two teams tied for first, the Brewers taking the East Division title with a decisive 10-2 victory. Harvey's Wallbangers overcame a 0-2 deficit in the best 3-of-5 ALCS to defeat California, and lost a heart-breaking game 7 to the Cardinals in the World Series. Kuenn managed Milwaukee one more year, fired after a very respectable 87 & 75, then scouted for the Brewers until passing much too young at 57 in 1988 of diabetes & heart disease. Posthumously, Harvey was elected to the Wisconsin Athletic Hall of Fame, honored with a plaque in the "Brewer's Honorarium" at Milwaukee's Miller Park, and with a place in the hearts of Tiger fans everywhere.

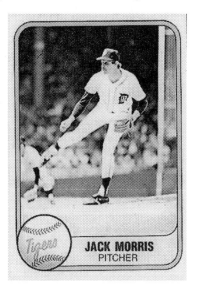

MLB's finest catcher-pitcher battery of the 1980's, Lance Parrish & Jack Morris

Although Detroit's winning percentage slipped from .550 in the strike-shortened 1981 (60 & 49) to .512 in 1982, there were several noteworthy '82 individual achievements, none more than those of Lance Parrish. Although he made the 1980 All-Star team, '82 was truly Lance's breakout year. Still one season away from winning his first Gold Glove, defensively he was already recognized as one of the game's best catchers, while offensively Parrish earned his first Silver Slugger, awarded to the finest league hitter at his position, posting a .284 average with 32 homers - establishing the single season home run record for

A.L. catchers - and 87 RBIs. Lance received his first MVP votes along with his 2nd All-Star team selection – and threw out 3 National League runners trying to steal, setting an All-Star game record.

Rookie utility man Howard Johnson proved the best surprise is no surprise: after hitting .317 in 366 at bats in AAA Evansville, he was promoted to the Tigers & hit a team-high .316 in 155 plate appearances.

DDDDDDDDDDDDDDDDDDDDDDDDDDDDDDDDDDDDDDDDDDDDDDDDDDDDDDDDDDDDDDDDDDDDDDDDDDDDD

The quiet 4 & 4 start to the 1983 season awoke with some big excitement in game number 9...

On April 15, a Friday evening, the Tigers played the White Sox in front of over 19,000 at Chicago's Comiskey Park. Milt Wilcox was on the mound for Detroit. The Tigers were roughing up Sox pitcher LaMarr Hoyt and two relievers for 6 runs on 15 hits. Wilcox, meanwhile, was cruising along, all of his pitches working, putting down the White Sox 1-2-3 inning after inning.

At the same time back in Detroit, Eastern Michigan University alum Chuck Porta, Marc Weaks, and the author were at Cobo Hall for a concert featuring the rock band Foghat. While no surprise that Foghat's decibel level would be somewhere near thunderous, on this night the volume was set *so* high that it did not allow us to identify any of the songs played. Deafened and bored, we retired to a concession stand where a TV was tuned to the Tiger game. Although Foghat's wall-of-sound eliminated the possibility of hearing game commentary from Kell & Kaline, strangers quickly brought us up to speed on the perfect game on which Wilcox was working.

We picked up the game with two outs in the Sox' 7th, the always dangerous Harold Baines stepping up to the plate. Sure enough, Harold stung the ball, but his liner was tracked down by Larry Herndon in left to end the frame. Detroit padded their 4-0 lead with two in their eighth when Glenn Wilson and Chet Lemon singled in runs, but as nice as that was, everyone was focused on Milt getting 6 more outs.

Wilcox fanned Big Greg Luzinski to open Chicago's 8th, then took out Ron Kittle on a flyball to Chester in center, and completed the inning as Greg Walker stood there like the house by the side of the road and watched strike 3 sail by. Tommy Brookens was stranded on 2nd as the Tigers ninth ended, and now Wilcox was back to the mound for the final 3 outs and baseball immortality. Carlton Fisk led off by flying out to Herndon in left-field. 2 outs to go. Milt next faced a pinch hitter and Kalamazoo native, Mike Squires, who grounded out to reserve first baseman Rick Leach, the old UM quarterback in his 3rd season with the Tigers. One out to go. Wilcox would have to face another pinch hitter, one of the finest in the majors, Jerry Hairston. The Chicago fans were on their feet, the majority cheering on the opposing pitcher in his quest.

No one had to wait long to see how this would end – Hairston lined the first pitch for a single that landed in front of Lemon in center. Michigan cursed as one, and many Sox fans at the game booed, disappointed at missing their chance to witness history. Chicago lead-off man Rudy Law, the player no one wanted to see bat in the ninth, was induced by Wilcox to ground out unassisted to Leach at first to complete his one-hit shutout. White Sox manager Tony LaRussa caught some heat for sending up his ace pinch hitter at the end of a game that Chicago was not going to win, for what seemed to many only to wreck a perfect game. Although Tony may not have said it, his reasoning might have been the same as Washington manager Walter Johnson's was 51 years earlier, his team behind Detroit 13-0, when he sent up his ace pinch hitter with two outs in the ninth to face Tommy Bridges who, like Wilcox, was one out from perfection: *"A hitter gets paid for hitting like a pitcher gets paid for pitching."*

On the 2018 TV show, *"Legends of the Olde English D"*, Kirk Gibson and Alan Trammell were talking about rain delays in Tiger Stadium in the early-1980s, and how during the delays the centerfield scoreboard would always show highlights from the 1968 World Series. Tram said, *"We were getting a little tired of that, and we wanted to make a name for ourselves."*

In 1983, the Tigers took a big step towards making their own mark. However, through the first two months of the '83 campaign, it was looking like every year since 1978 (except the '81 split-season), with just enough wins to be above .500, but not enough to challenge for the division title. After losing a 6-4 decision to Toronto on May 30, Detroit's record was 22 & 23 – but then, it all clicked. Dave Rozema went 4 & 0 in June while surrendering only 5 runs, and in all 4 Rosie wins, Aurelio *Senor Smoke* Lopez earned the save; by the end of June, Smoke's record was 5 & 3 with 11 saves and a 1.83 ERA; Jack Morris rang up a 5 & 2 June and, being Jack, all but 2 were complete games; at month's end, Parrish, Whitaker and Enos Cabell were all hitting over .300, with additional contributions coming from unexpected places – on the strength of rookie 3rd baseman Marty Castillo's June 28, game-winning, 9th inning home run, the 40 & 31 Tigers had clawed their way into a 3-way tie for first with Toronto & Baltimore.

DDDDDDDDDDDDDDDDDDDDDDDDDDDDDDDDDDDDDDDDDDDDDDDDDDDDDDDDDDDDDDDDDDDDDDDDDDDDDD

June 12, 1983 was officially *Greenberg-Gehringer Day* at Tiger Stadium, the numbers of the two Hall of Famers, #2 Charlie Gehringer and #5 Hank Greenberg, retired between games of the doubleheader. Richie Hebner, sold to the Pirates in August '82 to make room for the kids coming up, was the last to wear #2; Howard Johnson, sent down to the minors in May, the last to wear #5 (when recalled by Detroit in August, the number 5 no longer available to him, Tigers equipment manager Jim Schmakel said, *"Look at it this way, Howard, you're the first rookie to have his number retired"*). With both Hank and Charlie on hand for the ceremony, Gehringer was introduced as the greatest 2nd baseman in Tiger history, and a loud *"Looooo!"* rolled down from the stands - understandable as Charlie played his last game 41 years ago, and many in attendance today would not have seen the amazing Gehringer in action. The older fans in the crowd, though, nodded in agreement with the assessment.

June 14, 1983 at Michigan & Trumbull, Tigers versus Red Sox. Baseball fans witnessed what was arguably the most amazing combination of power AND speed by one man in one game. In the fourth inning, Kirk Gibson hit a ball over the right field roof that cleared the Ace Lumber Yard on Trumbull, traveling an estimated 523'. In the sixth inning, Gibson stepped up to bat with Lou Whitaker on 2nd base. Kirk drove the ball deep to center. Lou, unsure if it would be caught or not, ventured only a few steps off the bag. Gibson, on the other hand, had the after burners on since leaving home plate. Once the ball eluded the outfielder, on its way to the wall in dead center, Whitaker began running, no more than a few steps ahead of Gibson, who was quickly narrowing the gap between the two. Lou slid into home, arriving when the ball did, and Umpire Larry Barnett emphatically thumbs out Lou, his back to the Kirk Gibson freight train that in another second slams into both Barnett and the Boston catcher, knocking each to the ground, rendering the ump at a minimum, dazed, or at worst briefly unconscious. It was catcher Rich Gedman's good fortune that the umpire was between him and Gibson, serving as a cushion of sorts. The first base ump, Ken Kaiser, ran down the line towards home to make the call on Gibson, sees a ball lying on the ground and spreads his palms out while shouting *"safe!"* The only problem was that 5 balls were on the ground, spilled from the pockets of the prone umpire. The Red Sox' challenge of the call fell on deaf ears.

So… Lou is out, Gibson is safe, umpire Barnett is flattened and, for some reason, Gibby is only credited with a double instead of an inside-the-park home run, or at least a triple, & we see why it's said that Bill Lajoie stole Kirk Gibson from the National Football League. The fans are roaring with delight, knowing that they witnessed two of the most spectacular back-to-back at bats by a single player in baseball history. The only two Detroit runs in the 6-2 loss were well worth the price of admission; Boston 2nd year pitcher Mike Brown was the man Gibson hit both balls off of and, although Brown was the winning pitcher, he undoubtedly was hoping he'd never have to face Kirk Gibson again.

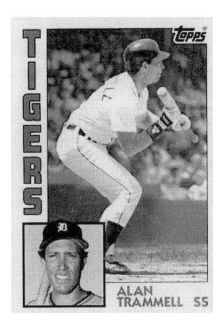 

Tram & Lou/Lou & Tram: on their way to establishing the MLB record for longest-running double-play combination of 1,918 games together, had a huge 1983… hit .319 & .320, respectively; both Gold Glove winners; Lou an All-Star

The Tigers went into the 3-day break for the All-Star game in fine fashion, after a July 3rd, 10-1 thrashing of the Orioles, broken open on a grand slam delivered by Johnny B. Wockenfuss, the finest hit 'n run man in the game (although clearly, he could do more than hit 'n run). Detroit was in a 5-team battle for 1st on the eve of a 4-game series at The Corner with the Yankees beginning August 11. The standings read: *Tied for 1st Detroit – Milwaukee – Baltimore, 1 game out New York, 2.5 games out Toronto*

In game 1 versus the Yanks, Detroit lost a tough one in 10 innings, but repaid the favor the next day, rallying for the tying run in the 9th on a dramatic 2-out Alan Trammell home run, winning in 10 when Parrish doubled & raced home on Herndon's single for the 7-6 win. 50,016 packed Tiger Stadium for the anticipated game 3 pitchers duel between Jack Morris and Ron Guidry, both aces going the full nine as Detroit came from 3-2 down on a Johnny Wockenfuss 2-run homer in the 7th, plus a Glenn Wilson 2-run double in the 8th, to account for the 6-3 final score. New York took the finale 4-1 before leaving town for the trip back to the Bronx, the wonderfully close standings now reading: *Tied for 1st Detroit – Baltimore, 1 game out Milwaukee – New York, 1.5 games out Toronto*

Although Detroit went 27 & 20 the balance of the '83 season, August 14 would be Detroit's final game in first place as the Orioles played at a blistering .700 pace (33 & 14) the rest of the way to surge ahead of the pack. From September 10 on, Detroit was in 2nd place every day thru the season's end, finishing 92

& 70, 6 games behind 98-win Baltimore. Despite falling short of the division title, the Tigers and their fans felt great about their young, improving squad, and how well they played the Orioles in two September series, including pounding Baltimore pitching for 9 runs in each of the last 3 games.

Besides chalking up the team's best winning percentage since that of the '68 Champs, the '83 Tigers had some of the finest individual performances in all of baseball...

For the 1st time in the history of the Gold Glove Award (given to the best defensive player at his position), 3 were awarded to the same team in the same year: Whitaker, Trammell, and Parrish.

Lou was #8 in MVP balloting, won his first of 4 Silver Sluggers, his .320 3rd in the A.L., won first of 3 Gold Gloves, and made first of 5 All-Star teams; Tram was #15 in the MVP race, won 3rd of 4 Gold Gloves, his .319 average an A.L. 4th; Lance came in #9 in MVP voting, made his 3rd All-Star team, won his 3rd Silver Slugger with a league 4th 114 RBIs, 9th 27 homers & 3rd 42 doubles, and won his 1st Gold Glove; Gibby and Herndon tied for A.L. 2nd with 9 triples; Herndon's 182 hits a league 8th; and in total bases Lou was 7th, Lance 8th, and Herndon 10th. Among the pitchers, Morris & Petry were a league 4th & 5th in wins with 20 & 19 respectively; Jack led the A.L. in both 293 innings & 232 strikeouts, 3rd in Cy Young voting (as in '81); Senor Smoke went 9 & 8, 18 saves & 2.81 ERA, earning his 1st & only All-Star team selection.

Optimism for the 1984 season was sky-high!

1984 Wire to Wire

There's a roar in ole' Motown
The Tigers are back and the word's going round
Summer's alive on Trumbull Avenue
Alan, Lance, Jack and Chet with sweet, sweet Lou
Bless you boys

("Bless You Boys" by Curtis Gadson & Loren Woods)

Coming off the 92-win season of 1983, the Tigers - rightly so - felt they were so close to their goal of a World Series Championship that only one or two transactions would get them there. So, the week before Christmas 1983, newly-promoted to GM, Bill Lajoie (Jim Campbell now President) announced Detroit's first significant signing of the free agent era, that of infielder Darrell Evans, coming off an All-Star season with the Giants. Evans knew how to get on base, excelled in the clutch, and – prior to '84 – hit 20 or more homers 6 times. Then, shortly before the 1984 season started, Lajoie pulled the trigger on the move the Tigers hoped would put them over the top: on March 26, they traded to the Philadelphia Phillies two popular and productive players, outfielder Glenn Wilson & man-who-plays-well-everywhere, Johnny B. Wockenfuss, for first baseman Dave Bergman & reliever Willie Hernandez. Bingo!

The 1984 *"Wire-to-Wire"* Tigers held first place from Opening Day until the regular season ended. The last major league team to stay in first from the schedule's start to finish was the 1927 Yankees, while the very first team to go wire-to-wire was the 1887 Detroit Wolverines of Charlie Bennett fame. Guided by Sparky Anderson, the '84 Detroiters were 35 & 5 out of the gate and never looked back, ending 104 & 58 – the most wins ever for a Tiger team. The faithful came out in droves to cheer on their record-setting heroes, only once after May 17 did the team fail to draw at least 26,000. The 2,704,794-attendee total set (until 2007) the all-time franchise high, while drawing more on the road than any other MLB team.

Jack Morris, Dan Petry, and MVP/Cy Young winner Willie Hernandez anchored the pitching staff, while Kirk Gibson, Lance Parrish, Alan Trammell, & Lou Whitaker led the top run producing offense in the league, driving Detroit into the World Series for a date with Tony Gwynn and the San Diego Padres. The '84 Tigers clinched the division at home, the pennant at home, and the World Series at home – the first team to do that since New York's 1969 *Miracle Mets*.

The Tigers opened the '84 season with 5 games on the road, and won all 5. The 4th game took place on the Southside of Chicago in Comiskey Park, Jack Morris on the mound for Detroit. Jack recalled years later for Fox Sports, *"There was one particularly drunk fan, havin' a few pops over the dugout. He was piling up the big 18 ouncers, and about the fourth inning he started getting real vocal. By the sixth inning he started giving me the heckle. I looked up and saw all these zeros on the scoreboard – I didn't even know at that point that I had a no-hitter going, and I couldn't remember any time in my career where I was that deep in the game with a no-hitter. So it was like, Wow! This is pretty cool! When I came off the mound in the seventh inning, the guy was just getting really belligerent, and I told him, 'Quit drinkin'. You're gonna see something great here today, and you gotta stick around for it,' but he didn't make it. He had one more and they kicked him out, so he didn't even get to see the end of it."* With two out in the White Sox 9th, Morris struck out Ron Kittle to complete the 5th no hitter in Tiger history, and first since Jim Bunning no hit the Red Sox at Fenway in 1958.

After the oh-so-close 1983 season, expectations of the team's fans were through-the-roof, and when our boys took the home field for the first time after their 5-0 road trip, the faithful were downright giddy! April 10, 1984, was a glorious, sun-soaked, day in Detroit for the Tigers Home Opener. 51,238 filled the Old Ballyard, sharing the excitement and anticipation of Tiger fans everywhere – and the script could not have been written any better. After visiting Texas grabbed a 1-0 lead in their first, the Tigers responded quickly: Lou & Tram began the bottom of the inning with a pair of walks, as number 3 batter Darrell Evans made his home field inaugural trip to the batter's box wearing the Olde English D. Darrell turned on a pitch from Dave Stewart and, in one of the sweetest sights ever witnessed at The Corner, deposited a 3-run moon-shot into the right-field upper deck overhang, immediately endearing Darrell Evans to Tiger enthusiasts. Detroit tacked on two more runs, including one on a run-scoring single by Tiger-only-two-weeks Dave Bergman, while Dan "Peaches" Petry, outstanding on the hill, went the distance in tossing a 4-hitter while striking out 7 in the Opening Day 5-1 victory.

On the evening of Opening Day 1984, ex-Detroit Lion & current auto dealer Mel Farr is in bed watching the 11 o'clock news. The head of his service department, Johnny Harcourt of St. Clair Shores, is being interviewed live by Channel 7's Diana Lewis in front of Nemo's Bar. The interview is not to promote Mel Farr Superstar's auto dealership, but rather to talk about the Opening Day John just attended. This was a bit of a surprise to Mel as Johnny had called in sick about 16 hours ago. The next morning, Mel walks through the work area of his slightly sunburnt employee. *"John, they say you went to the doctor's yesterday." "Yessir." "Is your doctor's office at Michigan & Trumbull?"* Without missing a beat, Johnny replied, *"First place I'd look for him."* Then Mel grinned at John & said *"Next time, if you want to go to the ballgame, just tell me you want to go to the ballgame."*

Detroit's 18 & 2 April tied the record for best ever MLB 20-game start, and made the Tigers national celebrities, as evidenced by the amazingly large number of Olde English D caps worn at the Kentucky Derby, a heart-warming scene to all Tiger fans in attendance that first Saturday of May '84 at Churchill Downs. On May 24 versus the California Angels, the Tigers won 5-1, and tied the 1916 New York Giants for the major league record of 17 consecutive road victories (Detroit had lost their final '83 road game before winning the first 17 in '84). When the Tigers left Anaheim that night for their flight to Seattle, they had begun the season 35 & 5 overall – the best ever major league record after 40-games.

With the 35 & 5 start, the folks from *Time* magazine paid a visit to Hoot Robinson's Bar. After partaking of some Stroh's 'n Hoot burgers, they sought the proprietor's view on everything from Mickey Cochrane & the Boys of '35 to the current season. Hoot obliged, and *Time* spent several hours chatting up the man & his clientele, shooting photos of everything from Hoot and his staff serving the thirsty patrons, to the Men's Room trough urinal filled with buckets of ice. The plan called for Sparky to grace *Time's* cover, the inside pages devoted to a piece about the Tigers and the tavern with whom the team shared Trumbull Avenue for 50 years, Hoot Robinson's Bar & Grill. And then came the Friday, Saturday & Sunday losses in Seattle: 35 & 5 became 35 & 8, and the magazine cover and the inside spread were cancelled.

DDDDDDDDDDDDDDDDDDDDDDDDDDDDDDDDDDDDDDDDDDDDDDDDDDDDDDDDDDDDDDDDDDDDDDDDDDDD

Detroit started that late-May series in Seattle with an 8.5 game lead over 2nd place Toronto. In 9 days, the lead had shrunk to 4.5 just as Toronto arrived at The Corner for a 4-game series. The June 4 opening battle was one of the most memorable games in a season of memorable games. Pitching were Blue Jays ace Dave Steib at 8 & 0, versus Detroit's Juan Berenguer, 3 & 3. Juan's last start was the 2nd of the 3 Seattle losses, when he was pulled in the 1st inning after surrendering 4 runs and recording only 1 out –

the Steib-Berenguer match-up did not have a calming effect on the jittery Tiger fans. Sure enough, going into the bottom of the 7th, Stieb had baffled the Tiger hitters, allowing only 3 well-spaced hits, while Juan was nicked for a solo shot & a 2-run homer, Detroit in a 0-3 hole. Tiger Johnny Grubb, a clutch-hitting veteran outfielder acquired in '83, hit a short fly for the first out, but then Chet Lemon was hit by a pitch and Dave Bergman singled to give the Tigers their first threat as up stepped Howard Johnson. Ho Jo drove a Dave Steib offering deep into the stands, bringing a roar from the tense crowd, the game suddenly tied at 3 all. Steib was relieved before the third out and, as Willie Hernandez had relieved Berenguer with 2 outs in the top of the inning, the game was now in the hands of the bullpen.

Willie Hernandez was a closer of a different kind, throwing 140 innings in his 80 appearances, tossing more than one inning 45 times. Today, he would be on the mound for 3 full innings, replaced by Senor Smoke with two outs, nobody on, in the top of the 10th. Lopez got the one man he faced, as the 3-3 game went into the bottom of the 10th. Lance Parrish singled off Jimmy Key to lead off, and was bunted to 2nd by Evans. Roy Lee Jackson replaced Key, getting Rusty Kuntz on a grounder back to the mound for out number 2 before issuing a walk to Chester. As Lemon reached first, Dave Bergman stepped up to the plate. *In one of the most dramatic Michigan & Trumbull moments that Tiger fans would ever see,* Roy Lee Jackson quickly got 2 strikes on Bergman, but then Bergie started fouling off pitch after pitch in a battle of wills lasting a full 7 minutes. Finally, Dave Bergman got all of Roy Lee's 13th pitch, sending it deep into the night, depositing it among the fans in the right field overhang for a game winning 3-run homer as the folks in attendance joined those listening to Ernie & Paul or watching Kell & Kaline in jumping up 'n down in jubilation! Coach Dick Tracewski, who by this time had been in the game as a player or a coach for over 30 years, called Bergman's moment, *"the best at-bat I've ever seen."*

Although Toronto won the next two games, Detroit won the series finale as the Tigers broke open a 1-1 tie with a 4-run sixth, the key hit a 3-run homer by Ruppert Jones. Jack Morris went the full 9, giving up only 1 earned run in the 5-3 win while improving his record to 11 & 2. The signing of free-agent Ruppert Jones, another shrewd move by Bill Lajoie, occurred on April 10 while Jones' new Tiger teammates were winning their Home Opener. The 29-year old, an All-Star once each with Seattle & San Diego, and his 215 at bats for Detroit, produced an outsized number of clutch hits – like today's game winner.

Surviving this challenge by the Blue Jays, Detroit expanded their lead to 10 by the end of June and by 12 at the end of July, missing by 1 winning 70 of their 1st 100 games. They were never seriously threatened again. In the midst of this wildly exciting summer, Tiger fans began to do the wave... game after game after game. The wave first gained national attention at Oakland A's home games during the 1981 ALCS, as one person - simultaneous with everyone seated directly in front and behind him or her - abruptly stood up, raised their hands skyward, and at the exact moment that they quickly resumed their seat, the person to their right sprang to their feet and so on, until a rippling wave made its way all around the stadium. Locally, UM football fans at the Big House were doing the wave by the fall of '83. Tiger fans began to make the wave a regular part of each game in '84, soon creating wave variations: slow-motion, double-time, and counter-clockwise. The upper deck might be going slow clockwise, while the lower deck went double-time counter-clockwise. As Detroit wins piled up, the more they appeared on national TV, increasing the number of sports fans nationwide exposed to the wave, and soon the wave exploded across the USA. So, you can credit or blame us, depending on one's perspective.

July '84 road trip to Cleveland: Loooo & daughter Asia post-game

In early-August with the Royals in town, 18-year old Lisa Vollmers of Ann Arbor joined her 4 older brothers for her first trip ever to Tiger Stadium. As the sixth inning was winding down, the brothers explained to Lisa the traditional "seventh inning shift". So, as the top half of the 7th concluded, and the crowd stood to sing "Take Me Out to the Ballgame", Lisa dutifully moved one seat to her left, thus executing the "seventh inning shift". Since she had an end seat, this entailed crossing the aisle into the next section and asking people to move down. As Lisa turned for a nod of confirmation from her siblings, she saw instead all four doubled over in laughter.

While the fun lasted all year in the stands, records continued to be established on the field: the Tigers set the league benchmark by staying in first place all alone for 177 consecutive days. On September 18, a Tuesday evening at The Corner, Milwaukee was in town for the 2nd of a 3-game series – and the Tigers magic number to clinch the East Division was one. The entire state was buzzing with excitement, and 48,810 were on hand, ready for a celebration. The honor of pitching this big game for Detroit went to rookie Randy O'Neal, just called up from AAA Evansville. O'Neal escaped a bases loaded jam in the third, but otherwise was brilliant, in 7 innings of zero runs, 4 hits, and 6 whiffs. The Tigers did just enough offensively, Lou scoring in the 1st on a Parrish grounder, Tram in the 6th on a Parrish single, while Tommy Brookens solo homer in the Detroit 7th increased the lead to 3-0 and had the big crowd howling with anticipation. Willie Hernandez relieved in the 8th and, with the fans refusing to leave their feet, secured the final 6 outs needed to crown Detroit the 1984 East Division Champions, Ernie exclaiming to the radio listeners, *"All of the excitement of the season has broken loose here at Tiger Stadium."*

Post-game, Southgate's Craig Weaks was engulfed in the throng of celebrants crowding Trumbull Avenue, when he looked across the street towards the top floor of the Tiger offices. There in the window, watching the party taking place below, stood Jim Campbell. Craig raised his arm, giving a thumbs up sign to Campbell, who noticed Craig and responded in kind, the team president and the fan sharing a moment of pure delight.

DDDDDDDDDDDDDDDDDDDDDDDDDDDDDDDDDDDDDDDDDDDDDDDDDDDDDDDDDDDDDDDDDDDDDDDDDD

At the conclusion of the regular season, the 104 & 58 Tigers finished 15 games ahead of 2nd place Toronto. Post-season play opened October 2 versus the A.L. West champion K.C. Royals. This was the culmination of an unbelievable season, the wire-to-wire Tigers never out of first place, a Jack Morris no-hitter, the 35 & 5 start, the team's 104 victories setting a single season club record. On September 24, the lead story on the noon news announces that, at 9AM tomorrow morning, tickets for both the American League playoffs AND the World Series would go on sale at Tiger Stadium.

210PM... 19 hours before ticket sales begin, better-half Maggie and I are standing with the hopeful at the ballpark. A USA Today reporter interviews a person in front of us, identified as number 50 in line from where all post-season tickets will be sold, Gate 9 at the intersection of Kaline Drive & Cochrane Avenue, at the northwest corner of Tiger Stadium (yes kids, this is how it was done before computers, smart phones, and Ticket Master). Those lined-up while away the time with small talk, reading, & prognosticating all-things-Tigers with newly-met acquaintances standing nearby.

1130PM... the line runs from Gate 9 east down Kaline Drive to Trumbull, and turns south, reaching a point directly across the street from the Brooks Lumber Yard.

1152PM... East Detroit's Chucky Porta has arrived. If you hope to slide into line at this point, the idea is to do it with little fanfare as fans in this section of the line have been waiting for close to 10 hours. But, the always-colorful Chucky begins shouting to us from 100 yards away, maintaining a loud exuberance until standing beside us. The weight-lifter a couple of folks away threatens to toss the next friend of ours who walks into line over the left-field wall to an early seat.

2AM... a football game breaks out among those in line. Within the shared experience, a fraternity of sorts has formed among the ticket seekers, and an honor system established allowing those who've been there for hours to step out and join the football game without losing their place in line. Chucky mentions that he's going to take a walk to the White Castle, a couple blocks west on Michigan Avenue, for some sliders, but a fella nearby tells him he might want to think twice since a friend of his was recently robbed there. Southgate's Marc Weaks knows none of this, the music turned up loud through his earphones, and he accepts Chucky's invitation to join him for the burger stroll.

237AM... while not yet in view, we smell the White Castles purchased by Chucky.

241AM... Chucky and Marquis return safely with the sliders, shared with Maggie and me.

350AM... with overnight temps in the mid-30s, Maggie has been stretched out on a chaise lounge we've brought, burrowed beneath several blankets. An hour after ingesting the grease-burgers, she turns over on her side, untucking the blankets, freeing the pocket of slider gas that had been ripening undercover. The impact on the pick-up football game is immediate. The guy closest to us had been going out for a pass, which sailed over his head when his knees buckled as the aroma assaulted his nose. Several *"What in God's name?"* were issued, and it was the first time any of us could recall the word "malodorous" used by someone other than a college professor or a janitor. There were no casualties.

701AM... the line now stretches from Kaline & Cochrane in the NW corner of the stadium, east down Kaline Drive to Trumbull, passing Hoot's as it turns south to The Corner at Michigan & Trumbull, and runs 150' west on Michigan. The fans are becoming a bit rowdy as dawn breaks.

845AM... the fella last seen at 3AM collecting empties from those in line, weaves through the crowd, cheered while pounding down a bottle of Wild Irish Rose, the reward for his middle-of-the-night efforts.

9AM... the Ticket Window opens! TV crews are back in force.

927AM... the tickets are in our hands! Pooling our 1 per person limit per game, we have 4 seats for each potential post-season home game, at a cost of $25 per ticket. In line for 19 hours & worth every minute! *Go Tigers! Bless You Boys!*

DDDDDDDDDDDDDDDDDDDDDDDDDDDDDDDDDDDDDDDDDDDDDDDDDDDDDDDDDDDDDDDDDDDDDDDDDDD

To get to the World Series, the Tigers, champs of the East Division, had to defeat the West Division winner, Kansas City Royals. The Tigers regular season win total of 104 was 20 more than the Royals number, so the 3-game sweep in the best-of-5 playoff was not a big surprise. Games 1 & 2 were in KC, the Tigers following up an 8-1 blowout win with a 5-3 victory keyed by Johnny Grubb's 11th inning 2-run double. The Tigers returned home for the A.L. Championship Series-clinching 1-0 victory, featuring a dominant 8-inning pitching performance by Milt Wilcox.

The National League West Division San Diego Padres were the Tigers unexpected Series opponent, not unexpected because they were inferior to the East champion Chicago Cubs in the regular season (92 wins San Diego versus 96 wins Chicago), but because the Padres found themselves in a National League playoff series hole to the Cubs of 2 games to none, and one loss away from elimination. Losing those 2 games by an impressive combined score of 17 to 2 lent an air of certainty to San Diego's demise. By the conclusion of the Cubs-Padres 2nd playoff game, much of Detroit talked excitedly about what seemed to be a certain Tigers-Cubs Series match-up, many checking the Detroit-Chicago Amtrak schedule. These two teams shared a World Series history going back to the early years of the 20th Century: in the 1907 and 1908 Series, the Cubs defeated the Tigers, clinching both times on Detroit's home field of Bennett Park (in fact, until the 2016 Series, Bennett Park was the only field on which the Chicago Cubs ever won a World Series), the Tigers returning the favor by defeating the Cubs in 1935 & 1945. The all-time Tigers versus Cubs Series record was knotted at 2-2, and '84 would be the rubber match. The San Diego Padres, however, spoiled the plan, storming back to win the final 3 wonderfully-entertaining games over the Cubbies, the Padres led by playoff MVP Steve Garvey's clutch hitting.

DDDDDDDDDDDDDDDDDDDDDDDDDDDDDDDDDDDDDDDDDDDDDDDDDDDDDDDDDDDDDDDDDDDDDDDDDDD

World Series 1984

Game 1 San Diego: Still high from the excitement of their heroes' comeback against the Cubs, 57,908 shoe-horned their way into San Diego's Jack Murphy Stadium to witness the first World Series game in San Diego's short (1969 expansion team) history. TVs all across Michigan were tuned to the game, and right out of the starting gate, the Tigers gave those watching reason to smile, courtesy the inseparable duo of Loooo & Tram. Lou Whitaker doubled to lead-off the game, and number 2 batter Alan Trammell singled him home. 2 batters into the Tigers first World Series in 16 years, and its 1 nothing Detroit! Although Lance Parrish & Larry Herndon singled in the first, Tram was thrown out on a steal attempt before those two hits, so Detroit settled for 1 against a shaky Mark Thurmond. Jack Morris, of course, was the Tigers game one starter, but he also had a rough 1st, giving up a 2-run double to Terry Kennedy, and the Padres took a 2-1 lead into the 2nd.

Thurmond & Morris settled down after that, Captain Jack particularly untouchable. Then came the Tigers 5th. The Quiet Man aka Mister Dependable, Larry Herndon, stepped to the plate and followed a Lance Parrish double with a mighty drive, deep into the right-field stands, putting the Tigers back in front, 3-2. That remained the score as San Diego came to bat after the 7th inning stretch, Kurt Bevacqua leading off. Bevacqua sent a line drive bouncing into the right field corner, where Kirk Gibson made a great play on the ball, making a cat-quick throw on the fly, no bounces, to cutoff man Lou Whitaker, who was perfectly positioned beyond the infield dirt in right. Just as Bevacqua was rounding 2nd base, Lou fired a no-bounce laser right on the money to third baseman Marty Castillo, who applied the tag on the head-first sliding baserunner. Instead of the potential game-tying run on third with nobody out, the Padres had one out and no one on. From here, Morris was unhittable, recording the final 8 outs to complete the one-run victory.

Game 2 San Diego: In front of another packed house in Southern California, it was 18-game winner Dan Petry against San Diego's Ed Whitson. Once again, the Tigers' offense showed their teeth in the opening inning, putting 3 runs on the board behind RBI singles from Kirk Gibson and Darrell Evans, sandwiched around a sacrifice fly by Lance Parrish. 7 batters and 5 hits into the game, and Whitson would not face an 8th batter. Reliever Andy Hawkins replaced Ed, getting the third out.

Back home in Detroit, the excitement was sky-high but soon muted, as the Bengal's offense could do nothing with the Padres bullpen, and San Diego batters chipped away at Detroit's lead with single runs in the first & fourth. And then there was the fifth. After getting Steve Garvey on a fly ball to center, Dan Petry walked Craig Nettles and gave up a single to Terry Kennedy. It was then that the entire Great Lakes State got to know Kurt Bevacqua just a little bit better. He deposited a Petry offering over the left-field fence, igniting in Tigers players and the faithful a slow burn by blowing kisses to San Diego fans as he rounded the bases, putting the Padres up 5-3, and launching the fanatics of Jack Murphy Stadium into ecstasy. Dan was immediately pulled, the Tigers' relievers untouchable but the damage was done, the Series all even at 1 game apiece heading to Detroit for the next 3 games.

Game 3 Detroit: History was made today, as Tiger Stadium became the oldest ballpark, at 72-years old, to host a World Series game. That tidbit was of little importance to the 51,970 rocking the revered structure. Today it would be Milt Wilcox facing San Diego's Tim Lollar. For the first time in this Series, the Tigers did not score in the first inning – an oversight they impressively took care of in the second. Tim Lollar must have wondered what Motor City vehicle ran him over. The inning started innocently enough. With two out, Chet Lemon made it to 2nd on his single and a wild pitch – and then the fun began. Marty Castillo had his shining moment with a home run that carried well beyond the left-field fence, putting the home team up 2 to nothing. The dynamic duo of Lou & Tram put another run on the board with a walk & a double. A walk to Gibson and a surprising infield single by Lance Parrish loaded the bases and sent Lollar to the showers. Greg Booker walked the first man he faced, Larry Herndon, forcing in another tally, and the Tigers headed into the third inning up 4 – zero.

Milt gave back a run in the third, but the Tigers immediately matched that run without a single hit, as walks were issued by Booker to Darrell Evans, Lou & Tram, before Gibby was hit by a pitch, forcing a run across the plate. Tigers 5, Padres 1 after 3. Wilcox was stellar after that, mixing his pitches and keeping batters off balance, gutting it out as he so often did, turning the game over to the bullpen after his 6 innings. Although Bill Scherrer was reached for one run, Willie Hernandez came in to get the last out in the 7th, and sailed through the 8th & 9th untouched, securing the Tigers 5-1 win, and 2-1 Series lead.

Game 4 Detroit: Captain Jack will get you high tonight – a natural high by a master at his craft. Game 4 found Jack Morris facing Eric Snow. Although the blustery day at the Corner was reminiscent of many home openers, the Jack Morris & Alan Trammell Show (coming to a Hall of Fame near you) was a fire that melted Snow and gave the Tigers a commanding 3 games to 1 lead. In both the first and the third innings, Alan Trammell hit a 2-run homer, each time – of course – chasing home Lou Whitaker. The 2nd Trammell home run knocked Eric Snow out of the game and, although once again the Padres bullpen was effective, the damage was done. Morris gave up single runs in the 2nd and 9th, in command the entire 4-2 Detroit victory. There would be one more game to play at The Corner.

'84 World Series scenes: GM Jim Campbell crossing Trumbull, Willie Horton in the nacho line

Game 5 Detroit: Owner Tom Monaghan's helicopter, with the Olde English D painted on its bottom, sets down on its Checker Cab Company rooftop pad, cheered by hundreds of fans milling about The Corner pre-game; the sausage stand near Hoot's smelled fantastic; entering the Grand Old Park, its gridlock inside; Willie Horton signed autographs by the nacho stand (retired for 4 years and he looked great! – hey Jim Campbell, need a DH?); Vice-President George Herbert Walker Bush was on hand, the University of Michigan Men's Glee Club beautifully singing our National Anthem, the nervous energy of 51,901 buzzing through the stands. Bush hands the first-pitch-ball to the man standing next to him, Tiger legend George Kell, and Kell tosses out the ceremonial first pitch to Lance Parrish. Let's Go Tigers!

The pitching match-up is Dan Petry versus San Diego's Mark Thurmond. The Tigers, as they have the entire Series, get to the starting pitcher early in the game. Lou opens the 1st with a line single to right, getting the fans crazed immediately, but is forced by Tram. One on one out. Up steps Kirk Gibson, and there it goes! Deep into the Upper Deck right-field stands, a 2-run home run, landing no more than 50' from the bleachers. Sparky sends Gibby out for a curtain call, and the fans go wild! When the 7th batter of the inning, Chet Lemon, hits a run-scoring single, Thurmond is pulled for Andy Hawkins. And, just as they have the entire Series, the Padre's relievers shutdown the Tigers offense. And, just like the earlier games, the barn door is closed too late, as Detroit has staked Petry to a 3-0 lead. When Hawkins enters the game, the Padres starters ERA is 13.94 & the bullpen ERA is 0.38.

The immensely likeable Dan Petry is having a rough go on the mound. As in game 2, the 3-0 lead he enjoys evaporates, and Dan is pulled in the 4th when San Diego knots the score at 3-all. Reliever Bill Scherrer takes over with 2 outs in the 4th, gets the third out and the first 2 of the 5th, when the call goes out to the bullpen for Aurelio Lopez, who makes quick work of the only Padre he faces in the fifth.

It's still 3-3 going into the Tigers' half of the fifth. Kirk Gibson is on third base with one out when Rusty Kuntz pops up to short right-field. RF Tony Gwynn seems to lose the ball for a moment, leaving second baseman Alan Wiggins to make the catch. Despite the fact that the pop is shallow, Gibby knows that Wiggins lacks a strong arm AND is backpedaling, his momentum taking him away from the diamond. Kirk sees his chance, tags up & roars home with a slide well ahead of the throw, giving the Tigers the lead once again, 4-3.

Goose Gossage comes in the ballgame in the 7th. He gets Gibby on a called third strike, a call that turns Kirk livid, and Gibby shares some deep thoughts with the umpire. Gossage is throwing nothing but 96 or 97 mph fastballs under the heading, *"I'll throw my best, you know what's coming, let's see if you can hit it."* The next batter, Lance "Big Wheel" Parish, times his swing beautifully and sends a rocket into the left field lower deck seats, bumping the Tiger lead from 4-3 to 5-3.

NBC announcers Vin Scully & Joe Garagiola and a large section of the crowd cannot believe that Sparky took Aurelio *Senor Smoke* Lopez out of the game going into the 8th inning, replacing him with Willie Hernandez. As great a year as Willie had (9 & 3, 1.92 ERA, 32 of 33 saves – the only saved missed was when an inherited runner on third scored on a sac fly), Lopez was on fire today – the last 14 pitches (21 of 25 total) he threw were strikes. *"You just wind him up, he threw you a strike,"* said Joe Garagiola. Lopez faced 9 batters, struck out 4, and allowed no runners.

The third batter that Willie faces, Kurt Bevacqua, hits a solo home run to draw the Padres within one run, 5 to 4. Nervous boos from the crowd cut their way through the stadium hum, filtering down to the field, in agreement with the announcers' assessment of Sparky's decision to pull Senor Smoke.

Former ('63-'66) Tiger manager, Charlie Dressen, gets nationwide mention on the Series broadcast: when a Padre chops a foul ball straight down at the batter's box, Scully & Garagiola both comment, *"That's a worm killer – that's what Charlie Dressen used to say."* Hernandez picks off Luis Salazar, the potential tying run, with 2 out in the 8th, and the ballpark explodes. The conga line of vendors, weaving their way through the upper deck bleachers, underscores the carnival atmosphere that has enveloped the Old Ballyard.

The 8th opens with the Detroiters clinging to their one-run lead. Neither players nor fans want to see this game slip away, and have to go back to San Diego for a 6th, and maybe a 7th, game. Marty Castillo works Goose for a walk to open the Tiger 8th. Lou lays down a sacrifice bunt towards Craig Nettles at third, who fires the ball to 2nd in an attempt to get the lead runner. The throw may have been to the base soon enough, but inexplicably Padre 2nd sacker Gary Templeton did not have his foot on the bag, so Castillo & Whitaker are both safe. Trammell bunts the runners over, leaving it 2nd & 3rd with one out and Gibby coming to bat.

Gibby waiting for THE pitch from Gossage!

With the base open, San Diego Manager Dick Williams signals to his catcher for an intentional walk to Gibson, to set up a possible double play. Broadcasters Scully & Garagiola have been calling that one, *"You gotta believe he's going to walk him."* Gossage, however, shakes off catcher Terry Kennedy, prompting a confab on the mound with Manager Williams, Kennedy & Gossage. Goose is telling them *"I've got this guy – I'm gonna strike him out."* While the meeting on the mound takes place, Scully is recalling, *"You know what's interesting. Kirk Gibson made his major league debut, his very first at bat in the big leagues, against Goose Gossage…"* Garagiola pipes in, *"That's a great way to break in,"* before Scully continues, *"and Gossage struck him out on 3 pitches."* Garagiola added, *"He blew him away, Sparky says."* Vin wrapped it up, *"Maybe because of that, Goose is telling Williams, 'I can get him' – well, we'll see."* Scully is back to the play-by-play, *"Ball one. The infield is up. They give Gibson the left-field foul line. And **THERE IT GOES**!!!"* Goose-busters! Gibson has absolutely crushed the Gossage fastball, a no-doubt-about-it, 3-run homer, into Norm Cash Country, deep in the right-field upper deck. 8-4 Detroit.

The Old Ballyard is going berserk! Gibby has his right arm victoriously raised, fist clenched, as he rounds 2nd for 3rd. All around is bedlam! At the plate, Gibby is nearly breaking wrists with his high-fives. Both arms are raised, and Gibby is jumping up 'n down on the way to the dugout from home plate, facing the crowd in the lower deck between home & third, shouting for joy! Now in the dugout, Gibby is still giving thunderous high-fives, almost taking off Tommy Brookens' hand, before being wrapped in a bear hug from Darrell Evans. What a beautiful sight to behold! Lost in the splendid madness, and of which he could care less at this moment, is that Gibby's 5 runs-batted-in for the day (a 2-run homer in the first, plus his 3-run missile in the 8th) is only one off of the World Series record.

"The saddest words of tongue and pen – what might have been for San Diego," Vin Scully paraphrases John Greenleaf Whittier's classic line as the crowd begins to cover the band Steam with the Michigan & Trumbull rendition of *"Na-na-na-na, na-na-na-na, hey-hey-hey, goodbye!"* The 9th inning is about to begin as variations of the wave – slow and to the left in the lower deck, while above the upper deck is fast and to the right – erupt.

The Tigers are 3 outs away from their first World Championship since 1968. Gary Templeton leads off San Diego's 9th and grounds to Trammell, who tosses to Dave Bergman at first. One down. Bruce Bochy, making his first appearance this Series, slaps a base hit to left-field. Alan Wiggins pops a foul that Lance Parrish catches right in front of the Tiger dugout. One out to go. Tony Gwynn hits a fly ball down the left-field line, and as Larry Herndon races towards the foul line, the final out of the 1984 World Series settles into his glove, clinching for the Detroit Tigers the 4th Series title in their history! Bless You Boys! A deafening roar serves as the backdrop as the Tigers race from the dugout to celebrate on the infield. How perfect that the first person future Hall-of-Fame pitcher Jack Morris hugs in this mob scene is the man who will be inducted into Cooperstown with him 34 years later, Alan Trammell.

Herndon snags the final out as the team explodes from the dugout   *Parrish douses mentor Freehan*

In the San Diego dugout, Champ Summers is the only Padre sitting on the top step, taking in all the commotion in the ballpark where he had the best playing days ('79 .313 with 20 homers, '80 .297 with 17 homers) of his career. Champ Summers was a Detroit fan favorite, and the man with the greatest baseball name of all-time, in the author's opinion. There is a sad look in Champ's eyes, likely because his team just lost the Series, but perhaps thinking he could be, should be, out there celebrating with his old teammates, had not the Tigers traded Champ before the '82 season for Enos Cabell. Today will be the last time that 38-year old Champ Summers will ever wear a major league baseball uniform.

The post-game celebration headlined newspapers across the country, the achievements of the team taking a back seat to the rowdy behavior in the streets and the police car flipped over and set on fire. The badly-behaved missed the special moments that took place, including those enjoyed inside the walls of 77-year old Hoot Robinson's bar. Celebrations among friends mixed with those among strangers, dear friend Chucky Porta and the author toasting with a Vietnam veteran we'd just met. The vet, intoxicated by the joy of the season, the day, and the endless rounds consumed, hugged us and declared, *"The Tigers winning tonight made that whole war worthwhile!"*...

Vietnam Vet's comments elicit expressive Chucky reaction at Hoots celebration

1985 – 1987; Norm Joins the Angels & One Last Post-Season at The Corner

I'm a swinger, and I'll swing, swing, swing
I'm a singer, and I'll sing, sing, sing

("Norm Cash Show Theme Song" sung by Norm)

As the sun broke through the clouds above Tiger Stadium, the chilled faithful watched the raising of the 1984 World Series Championship banner above the Old Ballyard. On a cold, April 8, Opening Day 1985 at The Corner, the joyous fans seemed oblivious to the occasional blowing snow and falling temperatures. Cleveland, the foe in the back-n-forth tussle, led 4-3 going into the Tigers' 8th, when Detroit scored two runs on a single by rookie Chris Pittaro, one of 3 hits by Sparky's latest "can't miss" prospect, and a sac fly by Lou Whitaker. In his 6th consecutive Opening Day start, Jack Morris went 8 innings to pick up the win as Guillermo (don't call me Willie anymore) Hernandez threw a perfect 9th.

Cleveland 100 003 000 – 4 runs/6 hits/1 error

Detroit   000 120 02x – 5 runs/10 hits/0 errors

Attendance 51,180; weather – partly sunny, snow flurries & 30; time – 2 hours & 49 minutes

In addition to the win & the raising of the banner, the game was notable for two reasons: (1) It was the start of Sparky's short-lived experiment of moving All-Star second baseman Lou Whitaker out of position to third base to make room at 2nd for Pittaro and (2) the entertaining spectacle of the local Channel 2 News Crew, while interviewing fans in the bleachers, asking Southgate's Marc Weaks his opinion of the Tigers new L.A. (i.e., Low Alcohol) beer policy.

First, Chris Pittaro: This young man made such an impression on Sparky during spring training that Anderson thought it wise to break up the finest double-play combination in the majors, moving (the amazingly cooperative) Lou to third while installing Pittaro at 2nd. Sparky told reporters that, *"Chris Pittaro has the chance to be the greatest 2nd baseman who ever lived!"*, a group that includes, to name a few - with their lifetime batting averages - Charlie Gehringer (.320), Nap Lajoie (.339), Rod Carew (.328), Jackie Robinson (.311), Rogers Hornsby (.358), and Lou Whitaker (.283 from his '77 rookie year through '84, plus A.L. Rookie of the Year & 2-time Gold Glove winner). The 1985 Opener was the high-water mark for Chris Pittaro, whose star and batting average fell quickly, limiting him to 28 games in '85, and earning Chris a ticket to Minnesota in a January 1986 trade for the slight upgrade of utility man Dave Engle. Pittaro would hit a combined .182 in two seasons of limited action for the Twins before retiring at the end of the 1987 season and falling a successful baseball career short of Cooperstown.

Second, Southgate's Marc Weaks: After the raucous behavior on the streets of Detroit six months ago, after game 5 of the '84 World Series, the Tigers decided to not only limit beer sales to two per person, but to also replace real beer with something called Low Alcohol or L.A. Beer. It was the unanimous opinion of all asked on Opening Day that L.A. Beer's 2 main characteristics were (1) a horrible taste and (2) giving headaches to those who drink it. Some folks felt a bit stronger than others about L.A. Beer, & one of those was Marc Weaks. Late in the game, as the TV 2 News crew moved through the bleachers looking to interview fans about this new ballpark beer, they asked Marc his feelings on the subject, and he obliged. In a proclamation completely devoid of expressions that could be aired on the upcoming 6PM newscast, Marc wove a colorful-cuss-word-tapestry into a commentary that ran close to a minute, as both the interviewer and the cameraman stood stunned, their mouths agape, with Marc's friends bent over in laughter. It has always been the assumption that this never-shown-on-the-air treasure is kept in a special place at TV 2, brought out for the amusement of the staff at retirements, holiday parties, and other special occasions.

DDDDDDDDDDDDDDDDDDDDDDDDDDDDDDDDDDDDDDDDDDDDDDDDDDDDDDDDDDDDDDDDDDDDDDDD

The '85 squad broke fast from the gate, sweeping the season opening series with Cleveland, concluded with a wild 11-10 affair that Detroit won with single runs in the 8th, 9th, and with no hits & 3 walks in the 10th. After traveling to Kansas City for a two-game sweep behind Jack Morris & Dan Petry, the team came home to host Milwaukee. Walt Terrell, acquired from the Mets for Howard Johnson late last year, pitched brilliantly in a game one, 2-1, win as Detroit improved to 6 & 0 on the young season. It started to look like 1984 all over again, a delightful prospect.

Dreams of an undefeated season were dashed the next day, a 2-0 Milwaukee victory, beginning a mediocre run of .500 ball through May and into early-June. The bullpen was not the weapon in '85 that it was in '84. Hernandez was good, but not the automatic machine of the championship season, while Aurelio Lopez & his 10 & 1 record in '84 to went south to 3 & 7, surrendering 5 runs every 9 innings. The starting staff was bolstered by the June 20 acquisition (for minor leaguer Duane James) of native son Frank Tanana. Frankie had lost the flaming fastball that he once possessed, and had become a crafty pitcher, relying on a variety of junk balls delivered at varying speeds with great movement high 'n low, and in 'n out, effectively keeping hitters off balance. Now known nationally as *Frankie Tanana Daiquiri*, thanks to that nickname bestowed upon him by ESPN's Chris Berman, he was an important cog in the rotation, along with Morris, Petry, & Terrell, producing a combined earned run average in the low 3s.

Walt Terrell replaced in the rotation 36-year old Milt Wilcox. After Milt's major league debut as a 20-year old for Sparky Anderson's Cincinnati Reds in 1970, trades to Cleveland and the Cubs preceded his mid-'76 purchase by the Tigers. From 1978 through 1984, Milt was a dependable third starter, producing victory totals of 13, 12, 13, 12, 12, 11, and 17. The 17 wins of '84 came at a high price, pitching through a terrible arm pain, made possible by taking 7 cortisone shots over the course of the season, risking his health and possibly any future chance of pitching in order to contribute to the special year Detroit was experiencing. After the 17 regular season victories, Milt was outstanding in the ALCS clinching game 3 over the Kansas City Royals, hurling 8 innings of 2-hit ball in the 1-0 win; he followed up the Tigers only World Series loss with a big game 3 performance, throwing 6 innings of 1-run ball in the 5-2 victory. About Milt's ALCS game, Darrell Evans commented, *"He was the third guy and different from the two power guys, Jack Morris and Dan Petry. Then Milt comes in and throws all his changing speeds. He knew when to walk a guy, when to challenge a guy, and then you get him in a big-game situation like that one and he pitches as good a game as has ever been pitched, probably. He went through so much for us and never complained."* Pitching through the pain of '84 took its toll on Milt's arm, and after only 8 games and a 1 & 3 '85, he was shut down for the year in June. The Tigers released Wilcox in December, and he gave it another shot with Seattle, signing with them in time for the '86 campaign. The Milt of old was no more, and after going 0 & 8 with a 5.50 ERA in 13 games, the Mariners released Wilcox on June 14, 1986, ending his major league career.

DDDDDDDDDDDDDDDDDDDDDDDDDDDDDDDDDDDDDDDDDDDDDDDDDDDDDDDDDDDDDDDDDDDDDDDD

The dissatisfaction with the L.A. Low Alcohol beer served at Tiger Stadium effective with the '85 Opener expressed itself most among the upper deck bleacher fans, best known by their nickname of "Bleacher Creatures". You mess with their beer, and trouble will follow. A restlessness among this segment of the faithful had been festering since Opening Day, and bubbled over during the Saturday, May 3, 7-1 win over the White Sox. As usual among these denizens, batted beach balls filled the air, insults shouted down upon the opposing team's centerfielder positioned directly below, and chants hurled back 'n forth among various Bleacher Creature sections. One such chant mimicked the popular Miller Lite beer commercial, shouts of *"Taste Great!"* eliciting a reply of *"Less Filling!"* But today, the Creatures were a bit more unruly than usual, the chant revised to *"F*** You!"* with a responding *"Eat S***t!"*

Livid, Jim Campbell issued a post-game press release noting, *"The Detroit Tigers will not condone such activities",* and that the upper deck bleachers were closed indefinitely. The team decided to reopen the closed bleachers before the end of May and, although this bad behavior would resurface every once in a while, Campbell never closed these seats again. Unfortunately, the L.A. beer policy lasted longer, a few seasons longer, then the shuttered bleachers did.

In the month leading up to the 1985 All-Star game, the Tigers were rolling, closing to within 3 & ½ games of East Division leading Toronto at the break. The big bats thundered, with Parrish, Gibson, and Evans all on a pace to knock in 90 to 100 runs, Tanana provided a dependable 4th starter, and the bullpen settled down. But from mid-July on, the Tigers cooled off and they could not keep pace with surging Toronto. As August turned into September, Detroit was 12 out and fading. 38-year old Darrell Evans tried to carry the club with his 40 home runs, becoming both the oldest player in MLB history to lead the league in homers AND the only player to hit 40 homers in a season in both leagues. But despite Darrell's heroics, 1985 would not be 1984, and when the season concluded, the Tigers 85 & 77 record was good for third place, 15 games behind the Blue Jays.

DDDDDDDDDDDDDDDDDDDDDDDDDDDDDDDDDDDDDDDDDDDDDDDDDDDDDDDDDDDDDDDDDDDDDDDDDDDDDD

Johnny Harcourt of St. Clair Shores and Michael McBride, a Son of Ireland, attended one of those hot August night games in '85. Perhaps cause-and-effect of the L.A. Beer policy, Mikey stowed a pint of whiskey down his butt crack to get it past security. In the 90-degree heat Mikey, a good 300 pounds, started to fidget 'n squirm, knocking Johnny out of his seat in the process. It turned out that the bottle cap had split and booze was running down Mikey's hind quarters. He was now getting an education on the effect of alcohol on open cracks. After Mikey excused himself, Johnny came upon him in the men's room, seeing Michael's pants down around his ankles and his butt wedged under the running cold water in the sink. Johnny figured nothing like a good alcohol burn to get the hemorrhoids up. Post-game, the two headed to the Anchor Inn Bar, where Mikey provided unscheduled entertainment for the regulars, perched on a bar stool with his bare behind up against the cold blasts from the air conditioner.

DDDDDDDDDDDDDDDDDDDDDDDDDDDDDDDDDDDDDDDDDDDDDDDDDDDDDDDDDDDDDDDDDDDDDDDDDDDDDD

As 1986 began, the Tigers played their first season since 1978 without Aurelio "Senor Smoke" Lopez. After his incredible 1984 regular season, 10 & 1/2.94 ERA/14 saves, he elevated his game in the deciding World Series game 5, toying with the Padres in as dominating a performance as you will see in a Series game, 2.1 innings of no hits, no walks, and 4 strikeouts. As impressive as those stats are, they did not do Smoke's performance justice. Conversely, Aurelio fared badly when called upon in 1985 and, at 37 years of age and his contract up, the Tiger decided not to pursue him for '86. Adios, old friend.

Gibson's two 1986 Opening Day homers were the first by a Tiger since Johnny Groth in 1949

The Tigers spun their wheels early in '86: April 10 & 9, May 13 & 13, June 14 & 15. A solid July through late-August, capped off with a 14-0 blasting of Seattle on August 23, brought them to 67 & 58 and within 6 games of first place Boston, but they then dropped 6 of 7, and could never make a serious run after that. The bullpen was the Achilles heel, and many fans were singling out for blame a hero of '84 and the face of the relief staff, Willie Hernandez. His ERA wasn't bad at 3.55, and there were a few blown saves, but mostly Willie was suffering from "Norm Cash Syndrome": he'd made the mistake of achieving near perfection his first year with Detroit, and that's what fans now expected. Sue Klaus of St. Clair Shores summed up the feelings of many towards Hernandez by '86, *"Willie is like an obscure rock band that has had one number 1 hit – we should never have heard from him again."*

Detroit's 87 & 75 earned them a 3rd place finish, 8.5 games behind the Red Sox and their ace, Cy Young winner & MVP, Roger Clemens (24 & 4/2.48), in the East Division. The Tigers had the unique distinction of having all 5 of their infielders hit at least 20 home runs each: catcher Lance Parrish at 22, 1B Darrell Evans 29, 2B Lou Whitaker 20, SS Alan Trammell 21, and 3B Darnell Coles 20 (in Darnell's first & only full season with Detroit). Along with Kirk Gibson's 28, Detroit led the majors with 198 homers. The American League All-Star roster featured 3 Tigers: Lance Parrish, Lou Whitaker, and for the third year in a row and the final time, Willie Hernandez. Glaring in the roster's absence was Jack Morris, who finished '86 at 21 & 8, 6 shutouts, with a 3.27 ERA.

DDDDDDDDDDDDDDDDDDDDDDDDDDDDDDDDDDDDDDDDDDDDDDDDDDDDDDDDDDDDDDDDDDDDDDDDD

5-time All-Star, only player in the American League to have over 20 homers every year from 1961-1969, Norman Dalton Cash...

October 13, 1986 was one week after the Tigers season finale and just a few months after Norm Cash made it one last time to Michigan & Trumbull, participating in an Old Timers Game. On that October 13 night, tear-choked sports reporter Larry Adderly announced to Detroit's Channel 7 viewers that Norm died the evening before on Northern Michigan's Beaver Island. Norm had been out with his wife and a friend, first to dinner and then on to the Shamrock Bar, afterward walking out to the dock to check on his cabin cruiser. It had rained that day and, wearing his traditional cowboy boots, Norm slipped on the soaked pier, hit his head, and drown in the waters of Lake Michigan. He was only 51 years old.

9 days before Norm died, he was inducted into the Hall of Honor of his college alma mater, Sul Ross State University, in his native Texas. Norm was All-Lone Star Conference in both baseball (batting .426 & .441) and football (setting the single season rushing record of 1,255 yards). After his senior year of 1955, Cash was drafted by both the Chicago Bears (as a halfback) & the Chicago White Sox, choosing baseball. In '61, Norm was inducted into the NAIA Hall of Fame; in '01, he was inducted into the Texas Sports HOF.

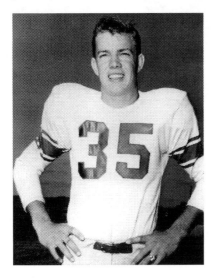

"I've never seen a first baseman any better at tracking foul fly balls down the line than Norm Cash"
– to quote just about everybody

Norm was one of the best defensive first basemen in major league history. All-time among American League first basemen, Cash ranked fourth in assists (1,317), tenth in double plays (1,347) and was fifth in games at first base (1,943). In the 1960s, Norm was the single season champ for putouts in '61, fielding percentage in '64 & '67, and assists '65-'67. Cash is the Tigers career defensive record holder at first base in games, putouts, assists, and double plays, breaking marks set by Hank Greenberg. Norman had a .991 fielding percentage at first base in his career.

The Tiger locker room from 1960 through 1974 was always a place where fine country & western songs could be heard, many emitting from the lungs of Norm Cash. Norman was loved by Tiger fans & he loved 'em right back, entertaining folks during and after his playing days. On WXON's early-70s *The Norm Cash Show,* besides singing his "I'm a Swinger" theme song, Cash chatted up friends from the world of sports. In 1976, Norm was a color commentator for ABC's nationally televised *Monday Night Baseball.* He suffered a stroke in 1979, recovering enough to resume providing color commentary from '81 through '83, this time locally for ON-TV broadcasts of Tiger games, until resigning after what may have been a 2nd stroke caused him to slur his words.

Al Kaline said of his old friend, *"Norm never let anyone get down. He was such a happy-go-lucky guy. He made everyone feel good."*

Whitey Herzog, before moving on to a successful managerial career, including a 1982 World Series championship with St. Louis, was an outfielder and first baseman for 8 major league seasons, ending his playing days with a single year as a Tiger in 1963 when he roomed with Cash. *"There was nothing Norm Cash couldn't do"* said Whitey. Alluding to Norm's late hours, *"When Norm is your roommate, its' like having your own room."*

A Lindell A.C. regular calls the bar, saying he's run out of gas on the highway, and could someone help. 40 minutes later, Norm Cash pulls up next to the man's car with a can of gasoline. Lindell bar co-owner Jimmy Butsicaris said, *"Norm had about a big a heart as you'll ever see on a person. Normie was one of the top 5 ballplayers as far as human goodness was concerned. When it came time to speak at a charity dinner, Norm was always there. He would just say 'when' & 'where' when it came to giving to others."*

John Steck of Ann Arbor had the honor of attending a University of Michigan football game with Norm. *"At our family house was a pre-game gathering of our good friends, Fat Bob 'the singing plumber' Taylor and his wife, Carol, and a couple of their friends... Mr. & Mrs. Norm Cash! Norm was in rare form, telling jokes in his Texas drawl and drinking to beat the band, as I was (just to be polite, of course). By the time we got to the game, we were all pretty happy (I'm sure that Michigan won, but that's just an assumption), and of course didn't stop drinking during the game. We brought beer, but ran out by halftime, so I was sent out of the stadium to buy more beer at a place across the street. We finished another six-pack by game's end, and thus solidified my opinion that Norm Cash was the greatest Tiger that ever lived!! At least that's what I remember."*

His old GM Jim Campbell once said of Norm, *"He might have gotten his nights and days mixed up now and then, but I've never known a ballplayer who got as much fun out of playing baseball. Norm was one of the more entertaining guys I've ever been around. He got along with the fans, the media... with everybody. Norm was one of the greatest players to ever wear a Tiger uniform."*

Willie Horton said of Norm, *"We used to call him the John Wayne of baseball – he always had a Marlboro and a Budweiser."*

Ray Lane told the story of when Norm had singled in a game against the Orioles, *"Boog Powell was playing first base for the Birds, Norm getting a bit of a lead... line drive to Powell. Cash is 20' off the bag. Before Powell steps on the bag to double-up Norm, Cash calls time-out* (Ray Lane making the "T" sign with his hands). *Powell was on his knees laughing"* (it's believed that Powell tagged the bag first).

The most famous Norm Cash story, of course, took place July 15, 1973. The California Angels were the opponents at The Corner, and Nolan Ryan was pitching what he described as, *"Of all the no-hitters I had thrown, that one by far was the most dominating"* (Ryan threw 7 career no-hitters, 3 more than Sandy Koufax, second on the list). When Norm came up to bat in the ninth, Nolan had already struck out 17 Tigers – including Cash twice – and had one more out to go for his 2nd no-hitter of the season. Umpire Ron Luciano noticed Cash wasn't using an authorized bat, but rather a table leg – or a piano leg, depending on what old teammate is telling the story. What everyone agrees on is that the ump informed Norm he could not bat with the makeshift lumber, and Norm replied, *"What difference does it make? I'm not going to hit him anyways,"* grabbed a regulation bat, and proceeded to pop out to short to end the game and seal Ryan's no-hitter. Norm turned to the ump and said, *"See, I told ya."* Norman's at bat against Nolan Ryan was honored in a 1992 episode of *"The Simpsons"* when a character named Carl Carlson brags to teammates about his piano leg bat in an episode entitled "Homer at the Bat."

In 2013, Gates Brown reminisced about his friend and teammate...

"He enjoyed every game... lived life on the field as well as off the field. Norm Cash... you know, a lot of days he'd come into the clubhouse, I swear, drunk... the first thing he'd do is go in the trainer's room, drink all the Pepto-Bismol, then in the shower, a hot shower then a cold shower, and he'd tell the

pitchers, 'If you can hold 'em for 7, I'll be ready', and I'll be damned if he didn't win a few games that way. He'd hit a home run... you don't know what it's like to play with a guy like Norm Cash. But I guarantee every team needs a guy like Norm Cash to win."

DDDDDDDDDDDDDDDDDDDDDDDDDDDDDDDDDDDDDDDDDDDDDDDDDDDDDDDDDDDDDDDDDDDDDDDDDDD

One old favorite returns, while a current one leaves: John Hiller visits Grand Rapids from his U.P. home, while Lance Parrish departs Detroit for Philadelphia

The Tiger Express opened 1987 missing a Big Wheel, the nom de guerre of Lance Parrish. Lance turned down Detroit's contract offer, became a free agent, and signed with the Philadelphia Phillies. Back issues had sent Parrish to the disabled list for a short time in '85 and longer in the 2nd half of '86, an issue cited by Detroit in contract negotiations that became contentious, prompting Lance to look elsewhere, and culminating with him becoming a Philly on March 13, 1987. Fortunately for the Tigers, while Lance was injured after the '86 All-Star game, they acquired a steady hand behind the plate from St. Louis, Mike Heath. Even more fortuitous for the team's 1987 fortunes, a young catcher in the organization had a fine 1986 at AAA Nashville and was ready to be promoted to Detroit, Matt Nokes.

Opening Day 1987 was a chilly, sunny, gorgeous day in Detroit. It was Monday, April 6, and Jack Morris was on the mound for his 8th consecutive Opener starting assignment, facing the visiting New York Yankees with 51,315 rabid fans cheering him on. The opposing pitcher was Dennis Rasmussen, coming off of an outstanding 18 & 6 season.

An unearned run in the 4th gave the Yankees a 1-0 lead, and it stayed that way until the Detroit 6th as Larry Herndon led off. What was about to happen would be talked about for years to come as one of the most memorable sports moments anyone attending that day would ever recall. Sitting among a group of 50 friends in the centerfield upper deck bleachers, we saw Larry swing at a Dennis Rasmussen offering, and the ball rocket off his bat, heading in our direction. It seemed to be picking up speed as we and everyone around us began yelling. Incredibly, the ball seemed to still be rising as it slammed into the facing of the upper deck right in front of us, making a sound on impact as if a cannon had been fired.

Herndon's monster shot tied the game at 1 and, although it could not save Detroit from losing 2 to 1 in 10 innings, the home run made headlines in the evening news and the next day's newspapers. *United Press International* reported the home run as, *"One of the very few to reach the dead center field upper deck in Tiger Stadium. In its own way it was as impressive as any of the over-the-roof shots."* The Detroit *Free Press* featured an overhead view of Larry's mammoth scorcher, with an arrow added to follow the path of the homer. *ESPN.com* listed the blow within its *Top Ten Legendary Sports Stories*, including many fans characterizing it as the hardest hit ball they'd ever witnessed, one calling it *"The hardest line shot I've seen in 40 years of watching baseball – I have no doubt that it was the longest home run EVER hit that did not exceed 100' in height off the ground"* and another saying *"Had it not hit the facade, the ball would've traveled 600'."*

Larry Herndon had an interesting 1987. Although losing playing time in the outfield to Pat Sheridan, a free agent acquisition, in his 89 games Larry hit a team-high .324 with a .520 slugging percentage. Of his 9 homers, the first and the last would be the subject of conversation for a very long time.

DDDDDDDDDDDDDDDDDDDDDDDDDDDDDDDDDDDDDDDDDDDDDDDDDDDDDDDDDDDDDDDDDDDDDDDDDDDDDD

The combination of Detroit's mediocre 7 & 11 start and Milwaukee's red-hot 17 & 1 start had the Tigers 10 games out of first before April was done. By May 11, 30 games into the '87 season, Detroit's record was an ugly 11 & 19, good for 9.5 games out of first. *Then the season changed suddenly.* The team won 13 of their next 15 games, capped off by a 15-7 slugfest win over the Twins, pulling within 5 of the first place Yanks and leaping past Milwaukee (who experienced an amazing turnaround, going 5 & 20 after opening the season 17 & 1). From Detroit's 30-game start of 11 & 19, they played .660 ball the rest of the way, winning 87 & losing 45; through June & July they inched closer and closer to the two division leaders, New York and Toronto. And, as in '84, the bullpen had become a strength: rookie right-hander Mike Henneman gained Sparky's confidence, pairing with Willie Hernandez to give Detroit a strong, righty-lefty, one-two punch. In 55 games, Henneman went 11 & 3 with 7 saves and a 2.98 ERA.

On August 7 at The Corner, the Yankees provided the Friday night opposition. The pitching match-up did not seem to be in the Tigers favor, with Detroit rookie Jeff Robinson squaring off against the Yanks 14 & 6 Rick Rhoden. In Robinson's previous outing, 5 days before against these same Yankees at the Bronx, Jeff was knocked out of the game before the end of the third inning as New York tagged him for 4 runs, his ERA rising to 5.15. Tonight, it started out like more of the same. In the 1st, the Yankees loaded the bases with 1 out, but Robinson struck out the next two batters to strand all 3 runners. In the second, he gave up singles to the first two hitters, but got the next 3 to leave those two runners stranded – those three 2nd inning outs represented the first of 24 consecutive outs that Jeff Robinson rang up, as he tossed perfect frames in the 3rd through the 9th innings in an 8-0 Tiger win that pulled them within 1.5 games of first place Toronto and 1 game back of second place New York.

For this Jeff Robinson gem, the vast majority of our group parked, as usual, at Irene Sember's lot on Elizabeth Street, behind Hoot Robinson's Trumbull Avenue bar. One friend, Brian "Life" Vittes of Oak Park, took a different tack, parking north of I-75. During the game, he was touting the virtues of his decision to seek out a free parking spot versus paying $3 to park at Irene Sember's, or any other pay-to-park, lot. No more forking over cash to park on game day for him. Meeting at a friend's later that same day, Life arrived a bit tardy, cursing *"the addicts who knocked out my driver's side window to get $3 in change,"* ironically the exact cost to park at Irene Sember's lot.

Born in 1922, Irene Sember resided at 1348-54 W. Elizabeth Street, one block east of Hoot's and one block north of Nemo's Bar. Surrounding Irene's well-kept home was her green-as-Tiger-Stadium lawn and her garden, a more gorgeous one in Corktown could not be found, and to the east of the garden, Irene's 60-car lot. Since 1970, parking at Irene's for a Tiger game had been a cherished tradition. Vid Marvin of Ann Arbor pulled in at Irene's with a couple of cold beers on the front seat. Irene said, *"Hon, I can put those in my refrigerator so they're good for you after the game."* Touched by her concern, Vid replied *"Thank you Irene, but I'm going to finish them now."* As Vid recounts the story with a warm, faraway, smile, one gets the impression that were Irene not 3 decades older than Vid, he might have proposed to her on the spot.

Irene is fiercely loyal to her regulars, always remembering each one, ensuring that they have a place to park at the busiest times, especially on Opening Day. One Opener, a 20-something, hot-shot stranger tried to muscle his fancy car into the lot, and Irene ran at him with a steady stream of barking to *"Get out! Today is for my regulars!"* with several customers right beside her, until he backed out to the cheers of her tailgating patrons. The loyalty Irene showed to her regulars came back to her several times over: Birmingham's Laz Surabian parked for a game somewhere other than Irene's, and recalled a one-way conversation later that evening with Southgate's Marc Weaks, *"He chastised me for parking at the Checker Cab Co. instead of at Irene's, letting me have it for a good ten minutes. I never made that mistake again."*

Irene Sember among just a few of her many fans

Bill Lajoie felt that one more piece needed to be added to the roster in order to push Detroit over the East Division finish line. So, on August 12, Lajoie sent 20-year old, minor league pitching prospect John Smoltz to the Atlanta Braves for veteran hurler Doyle Alexander. The trade was a difference-maker for the 1987 Tigers playoff hopes: as a Tiger, Alexander was an amazing 9 & 0 with a 1.53 ERA. Although John Smoltz would go on to have a Hall of Fame career with Atlanta, very few Tiger fans had ever heard of John when this trade was made, and even fewer questioned its wisdom at the time; what we do know is that Lajoie traded a promising prospect, but by no means a certain star, for a pitcher who went 9 & 0 for the Tigers in a year they won the division by one game.

Sparky Anderson sat for an August 1987 interview with WJR's J.P. McCarthy, with the Tigers one-game behind Toronto. J.P. said, *"Sparky, you told me in May, when the Tigers were floundering near last place, beginning the year 11 wins & 19 losses, that just wait, in September we'll be in it, Toronto will be in it, and the Yankees will be in it – well, it's not even September yet, and here you are".*

"Well Joe, when we left camp, the coaches and I had a very good feeling about this team as a group. Sometimes you can't go position-by-position. This is my best club ever for all-around people. They don't dwell on a loss – they have the best outlook. I think the best thing for me to do is stay out of their way. They know what their job is, and they know how to go about it."

The loss of catcher & clean-up batter Lance Parrish to the Phillies was covered nicely by the emergence this year of Matt Nokes (.289, 32 homers, & 87 RBIs earning him the Silver Slugger Award) & and the fine play of veteran Mike Heath as back-up catcher (in 270 at bats, .281, 8 homers, 33 RBIs), getting 40 home runs & 120 RBIs out of that position.

With the power loss of Parrish, Sparky decided to bat Alan Trammell at clean-up, leading many to think that Sparky was crazy. Trammell ended up with career highs in average at .343, homers with 28, and runs batted in with 105. When asked late in the season, how Sparky could know that Alan would have such a great year, he replied, *"With Lance's power lost, we needed someone in the four slot who could make contact. And I believe that Alan Trammell is someone we can lean on. He's worked to reach the highest plateau, and I can truly say he has become one of baseball's ten best players."*

DDDDDDDDDDDDDDDDDDDDDDDDDDDDDDDDDDDDDDDDDDDDDDDDDDDDDDDDDDDDDDDDDDDDDDDDD

On August 9, the Tigers pounded the Yankees 15-4, Dan Petry the beneficiary of an offensive explosion powered by home runs from Alan Trammell, Darrell Evans, Matt Nokes, and Bill Madlock. "Mad Dog" Madlock was a June 4 free agent signing by Lajoie that was paying big dividends for Detroit. At 36 years of age, the past 4-time National League batting crown winner still had plenty of pop left in his bat, and in 87 games as a Tiger DH & corner infielder had 14 homers and 50 RBIs, many of them at crunch time. With New York soon to slide out of the pennant race, the 15-4 win pulled Detroit to 1.5 games back of the Blue Jays. *Amazingly, that game & a-half was the most that would separate the two teams over the next 46 days*, thru September 24, when the Tigers arrived in Toronto for a crucial 4-game series.

Detroit was one-half game back going into the first of 4, and Sparky had Jack Morris ready to start this important contest. Morris had one bad inning, and that was enough, the Blue Jays 4-run fourth all that they needed in a 4-3 win. *Tigers 1.5 games behind*. In game 2, Detroit-born Frankie Tanana pitched brilliantly, leaving after 7 with a 2-0 lead. Dickie Noles, a reliever the Tigers acquired from the Cubs just 3 days earlier, tossed a scoreless 8th, then in the 9th got the first man out before yielding a single to Jesse Barfield, bringing old friend Rick Leach to the plate as the potential tying run. Sparky brought in Willie Hernandez who had nothing on this day, getting tagged for a double by Leach, putting runners on 2nd and 3rd, and then Willie gave up a game-tying triple to Manny Lee, only the 6th extra base hit all year for Lee. With the winning run 90' from home and one out, Mike Henneman relieved, intentionally walking the next two batters to set up a force at every base, before facing Lloyd Moesby. Lloyd hit a grounder that Lou Whitaker couldn't handle, allowing the winning run to score. *Tigers 2.5 games back*.

Game 3 in Toronto was more heartbreak of the same. The Tigers led 9-7 going into the bottom of the 9th, Mike Henneman - brought in to get the final out in the 6th – still on the mound. As Barfield led off with a double and Willie Upshaw singled him to third, folks in front of their TVs back in Michigan anxiously paced the floors. When Henneman hit Rick Leach with a pitch, loading the bases and still no one out, Sparky called on Dickie Noles for the 2nd day in a row. And, for the 2nd day in a row, a light-hitting Blue Jay, this time Juan Beniquez, hit a 9th inning triple – today a walk-off. _Tigers 3.5 games back._

Detroit had one last chance in Toronto before returning to Detroit for a season-ending 7 game series, including the final 3 versus the Blue Jays. Lose today, and the Tigers have to overcome a 4.5 game deficit. 8 & 0 Doyle Alexander was given the assignment to salvage the finale, and although again magnificent, Detroit was losing 1-0 and down to their last 3 outs. Toronto's ace closer, Tom Henke, was the challenge facing the Tigers as Kirk Gibson stepped to the plate, and Gibby hit the Tigers biggest home run so far this season, tying the game and allowing the team and their fans to breathe again. In the 11th, Darrell Evans homered to put Detroit up 2-1, but an unearned run in the bottom of the frame allowed the Blue Jays to pull into a 2-2 tie.

2-2 was still the score as the Tigers came to bat in the 13th. One of the more colorful men to ever put on the Olde English D, rookie 3rd baseman Jim Walewander, led off. In July, Jim saw his favorite musicians, punk rock band _The Dead Milkmen_, play in Hamtramck, met them backstage, and invited the Milkmen to the next day's Tiger game, where they posed with Sparky Anderson on the dugout steps. Sparky chatted with the band, saying later, _"One of them had on combat boots, a camouflage army shirt, and an earring. I told him, 'Son, don't take no prisoners.'"_ On that July 26 day, Walewander hit the only home run in his short, 4-year/162-game, career and it turned out to be the game-winner against the Angels. Post-game, Jim fielded reporters' questions: _"Did the Dead Milkmen give you inspiration?" "No, they gave me a T-shirt." "What did you do with the home run ball?" "I put it in my glove compartment with the one from my first hit. When I get enough balls to fill the glove compartment, I'll buy a new car." "What are your goals?" "I want to be on the Bozo the Clown Show in Chicago again. I was on it as a kid but I never got the bean bag in the third hole."_

Back to the 13th inning in Toronto… Jim Walewander drew a lead-off walk, and was bunted to 2nd by Lou before Gibson lined a single to center. Walewander ran through the stop sign of 3rd base coach Alex Grammas, and safely slid head-first across home plate with the lead run. In the bottom of the inning, relievers Mike Henneman, ex-Padre Mark Thurmond, and Dickie Noles each recorded one out to seal the 3-2 Detroit victory. _Tigers 2.5 games back and heading home._

Before Detroit hosted the October 2, 3 & 4 games vs. Toronto, Baltimore was in town for 4 contests. Morris & Petry dropped games 1 & 3, while Frankie Tanana held the O's to 1 run on 3 hits in a 10-1 win in game 2, and Walt Terrell won a huge game 4 on October 1. Terrell picked a wonderful time to have the best of his 4 seasons as a Tiger, setting personal highs with 17 wins, 244 innings, & 143 strikeouts. While the Tigers split their 4, the Blue Jays surprisingly lost all 3 of their games with Milwaukee, leaving Detroit 1 game behind Toronto on the eve of their big series.

DDDDDDDDDDDDDDDDDDDDDDDDDDDDDDDDDDDDDDDDDDDDDDDDDDDDDDDDDDDDDDDDDDDDDDDD

In an August radio interview, WJR's J.P. McCarthy told Sparky, _"I'm not going to give up my tickets for the 2nd, 3rd, or 4th of October. I'm keeping those, and I will be there for each one of those games because you have told me all year long, wait 'til October 4th – that's the day."_ Sparky the Clairvoyant correctly saw several months ahead how critical October 4 would be in the pennant race, but even George "Sparky" Anderson might not have been able to predict what an amazing day, and the two days before it, turned out to be...

Friday, October 2 – with Toronto one game ahead of Detroit, should the Tigers take 2 of 3, a one-game, winner-take-all, playoff game would be held on Monday in Tiger Stadium. So, many fans made two trips to The Corner on October 2, the first in the pre-dawn hours to stand in line for the possible playoff game in 3 days, and then back that evening, one of 45,167 in attendance for the opening game against the Blue Jays. Toronto drew first blood, as normally-light hitting Manny Lee followed up his big ninth inning triple of just 6 days ago with a 2nd inning, 3-run homer off Doyle Alexander. In the bottom of the frame, Detroit answered with a surprise of their own, as rookie Scott Lusader, called up from AAA Toledo just last month, hit his first major league home run, a 2-run shot, to make the score 3-2 Jays. A third inning Trammell solo shot coupled with a Chet Lemon RBI grounder put Detroit ahead 4-3, and Alexander – with a late-inning assist from Mike Henneman – made that stand up as the final score, shutting down the Blue Jays the rest of the way. *Detroit & Toronto are now tied for first place.*

Saturday, October 3 – Jack Morris & Mike Flanagan tangled in a classic pitcher's duel, each only giving up two runs, Jack over 9 innings, Flanagan over 11. It was still 2-2 as the Tigers came up in the bottom of the 12th with 45,026 on the edge of their seats. Jeff Musselman had relieved Flanagan and, after getting Mike Heath for the 1st out, surrendered back-to-back singles to Lou Whitaker & Mad Dog Madlock, as Jim Walewander went in to run for Whitaker at 2nd base. After a walk to Gibson loaded the bases, Mark Eichhorn came in to pitch to Alan Trammell and, with the entire stadium on their feet chanting *"M-V-P! M-V-P!"*, Tram greeted him with a walk-off RBI single, ending the 4-hour affair, sending the crowd wild, and *Detroit up 1 game on the Blue Jays*. With one regular season game to go tomorrow, even with a loss, the worst that the Tigers could do is host a Monday playoff game... but with a win, the division is theirs.

Sunday, October 4 – On an afternoon made for baseball at The Corner, the runs were hard to come by. Detroit-native Frankie Tanana was handed the ball to face Toronto's Jimmy Key. Both pitched brilliantly, Key throwing a complete game, striking out 8 and only allowing 3 hits, but one of those hits was a 2nd inning Larry Herndon solo shot into the lower deck left-field seats – the perfect bookend to Larry's mammoth Opening Day blow against the facing of the upper deck bleachers. Tanana kept the batters off balance all game, offering a menu of slow, slower, & slowest pitches, a bewildering breaking ball mix of sliders, curves, change-ups, and just for fun, the occasional 80 mph fast ball. Going into the 9th, Toronto was held scoreless. The first Blue Jay due up that inning was future Tiger Cecil Fielder, and he went down on strikes. The next batter, a man who had done so much damage to Detroit in the past few days, Manny Lee, bounced out to 3rd baseman (not the Doors) Jim Morrison, a late-season acquisition from the Pirates for Darnell Coles. The third batter of the inning, Garth Iorg, topped a weak grounder back to the mound, and Frank took a couple of steps towards first sacker Darrell Evans before softly tossing it underhand to him, *and the Tigers are the East Division Champions of 1987!*

As the Tigers emptied the dugout to rush the infield in celebration, one player was absent from the mob scene. Sweet Lou Whitaker had pulled 2nd base from its moorings, found a Sharpie in the clubhouse, wrote out an inscription on the base, and presented it to his long-time double-play partner...

1987 MVP Alan Trammell, Congratulations from your friend, Louis Rodman Whitaker

To this day, Trammell gets choked up when speaking of Lou's gift, displayed on Alan's living room wall.

Lou was wiser than the sportswriters who chose George Bell of the 2nd place Blue Jays as league Most Valuable Player. Alan Trammell of the 1st place Detroit Tigers finished second in the balloting.

DDDDDDDDDDDDDDDDDDDDDDDDDDDDDDDDDDDDDDDDDDDDDDDDDDDDDDDDDDDDDDDDDDDDDDD

The West Division champion Minnesota Twins opposed Detroit in the American League playoffs. The Tigers were heavy favorites over the Twins, Detroit's 896 runs scored the most in the majors in over 3 decades, and their 98 wins and 225 homers tops in all of baseball. Minnesota had a horrible road record of 29 & 52, but an MLB-best home mark of 56 & 25, and it was their good fortune that 1987 was the turn of the West Division champs to host games 1, 2 and – if needed – 6 & 7.

Game 1 Minnesota: Minnesota played in the Hubert H. Humphrey Metrodome, the polar-opposite of Tiger Stadium's perfect beauty. The Metrodome was a plastic, sterile, box-like structure that could be likened to a giant putt-putt golf course, and an ugly one at that. As the Tigers took this field for game 1 on October 7, they were greeted by jet-engine decibel sound levels. National TV broadcaster Al Michaels commented, *"Now we know what sound feels like."* The crowd noise was described in the *L.A. Times* as, *"54,223 Scandinavian James Browns."* At the end of the game, the sound was equated to standing behind a power lawn mower for 3 hours. It was believed by more than a few folks that contributing to the din was pre-recorded, amplified crowd noise piped into the stadium.

The game 1 pitching match-up pitted Doyle Alexander, who had been a perfect 9 & 0 for Detroit since his late-season acquisition, versus the Twins' Jeff Reardon. Minnesota's Gary Gaetti homered off Doyle in the bottom of the 2nd, and Mike Heath answered for Detroit with his rocket into the centerfield stands the next half-inning. It remained 1-1 until Gaetti led-off Minnesota's 5th with another homer, and in the process set an MLB record by homering in his first two post-season career at bats. When the Twins tacked on two more runs in the frame, folks in front of their TVs back in Michigan began to curse the "Homer Hankies" that every fan in the Metrodome was waving. Apparently, this was the debut of the Homer Hanky, an 18-inch cotton square & the brainchild of a local newspaper reporter that appealed to Minnesotans enough that thousands of Twins fans lined up to buy and then wave them non-stop once the game began.

A Kirk Gibson solo home run and a Mike Heath RBI single cut the lead to 4-3, and then in the 8th Detroit surged ahead 5-4 on back-to-back RBI sac flies by Dave Bergman & Chet Lemon. Just when it looked like another Tiger late-inning comeback had pulled victory from the jaws of defeat, the Twins tied it in their 8th on a Kirby Puckett double, knocking Doyle Alexander out of the game. Willie Hernandez brought no relief at all, surrendering an RBI single & 2-RBI double to the only 2 batters he faced to put the Twins up 8-5. Johnny Grubb led off Detroit's 9th with a single and, when Sweet Lou walked with one out, the tying run was at the plate. But Bill Madlock and Kirk Gibson go down swinging, and Minnesota takes game 1.

Game 2 Minnesota: Minnesota-born Jack Morris was called on today by the Tigers to even the series, with the Twins sending out Bert Blyleven. Chester Lemon followed a Matt Nokes single with a 2-run homer to give Morris a 2-0 lead in the 2nd, but this was not Jack's day. Although he tossed all 9 innings, the Twins scored 6 runs for a 6-3 win, to go up 2 games to none. The day after Doyle Alexander suffers his first loss in a Tiger uniform is the only time in Jack Morris's career as a Tiger that he loses a game in Minnesota. One might see this all as a bad sign.

Game 3 Detroit: 49,730 at The Corner had plenty to cheer about early as Detroit exploded for 5 third-inning markers charged to Twins starter Les Straker, the big blow a Larry Herndon 2-run double to greet reliever and ex-Tiger Dan Schatzeder. Minnesota chipped away at Tiger hurler Walt Terrell, with 2 runs in each of the 4th, 6th, and 7th to take a 6-5 lead. With Detroit facing a 3-0 series hole and down to their last 6 outs, Herndon led off the 8th with a single, and one out later, Detroit-native Pat Sheridan turned on a Jeff Reardon offering, depositing it into the right-field upper deck to put the Tiger ahead 7-6. Mike Henneman had to face 3 of the toughest Twins hitters in the ninth, and put down Kirby Puckett, Kent Hrbek, and Gary Gaetti for a 1-2-3 inning, cutting Minnesota's series lead to 2-1. At the game's joyful conclusion, the field was littered with placards passed-out to fans as they entered the stadium. An article in the next morning's paper said that the team would not be handing out posters for game 4.

Game 4 Detroit: To accommodate the TV networks and avoid a conflict with their slate of NFL games, *Sunday Night Baseball at Tiger Stadium* made its debut, Frankie versus Frankie, Tanana versus Viola. An unearned run gave the Tigers a 1-0 lead after one, but Tanana was not as sharp as his last outing versus Toronto, surrendering solo runs in the 3rd, 4th, 5th, and 6th, and it was 4-2 Twins going into the bottom of the 6th - but here comes Detroit. Chet Lemon & Darrell Evans led off with singles, before Dave Bergman singles home Chet to cut the deficit to one, sending Evans to 2nd. Mike Heath lays down a beauty of a sacrifice bunt, moving Darrell to 3rd & Bergy to 2nd with only one out. *Looooooo* is due up and the Twins make a pitching change, bringing in ex-Tiger Juan Berenguer, as the Old Ballyard rocked with excitement.

And then came the play that turned the ALCS.

After Berenguer delivered a pitch to Whitaker, Minnesota catcher Tim Laudner noticed Evans a little too far off the bag at third, and rifled a throw down to Twins' third baseman Gary Gaetti, who applied the tag as Darrell dove back, too late. After the ump called him out, Evans was on his knees, hands on hips, arguing the call, but to no avail. In the next day's *Detroit Free Press* photo, the look on the ump's face appears to be one of compassion for a player well-liked by all, but that did not change the call.

So now, rather than the tying run at third and lead run at second with one out, there are two down and Dave Bergman still on 2nd. A Juan Berenguer wild pitch moved Bergy to third, the tying run once again '90 from home, and then Lou draws a walk. However, a fly ball to center by Jim Morrison – instead of a sac fly that ties the game – ends the inning. The score remained 4-3 until the Twins 8th when a throwing error on a grounder to third baseman Evans makes his bad day even worse, leading to an unearned run and a 5-3 final score. Darrell later said, *"I was thinking that at least my kids still love me, and my dog still loved me, too, so I was going to be ok. It was one of the worst games of my life."* In less than 24 hours, we would be reminded that Detroit has the greatest sports fans anywhere.

Game 5 Detroit: 47,448 were in attendance at Tiger Stadium for game 5, their team down 3 games to 1, a single defeat away from elimination. Everyone in the ballpark knew that Darrell Evans, despite being a clutch hitter, a favorite of his teammates and the fans, a charismatic ballplayer who exuded joy every moment he was on the field, was the main reason they were in this position – and no one knew that more than Evans himself. However, what no one could foresee was that one of the classiest moments ever witnessed in a sports setting was about to take place.

In the bottom of the first inning, Darrell Evans walked from the on-deck circle to home plate. Not a boo was heard. Instead, some folks began to stand and applaud, then more, and then more. Soon every person in the park was on their feet, the applause accompanied by cheering. Eyes were filling with tears, including those of Darrell, who later told reporters, *"It was something I didn't expect. You can't pay enough money to have these things happen to you."* The easiest thing in the world for a fan is to jump up and down when your team wins, but this was an act of love, letting Darrell know that one mistake pales in comparison to how much they appreciated his contributions since becoming a Tiger in 1984. What a wonderful way to honor a man who never gave less than 100% and was always a class act, no matter what happened the day before. Looking back on all of the amazing events in Tiger history, for fans of a certain age, only two bring goose bumps every time they are recalled: almost anything about the Bird, and the standing ovation that Darrell Evans received the day after his critical base running blunder.

In that first inning at bat, Darrell drew a base-on-balls, and moved to 2nd on a Gibson single, but the rally died there. In the next half inning, Doyle Alexander imploded, the pitcher who had gone 9 & 0 replaced by an awful body double, giving up 4 runs & only retiring one of the 8 batters he faced, before 2nd-year man Eric King came in to strand the 3 runners he'd inherited. King did a fine job in relief, keeping Minnesota at bay for 5 innings, and in Detroit's 4th a Trammell RBI single & Matt Nokes 2-run homer cut the deficit to 4-3. But King allowed a sac fly RBI and Mike Henneman relieved him, but had a terrible outing, allowing 4 runs, the difference in the Tigers season-ending 9-5 loss.

DDDDDDDDDDDDDDDDDDDDDDDDDDDDDDDDDDDDDDDDDDDDDDDDDDDDDDDDDDDDDDDDDDDDDDDDDDDDDD

The Minnesota Twins went on to defeat the St. Louis Cardinals in the 84th Fall Classic, 4 games to 3. Reflecting their regular season trend, the Twins won all 4 home games and lost all 3 road games.

Detroit, although falling short of winning it all in '87, were excited about the contributions of several youngsters in their first full seasons with the team including All-Star catcher Matt Nokes, rookie pitchers Mike Henneman & Jeff Robinson (9 & 6), and rookie outfielder Scott Lusader (.319 in 23 late-season games). The promise of these kids, along with a strong veteran foundation, had fans encouraged about the upcoming season.

But 1988's optimism took a big hit late in '87 when a labor arbitrator declared baseball's owners had colluded in restricting the movement of free agents. This decision freed the effected players from their contracts including Kirk Gibson. Gibby then began negotiating with the Tigers on a new contract, but team owner Tom Monaghan seemed intent on lashing out at Gibson, perhaps in part stung by the labor arbitrator's decision, stating in an interview that Detroit would be better without Gibson (a ridiculous assertion) and calling Kirk *"a disgrace to the Tiger uniform with his half-beard, half-stubble."* Pushed along by Monaghan's sabotage, Gibson signed a 3-year contract with the L.A. Dodgers in January '88.

Gibby's combination of power and speed was reflected in his homers/stolen bases from '84 to '87: 27/29, 29/30, 28/34, and 24/26. As difficult as it would be to replace that production, more difficult would be replacing someone who came up big time at crucial moments as consistently as Kirk did, best exemplified in the World Series of '84 and, for the Dodgers, in the '88 playoffs & Series.

Without Kirk Gibson, 1988 would be a much taller mountain to climb.

1988 – 1990 The Pennsylvania Poker, Herbie Redmond, Bo, Big Daddy, Not Ernie!

Well I got me a fine wife I got me an ole fiddle
When the sun's comin' up I got cakes on the griddle
Life ain't nothin' but a funny funny riddle
Thank God I'm a country boy

("Thank God I'm a Country Boy", aka the Herbie Redmond Theme Song, by John Denver)

Detroit's 1988 season opened with a new lead-off man and a new-look outfield.

Anticipating the departure of Kirk Gibson during contract negotiations with him in late-1987, the Tigers made an early December trade, sending pitcher Dan Petry to California for fleet center-fielder Gary Pettis. The two-time Gold Glove winning Pettis was only a .242 hitter in 6 years with the Angels, but did average 52 steals per 162 games over that time. While lacking Gibby's power and big game impact, Gary was an improvement defensively and even an upgrade in speed. He would lead-off, with Lou moving to the number two slot. On defense, Pettis took Chester's spot in center, pushing Lemon to a new position, right field, with Pat Sheridan playing left.

The departure of Dan "Peaches" Petry was a sad event for the Tiger faithful. A great teammate, a warm soul, and a fine pitcher, Dan averaged a record of 17 & 10 for Detroit from 1982 through his lone All-Star year of 1985, but slid to 5 & 10 in '86 and his 9 & 7 of '87 came with a 5.61 ERA. Combined with the late-'87 acquisition of Doyle Alexander and development of Jeff Robinson, Detroit felt Dan expendable.

The Tigers opened '88 with 6 games on the road, the first 3 at Fenway Park and the next 3 at Kansas City's Royals Stadium. Game 1 of 162, April 4 in Boston, featured a classic pitching match-up, Jack Morris against the Cy Young Award winner the last two years, Roger Clemens. After the previous 4 Tiger batters went down on strikes, Tommy Brookens drew a one-out walk in the third, moved to 2nd on a balk and raced around to score on a Sweet Lou single. An inning later, Chet Lemon followed a Pat Sheridan base-on-balls with a triple into the right-field corner, making it 2-0 Detroit. The lead only held up a half-inning as Boston reached Jack for 3 runs in their half of the fourth. But Morris was untouchable after that and, after a Matt Nokes solo homer in the 6th, the game stayed tied at 3 into the 10th, when Trammell's 2-run homer off of ace reliever Lee Smith gave Black Jack & Detroit the win.

DDDDDDDDDDDDDDDDDDDDDDDDDDDDDDDDDDDDDDDDDDDDDDDDDDDDDDDDDDDDDDDDDDDDDDDDDDD

When Detroit played their final game of May, they found themselves in third place, 4.5 games behind the division-leading New York Yankees. The Tigers then caught fire, including a 4-game sweep of the Indians in Cleveland that vaulted Detroit into 2nd place and closing in on New York. When the Bronx Bombers arrived at The Corner for a 3-game series starting June 20, the Tigers were only one-half game behind. A nice-sized crowd of 33,660 turned out for the 8:05PM Monday series opener, Tommy John of the Yanks on the mound against the Tiger fresh off a 1-0 shutout of the Orioles, 8 & 2 Jeff Robinson. In the Detroit 2nd, 35-year old first baseman Ray Knight, acquired in a pre-season trade with the O's for pitcher Mark Thurmond, and wrapping up a nice 13-year career with a single season as a Tiger, lined a single to right before scoring on a Darrell Evans double to straight-away center. With the game 1-0 Detroit after 2, both hurlers settled into an outstanding pitchers duel lasting into the 9th. Jeff Robinson was one out away from his 2nd consecutive white-washing when New York's Dave Winfield knocked in the tying run with a double to center. Mike Henneman took over on the hill and tossed a scoreless 10th before Detroit came up to bat, facing Yanks' reliever Cecilio Guante. After Gary Pettis struck out, up stepped Tom Brookens who turned on a Guante fastball, sending it deep into the left-field stands for a walk-off victory for the suddenly-in-first-place Detroit Tigers. The crowd screamed themselves hoarse as Brookens' teammates mobbed him at home plate.

Despite the dramatic victory over the despised rivals the night before, only 26,535 were enticed to come downtown for the 2nd game versus the Yanks. By the time this memorable affair concluded, many more wished they would've made the journey. The Tigers, surprisingly, made their run to first place with Jack Morris in a first-half funk, and he entered tonight coming off of a 13-5 drubbing at the hands of Toronto, his record falling to 6 & 8. This evening was even worse, the New Yorkers using Jack for batting practice in the 2nd, smashing 3 doubles and a home run before he could get 3 outs, and sending Morris to an early shower. The Tiger bullpen did a fine job, Paul Gibson and Eric King holding New York to 1 run over the final 7 innings, but the Tigers trailed 6-1 going into the bottom of the ninth.

Down to their last 3 outs, Detroit showed signs of life. Dave Bergman led off with a single and Darrell Evans worked Yankee pitcher Neil Allen for a walk. New York Manager Billy Martin didn't want to take any chances, and brought in closer Dave Righetti. The first man to face Righetti was Matt Nokes who singled to load the bases, but when Pat Sheridan lined out and Brookens fanned, it looked bleak for the Motor City Nine. However, Dave Righetti started to have problems with his location, first issuing a free pass to Lou to force in the run that made it 6-2, then walking free-swinging utility man Luis Salazar to push the 6-3 run across the plate. With 2 runs in and Alan Trammell due up, the fans were starting to make serious noise as Billy Martin was on his way to the mound once more. The manager surprised everyone by taking his closer out of the game and replacing him with Cecilio Guante, the very same man who gave up the game-winning home run to Tommy Brookens just 24 hours earlier.

Bottom of the ninth, Yankees 6 Detroit 3, 2 outs, bases loaded, the batter at the plate representing the winning run, and now the count is full. Detroit loses, they fall to 2nd place. BUT... Guante's pitch gets a little too much of the middle of the plate, and Alan sent it far into the night, slamming it into the facing of the left-field upper deck for *a walk-off-grand-slam-home-run!* The fans are screaming, going out of their minds as Trammell is engulfed by his ecstatic teammates! Detroit now moves to 1.5 games up on New York. Years later, Alan was asked for his most memorable hit. He smiled and said, *"Of course, the two, two-run homers in game 4 of the '84 World Series are at the top, but... I think the most fun was the walk-off grand slam against the Yankees in 1988."*

After suffering two crushing defeats to Detroit, the Yankees had to get ready for one final game at The Corner before leaving town. The House of Horrors continued for New York as Tommy Brookens singled in the 10th and scored the winning run on Luis Salazar's long hit to right-center off reliever Charlie Hudson, giving Detroit a 3-2 victory. 3 games, 3 walk-off hits, and a series sweep for the Tigers over the Damn Yankees, Detroit now in first by 2.5 games (and the names of Tommy Brookens & Charlie Hudson will be linked again in 1989). When the Yankees returned to New York, George Steinbrenner announced that he had fired Billy as manager to be replaced by Lou Piniella. This marked the fifth and final time that George hired and then fired Martin as Yankee manager. 1988 may have been the most volatile of Billy's years as skipper: fined twice, suspended once, involved in one bar fight – and it's not even July.

Since the June sweep of the Yankees, the Tigers were in first place all but 2 days through September 4, holding off New York and Boston in a 3-team fight for the division lead. After defeating the Red Sox for the fourth game in a row on August 6, Detroit was 66 & 43 and 4 games up on both opponents, the

Bengals high-water mark of 1988. The Tigers would reach this mark one more time this season, after Morris – back to his old self in the season's 2nd-half - tossed a 5-0 shutout at the White Sox on August 21, improving Detroit to 73 & 50 and 4 up on Boston, 6 up on New York.

And then, the bottom fell out. From August 22 through September 14, Detroit went 4 & 19. On the morning of September 15, the team was 77 & 69 and 5.5 games back of first place Boston, 1 back of the 2nd place Yankees. The Tigers were able to overcome the loss of Kirk Gibson to free agency as long as everyone stayed healthy, but the 1988 Detroit Tigers starting 9 and pitching staff was the oldest ever fielded, before or since, in the team's history – and those old men began to break down. Some was self-inflicted: at the start of September, Lou Whitaker was dancing at a party and did the splits when he tore cartilage in his right knee, ending his season; Alan Trammell missed almost 2 months of action after the All-Star break with shoulder & groin injuries; the replacements for the greatest double play combination in baseball history were Jim Walewander and Luis Salazar. An injury every bit as impactful but having nothing to do with age was the loss of 26-year old Jeff Robinson, who's .684 winning percentage (13 & 6) and 2.98 ERA were tops on the pitching staff, but arm troubles shut him down completely by mid-August, his last win an August 2, 1-0 shutout of the Royals.

Detroit rallied to win 9 of their final 12 games, but were eliminated on September 30. The final standings for 1988 read: 1st place Boston 89 & 73 _and one game back_ 2nd place Detroit 88 & 74. When a team loses Kirk Gibson for an entire year, Alan Trammell for 2 months, and Lou Whitaker for one month – yet only finishes ONE game out of first place... the fans ask what might have been.

Kirk Gibson, the man who Tom Monaghan suggested the Tigers would be better off without, had an immediate impact on his new team, the Los Angeles Dodgers. He called a meeting in spring training for the team that finished 4th in their division the prior year, letting everyone know that he was there to win a championship, and would do whatever it took to make that happen. Gibby sparked the Dodgers to the N.L. West Division title, topping L.A. in home runs, doubles, runs, slugging percentage, and on-base percentage. In the NLCS versus the Mets, his 12th inning homer won game 4, and his 3-run homer proved to be the margin of victory in game 5. Kirk was injured late in the NLCS, and when the World Series began versus Oakland, it was questionable if Gibson could play at all. But he was able to hobble to the plate for his lone '88 Series at bat at the end of game 1, _2 outs – 1 man on – L.A. down 4-3_, to face Dennis Eckersley, the finest relief pitcher in the game. Kirk swung on the full count pitch, broadcaster Jack Buck shouted, _"I can't believe what I just saw,"_ and Gibby circled the bases with a walk-off, 2-run homer, the key play in the Fall Classic as the Dodgers upset the favored Athletics, 4 games to 3. For the 2nd time in 5 years, Kirk Gibson hit one of the most memorable home runs in World Series history.

After the 1988 season concluded, and the Baseball Writers' Association of America voted Gibson the National League's Most Valuable Player award, Kirk received a phone call from Tiger owner Tom Monaghan, congratulating Kirk on his season, and apologizing for his past behavior.

DDDDDDDDDDDDDDDDDDDDDDDDDDDDDDDDDDDDDDDDDDDDDDDDDDDDDDDDDDDDDDDDDDDDDDDDDDDD

Two days before Christmas of 1988, 41-year old Darrell Evans left the Tigers to sign as a free agent with the Atlanta Braves, the team that he began his major league career with as a 21-year old in 1969. In five seasons wearing the Olde English D, Darrell hit 141 home runs & knocked in 405 runners – a nice 162-game average of 32 HRs & 91 RBIs - and won the life-long affection of Tiger fans everywhere. It was in Atlanta in 1973, that Darrell Evans, Davey Johnson & Hank Aaron became the only 3 teammates to ever each hit 40 or more home runs in the same season. Darrell went on to hit 11 homers as a part-time player for the Braves in 1989, finishing his career with 414 home runs.

DDDDDDDDDDDDDDDDDDDDDDDDDDDDDDDDDDDDDDDDDDDDDDDDDDDDDDDDDDDDDDDDDDDDDDDD

Unfortunately, in spring training of 1989, it was apparent that Sparky had settled on Rick Schu as his main guy at third base, and on March 23 of that year, Tommy Brookens was traded to, of all teams, the New York Yankees for pitcher Charlie Hudson. Tommy played one year in New York and one more in Cleveland before retiring from the game at age 36.

Fortunately, Tommy came back to the Detroit organization as a minor league manager from 2005 thru 2009 and in 2010 returned to the parent club as a coach under Manager Jim Leyland. It was a special moment to see Tommy on the baseball diamond in Detroit once again in the jersey sporting the Olde English D, a jersey he was always meant to wear.

12 days after the 1989 trade of Brookens to the Yankees, I sent my thoughts on the matter to Tiger G.M. Bill Lajoie (the "Prohibition" mention in the letter was a jab at the team's Low Alcohol beer policy)...

April 4, 1989

Detroit Tiger Baseball Club
2121 Trumbull
Detroit, Michigan 48216

Attn: Bill Lajoie

Bill,

Please consider...

From a purely pragmatic point of view, what are we to do when mid-May rolls around & this year's edition of "the new third baseman" sees his average free falling down through the .220s & finds his Enos Cabell model iron glove cannot pick up the screamer down the 3rd base line to start the key around the horn double play that is crucial to the success of a team who will live or die by pitching & defense? And for what do we find ourselves in this nasty situation? For a pitcher from New York whose very entry into a ballgame was cause for rejoicing among all opposing fans & alerted all those sitting in the deepest sections of the ballpark to set down their beers (except, of course, at Tiger Stadium where Prohibition reigns) & ready themselves for the stinging sensation one feels as an arching home run settles into their hands.

From an emotional point of view, how can you so lightly discard the very heart of OUR ballclub, a man who is the very essence of class & whose work ethic is an example that any person can look to as a model? And to exile Tommy to New York!?! What, were all the jails already full? To a fan who was willing to brave 19 hours in 36-degree weather for Series tickets, subsisting only on White Castles, who was willing to gladly visit the old ballyard even during the 90 to 100 loss seasons under the Ralph Houk era, your total disregard for the feelings of the thousands of fans whose loyalty equal or exceed mine is impossible to comprehend. Such a reward for Tommy's 100% effort guaranteed everyday & not one complaint in 10 years seems somehow to fall short.

Doc Fletcher

Tommy baseball card alongside Corktown-neighborhood artist rendering of
a Brookens skeptic and a Brookens fan, Sparky & Ernie

Ernie Harwell also thought Tommy one of his all-time favorite Tigers, calling this man from the Quaker State town of Chambersburg, "The Pennsylvania Poker", in a nod to The Andrews Sisters *Pennsylvania Polka* song. Thomas Dale Brookens was the sum of desire, hustle, defense, clutch hitting & likability. It seems like everyone thought highly of Tommy Brookens – except Sparky Anderson. Tommy was brought up from the minors to Detroit midway thru the 1979 season, shortly after Sparky became skipper, and wore the Olde English D through the '88 season, each of his 10 years in Detroit with Sparky as manager. No matter his defensive excellence at the hot corner, or how many big hits he had, there was always another third baseman that was going to be Sparky's next Mike Schmidt or Eddie Matthews, someone who would come out of spring training manning the hot corner while Brookens sat...

1980 was Tommy's first full season with Detroit, he was the guy at third, excellent at turning rockets hit down the line into a 5-4-3, 3rd-2nd-1st, double play. Brookens was number 4 on a big hitting team in runs-batted-in, 2nd in doubles, and a tough out in the clutch. On August 20, 1980, Tommy went 5 for 5 including a home run and a triple, and grabbed a scorcher down the third base line to start a triple play – he had 9 more hits over the next 3 days, and was chosen as the American League Player of the Week. But the '81 season opened with Mick Kelleher on third, then some time there for Stan Papi, before Tom Brookens reclaimed his position, outhitting both Kelleher & Papi. It was the same story in 1982, when Sparky traded Champ Summers to the Giants for Enos "Old Dude" Cabell. Although Brookens was at third for Opening Day, Cabell started there game 2, recording the first of his many errors for Detroit, a man much safer defensively at first base. Over Enos' two years with the Tigers, safety cones should have been set-up around third when he played the hot corner. It got to the point that fans hoped any ball hit to Enos at 3rd, after making that distinctive clanging sound off his glove, dribbled just far enough away that Cabell would not be tempted to try to pick it up, throw wildly to first, and end up with the hitter at 2nd, if not 3rd, base. In both '82 & '83, Brookens was back as the regular at 3rd by mid-season.

And on and on it went... in '84, it was Howard Johnson and Marty Castillo who nudged ahead of Tommy in the 3rd base pecking order, as did Barbaro Garbey, whom Sparky called "the next Roberto Clemente."

Barbaro had a different career path than Roberto, and was in the Mexican League by '86. Throughout all of this, Tommy became a fan favorite. On a muggy July night in 1985, Johnny Harcourt of St. Clair Shores joined me at The Corner for a game with Texas. The Tigers found themselves going into the 11th inning without a catcher - Lance Parrish was out with a bad back, and Sparky had pinch hit for Bob Melvin & 3rd string catcher Marty Castillo. To the delight of 36,802, on their feet and cheering, who came out of the Tigers dugout wearing the catcher's gear, but Brookens! It looked like the shin guards came up to his waist. After the game, Tommy admitted his nervousness, *"I didn't know if I could do it. I warmed up pitchers in the bullpen, but never caught a game in my life."* Initially, there were no baserunners for Brookens to contend with as Texas went down 1-2-3 in both the 11th & the 12th. When the first man to get on for Texas in the 13th broke for second, Tommy popped up from behind the plate and fired a ball that, at first glance, looked like it would beat the runner to 2nd. But when the ball cleared pitcher's mound, it appeared to fall off a table. John & I looked at each other with the same unspoken "oh oh". However, of the 3 additional Texans that reached base during Tommy's time behind the mask, only one stole a base. Brookens caught the final 5 innings of the 15-inning affair, a game finally won in the bottom of the 15th when Barbaro Garbey had his Clemente moment, singling in Tram with the game-winner. The crowd was on their feet, with the loudest cheers & shouts reserved for Tommy Brookens who told reporters, *"It was a lot of fun back there, but I don't want to get back there often."*

In '85, outside of his star turn as an emergency catcher, Tommy regained his place as the number one third sacker, playing his usual top-notch defense, and delivering key hits while contributing 34 doubles, behind only Kirk Gibson on the team. For '86, Sparky's wandering eyes landed on Darnell Coles for the starting role at third, but Brookens forced his way into the line-up with his defensive versatility as one of the league's finest utility players, hitting a solid .270. In '87, Tommy won his third base job back from Darnell Coles, and kept his starting role through 1988 – until his exile to the Bronx.

Sparky's 1989 replacement for Brookens, Rick Schu, hit .214 and was released at the end of the year. Charlie Hudson, the pitcher Detroit received for Tommy, posted a record of 1 & 5 with zero saves and a 6.35 ERA. Charlie's single year with Detroit, his final year in the majors, ended in August when he drove his car into a telephone pole and broke his leg and knee.

DDDDDDDDDDDDDDDDDDDDDDDDDDDDDDDDDDDDDDDDDDDDDDDDDDDDDDDDDDDDDDDDDDDDDDDDDD

The Tigers and their fans were optimistic about the 1989 season. After coming so close in '88, despite missing Trammell & Whitaker for much of the 2nd half, the feeling was that a healthy squad could be a championship squad. For the 10th consecutive season, Jack Morris took the mound for the first game of the year, this time at Arlington Stadium in Texas. Although he pitched well, tossing a complete game 6-hitter with 8 strikeouts, he lost a 4-0 pitchers duel with Charlie Hough. Dancing in the minds of Tiger fans were echoes of Chris Pittaro in 1985, as Sparky's latest "can't miss kid", Torey Lovullo, started at first base and batted 2nd today, going hitless in four at bats. The year before, Torey was called up to Detroit late-season and played in his first 12 major league games, hitting .381. Sparky was impressed enough that, going into 1989, he proclaimed of Torey, *"I'll die before he comes out of the lineup."*

George "Sparky" Anderson didn't die, but he may have felt something almost as painful. And, so did Torey. The two shared a miserable April & May '89. The Tigers stumbled badly out of the starting gate, going 14 & 24 in their first 38 games. During that time, Torey Lovullo played in 29 games & looked lost, batting .115 while fanning 20 times in 87 at bats. Although, while Sparky managed baseball's winningest team in the 1980s, he'd experienced rough moments like 11 & 19 in the first 30 games of '87, this felt different. The losses were piling up and he couldn't sleep. Anderson spoke of suffocating feelings, a sensation like that of being locked in a closet, unable to breathe until he could get out, & shared these experiences and his concern about them with Jim Campbell, who arranged for doctors to put Sparky through a battery of tests. The physicians concluded that the skipper suffered from depression and a lack of energy due to being mystified at his inability to stop the losses – his only losing season in 20 years as a manager was 1971 with Cincinnati. On May 19, Anderson was sent home to Thousand Oaks, California for rest & relaxation; around this same time, Torey Lovullo was sent to the Toledo Mud Hens to regain his swing & confidence.

A Tiger executive said of Sparky, *"Here was a guy who had basically never lost, and suddenly he was riding a treadmill of losses with no end in sight. It was a shock, and every time there was a hint of improvement, someone else got hurt."* Twenty Tigers found their way on to the disabled list in 1989 and no help was coming from the organization's minor league teams: of all the players on the current squad, only Mike Henneman developed in the farm system from the time Sparky became manager in 1979. Since Bill Lajoie, the genius that discovered and signed so many of the heroes of '84, was bumped up from Scouting Director to General Manager once Monaghan bought the team in '83, five different men had served as Scouting Director, disrupting any continuity among Tiger scouts. On top of all of that, the Tigers employed insults as a negotiating tactic with top performers Gibson & Parrish (so much so that Lance took less cash to sign with the Phillies), pushing these winning players out the door.

While Torey Lovullo would remain in Toledo the balance of 1989, Sparky returned to the dugout after 17 days away from the Tigers. Anderson's time away allowed him to re-evaluate his value to the game, *"Sure, I think I've contributed to my teams with honesty, fairness and an understanding of pitching, but I'm no genius and I don't want to hear that I am. I didn't invent the game. There were a hell of a lot better before me and there will be a hell of a lot better after me."* Everyone was happy to see Sparky back and looking good, but on the field the losing continued. After ending May on an 8 & 4 run to climb from last place to fifth in the 7-team East Division and close to 5 games behind, a 2 & 10 opening to June plunged the Tigers to 10.5 out of 1st and back into the cellar, where they would stay until year's end. In the league, Detroit was last in batting average & earned run average, second-to-last in runs scored. The 59 & 103 Tigers had the worst 1989 record in the majors, the 2nd most losses to date in team history, and were a distant 30 games behind 1st-place Toronto.

In 1988 & 1989, Gary Pettis gave Detroit what they sought - great center-field defense that earned him Gold Gloves each year, and speed on the base paths, swiping 44 & then 43 bags. But with his contract up, Pettis decided to leave the Tigers and sign with Texas in November of '89. In December, Detroit signed an ex-Toronto Blue Jay, agreeing to terms with free agent Lloyd Moseby, to become the new centerfielder. A 2nd December free agent signing took place, this one to plug the hole at third existing since Brookens' departure, with a man exhibiting Tommy's hustle & determination, Tony Phillips. Of Tony, Paul Carey later said, *"Tony was just what Sparky was looking for… perhaps the most versatile player he ever managed. Feisty and cocky, yes, but a gamer. I can still hear that cackle of a laugh."*

DDDDDDDDDDDDDDDDDDDDDDDDDDDDDDDDDDDDDDDDDDDDDDDDDDDDDDDDDDDDDDDDDDDDDDD

On January 1, 1990, at the 76th Rose Bowl in Pasadena, California, the University of Southern California defeated the University of Michigan by a score of 17-10 in what was the final game as UM Football Coach and Athletic Director for 60-year old Glenn "Bo" Schembechler. In 21 years at Michigan and 6 before that at Miami, Ohio, the legendary Bo compiled a head coaching record of 234-65-8. Only Joe Paterno, Tom Osborne, and Nick Saban won 200 times in fewer games as a major college head coach.

Bo was not retired for long.

On January 8, 1990, Tom Monaghan announced that John Fetzer, who had been named chairman of the board after selling the Tigers to Monaghan in late-1983, would become chairman emeritus, replaced as chairman by Jim Campbell, the previous team president. Campbell's vacated position of president would be filled by a person new to the organization, Bo Schembechler. A my-way-or-the-highway, no-nonsense man taking over a job that, in large part, entails the diplomatic chore of dealing with the public. What could go wrong? According to Richard Bak's book, *A Place For Summer*, Monaghan included in the job offer to his long-time friend a 10-year deal that included $220,000 annual compensation, a $200,000 condominium, two Cadillacs, and country club memberships.

One week after Coach Bo became President Bo, Detroit signed to a contract an old adversary, one best known to Tiger fans as a strikeout victim in the 9th inning of Frank Tanana's 1987 1-0 finale masterpiece over Toronto, Cecil Fielder. The bit slimmer Cecil of '87 looked to have beefed up while playing in 1989 for the Hanshin Tigers in Japan, where his nickname was "Wild Bear". The only 1989 Detroit Tiger with more than 11 home runs was Sweet Lou Whitaker's 28 and it was hoped that Fielder could come close to the 38 he hit last year in Japan. Sparky told the media, *"I know he can hit the ball a long way and in this ballpark that can mean something."* Exactly one week later, on January 22, 1990, it was announced that an old friend was coming home. After two uneventful years with the Angels, one as a starter & one as a reliever, free agent Dan Petry signed with the Tigers.

The excitement of all this January *hot stove league* news was tempered with word of a MLB lockout. The 7th work stoppage since 1972 began in February and, by the time it was resolved 32 days later, spring training was cancelled and Opening Day moved back one week to April 9. No games would be lost as it was agreed that the season would be extended 3 days so that all teams could get in their 162 games.

While Tiger fans waited for the delayed '90 season to begin, they received sad news. On April 4, 61-year old Herbie "the dancing groundskeeper" Redmond, passed away. At the end of the fifth inning each game, the grounds crew would drag their brooms across the infield dirt, smoothing it out for the game's last 4 innings. From the time Herbie joined the Tigers ground crew in 1969 through 1989, he entertained fans as he danced while rounding the infield. When asked to explain his *Herbie Shuffle*, he said, *"First you strut to third, then you wave your cap, next you shake those hips and jump for joy, then kiss that cap and salute the team."* For the longest time, the only song Detroit would play on the p.a. system during this fifth inning tradition was *"Thank God I'm a Country Boy"*, but when Herbie would break stride from his fellow groundskeepers, launching into a soft shoe routine while waving his cap at the adoring fans, this John Denver song became the happiest tune you ever heard. When Jim Campbell banned Herbie's dancing in '84, it felt like somebody died at The Corner, and the booing lasted long and loud. Tiger management relented and once it was announced that Herbie's dancing ban was lifted, the fans eagerly anticipated Herbie's next dance almost like an upcoming Bird game from '76: when the grounds crew next dragged their brooms, and Herbie began his so-familiar dance, the place went crazy. In Redmond's obituary, Ernie Harwell said, *"Herbie was an original. The irony is that the Yankees tried to hire a man to imitate him, and he failed. You couldn't imitate Herbie. It was all spontaneous."* Herbie Redmond aka Short Dog aka Herbie the Love Bug, the man who made us love *"Thank God I'm a Country Boy"*, will always have a special place in our hearts…

Jack Morris, for the eleventh consecutive season, from 1980 to 1990, a team record, was once again handed the ball to start Opening Day for the Detroit Tigers. It's a well-earned distinction for the man who won the most games in the major leagues over the course of the 1980s. Detroit opened at Fenway Park this year, Morris & Roger Clemens both tossing a fine game, but Tiger errors led to 3 unearned runs in a 5-2 loss. Kevin Ritz, a young pitcher in his 2nd year with Detroit, who would spend all but four 1990 games in AAA Toledo, started the next day's game and was pulled after giving up 4 hits & a walk in the 3rd inning. Dan Petry relieved, playing for Detroit for the first time since '87, and was excellent, pitching through the end of the 7th, shutting out Boston on 3 hits. The Tigers, however, lost 4-2. The Red Sox completed the sweep the next day, before both teams – in a scheduling quirk caused by the 32-day strike – flew to Detroit to play just one game at The Corner. To quote Dave Bergman, *"The guys who made up this schedule must have been in a room with a bottle of Wild Turkey and 40 straws."*

The 1990 Home Opener was played before 44,906, and Detroit got everyone in a fine mood by bursting out to a 10-1 lead after 3 innings. New lead-off man Tony Phillips gave fans a preview of the high on base percentage, hustle, and run scoring they could expect from him over the next 5 years: Tony began his 4 for 4 day by bunting his way on in the first, stealing 2nd, and then scoring run #1 of his 97 for the year, when he came home ahead of Lou's homer. Phillips followed that up with a 2-RBI single in the 2nd, and a RBI single in the third. Frankie Tanana weakened in the top of the fifth, leaving with the Tigers up 10-5, relieved up newly-acquired Urbano Lugo. It was Lugo's finest moment in his short Detroit career, allowing Boston 1 run on 2 hits through 3 & a third innings, picking up one of two wins he'd chalk up in 13 games before his 7.03 ERA motivated the Tigers to send him to Toledo. Final: Detroit 11 Boston 7.

Meanwhile, the Wild Bear from Japan, aka Cecil Fielder, took some time to heat up. In the first 5 games of the young season, he was 3 for 19 with 8 strikeouts and no home runs. In game 6, played in front of a small gathering of 11,294 at The Corner, the Tigers found themselves down 5-0 to Baltimore in the sixth. Alan Trammell led off the inning against the Baltimore starter, Dave Johnson, and lined a double to deep right field. Cecil stepped into the batter's box, and the right-hand slugger sent a fastball deep into the right-field upper deck seats, an amazing distance especially considering it was an opposite field blast. Although Detroit fell 7-4, Fielder's prodigious smash was a welcome sight to the team that hit 116 homers total the prior year. 4 days later at home against the Yankees, Cecil hit his 2nd homer as a Tiger, another monster shot, this one well into the left-center upper deck, as Sparky noted, *"That's where the big boys hit 'em,"* in Detroit's 8-4 win.

Cecil had 7 homers at the end of April & 18 by the end of May – the most Fielder had in any of his four years as a reserve with Toronto was 14. Despite Cecil's production, the Tigers record at the end of May was 20 & 29, a game & a half back of their pace in the awful 103-loss campaign of the previous year. Tiger fans, though, loved the stunning power show that Cecil was putting on. Trammell exclaimed, *"As soon as he steps to the plate, he's in scoring position."* The hitting display, combined with Cecil's 6'3" & 280-pound frame, quickly had Fielder's teammates replacing his Japanese league "Wild Bear" moniker with a new one: *Big Daddy.*

The wins gradually began to come, starting with a 16 & 12 June. By the July 9 All-Star game break, Detroit improved to fourth-place, 6.5 games behind first-place Boston, with Cecil's league-best 28 homers & 75 RBIs leading the way. The Midsummer Classic was played at Wrigley Field, a 2-0 A.L. win. Fielder earned his 1st of 3 All-Star team selections as a Tiger, and Trammell – on his way to a third Silver Slugger award and a fourth-place finish in the batting race at .304 - received his 6th & final selection.

The 1990 Tigers were never a real threat to win the division, sitting all except a handful of dates the rest of the way 5 to 10 games below .500. Cecil's home barrage, however, kept fans all across the country entranced. Into mid-summer, Fielder was considered likely to hit 50 home runs, a bar previously reached only 10 times in the history of the game, and a long-shot to catch Roger Maris' all-time record of 61. At home and on the road, the national media was on hand to tell the story of Big Daddy's historic bid. And it wasn't just the number, it was the distance that many of his homers traveled...

On Saturday, August 25, Oakland was in town for an afternoon game. 17 & 9 Dave Stewart, one of the game's finest pitchers, squared off against Frank Tanana. In the bottom of the first, Tony Phillips was on 2nd with a double as Cecil strode to the plate. Big Daddy hit a titanic blast that landed on top of the left-field roof and bounced over. Ex-Tiger Jim Northrup, handling PASS Sports color commentary for this game, told the listening audience that this made Fielder only the third player to have a ball land on top of, and then bounce over, the left-field roof, joining Harmon Killebrew and Frank Howard in the select trio. In the fourth inning, Cecil hit another 2-run homer, driving in 5 runs in the 14-4 victory. As August came to a close, Fielder had 42 homers and 111 RBIs.

Sunday, September 23, drew 43,666 to the Oakland A's Coliseum, many to see Cecil Fielder in person. Detroit opened the scoring in the 2nd, when fleet 21-year old center-fielder, Milt Cuyler, brought up for his first look at the majors this month after stealing 52 bases in AAA Toledo, singled in a run. Tony Phillips and rookie third baseman Travis Fryman, hitting an outstanding .317, followed with singles to load the bases and the Oakland fans roared as Big Daddy came to bat. He didn't disappoint, putting a charge into the pitch from future-Tiger Mike Moore, sending it deep into the left-field stands for a grand slam, home run number 48 and RBIs 123, 124, 125 & 126 in the Tigers 6-0 win.

During Detroit's final home stand of 1990, Cecil hit home run number 49, but no more in the 6 games. Number 50 would have to be hit in the season's final 3 games, all at Yankee Stadium. In game 1, Frank Tanana threw shutout ball into the 8th, and Jerry Don Gleaton (more about him in a minute) picked up his 13th save, the game's only runs coming home on a Travis Fryman 2-run homer. In game 2, Detroit fell 4-1, still no 50th homer. If it was going to happen, it would have to be in game number 162, Yankee rookie hurler Steve Adkins against Jack Morris. A Tiger hit a grand slam in the first, not Cecil, but rather 36-year old outfielder Gary Ward, a 1989 free agent signee playing the last game of a nice 12-year career (last 2 years as a Tiger platoon player with 18 homers). Finally, in the 4th, it happened. Tony Phillips was on first with a walk when Big Daddy walloped number 50 deep into the left-field seats. Cecil later said, *"I started pressing quite a bit. It was something that hadn't been done for a while. For me it was an unbelievable feeling at that time."* With the 50th now achieved, Fielder came up in the 8th with two men on, and reliever Alan Mills on the mound. Big Daddy crushed a fast ball on a line into the left-field seats for his 51st and final home run of 1990, as the Tigers rolled 10-3 in the Bronx, ending a 1990 that provided many more great memories than a 79 & 83 record would indicate.

After the '89 team hit only 116 homers, the '90 Tigers led the A.L. with 172. Cecil Fielder became the first major leaguer to hit 50 or more homers since Cincy's George Foster hit 52 in 1977, and the first in the A.L. since Roger Maris hit 61 in '61. It was the beginning of an outstanding 3-year run for Big Daddy, leading the league in homers back-to-back years, the 51 in '90 followed by 44 in '91, and topping the league in RBIs with 132 in '90, 133 in '91, and 124 in '92 – joining Ty Cobb and Babe Ruth as the only players with three consecutive RBI titles in American League history.

Cecil reflected on his 1990 season for mlive.com in 2018, *"Oh, it was great! Did some real damage that season and it was fun because there were some consummate professional cats on that team... Lou Whitaker, Alan Trammell, Chet Lemon and Dave Bergman. It was good for me to be around them and be able to rap with those cats."*

DDDDDDDDDDDDDDDDDDDDDDDDDDDDDDDDDDDDDDDDDDDDDDDDDDDDDDDDDDDDDDDDDDDDDDDDDDDD

Jerry Don Gleaton was the reliever who saved the October 1 game at Yankee Stadium for Frankie Tanana. It would be Gleaton's final appearance of the '90 season for Detroit, and it was a dandy, allowing no hits in 1 & 1/3rd innings as he racked up save number 13 and lowered his ERA to 2.94.

Detroit acquired Jerry Don Gleaton from Kansas City one week before Opening Day for a career minor league pitcher. At our sponsor bar, Canton's Mobil Lounge, after an evening of play by our softball team, the Gleaton transaction could not pass without comment from old friend and life-long Yankee fan, Mark Alwood. *"Jerry Don Gleaton!"* he yelled derisively over his beer across the table at his teammates, Tiger fans all, *"another typical crappy pick up by the Tigers."* Sure enough, Jerry Don started out slow, seeing limited action the first couple of months, but as the year progressed, so did Sparky's confidence in him at critical moments. 3 saves in July were followed by 4 in August and 4 more September-October. From the All-Star game on, he seemed to be pitching every 2 to 3 days, and during the year appeared in 57 games, on the mound at the end of 34 of those. As Gleaton's innings piled up and his ERA lowered, softball nights post-game in the bar became even more joyful than usual – quite an achievement - making sure that Yankee Mark was between two guys yelling back 'n forth about Jerry Don's latest conquest, as 6 simple words, *"How 'bout that Jerry Don Gleaton!"* seemed to magically cause steam to rise from our target's ears. And the coup de gras? Gleaton's final save of the season, lucky number 13, was at Yankee Stadium. Really, does it get any better than that? A long-running retort to a Yankee fan's obnoxious statement is a delightful example of what makes baseball the Great Game that it is.

DDDDDDDDDDDDDDDDDDDDDDDDDDDDDDDDDDDDDDDDDDDDDDDDDDDDDDDDDDDDDDDDDDDDDDDDDDDD

Ernie Harwell's contract as WJR radio broadcaster for Tiger Baseball expired at the end of 1990. At season's end, Ernie set up a meeting with Tiger President Bo Schembechler to negotiate a new 5-year deal. It was during this confab that Ernie discovered the WJR-Tiger position: to let the 72-year old Harwell go and hire a new broadcast team in an attempt to reach a younger audience, acting on the advice of a Chicago consulting firm hired by the Tigers. Bo did agree that Ernie could broadcast one final season, offering him a contract that would run through 1991, and Harwell requested that the Tigers set up a press conference for him at The Corner. Bo acquiesced and even agreed to broadcast it – a move he soon came to regret.

On December 19, 1990, live from the offices of the Detroit Tigers, Ernie Harwell told the assembled press that he had one last year in the booth, *"I wanted to go on longer, but the Tigers decided they didn't want me to go on longer. Bo was very forthright. He told me, 'We don't want you to come back.' I have no bitterness. I was surprised when the one-year deal came up. My health is fine. I was told they wanted to go in a different direction. I would have preferred to have the decision on my shoulders rather than have somebody tell me."* Also attending the news conference was the stunned Paul Carey, Ernie's partner in the booth since 1973. Carey aka the Voice of God told the press that he'd decided 3 weeks ago 1991 would be his final season in the booth, but he was just learning of Ernie's firing along with everyone else today.

Immediately realizing how bad Ernie's comments sounded, Bo addressed the writers, taking things from bad to worse, letting them know the reason WJR & the Tigers decided to fire Harwell is they feared Ernie would retire suddenly (if that's the case, why was Harwell asking for a 5-year extension?) and there'd be little time to get a quality replacement. A *Detroit News* December 20 story quoted Bo, *"It's our judgment that he's coming down close to the end of his career. We didn't want to have to go out and search."* Despite the immense amount of love that Coach Bo earned from UM fans, even folks in Ann Arbor thought this whole episode stunk. Inspired or depressed by the news, Ann Arbor comedy troupe the Stunt Johnson Theatre penned a play entitled *"Bo & Woody"* featuring Woody Hayes coming back from the dead & instructing Bo to do all sorts of stupid things, firing Ernie at the top of the list. *The Sporting News* reported a Grosse Pointe hospital volunteer as saying, *"When the nuns working at the hospital heard of Ernie's firing, they said some words I didn't think they knew."*

The depths of the fans anger grew over the winter, reaching a new level of disgust in the new year.

1991 - 1994 Bats Be Booming; New Ownership & Ernie's Back; World Series Strike

"I am a mild & lazy guy. I was that way long before Steve Martin became a wild & crazy guy."

(Ernie Harwell)

1991 opened with two transactions that greatly impacted the Tiger franchise.

On January 11, Detroit pulled off one of the finest trades in team history. Pitcher Jeff Robinson had been struggling with arm problems over the last two seasons, unable to regain the form that made him staff ace in 1988, and was traded to the Orioles for catcher Mickey Tettleton. After departing the Tigers, Jeff had two more rough years, going a combined 11 & 14 with a 5.17 ERA, before retiring. In Mickey's four years in Detroit, he came to be considered one of the top catchers in the team's history. From '91 – '93, Tettleton hit 31, 32 & 32 home runs and won two Silver Slugger Awards as the best hitter at his position. In his 4th year with the team, Mickey earned his 2nd All-Star team berth (his first with Baltimore in '89).

The 1990 day that Cecil Fielder hit homers 50 & 51, the final game of the season, was also notable for being Jack Morris' final day as a Detroit Tiger. On February 5, 1991, free agent Morris signed with his hometown team, the Minnesota Twins. From 1991-1993, the Tigers were a league best in scoring runs & a league worst in giving 'em up. Minus Jack, and his 46 wins, over these 3 years, may have meant the difference between the entertaining team it was & the championship team it might have been.

Team President Schembechler first infuriated fans in December '90 as the hatchet man sending Ernie Harwell packing once the '91 season concluded. Then, Tom Monaghan, who echoed generations of Tiger fans by calling Tiger Stadium a "shrine" when he bought the team in 1983, began in the late-80s to give voice to the need for a new ball park, eventually adding the threat of moving the team out of Detroit if that did not happen, and it was Bo who beat this unpopular drum on Monaghan's behalf. Although the threat of a widespread boycott of Opening Day 1991 did not materialize to any great degree with 47,382 still making their way thru the turnstiles, a general discontent and distrust of those running the team was thick in the air.

Whether it be in Bo's presenting the case for Ernie's departure or the need for a new stadium, the forceful personality that was so successful in motivating 20-year old football players to victory, did not produce the same results with the general public. As Bo was preparing to address the Detroit Economic Club in April of '91 on the stadium issue, Monaghan proved that timing and diplomacy were not in his wheelhouse, telling a reporter, *"Detroit is one of the worst baseball cities in America, and the fans' perception about crime make the (current) location a liability."* The *Metro Times* likened Monaghan's remarks part of "Fan Alienation Week." In this environment, Schembechler informed the area civic & business leaders of the Economic Club that, *"It's unfair for you to think that you can shackle us to a rusted girder in Tiger Stadium and expect us to compete & win, because it's not going to happen."* It's almost like the '84 & '87 successes took place decades ago. Bo's Economic Club presentation included the startling comment that *"over half of all Tiger Stadium seats have obstructed view"* versus the 3,000 that actually did, not a statement that built support & trust among the community for the Monaghan team. *Esquire* magazine included Tom & Bo on their July '91 list of *Most Annoying People in America*.

Although disgust with the club's position to rid us of our beloved stadium AND our beloved announcer did little to keep fans away from The Corner on Opening Day, the man who had been Detroit's starter for the last 11 Openers did decide to stay away from Tiger Stadium today. For the first time since 1979,

Jack Morris was the Opening Day starter for another team, the St. Paul-native signing an off-season free agent contract with the Minnesota Twins. 1991 was his 12th consecutive Opening Day assignment, and when Jack earned the same honor for the Toronto Blue Jays in 1992 & 1993, Morris held the all-time MLB consecutive record for Opening Day starts at 14. Jack's longevity & durability were also reflected in his lifetime 175 complete games, the most for any pitcher since 1975. With Jack now a Twin, Frank Tanana was handed the ball in Detroit's 6-4 Opener win over the Yanks, the victory powered by a Trammell 2-run homer & 2-run double, and a 7th inning Big Daddy tie-breaking 2-run double.

This 1991 edition of the Detroit Tigers had a muscle beach look about it, including big boys Cecil Fielder, Mickey Tettleton, and free agent signings Pete Incaviglia & Rob Deer. Sparky was impressed by the time Deer spent in the weight room preparing for the '91 season, *"Rob showed up this year looking like Venus de Milo."* Likening Rob to a famous statue that has no arms may account for all of the strikeouts he piled up in '91, a league-leading 175 or once every 3 times at bat, to go with his 25 home runs & .179 average – he pretty much either struck out or homered. In fact, the team as a whole was tops in both categories with 209 homers & a then-A.L. record 1,185 Ks. Sparky saw the bright side of whiffing, *"The good thing about all of these strikeouts is that we hit into less double plays."* Much as the toothless man has no need for floss.

With Jack Morris gone, the Tigers spent money on yet another free agent, pitcher Bill Gullickson. On a team sorely in need of quality pitching, this was an excellent signing, as Gullickson led not only the Tigers but also the league in wins with 20 and starts with 35, finishing 8th in Cy Young balloting. Even with Bill on the staff, the team's 4.51 ERA left them an A.L. 12th out of 14. The weak pitching (796 runs given up)/big hitting (2nd in the majors with 817 runs scored) Tigers experienced many series scores like the one with Texas in early May: win 7-6, lose 6-5, & win 8-7. One fan said watching this team was like watching an Earnie Shavers fight – win or lose, there'd be fireworks *(interestingly, in the run-up to his '77 fight with the bald Shavers, Muhammad Ali held up an 8 x10 of Earnie's head for reporters, covered all but the top of Shavers' head with a piece of cardboard, and shouted, "I'm fightin' an acorn! I'm fightin' an acorn!").* Five players hit over 20 homers, led by 44 from Big Daddy, 31 Mickey Tettleton, 25 Deer, 23 Sweet Lou and 21 Travis Fryman. There always seemed to be runners on base when these homers were launched, as Detroit also led the A.L. in walks with Tettleton (#2 at 101), Lou & Rob Deer in the top 10.

This was the prototypical .500 team, in April going 10 & 9, May 13 & 14, June 14 & 14, and July 14 & 12. The home run barrage was keeping the fans excited, including when Mickey Tettleton hit two balls over the Tiger Stadium right field roof within 5 days of each other in June. Mickey became the 5th player to hit 2 or more homers over Tiger Stadium's right field roof, joining (4 times) Stormin' Norman, (3) Mantle, (2) Jason "Rooftop" Thompson and (2) Kirk Gibson. Tettleton's 2nd shot over the roof occurred in a Tiger victory with a very-normal-for-'91-score of 8 to 7; the Tiger pitcher in this shootout was Dan Gakeler, a very-normal-for-'91-starter, one of ten tried by Sparky, who in his only major league season started 7 games, completed none, relieved 24 times, posting a record of 1 & 4 with a 5.74 ERA with 2 saves.

Despite treading water the first 4 months of '91, going into August, 51 & 49 Detroit was alone in 2nd place, only 6 games (5 in the loss column) behind Toronto. Opening August on a 10 & 6 run, the Tigers closed to within two games of Toronto as the Blue Jays arrived August 16 at The Corner for a 3-game weekend series. Although Detroit lost 2 of the 3, the Bengals won their next 7 in a row, allowing them to catch Toronto in a first-place tie. The two teams would share first for 3 days, through August 26, but that would be Detroit's high-water mark of 1991. The Tigers dropped their final four of the month, and were 3.5 behind as September began. A September 2, Tiger 12-5 win in Seattle, pulled the team to within two in the loss column, but Detroit could only take 13 of the final 28, finishing 7 back in 2nd place, 84 & 78.

The Tiger finale of '91 was against the Orioles and played at Baltimore's Memorial Stadium. Not only was it the final time that Ernie & Paul would work a game together in the broadcast booth, but it was the last time a ballgame would be played at Memorial Stadium, the O's moving to brand new Camden Yards for the '92 season. The 7-1 Tiger win had no effect on the standings, but it was a fine, complete game tossed by 38-year old Frankie Tanana, who improved to 13 & 12 while lowering his ERA to 3.77. 50,700 Orioles fans came out to say goodbye to the park built in 1954, a babe compared to 1912 Tiger Stadium, and honor those who played there. Pre-game, two graying, revered athletes walked in street clothes to the foul line near 3rd base, described by the p.a. announcer as the greatest third baseman in MLB history & the greatest quarterback in NFL history, #5 and #19, Brooks Robinson & Johnny Unitas, who both made picture-perfect, ceremonial first pitch baseball & football tosses, towards home plate.

Post-game, Oriole greats from over the years, wearing their uniforms, exited the dugout one-by-one, and trotted to their old defensive positions. The first to take his place on the field was a beaming Brooks Robinson, the 20-year old protégé of 34-year old George Kell back in 1957, two good old boys from Arkansas. Frank Robinson was next, running out to his old right field position. The third Oriole was first sacker Boog Powell, the *Boooooooog* cheer rolling thru the stands, followed by a tearful Jim Palmer, one great pitcher and the man who 9 years before playfully joined in our fun at The Corner, tossing a wet towel into the chest of Lambertville's Greg Sulewski - and on the players came and the adulation rose. The chills and tears flowing 10.6.91 at Memorial Stadium would be repeated at Tiger Stadium 9.27.99.

How emotional it must have been for Ernie & Paul, to be wrapping up their 19 years together, no matter where the game was at, but for Ernie was the added fact that he was the first radio announcer in the history of the Orioles, broadcasting their Opening Day 1954 game, the inaugural game when the team known as the St. Louis Browns became the Baltimore Orioles – a game played at Briggs Stadium. Two days before the Memorial Stadium finale, the Orioles honored Ernie during a pre-game ceremony.

As the final Memorial Stadium game began, Ernie opened the WJR broadcast reminiscing, *"I remember the first game in Memorial Stadium. It was a day much like today. Rained on the parade in the morning, but when we got to the ballpark, the sun came out."* Then, later in the game, Ernie turn to his dear friend and broadcast partner, Paul Carey, *"I've been asked to read a marriage proposal, Paul, 'Rachel Rozmys, will you marry me?' I wonder if she knows from whom the proposal is coming. Anyway, we await the outcome."* As Frank Tanana was keeping Oriole bats under lock 'n key, Ernie kept the listeners' interest, *"Did you know that a Cubs groundskeeper invented the bat rack?"* Baltimore native and ex-NFL star running back, Calvin Hill, stopped by the booth, telling Ernie, *"You make me feel young when I hear your voice."* Although Paul handles the play-by-play for the middle 3 innings, Ernie has a 6th inning update for the audience, *"The young lady said yes. Rachel Rozmys will marry you, John Miller."* As the game nears its conclusion, Paul asks Ernie what he intends to do with an old hound's tooth overcoat that Harwell keeps in the broadcast booth, just in case, *"I don't know. I tried to give it to the Salvation Army, but they wouldn't take it."* The scene is 1 out in the O's ninth, the Tigers comfortably ahead, Cal Ripken at the plate with a man on first... Tanana winds and pitches... Ripken hits a grounder down to Tony Phillips at third, Tony fires to Lou for the force at 2nd and Lou rifles a throw to Dave Bergman at 1st to nab Ripken, granting us all a final Ernie-ism from our radios, *"Two for the price of one!"*

With the game over, Oriole fans excitedly readied themselves for the Memorial Stadium celebration they know is coming, while Ernie says a few final words to the folks back home, *"I've had a gratifying career as your Tiger announcer, and now I say goodbye. I'll never be able to repay all the warmth and affection you fans have shown me. I agree with Satchel Paige and William Shakespeare. Old Satch said, 'Don't look back, something may be gaining on you.' And Mr. Shakespeare once wrote, 'To have done is to hang quite out of fashion.' Thank you very much, and God bless all of you."*

The 1991 Tiger finale marked the final time dear friends & lengendary broadcast partners, Ernie & Paul, worked a Tiger game together; this 2006 photo was from Nancy Carey's 60th party

DDDDDDDDDDDDDDDDDDDDDDDDDDDDDDDDDDDDDDDDDDDDDDDDDDDDDDDDDDDDDDDDDDDDDDDDDDD

1992 news...

The Good News: Jack Morris is pitching at The Corner on Opening Day! The Bad News: he's pitching for the Toronto Blue Jays. The Real Bad News: the Tigers have banned smoking at the stadium, so no more White Owl cigars while cheering on our Tigers. Tech News: Detroit began taking credit card ticket orders.

Black Jack's first year a non-Tiger worked out well for him, as his Minnesota Twins won the World Series over the Atlanta Braves and Morris was named the Series MVP, with Jack winning Game 7 on a 10-inning complete game, 1-0, shutout. After the Series, Morris exercised his option to become a free agent, weighed offers from both Minnesota & Toronto, said the Twins' proposal *"wasn't close"*, and soon became a Blue Jay. Before 51,068, on a Monday afternoon, Morris pitched against Detroit's 20-game winner of a year ago, Bill Gullickson, and despite Jack surrendering 9th inning solo homers to Big Daddy Fielder and Rob Deer, Morris threw 144 pitches as he went the distance in Toronto's 4-2 victory. In the 2nd game versus the Blue Jays, starters Tanana & Todd (son of Mel) Stottlemyre were both gone before the fifth inning was done and, despite 2 more homers by Fielder and a nice MLB debut of 25-year old Tiger pitcher John Doherty (3 hits in 2.1 innings), Detroit lost 10-9.

The Tigers did not win once in their season opening 6-game home stand, sitting in last place 6 games out of first. Despondent fans viewed the Tabbies on a pace to go 0 & 162 and finish 162 back, a view dashed in Detroit's first road game, Detroit outscoring Cleveland 7-5, in a contest featuring Rob Deer's 2nd hit of the season aka his 2nd home run of the season. The next day, Rob had one more hit, also a home run. On April 16, the final game before leaving Cleveland, Rob Deer went 2 for 5, both hits home runs. After 10 games in the '92 season, Rob Deer's first 5 hits of the season were all home runs, making him the only major leaguer in history to ever pull off this feat, and Rob was on his way to a full year total of 32 homers (with just 64 RBIs) & 131 strikeouts.

The '92 Tigers were much like the '91 Tigers, with a little less pitching (egad!). Detroit was #1 in the A.L. with 182 homers (Big Daddy 35, Tettleton 32, Deer 32, Fryman 20), #1 at 791 runs (Tony Phillips tops in the league with 114). Detroit batters struck out 1,055 times, more than any other A.L. team, and the pitching staff was last with a 4.60 ERA. The Tigers and any team they were playing at a given time were likely scoring runs at a pinball machine-pace and, though entertaining, the Tigers could not overcome the poor start to their season. From June 20th on, Detroit was never closer than 10 games to first place.

But even when the team is having a rough time, the characters of the game draw you in. One such individual was Skeeter Barnes. The fans had taken a real liking to this 35-year old, in his 2nd year with Detroit. Skeeter just seemed like a happy sort, and might show up anywhere on the diamond, playing 6 different positions (3 OF, 1B, 2B, 3B). Wearing the Olde English D from '91 to '94, Skeeter hit a fine .281. And then there was John Doherty. The rookie stood out as one of the few pitchers having a good year, in 47 games including 11 as a starter, going 7 & 4 with a 3.88. Tavern owner Hoot Robinson spoke highly of John, who had become the current Tiger to most frequent Hoot's establishment. John Doherty's most memorable '92 outing was also his shortest at 2 pitches. On June 8 at The Corner, Tiger starter Mark Leiter, 23 & 18 with Detroit from '91 thru '93, left after tossing 5 innings with the Tigers up 8-1. Before Doherty entered the game, Cleveland hurler Dennis Cook almost hit Tettleton on back-to-back pitches in the bottom of the fifth, sparking a lot of back 'n forth barking between the dugouts, the atmosphere as Doherty took the mound. The first batter he faced was Glenallen Hill, and on John's first pitch he drilled him on the arm. As Hill took his base, Sandy Alomar stepped in to bat. John's 2nd pitch sailed directly over the head of Alomar, who charged the mound and launched a flying Kung Fu kick at Doherty. Both dugouts and bullpens emptied, the ensuing scuffle beyond the usual baseball grab-your-partner that takes place on such occasions. Tony Phillips and the Tribe's Carlos Baerga didn't want the clash to end, and had to be restrained by teammates. Doherty & Alomar were tossed, probably not on their way to share a few beers & laughs at Hoots, and I headed for a stadium pay phone *(like a cell phone, except you have to hunt one down, and possibly wait your turn in line, to use it, then have the correct amount of coins for the privilege)* to a call Laz and Connie Surabian, Birmingham MI transplants now in Tuckahoe, N.Y., to give them the blow-by-blow details one can only witness on a night out in the big city.

DDDDDDDDDDDDDDDDDDDDDDDDDDDDDDDDDDDDDDDDDDDDDDDDDDDDDDDDDDDDDDDDDDDDDDDDDDD

At 71 years of age, Detroit native & legendary Tiger pitcher Hal Newhouser was inducted into baseball's Hall of Fame in 1992 along with Rollie Fingers, Tom Seaver, and an umpire from 1925 through 1954, Bill McGowan. Prince Hal was voted in by the Veterans Committee, and had a wait of 39 years after retiring to get the call. In looking at Hal's record, one item that had to jump out at the Committee: Newhouser led the majors in wins for one entire decade, the 1940s. There was a parallel Detroit story when Jack Morris also had to wait for the Veterans Committee to vote him into the Hall in 2018 (though his 14 year wait from retirement to induction was much shorter than Newhouser's 39 years), and one item that must have impressed the Committee was that Jack led the majors in wins for the decade of the 80s.

Hal Newhouser posted a lifetime record of 207 & 150 with a 3.06 ERA, was a 6-time All-Star, 2-time A.L. MVP, topped the A.L. in wins 4 times, strikeouts & ERA twice each, won the pitching Triple Crown (wins, ERA, strikeouts) in '45 and was a World Series champion with Detroit that same year.

Newhouser's induction speech was a rarity, under 2 minutes, dedicated to thanking those who made it all possible for him, primarily his parents, *"Although my dad could not be here today, somehow I think that he is."* Hal's 95-year old mother, Emilie, was on hand, and when Hal thanked his Mom, he said, *"May I say this – she's still healthy and she still drives her own automobile."* No single line received more applause on this glorious day.

DDDDDDDDDDDDDDDDDDDDDDDDDDDDDDDDDDDDDDDDDDDDDDDDDDDDDDDDDDDDDDDDDDDDDDDDDDD

On August 3, 1992, Bo & Millie Schembechler were in their Ann Arbor home celebrating their wedding anniversary when the fax machine began to hum. The fax was a poor excuse for an anniversary message. It was from Tom Monaghan, letting Bo know that he was being fired as Tiger president. Schembechler's reply was pure Bo, *"The hell with them. I'm celebrating my 24th wedding anniversary tonight."* Bo was not the only executive to receive the axe. Jim Campbell, with the Tigers for 53 years, was also let go. In a press release, Monaghan said, *"Jim has been a valuable ally, confidant and consultant throughout my years as the Tiger owner. I will miss working with him very much."* Monaghan was quoted about Bo in less sentimental terms, noting of his long-time friend that there were *"personal differences."*

From one pizza king to another, Domino's Tom Monaghan had been negotiating a sale of the Tigers to Little Caesar's Mike Ilitch. It was believed that the deal negotiated hinged on the departure of Campbell & Schembechler from the executive team. Jim Campbell will be remembered as the guiding hand in building championship teams in 1968 & 1984. In his time with the Tigers, Bo Schembechler will be remembered for his farm system successes in upgrading training facilities, introducing conditioning & strength programs, and improving the coaching & medical staffs. But Bo is mostly remembered for his overbearing attempt to secure a new stadium, and as the man who fired Ernie Harwell.

DDDDDDDDDDDDDDDDDDDDDDDDDDDDDDDDDDDDDDDDDDDDDDDDDDDDDDDDDDDDDDDDDDDDDDDDDDD

On September 25, 1992, a Friday night at Michigan & Trumbull, Cleveland was in town to open a 3-game series. A sparse gathering of 13,624 cheered on Detroit as, one out from defeat, Cecil Fielder hit a 2-out double to score Tony Phillips and force extra innings. When Skeeter Barnes raced home from 2nd base in the 10th on a Chad Kreuter pinch hit single, it completed Detroit's 6-5 come-from-behind victory. The win was number 1,131 for George Sparky Anderson as Tiger skipper, tying him with Hughie Jennings for most victories as Tigers manager. When Detroit crushed Cleveland 13-3 two days later, Sparky had the title of winningest Tiger manager to himself.

The Tigers ended the '92 season in sixth place, 21 games behind Toronto, at 75 & 87. During the final 5 months of the year, an ex-Tiger had, in a word not usually associated with him, *quietly* returned to his home state of Michigan. In March, Kirk Gibson had been traded by the Royals to Pittsburgh for pitcher Neal Heaton, reuniting Gibby with his first professional manager back in '78 with the Lakeland Tigers, Jim Leyland. On Opening Day for the Pirates, Gibson led-off and played right, and was in that spot 3 of the first 5 games, but started the season slowly, and after hitting just .196 in 16 games, was given his unconditional release on May 5. At the age of 35, Kirk came home to spend the summer with his family, where he was when Mike Ilitch became the owner of the Tigers. Ilitch loved Gibson's style of play, could not understand how Detroit ever let him leave after '87, and on February 10, 1993, signed Kirk to come back to the Tigers for the upcoming season.

The new owner made another early '93 move that excited the fans. Ilitch thought it important that Ernie Harwell leave the Tiger radio booth under more respectful circumstances than the messy exit under Bo Schembechler at the end of 1991, and asked Harwell to come back for one more season. So, the 1992 rookie broadcast team of Rick Rizz & Bob Rathbun would in '93 make room for a legend in the booth, as Ernie's joined the two for play-by-play in the third, fourth & fifth innings.

DDDDDDDDDDDDDDDDDDDDDDDDDDDDDDDDDDDDDDDDDDDDDDDDDDDDDDDDDDDDDDDDDDDDDDDDDDDD

Detroit's 1993 Home Opener took place on Tuesday, April 13. The boys had just returned home from a 6-game road trip, dropping 4 of 6 to the A's and the Angels. Although they'd averaged 5 runs a game out west, the fans ain't seen nuthin' yet. The Detroit 9 was a blur of players crossing home plate in a 20 to 4 crushing of Oakland, kicking off a run of 11 wins out of 12. These 12 games included some of the most delightful April baseball in memory: a weekend of fun with Seattle started with a 5-0 shutout as newly-signed free agent lefty David Wells outdueled Randy Johnson; another 20-run explosion on Saturday (pushing Chad Krueter's average to .526) produced a 20-3 win; and on one of the most gorgeous Spring Sundays you'll ever see, the Tigers pulled out victory from the jaws of defeat on a Travis Fryman ninth inning, two-run, walk-off homer in a 8-7 Tiger win. The cheers prompted by Fryman's blast shook the old ball yard, sending the bleacher creatures on a conga line down the stadium ramps, out into the middle of Trumbull Avenue, and the booty shaking did not stop until winding its way into Hoot Robinson's Bar for a celebratory round or two.

Tiger pitchers by the vague to unfamiliar names of Bob Macdonald, Tom Bolton, Mike Munoz, and John Kiely were pitching, but it hardly seemed to matter who was on the mound the way the bats were booming. The Tiger Wrecking Crew paid a visit to the Hubert H. Humphrey Metrodome in Minneapolis, and did not leave until pounding Twins pitching for victories of 12-4, 17-1, and 16-5. The only Homer Hankies waved were by those folks who had cars in the parking lot with Michigan license plates. The Minnesota Massacre catapulted the Tigers into the totally unexpected position of first place, where they would stay for the next two months. As of mid-May, Detroit's offense was averaging 8 runs per game, on a pace to set the all-time MLB record for runs scored. Sparky let folks know of the opponents, *"If they're punishable, we'll punish them."*

DD

Members of the 1968 team gathered at The Corner in '93 for an Old-Timers game and a celebration of the 25-year anniversary of their World Series Championship. Dick "Trixie" Tracewski was talking to a reporter as he reminisced about those days, pointing out that Dick "Mad Dog" McAuliffe was the real leader of the team. Mac was standing nearby & replied, *"Well, they always followed me into the bar, if that's what he means."*

1993 Father's Day was a very special day for the author, the only time I ever attended a game at Michigan & Trumbull with both my Mom & Dad, Mary & Herb Fletcher. Good thing we were in our seats early, as Detroit ran across home plate 5 times in the first off Milwaukee's Ricky Bones, capped off by a spectacular grand slam courtesy of Mickey Tettleton. Righty John Doherty was on cruise control today, departing after 7 innings with a 7-0 cushion, improving his record to 7 & 2 while lowering his ERA to 2.74. The 7-3 Tiger win left first-place Detroit at 43 & 25, two games up on Toronto & 3 up on New York. Post-game, the 3 of us wandered across Trumbull Avenue to Hoot's in order to introduce the folks to the Man himself. Hoot was missing from his usual spot behind the beer tappers, sitting instead in the back-right corner booth, breathing with the help of a newly-acquired oxygen machine. He was his usual cordial self while meeting my parents, explaining the need for the machine, *"Doctor said I shouldn't work where there's smoke, said I'm allergic to it. I've run a bar for 60 years – how allergic can I be?"*

The Father's Day win was the peak for the '93 Tigers. The next day, the team embarked on a 9-game road trip, and lost every one of them. The Tigers came home to meet Texas on July 1, and lost that one, too, falling to third place, 4.5 games back of the Blue Jays. July 2 was a 7:38PM start time against Texas, and to the 29,330 who came out to cheer their Tigers on, it looked bleak. Bill Gullickson didn't pitch badly, only surrendering 6 hits, but left after the top of the 8th in a 4-0 hole. If Detroit was going to mount a comeback, they had the right man leading off, Tony Phillips, who this year led the A.L. with 132 walks while enjoying a career-high .443 on base percentage. Sure enough, Tony singled off the tough Kevin Brown. Dan Gladden, turning 36 in 5 days, in his 2nd year with Detroit & final year of his career, also singled. With Brown tiring, Matt Whiteside relieved, and Travis Fryman greeted him with a double into the right-center gap, scoring both runners. It's Texas 4 Detroit 2 and the fans are now on their feet & getting loud 'cause here comes Big Daddy to the plate. Fielder swung at the very first pitch, and sent an absolute monster of a drive to left field. For the second time in his career, Cecil Fielder landed a baseball on the left-field roof, where it bounced before falling back into the sea of howling fans below. You cannot hear yourself think. It's a brand-new ballgame, all tied up at 4. That was the score as the game moved to the bottom of the 10th. With one out, Texas reliever Bob Patterson pitched carefully to Big Daddy, issuing a base on balls to him. Patterson was able to get Kirk Gibson on a fly ball to center, and with two out, Mickey Tettleton dug in. Mickey swung, the ball disappearing deep into the left field seats as the crowd shouted as one with plenty of high fives, hugs, back-slappin' and jumping up 'n down. Final score, Detroit 6 Texas 4.

The reprieve was a brief one. The losing picked right back up the next day, the team still hitting but the pitching not able to keep up, coming in on the short end of too many 9-6 & 12-7 games. Detroit lost 17 of 26 the rest of July. A 7-game winning streak in late-August increased readership of each morning-after's sports page, drew the Tigers to within 4 games of 1st on August 28, and included an incredible game against Oakland by pitcher Mike Moore: on August 23 at The Corner, Moore pitched to 28 men – 27 outs and 1 single – in a 9-0 win that improved his record to 10 & 6 and dropped his ERA to a number that underlined the Achilles heel of the 1993 Detroit Tigers, 5.20. The Boys of Summer were 5 out as late as September 10, but could get no closer, finishing 85 & 77, 10 behind first-place Toronto, leading the league with 899 runs, 765 walks, a .362 on base percentage, & .796 on base plus slugging percentage.

DDDDDDDDDDDDDDDDDDDDDDDDDDDDDDDDDDDDDDDDDDDDDDDDDDDDDDDDDDDDDDDDDDDDDDDDDDDD

With the 1993 season concluded, Ernie was asked by the pay-cable station PASS if he would be willing to share their booth with ex-Tigers Jim Northrup & Jim Price. Harwell accepted, and worked for PASS from '94 thru '96, and then – after George Kell retired - at TV station WKBD in '97 & '98, sharing the booth with Al Kaline. Ernie's old 1993 radio partners, Rick Rizz & Bob Rathbun, had an impossible act to follow, made worse by replacing Ernie at a difficult time through no fault of their own, and were never fully accepted by the majority of Tiger fans. The two found themselves fired at the end of 1994, replaced on radio by Frank Beckmann & Larry Sorenson.

In 1999, Ernie Harwell was finally back where he belonged, back where he should've never left, covering Detroit Tiger games from the WJR radio broadcast booth. The only piece missing was Ernie's old friend & sidekick, Paul Carey, who left with Harwell at the end of the 1991 season when Ernie was forced out. In '99, Ernie shared the booth with Jim Price, and then from 2000 thru 2002 with Price & Dan Dickerson. Ernie celebrated his 84th birthday on January 25, 2002, and announced that this would be his final season behind the mike. The outpouring of love in this final year came not only from the Tiger faithful, but from teams & their fans all over the league – it was one, beautiful, goodbye tour. Opposing teams asked Ernie to throw out the first pitch during Detroit's last 2002 series at their ballpark. The visitors broadcast booth in Cleveland was renamed in his honor. The press box at Comerica Park was christened the Ernie Harwell Media Center.

Near the end of 2002, Ernie was a guest on WJR's Paul W. Smith morning show. Many old friends, ball players and others, called into the show to share memories with Ernie. Near the end of the program, Ernie was told there was time for *"one final call, from a special guy. There's a man on the line, he was a third baseman, and I think he was one of your all-time favorite Tigers, wasn't he?" "Oh, absolutely"* Ernie said. *"Who was that Ernie?" "Tommy Brookens!" "Yeah, I think he's calling from Pennsylvania..."*

Tommy is on the line, *"Ernie, how you doin' today?"* Ernie clearly loves hearing from his old friend, and kids him, *"Hey, aren't you out fishin' or huntin' or doin' something worthwhile?" "Well, I'm sittin' here with a buddy, and we're makin' some spaghetti sauce. He's got the rifle pointed out the window, you know we need some venison to put in there."* Ernie laughs, *"I'll tell ya."* Tom continues, *"So that's what we're doin' here today. I wanted to call and say hello to you, and wish you all the best. I'm gonna come out and visit you here next weekend, we're havin' an Old Timers Game. I really like the fact that now they're calling 'em a Legends Game, that means we don't have to be Old Timers anymore, we can just be legends."* Ernie sez, *"Hey, you can be a legend – you're my man!" "Well, you're the real legend out there, I'll tell ya that. I can remember when I was playin' & you give me the nickname 'the Pennsylvania Poker', and WJR carried clean in here to Pennsylvania, part way, and I had an aunt and she said, 'I want you to tell Ernie something for me. Every time it seems like you come up Tom, the radio fades in or out. Could you tell Ernie to talk just a little bit louder when you get up to the plate?' So I'll never forget that."* Ernie laughs, *"I'll tell you, you're great! I love you and thanks for calling."*

On Sunday, September 29, 2002, the Tigers played the season's final game in Toronto. At the end of the game, Ernie emotionally signed off, *"I have just finished my baseball broadcasting career. And it's time to say goodbye, but I think goodbyes are sad and I'd much rather say hello. Hello to a new adventure. I'm not leaving, folks. I'll still be with you, living my life in Michigan—my home state—surrounded by family and friends. And rather than goodbye, please allow me to say thank you. Thank you for letting me be part of your family. Thank you for taking me with you to that cottage up north, to the beach, the picnic, your work place and your back yard. Thank you for sneaking your transistor under the pillow as you grew up loving the Tigers. Now I might have been a small part of your life. But you've been a very large part of mine. And it's my privilege and honor to share with you the greatest game of all."*

DDDDDDDDDDDDDDDDDDDDDDDDDDDDDDDDDDDDDDDDDDDDDDDDDDDDDDDDDDDDDDDDDDDD

The team that the previous April pummeled opponents at a historic rate was missing in action as the 1994 season began. The Tigers sat 7 & 14 going into May, 8 games back of East Division-leading Boston. Despite rallying for a 16 & 11 May, behind a month-long offensive explosion led by Cecil Fielder & Kirk Gibson, Detroit opened June further off the pace, 10 games behind the surging New York Yankees.

Going into the July 12 All-Star game, Detroit was 11 out of first. Gibby continued his fine season, on his way to being named Tiger of the Year by Detroit sportswriters, ending with a .276 average, 23 homers and 72 RBIs. At just 25 years of age, Travis Fryman made his third consecutive All-Star game. In each of his first 3 full seasons, 1991-1993, Fryman averaged 21 homers & 95 runs batted in, and after only 115 games in '94, he had already put 18 balls into the seats and driven in 85 runs, on a 162-game pace for 25 homers & 119 RBIs. But in 1994, there would be no 162 games. The 8th work stoppage to date in MLB history made August 11, a 10-5 loss to Milwaukee at The Corner, the 53 & 62 Tigers 115th and final game of the year.

The 1994 Strike was the one that drove away many fans from the game of baseball, some for a short period of time, some for years, and a relatively small amount yet to return. The strike's cause was a common theme: the battle between owners, attempting to rein in rising salaries they claimed would ruin them, and the players opposing these efforts. Not only did the strike force cancellation of all regular season games after August 11, but also the post-season including, what really upset the game's acolytes, the World Series. For the first time in 90 years, a World Series would not be part of Fall in America.

1994 Hoot Robinson

Hoot Robinson's Bar, 2114 Trumbull at Elizabeth Street, (313) 965-4855

The Major League Baseball strike that had begun on August 12, 1994, came to an end on April 2, 1995. When fans arrived 4 weeks later at The Corner for the delayed 1995 Opening Day, and glanced across Trumbull Avenue, the piece of history lost during the strike could not be missed...

Hoot Robinson officially closed his bar on Friday, September 2, 1994. A combination of crippled business from the baseball strike that began the month prior, and Hoot's declining health, forced the decision. Then, just over 3 months later, on December 15, 1994, Hoot passed away. Gone with him was one of the last links to long-ago Tiger legends and Hoot's customers, like Hank Greenburg and Rudy York. To quote the *Detroit Free Press*, *"The death last week of Hoot Robinson, 87, who put a smile on the faces of everyone who entered his famous bar & grill for more than 60 years, brought a tear to the eyes of his fans & customers. Baseball greats from Babe Ruth to Kirk Gibson enjoyed visiting Hoot, who closed his bar September 2. Won't seem the same around Tiger Stadium without him."*

Located on Trumbull, just north of Michigan Avenue and across the street from, at first, Navin Field, then Briggs Stadium, and finally Tiger Stadium, stood the bar & grill of Hoot Robinson, who was, in his words, *"a proprietor on the block"*. For tens of thousands of Tiger fans from the 30s through the 90s, a pre and/or post game stop at Hoot's bar was a mandatory part of the fun at the Old Ballpark. The 1970s through 1990s bar staff of Kim, Maurice, Geri, Saul, Elsie, Kay, Donna, Linda, and the owner himself was as much a part of the Tiger experience as Stormin' Norman, the Bird, Tommy Brookens, and on and on.

Maurice looks around, refuses our money, then smiles saying, "Don't tell Hoot," before sliding shots across the bar to Ann Arbor's Vid Marvin and the author. In a few moments Kim sez, "Your money's no good here," then, after looking around for Hoot, sets beers in front of us; 15 minutes later Hoot slides us beers & repeats Kim's, "Your money's no good here," statement. Now that's a good day, the kind that inspires one to write in Hoot's name for Governor then, in the next election, President. He should've been elected both times.

For over a quarter of a century of attending Opening Days, our group of 40 to 50 included a pre-game gathering at Hoot's. We had calculated that the average time when all tables & chairs at Hoot's would be spoken for on Opening Day was 10:17AM, a fun tidbit that guaranteed nothing, much like when a routine grounder was hit to Chico "I got a hole in my glove" Fernandez at short.

"I've been on the block since 1928, when I turned 21, opening a restaurant in the Checker Cab building."

When Hoot first welcomed customers, it was in a coffee & donut shop, 'til shortly after Prohibition was repealed (aka 1 week before Mickey Cochrane became a Tiger) and Hoot picked up his liquor license in time for the 1934 Tiger season. Hoot's had customers during all 4 Tiger World Championship seasons, '35, '45, '68, and '84. In game 7 of the 1934 Series, when fans tossed bottles and other projectiles at the Cardinals' Ducky Medwick, quite a few may have picked up a pre-game head of steam over at Hoot's.

"Rudy York was a regular – a lot of the Tigers were, but not like Rudy. When he hit his 17 homers that year in August, it was packed in here. I made sandwiches for the team before they boarded their train at Central Station for road trips."

For one glorious season, two huge events overlapped. 1934 was both the first year that Hoot had his liquor license AND the last for Babe Ruth as a Yankee, and anytime the New Yorkers were in town for a series at The Corner that year, you could find the Babe at Hoot's. Hoot got a kick out of talking about the summer when you could often see the Babe bellied up to his bar. Talk about timing: 1934 was also the year that Detroit won their first pennant since 1909, and Navin Field attendance improved from 320,972 in '33 to a league-leading 919,161 in '34. Great time to open a bar across the street from The Corner!

One of Hoot's most loyal customers was Tiger pitcher Dizzy Trout, during his 14 seasons in Detroit, 1939 into 1952. According to former batboy Dan Dillman, late on the mornings of when Dizzy was scheduled to take the mound, his ritual was to send the batboy over to Hoot's to pick up two of their generously-sized pork chop sandwiches and two soda chasers. Dillman recalled the result of one of those meals, *"Trout bent over to get the catcher's sign. Then it happened – a prodigious belch erupted from his mouth, spewing tobacco juice across the front of the white home jersey with the Olde English D."* Catcher Bob Swift asked Trout if he'd just thrown up, eliciting a big grin from Dizzy, *"No, but Hoot's pork chops sure taste better the second time around."*

DDDDDDDDDDDDDDDDDDDDDDDDDDDDDDDDDDDDDDDDDDDDDDDDDDDDDDDDDDDDDDDDDDDDDDDD

Agnes DeBono, better known to the bar's clientele as Kim, is a native of the island nation of Malta. Shortly after immigrating to the Detroit area in 1959, Kim began over 30 years of working at Hoot's, a friend to both Hoot and his wife Mary, and she served the bar's customers through its final day. Kim shared stories of Hoot as a go-getter even before he was a teenager, first hawking newspapers, then later candy and, as he got older, cigars & cigarettes, in front of Henry Ford's Highland Park auto plant from the mid-1910s into the 1920s.

Kim knew how to treat Hoot's patrons right, and also had a courageous feistiness, taking no guff and tossing the unruly. Her pluck, a huge asset to Hoot in running his tavern, frequently collided with that same spunk in Hoot himself. Kim told Hoot, *"You remind me of my father. He didn't cuss, but he made other people cuss."* Kim wore a baseball cap into work the next day. Hoot was on the other end of the bar, looks at her funny and asked, *"What the hell are you doing wearing a baseball cap?"* Kim walked close to Hoot so he could read what was spelled out on the front of the cap, *"You Piss Me Off!"*

Kim was behind the bar one day when a busload of about 20 guys pulled up to the tavern, each ordering a shot. She set 20 glasses out on the bar, all laid out in a row and measured the liquor for the first one. Eyeballing the rest, Kim took the bottle and ran it across each shot glass. When Hoot saw she wasn't measuring each as he always did, he shouted, *"What the hell are you doing?!"* Kim told him, *"Just get out of my damn way so I can make some money for you."*

Kim wasn't the only Hoot employee that bumped heads with Hoot. One day Elsie, an older but strong gal, was carrying a keg in each hand out of the cooler. Hoot and Elsie were having a running argument, Hoot following Elsie back into the cooler. When Elsie emerged with more beer, with Hoot still in the cooler, Kim yelled to Elsie, *"Lock it!"*

Hoot's right-hand woman, Agnes DeBono aka Kim, back row left

Once a female patron was physically threatening Elsie. Kim got right in her face, telling her to, *"Get the f' out of here!"* When that lady made the mistake of leaving her purse behind, Kim grabbed it, stepped out the bar's front door, and flung it across the street. Kim proudly said, *"It landed at Gate 1,"* noting that she was always athletic. *"When I arrived in the US, I said of the men, 'What the hell are those sissies doing playing basketball?'"* Kim thought it was just women who played the game, like she did in Malta.

Many Tigers were regulars at Hoots until the lights went out in 1994. Kim talked about their various personalities and held up Dave Rozema, a bar fixture during his 1977-1984 Tiger years, as one of the nicest persons she'd ever met – to quote Kim, *"He's cool"*. Kim had the perfect job for someone who loved Tiger baseball as much as she did, and often took her lunch break strolling across Trumbull to the stadium as the ballgame was heading into the 7th inning. A friend manning one of the turnstiles would let her in. One year when the Tigers were struggling, there was a string of games where Kim's entry always seemed to coincide with a Detroit game-saving rally. As word got out about Kim as a good luck charm, a large group of Tiger players came into Hoot's post-game and urged Kim to continue to *"Go across the street! Go across the street!"* She recalled that the players included Lou Whitaker and Alan Trammell, whom Kim greeted with a *"Boy, you are short."*

Despite Hoot's & Kim's personalities clashing while working together at the bar, their fondness for each other came through – Kim as she speaks now of Hoot, and Hoot who, as he neared the end, frequently calling her to talk, sometimes as late as 1 in the morning. After one such early morning call, as Hoot was rehabbing after a stay at Henry Ford hospital, Kim hopped in her car to find him something to eat, and was on the rehab's ground floor ready to board the elevator. As the doors opened, out stepped Hoot's best friend, restauranteur Joe Muer (Hoot had a special table at Joe Muer's) – Hoot had called him, too, and Kim figured that whatever the hell she could find for Hoot in the middle of the night wasn't going to be anywhere near as good as what Joe just brought him.

DDDDDDDDDDDDDDDDDDDDDDDDDDDDDDDDDDDDDDDDDDDDDDDDDDDDDDDDDDDDDDDDDDDDDDDD

In the mid-50s, Hoot moved his Trumbull Avenue tavern a few feet south to the location it would remain the rest of its days, 75' across the street from Briggs/Tiger Stadium gate 1. There, Hoot's was housed in a long & narrow building, the Trumbull Avenue door opened to the back bar on the left, the kitchen just beyond it. The walk to the restrooms took you past both the bar & kitchen and always, always, past stacks of beer cases – Stroh's, Pabsts, Falstaff, Goebel's, Carling – leaning against the wall leading to the johns. 2-3 steps past the head, the bar floor rose up to meet Hoot's back door. If you entered through that door, you'd damn near sprain an ankle on the steep drop from outdoors to the bar floor.

Early Opening Day '86: Hoot out front of the bar, & out the back door, just beyond that steep drop, with Maggie

Laz Surabian of Birmingham had Hoot on his beer truck route in the 70s, "Hoot was a great man, Hoot Robinson's a great bar. I recall the time I tried to deliver beer at lunch time. The kegs needed changing & I made the mistake of turning the taps off with the lunch crowd in. Oh boy. Hoot went ballistic, running me out of the bar and screaming after me, 'I have customers to take care of! You get the heck out of here, and don't ever come in here after 11AM - unless it's after 2PM!'"

It wasn't all baseball at Hoot Robinson's. Bobby Layne would drink at Hoot's to get himself in the right frame of mind a few hours before that day's Lions' game. When we'd go downtown for Wings' games at the Joe, it was a mandatory stop at Hoot's beforehand – the baseball off-season was the perfect time to go to Hoot's. With the stress of handling large crowds of Tiger fans gone, Hoot was relaxed, and would either lean against the taps or pull up a chair and share his stories with us on cold February nights, *"In the 30s, we'd travel to Montreal to watch the Wings play the Montreal Maroons. This was back when Wings fans were really crazy, and they'd throw fifths on the ice – who would want to waste a FULL fifth that way?"* or Hoot would tell of 1940s train trips to see the Lions play the Chicago Bears or Chicago Cardinals at Wrigley Field, *"We'd always leave this one guy behind who was too drunk to find the train home."* If Hoot was on a roll, we'd stay for hours and eat that evening's Wings tickets.

After a Tiger game in 1979, Hoot was standing at one of his booths, talking to Dave Rozema and Alan Trammell who were sitting there – and the ladies were lined up 6 or 7-deep behind Hoot, anxious to meet the young Tigers. Before a ballgame in the 80s, EMU brothers Marquis Weaks, Chucky Porta and I asked Hoot for shots of Tequila. *"I don't have that, but this Old Grand Dad Whiskey will curl your toes."* Hoot poured out 3 healthy shots of Old Grand Dad, and we floated across Trumbull to the game.

Bernadette Kearns of Ann Arbor remembers, "I can smell the place right now. There's something special about the bar-smell that never quite goes away... the spilled beer and booze become part of the floor and the woodwork."

Johnny Harcourt of St. Clair Shores and his nephew Larry joined me for one of those days at The Corner that were so wonderfully commonplace in 1984, sun shining on the packed house as the Tigers win yet another game. We moseyed across Trumbull to Hoot's post-game, and found the bar crowd overflowin' out on to the sidewalk, 4 or 5-deep. Larry said, no way we'll get a drink here. I sized up the situation & said give me a minute and I'll be right back... made my way through the horde, squeezed up to the bar, staked a couple square inches with my elbow, and yelled to my man behind the bar, Saul, who knew a thirsty regular when he saw one, *"Whatcha need Doc?"* he smiled. I traded Saul enough currency for 3 Stroh's, 3 shots, borrowed a tray, and wound my way back outside. As Johnny tells it, he & Larry see this arm sticking out above the fray, holding up a tray with drinks on it, zig-zagging towards them. Clearing the crowd in the tavern, then the one out on the street, I pulled my arm & the tray on it down, handed Johnny & Larry a beer 'n a shot each, grabbed mine off the tray, gave my best Belushi-arched eye brow look at the United States Post Office box next to us, opened its door with one hand & fired in the now empty tray with the other. The perfect end to a perfect day! *Post-script:* telling Hoot the story my next visit, offering to pay for the tray, he told me, *"your money is no good here",* and I gladly accepted the no charge Stroh's he then slid my way. Some days my money was good at Hoot's, some days not, but every day spent in his bar was a ridiculously good day.

"Tiger players don't come in as often as in the old days, but Chet Lemon is in here all the time."

On a fine 1992 night at The Corner with Ann Arbor's Jimmy Vollmers, Vid Marvin, and Johnny Steck, I got up from my Upper Deck seat to quench a hunger 'n thirst. I walked down the long Tiger Stadium ramp that took you from the upper deck down to ground level, a ramp located across Michigan Avenue from the auto repair *Limp-In, Leap-Out* neon sign, and asked the stadium security fella if I could go over to Hoot's to make a phone call. He said yes. I strolled into Hoot's, just a couple of folks there besides Hoot himself, walked to his pay phone, and placed an order with the pizzeria located in the Checker Cab Company building just a few steps away. Pulled up a bar stool, the bar quiet and not needing much of Hoot's attention, had a Stroh's and a nice chat with the man himself, soon left for the pizza before circling back to Hoot's for another Stroh's to enjoy while chatting with Hoot and wolfing down the pie, let Hoot know the boys were waiting for me back at the ballyard, ordered 4 shots to go, and said see you after the game with the 3 guys and 4 empty glasses.

Being a chilly evening, I had a long black coat with me that had *Schoolboy Rowe-big pockets* (see 1937 chapter). Put the coat on and placed the 4 shots into the pockets, 2 inside and 2 outside the coat, and walked gingerly but steadily across Trumbull to where the security fella was that let me out about 45 minutes ago. *"Did you make your call?"* *"Yes I did, thank you."* I now had my biggest challenge – walking up the looooong ramp to the Upper Deck, then up the steps to our row, without spilling the shots. The endeavor was a success! Before sitting down, I pulled shots from my two outer pockets, handing them to the boys, then pulled shots 3 & 4 from the inner pockets, handing one to the fellers & placing the 4th shot on the ground next to my seat. No drops spilled, we toasted Hoot, and a grand time was had by all.

In '93, Hoot's doctor advised him to cut back on his bar hours, "He said I was allergic to smoke. I've run a bar for 60 years – how allergic could I be?"

The December 1994 funeral was a celebration of Hoot and what he and his pub meant to Tiger fans everywhere. The magic formula was the man himself, his supporting cast, and the tavern's location to the ballpark. Hoot Robinson's was an institution and a pearl in the City of Detroit. It seemed to be here forever – and it always will be in the hearts & memories of Hoot's long-time patrons.

USMC's BJay Wright needs no words to describe the joy of time spent in Hoot Robinson's

1995 – 1999 Back to Work; Lou & Tram; the Brow; One Game to Go at The Corner

"Like the assembly-line town it represented, the ballpark was more workmanlike than elegant – full of imperfections but entirely lacking in pretense."

(Essayist Peter Hyman)

In February of 1995, the MLB Players strike of 1994 lingered on. As the 1995 season approached, and a cancellation of at least part of the schedule loomed, management of many teams declared their intent to recruit substitute players to fill in for the strikers. Sparky refused to manage the Tigers with these replacements, leading to a life-long riff between Sparky and owner Mike Ilitch. The Canton, Michigan-based *Mobil Lounge Softball Team & Beer Swillers Club* staged a rally at The Corner, to protest in equal parts the childish actions of management, of the players, & the inaccurate weather forecasted by Sonny Eliot *("Please tell Sonny that I had to shovel half-a-foot of 'partly cloudy' off of my driveway.").* The rally was a great off-season excuse to gather the softball team, their families 'n friends together at Michigan & Trumbull, while ridiculing rich owners & players who did not know how to divide their good fortune.

The Beer Swillers carried placards, including one announcing we "WILL PLAY FOR BEER", outside of the stadium, while several teammates tossed a ball around in front of the Trumbull Avenue entrance. The display underscored how silly the whole replacement player concept was. To continue the protest a couple of blocks away at a proper meeting hall (may Hoot's R.I.P.), we convened at Nemo's Bar. Ann Arbor's Vid Marvin, appropriately for a softball team's lead-off man, was first to arrive, mostly 'cause he ran all the way there. Vid shared the story of our protest with Nemo's owner Tim, who brought out 3 fifths, and began pouring quite a few drinks. Vid asked what's going on, and the barkeep replied, *"Well, I think you earned free shots."* Surveying the 20 shot glasses being filled, Vid informed Tim, *"I don't think I can drink that many."* Tim laughed, *"No, no – wait for your buddies, wait for your buddies!"* After the owner's initial free shots, and several purchased rounds, we thanked Tim for his hospitality, letting him know that we were going to Miller's Bar in Dearborn for some burgers, absent-mindedly overlooking the fact that Nemo's sells great burgers themselves. Tim looked at Vid, shook his head, and Vid what said, *"What?!"* Tim said, *"Well, I shouldn't tell you this, but they buy all our rejected meat."*

The Great Strike of '94 & '95 halted at the end of March with a ruling from a U.S. District Court, just as owners were prepared to start the season using replacement players. An agreement was forced upon the owners & players, the 1995 season finally beginning at the end of April with a schedule shortened to 144 games. Amazingly, the umpires decided to go on strike just as the season was to begin, so 1995 opened with regular players, but replacement umpires. Detroit won the season opener in California, 5-4, powered by a 3-run homer off the bat of '94 acquisition Juan Samuel & a 2-run shot by Big Daddy, while oft-forgotten rookie Rudy Pemberton had a day he will always cherish, picking up 3 of the 9 hits he'd have in a Tiger uniform, as Buddy Groom earned his only save of '95. After this single game against the Angels, the Tigers traveled to Seattle, losing 3 of 4, before coming home to The Corner for the delayed May 2nd Opening Day. 39,398, an unusually small crowd for this annual holiday, were introduced to rookie right fielder Bobby Higginson and saw 4 Tiger pitchers get raked in an 11-1 loss to Cleveland.

Exasperated by the squabbling MLB players & owners, a group of 40 friends bypassed the Tiger Home Opener, breaking with a tradition running from 1975-1994, instead heading an hour south to another historic ball park, Ned Skeldon Stadium in Maumee, Ohio, to see the Toledo Mud Hens Opener. In the year of (almost) replacement players and (actual) replacement umpires, it was appropriate that during an August '95 trip to once again cheer on the Mud Hens, we met the "Replacement Muddy", forced into service when the usual "Muddy" team mascot, while dancing on the Hens' dugout, fell on to the dugout floor, suffering a banged head and a broken arm.

DDDDDDDDDDDDDDDDDDDDDDDDDDDDDDDDDDDDDDDDDDDDDDDDDDDDDDDDDDDDDDDDDDDDDDDDDD

The Tigers 1995 brain trust hit .000 in 3 trades that baseball historians are still trying to figure out…

1. On April 13, the Tigers traded Tony Phillips to California for outfielder Chad Curtis. Chad was ten years the younger man, providing both power & speed with 21 homers & 27 stolen bases in '95, but Detroit would miss Tony. His play let everyone know that, at age 36, Phillips was not slowing down: after being traded, from 1995 through 1997, Tony had a .400 on base percentage, averaging 16 homers & 111 runs scored in each of the 3 seasons. Chad Curtis, on the other hand, was traded by Detroit in July '96 for two journeyman, middle-inning relievers. Sadly for the victims, Chad became best known for his sentencing in 2012 for sexual misconduct with several under-aged girls in Lake Odessa, Mi. The prosecutor said Chad's sentencing statement *"was the most selfish, self-serving, victim-blaming statement I've heard in my career as a prosecutor. It speaks volumes about his character, or lack thereof."*

2. On a team with a 5.49 ERA and desperate for pitching, the Tigers traded relief ace Mike Henneman to the Houston Astros for utility man Phil Nevin. On the August 10 day Henneman was traded, he had a 1.53 ERA with 18 saves, 12 more than the next man. In 1996, Mike had a career-high 31 saves for Texas – the entire 1996 Tiger team had 22 saves. When he left the Tigers, Henneman was their all-time career saves leader with 154 (to later be passed by Todd Jones at 235). In 2.5 years as a Tiger, Nevin hit .246. Traded by Detroit at the end of '97 for a career minor league pitcher, Nevin then went on to become an All-Star for San Diego.

3. One Detroit Tiger made the 1995 A.L. All-Star team, pitching staff ace David Wells. Far & away the best pitcher on the team, by the end of July David's record was 10 & 3 with a 3.04 ERA. It was then that Detroit traded Wells to Cincinnati for C.J. Nitkowski, Mark Lewis & a career minor-leaguer. During David Wells next 10 seasons, at a time when the Tigers had some of the worst pitching in their history, he consistently was one of the majors best, averaging each of those years a 15 & 8 record. Of those that Wells was swapped for, 2nd sacker Mark Lewis hit .270 with modest power in his one year in Detroit, while in 5 years as a Tiger, C.J. Nitkowski went 11 & 24 with a 5.68 ERA.

DDDDDDDDDDDDDDDDDDDDDDDDDDDDDDDDDDDDDDDDDDDDDDDDDDDDDDDDDDDDDDDDDDDDDDDDDD

At the All-Star break, 37 & 33 Detroit was in 2nd place, 3 games back of first place Boston. By the end of July, the Tigers slid to 8.5 games behind, and the subsequent trades of David Wells on July 31 and Mike Henneman on August 10 showed players & fans alike that management had thrown in the towel for the season. Kirk Gibson was among those who saw the writing on the wall and on August 11, at 38 years of age, he decided it was time to hang it up, telling the press, *"I've been traded to my family"*. Gibby played with a fire and passion that excited fans and willed his teammates to success. On the biggest stage, Kirk was the man you wanted at the plate. His lifetime numbers are impressive, but do an inadequate job in telling the whole story: in 1,635 games over 17 seasons, Gibson batted .268 with 255 home runs, 284 stolen bases, 985 runs scored, and 870 runs batted in.

On September 13, 1995, Lou Whitaker & Alan Trammell played their 1,915th game together as a double play combination, establishing a new Major League record. How perfect that in this game, with the

Tigers down 3-2 going into the bottom of the ninth, Detroit won 5-3 on a Sweet Lou 3-run, walk-off, homer. Lou's home run, off Milwaukee relief pitcher Mike Fetters, was the 2,369th and final hit of his career – one year and 16 days later, Alan Trammell's 2,365th and final hit of his career would also be off of Mike Fetters.

By the time 1995 came to a close, Whitaker and Trammell played together 1,918 times. Lou closed out his 19-year career strong, in the last 3 seasons hitting .290, .301, & .293. Although Lou's contract had run out, the Tigers wanted him to continue playing, and offers also came in from Boston, Oakland, Atlanta, and the Yankees, but Whitaker was ready to call it quits. Louis Rodman Whitaker had always been confident in his baseball abilities, the minor leaguer telling Tigers general manager Jim Campbell when he met him in 1976 spring training, *"I'm Louis Whitaker and I'll be playing for you soon."* Sweet Lou would go on to join Rogers Hornsby and Joe Morgan as the only second basemen in MLB history with at least 2,000 hits, 200 home runs, 1,000 runs, and 1,000 RBIs. Lou's fielding percentage was .984 and batting average .276. He was the American League Rookie of the Year in 1978 (Tram was 4th), a 5-time All-Star, 4 time-Silver Slugger winner, and 3-time Gold Glove recipient. Along with Trammell, who would play one more season, the two became the 8th double-play combination to win Gold Gloves in the same season and they did it twice ('83 & '84). Lou Whitaker will one day be inducted into baseball's Hall of Fame.

The 1995 Tigers ended the shortened 144-game season at 60 & 84, 26 games behind the Red Sox. After being the top home run hitting team in the league over the last 5 years, Detroit slipped to 159 homers, only 7th in the 14-team league. On May 28, however, the Tigers and the White Sox put on a long-ball exhibition for the small crowd of 10,813 who came out to The Corner. The two teams combined for 12 home runs to set a major league single game record. Although Detroit hit 7 of the 12, including 2 each by Big Daddy and Gibby, Chicago won 14-12. On July 2, 2002 at Comiskey Park on the South Side of Chicago, the same two teams would tie the record that they set on that Sunday afternoon in May '95.

At 4PM on Sunday, October 1, 1995 in Camden Yards, the curtain closed on the managerial career of George Lee "Sparky" Anderson, the only manager the Tigers had known since June 12, 1979. The 4-0 loss to Baltimore was no. 1,834 against 2,194 victories, a .545 winning percentage. The Bridgewater, South Dakota native and 2nd sacker for the '59 Philadelphia Phillies ended with the 6th-most wins for a manager in MLB history, and his 1,331 victories in Detroit make him the winningest Tiger manager ever. Considered to be one of the game's greatest, he became the first skipper to lead teams to World Series Championships in both leagues, first with the National League Cincinnati Reds in 1975 & 1976, and then with the Detroit Tigers in 1984. Five teams he piloted won pennants, four won over 100 games in a season, and in six other seasons his teams won at least 90 games. And he entertained us countless times with a long list of Sparky-isms including...

"I've got my faults, but living in the past is not one of them. There's no future in it." "I only had a high school education, and believe me, I had to cheat to get that." "Just give me 25 guys in the last year of their contracts & I'll win a pennant every year." "If I ever find a pitcher who has heat, a good curve and a slider, I might consider marrying him, or at least proposing." "The great thing about baseball is when you're done, you'll only tell your grandchildren the good things. If they ask me about 1989, I'll tell them I had amnesia." "Pain don't hurt." "Me carrying a briefcase is like a hotdog wearing earrings." "The problem with John Wockenfuss getting on base is that it takes 3 doubles to score him."

Walt Terrell said, *"When Sparky took you out, you weren't allowed to say anything. You had to put the ball in his hand softly and walk quietly off the field. That was the rule. I remember one time in the 8th inning, I had given up 4 runs or so when he came out to get me. He took two or three steps onto the field and I said, 'What took you so long?' And he said, 'I was in the bathroom. I didn't know you were getting beat so bad.'"*

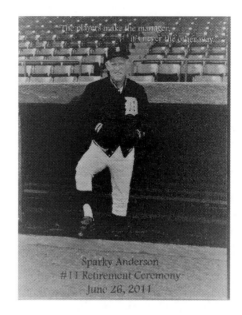

Sparky Anderson
#11 Retirement Ceremony
June 26, 2011

Sparky Anderson and Ernie Harwell quickly became close friends after Sparky arrived in Detroit in 1979. A favorite Sparky story of Ernie's was told by Harwell in a newspaper column he wrote: *"In 1984, the year the Tigers started 35 & 5, Sparky's team had won 16 (on their way to 17) road games in a row. His picture graced the cover of magazines, and his name was in headlines across the country. (The morning after the Tigers 16th consecutive road win) He and I were having breakfast at our Anaheim, California hotel when a fan approached our table. 'Hi Sparky,' he said, 'I'm a great fan of yours. I live in San Diego now, but I was living in Cincinnati when you managed that Big Red Machine. You have always been my hero. Without a doubt you are the greatest manager ever.' Sparky beamed. Silently, he listened and just nodded his head. Then, the man spoke again. 'And by the way, what are you doing these days?'"*

DDDDDDDDDDDDDDDDDDDDDDDDDDDDDDDDDDDDDDDDDDDDDDDDDDDDDDDDDDDDDDDDDDDDDDDDDDDDD

1996 begins... and then there was one. Only one active player remains from the 1984 World Champions, as 38-year old Alan Trammell decides to push those slightly-older muscles & bones through a 20th year of major league ball. As the newspapers reported, Tram applied heat to his shoulders before a game and ice to his body afterwards. His presence would be a balm to a 5-time All-Star player in his first year of big league managing, old Cleveland nemesis, Buddy Bell. 1996 would not be an easy season for either man. With the low expectations of a team that traded away last year their best starting pitcher, their best relief pitcher, and their 100-runs-a-year lead-off man, and a team that saw Sweet Lou and Gibby retire, the fact that Detroit's first game, taking place in Minneapolis, was scheduled for April Fools' Day seemed perfect. As did being outscored 8-6, with Tiger starter Felipe Lira giving up 6 runs in his 3 innings. During the 7-game road trip to open the season, 2 of Detroit's 3 wins required them to score 10 runs to best the opposition as their pitching was getting pounded, a preview of things to come.

42,932 came thru the turnstiles to celebrate the April 9, 1996 Home Opener. In a bizarre game, Tiger starter Scott Aldred surrendered 7 runs in his 3.1 innings and Detroit only managed 4 hits, but one was a 3-run homer by Travis Fryman and another a Big Daddy grand slam, as the Tigers outscored Seattle 10-9. The concession stands were another story: although the Tigers returned to selling real beer instead of Low Alcohol brew, they thought it appropriate to thank the fans who stuck with them through the '94-95 Strike by shutting down Opening Day beer sales in the 4th inning. Unbelievable. BUT, compensating for that breech of common sense & courtesy, a fella named Pete re-opened Hoot Robinson's! Just to be back inside the grand old tavern, closed for the last 1 year & 7 months, with many of Hoot's photos still up on the walls, was a wonderful gift to long-time Tiger fans.

On April 16 in Toronto, Detroit piled up 13 runs to overcome the 8 given up by Tiger pitching, pushing the team to 8 & 7 and over .500 for the 2nd & last time in '96. In the 12 remaining April games played, Detroit lost 11, including a 24-11 thrashing at the hands of the Twins – the only win in the 12 was when the Tiger offense scored 14 runs. The month's one respite was when Tiger fans took time to recognize April 28, 1996, the 100th anniversary of the first game ever played at The Corner.

The 1996 numbers were historic, and not in a good way: in May, Detroit won only 4 of 27 games, the worst stretch taking place when Chicago came to The Corner for a 3-game series May 17-19, the White Sox pounding Tiger pitching 11-6, 16-4, and 14-3. After the weekend series with the Sox, the Tigers traveled down to Toledo to play an exhibition game versus their Mud Hens farm club – and *lost* 14-1. *Yikes!* Its moments like these that may have had Trammell questioning his decision to play this season. After Alan experienced the delight of the 35 & 5 start of '84, the '96 team was the fun house mirror version of those champions: from April 16, when Detroit was last over .500 at 8 & 7, the team spiraled into a 5 & 39 skid (not including the 14-1 loss to the Mud Hens) that ended when the starving fans were treated to back-to-back wins over the Yankees on June 7 & 8, by scores of 6-5 & 9-7. *The June 7 victory was the first Tiger win at home since defeating Texas 5-2 on May 2, 36 days ago!*

Underscoring just how atrocious the '96 team was: Tiger hurlers entered the June 7-9 Yankee series with a 7.18 earned run average. By surrendering 12 runs total in the two games, the pitching staff actually lowered that number. They seriously challenged the major league mark for the worst team ERA ever, 6.70 set by the 1930 Philadelphia Phillies. The 1930 Philly team, at least, had the excuse of playing in the old Baker Bowl with a right field fence only 281' from home plate (although with a 40' tall tin wall built to compensate for the short dimension). Of the '96 Tiger pitchers, Understatement King Big Daddy Cecil Fielder observed, *"I think we have to find some good arms if we're going to win."* First-year pitching coach, Jon Matlack, the old New York Met lefty, said, *"I've had friends leave messages telling me to stay away from sharp objects or to stay on a low floor."* Better yet, let's have the 46-year old, 3-time All-Star, Matlack suit up and join the pitching staff. Inserting Matlack into the rotation is something that Manager Buddy Bell may have considered, based on his comments to the press when asked about an upcoming pitching schedule, *"We'll probably go with Lolich on Thursday, and if we can get McLain, which I don't think is possible* (being in prison & all)*, he'll pitch on Friday."*

Detroit was not only on a pace for the worst team ERA ever, but also to lose more games than the 120 of the record-holding 1962 New York Mets. Losing too much money and too many games over the last 2 seasons, owner Mike Ilitch hired Randy Smith away from San Diego in late-'95 to become the new Tiger general manager. The directive given Smith by Ilitch and team president John McHale was to overhaul the farm system, which had not produced a star player since 1979 outside of the recently-traded Mike Henneman, pass on big money free agents, and build from within. The team and their fans knew the process would be painful, but nobody could have foreseen awful on this scale. By the July 9 All-Star game, the Tigers were 27 & 61, 26.5 games behind first place New York. With the pitching staff well-rested from the 3-day Midsummer Classic break, regular season play resumed as they were lit up for 11, 11, 10, & 6 runs in a 4-game sweep at The Corner by Boston.

In this environment, July 31 came as a relief to Cecil Fielder as the day that Big Daddy was traded to the Yankees, in what clearly was a cost-cutting measure, for minor league pitcher Matt Drews, who never made it to the majors, and 4-time All-Star but well past his prime, Ruben Sierra (as a Tiger, Ruben hit .222 with 1 home run in 46 games, then was traded at year end to the Reds for two players who never made The Show). Cecil had 26 homers & 80 RBIs for Detroit in 107 games, then in 53 games with New York hit another 13 home runs with 37 RBIs, helping the Yankees to their first World Series crown since 1978. Tiger fanatics were gloriously entertained in Fielder's 6 & ½ seasons with Detroit. During those years, fans at The Corner timed their trips to the concession stand or bathroom to ensure being in their seats when Big Daddy was due to hit, and he delivered with 245 homers & 758 RBIs. With Cecil gone from a horrible team, the last big draw to a '96 game was to see Alan Trammell play one last time.

DDDDDDDDDDDDDDDDDDDDDDDDDDDDDDDDDDDDDDDDDDDDDDDDDDDDDDDDDDDDDDDDDDDDDDDDDDDDDDDDD

With just two months left in Tram's 20-year career, newspapers kept up a constant stream of articles reminiscing about Alan's playing days, always tied to Sweet Lou Whitaker as if they were blood brothers, the memories a comforting diversion for the shell-shocked Tiger faithful of '96...

How in '76, at the Fall Instructional League at St. Petersburg, Florida, Alan Trammell & Lou Whitaker first met, roommates at the same hotel. Tram was a shortstop from the start, Lou initially a third baseman reluctantly converted to second base, the two working that fall under the guidance of recently-retired Eddie Brinkman, now an instructor for Detroit. After the Instructional League season, Eddie told Detroit that they had something special in the young double-play duo.

How in '77, Tram and Sweet Lou played together at minor league Montgomery; how they made their Detroit debut together that same year on September 9, in the back half of a twin bill at Fenway, the first of their 1,918 games together; how that day they both got singles in their first major league at bat off the same pitcher, Reggie Cleveland, Lou in the first & Tram in the third.

How in '78, Tram & Sweet Lou both had such an outstanding spring training that Manager Ralph Houk had no choice but to bring the two north with the parent club, their first full season in the Show; how Houk compared the two to his former Yankee double-play duo, SS Tony Kubek & 2B Bobby Richardson, saying, *"It's the damnedest thing. You tell one of them something and he says, 'We can do it.' Like they're a team."* In 1977, Tram wore number 42 and Lou 43, but for 1978 and the rest of their careers, Whitaker wore number 1 and Trammell number 3.

How in '79, the cover of the Tiger Yearbook featured a photo of Tram & Lou sitting back-to-back on 2nd base. The two were now part of a band of brothers with fellow Tiger draftees Gibson, Brookens, Parish, Rozema, Morris, and Petry; teammates that grew together, just like the '68 guys did, maturing, talking baseball & game strategies over dinner or a beer, challenging each other and gradually transforming themselves into the 1984 Champions.

DDDDDDDDDDDDDDDDDDDDDDDDDDDDDDDDDDDDDDDDDDDDDDDDDDDDDDDDDDDDDDDDDDDDDDDDDDDDD

The 1996 Tigers were able to avoid the two dreaded MLB records that, in mid-Summer, it appeared they might break. The N.Y. Mets '62 futility mark of 120 losses remained safe as Detroit ended 53 & 109 – they did not catch the Mets, but they did establish the bottom rung in Tiger history. Likewise, the '96 fellas were able to avoid passing the 1930 Phillies all-time worst 6.70 ERA by coming in at 6.38, but this number did set the Tiger team mark.

The season's final game played September 29, and 13,038 came out to The Corner to say goodbye to Alan Trammell. In the 10th inning of a 5-5 tie, visiting Milwaukee took a 7-5 lead as Detroit came to bat. Mike Fetters, the Brewer pitcher, took care of Ruben Sierra on a fly out. The next batter was Curtis Pride, the man who accepted being born deaf as a challenge to overcome, and Curtis singled to push his season-ending average to .300, a bright spot in an ugly year. Now the crowd rose to its collective feet as up stepped Alan Trammell, and Tram thanked them by slapping a single to center. Detroit's rally fell short, but the crowd continued to cheer as Alan walked back out on to the field for the final time as a player. A 15-minute ceremony took place as Trammell was presented 2nd base before speaking to the fans, *"Today is my last day. As much as it hurts to say it, it's somewhat of a relief. Every one of us here had a dream, and I feel very fortunate to have been able to do it longer than most. And I'm very proud that I have been able to do it all with one ballclub."*

In Alan's career, he was a 6-time All-Star, 4-time Gold Glove, 3-time Silver Slugger, and finished in the Top 10 in MVP balloting 3 times. Trammell had a batting average of .285, a fielding average of .976, hit 185 homers with 1,003 RBIs & 1,231 runs scored. In Tram & Lou's 1st Tiger game, they had their 1st major league hit, both off of Boston's Reggie Cleveland. Tram & Lou's final hits, 1 year & 16 days apart, were both off of Milwaukee's Mike Fetters. And both, of course, were World Series Champions.

Kirk Gibson spoke about Tram & Lou in a 2010 *Baseball Prospectus* interview...

"I first saw them in 1979 when I went to spring training. They were already in the big leagues—they came up in 1977—so we became teammates when I came up in 1979. My whole career in Detroit, both my first trip there and my second trip, there was never, ever another double-play combination than Alan Trammell and Lou Whitaker. And you don't realize until you go and play for another team, and watch somebody else, just how important that is for a team to be a successful club. I mean, they were together for virtually every game I played for the Tigers. And they were damn good.

"I retired in 1995, so they'd have been there for 18 years at that time and I think it's safe to say that they knew each other's mannerisms as well as anyone ever has in the game. They made plays. I remember one time I hit a home run to win the game. It was in the bottom of the ninth inning, or something like that—we were in Detroit—and Sparky called me in. He said, 'Hey, Gibby. You did a good job on the home run, but let me ask you a question.' They had the bases loaded with one out, & Lou made an unbelievable play and he and Trammell turned it, so Sparky goes, 'If Lou doesn't make that play, does your home run mean anything?' So, when the media came over to talk about the home run, I said 'You're at the wrong locker, because if Lou doesn't make the play, I don't get the opportunity.' That's the type of player both of those guys were.

"They weren't flashy; they were just damn good. They were big-time playmakers when it counted. They were very consistent and steady. And both were very, very, very good hitters. They were simply big-time players. Maybe I'm partial—in fact, I'm sure I am—but there have never been two people to play like that, together, in the history of the game. I don't know why they wouldn't be (in the Hall of Fame). I don't know why baseball wouldn't want them in the Hall of Fame, or why they wouldn't want to promote that, because it's exceptional, what they did. It's just exceptional. They should be in there together."

DDDDDDDDDDDDDDDDDDDDDDDDDDDDDDDDDDDDDDDDDDDDDDDDDDDDDDDDDDDDDDDDDDDDDDDDDDDD

On February 13, 1997, Joe Diroff aka the Brow passed away.

One night at the Old Ballyard in the early-90s, things weren't going well for the home team, and we were talking about how dead it all felt. And then, emerging from the tunnel into the lower deck seats, a cyclone of energy swirled through the crowd. It was, of course, the Brow! Hoo-ray! He was all flailing limbs & crazy signs, bouncing on one leg, the other kicking the air as if he were Kung Fu fighting, Brow's arrival was an adrenaline rush for all lucky enough to be in attendance. Joy and laughter infected every fan within sight or sound of him. When the Brow is at the park, there is no such thing as a bad time. Joe Diroff had two big, bushy, eyebrows that met right above his nose, creating one huge, beautiful, arching eyebrow. And that's how you become known as "the Brow".

There's the Brow hoping around on one leg, trying to get the folks fired up to cheer on our Boys of Summer, *"Strawberry Shortcake, Gooseberry Pie, V-I-C-T-O-R-Y!!!"* A few minutes later, in another section of Tiger Stadium, there he is again, by the bottom of the concourse tunnel, a ketchup bottle in his right hand, a mustard container in the left… if behind, the right hand rises and Brow shouts, *"We WILL Ketchup!"* If the bad guys are at bat, the left hand rises & he hollers, *"They Can't Cut the Mustard!"*

The Brow set up shop for a few minutes by the Tigers dugout. He has a handful of colorful signs for props to support whatever cheer he thinks is appropriate to get us and the team going. Now he does a jig, shaking a large, plastic banana, and then, *"Let's Go Bananas!!!"* explodes from the man under the beat-up, old fishing hat, always matched with his white shirt & black tie.

Mister & Missus Diroff raised 10 kids before Joe retired as a school teacher at the start of the 80s. After two years of fishing, he was going stir crazy, and asked for divine direction. The Brow soon began leading cheers at sports venues, and didn't stop until a stroke slowed him in 1995. *"God gave me a talent to do this, to make people feel good."* It wasn't only at home games, although Brow missed very few of those, but he'd often travel to support the Tigers and other Detroit-based teams when they hit the road. If it was a trip that his old Dodge couldn't make, he'd make other plans…

During the Red Wings 1987 playoff series versus Edmonton, Brow bought an airplane ticket to the Canadian city, the players shocked to see him in their hotel lobby, cheering them on as they walked by. The Wings were eliminated on that Edmonton trip, but the Ilitch family invited Brow to fly back on the team charter. As Brow led cheers in the aisle, the defeated players couldn't help but brighten up, and they soon found themselves joining in with whatever crazy, fun cheer that the Brow was leading. The Wings passed the hat on the flight, to pay for Brow's ticket he bought to get to Edmonton.

There was the Brow that thousands of fans would see at any given game, and then there was the Brow that made time to greet players returning from road trips, especially if they had a rough game or series. *"I figured the boys could use some cheering up."* There he'd be, the Brow on his lawn chair in a deserted airport, jumping up to greet the players as they came off the plane. Even if dejected, they couldn't help but smile. *"Brow,"* said Kirk Gibson, *"you're a true fan."*

There he is now, down in Kaline's Corner, imploring the team & the fans both: *"Let's Get PUMPED UP!"*

The Brow has left us and a sad quiet has descended over the old ballyard.

DDDDDDDDDDDDDDDDDDDDDDDDDDDDDDDDDDDDDDDDDDDDDDDDDDDDDDDDDDDDDDDDDDDDDDDDDDDDDDDD

After what he went through as a rookie manager in '96, Buddy Bell must have felt like he was skippering the 1984 Tigers in '97. Not only did the team match their previous year's full-season, 59-win, total by August 21 (with 36 games yet to play), they won number 59 in a 2-1 pitcher's duel, as rare in '96 as a dull day with Norm Cash. After the entire '96 team had only 22 saves, the August 21, 1997, 2-1 win earned save number 24 for one man (on his way to a full year 31), Todd Jones, an outstanding acquisition, picked up in a 9-player trade with Houston on December 10, 1996 (a trade that sent Brad Ausmus, after only 75 games as a Tiger, to the Astros; Brad will return to Detroit by '99). As the Tiger closer from 1997-2001 and 2006-2008, Todd was Houdini, with an amazing ability to take the mound in the 9th with the game on the line, put the tying and/or winning runs on base, but escape with the save. Just knowing that Todd Jones was warming up was enough to send fans into various stages of angst, his entry prompting those watching at home to pace the floor, and earning from Ernie Harwell the nickname *"Roller Coaster"*. Expect a long 9th inning when he entered the game, Todd advised the fans, suggesting they go into the kitchen and make themselves a sandwich, 'cause it's gonna be awhile. Despite the high-wire act, Todd converted 319 of the 394 games he came in to close in his 16 major league seasons, including a Tiger team-record 235 (out of 274, 86%) in his 7.5 years wearing the Olde English D. In 2000, Todd led the league with 42 saves to earn a spot on the All-Star team and finished 5th in voting for the Cy Young Award. As mentally tough as Jones was while on the mound, he was a fun individual who loved the fans and endeared himself to them (when he wasn't giving the faithful an upset stomach) by actions like sharing an order of nachos with those seated by the bullpen or sleeping overnight in the Tiger clubhouse the night before the last game ever at The Corner.

In '97, finally, some homegrown Tigers blossom. Justin Thompson broke in with the class A Bristol Tigers as an 18-year old in 1991, arm problems slowing his development until he made his MLB debut in '96. Injuries contributed to a rough 1 & 6 rookie year, but he was healthy in '97, and what a difference it made. The 6'4" Thompson had a tremendous arm and seemingly limitless potential, said by analysts to be another Roger Clemens. On June 1 in Seattle, Detroit fell 4-1, although Justin struck out 9 Mariners including All-Everything Ken Griffey Jr. 3 times. 6 days later, this time at The Corner, Justin was once again pitching vs. Seattle, once again struck out 9, and once again whiffed Griffey Junior 3 times, but this time Detroit won 3-1. Over the two games, Justin Thompson struck out Ken Griffey Junior in six-consecutive at bats, the only time any pitcher has ever done that to the future Hall of Famer. Mariner Manager Lou Pinella said, *"Nobody's had that type of mastery over Junior. He is impressive, a good-looking young pitcher."* Justin Thompson sounded confident speaking to reporters, *"I approached Griffey the same way I did last week. I started him hard and away and showed him the curve for something different, and then went hard and away again. I'm going to keep doing that until he shows me he can hit it."* Griffey left without speaking to reporters. The Tiger victory was powered by two home runs, both by 2nd year players, a 2-run shot by catcher Raul Casanova, and first sacker Tony Clark's monster blast over the right field roof, the blow entering him into a select fraternity. Tony was another quality youngster that came up through the farm system. A '90 first round draft pick by Detroit, his rookie year in the big leagues was a good one, overlooked in the mess that was 1996, as in just 100 games he hit 27 home runs and knocked in 72 runs. In '97, Clark began a 3-year run for the Tigers in which he averaged 32 homers & 106 RBIs from '97-'99.

In one year, Tiger pitching went from zero staff stoppers to a nice 1-2 punch. Joining Justin Thompson in the rotation was Willie Blair, acquired by Detroit at the end of 1996 in what was thought to be a minor transaction. In Willie's first 7 major league seasons, Blair averaged 4 wins a year. In '97, his 8th year, Willie posted a 16 & 8 record with a 4.17 ERA that looked great put up against the '96 team's 6.38 ERA.

June 7, 1997, the 2nd night in a week that Justin Thompson struck out Ken Griffey Junior 3 times, a large group of friends attended the game, but not one stayed to the end. At first, a couple left here and there, and then several at a time. The draw was across Trumbull Avenue from Tiger Stadium gate 1 and the TV at Hoot Robinson's, tuned to Game 4 of the Stanley Cup Finals. The Detroit Red Wings, playing just one mile away at Joe Louis Arena, were attempting to complete a sweep of the Philadelphia Flyers and earn their first Cup in 42 years. The late Hoot's first lieutenant, Kim DeBono, had returned to her old job in '96 when the new owner re-opened the bar, and was holding a table for us as long as possible at the increasingly packed pub. A 2nd period goal by grinder Darren McCarty proved to be the Cup-winner in the Wings 2-1 clincher. The 4-game sweep changed the "Legion of Doom" nickname of the favored Flyers to the "Legion of Broom". Hoot's patrons spilled out on to the sidewalk to celebrate as cars circled the neighborhood, brooms sprouting from each window, horns honking as bar customers high-fived fans leaning out from the passenger windows. How are Ken Griffey Junior and the Philadelphia Flyers alike? They both got their butts kicked by Detroit tonight!

DDDDDDDDDDDDDDDDDDDDDDDDDDDDDDDDDDDDDDDDDDDDDDDDDDDDDDDDDDDDDDDDDDDDDDDDDDDDDDDDDD

Although the '97 Tigers never challenged for first place, ending the year 19 games behind the Orioles, after the disaster of the 109 losses/6.38 ERA of 1996, a 79 & 83 record looked mighty good. Especially exciting was how quickly Detroit turned things around from what looked to be a long-suffering situation, and where did all these promising young players come from? Pitchers Justin Thompson, Willie Blair, and Todd Jones shined, supported by 100+ RBI seasons of Tony Clark, Bobby Higginson, and Travis Fryman, while centerfielder & lead-off man Brian Hunter, who arrived from Houston along with Todd Jones, topped the league with 74 stolen bases. GM Randy Smith, his name dragged through the mud just last year, was now being hailed as a genius who knew talent & how to acquire it.

In the summer of '97, five years after his induction into the Hall of Fame in Cooperstown, the Tigers retired the number 16 of Hal Newhouser. Around his jersey retirement festivities, Hal was interviewed in the Tigers broadcast booth, and asked his thoughts about Justin Thompson. Hopes were high among the team and its fans that Justin would be the staff's long-term ace after his outstanding '97 first half and selection to the All-Star team, while on his way to finishing with 15 wins and a league-fifth 3.02 ERA. Newhouser didn't have to study Thompson for long when he explained that Justin's throwing motion put so much stress on his arm that he wouldn't last 3 years. In the midst of the excited hopefulness experienced by Tiger fans in '97, Hal Newhouser's words were, for most, quickly forgotten.

DDDDDDDDDDDDDDDDDDDDDDDDDDDDDDDDDDDDDDDDDDDDDDDDDDDDDDDDDDDDDDDDDDDDDDDDDDD

"Historic preservation is about keeping us in active contact with our past – the good and the bad – so that we will never forget it, and learn from it. In the long run this is why it is vital that we preserve historic places like Tiger Stadium, for what they teach us about ourselves, as well as about the game. When we preserve our past, we preserve what unites us, not what divides us, which is why cities that do preserve the best of their heritage and culture have more soul and community spirit than those that do not." So spoke Jack Walter, president of the National Trust for Historic Preservation.

Monaghan & Schembechler may have been bulls in a china shop in how they went about their business, but what they sought was exactly what the next owner wanted – a new stadium. Mike Ilitch was just less blatant and more diplomatic in going after his goal. While losing in the neighborhood of $30M annually since his first full season of ownership in 1993, Ilitch saw how revenues jumped for teams in the first few years when new stadiums opened in towns like Baltimore, Denver, and Cleveland, and he wanted in. Historic preservation would finish a distant second to pocketbook preservation as Ilitch negotiated successfully for a new stadium. Funding would be shared between the team, the city and the state. The clock was now ticking towards the end of Tiger Stadium.

DDDDDDDDDDDDDDDDDDDDDDDDDDDDDDDDDDDDDDDDDDDDDDDDDDDDDDDDDDDDDDDDDDDDDDDDDDD

1998 began with a bad omen: 16-game winner Willie Blair was lost to the Tigers as the free agent signed a contract with the Arizona Diamondbacks.

The year opened unusually early, the Tigers first game on March 31 at Tropicana Field versus the Tampa Bay Devil Rays. Detroit bats were booming, the team taking an 11-0 lead by the fifth, coasting to an 11-6 win behind 8 innings of 2-run ball by Justin Thompson, and 3 hits each by newly-acquired free agent and left-fielder Luis Gonzalez and 2nd baseman Damion Easley. Damion was in his 2nd full season as a Tiger, and '98 would be his career year with 27 homers, 100 RBIs, a Silver Slugger award and an All-Star team selection. From this March victory, an awful April followed, the Tigers dropping 18 of 23. The pitching staff was raked for 10 runs twice and 11 runs four times. The one nice surprise in the rotation was Brian Moehler. A 1993 6th-round draftee, Moehler was in his 2nd full year in the majors, and topped the staff with 14 wins & a 3.90 ERA, the only starter with an earned run average below 4.

Although April ended on a positive note, a 7-2 victory over Texas, behind a complete game 6-hitter by Moehler and Easley's 3 hits & 4 RBIs, Detroit's record as they began May was only 6 & 18, leaving them 7 games behind the Central Division leading Indians (1998 marked the Tigers first year in the Central after residing in the East Division since the league was split into 2 divisions in '69, 3 divisions since '94). The team play improved in May, but their ace was struggling. Justin Thompson ended the month 3 & 5 and was not the commanding force on the mound that he was in '97.

At the All-Star break, 34 & 50 Detroit was a distant 15.5 games out of first and going nowhere. After an 8 & 22 August left the team at 52 & 85, manager Buddy Bell was fired and replaced by Larry Parrish, an old ballplayer who, after a fine 14-year MLB career, had coached & managed in the Tiger organization since 1992. Only by winning 7 of the year's last 10 games did the last-place Tigers avoid 100 losses, closing '98 at 65 & 97, 24 games behind Cleveland. And as the year progressed, it seemed more & more likely that when Hal Newhouser expressed alarm about how Justin Thompson's throwing motion would shorten the young star's career, he knew what he was talking about. Justin ended '98 on a 2 & 6 dive, winding up the full year at 11 & 15, arm troubles hampering Thompson as the dominance he'd displayed in '97 gradually slipped away, reflected in his ERA jumping to 4.05 in '98 & 5.11 in '99.

On November 10, 1998, 77-year old Prince Hal Newhouser died from emphysema and heart problems.

DDDDDDDDDDDDDDDDDDDDDDDDDDDDDDDDDDDDDDDDDDDDDDDDDDDDDDDDDDDDDDDDDDDDDDDDDDD

Detroit opened 1999 in Texas, winning 11-5. Tiger leftfielder Juan Encarnacion, in his first full season in The Show, homered and did so 18 more times this year. Newly-acquired free agent, 3rd baseman Dean Palmer, had the first two hits of a fine '99, leading Detroit with 38 homers & 100 RBIs, just ahead of Tony Clark's 31 & 99. Behind the plate for the Tigers, once again, was Brad Ausmus, who probably should have kept a home in Houston <u>and</u> in Detroit: traded by the Tigers to Houston after '96, then traded by the Astros back to Detroit at the start of '99. Ausmus, a defensive stalwart, hit .275 & made the All-Star team in 1999, was traded back once again to Houston after the 2000 season, where he won Gold Gloves in '01, '02, and '06. Retiring as a player after the 2010 season, 4 years later he was back in Detroit as the Tigers manager.

After their Opening Day victory in Texas, the Tigers dropped their next 5 road games before flying to Detroit to open the home portion of the schedule...

1999 Opening Day... the last one at Michigan & Trumbull... where baseball has been played since 1896. 47,449 fans came out to be part of *the Final Opening Day Ever at The Corner*. For the Eastern Michigan University-based band of brothers & sisters known as "ETT", April 12 of '99, a day described by George Kell as a sunshiny afternoon, was their 24th Tiger Home Opener out of the last 25 years. In that quarter-century, ETT missed only the 1995 Tiger Opener, choosing to attend the Toledo Mud Hens Opener in lieu of watching the MLB players, whose strike cost fans the 1994 World Series.

How sad it will be to see the Detroit Tigers leave 2121 Trumbull Avenue, the oldest address in American Professional Sports, home to Ty Cobb, Mickey Cochrane, Hank Greenberg, Al Kaline, Ernie Harwell, Norm Cash, Willie Horton, Mark Fidrych, Herbie Redmond, and on & on.

But how wonderful it was to be in the stands for one more Opening Day in this Grand Old Ballpark, despite a tough, 1-0, loss to Minnesota in 12 innings. After losing 2 of 3 to the Twins, the home stand improved greatly with a 3-game sweep of the Yankees (just for the pure joy of typing this once again... *a 3-game sweep of the Yankees*) followed by taking 2 of 3 from Boston. However, little went well after the Red Sox left town.

The '99 Tigers struggled early, mid-season, and late in the year. In the 14-team American League, Detroit was 12th in both runs scored and earned run average. The only month they played over .500 ball was September & by then it was way too late: as August ended, Detroit was 28 games back with 30 to play.

DDDDDDDDDDDDDDDDDDDDDDDDDDDDDDDDDDDDDDDDDDDDDDDDDDDDDDDDDDDDDDDDDDDDDDDDDDDDD

Mark Alwood of Lambertville invited his dad, Woody, to The Corner for Father's Day 1999, and also in celebration of two impending events: dad's 80th birthday and the Old Ballyard's final season. *"Dad was a lifelong St. Louis Cardinal fan primarily because of Stan Musial. My father was also from the generation that constantly had work to do after he got home from work, and pretty much felt to pay money to sit at a sporting event was time and hard-earned income spent a little too frivolously. However, as far back as I can remember, the ball game was always on his portable radio in the garage loud enough to be heard whether he was doing yard work, at his workbench, or wrenching on one of the cars."*

"That game sitting in two box seats in the upper deck overhang between home and first base has become my fondest Tiger Stadium memory! It was my earliest arrival before a game, which the two of us spent leisurely talking about everything and nothing in particular. We also stayed and watched the post-game fireworks display, which was the first of this caliber my dad had ever seen. Our section was peppered with foul balls and after several close calls a young girl sitting next to dad reached over him for a ball that saved him from a beaning, but also knocked his glasses into his lap. This elicited a casual replacement of his eyewear and an inquiry from dad, 'Is it always like this here?'"

DDDDDDDDDDDDDDDDDDDDDDDDDDDDDDDDDDDDDDDDDDDDDDDDDDDDDDDDDDDDDDDDDDDDDDDDDDDDD

The 1999 Detroit Tigers picked a good year to have a bad season. Fans were coming down to The Corner to celebrate the history more than the present. Representative of what '99 meant to the faithful was what brought them to Michigan & Trumbull on Sunday, July 11. Although the 36 & 51 Tigers sat 20.5 games behind first place Cleveland, and were facing Milwaukee, another team going nowhere this year, 32,974 came through the turnstiles. The draw? The Bird was in town, 23 years after his amazing 1976 season, visiting with fans pre-game at the Tiger Stadium plaza, signing autographs and telling stories to the enthralled attendees. In the sideshow, Detroit fell to the Brewers 3-2, Brian Moehler pitching well, but undone by 2 unearned runs. This game was the finale of a 3-game series vs. Milwaukee, including the Bird's visit, each game noteworthy for different reasons...

The day before, Justin Thompson tossed 8 innings of 5-hit ball in the 9-3 Tiger victory, improving his record to 8 & 8. After such a fine outing, it was hard to believe Justin would only win once more in his major league career, going 1 & 3 the balance of '99, not to return to the big leagues until a short 2-game stint with Texas in 2005, constant arm injuries convincing Justin to hang up his glove.

On July 9, two days before the Bird's visit, Milwaukee's Jeremy Burnitz hit a ball over the right-field roof. The Upper Deck was completed in both right & leftfields at then Briggs Stadium by 1938. Since then, 36 balls cleared the Upper Deck roof and left the ballpark. The first was on May 4, 1939, when Boston Red Sox rookie Ted Williams deposited a pitch from Tiger reliever Bob Harris on to Trumbull Avenue, hitting the Checker Cab Company building on its first bounce. Burnitz' July 9, 1999 towering homer, off of Tiger starter Nelson Cruz, was the 36th and last to leave the park, 4 over the left-field roof, 32 over the right-field roof.

DDDDDDDDDDDDDDDDDDDDDDDDDDDDDDDDDDDDDDDDDDDDDDDDDDDDDDDDDDDDDDDDDDDDDDDDDDDDDDDD

1999 at The Corner: the 104th & final season for the Tigers, the first for 2-year olds
Spencer Vollmers of Dexter and Katrina Harcourt of Jacksonville

The final home stand in the history of Tiger Stadium began on Monday night, September 20, the start of a 4-game series against first place Cleveland. Detroit won game 1 in a 10 inning, 4-3 thriller, the winning run coming home on Juan Encarnacion's 1-out single. Outscored 15-2 in games 2 & 3 combined, the Tigers won an entertaining 7-5 game 4 battle, coming back from a 3-0 deficit on clutch RBIs by Tony Clark, rookie outfielder Gabe Kapler, Encarnacion, and Luis Polonia. Journeyman Polonia, a 35-year old with his 6th team not including two years in the Mexican League, was still showing the kids how it gets done, batting .324 in 333 at bats in his one full season in Detroit.

The final series ever at Tiger Stadium, 4 games versus the Kansas City Royals, began on September 24, a Friday, before 39,030 who witnessed a Tiger 7-3 loss. 41,164 on Saturday saw a much happier outcome, Tiger bats putting an 11-3 whipping on the Royals behind Brad Ausmus' big day of 1 homer, 3 hits & 3 RBIs. Sunday was as perfect a day for baseball as the Good Lord ever made, enjoyed by 41,586 fans who watched rookie pitcher Dave Borkowski, in an outing that was likely his finest, and certainly the most personally-satisfying, in an 8-year, 13 & 20/5.87 ERA career, whiff 6 in 8 innings of 4-hit, 1-run ball, as the Tigers coasted to a 6-1 triumph behind homers by shortstop Deivi Cruz, Dean Palmer, & Gabe Kapler.

Although the 2nd to the last game at Tiger Stadium was over, Detroit-native Dave Borkowski's greatest day ever continued, as he was interviewed on the WJR post-game show by Ernie Harwell himself, the man Borkowski listened on the radio to as far back as he could remember while following his hometown team. Chatting with Ernie, Borkowski seemed more interested in telling him about growing up in Detroit and going to Tiger Stadium as a kid than about the game Dave threw today. Harwell spoke of this being his 4th decade of broadcasting Tiger games, beginning in 1960 with George Kell as his booth partner, and then informed the listening audience that Monday's Tiger Stadium finale would not be the last trip to the old ballyard for him: on Tuesday, Ernie would have lunch with 1933-1938 Tiger pitcher Elden Auker and Jo Gehringer, Charlie's widow. They would then visit the empty stadium, sit in the stands, and share their memories of so many wonderful days of old.

As the field emptied after his Tiger teammates congratulated Dave Borkowski on his gem, fans lingered in the ballpark as long as the ushers & stadium security allowed, and then stretched out their time on the streets and in the Ma & Pa parking lots surrounding Tiger Stadium, soaking up the glorious weather, but mostly just wanting to stay as long as possible next to an old friend who would soon be leaving us.

Baseball for Tiger fans would never be the same in a different ballpark, no matter how beautiful it may be, and the good-bye was a difficult one, more so for some than others. But it wasn't goodbye yet, as there was one last game to play at the Old Gal.

One last game to play at Michigan & Trumbull.

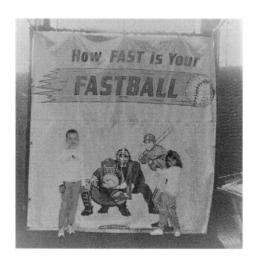

Lunches with Paul Carey

"Detroit Tiger Baseball is on the air!"

Paul Carey's dramatic signature broadcast, followed by a growling Tiger, was delivered in a baritone that brought goose bumps to years of Detroit Tiger fans, and will so long as it can be heard on the Internet. Listening to it brings us back to our youth, to summer days, and to transistor radios tuned to Ernie, Paul, George Kell, & Ray Lane. Paul said, *"I think I recorded 'Tiger Baseball is on the air' when I was producing the Tiger network, either in '64 or '65."* In 1956, Paul joined WJR's announcing staff, and from '64 to '71 produced the Detroit Tigers Radio Network, made up of WJR and all affiliates carrying Tiger games.

Ernie Harwell & Paul Carey. Just saying the two names together brings a smile to Tiger fans everywhere. As the end drew near for baseball at Michigan & Trumbull, fans frequently flashed back to treasured memories while following their team, and couldn't help but fondly think of this radio duo. 1998 marked a quarter century since *The Greatest Radio Broadcast Team in the history of sports* first shared the Tiger Stadium booth in 1973, a baseball announcer marriage made in heaven that would last through 1991.

Years later, Tim Patrick, a friend and teammate of mine on the Canton, Michigan-based Mobil Lounge Softball Team, and his wife Barb, met Joe Sayers. Joe, a former Chicago Cubs scout, lived next door to Paul and Nancy Carey. Tim, shortly after meeting Paul, gave me a copy of Ernie Harwell's *"Tuned To Baseball"* book, with a note that read, *"In 2008 I'm going to set up a luncheon with Paul Carey and we'll have him sign the book."* Hot dog! Take me out to the ballgame!

Good fortune smiled that August, bringing together four baseball fanatics, Paul, Joe, Tim, & the author, for a luncheon that ran the bases nearly 4 hours. The conversation spanned the history of Detroit Tiger baseball & beyond, time spent that could be characterized by any long-time, dyed-in-the-wool, Tiger fanatic as perfectly wonderful. No one wanted to leave, and thus began an annual (twice-a-year when lucky) lunch tradition through 2015, the year before Paul left us. During that first lunch in 2008, Paul inscribed my copy of the book authored by his dear friend Ernie, *"Doc! Great to have lunch & talk baseball – Paul Carey"*. The man whose golden pipes so beautifully complimented his broadcast booth partner, Ernie Harwell, for almost two decades, was as gracious, kind, funny, and cool in person as he sounded over our radios for lo those many years. As that first conversation began, it was immediately clear how passionate this Mount Pleasant native and life-long Tiger fan was about his baseball team. Paul emailed the 3 of us the next day...

"I thoroughly enjoyed our conversation about softball, baseball, old taverns, scouts, and rivers. We almost made it to dinner-time. The conversation prompted me to hit the Baseball Encyclopedia to check on old Tiger teams. I can name the lineup for the '35 Tigers but not quite the '61 team, so I found that Cash, Wood, Chico Fernandez, and Boros made up that infield with Kaline, Bruton and Colavito in the outfield, and Brown and Roarke sharing catching duties. It was Lary, Bunning, Foytack, Mossi and Regan with Aguirre and Fox in relief. Don Demeter played in '64 and '65 while Bill Tuttle was CF in '54-'57. And I'd forgotten that '61 was Dick McAuliffe's first year... and remember? He was a shortstop then. And, it came to me that the Cleveland GM who traded Colavito was Frank Lane. Isn't this fun?"

At that lunch, I gave each of my 3 companions a copy of my book, *"Weekend Canoeing in Michigan: the Rivers, the Towns, the Taverns"*. Paul concluded his 2008 email with a comment on the book, *"Doc, I've already checked out several taverns. To Hell with the rivers."* In his younger days, Paul was a regular at the Green Spot Tavern in Mount Pleasant, a lover of Altes, Pfeiffer, Goebbels and Stroh's beer. In 2011, Paul's familiarity of pubs contributed to one of my canoeing & kayaking books, making him an official member of the crack research team. Paul attributed many fine days to Rochester's Paint Creek Tavern, spent sitting alongside Paint Creek, a tributary of the nearby Clinton River. Naturally, our next lunch found us at the Paint Creek Tavern, where we unanimously voted Paul's suggestion an excellent one, & enjoyed a back-in-the-day-story shared by ex-Chicago Cub scout Joe Sayers. Joe told of a fellow scout in attendance at a minor league game when a lightning bolt split a fly ball in two. The outfielder caught one-half of the ball – is it an out? The ruling is that any portion of a caught ball results in an out.

Paul at the Paint Creek Tavern alongside flowing Paint Creek

Paul Carey was 7 years old when he became a fan while listening to Harry Heilmann's broadcasts of Detroit Tiger games in 1935, the year of their first World Series crown. Carey's favorite Tiger of them all was an important contributor to that '35 team, always a threat to steal a base, outfielder Gerald "Gee" Walker. The first game Paul attended took place in '37 at Navin Field, Yankee Red Ruffing outdueling Tommy Bridges, and Carey said, *"I cried all the way home."* From listening to Heilmann describe the action on the radio, young Carey decided he wanted to be a sportscaster. His dream realized, the deep voice going out over the airwaves earned several nicknames including "Mister Pipes" and "The Voice of God", while one newspaper columnist compared him to baritone singer Vaughn Monroe of "Ghost Riders in the Sky" fame. Ernie said of his friend, *"Paul has got a fantastic voice, the best voice I've ever heard on anybody. He makes anyone who works with him sound like a soprano."*

Excited about the impending 2012 Tiger Home Opener, I regaled friends including Paul with an email of Openers of Old. Featured was one story from '78, about the Bird on the hill, recovered (temporarily, it sadly turned out) from his arm ailments, spinning a 5-hitter over Toronto, with a link to a 1985 Steve Stone interview with Fidrych. Paul replied, *"Thanks for the memories, Doc. I'm sipping my second Crystal Palace (cheap booze) gin martini, having enjoyed watching Steve Stone's piece on Mark Fidrych. Can't handle beer any more (even Altes). That "Year of the Bird" was magical and it's so sad seeing him reminiscing about that glory year of '76 and what might have been. Just this morning at cardiac re-hab, another fellow told me about watching Mark that season. I don't think true Tiger fans of that era will ever forget that year. I went to the Opener last year for the first time since I last worked an Opener in '91, but will be sitting in a recliner on Thursday. Real Tiger fans, as you know, turn out in mid-September when it's 40 degrees and the club is 20 games out. I don't think we'll be 20 out this year."*

The joy of our lunches with Paul lasted through a final gathering on Wednesday, April 29, 2015. One year later, on April 12, 2016, 88-year old Paul Carey passed at home from chronic obstructive pulmonary disease and heart disease. Neighbor Joe Sayers said that Paul was determined to stay alive through his dear wife Nancy's birthday celebration. True to his word, that weekend Paul was cheerful & full of life, Joe describing Nancy's party as a great day for everyone. Carey successfully delayed his departure until the following Tuesday. Nancy Carey told the Associated Press he died *"very peacefully"* and that Paul was *"the love of my life and anybody that knew him was better off for knowing him."*

Amen.

9/27/99: The Final Home Game Ever To Be Played At Tiger Stadium

And there used to be a ballpark
Where the field was warm and green.
And the people played their crazy game
With a joy I'd never seen.
And the air was such a wonder
From the hot-dogs and the beer.
Yes, there used to be a ballpark right here.

("There Used To Be a Ballpark" by Frank Sinatra)

Early in the morning of September 27, 1999, Todd Jones awoke on a cot in the darkened Detroit Tiger clubhouse. As someone who loves the history of baseball, Todd decided how cool it would be on the night before the final game ever at The Corner, to sleep in Tiger Stadium.

As many games as I was blessed to have attended at The Corner since the 1965 inaugural with my Dad, 1999 was the one season that I purchased season tickets for Tiger baseball, in order to attend as many games as possible in this final year of play at Tiger Stadium AND ensure tickets for The Last Game. Our season ticket holders group included dear friends Laz & Connie Surabian of Birmingham, Ann Arbor's Jimmy Vollmers, and Taylor's Chris Weaks. It was our great fortune that available to us were seats in the famous right field overhang, seats that actually hang over the field of play by 10', suspended in mid-air. The upper deck was added in right field in 1936, the limited space between the right field fence & Trumbull Avenue, the street running behind the stands, necessitating the upper deck to overhang the field AND the sidewalk alongside Trumbull, to fit in the quantity of seats that owner Frank Navin requested.

Arriving downtown several hours before the ballpark gates opened for the 4:05PM first pitch, Jimmy & I walked the neighborhood around the stadium. We were only 2 among the thousands who felt the pull to be in the vicinity of The Corner by mid-morning, a fraternity of the faithful, direct descendants of those who 103 years ago attended the first game ever at overflowing 5,000 seat Bennett Park, plus another thousand standing behind roped-off areas and those hanging from the old oak & elm trees dotting the deepest outfield. On that April 28, 1896 day, many had tears in their eyes as they watched their hero, Charlie Bennett, make his way towards home plate on two artificial legs to catch the ceremonial 1st pitch, a duty Charlie performed at every Tiger Home Opener until he passed before the 1927 season began.

As if the 9.27.99 emotions weren't amplified enough, a roar spread through the growing crowd outside Tiger Stadium's walls. Their cheering was an involuntary reaction to the sight of the big convertible slowly making its way south on Trumbull towards Michigan Avenue, with Gordie & Colleen Howe smiling 'n waving from the front seat. Gordie loved baseball, becoming a big Tiger fan shortly after breaking in with the Red Wings in '46. Howe spent his summers from 1947 thru 1953 playing semi-pro ball in his native Saskatchewan, where he hit the longest home run ever at Cairns Field in Saskatoon, the ball landing on a moving flatcar beyond the right field fence.

Gordie Howe and Al Kaline, known famously as Number 9 and Number 6, respectively, first met after Al attended a Red Wings game with a mutual friend, before the men shared a post-game dinner at Carl's Chop House. Many rounds of golf together at Southfield's Plum Hollow course and a life-long friendship followed. Howe invited Kaline to a skate on the Olympia ice once, and as Al joyfully described it for the *Detroit News*, *"I hadn't skated in my entire life. I was a one leg pusher and Gordie was right by me. He gave me one of his famous elbows. I can always say Gordie gave me one of those elbows and knocked me into the boards."* Kaline, in return, invited Howe to work out with the Tigers at Briggs Stadium in 1957. Al said, *"Gordie put on a Tigers uniform and when he took his shirt off, he didn't have any shoulders. His arms went right into his neck. The other Tigers said 'What a beast!'"* Gordie stepped up to home plate at Briggs Stadium, took some batting practice swings, and when he was finally able to put one into the left field seats, Kaline said, *"From the expression on his face, it looked like he won the Stanley Cup,"* then Gordie hit a few more over the fence. Over the years, the distance that Gordie's batting practice hits traveled that day at Briggs grew each time the story was repeated, eventually having Howe clearing the roof in left, something that had only been done four times (once each by Harmon Killebrew, Frank Howard, Cecil Fielder, & Mark McGwire). To get to the bottom of the legend, Mitch Albom asked Gordie who answered his long hits were *"not out of the park, but several into the seats."* Al Kaline said of his friend, *"How great he was off the ice, how great he was around people, around kids, he never turned people down. He was always friendly to them, and to me that was why the people in Detroit and people in hockey everywhere loved Gordie Howe."*

Some of the biggest cheers at The Corner game #1 and game #6,911 were saved for two men not playing: Charlie Bennett in 1896 and Gordie Howe in 1999 ('57 Gordie photo hanging in Nemo's Bar)

DDDDDDDDDDDDDDDDDDDDDDDDDDDDDDDDDDDDDDDDDDDDDDDDDDDDDDDDDDDDDDDDDDDDDDDD

The Tiger Stadium dugouts were connected by tunnels to each clubhouse, the visitors on the first base side, the Tigers on the third base side. A sign above the visitor's clubhouse read, *"Visitors Clubhouse / No Visitors Allowed"*.

DDDDDDDDDDDDDDDDDDDDDDDDDDDDDDDDDDDDDDDDDDDDDDDDDDDDDDDDDDDDDDDDDDDDDDDD

Entering the stadium for the finale, each fan was met by a Tiger representative who embossed their game ticket with the words "Tiger Stadium" arched above "Sept. 27, 1999". I asked my ticket stamper to instead emboss the Topps 1963 Norm Cash card I'd brought for the occasion. *"Are you sure, sir?"* *"Oh yes, Norm would've wanted it this way."* We entered the stadium as soon as the gates opened, providing us with a relatively empty park & thus a better view for our planned walk through the stands around the entirety of the upper & lower decks. In an East Side Kids' moment, youngsters chipped off and pocketed concrete souvenirs from the bleacher wall beneath the giant centerfield scoreboard. Early arrivals heard Al Kaline, standing on the infield grass, give a pre-game, tear-jerking speech about the Grand Old Ballpark. Al told of 1953, when he was 19, the first time he ever saw the stadium, and how security at first wouldn't allow him in, figuring that he was just a fan, too young to be the newest Tiger; how Kaline's love of Tiger Stadium left him overwhelmed and humbled, and spoke of the park's *"character, charm, and history"*, and that *"the family memories of their visits to Tiger Stadium were the cement holding the park together."*

43,356 settled into their seats as Hall-of-Famers from both the Tigers and the KC Royals, Al Kaline and George Brett, walked out to home plate in their old uniforms, looking fit enough to play this afternoon, embracing and exchanging line-ups cards. Billy Rogell, the Tigers 1930-1939 shortstop, threw out the ceremonial first pitch, kind of a doubtful proposition to even Billy that this would happen. In the morning he was interviewed saying, *"First pitch? Hell, I'm 95! I can barely stand up!"* The feisty in Billy didn't check itself at the nonagenarian door, *"I hate to see this place go. The first game I played in this park was in 1925. As far as I'm concerned, there's nothing wrong with this ballpark."* All of the current Tigers wore the uniform numbers of famous Tigers of the past, except centerfielder Gabe Kapler, who did not wear a number in tribute to Tyrus Raymond Cobb as Ty played before numbers were issued. Rookie Rob Fick, called up to the parent club after a successful .309 year in the minors, was today's designated hitter. Fick had swapped his uniform number 18 for Norm Cash's 25. When Kaline saw Fick wearing Stormin' Norman's old number, he told Rob he'd hit one out today.

Brian Moehler, who had the honor of pitching the season opener, April 5 in Texas, would again be so honored today. Hopefully, that April victory in Texas could be repeated this afternoon. Facing Moehler was KC's best starter, Jeff Suppan. Before Brian tossed the game's first pitch, he turned away from the Royals' lead-off batter to face the flag in centerfield, kneeled down on the mound, and etched late father Fred's initials in the dirt. And the game was on. Moehler escaped a bases-loaded, one out, first inning jam. Luis Polonia led-off the bottom of the first with a blast deep into the center field stands, sending the already-jacked up crowd into orbit, the cherry on top of Polonia's .324 season. The Bird was spotted taking in the game in the lower deck seats behind home plate, and when fans would snap a photo or video tape Fidrych, he'd wave 'n smile like it was the nicest thing that ever happened to him. Kansas City single runs in the 2nd & 3rd were sandwiched around a Rob Fick bottom of the 2nd sac fly, the game tied 2-2 after 5 innings.

In the Tiger sixth, Dean Palmer showed speed to go with his power in beating out a grounder into the hole. Hustling to 2nd on Damion Easley's bunt, Palmer was in scoring position as Karim Garcia strode lively to the batter's box. Through an uneven year of struggle, this was Garcia's moment, driving his 13th homer of the year deep into the left-center field seats, his excitement surpassed by a sense of relief, as the festive crowd roared with emotion so strong you could feel it. Karim's tie-breaking smash changed the scoreboard to Tigers 4 Royals 2.

Tiger relievers Francisco Cordero and Doug Brocail tossed a scoreless 7th and 8th, keeping the lead at 2 runs going into the bottom of the 8th (for the weekend series, Brocail flew his father Ray in from Colorado, *"I just want to play catch with my father on this field before they close this place down. Without his help, I wouldn't be here."*). With KC reliever Jeff Montgomery now on the hill, Dean Palmer led off with a double to left. When Easley followed with a single, Palmer took third, and Damion advanced to 2nd on an errant KC throw. Karim Garcia was intentionally walked to set up a force at every base, and the strategy worked with the next batter, when a Gabe Kapler grounder back to the pitcher forced Palmer at home. With one out, the bags still loaded, Rob Fick moved from the on-deck circle towards home plate.

Setting the scene for the folks at home, TV announcer Frank Beckmann said, *"Here's Robert Fick, wearing Norm Cash's 25. Remember, Al Kaline told him that* (wearing Norm's number) *he'd hit a home run today"*. At this exact moment, Fick belted a pitch down the first base line, high into the now dark early evening, over our seats in the famous right field overhang, and on to the very same roof that Norm Cash sent home runs over on 4 occasions. *"He did it! There she goes, and it is... on the roof! Robert Fick, a grand slam that hits the roof and comes back! Kaline called it! How do you like that? Look at these flash bulbs! What a moment! Look out for the lumber yard!* (across Trumbull Ave.) *Oh, would Stormin' Norman have loved that!"* Ray Lane continued, *"Norm, if you're looking down... it reminds me of a stroke Norm Cash would take."* (Ray, we KNOW Norm is looking down!)

Rob Fick's grand slam, making the score 8-2 Tigers, appeared to have sailed into the Milky Way, so many camera flashes were going off. Fick's blast was the 11,111th home run ever hit at Michigan & Trumbull — and the last. Charles Fick, Rob's Dad, passed away just 10 months earlier. Rob said, *"I looked up in the sky and thought of my Dad. I know that he had something to do with all this."* That may well be, but among long time Tiger fans, they knew that Norm Cash did, too. Interestingly, the bat that Rob Fick used for the home run that represented the spirit of hard livin' Stormin' Norman was given to Dmitri Young by Fick 10 years later as a gift. The two, teammates in Detroit in '02, were compadres in their excessive drinking, but together, Fick & Young abandoned that kind of living. As a thank you, Fick gave the bat to Dmitri in 2009.

When Deivi Cruz followed Fick's blast with a groundout, the fans were too busy celebrating the grand slam to notice. The beautiful, deafening din made it impossible to hear the person next to you. Pinch hitter Kimera Bartee, the next batter due up, spent much of his pre-game filling empty film canisters with infield dirt near third base, handing the souvenirs to fans leaning over the railing, then stayed to sign autographs. That made much more of an impression on the new friends he'd made pre-game than the fact that Kimera grounded out to end Detroit's 8th.

"Well, here we go folks. It's been a grand day so far, 8 to 2 the Tigers lead, and here comes 'Roller Coaster Jones,'" Ernie tells the WJR radio listeners as Todd Jones is called on to secure the victory. Todd carried to the mound a well-worn glove, yet one that he'd never used before. Jones was wearing the last glove from Al Kaline's playing days, after Al graciously went along with the pitcher's request to borrow it for this special occasion. What a last 24 hours it had been for the man who would eventually be the team's all-time saves leader: sleeping last night in the Tiger clubhouse, being called on to close out the Final Game Ever at Tiger Stadium, and doing so while wearing Al Kaline's last glove. And Todd did it right, putting down the Royals 1-2-3 to end the Grand Finale properly, the last pitch called by Harwell, *"Jones is ready, he delivers... here's a **swing and a miss**! The game is over, and Tiger Stadium is no more."*

The Final Pitch at Michigan & Trumbull

Not a soul moved to leave at the end of *this* game. After players from both teams departed the diamond, Ernie Harwell took his place on the infield as the Master of Ceremonies. Recovering in his Thousand Oaks, California home from surgery, Sparky's face suddenly filled the giant center field screen to cheers from the assembled. The Anderson voice that would never be confused with another began talking about the great stadium & how when he returns, he wants to sit in the bleachers. Next, 65 former Tigers, each dressed in their Olde English D uniforms, entered the field one by one, spaced several seconds apart, through the centerfield gate, 440' from home. The fact that no names were announced over the p.a. system lent an otherworldly feel to it all, enhanced by the "Field of Dreams" music played in the background, as Tigers from as far back as the 1930s began to run, walk, or hobble to their old defensive positions. When needed, a golf cart brought them. In their first steps on to the field through the centerfield gate, the names on their backs were visible only to those in the lower deck bleachers, and the roar from the fans grew as more & more could see the jersey backside. Some were recognized when their images appeared on the centerfield screen, some recognized by their stride, bearing, or size without need of a name on a uniform or face on a screen. Once identified, that Tiger's name was shouted repeatedly though the stands, the jersey owner & their exploits of old cheered and discussed among the faithful, as if the person next to them could actually hear their words.

Mark Fidrych, the Bird himself, was the first to enter through the centerfield gates, having changed from his fan-in-the-stands clothes to his Tiger uniform, sprinting the 380' to the pitcher's rubber and doffing his cap before getting down on one knee to manicure the mound, just like back in 1976. This time his gardening work on the hill was not to get it perfect for pitching, but rather to scoop up some souvenir dirt which goes into a baggie the Bird produces from his back pocket. Bill Freehan is next through the gate, raising goose bumps in both '99 and thinking about it now. The current Tigers looked on in awe, lined up on the ground adjacent to their dugout, some recording the scene enveloping.

Following Freehan was Dave Bergman, Dick McAuliffe, Tommy Brookens, Dick Tracewski, Larry Herndon, Mickey Stanley, Don Lund, Dan Petry, Harry Eisenstat (nice trot for a late-1930s player), John McHale Sr., father of the current team president, Ed Mierkowicz, John Hiller (who does a little skip in the outfield to the cheers of the crowd), then 3 Detroit-natives & pitchers in a row in Steve Gromek, Billy Pierce (lost in one of the worst Tiger trades ever), & Frankie Tanana; and what an ovation for '68 Series hero Mickey Lolich (an announcer said, *"I don't think Freehan would want to have to pick him up now!"*); speaking of '68, here comes Willie… of all the great Willie Horton memories we have - throwing out Lou Brock at home in the 1968 Series game 5 at the top, of course - a favorite for many took place this night, when Willie ran out to his old defensive position in left and covered his face as he cried tears of joy; Don Wert, Doug Brocail, the 1st of 3 from the current team; Jim Northrup, Mike Henneman, & (the Duke of) Earl Wilson.

Billy Rogell, the oldest living Tiger at 95, brought a roar from the crowd as he took his place at short; Les Mueller, Ray Herbert, and Ray Boone greeted by a long *"Booooone!"*, Jimmy Outlaw, Joe Ginsberg, and how wonderful it is to see George Kell standing at third base one more time!; pitching great Virgil "Fire" Trucks makes his appearance, and I pull out of my pocket his Topps 1956 card, passing it among folks standing nearby – it travels 5 rows away before love of the Tigers brings it back; Jake Wood, Reno Bertoia, Senator Jim Bunning, Billy Hoeft, Brad Ausmus, the 2nd of the current Tigers, pitcher Elden Auker does a fine shuffle for an 89-year old, Jim Price, Steve Kemp seen doing something rarely seen in his playing days – smiling, Ron LeFlore who gets a nice hug from Mickey Stanley, Jason Thompson, what a roar for Darrell Evans, Dave Rozema, and the 3rd & final current Tiger, Damion Easley, Lance Parrish and battery mate Jack Morris get a big ovation, Charlie Paw Paw Maxwell, the Gater who looks like he might've snuck more hot dogs by Mayo Smith than one might think, Milt Wilcox, Johnny Wockenfuss, Chester Lemon, Aurelio Rodriguez, Willie Hernandez; Kirk Gibson ran several steps out of the centerfield gate before stopping to strike the pose he made famous after his "Goose-busters!" '84 Series-sealing upper deck shot off of Goose Gossage, then completed his run to right field like a man looking for someone to tackle; Cecil Big Daddy Fielder is next.

And now Number 6… wow! The ballpark explodes as Al Kaline takes his spot at Kaline's Corner, the emotions running high. Everyone expects that Kaline would be honored as the final Tiger to take the field tonight, but there is one last introduction to be made after Al: the only two players to enter the field as a pair, Alan Trammell & Lou Whitaker. How perfect for not only the longest second base & shortstop pairing in major league history, but also *the two who were the all-time longest MLB teammates!* Tram & Sweet Lou ran to the 2nd base bag, Whitaker feigning a leg cramp on the way, shook hands and took their short and 2nd base positions, respectively, as the crowd went wild! Once all 65 players were assembled, 43,000 fans begin to chant *"Let's Go Tigers!"* sending goose bumps, once again on a day of plenty, through the crowd.

An outfield sign hangs with the message, *"Today, there is crying in baseball"*.

The final two Tigers to take their old positions on the field:
Lou & Tram (both waving, bottom right corner)

Ron LeFlore arrived for the celebration owing over $80,000 in child support payments. His wife and the law had been unable to track him down, until the word of his 9.27.99 participation got out. Kindly, they allowed LeFlore to have his moment with his teammates on the field, but were waiting for Ron in the locker room. The kids got their money.

Though some ex-Tigers still in this world did not make it to Tiger Stadium today, once all 65 who did participate in the post-game ceremony were stationed at their old defensive positions, they left those positions and created a line that ran from the centerfield flag pole to home plate. As Beethoven's haunting "Moonlight Sonata" filled the stadium, the flag was lowered and passed from player to player. Next to home plate stood the 2nd to last player in this procession, great 1930's pitcher Elden Auker, who handed the flag over to current team catcher Brad Ausmus. Auker then took the microphone, *"66 years ago, I threw my first pitch as a Tiger, from this very pitcher's mound that we see tonight,"* eliciting a huge cheer from the fans, and Elden then spoke of what the team, the ballpark, and the fans meant to all who've been Tigers. The touching moment was briefly interrupted when Elden directed Ausmus to *"take this flag to Comerica Park, your new home"*. These last words brought down such an impressive cascade of boos from the stands that a huge smile broke out on Al Kaline's face and many of the Tigers honored today had to laugh. As Elden continued to speak with such passion about being a Tiger, the crowd was quickly his again. *"Never forget us, for we live by those that carry on the Tiger tradition, and who so proudly wear the Olde English D. To wear this uniform is a great privilege and an honor."* Kaline, standing between Bill Freehan & Jim Price, has his arms around them both, intently listening to Elden's words. *"On behalf of the old Tigers, we ask the young Tigers of today and tomorrow, to wear this uniform with pride. And never, on the field or off, allow your personal conduct to defile or disgrace the great tradition the uniform represents. And always remember, once a Tiger, always a Tiger. God bless all the Tigers of the past, present, and future, and God bless our fans who make this whole affair possible".*

In an interview later with Bill Dow, Elden said *"It was truly a touching day for me and hard to think this was the last game there. It was a great honor to have been chosen to speak on behalf of former players, but it wasn't easy. One time I had to stop when I was speaking because I choked up a bit when I saw Ernie Harwell looking at me with tears in his eyes. A couple of times I didn't think I'd make it through."*

Each of the Tiger alumni threw a souvenir baseball into the stands, before slowly walking off the field, disappearing ghost-like through the centerfield gate through which they came. It was then that George Campbell, great-nephew and oldest living relative of Charlie Bennett, the man for whom the first ballpark at The Corner was named after, the 1896 "Bennett's Park" becoming "Bennett Park", threw a ceremonial finale pitch to Brad Ausmus, with the ball that would be used for the first pitch at Comerica Park.

The game was now done, the post-game ceremony concluded, except for one final, beautiful, sad, goose-bump, golden moment to be forever treasured. One-by-one, rows of bulbs went black on the 8 light towers high above us, 1,428 lamps of 1,500-watt bulbs going dark in an eerie, emotional procession, and as the crowd stood silently only one was left on the field of play. Our dear Ernie Harwell, fighting the tears all Tiger fans felt, was at home plate, and spoke into the microphone for the last time ever at The Corner…

"Ladies and gentlemen, less than six months ago, we began a warm season of farewells, and with each passing day we came a little bit closer to this historic occasion, September 27, 1999. The Lions, Joe Louis and Nelson Mandela. Six-thousand eight-hundred and seventy-three regular-season games, 35 postseason contests and a trio of spectacular All-Star Games, Tiger Stadium has been home to this great game of baseball. But more than anything, it has been a cherished home to our memories. Will you remember that last base hit? The last out? How about that last pitch? Or maybe it's the first time as a child when you saw that green, green grass that will forever be etched into your mind and soul. Tonight, we say good-bye. But we will not forget. Open your eyes, look around and take a mental picture. Moments like this shall live on forever. It's been 88 moving years at Michigan and Trumbull. The tradition built here shall endure along with the permanence of the Olde English D. But tonight, we must say good-bye. Farewell, old friend Tiger Stadium. We will remember."

Epilogue

It's Tiger Stadium – built in One-Nine-One-One
It's Tiger Stadium – lookit Jake Wood run!
It's Tiger Stadium – little mustard on that bun
It's Tiger Stadium – as big as Cecil's son

70 and sunny bleachers Opening Day
Mickey Stanley on the run – what a play!
A good time for all, we might stay until May
Beer vendor pulled up a seat, & he's a gonna stay

("It's Tiger Stadium" – Doctoones 1993)

Without the connections that Todd Jones had, I was unable to sleep inside Tiger Stadium after the Last Game Ever Played at The Corner. So, I honored the ending of the ballpark we loved instead by spending the night a (very long) fly ball away from Michigan & Trumbull at a Porter Street Bed & Breakfast. In the pre-dawn hours of the morning after, walking to my car parked at, of course, Irene Sember's lot at 1348-54 W. Elizabeth Street, one block east of Hoot's and one block north of Nemo's Bar, I took the long way to Irene's, strolling by The Corner. There, under artificial lighting, each of Detroit's local morning news teams shared the story of yesterday, including a feature about *The Last Fan to Leave Tiger Stadium*. The subject of the feature was friend of many, pizzeria owner and former Ypsilanti mayoral candidate, Faz Husain of Ann Arbor. With the ballpark emptying out last night, Tiger security requested that Faz leave, but he informed them that he was waiting for a friend, Mitch Albom, to arrive before he could depart. It would be awhile as Albom was busy with interviews surrounding the finale story.

A WJR intern who also worked stadium security told *Detroit Free Press* columnist, author, and WJR radio host Mitch Albom that someone told security *"I'm waiting for Mitch"* to avoid getting tossed out. The Day After the Finale, while listening to Albom's radio show, I hear Mitch say he wants to know who this person is who used his name to become *The Last Fan to Leave Tiger Stadium*. I shout to the next room, *"Hey Maggie, Albom wants to talk to Faz!"* and I call Faz who says, *"Doc who?"* I told him, *"You know, Maggie & Doc"*. Faz says, *"Oh yeah, I love you bro."* *"I love you, too, Faz. Anyway, Mitch Albom would like to talk to The Last Fan to Leave Tiger Stadium."* *"Really bro? Do you have WJR's phone number?"* *"Sure Faz, here you go."*

5 minutes later, Albom says on the air, *"We have the man on the line"* *"Hi Mitch – you the best, bro!"* *"Faz, you used my name to stay…"* *"No bro, we're old friends, we met once."* *"Faz, I don't know you and…"* *"No Mitch, I know Mother Teresa, and about my new book, 'I Love Everyone'…"* Mitch and his crew are cracking up, *"Do we need anyone in our Marketing Department? We have a real self-promoter here."* *"No Mitch, you're all wrong, and if you call me at Hello Faz Pizza, 734-741-7777, I'll show you."*

Faz Husain, as kind-hearted & generous an individual as he was an outstanding pizza maker & marketing genius, was able to get his pizzeria's phone number – at no charge - on the air at Midwestern radio powerhouse WJR <u>AND</u> become *The Last Fan to Leave Tiger Stadium*. What an amazing two days!

DDDDDDDDDDDDDDDDDDDDDDDDDDDDDDDDDDDDDDDDDDDDDDDDDDDDDDDDDDDDDDDDDDDDDDDDDD

In the year 2000, 1 mile east of old Tiger Stadium, for the first time in 104 years, the Tigers home field resided somewhere other than at Michigan and Trumbull. Though Comerica Bank paid $66M so that, for the next 30 years of the new park's existence, it would be called Comerica Park, fans still frequently call the place the Tigers play ball, Tiger Stadium.

DDDDDDDDDDDDDDDDDDDDDDDDDDDDDDDDDDDDDDDDDDDDDDDDDDDDDDDDDDDDDDDDDDDDDDDDDDDDDD

Summer 2000 featured a college all-star game played at The Corner, a squad from Michigan facing off against one from Ohio. The outcome of the game, irrelevant. Fans would have purchased tickets for a stamp collecting seminar if it meant getting inside the hallowed grounds once again. As a delightful bonus, 96-year old Billy Rogell threw out the first pitch. Billy's throw fell almost straight down to the ground instead of reaching the catcher, as his shoulders slumped & head dropped – until the crowd began chanting *"Billy! Billy!"* and a big ole grin spread across his face as he left the field of his youth.

DDDDDDDDDDDDDDDDDDDDDDDDDDDDDDDDDDDDDDDDDDDDDDDDDDDDDDDDDDDDDDDDDDDDDDDDDDDDDD

The Corner Ballpark & the Willie Horton Field of Dreams

Since the final Tiger game at Michigan & Trumbull was played in 1999, and since the final piece of the demolished old stadium was hauled away in 2009, debates took place about what to do with the grounds at The Corner. One of the ideas, allowing Walmart to build a store on this treasured earth, had at least one Tiger fan with my name, born on my birth date, and with the same Mom & Dad, consider resorting to urban terrorism. Fortunately for all of us, the idea of Kaline's Corner sharing space with a Walmart did not come to fruition.

Devised and discarded were a series of proposals for The Corner's future put forth by government and business leaders. While their debate dragged on, our Field of Dreams became overgrown and haggard, until a group of volunteers stepped into the grooming void. The *Navin Field Grounds Crew*, formed in 2010, dedicated themselves to restore & maintain the historic field. Thanks to the labor of love by this army of groundskeepers, their work frequently visible to folks traveling down Michigan or Trumbull, baseball fans were able to be a part of history by playing their own baseball or softball game where those wearing the Olde English D once roamed.

The efforts of the Navin Field Grounds Crew continued until 2016, when a determination was finally reached on what to do with The Corner: to continue playing baseball where it had been played from 1896 through 1999. With ground broken in 2016, on Saturday, March 23, 2018, "The Corner Ballpark" was unveiled, the inaugural event a high school baseball doubleheader on its' "Willie Horton Field of Dreams": game 1 Detroit King vs. West Bloomfield, game 2 Detroit Western vs. Saline.

The Corner Ballpark serves as the new home to PAL, the acronym of Detroit's Police Athletic League. The new PAL headquarters was created at a cost of $21M. The "Willie Horton Field of Dreams" baseball field is located on the same footprint with the same dimensions as that diamond played on by Ty Cobb, Hank Greenberg, Al Kaline, Norm Cash, Mark the Bird Fidrych and, of course, Willie Horton himself. Within the field of play remains the flag pole in dead center, the same one where Chet Lemon tracked down so many 435' fly ball outs for pitcher & Detroit native, former flamethrower turned junk ball artist, Frankie Tanana. The only change from the old Tiger Stadium field is that live grass is replaced by artificial turf. Oh well, perfect can wait for heaven, but this is still a fantastic place to visit and one where you can put yourself back in that place where so many of our memories were made.

The Corner Ballpark & the Willie Horton Field of Dreams

The Corner Lives!

Doc Fletcher has had 9 books published about the joy of canoeing & kayaking, primarily on rivers running through his beloved Michigan. Moving to dry land, this book - his tenth – revolves around the passion, passed down through the generations, that folks in the Great Lakes State have for our Detroit Tigers. Go Get 'Em Tigers!

Doc's website is www.canoeingmichiganrivers.com

*Doc (middle of dugout) and Maggie (on dugout, 2nd from left)
surrounded by the love of family & friends (2002 Tiger Stadium)*

Printed in the United States
By Bookmasters